D1797094

Eva Zehentner

Competition in Language Change

Topics in English Linguistics

Volume 103

Eva Zehentner

Competition in Language Change

The Rise of the English Dative Alternation

DE GRUYTER
MOUTON

ISBN 978-3-11-063034-3
e-ISBN (PDF) 978-3-11-063385-6
e-ISBN (EPUB) 978-3-11-063044-2

Library of Congress Control Number: 2019934671

Bibliographic information published by the Deutsche Nationalbibliothek
The Deutsche Nationalbibliothek lists this publication in the Deutsche Nationalbibliografie; detailed bibliographic data are available on the Internet at http://dnb.dnb.de.

Printing and binding: CPI books GmbH, Leck

www.degruyter.com

To S.

Acknowledgements

I am incredibly grateful to a number of people who have accompanied me through my PhD thesis, on which this book is based, and everyone who has become part of my academic (and non-academic) life since. First, I would like to thank the editor of the TiEL series, Elizabeth Traugott, for her great help in revising the manuscript, and bringing it to completion – her comments, suggestions, and general support have been immensely valuable to me, and have certainly had a more than positive impact on this book. Many thanks are also due to the two reviewers of my thesis, Timothy Colleman and Gunther Kaltenböck, whose remarks were greatly appreciated and have guided many changes made to the original manuscript. Any remaining shortcomings are of course my own.

Niki Ritt has played an enormous role in supervising and shaping my PhD, and continues to be a huge inspiration. Not only would this book not exist in its present form without him, my entire way of thinking about linguistics – and life in general – would be entirely different. Niki has been the greatest of mentors, and I feel very lucky for it. I am furthermore deeply grateful for the ideas, cooperative-ness and friendship I have received from my former colleagues in Vienna, most importantly Andreas Baumann, Nora Dorn-Verlooy, Kamil Kaźmierski, Christina Prömer, Lotte Sommerer, and Lotti Viola.

My new colleagues in York, above all Ann Taylor and Julia Kolkmann, deserve huge thanks for welcoming and looking after me in the best possible way – I am very happy to be part of this department, and to be surrounded by so many excellent people (on both an academic and personal level). York is also where most of the transformation from thesis to book took place. Zurich has opened up possibilities for new endeavours; here, I would like to express my sincere gratitude to Marianne Hundt, who has been a great source of encouragement and support, and who is generally a remarkable person. I look forward to things to come. Finally, I am thankful for the inspiring input from, and fun times with, a range of linguists all around, in particular Lauren Fonteyn. My family and (non-linguistic) friends are equally amazing.

https://doi.org/10.1515/9783110633856-202

Contents

Tables

https://doi.org/10.1515/9783110633856-204

Figures

https://doi.org/10.1515/9783110633856-205

List of abbreviations

abstrTrans	abstract transfer
Acc	accusative
Addr	addressee
Adv	adverb
Aff	affectee
Agt	agent
Aux	auxiliary verb
Ben/Mal	benefactive/ malefactive
bmLV	benefactive/ malefactive light verb pattern
CAS	complex adaptive system
comm	communication
comm.revTrans	communicated reverse transfer
concrTrans	concrete transfer
DCxG	Diachronic Construction Grammar
Dat	dative
Depr	deprivee
DO	direct object
DOC	double object construction
EGT	Evolutionary Game Theory
EM	East Midlands
eME	early Middle English
eModE	Early Modern English
ESS	evolutionarily stable strategy
Exp	experiencer
f	feminine
Gen	genitive
intTrans	intended transfer
IO	indirect object
lME	late Middle English
lModE	Late Modern English
LV	light verb
m	masculine
ME	Middle English
Neg	negation/ negator
NE	Nash equilibrium
Nom	nominative
NP	noun phrase
Obj/ O	object
Obj$_1$	object 1 (indirect object)
Obj$_2$	object 2 (direct object)
Obl	oblique
OE	Old English
Pat	patient
PDE	Present Day English

https://doi.org/10.1515/9783110633856-206

Poss	possessive
PP	prepositional phrase
PRC	prepositional recipient construction
Pred	predicate
prep	preposition
pron	pronoun
ps.	person
PTC	prepositional theme construction
Rec	recipient (recipient-like argument)
revTrans	reverse transfer
Sem/ Sem	semantics
sg.	singular
SNE	strict Nash equilibrium
Subj/ S	subject
Syn/ Syn	syntax
Th	theme
V	verb
V_{cm}	caused motion verb
V_{comm}	communication verb
V_{disp}	dispossessive verb
V_{ditr}	ditransitive verb
V_{fin}	finite verb
$V_{Int.Trans}$	intended transfer verb
V_{mal}	malefactive verb
$V_{non\text{-}fin}$	non-finite verb form
VP	verb phrase
V_{trans}	transfer verb
WM	West Midlands

1 Introduction

This book addresses one of the most pervasive questions in historical linguistics, namely, under which conditions variation in a language system is maintained rather than being reduced. It does so by zooming in on one particular case of stable and predictable variation between argument structure constructions in English. More specifically, the book reconstructs, describes, and explains the historical emergence of the English 'dative alternation', which is illustrated in (1).

(1) a. John *gave* **Mary**$_{\text{REC}}$ <u>a book</u>$_{\text{TH}}$
 b. John *gave* <u>a book</u>$_{\text{TH}}$ **to Mary**$_{\text{REC}}$[1]

As can be seen, what alternates in these construction types is the position and the syntactic encoding of the indirect object (the recipient argument). It can either be expressed as a noun phrase (*Mary*) that precedes the theme (*a book*) – as in (1a) – or as a prepositional phrase (*to Mary*) that follows the theme (1b).

Inquiring into the past of this phenomenon is worthwhile for the following reasons: For Present Day English (PDE), the complementation pattern(s) occurring with ditransitive verbs such as *to give*, *to send*, or *to sell* have been studied extensively. Indeed, they have come to constitute "a popular test case for theories of argument structure and the syntax-semantics interface" (Colleman and De Clerck 2011: 186). Despite this exhaustive research interest in PDE ditransitives, however, the history of the verbs and of the construction(s) available to them has only rather recently begun to receive some attention (cf. Allen 1995; McFadden 2002; De Cuypere 2010, 2015a, 2015c; Colleman 2011; Colleman and De Clerck 2011; Wolk et al. 2013; Yáñez-Bouza and Denison 2015; Zehentner 2018; *inter alia*). In addition to a general lack in research on the phenomenon, there are a number of issues in the diachronic development of the forms which have not really been dealt with based on empirical data at all. These include e.g. the range of verb classes associated with ditransitive constructions at earlier times, the fate of non-prototypical ditransitive verbs, or the role of other, additional variants. To fill these gaps is one of the major goals of this book.

1 If not indicated otherwise, the examples presented were either invented or drawn from various corpora (*PPCME2, COCA, BNCweb*) by me. In all examples, the verb is marked by italics, the recipient (indirect/prepositional object) is in bold, and the theme (direct object) is underlined.

https://doi.org/10.1515/9783110633856-001

The present book therefore aims to tackle some remaining open questions, and to provide a more comprehensive account of the history of the English dative alternation by means of a quantitative investigation of ditransitive patterns in a corpus of Middle English. For the purposes of explanation, it combines the descriptive machinery of construction grammar with evolutionary thinking, meaning an understanding of languages as essentially historical systems, whose constituents exist because they have been successfully transmitted among speakers and speaker generations. It tests the validity of an 'evolutionary construction grammar' approach to language and language change, in which the notions of competition and cooperation between form-meaning mappings are of central importance.

The main contribution of the book is that it furthers our understanding of the PDE dative alternation and its features by providing a historical explanation for it. It demonstrates that taking a diachronic perspective to a synchronic phenomenon is highly fruitful. Since the development of the dative alternation is viewed as representative of a more general scenario type, the monograph is relevant to the study of language variation and change in general, specifying when two or more alternative "ways of saying the same thing" (Labov 1972: 271) can come to form historically stable relationships. Furthermore, it takes an innovative approach to language change in merging two theoretical frameworks, and in applying two different methodologies, corpus analysis and evolutionary game theory.

1.1 The phenomenon

English ditransitives – defined here as verb structures including three semantic roles, namely an agent argument (AGT), a recipient-like argument (REC), and a theme (TH) – have been widely studied in the linguistic literature and have been approached from a range of theoretical and methodological angles. The most prominent feature of such verbs is their ability to appear in both a nominal pattern, usually referred to as the 'double object construction' (DOC), and a prepositional construction with *to* (see sentences [1a-b] above). The examples also indicate that the choice of construction types strongly correlates with a choice of word order, in that the theme either follows the recipient or precedes it. While the former order is prototypically associated with the DOC (*John gave Mary*$_{\text{REC}}$ *a book*$_{\text{TH}}$), the latter is the common order for the *to*-prepositional recipient construction (*to*-PRC): *John gave a book*$_{TH}$ *to Mary*$_{TH}$.[2] The phenomenon of ditransitive verbs occurring mainly in these two patterns is now broadly known as the 'dative alternation' (earlier 'dative shift'), and its emergence and establishment in the history of English is what is at the heart of this book. Before delving further into this issue, however, a few additional introductory notes, particularly on terminology, are in order.

In general, the notion that the DOC and the *to*-PRC are 'in alternation' is here taken to imply a strong and transparent relation between them. As will be shown, this relationship is determined by the fact that the correspondences between the constructions are highly systematic, and that productivity and priming effects between the constructions seem to hold. A similarly close connection has been observed to exist between the DOC and a prepositional pattern involving *for* (*for*-PRC). This 'benefactive alternation' is illustrated in (2) below (Theijssen et al. 2010: 115; also Kittilä 2005). When reference to both alternations is intended, the book uses the superordinate expression 'ditransitive alternation(s)'. However, for the sake of formal brevity, I will often refer to the *to*-pattern only.

(2) a. John *baked* **Mary**$_{REC}$ a cake$_{TH}$

b. John *baked* a cake$_{TH}$ **for Mary**$_{REC}$

The robust relationship between the members of the ditransitive alternation(s) distinguishes these two PRC-types from other prepositional paraphrases, whose association with the DOC is less systematic and much weaker, even though they also share the semantics of the DOC to a certain degree. Examples of such alternative periphrases are given in (3) and (4).

(3) a. John *cast* **Mary**$_{REC}$ a glance$_{TH}$

b. John *cast* a glance$_{TH}$ **at Mary**$_{REC}$

---

2 The terminology used in this book differs from that of some other accounts of ditransitives in PDE or earlier stages. For example, Goldberg (1995) and others following her, use 'ditransitive' to refer exclusively to the DOC, while leaving the *to*-PRC unlabelled. A further term frequently used to refer to either the DOC, the *to-*/ *for*-PRC, or both, in PDE is 'dative' (e.g. Bernaisch, Gries, and Mukherjee 2014; Campbell and Tomasello 2001; Davidse 1996; Emonds 1993; Green 1974; Polinsky 1998; Wierzbicka 1986, among others). I prefer to avoid this, however, since "there [clearly] is no overt dative case in English [anymore]" (Jackendoff 1990: 195; also Jespersen 1927: 278). My use of 'dative' is thus strictly limited to discussions of case morphology in earlier periods of English. Even then, however, dative cannot be equated with the semantic function of recipient, since this role could be expressed by various cases, and dative case was in turn not restricted to recipients (within ditransitive constructions). A list of terms as used by various authors can be found in Gerwin (2014: 7–8, fn5).

(4) a. John *asked* **Mary**$_{\text{REC}}$ <u>a favour</u>$_{\text{TH}}$

b. John *asked* <u>a favour</u>$_{\text{TH}}$ **of Mary**$_{\text{REC}}$

These patterns are subsumed under the umbrella term 'prepositional recipient construction' (PRC); in analogy to the *to*-PRC and *for*-PRC, the specific preposition type involved is simply added to the label in cases where it is necessary and relevant to distinguish between the various prepositions. For example, (3b) above illustrates an *at*-PRC, meaning that REC is marked by the preposition *at*, while (4b) represents an *of*-PRC. To refer to the PP alone, the label '*prep*REC' is used; the generic 'prep' can here again be substituted by the specific prepositions (e.g. *to*REC or *of*REC).

Although the evolution of these alternative PRCs (whose frequency and semantic range were significantly greater in earlier periods than in PDE) will be shown to differ markedly and in many respects from that of the *to*-(*for*-)PRC, the study of their fate is deliberately included in this book. This is because I argue that they played an important role in the history of the alternation.

For similar reasons, the book also contains a discussion of 'prepositional theme constructions' (PTC), which will provide us with further insights into the diachronic development of ditransitives as well as of the alternation and will add another layer to the story. These patterns correspond to the PRCs described above in that one of the arguments is marked by a preposition. However, as the label says, it is not the recipient but the theme that is prepositional in this case (*prep*TH). Furthermore, PTCs prototypically exhibit the same word order preferences as DOCS, i.e. REC-TH order, rather than the other way round. Examples include the following:

(5) a. John *told* **Mary**$_{\text{REC}}$ <u>the news</u>$_{\text{TH}}$

b. John *told* **Mary**$_{\text{REC}}$ <u>about the news</u>$_{\text{TH}}$

(6) a. John *asked* **Mary**$_{\text{REC}}$ <u>a favour</u>$_{\text{TH}}$

b. John *asked* **Mary**$_{\text{REC}}$ <u>for a favour</u>$_{\text{TH}}$

Such paraphrases are not available for all ditransitive verbs, and the variation is again not as pervasive. Nevertheless, their role in shaping the alternation's establishment should not be ignored.

Finally, I will draw on evidence for an additional (though highly restricted) pattern which can also be taken to have had some impact on ditransitives – as shown below, certain verbs originally found in the DOC typically shifted to exclusive use in a possessive construction (POSS) over time (7).

(7) a. *John *broke* **Mary** <u>the shoulder</u>[3]
    b. John *broke* **Mary's** <u>shoulder</u>

The inclusion of a range of alternative patterns represents a major methodological difference between this book and most extant work on ditransitives in English. The main reasoning behind this decision is that looking at the members of the dative alternation in isolation – as earlier studies have typically done (e.g. McFadden 2002; De Cuypere 2015a, 2015c) – is highly problematic. This is also argued for in Arppe et al. (2010: 12), among others: "Most linguistic decision that speakers make are more complex than binary choices" (cf. further Mukherjee 2005). I demonstrate that casting a wider net, and more importantly, approaching ditransitives as a network of related constructions, facilitates the understanding of their diachronic development as well as the status of the alternation(s) in PDE. In particular, it brings the specific status of the *to*-PRC into sharp focus, and thereby helps to account for the phenomenon that represents the focus of this work: the emergence and the history of the dative alternation in the narrow sense. It should be noted that despite the empirically broader approach taken here, much of the discussion of previous literature is nevertheless centred around the dative alternation. This is to a large part due to the significantly more limited coverage of other patterns in earlier research, but also reflects limitations in scope of coverage.

1.1.1 Ditransitives and the dative alternation in Present Day English

Present Day English ditransitives have been frequently adduced in theoretical arguments and have been approached from various perspectives. Both their formal and their functional characteristics have received a great deal of attention. Among the issues most relevant to the present book are first and foremost the question of what the term 'dative alternation' actually refers to, and connected to this, the question of how large the functional/semantic overlap between the two constructions actually is (see e.g. Ozón 2009: Ch. 2.2 for an overview). As will be shown below, these are also the main points of interest in constructionist accounts, where the DOC and its prepositional paraphrase feature prominently.

3 Following common practice, ungrammaticality in PDE is marked with an asterisk (*) in this book, while questionable acceptability is indicated by a pre-posed <?>.

Generally, one problem that has repeatedly and abundantly been discussed in the literature is the nature of the two arguments (or objects) involved in ditransitive events; here, it has been noted that apart from assuming different semantic roles, they also show striking asymmetries in their syntactic behaviour. For example, in the DOC the theme-argument is not usually accepted as the subject of a passive clause, whereas the recipient-argument is fine (8). With the *to*-PRC, on the other hand, the exact opposite holds. While the TH-argument can felicitously be used as a passive subject in this case, the use of REC as a subject is markedly more awkward (9).

(8) a. **Mary**$_{\text{REC}}$ *was given* a book$_{\text{TH}}$
  b. ?A book$_{\text{TH}}$ *was given* **Mary**$_{\text{REC}}$

(9) a. ?**To Mary**$_{\text{REC}}$ *was given* a book$_{\text{TH}}$
  b. A book$_{\text{TH}}$ *was given* **to Mary**$_{\text{REC}}$

For this and other reasons, the arguments are typically said to fulfil different syntactic functions or grammatical roles in the clause: The REC-argument takes the role of 'indirect object', whereas the TH-argument functions as the 'direct object' of a verb.[4] Thus, the TH-argument in ditransitive constructions is assumed to correspond closely to direct objects of mono-transitive verbs, while the REC-argument differs from them both syntactically and semantically (Huddleston and Pullum 2002: 250; cf. also Quirk et al. 1985: 727, n.[a]). In this book, I will largely stick to the practice of labelling semantic role instead of syntactic function. The first object of ditransitive verbs will consistently be referred to as the 'REC-argument' rather than as the 'indirect object', whereas the second object is mainly labelled 'TH-argument' instead of 'direct object'. One problematic issue with this method is that the first argument of ditransitives in earlier English (and to some extent still today) could encode a wide range of roles that are not compatible with prototypical 'recipients' (e.g. deprivees in a stealing event). These will nevertheless indiscriminately be marked as 'REC' here.

Because of the syntactic (and possibly also semantic) differences between the nominal recipient in DOCs and the prepositional recipient in the *to*-PRC – such as the distinct ordering preferences, and the different degrees of passivisability as indicated above – it has also been debated whether they in fact qualify as alternatives of each other or not. This issue is of key relevance for this book, and importantly also ties in with the question whether the two constructions as

4 Cf. Jespersen (1927); Quirk et al. (1985: 726–728); Barss and Lasnik (1986); Larson (1988); Jackendoff (1990); Hudson (1992); Polinsky (1998); Biber et al. (1999); Ozón (2009: 24, 39, 41–43); Huddleston and Pullum (2002: 249); Gerwin (2014: 10–11); among others.

a whole should count as (at least roughly) equivalent to each other (Ziv and Sheintuch 1979: 398–399; Anderson 1988: 291; Huddleston and Pullum 2002: 248; also Hudson 1990). As I show below, my answer to this question is strongly affirmative: The first arguments in both constructions index the same semantic role, namely that of recipient, or a recipient-like participant. In addition, they also serve the same syntactic role in the clause, i.e. that of indirect object. (I nevertheless occasionally refer to PP-recipients as 'prepositional objects' [PO]. This is, however, not intended as a statement on their status, but is only done in order to distinguish between nominal and prepositional REC-arguments where relevant). One of the major aims of the monograph is then to investigate whether this correspondence between the prepositional argument and the NP-argument in ditransitive constructions was always given, or only emerged at a certain point in the history of English.

In addition to the syntactic and semantic status of the individual parts of the constructions, the relationship between the members of the dative alternation, the DOC and the *to*-PRC, has been much debated (e.g. Fillmore 1965; Emonds 1976; Langacker 1991; Goldberg 1995, 2002). While most accounts acknowledge that there is some link between the patterns, the precise nature of this link as well as the focus put on it differ quite substantially between theoretical frameworks.[5] For example, functional or functionalist approaches have typically concentrated on investigating the discourse-pragmatic and semantic factors influencing or determining the choice of one construction over the other (Mukherjee 2005: 33). These studies suggest that the factors at play most prominently include the animacy or pronominality of the objects, their discourse-status, or their relative length (cf. De Cuypere 2015a: 227 for a comprehensive list of influential factors; also Ozón 2009; Gerwin 2014). While the DOC, for instance, is the preferred choice with animate, pronominal, given, or definite recipients, the *to*-PRC is favoured when non-topical (inanimate, nominal, new, indefinite) recipients are involved. Although the specific factors that have a role in the choice between constructions as such are not investigated in this study, the fact that the DOC and *to*-PRC seem to stand in a complementary distribution in regard to a range of features is important to the argument that I put forward.

In constructionist approaches, the members of the alternation have traditionally been seen as independent, co-existing constructions, i.e. form-meaning

5 Because of the rich (and vast) amount of literature on the topic, several comprehensive overviews exist of how PDE ditransitives and the dative alternation are treated in different frameworks and traditions. I will refrain from reproducing such an overview here but refer the reader to those in previous works (e.g. Mukherjee 2005: Ch.1; Ozón 2009: Ch.2.2).

pairs (e.g. Goldberg 1995). Although the patterns are supposed to be more or less semantically synonymous, the relationship between them has long been considered an epiphenomenon of the large overlap in verbs found in them. Accordingly, the alternation by itself has been paid little heed in earlier works in this framework (Goldberg 1995: 89; cf. also Langacker 1991: 326; Goldberg 2002). More recent construction grammar accounts have, however, re-introduced a focus on the alternation and argue for a link between the constructions that is stronger than a mere partial paraphrase relationship (Cappelle 2006; Perek 2012, 2015). As pointed out in the following, constructionist, 'alternation-friendly', treatments of ditransitives are particularly interesting for the present account, since usage-based construction grammar constitutes one of its theoretical bases. I here follow those constructionist accounts that emphasise the alternation in assuming an intimate connection to hold between the two constructions in PDE and aim to explore when and more importantly how and why it came into being.

1.1.2 Ditransitives and the dative alternation in the history of English

With regard to the historical development of the members of the dative alternation, the first thing to observe is that much has changed since the earliest attestations of English. Most significantly, the alternation was not yet present at all in Old English. It is of course true that certain ditransitive verbs and verb classes – such as communication verbs like *tell* – could not only take two object NPs (typically in different cases) but could occur in prepositional constructions as well. However, no obvious and strong association between the DOC and the *to*-PRC can yet be found in texts from this period (Cassidy 1938; De Cuypere 2013, 2015c). In addition, prepositional alternatives to object noun phrases were not limited to *to* or *for* in Old English but varied across and even within individual verb classes. This is evident from the examples in (10), which illustrate a range of PRCs other than *to* with verbs of dispossession like *afyrran* 'take away' or *bereafian* 'steal, despoil'. (Note that as discussed below, the fact that such verbs could be used in the DOC in the first place – see e.g. the examples in [11] – is a further striking difference to PDE).

(10) a.	*afyrde*	**fram**	**hire**$_{REC}$	þa	leohtnesse$_{TH}$
	took	from	her	the	brightness

'took the brightness away from her'
(Wærferth, Dial. Greg 288; Visser 1963: 633)

b. Đu *afyrdest* **of** **Jacobe**$_{REC}$ ða graman hæftned$_{TH}$
you took away of Jacob the troublesome captivity
'you took the troublesome captivity away from Jacob'
(Ps. Th. 84, 1.; Bosworth-Toller, s.v. *a-fyrran*)

c. him ageafe þæt$_{TH}$ he ær **on** **him**$_{REC}$ *bereafode*
him restored what he before on him stole
'restored him what he had before stolen from him'
(Ors. 3, 11; S. 146, 30.; Bosworth-Toller, s.v. *be-reafian*)

(11) a. Đu **me**$_{REC}$ *afyrdest* frynd ða nyhstan$_{TH}$
yo me took away friends the closest
'you took my closest friends away from me'
(Bd. 2, 20; S. 522, 23; Bosworth-Toller, s.v. *a-fyrran*)

b. Heo **hit**$_{REC}$ ne *mæ* his gewittes$_{TH}$ *bereafian*
she it not may its faculty steal
'she cannot steal its faculty from it'
(Bt. 5, 3; Fox 12, 25; Bosworth-Toller, s.v. *be-reafian*)

A clear and intimate link between the double object construction and one particular prepositional periphrasis (namely that with *to*), i.e. the dative alternation proper, only emerged Middle English. This took place against the background of a concomitant and general spread of PP-patterns at the expense of nominal structures (cf. e.g. Mustanoja 1960; McFadden 2002).

Furthermore, the development is often seen as linked to a number of other changes which took place around the same time (at the turn from Old to Middle English), such as the loss of case inflections and the gradual emergence of fixed word order. These major changes also strongly affected ditransitive constructions. Their impact becomes apparent if we compare Old English ditransitives to Present Day English ditransitives. Among the obvious differences are the following: First, not only one but various case frames or case patterns were still available for ditransitive verbs in Old English. REC and TH arguments could carry either genitive, accusative or dative case marking in various combinations. The DOC sentences in (12) show some of these patterns, including the most frequent one, namely [DAT$_{REC}$-ACC$_{TH}$].

(12) a. *dældon* heora æhta$_{ACC-TH}$ ealle **þearfum**$_{DAT-REC}$
distributed their belongings all poor
'distributed their belongings to all the poor'
(coaelive, ÆLS_[Basil]:54.479; De Cuypere 2015a: 7)

b.

Se	Halga	Gast	**hie**ACC-REC	æghwylc	<u>god</u>ACC-TH	*lærde*
the	holy	spirit	them	every	good	taught

'The holy spirit taught them every good thing'
(Blickl. Homl. 12: 13121.1613; De Cuypere 2015a: 233)

c.

hineACC-REC	<u>wædum</u>DAT-TH	*bereafian*
him	clothes	steal

'to steal his clothes from him'
(ÆCHomI, 29 426.4; Allen 1995: 29)

d.

and	*forwyrnde*	**him**DAT-REC	ingangesGEN-TH
and	denied	him	entry

'and denied him the entry'
(coaelive, ÆLS_[Maur]:304.1673; De Cuypere 2015a: 232)

Similarly, the arguments of the prepositional constructions featured a variety of case frames as well, although prepositions generally showed a predilection for dative case, and the PRC [*prep*DATREC-ACCTH] (13) was probably more frequent than other prepositional patterns (Mustanoja 1960; Visser 1963).

(13)

and	*sende*	<u>þis</u>	<u>ærendgewrit</u>ACC-TH	**him**	**to**DAT-REC
and	send	this	letter	him	to

'and sent this letter to him'
(coaelive, ÆLS_[Abdon_and_Sennes]:86.4777; De Cuypere 2015c: 8)

By contrast, in PDE there is no overt morphological case marking on the object arguments anymore, and both the DOC and the prepositional patterns involve two uninflected NPs. Although traces of the old system are visible in the subject vs. object forms of personal pronouns (*he* vs. *him*), the indirect and direct objects of ditransitive verbs (neither pronominal nor NP ones) are not formally distinguished in any way today. The general loss of inflectional morphology that hit the English language system at the turn to Middle English accordingly affected the way in which ditransitive constructions are expressed quite substantially. It is plausible to assume that this may have triggered, or at least supported, the rise of prepositional patterns at the expense of the morphologically indistinct descendants of nominal constructions such as the DOC (e.g. Fischer 1992: 233; Allen 1995: 158; also Mustanoja 1960: 95).

Another difference reflects the fact that word order in Old English was generally freer than it is in PDE. That is to say, the order of the objects in the DOC was variable, with REC either preceding (14a) or following TH (14b) (e.g. Fischer 1992: 370–382; Trips 2002).

(14) a. and þær *geoffrode* **Gode**$_{\text{REC}}$ <u>menigfealde</u> <u>lac</u>$_{\text{TH}}$
and there offered God manifold gifts
'and offered God manifold gifts there'
(Ælfric, AS Hom. 578; De Cuypere 2010: 340)

b. Ðu *cyðest* <u>mildheortnysse</u>$_{\text{TH}}$ **ðinum** **ðeowan**$_{\text{REC}}$
you show mercy your servant
'you show mercy to your servant'
(Ælfric, AS Hom. 146; De Cuypere 2010: 340)

The same applied to the available Old English prepositional paraphrases, in which the PP-argument could also take up practically any position in relation to the NP-argument. While, for instance, the prepositional REC-argument in (13) above follows the NP-theme, it precedes it in (15).

(15) min God **me**$_{\text{REC-1}}$ *asende* **to**$_{\text{REC-2}}$ sona <u>his</u> <u>engel</u>$_{\text{TH}}$
my God me sent to soon his angel
'my God soon sent to me his angel'
(coaelhom, ÆHom_11:343.1662; De Cuypere 2015c: 8)

Although PDE ditransitives of course still display variation concerning the constituent order, word order is now conditioned by the type of construction, instead of all orders being available for all patterns.[6] That is, the two members of the dative alternation are now complementarily associated with two different canonical orders. On the one hand, there is the DOC with a fixed [REC-TH] order (16a), and on the other hand, the *to-/for*-PRC, where *prep*REC typically follows the nominal theme (16b). Prepositional theme-constructions, as mentioned above, show a standard order of [REC-*prep*TH], thus providing a third option (*John provided Mary*$_{\text{REC}}$ *with an apple*$_{\text{TH}}$).

(16) a. John *gave* **Mary**$_{\text{REC}}$ <u>an apple</u>$_{\text{TH}}$ vs. ?John *gave* <u>an apple</u>$_{\text{TH}}$ **Mary**$_{\text{REC}}$
b. John *gave* <u>an apple</u>$_{\text{TH}}$ **to Mary**$_{\text{REC}}$ vs. ?John *gave* **to Mary**$_{\text{REC}}$ <u>an apple</u>$_{\text{TH}}$

Even though they differ with regard to the order of the two objects within them, the constructions nevertheless show the same behaviour in respect to word order in the rest of the clause: Both components of the constructions occur postverbally and thereby fit the general SVO order that has become established in English. The fixation of word order on the clause level as well as the develop-

6 This tendency is statistical rather than categorical, and especially with two pronominal objects, there is considerable regional variation (cf. e.g. Gerwin 2014).

ment of fixed object placement are usually located around the same time as the emergence of the alternation and are likewise often related to the erosion of case morphology (e.g. Allen 1995; Bech 2001; Trips 2002; De Cuypere 2010, 2015a, 2015c).

Finally, there are semantic differences between Old English and PDE ditransitive constructions. In the case of the DOC, the Old English construction seems to denote a wide range of meanings that fall into the category of indirect affectedness. The REC-argument typically refers to "an individual affected by a process or state which obtains in some part of his personal sphere" (Dąbrowska 1997: 68). This includes, for example, the semantic roles of addressee (communication verbs), but also those of deprivee (dispossession verbs) or affectee of a benefactive or malefactive action (cf. Rohdenburg 2007; Colleman and De Clerck 2011).[7]

In PDE, in contrast, only some verb classes, such as verbs of transfer (e.g. *give, hand, sell*), intended transfer (*offer, promise*), or communication (*tell, show*), are still perfectly acceptable in the construction. The use of others, like verbs of dispossession (17a) or 'pure benefaction/malefaction' (17b-c), is ungrammatical in standard PDE.

(17) a. For dronkenesse *bireveth* **hym**$_{REC}$ the discrecioun of his wit$_{TH}$
for drunkenness robs him the discretion of his wit
'because drunkenness robs him of the discretion of his wit'
(CMCTPARS,316.C2.1212; PPCME2: M3)

b. *softe* **me**$_{REC}$ mi sar$_{TH}$
soften me my pain
'alleviate my pain for me'
(CMMARGA,62.120; PPCME2: M1)

c. *ibroken* **ham**$_{REC}$ þe schuldren$_{TH}$
broke them the shoulders
'broke their shoulders'
(CMJULIA,114.303; PPCME2: M1)

Rather than expressing indirect affectedness of a participant, the prototypical PDE DOC accordingly refers, much more specifically, to the successful transfer of an entity to a recipient. This is also clear from the verbs that it is most fre-

7 As pointed out before, the label 'REC' is therefore also not limited to prototypical recipients in the earlier periods but stands in for a comparatively broad category of semantic roles.

quently instantiated by (Malchukov, Haspelmath, and Comrie 2010: 2; also e.g. Goldberg 1995; Croft 2003; Stefanowitsch and Gries 2003).

What we can infer from this is that during Middle English and beyond, a noticeable reduction in the range of verb classes or meanings associated with the construction must have taken place, through which the DOC became more and more strongly linked to the concept of 'caused possession/ transfer'. This decrease in associated meanings through the loss of (peripheral) sub-senses has recently been argued to constitute a case of constructional semantic narrowing. It is also thought to have been triggered by the loss of case marking at the transition from Old to Middle English, and by the rise of prepositional competitors to the older constructions (Colleman and De Clerck 2011: 183; cf. also Barðdal 2007; Barðdal, Kristoffersen, and Sveen 2011). It is worth noting at this point already that the verb classes lost from the DOC typically become restricted to one or more of the alternative patterns included in this study – verbs of dispossession occur in both PRC and PRT patterns today (17a-b), and one option for malefactive verbs is to indicate the affectee by a possessive pronoun/NP (18). Investigating the link between these developments will be of central importance in this book.

(17) a. John *stole* a book$_{\text{TH}}$ **from Mary**$_{\text{REC}}$

b. John *robbed* **Mary**$_{\text{REC}}$ of a book$_{\text{TH}}$

(18) John *broke* **Mary's**$_{\text{REC}}$ shoulder$_{\text{TH}}$

The opposite development to the DOC's narrowing is seen with the prepositional patterns, in particular with the PRCs, and even more specifically with the *to*-PRC: Here, verb classes seem to have been added rather than lost. (A prime example for this development is the case of verbs like *deny* or *refuse*, which can be used in a *to*-PRC in PDE, something they could not do in Old English.) The prepositions appear to have expanded in contexts of use and have taken on more general or wider meanings. For instance, *to* has come to index more abstract (animate) recipients in addition to spatial, concrete goals, while *from* now indexes abstract, animate deprivees as well as spatial sources.[8]

In conclusion, what needs to be explained about the history of the dative alternation in English are (i) the emergence of the alternation per se, (ii) its historical stability, and (iii) the evolution of the specific properties exhibited by its members in PDE. This book reassesses these issues from a clearly defined perspective, and thereby provides a historical explanation of a PDE phenomenon.

8 This change has frequently been addressed in terms of grammaticalisation theory, with varying conclusions (Colleman and De Clerck 2009: 13).

It specifically concentrates on the history of ditransitives and the emergence of the dative alternation in Middle English, but at the same time takes into account broader developments in the English language, as well as other connected patterns. The precise research questions the book addresses are presented in the following section.

1.1.3 Main research questions to be addressed

The main research interest of this monograph is clearly the diachrony of the dative alternation in English. That is to say, the most basic questions it attempts to answer is when, how and why the PDE dative alternation came into being, why this variation has been maintained in the system over time, and when, how and why its members came to have the particular formal and functional features they show today. These larger issues can be broken down into several smaller questions, given in the following:

i. When did the prepositional patterns appear and/or become more frequent, and how did they become established as alternatives to the DOC?
   - Which types of prepositional patterns (PRC patterns including prepositions other than *to*, as well as prepositional theme patterns) can be identified?
   - Are these different patterns systematically distributed (e.g. according to individual verbs or verb classes), and are there any changes in their distribution over time?
   - How can we describe and explain the interaction between the constructions in a principled way?

ii. Can we observe any changes in the features of the members of the dative alternation in the period under investigation?
   - Is case marking on the arguments of ditransitive verbs lost during Middle English, and if so, how does this change proceed?
   - When, how and why did the complementary distribution of object orders in the dative alternation develop, and are there any conspicuous changes in the clausal word order of ditransitive patterns?
   - Is there a semantic specialisation towards a basic meaning of transfer in the DOC in Middle English, and how does the development of the prepositional pattern(s) compare to this?

iii. Do these developments directly reflect system-wide changes taking place at the same time (such as the general fixation of word order), and can we assume these developments to correlate, or even be linked causally?

Finally, the book asks whether and how the development of the dative alternation can be successfully modelled in a joint framework of construction grammar and evolutionary linguistics, which I refer to as 'evolutionary construction grammar'. I briefly discuss this in the next section.

1.2 Theoretical framework(s)

Concerning the theoretical framework, this study applies two distinct approaches to language and language change (and especially to changes in ditransitive complementation in the history of English). These are a) construction grammar and b) evolutionary linguistics. Usage-based construction grammar, as a bottom-up and decidedly data-driven approach to language, is used to identify and define the patterns in question. Regarding it as self-evident that the patterns which characterise or constitute languages are there because they have managed to replicate successfully, evolutionary linguistics is in contrast employed as an explanatory framework, to account for the emergence and, more importantly, the maintenance of variation and the success of individual variants. In the following, an outline of the main tenets of usage-based construction grammar and their implications for diachronic linguistics is provided. – By contrast to evolutionary linguistics, no exhaustive general introduction to (diachronic) construction grammar will be included in the main parts of the book; therefore, this is done in some detail already at this point. Focussing first on the concepts of constructions and constructional networks, the section afterwards deals with the principle of usage-basedness. This is followed by a short outlook to evolutionary linguistics. The central aims in merging the two frameworks are presented in the subsequent section on the main aims of the book (1.3).

1.2.1 (Diachronic) usage-based construction grammar

As Goldberg claims in the *Oxford Handbook of Construction Grammar*, "the constructionist approach is the fastest growing linguistic and interdisciplinary approach to language" (2013: 30). Accordingly, it has generated an already comparatively large body of literature on a variety of issues. Among other things, it has been applied to first/second language acquisition (e.g. Tomasello 2003; Ambridge and Lieven 2011; Diessel 2013; Ellis 2013), language contact (Höder 2012), diachronic change (e.g. Hilpert 2013; Traugott and Trousdale 2013; Barðdal et al. 2015, Sommerer 2018; Traugott 2016, forthc.), phonology (Välimaa-Blum 2011), morphology (Spencer 2001; Booij 2002a, 2005, 2013), syntactic theory (e.g. Fillmore, Kay, and O'Connor 1988; Goldberg 1995, 2006; Croft 2001; Hoffmann 2013), and artificial intelligence research (e.g. Steels 2012a, 2012b, 2013).

Most generally, constructionist approaches define themselves by delimitation from (mainstream) generative grammar. For example, they reject the assumption of an innate language faculty, and focus on language as reflecting domain-general cognitive processes (Goldberg 2006: 92, Ch.7, 9; 2013: 6, 23–25; Traugott and Trousdale 2013: 3).[9] Furthermore, language is considered to be non-componential; lexicon and syntax are therefore not neatly separated, but rather form a continuum (Hoffmann and Trousdale 2013: 1; also e.g. Fillmore 1988; Goldberg 2003). In contrast to transformational or derivational grammars, the framework is monostratal in that a distinction between surface/S-structure and deep/D-structure such as is made in Chomsky (1981) is dismissed (Goldberg 2002, 2013: 20; Culicover and Jackendoff 2005; *inter alia*).

The most fundamental and most basic tenet of all constructionist approaches is that all linguistic units are "learned pairings of form and function", i.e. constructions (Goldberg 2013: 15–16). These constructions are assumed to be psychologically real entities, organised in a larger taxonomic network. Among the principles not followed by all construction grammar theories is usage-basedness, which stresses the importance of language use and frequency in usage (compare also *exemplar theory* as proposed by e.g. Pierrehumbert 2001; Bybee 2006, 2010, 2013).[10] Among the constructionist frameworks which explicitly adopt a usage-based approach are Cognitive Construction Grammar, Radical Construction Grammar, and Cognitive Grammar; some recent constructionist accounts emphasising this aspect include Traugott and Trousdale (2013), Hilpert (2014), as well as Perek (2015). These are also the frameworks focussed on here: A bottom-up, data-driven account giving particular attention to the role of frequency in language representation and change is best compatible with evolutionary linguistics. It also presents itself as the best choice considering the empirical approach taken in the project.

While construction grammar (in its many different versions) is a fairly well-established framework in the theoretical linguistic landscape by now, applying constructionist ideas to historical linguistics and language change is a slightly

9 See also e.g. Croft (2001); Haspelmath (2008); Evans and Levinson (2009); Boas (2010).

10 Goldberg (2013: 16) furthermore provides a list of "several additional tenets traditionally associated with Cognitive Linguistics", such as semantics being based on 'construals' of a situation by the speakers.

more recent venture. However, diachronic construction grammar (DCxG)[11] has begun to prove increasingly productive in recent times. Even more so, the field "has experienced a dramatic explosion of interest" in the last two decades, as Traugott and Trousdale (2013: 39) assert. One of the earliest works to be mentioned in this context is Israel's (1996) explicitly constructionist account of the English *way*-construction. Since then, the field has been growing steadily and rapidly, with a large amount of publications on various theoretical aspects of the issue as well as applications to specific historical changes being found. An overview of work in diachronic construction grammar (although certainly not exhaustive) is given in Traugott and Trousdale (2013: 39–40). Among the more recent additions to the body of literature are e.g. Hilpert (2013, 2014) or the relevant contributions in Bergs and Diewald (2008), Boogaart, Colleman, and Rutten (2014) and Barðdal et al.'s (2015) edited volume *Diachronic Construction Grammar*. As briefly discussed in the following sub-section, the main focus in this tradition has been on changes to parts of constructions (constructional change) and the emergence of new constructions (constructionalisation), as well as the relation between the latter and grammaticalisation and lexicalisation (cf. e.g. Noël 2007; Patten 2012; Traugott and Trousdale 2013). Current key open questions within constructional approaches identified by Hilpert (2018) include "the status of constructions as mental representations of language, the emergence of new constructions, and the way in which nodes and connections are viewed as parts of the constructional network". Particularly the last issue is highly relevant to the present work.

In the next sections, I give a short overview of the main principles of construction grammar and their implications for historical linguistics and diachronic change. I start with the concept of constructions, before moving on to constructional networks and entrenchment and productivity.

1.2.1.1 Constructions, constructional networks, and language change

The 'construction', which is the most fundamental concept in construction grammar, in this approach has an independent theoretical status, and is defined as a conventional and learned "form-meaning or a form-function pairing, with symbolic links found between the form and the meaning" (Barðdal and Gildea 2015: 8; cf. also Goldberg 2013: 17).[12] While the 'form'-part (often labelled

11 The term 'diachronic construction grammar' is ascribed to Rostila (2004) and Noël (2007).

12 This is not the case in e.g. generative grammar, as can be gleaned from Chomsky's (2000: 8) statement that "grammatical constructions are taken to be taxonomic artefacts, useful for informal description perhaps but with no theoretical standing".

'SYN') comprises the phonological, morphological and syntactic properties of a pairing, the 'function'-part ('SEM') specifies the semantic and pragmatic features of a construction (e.g. Croft and Cruse 2004: 258–261; Goldberg 2006: 10, 53). For instance, the PDE double object construction, which pairs a syntactic form of [NP_X V NP_Y NP_Z] with a meaning of [X causes Y to receive Z], also includes information about the morphological make-up of the individual elements. Furthermore, it identifies discourse-pragmatic features of the construction and its components, such as the fact that the recipient referent is typically discourse-given. While the definition of constructions was earlier restricted to form-meaning mappings that were in some aspect idiosyncratic or unpredictable, it has since been extended to fully compositional patterns. The only precondition is that they be frequent enough to be recognised and stored as patterns (Goldberg 1995: 4 vs. Goldberg 2006: 5, 12–13).[13 14] Similarly, although most attention in constructionist research has so far been given to complex constructions such as whole clauses, smaller-sized, more atomic units like single categories, words, morphemes or even phonemes are now typically included in the definition (Croft and Cruse 2004: 255; Barðdal and Gildea 2015: 19–20). Neither idiosyncratic nor atomic constructions are, however, at the centre of this book; both the DOC and the *to*-PRC constitute constructions with relatively predictable semantics and are evidently complex rather than atomic. More specifically, both patterns represent 'argument structure constructions' in that they comprise a verb together with its syntactic arguments/semantic roles.

Apart from size and idiosyncrasy vs. generality, constructions are typically located on several other continua, including degree of phonological specificity (substantive/ lexically filled vs. schematic), and type of concept (lexical vs. grammatical). As to the first of these, constructions such as *book*, *-s* or *John gives Mary a book* are fully specified phonologically, whereas categories such as [NOUN], [-3rd ps. sg] or the abstract DOC [NP V NP NP] constitute highly schematic constructions. Partially lexically-filled or in-between constructions include e.g. [NOUN-*s*] or [NP *give* NP NP]. This cline from fully specified to fully

13 See further Langacker (1988); Losiewicz (1992); Goldberg (1999); Barlow and Kemmer (2000); Bybee and Hopper (2001); Tomasello (2003); Thompson and Fox (2004); Diessel (2011); Hilpert (2014).

14 As Traugott and Trousdale (2013: 11) argue, non-predictability is in fact no reliable indicator of construction status anyway, because "[s]ince the arbitrariness of the sign entails idiosyncrasy, idiosyncrasy is present in a construction by default". In a similar vein, Diessel (2015: 301) states that "there is evidence that even the most productive and most variable clause types, e.g., the transitive SVO, have holistic properties, i.e., properties that are associated with the entire structural pattern".

schematic also plays an important role in Croft's (2003) analysis of the DOC in PDE. His model, which distinguishes between DOCs on different levels of schematicity, ranging from verb-specific to verb-class-specific sub-constructions up to the abstract, underspecified DOC, is discussed in more detail in chapter (2) below and will later also be applied to the history of the constructions.

Regarding the second continuum, the gradient distinction between 'lexical' or contentful components on the one hand and grammatical, 'procedural' concepts on the other hand draws on the varying degrees of referentiality of constructions. On the lexical end of the cline, we find nouns, verbs and adjectives, whereas fully procedural constructions have "abstract meaning that signals linguistic relations, perspectives and deictic orientation" (Traugott and Trousdale 2013: 12). Constructions are usually found on various clines at the same time: For example, the syntactic category of [NOUN] is atomic and contentful, yet highly schematic, whereas the construction [NP *give* NP NP] is complex, partially filled, i.e. mostly, but not fully schematic, and mainly procedural. Furthermore, the clines are taken to be interdependent; an increased schematicity is e.g. associated with more procedural semantics (Croft and Cruse 2004: 255; Barðdal and Gildea 2015: 21).

A further crucial tenet of construction grammar approaches is that they reject the generative view of language as a combination of a grammar (as a set of rules) and a dictionary. Instead, they follow Langacker (2008: 222) and other cognitive linguists in taking language to be "a **structured** inventory of conventional linguistic units" [original emphasis]. Thus, all constructions, whether lexical or grammatical, atomic or complex, specific or schematic, are organised into networks and assemblies.[15] The networks of interconnected constructions, or 'constructional families', in which each construction constitutes a separate node, are stored in the so-called constructicon(s), defined as the inventory/ies of all constructions (Croft 2007: 463; Traugott and Trousdale 2013: 8–11, 50–51).[16]

The basic constructionist assumption that language is not independent from other cognitive capacities is, according to Boas (2013: 242–244), also reflected in other claims. More specifically, the particular structure of the constructional inventory, as well as the existence of individual constructions, are

15 By positing such networks, construction grammar aims to account for the entirety of language. This view is famously summed up in Goldberg's statement "It's constructions all the way down!" (2003: 223, 2006: 18), recently rephrased and extended as "It's constructions *all the way everywhere*" [original emphasis] by Boogaart, Colleman, and Rutten (2014: 1).

16 See also Jurafsky (1992); Evans (2007: 42).

taken to be motivated by general cognitive principles such as iconicity or prototypicality (cf. also Goldberg 1995: 67; 2006: 166–182; Diessel 2015: 302). For instance, both chairs and pianos can be conceptualised as part of the conceptual network of 'furniture items'; however, chairs arguably represent more prototypical, iconic category members than pianos (Traugott and Trousdale 2013: 10). Constructional networks are then taken to be organised in a similar way to conceptual networks, with their members differing in degree of prototypicality (Diessel 2015: 302). An example of such a network is presented in Fig. 1 below, which features the DOC as one clause type in the middle. As indicated by the bold lining around [SUBJ *give* OBJ1 OBJ2], DOC uses with *give* constitute more prototypical members of this construction, while DOC uses of *refuse* or *deny* are arguably less prototypical (Goldberg 1995).

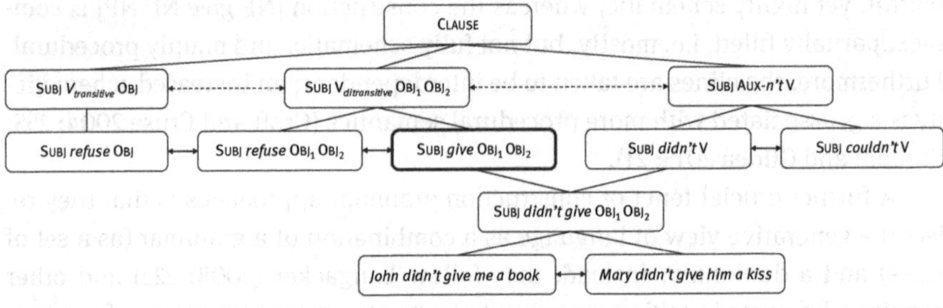

Fig. 1: Network of argument structure constructions in PDE (loosely based on Croft and Cruse 2004: 264)

It should be noted that although systematic relations are supposed to hold between both form and meaning on various levels, it is often next to impossible to do justice to this multi-dimensionality of the network on paper (Goldberg 1995: 99). Depictions of constructional networks are therefore almost always to some extent simplified, and typically focus on one dimension only (e.g. either form or meaning). For example, the constructional family of the DOC in Fig. 1 is based mainly on structural correspondences. Furthermore, no clear and widespread conventions for visually representing constructions, and more so, features like degree of prototypicality or entrenchment in constructions seem to exist; this at least holds true for 'vanilla' constructionist approaches. However, stricter formalisms do exist in certain constructionist versions such as Sign-based Construction grammar (e.g. Michaelis 2013) or Fluid Construction Grammar (e.g. Steels 2017).

Regarding links between the constructions in a network, a number of different types of relations are usually distinguished (Diessel 2015: 414). Among these are taxonomic, or vertical links, which connect constructions on different levels of schematicity, and paradigmatic, or horizontal links, which relate constructions at the same level of abstractness.

The first type of vertical links mainly draws on the lexicality-schematicity cline emphasised by Croft (2003). This means that there is a hierarchy of constructions from the most substantive, item-specific constructions at the bottom (*John didn't give me a book*) to the most schematic, generalised knowledge such as [SUBJ V OBJ$_1$ OBJ$_2$] or [CLAUSE] at the top (Goldberg 2006: 98). Lowest-level constructions are often referred to as 'micro-constructions', and are instantiated in use by 'constructs', i.e. actual token expressions. The term 'subschema' or sub-construction is, by contrast, used for individual type constructions at various degrees of schematicity like [SUBJ *give* OBJ$_1$ OBJ$_2$] (Fried 2010; Boas 2013: 239). The most abstract, higher order representations, defined by Kemmer (2003: 78) as "essentially routinized, or cognitively entrenched, patterns of experience", are labelled 'schemas'. In usage-based approaches such higher-level constructions crucially represent generalisations over different (sets of) lower level, more concrete patterns which are identified as in some aspect similar (Traugott and Trousdale 2013: 13–14; cf. also Tuggy 2007; Barðdal 2008).[17]

Vertical links are also often called 'inheritance relations', indicating that each construction gets its specific features from the higher-level construction dominating it. The higher-level construction specifies or 'sanctions' the structure of its daughter constructions (Croft and Cruse 2004: 264; Traugott and Trousdale 2013: 61; also Langacker 1987).[18] Both the transitive construction and

17 Other terms found in the literature include 'macro-' and 'meso-constructions' (e.g. Traugott 2008a, 2008b; Trousdale 2008, 2010). These are not applied in the present book.

18 Different versions of construction grammar disagree as to how precisely information is stored in the constructional taxonomy. Some accounts adopt a complete inheritance model and assume non-redundant representation of information only once, at the highest node possible. In contrast, others, including cognitive, usage-based construction grammar approaches, presume a default or normal inheritance model. In the latter, "all of the attributes of a dominating higher-level construction will be inherited by the lower-level construction unless there is conflict" (Patten 2012: 19; Barðdal and Gildea 2015: 18). Accordingly, the default model, contrary to the complete inheritance model, is able to capture lower-level idiosyncrasies as well as potential complexity or content mismatches (cf. Francis and Michaelis 2003). A sub-type of the default model is the full-entry model postulated by Goldberg (1995: 73–74). Here, information is represented redundantly at all levels in the hierarchy; rather than being inherited, it is specified at every node (see also Croft and Cruse 2004: 275–278; Patten 2012: 19–21). I remain largely

the DOC, for instance, get their subject-verb order specification from the highly abstract 'clause' (or 'Subject-Predicate') construction they are linked to (Goldberg 1995: 109). Importantly, however, constructions are not restricted to inheriting from one single construction but are usually linked to several higher-level constructions. This property, which Goldberg (2003) termed 'multiple inheritance', is illustrated by the example of [SUBJ *didn't give* OBJ_1 OBJ_2] in the figure above. This construction has multiple parents –namely the DOC and the negative auxiliary construction – which contribute different aspects to its structure. In this case, the daughter construction inherits the structure associated with the auxiliary from the negative construction, while the presence of two objects is specified by the DOC (Croft and Cruse 2004: 264).

By contrast to vertical relations, horizontal links are defined as links between constructions at the same level of schematicity (Diessel 2015: 414). In that, horizontal links between constructions, including more complex, syntactic ones, correspond to the well-established concept of paradigmatic relations between phonological or morphological elements (van de Velde 2014: 147). As also discussed by Hilpert (2018), the importance of horizontal links, and their role in the general make-up of constructional networks, have recently been put in the spotlight. Horizontal links e.g. feature explicitly in Diessel (2015), Traugott (forth.), as well as Zehentner and Traugott (forthc.).

In Fig. 1, horizontal connections are indicated by double-arrowed lines, supposed to hold e.g. between different verbs or verb classes used in the same construction (e.g. *give* and *refuse* in the DOC). Interpreted as different 'variants' of the same abstract construction – in this case the DOC – they make up paradigms in a way that is similar to e.g. the different morphological plural markers in English. Such variants are typically semantically related in some way: For example, the DOC uses of 'communication' verbs like *tell* are assumed to be related to 'transfer'-DOCs (featuring e.g. *give*) through a specific metaphorical mapping, that of 'communication is information transfer' (Goldberg 1995). Most importantly for the present account, however, horizontal links may also hold between different constructions an individual verb (or verb class) can be used in. In Fig. 1, transitive uses of *refuse* are horizontally related to DOC uses of the verb, and the different *refuse*-constructions can be thought of as constituting paradigms as well. This notion is particularly interesting for discussions of cases of systematic variation like the dative alternation: Its members are accordingly treated as likewise being related on the horizontal axis [DOC ↔ *to*-PRC].

---

agnostic on this particular issue here, and the notion of inheritance does not play any major role in this book.

Such alternation relationships originally did not receive much attention in construction grammar; quite the contrary, the (semantic, pragmatic, or discourse-functional) differences between the variants have long been highlighted in support of their status as individual, independent constructions (e.g. Goldberg 2002; Gries 2003). While Goldberg (1995: 91) does refer to 'S-synonymy' links holding between the members of the dative alternation, for example, the particular nature of these links is not specified, and little information is revealed about their role or emergence in the system (see further Perek 2012: 606). This has, however, clearly changed in recent years, with interest in alternation relationships and the appropriate way to model these rising again.

In this book, the links between the alternating constructions and the alternation as such, but also the (horizontal) connections between the patterns and additional variants, are at the centre of attention. More precisely, I follow Cappelle (2006) and Perek (2015) in arguing for an intimate connection between the members of the alternation, and the existence of an 'alternation-based abstraction', i.e. a higher-level generalisation over formally distinct but semantically similar constructions. This 'allostructions'-model is introduced in more detail below (section 2.2). In general, I view ditransitive patterns of any sort as part of a larger network, although the strength of the links between individual constructions may vary.

Change can then affect constructions and constructional networks in a variety of ways. Most basically, diachronic constructionist accounts differentiate between changes to parts of a construction (constructional change) on the one hand, and the creation of new constructions on the other hand (e.g. Hilpert 2013; Traugott and Trousdale 2013). Constructional change can either involve alterations of the function/meaning of a construction or include changes to the construction's form.[19] In both cases, changes can impinge either on one particular sub-part of a (larger) construction, or on the (complex) construction as a whole. Furthermore, both types of changes usually entail moving location along various clines, with constructions e.g. increasing in substantivity or schematicity, or developing towards greater idiosyncrasy or generality (cf. Traugott and Trousdale 2013: 116; also Bybee and Beckner 2014: 510–511). Torrent (2015) investigates the consequences of such changes for the configuration of the entire constructional network.

While constructional change concerns the internal dimension of a single construction only, constructionalisation is, by contrast, defined as "the creation

19 It can also theoretically impact the link between the form and the meaning of a construction; however, this issue will not be dealt with here.

of a form$_{new}$-meaning$_{new}$ pairing" (Traugott and Trousdale 2013: 22; Traugott 2015). Thus, it entails changes to both the semantics and the form of a construction. Nevertheless, constructional changes are involved in the creation of new constructions, in that they constitute necessary pre-stages of this process, and typically also impact the new construction after its emergence.[20] The emergence of a new construction is assumed to proceed via three stages: First, a change to the semantics of a construction occurs (e.g. pragmatic inferences become semanticised), which leads to two different meanings being linked to the same form (SYN$_1$ – SEM$_1$/SEM$_2$). The second step then sees the resolution of potential mismatches between the innovative meaning and the old form; the formal component is re-analysed. Observable evidence for this change only becomes available by the third step, when the new meaning and a new 'SYN'-component combine to form a new construction, which exists next to the old one: SYN$_1$-SEM$_1$ vs. SYN$_2$-SEM$_2$ (Barðdal and Gildea 2015: 13–14).

The strict distinction between constructional change and constructionalisation, as well as the concept of constructionalisation as advocated by Traugott and Trousdale (2013) have come under considerable criticism and the issue has since been further developed in different directions (e.g. Börjars, Vincent, and Walkden 2015; Hilpert 2018). As I argue below, their definition and (two-)stepwise model of constructionalisation is also difficult to combine with an evolutionary approach to language change, in which changes to any aspect of a unit result in the emergence of a new variant. A potentially more compatible conception of constructionalisation as the formation of new constructions is presented in Smirnova (2015, among others; also Rostila 2004, 2006; Noël 2007). Smirnova views constructionalisation as "a gradual accumulation of contextual restrictions followed by a structural reorganization of language material, whereby pieces of relevant contextual information are integrated into a new construction type" (2015: 81). The main focus in her account is on 'critical contexts'; more specifically, pragmatic implicatures arising in untypical, innovative contexts are gradually semanticised, which provides the precondition for structural reanalysis to occur in critical, structurally and semantically ambiguous, contexts and leads to the creation of a new construction type (further Diewald 2008; Diewald and Smirnova 2012). An example of constructionalisation, essentially following Smirnova (2015), is the emergence of the *to*-PRC as the semanticisation of an implied 'recipient' meaning and subsequent reanalysis of a former caused motion-pattern as a 'ditransitive construction'. These processes could take place in

20 Cf. the distinction between pre- and post-constructionalisation constructional changes advocated by Traugott and Trousdale (2013: 27–28); also Colleman (2015).

contexts involving untypical locational goals and later critical contexts with participants ambiguous between (inanimate) goals and (animate) recipients. The new construction differs from the old type in that it typically shows restrictions of some sorts, as well as reduced analysability and compositionality (Smirnova 2015: 102). In our case, the *to*-PRC is seen to be less flexible in regard to object ordering than the original *to*-GOAL ('caused motion') pattern.

Regardless of the precise conception of constructional change and constructionalisation, the processes involved evidently greatly impact the network as a whole, as any change to a part of the network will affect parts connected to it. Most relevantly for us here, new links between constructions can emerge, or existing links can decay. I propose below that the former process e.g. took place in the emergence of the dative alternation: With *to* coming to mark recipients through reanalysis, a horizontal connection develops between the *to*-PRC and the DOC. The emergence of new links can in turn lead to the emergence of new constructions, such as a cross-constructional higher-level generalisation over the DOC and the *to*-PRC once they had become horizontally linked. By contrast, loss of links is illustrated by the case of the DOC and verbs of dispossession; the link between the abstract DOC and this particular sense supposedly faded and was eventually lost entirely in the history of English. Such changes to the structure of a network and the relations within it are captured by and discussed in detail in Torrent's (2011, 2015) 'Constructional Network Configuration Hypothesis'. Other accounts in this vein are Patten (2012) on changes in the constructional network of *it*-clefts in the history of English and van de Velde (2014) on shifting links between formal strategies and specific functions in degenerate (many-to-many) systems. Connected to the issue of additions or losses of links, Torrent (2015) furthermore comments on constructional mergers, suggesting that previously unrelated constructions may come to converge either functionally, formally, or both ('Constructional Convergence Hypothesis'). Constructional splits, in contrast, would correspond to constructionalisation processes as just outlined.

To sum up, a major principle of constructionist approaches is that all grammatical knowledge is equivalently represented by form-meaning pairings which only differ in respect to various clines (Croft and Cruse 2004: 225). These constructions are not stored in isolation, but link to each other in a network, both vertically and horizontally. That is, constructions are organised hierarchically, ranging from item-specific, lexically filled constructions at the bottom, to highly schematic, abstract constructions at the top. Furthermore, paradigmatic, horizontal relations can hold between constructions at the same level of schematicity. The diachronic implications of these assumptions are that constructions (and their components) can change, and that new constructions can emerge or disappear. Moreover, the links between constructions in the network are subject to change, with new relations potentially forming while existing ones may be lost.

1.2.1.2 Usage-based constructionist approaches (to language change)

This book adopts a usage-based construction grammar approach to language and language change (e.g. Diessel 2011, 2015; Bybee 2013; Traugott and Trousdale 2013). The main tenet of this approach is, as Perek (2015: 6) contends, that "the cognitive representation of language emerges through, and is shaped by, language use".[21] Constructions and the configuration of the constructional network result from linguistic experience. Rather than being independent and static, language on this view hence constitutes a highly dynamic system; its constituents and the relations between them are emergent as well as flexible, gradient/fuzzy rather than strictly discrete, and constantly changing (De Smet 2010: 96; Bybee 2013: 49–52). A further principle of usage-based accounts is that language is grounded in, and influenced by, domain-general cognitive processes: These include categorisation or cross-modal association as well as neuromotor automation, analogy, chunking, and others (Bybee 2013: 49–50). Categories, or abstractions in general, are viewed as based on concrete, actual tokens in language use, meaning that abstract linguistic structure (such as schematic constructions) emerges from the use and storage of concrete lexical tokens in a bottom-up manner. The process of abstracting a schema is dependent on schematicisation processes; features common to a range of concrete tokens are extracted, abstracted over, and associated with a larger construction (Perek 2015: 168; Bybee 2013). Once abstractions or categorisations have come about, they are then stored alongside the more specific, lower-level representations rather than ousting them, as both the acquisition of particular instances and the generation of abstractions are cognitively beneficial (Traugott and Trousdale 2013: 53). Note that although a usage-based view on language inevitably prominently features the speaker/hearer as the 'users' of language, this does not necessarily mean that this approach is 'speaker-centric' – the present book focuses on constructions as shaped by usage without emphasising the role of speakers as rational agents.

21 Cf. furthermore Langacker (1987, 2000); Hopper (1987); Barlow and Kemmer (2000); Bybee and Hopper (2001); Bybee and McClelland (2005); Bybee (2006, 2010, 2013); Bybee & Beckner (2011), among many others.

A crucial factor in language use and cognition is frequency, as categorisation, among other processes, fundamentally depends on elements being repeated (Bybee 2013: 50–51; also e.g. Ellis 2002; Diessel 2007). Frequency is also taken to determine the degree of entrenchment of a construction, commonly defined as "the strength or autonomy of representation of a form-meaning pairing at a given level of abstraction in the cognitive system" (Blumenthal-Dramé 2012: 4). This is because whenever a particular construction is used or perceived, it is activated. Frequent activation of a construction in turn means it can be more easily accessed and activated in the future, i.e. it becomes better connected and increases in 'linguistic strength' (Blumenthal-Dramé 2012; Traugott and Trousdale 2013: 54–55; Barðdal and Gildea 2015: 24–25).

While both type and token frequency play a role in entrenchment, they do so on different levels of schematicity. High token frequency leads to lexically-filled, lower level constructions being entrenched, whereas high type frequency can result in the emergence and increasing entrenchment of a higher-level, more abstract construction (Langacker 1987: 59–60; Croft and Cruse 2004: 292–293, 308–320). For example, low-level constructions such as *Give it me!* are presumably highly entrenched (in certain dialects) due to their frequent text occurrence (Gerwin 2014). However, the degree of entrenchment of a higher-level, more abstract [V Th Rec] construction is probably rather low, since the pattern is restricted in type frequency. Apart from being largely confined to uses with two pronominal objects, it is also presumably not attested with a large range of verb types (cf. e.g. ?*Refuse/forgive it me*!). In contrast, the DOC as such (with a form of [V Rec Th]) is highly type frequent, being instantiated by a large number of different verbs and also verb class types and is accordingly expected to be highly entrenched.

Degree of entrenchment and schematicity, and consequently type and token frequency, also have an impact on the productivity of constructions. In usage-based approaches, productivity is commonly defined as a construction's success in attracting new elements, i.e. a construction's extensibility to lexical items it has previously not been witnessed with (Barðdal 2008: 18–19; Perek 2015: 167–169; *inter alia*).[22] It is generally agreed upon that type frequency contributes to productivity, since a large amount of different types means more

22 As Perek (2015: 168) points out, productivity in this sense "not only covers obvious cases of genuine syntactic creativity, whereby a verb is used in an unusual argument structure, but it is also meant to explain how children acquire a language under the well-warranted assumption that the input provided to them is inherently limited and does not necessarily contain all possible forms of the language".

bases for analogical extension. This is clearly given in the case of the PDE DOC: The high number of types associated with the construction means that it can readily be extended to new verbs (such as the new communication verbs *skype*, *whatsapp* or *snapchat*). Individual types with low token frequency, e.g. formal giving-verbs like *bequeath*, are supposed to further add to the construction's productivity. This is because their processing makes the activation of the more abstract representation necessary, thereby again increasing the strength of the construction (Bybee 2013: 62; cf. also Baayen 1993). In contrast, high token frequency (but low type frequency) is seen as disadvantageous, since individual tokens being highly frequent in fact reduces the probability that the more abstract type is productive on its own (Barðdal and Gildea 2015: 25). For instance, if *give* was found highly frequently in the DOC, but very few other verb types were used with it, the more abstract schema of 'DOC' would probably fade in favour of the more entrenched lower-level construction specific to the verb *give*. Barðdal (2008, 2011, 2012) adds the 'degree of constructional coherence' as a further factor in determining productivity. Fully productive constructions on this account have a low degree of semantic coherence, and, correlated to this, a high schematicity and high type frequency. However, low type frequency and low degree of schematicity, i.e. a high degree of similarity between the members of a construction can also result in some productivity ('semi-productive' constructions) (cf. Barðdal 2008; Traugott and Trousdale 2013: 119; Bybee and Beckner 2014: 507–508). This book mainly determines productivity based on type and token frequency, but also takes up and investigates Barðdal's suggestions concerning semantic coherence. Additionally, the measure of potential productivity of a construction – as the number of hapax legomena divided by its number of tokens – is taken into account (Baayen 2009). Following Baayen and Lieber (1991: 819), type frequency in combination with potential productivity is taken to yield the "global productivity" of a construction (cf. also Hilpert 2011).

Assuming a usage-based constructionist perspective to language change implies that language constitutes a dynamic system which is subject to change through experience, and that constructions are also flexible rather than static (Bybee and Beckner 2014: 504). Variation and change are therefore constantly produced, in adult communication as well as in child language acquisition. Further principles of usage-based views on language change are that the locus of innovation is the construct/ micro-construction level, and that change is gradual and incremental.[23] This follows from the basic claim that all experience, i.e. every single usage event (a 'construct' in Traugottian terms), is stored and thus has an effect on cognitive representation (Bybee and Beckner 2014: 503–504). It is here assumed that in encountering tokens in usage, a 'best-fit' principle is applied, meaning that the token is compared to stored instances. In this process, mismatches can occur, and variation is produced. Such small-step, lower-level changes can then accumulate and become larger-scale changes, affecting higher-level representations. While more schematic constructions are accordingly subject to change as well, such changes are epiphenomenal; they are caused by the accrual of lower-level changes originating in concrete tokens (Traugott and Trousdale 2013: 47–53).

The strong emphasis on frequency of use in usage-based approaches means that frequency is also taken to be a crucial factor in language change, shaping the trajectories of change (Bybee and Beckner 2014: 404). As to processes influencing frequency of occurrence, those most relevant to the present study are those of 'spreading activation', analogy, and reanalysis. The first of these refers to the mechanism of closely related constructions in a network being activated (near-)simultaneously in usage events; the activation of a particular pattern will also to a certain extent activate constructions that are vertically or horizontally connected to it (Hudson 2010: 95). Spreading activation is then furthermore viewed as responsible for priming effects, since the possibility of preceding constructions having an impact on following ones requires the pre-activation of shared or closely related features of these constructions (cf. also Jäger and Rosenbach 2008).

Analogical extension means that a construction can come to be used with types or tokens it was previously not associated with, but which are in some aspect similar to its existing members (Traugott and Trousdale 2013: 35). For example, the recently attested DOC uses of *provide* might be motivated by the verb's semantic similarity with other giving-verbs, which frequently occur in this construction. Thus, the type frequency of the DOC increases through analogical extension. Since increases in type frequency typically strengthen the cognitive representation of the higher-level construction, this may in turn lead to even more types being added. Reanalysis processes, on the other hand, involve differences or mismatches between interpretations, such as when *to* was reanalysed from allative goal-marker to recipient marker, and thereby raised its

23 See e.g. Traugott and Trousdale (2013: 74): "A succession of small discrete steps in change is a crucial aspect of what is known as 'gradualness' [...] a phenomenon of change, specifically discrete structural micro-changes and tiny-step transmission across the linguistic system".

token frequency (Barðdal and Gildea 2015: 5). While such new uses usually constitute non-prototypical, less entrenched instances of higher-level schemas in the beginning, they can develop into more central members over time. To illustrate: The earliest *to*-prepositional recipients were probably highly marked in comparison to the NP-recipients but became more regular in the course to PDE.[24]

In general, marginal and non-prototypical constructions are more prone to loss, since infrequent (or lack of) activation bears the risk of decreasing entrenchment, meaning that the construction is also less readily activated in the future. This can in time lead to the construction fading and becoming obsolete (Traugott and Trousdale 2013: 55, 65; Bybee and Beckner 2014: 507). I show below that this is precisely what happened in the history of the English DOC, when uses further removed from its prototypical meaning of transfer, such as verbs of dispossession, were ousted from the construction. The loss of more schematic constructions is typically the result of low type frequency (in terms of number of sub-constructions). While lower-level, more substantive constructs, which represent single types, might be highly token frequent, this will only serve to reinforce these particular constructions; it will not be conducive to the entrenchment of a higher-level generalisation. As Patten (2012: 22) claims, "the entrenchment of individual instances is [consequently] often found occurring alongside a concomitant loss (or weakening) of the overarching schema, which is no longer type productive" (also Bybee 1985). Such a development in turn often results in the fossilisation of the token frequent subordinate instances, whereas less frequent specific instances associated with the schema might be lost entirely. For example, if the micro-construction of *Give it me!* is very token frequent, but other types such as *tell it me / give this him / tell that her* are not, or only rarely used, this will probably lead to reduced entrenchment and possibly loss of the infrequent types as well as the more general schema [V Th Rec]. At the same time, *Give it me!* is reinforced, and survives as a fossilised use. Members of low type-frequency constructions are furthermore often attracted by more productive constructions; in the example just given, uses such as *tell it me* might e.g. change into *tell it to me*, instantiating a construction with higher productivity (Barðdal and Gildea 2015: 29–32). Nevertheless, infrequent use does not necessarily entail ousting, but constructions can remain stable, most commonly by developing specialised uses. The construction of [V Th Rec] is, for

24 On the topic of analogy and reanalysis see further Anttila (2003); Hock (2003); Fischer (2007); De Smet (2009); Gisborne and Patten (2011); Bybee and Beckner (2014); Sommerer (2018); among many others.

instance, now associated with particular dialects, meaning that it has acquired socio-regional values (cf. also S. Hoffmann's 2005 discussion of complex prepositions). Loss or decline typically does not affect all members of schemas at the same time or speed in any case. Instead, great variability is the norm.

To conclude, usage-based constructionist approaches are fundamentally 'bottom-up' rather than 'top-down', presuming that language use affects (or indeed forms) linguistic structure. Crucially, language change therefore also originates in language use. What follows from this is that the analysis of linguistic usage data, and of frequency in usage, is essential in determining the nature of cognitive representations (cf. Bybee 2013: 50–51; Goldberg 2013: 16). Such a 'what you see is what you get' view of language use and representation is particularly apt for this book: It is mainly based on an empirical analysis of ditransitive attestations and their frequency distribution in a corpus of Middle English and takes these data to directly reflect mental representation.

1.2.1.3 Summary

The previous sections have given an overview of the main tenets of usage-based constructionist approaches to language: On this view, the language system constitutes a network of form-meaning pairings at various levels of schematicity, stretching from fully substantive/filled to highly abstract, encompassing atomic as well as complex constructions, and so on. These constructions are related via different types of links, both vertical and horizontal. The diachronic implications of these assumptions are that both individual constructions and the connections between them can change; diachronic constructionist accounts distinguish between constructional changes which only affect parts of a construction, and constructionalisation, which involves changes to both form and meaning of a construction and leads to the formation of a new pairing (out of an older construction). However, it should be noted that this distinction is debated, and will also not be strictly followed in this book. Finally, the links between constructions are subject to change, meaning that new links can emerge, and existing ones can be lost.

The particular version of construction grammar used here is usage-based (diachronic) construction grammar: All linguistic knowledge and representation is crucially grounded in, and emerging from, usage. This entails, first, that change occurs at the construct and micro-constructional level. If such micro-changes accumulate, higher-order constructions in the network can be affected as well. Importantly, changes on more abstract levels are always epiphenomenal to lower-level alterations, i.e. are not directly caused by language use. Second, this means that frequency of occurrence and connected to this, entrenchment and productivity, are considered central factors in language representation and language change. This is particularly relevant for the present study whose empirical focus is on attested patterns in a historical corpus.

In the following section, the second framework applied in the book, namely evolutionary linguistics is very briefly presented – as will be seen, this approach clearly aligns with usage-based construction grammar in its emphasis on frequency. A more detailed overview of the approach is provided in Part II of the book (section 5.1).

1.2.2 Evolutionary linguistics

'Evolutionary linguistics' subsumes a number of approaches which differ in minor and not so minor ways, and itself may constitute a sub-theory of 'Generalised Darwinism', 'Universal Darwinism' or 'Complex adaptive systems theory' (e.g. Croft 2000, 2006b, 2013a; Ritt 2004; Rosenbach 2008; Beckner et al. 2009). The basic assumption here is that a variety of different systems, including biological and cultural ones, are subject to the same domain-general evolutionary mechanisms. Language change, as part of cultural evolution, is accordingly considered to be one specific manifestation of evolution, just like stock market movements or changes in immune systems (Rosenbach 2008: 25). This is because languages display the following features, characteristic of evolutionary systems.

First, languages are made up of constituents that are transmitted/ replicated. Potential examples of such replicating units are words, but also morphemes or, most relevantly for this book, constructions such as the DOC or the *to*-PRC. Second, variation is constantly produced in the population of linguistic constituents, as the replication process can be (and frequently is) unfaithful (Dennett 1995: 343). That is, copying mistakes can occur in each replication event. We can see such emergent variation e.g. in the reanalysis of a prepositional goal-construction to encode a recipient-meaning. This new prepositional recipient-construction (the *to*-PRC) counts as a variant of the DOC, and therefore enters into competition with it. Finally, the transmission/replication is differential – meaning that not all variants replicate equally well – and is subject to constraints that can be construed as environmental (Ritt 1995: 54; Croft 2000: 23, 2006b: 94, 2008: 221; Rosenbach 2008: 26). These constraints include physiologically grounded factors, i.e. cognitive or physiological biases, factors grounded in the system of co-constituents, and factors grounded in socio-historically contingent factors, such as prestige or identity (Ritt 2004: 221–229). Languages will then consist of those patterns which have replicated successfully under these locally given constraints. That is, replicators which are better adapted to these different types of factors will be more successful than other variants and have the potential to oust them. An alternative scenario to loss of one variant in favour of the other is the development of a cooperative relationship in which both variants construct their own (e.g. functional or social) niches; they adapt to each other in a mutually beneficial way (e.g. Petré 2014). Although social factors undoubtedly play an important role in language change, the present book will concentrate heavily on the first two types of factors, namely physiologically or systemically grounded pressures. As to cognitive-physiological factors, this for me includes issues such as expressivity or disambiguation power of linguistic constituents, as well as economy in production. For example, the DOC is clearly shorter; it is thus arguably more economical than its *to*-paraphrase, which in turn can be thought of as more distinctive. Intra-systemic factors may by contrast be responsible for the greater success of an inflection-less DOC in a language where morphological case marking is not very salient and indicative of semantic role any more.

In sum, languages meet the criteria of consisting of replicating units, of showing continuous and abundant variation at all times, and of displaying signs of differential replication under specific linguistic and extra-linguistic constraints (Dennett 1995: 343; Lass 1980; Rosenbach 2008). They can therefore be taken to represent historical systems of constituents that need to be adapted to constraints on their transmission. This means that they can or indeed must be studied in terms of evolutionary theory. That this should be the case is increasingly recognised in linguistic research, and evolutionary approaches to language and language change have begun to be applied more widely also in more traditional historical linguistic accounts (Ritt 2004; Petré 2014; van de Velde 2014; Kaźmierski 2015; among others). Taking an evolutionary perspective also in this book seems highly appealing for several reasons, including the fact that it allows us to address questions concerning language change in general, and particular changes in the history of a language, in a systematic and more enlightening way. By shifting away the focus from the speaker as an active, rational and intentional agent in language use and change, and instead taking the 'perspective' of the replicating patterns (so to speak), applying an evolutionary approach also forces us to take a more analytic, and less hermeneutic approach. Thus, evolutionary linguistics provides a better explanatory basis for linguistic investigations. Moreover, adopting an evolutionary framework, its terminology and conceptual inventory as well as methodology allows for interdisciplinary investigations, which can certainly yield interesting insights. – This is illustrated by means of an evolutionary game theoretic account here.

Importantly, the evolutionary approach also appears to be (intra- disciplinarily) perfectly compatible with a variety of more specific theoretical linguistic frameworks, especially cognitive, usage-based theories of language such as construction grammar (cf. e.g. Hurford 2012b: 176; Arbib 2012: x; Croft 2013a: 40). In the present work, I investigate to what extent this holds true, where potential problems might arise, and which specific assumptions a joint framework entails. The proposed framework of evolutionary construction grammar is then used to describe, analyse and explain the history of the Present Day English dative alternation.

1.3 Aims and main arguments

There are two major goals to this book: Its first central aim is to investigate the diachronic development of various types of ditransitive constructions in English, and to thereby help to explain the synchronic phenomenon of the dative alternation. This also involves exploring the rise of certain idiosyncratic features of these patterns, especially the members of the alternation, in PDE. The book strives to provide a sounder empirical basis for many assumptions in previous literature, which have so far not been adequately tested against language data.

The gist of the proposal put forward for the development of the dative alternation is that it constitutes a story of constructional innovation, competition and cooperation, as well as co-evolution. I expect that the discussion and analysis of the history of the dative alternation in such terms, i.e. conceptualising the history of the patterns involved as one of constructionalisation, competition, cooperation and co-evolution, will be highly fruitful in explaining the synchronic features of the constructions and the relationship between them. As to the first of these, I show that the diachrony of the dative alternation can be explained as a sequence of changes to a constructional network. Prominent changes here include the emergence of new constructions on different levels of schematicity or abstractness – either through mergers or splits of other constructions. Most importantly, such processes can be observed in the development of a range of prepositional ditransitive patterns out of older, more adjunctival (spatial) prepositional constructions (e.g. a *to*-GOAL construction changing into a *to*-RECIPIENT construction). Other cases are the establishment of an abstract, underspecified, alternation-based generalisation over the DOC and the *to*-PRC (see Cappelle 2006; Perek 2012, 2015).

The second crucial concept I focus on is competition, most significantly competition between variants in the constructional network, i.e. paradigmatic choices in language systems. Constructional competition presupposes variation, typically produced by constructional innovation. For instance, once the new 'ditransitive' prepositional patterns constructionalised and became viable alternatives to the resident nominal ditransitive constructions, and once (horizontal) links between the constructional variants developed, they entered into competition with each other. This process is taken to operate in a bottom-up manner, meaning that competition first arises on lower levels of the network, between lexically filled, verb-specific constructions. Over time, however, the competition can rise to higher, more schematic levels.

Competition is resolved in two major ways: Either, one variant wins out, while the other is lost, or, a state of co-existence and cooperation is reached. The former scenario holds for the development of a range of ditransitive verbs like the English dispossession verbs. Originally found in both the DOC and various PRCs, they are largely restricted to the prepositional variant in PDE (**John stole Mary a book* vs. *John stole a book from Mary*). In contrast, stable cooperation has emerged in the development of the PDE dative alternation proper. While the DOC (with a prototypical meaning of transfer) and the *to*-PRC competed against each other for some time, they eventually came to form a cooperative, mutually beneficial relationship; in this, the two constructions stabilise each other and profit from being associated. Evidence that the relationship between the variants is profitable for both rather than antagonistic comes from productivity and priming experiments. For example, Perek (2015) has demonstrated that the alternation is productive, with the use of a novel verb with one variant being facilitated by its use in the other. Positive priming effects between the two variants of the dative alternation have been confirmed by e.g. Goldwater et al. (2011). Moreover, the development of a complementary distribution of object orders according to discourse-pragmatic factors such as givenness or definiteness can be interpreted as a sign of constructional cooperation in the sense of a 'division of labour' (complementary niche construction).

One of the central arguments of the proposed book is thus that the emergence of the dative alternation constitutes a case of constructional competition resulting in constructional cooperation or symbiosis. Furthermore, and highly importantly so, the results of the evolutionary game theoretic account described below suggest that the dative alternation can be viewed as an evolutionary effect of or an adaptive response to changes in the environment of the constructions, i.e. changes in parameters like case marking prominence and word order flexibility.

Finally, the specific formal and functional features of the members of the alternation and their (further) development over time are taken to constitute instances of constructional co-evolution and mutual adaptation between the constructions involved. This means that the ditransitive allostructions, the DOC and the *to*-PRC, have come to stand in a mutually adaptive relationship to each other, in which changes in one pattern will inevitably be followed by changes in the other. It also entails that there is typically no simple one-directional causal influence of one discrete, large-scale change on another, but that causal effects are two-way, step-wise, and gradual developments, with many small adaptations on both sides. Such a mutually adaptive development can be seen in regard to the semantics of the DOC, as well as in respect to clause-level word order, with the constructions increasingly aligning with each other, and becoming formally and functionally more similar over time (cf. also the concept of 'attraction' in De Smet et al. 2018). On the other hand, co-evolutionary effects can appear in form of 'differentiation' processes, meaning that co-evolving constructions standing in an alternation relationship often diverge formally and/or functionally, and create their own respective niches. We can observe this in the complementary distribution of DOC and *to*-PRC according to discourse- functional factors in PDE, reflected in their word order preferences.

With regard to theory, the volume combines and integrates two frameworks that have gained wide currency in the study of language, cognition and culture, namely construction grammar and evolutionary linguistics. While the former is applied for description and analysis, the latter is mainly employed for its explanatory potential. The specific constructionist approach chosen here is usage-based, cognitive (diachronic) construction grammar as outlined above. This framework sees language as fundamentally shaped by language use in a bottom-up way; therefore, data-driven methods and frequency effects play a central role. Evolutionary linguistics, on the other hand, views language as a particular type of evolutionary system. Like evolutionary systems in general, it consists of populations of replicating units, shows continuous and abundant variation at all times, and exhibits signs of differential replication under linguistic and extra-linguistic constraints. Since evolutionary change always means change in variant frequency, evolutionary theory represents an especially suitable meta-framework for analyses in terms of construction grammar, where frequency is of similar importance. Furthermore, the conceptualisation of lexico-grammatical knowledge in terms of constructional networks facilitates the identification of constituents that count as variants of one another and that may therefore be in evolutionary competition for specific slots in a network. The crucial role that clearly defined form-meaning pairings (i.e. constructions) play in construction grammar makes the framework very compatible with evolutionary thinking, in which the notion of transmittable units, or 'replicators' is of foremost importance. A distinct benefit of taking an evolutionary perspective, on the other hand, is that it invites and aids the adoption of methodologies developed for the study of evolution in other domains. A specific method employed in this book is evolutionary game theory. The monograph hence outlines 'Evolutionary construction grammar' as a suitable framework for the study of language variation and change, demonstrates its potential, and suggests directions for its further development (see Croft 2000; Petré 2014, among others, for comparable approaches).

The chief contribution of the book is that it provides further insights into the specifics of the PDE dative alternation based on a rigorous quantitative corpus investigation in combination with other methods. It offers a plausible and encompassing scenario for this case of persisting variation. The book presents an original and new account of the history of this phenomenon in that it joins evolutionary and constructionist perspectives on language change and uses two different methodologies to test its assumptions. However, the proposals made in the book are assumed to not only hold for this case of stable linguistic variation, but to be of general interest to historical linguistic research into the conditions under which variation in the linguistic system is maintained instead of reduced. That is, the dative alternation is considered as representative of a general type, and the book thus addresses a problem of wider relevance to the study of variation and change.

1.4 Data and methodology

The project primarily employs two methods, which are explained in detail in the relevant chapters. The main part of the book reports on an empirical investigation of ditransitives in the *Penn-Helsinki Parsed Corpus of Middle English, 2nd edition* (PPCME2). This database is approximately 1 million words large, and to date the most representative and best-prepared corpus for the period.[25] The principal reason for focussing on Middle English data is that the emergence of the dative alternation and the major changes influencing its members are locat-

25 Corpus linguistics is understood here as a method (of both data collection and data analysis) rather than a theory in its own right, and that the corpus data is used for the assessment, validation, refutation or refinement of particular hypotheses or theories (e.g. McEnery and Hardie 2012: 6). The study thus takes a corpus-based rather than a corpus-driven approach.

ed primarily in this period. However, the discussion of the results evidently also comprises extant research on other stages.

The quantitative study includes double object constructions on the one hand, and prepositional patterns (involving all possible types of prepositions marking either of the objects) on the other hand; furthermore, alternative possessive patterns are taken into account. It should be noted that clausal objects, as well as passive ditransitive constructions were excluded from the data for reasons of practicability and difficulties in operationalising the corpus searches. Especially the issue of passives is highly important for the present book, among other things for questions of word order fixation as well as the emergence of a prototypical subject/object slot in the diachrony of English. However, the history of passives in English is too big an issue to be dealt with in the scope of this book in any meaningful way, and the instances were therefore dismissed altogether. All active tokens including non-clausal NP or PP-objects were classified according to a number of extra-linguistic and language-internal criteria, and statistically analysed by means of logistic regression models (e.g. Levshina 2015) as well as the tool of 'dinstictive collexeme analysis', used to detect distributional preferences in the data (Gries and Stefanowitsch 2004).

Corpus data can elucidate only some aspects of the highly complex developments the project deals with. Therefore, the analytic tool of evolutionary game theory (EGT) is employed to complement the insights gained from the corpus study (see Hofbauer and Sigmund 1998, 2003; Nowak and Krakauer 1999; Nowak 2000, 2006; Jäger 2004, 2007; Benz, Jäger, and van Rooij 2006; Deo 2015, among others). In the game theoretical model, I test the hypothesis that under universal pragmatic constraints such as end-focus, changing environmental conditions can result in the emergence of a system in which a semantic role is either expressed by an NP or a PP (e.g. Steels 2012c). Such conditions may be a decrease in salience of case inflections or a decrease in word order freedom. The combination of game theoretical modelling and more traditional corpus analysis is one of the major assets of the book and confirms that "methods that ha[ve] previously been tested and successfully applied in the natural sciences can enrich [...] the study of cultural language transmission and thereby increase our understanding of the historical development of specific languages" (Ritt and Baumann 2014).

1.5 Limitations

While my investigation can shed light on some issues that have so far been not been dealt with in sufficient detail, it is clear that there are also limitations to the study. On the one side, the discussion is entirely based on data from Middle English only, although the changes dealt with extend over a much larger time span from Old English (or even before) to Early/ Late Modern English and beyond. This issue can be resolved to a certain extent by drawing on data collected and analysed by other linguists (cf. above all Allen 1995 and De Cuypere 2010, 2013, 2015a, 2015c on Old English; Colleman and De Clerck 2011 or Wolk et al. 2013 on Late Modern English). Nevertheless, many suggestions and conclusions put forward will have to remain somewhat speculative; to further test these is left for future research. Focussing on Middle English is nevertheless valuable, as this period saw the greatest deal of change.

On the other side, sociolinguistic questions, including contact issues, are beyond the scope of the book. That is, the book does not address the impact of genre and regional variation on the data in any detail. This restriction is mainly due to the PPCME2's design, as certain dialects and genres are greatly overrepresented at the expense of others, but also reflects the 'bad data' problem inherent to historical linguistics in general (Labov 1994; Nevalainen 1999). This means that historical investigations typically suffer from limited numbers of texts being available and the fact that those available are typically written and of certain types only. However, conclusions can still be drawn from the data investigated here. Furthermore, the likely influence of language contact on the development of ditransitives in English is not explored. For example, it is often assumed that the income of French ditransitive verbs played a role in the rise of the *to*-PRC, since the recipient was typically marked by *à* in the donor language (19). Borrowed together with their French argument structure (or rather, in their construction), these verbs might have influenced the behaviour of the 'native' ditransitives and increased the frequency of PP-patterns (e.g. Ingham subm.; also Gerwin 2014: 41).

(19)	Jean	*donna*	le	livre$_{TH}$	**à**	**Marie**$_{REC}$
	John	gave	the	book	to	Mary
	'John gave the book to Mary'					

In addition to impact from French, Scandinavian is sometimes mentioned as an influencing factor in the development of ditransitives in English. This concerns above all the more general word order changes observable at the transition from Old to Middle English, and regional idiosyncrasies in object ordering (cf. e.g. Trips 2002; Gast 2007; Gerwin 2014). Although it is plausible that there was at least a reinforcing effect of incoming language structures, this is not part of the present book.

1.6 Structure of the book

The book is divided into three major parts. The first main part introduces some key issues in constructionist approaches to PDE ditransitives (chapter 2). It features a discussion of how argument structure in general, and the two constructions in question (DOC and *to*-PRC) are treated in this framework (section 2.1). Importantly, this chapter also outlines the constructionist approach to argument structure alternations the rest of the book is based on. Following Perek (2015), the dative alternation is not viewed as a mere epiphenomenon of a partial overlap in verbs instantiating the constructions, but receives an independent theoretical standing and is taken to be represented in the minds of speakers (section 2.2).

Chapter (3) starts by reviewing previous literature on the history of the dative alternation as well as the major changes which took place in the history of English and affected the constructions. Focussing first on the emergence of the dative alternation (3.1), it then proceeds to discussing – at least to some extent – the loss of case marking, the increasing fixation of word order (concerning both constituent order in the ditransitive clause and the order of objects), and changes in the semantics of the constructions involved (section 3.2). Finally, the chapter remarks on suggested correlations and causal effects between all of these changes (3.3). This overview of the state of research forms the basis of the empirical investigation presented in chapter (4) on 'Ditransitives in a corpus of Middle English'. After I briefly introduce the corpus used in the study and the methodology applied in extracting and analysing the data (4.1), I show and discuss the main results of the investigation (4.2). This chapter essentially lays the foundation for much of the argumentation put forward in the final discussion chapter.

Chapter (5) constitutes at the same time the second major part of the monograph, presenting the second framework and method employed in the study. It is primarily geared towards a readership interested in (but possibly as yet unfamiliar with) evolutionary linguistics. In section (5.1), I first introduce the framework, and briefly outline the history of the field. Afterwards, the key points and main questions in approaching language from this perspective, i.e. in viewing language as a cultural evolutionary system, are dealt with. Section (5.2) describes *Evolutionary Game Theory* (EGT) and presents the results of an application of this method to the history of the dative alternation. Although the findings gained from this approach are also important for the major claims made in the book, a further motivation for including it is to show that introducing innovative methods from other disciplines to linguistics can yield interesting insights.

The third part includes the central discussion chapters of the book, featuring both an overview of the new fused theoretical framework of 'evolutionary construction grammar' and its main tenets, and an account of the history of the dative alternation approached from this perspective. Chapter (6) first deals with the key questions that arise in attempting to combine the two approaches and offers possible solutions to these issues, before assessing the central concepts of constructional innovation, competition, cooperation, and co-evolution. It also briefly comments on the distinction between language strategies and language systems as presented e.g. in Steels (2011b) and closes by providing the basic set of principles of evolutionary construction grammar to be applied in the remainder of the book. In chapter (7), the history of the dative alternation in English is discussed from an evolutionary construction grammar perspective, with a focus on the four processes just mentioned. In section (7.1), I argue that the emergence of the dative alternation first involved constructional changes in adjunctival prepositional constructions, leading to the establishment of new prepositional object constructions, where the preposition marks an animate recipient-like participant rather than an inanimate location (e.g. goal or source). These new constructions then enter competition with the resident DOC(s). The competition is eventually resolved in different ways: Most strikingly, DOC uses of some verb classes, such as dispossession verbs, are ousted in favour of the corresponding prepositional uses. However, in other cases, e.g. with transfer- and transfer-related verbs, the construction types reach a state of co-existence in which they cooperate rather than compete with each other. Section (7.2) follows this line of argumentation but adds the concept of co-evolution – many of the formal and functional changes observed in the constructions can be explained as adaptive responses to changes in the other member. Such co-evolutionary effects include, on the one hand, differentiation processes, as in the movement towards a division of labour situation in settling on a complementary word order distribution, and a shared workload in respect to discourse-pragmatic factors such as givenness or newness. On the other hand, co-evolution can also be seen in semantic or syntactic alignment between the constructions, a phenomenon which has recently been dubbed 'constructional attraction' (De Smet et al. 2018). Section (7.3) comments on the issue of strategy selection vs. system selection in the case of the dative alternation, before the chapter is wrapped up by a summary of the proposed scenario for the development of ditransitive constructions (section 7.4).

Chapter (8) concludes the book, presenting first a short synopsis of its contents and its goals, followed by a summary of the main results and claims made. Furthermore, the chapter includes a brief remark on the theoretical implications of the book's arguments, and an outlook reviewing the study's limitations and suggestions for further research.

2 PDE ditransitives in usage-based construction grammar

Having briefly introduced the most basic tenets of the version of construction grammar I use in this book in (1.2.1) above, this chapter zooms in on construction grammar approaches to the specific topic at hand. It elaborates on how verbal argument structure, ditransitives and the DOC, as well as syntactic alternations such as the dative alternation, have been treated in constructionist accounts. The chapter starts with a discussion of the relationship between verbal and constructional meaning, giving special focus to Perek's (2015) theory of usage-based verb valency, and the lexical origin of constructional semantics (2.1.1). While this discussion is of course not restricted to the DOC but pertains to argument structure constructions in general (or even constructions in general), the DOC is used to illustrate the arguments made. In the subsequent section (2.1.2), varying constructionist approaches to the semantics of the PDE DOC, meaning the construction's prototypical and more peripheral sub-senses, are presented. In section (2.2), I review differing standpoints concerning argument structure alternations. This starts with views against independently represented alternations (2.2.1) and is followed by an introduction of pro-alternation approaches, most importantly Cappelle (2006) and Perek's (2012, 2015) 'allostruction/constructeme' model (2.2.2). The section also brings in the concept of 'alternation-based productivity'. Last, section (2.3) restates the most relevant points in taking a construction grammar approach to the dative alternation and its members in PDE.

2.1 Argument structure constructions (and the DOC)

The first part of this section on the one hand serves as a general (although of course not comprehensive) introduction to the main principles of construction grammar approaches to argument structure constructions, and to the DOC and the *to*-PRC in particular. This is certainly important for the present study, since it is concerned with the history of these patterns. On the other hand, the section advocates and further elaborates on usage-based construction grammar: Assuming linguistic representation to be essentially shaped by linguistic usage (and inversely, takes usage to directly reflect representation) is useful for historical linguistic investigations such as the present one, because the empirical focus in such studies is necessarily on the textual evidence that is available.

https://doi.org/10.1515/9783110633856-002

Taking a bottom-up approach, which views units identifiable in texts as indicative of cognitive patterns, is therefore clearly of advantage.

The second part concentrates more explicitly on the semantics of the double object construction in PDE, briefly dealing with the different sub-senses that have been proposed for the construction. The main aim of this section is to determine whether a basic meaning of 'transfer' is associated with the DOC, or whether its meaning is more diverse and idiosyncratic. Having a clear idea of what the semantics of the DOC in PDE entail is relevant for us insofar as changes to the meaning of the construction play a crucial role in the development of the dative alternation in the history of English and constitute one of the major foci of this study. The section closes by relating the issues under discussion in the two parts to each other. More precisely, I show that the semantics of the PDE DOC can be captured in a lexicality-schematicity hierarchical network as proposed by Croft (2003), representing both item-specific and more abstract knowledge.

2.1.1 Argument structure as a joint venture between individual verbs and constructions

In contemporary approaches to argument structure, the question continues to spark great interest of what precise role verbs play in determining how many (and which types of) arguments are realised. Essentially, there are two viewpoints on the issue, joined by an intermediate perspective (see the discussion in Perek 2015: 16). On the one side, there are so-called 'projectionist' or 'verb-centric' (non-constructionist) approaches, which emphasise the part of the verb, and consider the realisation of arguments to represent projections of the constraints of the lexical items (e.g. Gropen et al. 1989; Pinker 1989; Levin and Rappaport Hovav 1995, 2005, 2008).[26] Specifically, speakers are taken to store verbs with direct specifications as to the number, type, etc. of arguments they typically take. On the other side, we find more recent, constructionist, approaches which pay much attention to the contribution of schematic argument structure constructions, while the input of lexical verbs is restrained (Goldberg 1995). – This is not to say, of course, that verbs are irrelevant or dispensable on this viewpoint, it is only the precise extent of their semantic contribution that is

26 For an overview as well as critique of the main tenets of these approaches see Goldberg (1995: 9–23), Croft (2003: 50–53), as well as Perek (2015: Ch. 2.1.1); also Müller and Wechsler (2014) vs. Goldberg (2013, 2014); Boas (2014).

questioned. Finally, accounts such as Perek (2015), *inter alia*, constitute mixed approaches, since although many assumptions underlying it are explicitly in line with a constructionist framework, the need for richer lexical knowledge and a 'division of labour' relationship between verbs and constructions is highlighted (cf. also e.g. Herbst 2011). Such a usage-based constructionist perspective on argument structure furthermore points out the importance of lexical material in the emergence of constructional meaning, thus stressing the interrelatedness of both sides of the coin even more. As will become clear in this section, this book agrees with Perek (2015) in taking a usage-based, joint-venture approach to argument structure.

The central issue that lies at the heart of this debate is the fact that most verbs show the following characteristics: First, general patterns can be observed with similar verbs. There seems to be a systematic correlation between aspects of verbal semantics and syntactic behaviour. For example, as illustrated by the examples in (22), transitivity is typically associated with an agent affecting a patient/theme (e.g. Hopper and Thompson 1980: 251). However, the same verb can also appear in more than one pattern, evidenced by *bake* in the examples under [b] in (21)–(23), representing intransitive, transitive and ditransitive uses of the verb. These properties present a challenge for projectionist approaches as they cannot adequately capture the correspondences between different verbs and have to account for multiple argument patterns of one verb by assuming verbal polysemy.

(21) a. John *ran*
     b. John *baked*
(22) a. John *made* <u>a sandwich</u>
     b. John *baked* <u>a cake</u>
(23) a. John *gave* **Mary** <u>a book</u>
     b. John *baked* **Mary** <u>a cake</u>

The main tenet of constructionist approaches to argument structure now is that the patterns observed with verbs are not fully and exclusively determined by the verbs themselves. Instead, speakers store highly abstract, schematic argument structure constructions (featuring a more abstract category of 'VERB') in addition to patterns specific to individual, concrete verbs. On this perspective, 'skeletal syntactic constructions', which map a range of argument roles specified by an abstract event description onto morpho-syntactic form and functional categories, are recognised "as meaningful in their own right" (Goldberg 1995: 21). For instance, we can posit a schematic double object construction as shown in Fig. 2 – here, the roles of agent, recipient, and patient/theme in a scene of 'causing to receive' are linked to a verb denoting this broad meaning and the syntactic functions of subject and objects.

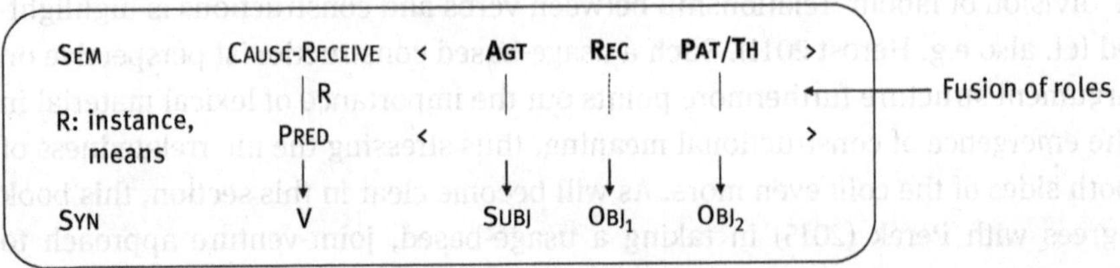

Fig. 2: The schematic double object construction (model adapted from Goldberg 1995: 50)

The schematic construction accordingly consists of an abstract predicate and particular argument roles and can also be represented as [[AGT *cause-receive* REC PAT/TH] / [SUBJ V OBJ1 OBJ2]]. By contrast, individual verbs are related to particular participant roles defined on the basis of their frame-semantic meaning. The latter type of roles is said to 'fuse' or integrate with the former "[i]f a verb is a member of a verb class that is conventionally associated with a construction" (Goldberg 1995: 50). The fusion of roles is determined by two principles: the semantic coherence principle as well as the correspondence principle. The former states that roles need to be semantically compatible in order to be fused (Goldberg 1995: 50). In more general terms, this means that the semantic frame that is associated with a verb needs to be congruent with the meaning of the abstract construction (cf. also Perek 2015: 24). The correspondence principle, on the other hand, is concerned with profiling of arguments in that lexical profiling and expression of a participant role necessarily entails fusion with a profiled argument/ semantic role that is specified by the construction (Goldberg 1995: 50).[27] If both principles are fulfilled, and there is perfect agreement between the constructional and verbal roles, we can speak of 'inherent compatibility' (Perek 2015: 28). In the case of the DOC, both semantic compatibility and correspondence of profiled roles are straightforwardly given with verbs that express 'giving' events, such as *give* or *hand*. This is because the meaning of the construction 'X causes Y to receive Z' is comprised (or elaborated) by the verbal semantics. Furthermore, as indicated in Fig. 3, there is a one-to-one correspondence between the profiled semantic roles of the construction (agent, re-

27 'Profiled' here refers to argument roles being highly prominent and always accessed (Goldberg 1995: 44; also Langacker 1987).

cipient, patient) and the participant roles associated with the verb (hander, handee, handed), which are then mapped onto the respective syntactic positions in a clause (subject, objects).

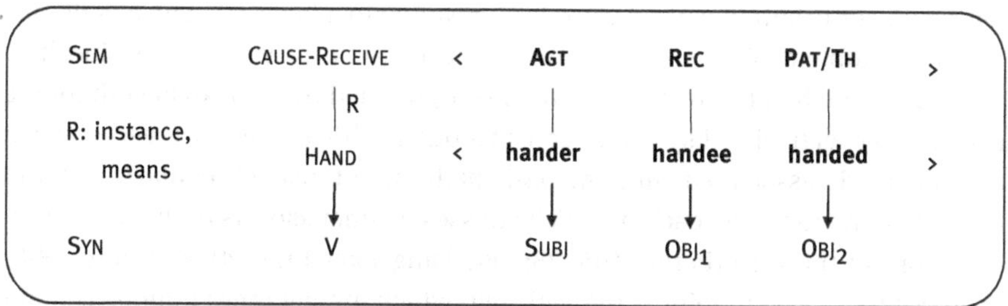

Fig. 3: Composite fused structure of the DOC and the verb *hand* (adapted from Goldberg 1995: 51)

As Perek (2015: 25) points out, the "stipulation that the participant roles of the verb must be *construed as*, though not necessarily *be*, instances of the argument roles of the construction, allows for some flexibility in determining semantic compatibility" [original italics]. Such imposed construals are, for example, responsible for the interpretation of goals as recipient arguments in clauses like *Joe sent Chicago a letter*. Similarly, the appearance of verbs of future transfer or communication in the DOC (cf. also section 2.1.2) can be explained as metaphorical extensions or mediations of verbal meaning, with the communicated messages being construed as transferred objects. Other issues that can occur in the fusion of verbal and constructional roles are mismatches in profiling or number of roles (as well as other violations of constructional constraints). In these cases, the construction may contribute 'unusual' or normally absent meaning aspects to a clause; it thereby semantically enriches it. As to the first, consider the example of *mail*, which involves two lexically profiled participant roles ('mailer' and 'mailed'), and an unprofiled third role of 'mailee'. The DOC, by contrast, does not show any asymmetry in profiling, as all argument roles are of equal salience. Therefore, the mailee is elevated to profiled status in a composite fused structure of DOC and verb. In other instances, a whole new meaning component might be added to a verb's meaning: For instance, the roles of 'kicker' and 'kicked' (or 'baker' and 'baked') are regularly associated with the semantics of the verbs *kick* (or *bake*). However, the additional recipient argument in sentences like *John kicked Mary the ball*, is not linked to an independently existing participant role, but is provided by the construction itself (Goldberg 1995: 52–

56; Croft 2003: 50–53; Boas 2013: 236–237). This phenomenon is often referred to as constructional 'coercion' (Michaelis 2005; Lauwers and Willems 2011).

Standard construction grammar thus views argument structure as a joint venture between individual, concrete verbs and abstract verbal constructions, with both contributing certain aspects of meaning to a licensed clause. Still, one intrinsic problem of this perspective is the possible ways to determine how many and which participant roles are in fact provided by the lexical verb (or the schema, respectively). Especially conspicuous in this context are verbs which are not clearly associated with one basic pattern, but instead regularly occur in different constructions, each of which stresses distinct aspects of the 'conceptual import' of the verb (Perek 2015: 28; also Langacker 1987, 2008; Talmy 2000; Croft 2012). A case in point is the verb *sell*, which among other options can appear with both mono-transitive and ditransitive (DOC) syntax. These uses differ in terms of profiling. In the former, only the onset of the transfer (*John sold a book*) is profiled, while the latter profiles the entire event of 'seller causes buyer to receive goods' (e.g. *John sold Mary a book*). Since both of these patterns are very frequent, two ways of conceiving of the basic valency of the verb are possible. On the one side, it can be taken as a two-participant verb, with the DOC providing the additional component of recipient and indirect object argument in a three-participant construal. On the other side, we could argue that it inherently specifies three participants. In the latter scenario, coercing the verb into a mono-transitive construction would involve the subtraction of an argument rather than adding meaning facets, which intuitively strikes one as awkward. Also, it seems that most speakers rarely express all possible participant roles associated with the verbs (Perek 2015: 30–31, drawing on Langacker 2008). Therefore, assuming that the default situation is one of profiling the whole semantic frame, i.e. all roles, even though they will not be evoked in a majority of cases, seems counter-intuitive, and not too conducive to cognitive effectiveness.

In general, when taking into account the role of different construals of an event, the postulation of a single verb sense with much information contributed by the schematic construction is difficult to maintain (Perek 2015: 33; also Langacker 2009). This is further supported by the fact that many verbs show a considerable degree of idiosyncratic behaviour, which can hardly be captured by highly abstract constructions. This indicates that a large amount of item-specific knowledge needs to be stored alongside the schematic argument structure constructions (cf. Perek 2015: 33–37; Faulhaber 2011; Herbst 2011; *inter alia*).[28]

28 Compare e.g. the unacceptable (or at least unusual) use of *donate* or *whisper* in the DOC, as discussed in section (2.1.2).

Based on these issues, Perek puts forward a usage-based account of argument structure, with the main tenet that a verb is not restricted to one precise construal of its semantic frame but can be conventionally associated with a variety of them. This means that a verb can have more than one lexical entry with corresponding participant roles (Perek 2015: 43). However, and crucially for his approach, new entries are not established each time a verb is used in an innovative pattern, but everything is dependent on frequent usage. The number of entries for a lexical item therefore results from usage rather than being entirely arbitrary (Perek 2015: 43).[29] This perspective reduces the role of abstract constructions and foregrounds the part played by individual verbs to a higher extent than other constructionist accounts. Nevertheless, the fundamental principles of construction grammar are maintained. Incidentally, much of this discussion is reminiscent of and also implicitly or explicitly present in a number of constructionist approaches, namely those which rely on the postulation of a schematicity cline or hierarchy, able to capture both item-specific knowledge and generalisations (Croft 2003; Goldberg 2006; Boas 2008). I discuss the specific assumptions that these approaches make in the following section.

The usage-based approach to the relationship between lexical verbs and abstract constructions is summed up nicely by Diessel (2015: 314) as follows:

> One can think of the relationship between lexemes and constructions as part of a probabilistic network shaped by language use. On this account, verbs (and other lexemes) and constructions are related to each other by connections with graded activation values that are determined by the combined effect of general semantic criteria and the language users' experience with particular lexical expressions and constructions.[30]

As already discussed in the introduction, usage-based constructionist approaches furthermore view lexical material as essential in the emergence of constructional meaning, suggesting that speakers' experiences with concrete, 'fully filled' patterns provide the fundamental basis for linguistic structure (Diessel 2015: 312). The close relationship between the meaning of an argument structure construction and its usage is evidenced by several issues, including

---

29 The main benefit of Perek's account (apart from the elaboration and refinement of a constructionist view on argument structure) is that he takes great care to ground his assumptions in empirical evidence. Conducting reaction time experiments coupled with corpus analyses, he tests the hypothesis that the cognitive status of valency patterns (that is, the frame of participant roles associated with a certain verb) is related to frequency of occurrence and finds that this indeed seems to be the case.

30 See also Croft (2003: 65): "Speakers are not exposed to verbs in isolation, nor are they exposed to schematic argument structure constructions without verbs in them".

distributional as well as acquisition biases. For example, it has been noted that constructions are typically associated with specific (frequent) words or even one single verb whose semantics very closely match the meaning of the schematic construction (Diessel 2015: 312; Perek 2015: 80; also Rostila 2007). Moreover, constructions tend to be used predominantly with verbs that are semantically compatible or at least connected in meaning to the construction as a whole. This is of course not accidental. Rather, it is taken to support the assumption that the meaning of the argument structure construction is in fact abstracted from the verbs instantiating it.

Empirical evidence for these postulations comes from corpus studies, more precisely from collostructional analyses as introduced by Stefanowitsch and Gries (2003), and as also included in this book. As Stefanowitsch and Gries point out, such analyses can be used to "determin[e] the degree to which particular slots in a grammatical structure prefer, or are restricted to, a particular set or semantic class of lexical items" (2003: 211). Taking collostruction strength as pointing towards the extent of semantic compatibility of a verb with a construction, they find that the verb most strongly attracted to the DOC in the ICE-GB corpus is, as expected, *give*. This verb can thus be considered a good prototype of verbs with the same structure (Stefanowitsch 2006, 2013). Further verbs clearly associated with the DOC in Stefanowitsch and Gries' (2003) as well as Stefanowitsch' (2006) data include communication verbs such as *tell*, *ask* or *show* as well as other verbs of transfer (concrete transfer in the case of *send*, and intended/future transfer in *offer*). This substantiates the often-found proposal that the meaning of the DOC is one of 'transfer' (see section 2.1.2 below; also e.g. Goldberg 2013: 19, and many others). What is also interesting is that those collexemes that are strongly repelled by the DOC despite occasionally being used in it (such as *make*, *keep*, *do*, or *have*) evidently do not inherently express transfer. Most of them are restricted to fixed phrases (*do someone a favour*). Accordingly, the probability of them strongly determining the constructional semantics is relatively low (Stefanowitsch 2013: 294). However, the fact that verbs are capable of appearing in constructions that they are not typically associated with, does suggest that verbs and constructions are at least partly independent of one another (Stefanowitsch 2013: 5; cf. also Stefanowitsch 2006: 65).[31]

The idea that there are distributional biases in the use of constructions towards certain, semantically highly compatible, verbs also finds corroboration in

31 As will be discussed in section (2.1.2), repelled items do include semantically compatible verbs such as *say* as well. The non-occurrence in or at least strong resistance to the DOC of such items requires explanation.

studies on language acquisition. For instance, Goldberg (2006: 92) states that "[t]he dominance of a single verb in the construction facilitates the association of the meaning of the verb in the construction with the construction itself, allowing learners to get a 'fix' on the construction's meaning". As to the DOC, Goldberg, Casenhiser, and Sethuraman (2004: 298) find that the most frequent verb in this construction in a corpus of child-directed speech is again *give* (accounting for about 20% of all DOC tokens). Tests on the cue validity of the DOC as a predictor of transfer meaning further substantiate the assumption that constructional meaning is derived from the semantics of the verbs that typically appear in this construction. These verbs are consequently also essential in the acquisition of constructional meaning (Goldberg 2006: 109–111).[32] Such effects are not limited to child language acquisition but are found in second language acquisition and adult speech in general as well: Perek and Lemmens (2010), among others, show that up to 50% of DOC tokens in the ICE-GB corpus in fact feature *give*. This corresponds to Stefanowitsch and Gries' (2003) results.[33] It is then assumed that from such highly-frequent, prototypical instances, speakers abstract more general constructions at various levels of schematicity. These may link to a number of semantically highly compatible, but also to less compatible verbs. The abstractions are stored and processed together with more substantive exemplars, rather than replacing them (Stefanowitsch 2013: 9; Perek 2015: 111; *inter alia*).

In the following section, the semantics of the DOC are dealt with in still more detail, including a brief review of idiosyncratic or unusual DOC uses. This links the preceding discussion to Croft's (2003) proposal of verb-specific, verb-class-specific and abstract constructions in the case of the DOC.

2.1.2 Determining and modelling the semantics of the DOC

The precise semantics of the PDE DOC have received considerable attention in both non-constructionist and constructionist approaches. Within the latter, probably the best-known account is Goldberg (1995). In her view, the English DOC constitutes a prime example of constructional polysemy, meaning that

32 See Casenhiser and Goldberg (2005) and Boyd, Gottschalk, and Goldberg (2009) for similar studies.

33 Cf. also Tomasello's 'verb island hypothesis', stating that a child starts out with item-specific knowledge, and only gradually abstract over similar instances (e.g. Tomasello 1992).

"the same form is paired with different but related senses" (Goldberg 1995: 33).[34] These different senses vary in degrees of prototypicality: The central sense is thought to be one of 'an agent volitionally and successfully causes a willing, animate recipient to receive an object'. In accordance also with the discussion above, *give* is the verb most prototypically associated with the DOC. This is because its semantics correspond most closely to this basic meaning. Apart from verbs which inherently denote acts of giving, the central sense of 'successful transfer' also includes verbs of ballistic motion (*throw, kick*) and verbs of deictically specified direction (e.g. *bring, send*). Drawing on previous work on ditransitives such as Green (1974), Gropen et al. (1989), Pinker (1989), and Levin (1993), Goldberg (1995: 75) proposes the following additional sub-senses of the DOC. A further, sixth sense is added in Goldberg (2002: 333):[35]

i. Conditions of satisfaction imply 'X causes Y to receive Z' (e.g. *promise, owe*)
ii. 'X enables Y to receive Z' (e.g. *permit, allow*)
iii. 'X causes Y not to receive Z' (e.g. *refuse, deny*)
iv. 'X intends to cause Y to receive Z' (verbs of creation or obtaining, e.g. *bake, get*)
v. 'X acts to cause Y to receive Z' (verbs of future giving, e.g. *leave, bequeath*)
vi. 'X causes Y to lose Z' (e.g. *cost*)

All of these senses are linked to the central sense by so-called 'polysemy links', specifying the kind of semantic relation between them. Several other uses of the DOC relate to the central sense via metaphorical extension links, which define the nature of the metaphorical mapping between two constructions. That is, expressions such as *John gave Mary a kiss* or *John told Mary the news* constitute extensions from the central sense, the source domain (Goldberg 1995: 33, 75–77, 141–151). For example, the first of these is licensed by the metaphor 'actions that are intentionally directed at another person are entities transferred to the per-

34 The notion of 'constructional polysemy' is not to be confused with 'verbal polysemy' in the sense of one verb having several lexical entries, as proposed in projectionist accounts (see section 2.1.1).

35 Further Wierzbicka (1988: 359–387); Hunston and Francis (2000). As Colleman and De Clerck (2011: 190) remark, "the majority of in-depth semantic analyses of the present-day DOC include a more or less fine-grained overview of double object verb classes as a crucial part of the overall analysis, regardless of their exact theoretical orientation". This means that the assumption of an inventory of verb-classes associated with the DOC is not restricted to constructionist thinking but has been recognised for quite some time.

son' (Goldberg 1995: 149). The latter, by contrast, is an instance of the 'conduit metaphor', which understands communicated messages as travelling towards and being 'received' by the listener (Reddy 1979). Similarly, *John showing Mary a picture* can be conceptualised as a perception moving towards the perceiving person (Goldberg 1995: 148). Cases that violate certain constraints of the DOC, namely that the agent be volitional, and the recipient be animate (as in e.g. *John gave Mary the flue* or *The music lent the party a festive air*), can be explained as instantiating metaphorical extensions of 'causal events are transferred entities'. The last instance furthermore illustrates coercion of inanimate elements into the construction (Goldberg 1995: 143–148). Although such coercions are certainly possible (and potentially also frequent), cases like these are not covered in this book; this is mainly due to issues of feasibility in the empirical study.

Colleman and De Clerck (2008) follow Geeraerts' (1998) analysis of the Dutch DOC as involving semantic extensions from a source meaning of 'beneficial transfer of a material entity from an agent to an active recipient'. This happens along various dimensions like direction, effect of the transfer on the animate participants (beneficial, maleficial, neutral) as well as nature of the transferred entity and ensuing possessional relation (concrete, abstract, communicative, or else).[36] Furthermore, they provide an elaborate account of how the seemingly idiosyncratic DOC verbs *forgive*, *envy* and *(not) begrudge* are linked to the construction's semantics (cf. also Colleman 2006). In contrast to Goldberg (1995: 131–132), who argues that the use of these verbs in the DOC is due to etymological reasons (with both verbs originally meaning 'give'),[37] the authors claim that their use is motivated by several shifts (on more than one semantic dimension). These include:

> (i) a metaphorical extension from **material** to **abstract** transfers with (ii) a shift in direction from a transfer **towards** the indirect object to a transfer **away from** the indirect object and/or (iii) an extension from the **actual causation** of a possessional transfer to an **attitude** towards such a transfer [original boldface]. (Colleman and De Clerck 2008: 202)

---

36 Importantly, Geeraerts (1998) "advocates a representation with semantic extensions along various dimensions, each of which corresponds to a particular component of the construction's semantic core" rather than Goldberg's "radial set representation with a basic sense and a number of individual additional senses which are directly linked to this basic sense" (Colleman and De Clerck 2008: 201).

37 While *forgive* earlier meant 'to give, to grant', *envy* denoted 'to give grudgingly' or 'refuse to give' (cf. OED, s.v. *forgive/envy*; Goldberg 1995: 132). It should be noted, however, that this sense of *envy* is in fact attested only rather late.

A similar explanation is used to account for the continuing appearance of verbs of dispossession such as *cost* in the DOC (24). This occurrence implies that John caused Mary to LOSE rather than receive a job. A possessive relationship is not established but cancelled by the event. Colleman and De Clerck (2008: 204–206) point out that the DOC use is untypical for verbs of dispossession insofar as the subject is not volitional and agentive and does not necessarily come to actually possess the theme. Nevertheless, it is clearly dispossessive in that the animate object is caused to lose something (cf. Colleman and De Clerck 2009: 34; also Pinker 1989: 111; Goldberg 2002).

(24) John *cost* **Mary** <u>her job</u>

This sense could be considered as entirely idiosyncratic due to its great semantic distance to the central sense of transfer. However, it is to some extent expectable that a construction evoking frames of giving (or blocked giving as in the case of *deny*) may encode antonymic relations as well (Colleman and De Clerck 2008: 204–205).[38] The use of *cost* is accordingly analysed as an extension of the basic sense of the construction along the dimension of directionality. Incidentally, *forgive* similarly involves the 'taking away' of an entity, since being forgiven can be construed as losing the burden of negative actions etc. one has to carry. 'Verbs of communicated reverse transfer' such as *ask* in patterns like *John asked Mary the time/ a favour*, which express an inquiry or requirement towards the REC-argument pose a related issue (Colleman and De Clerck 2008: 196–198, 204–205, 2009: 34–36; cf. also Goldsmith 1980: 439; Goldberg 1995: 131–132).

Uses of this kind are clearly part of the semantic range of the DOC in (at least written formal British) English. Still, it should be noted that there is a striking difference in productivity and position in the semantic network of the DOC between such verbs and classes such as *giving*-verbs (Colleman and De Clerck 2008: 210; Mukherjee 2005). While the latter show a tight connection to the construction's core meaning – as demonstrated by e.g. Stefanowitsch and Gries' (2003) collostructional analysis – attitudinal verbs like *forgive* or *envy* are undoubtedly in the periphery of the network. Hence, they also have a higher prob-

38 See also Goldberg's (2002: 333) claim that "a concept and its antonym typically serve as strong associates for one another in psycholinguistic studies". Note that the use of *cost* in the DOC could also be motivated by a metaphorical interpretation of the event as 'X causes Y to receive the cost of Z'; cf. also e.g. *to charge so. an amount of money* as 'transferring so. the obligation to pay an amount of money'.

ability to be affected by change.[39] Apart from divergences in frequency, less prototypical verb classes also differ noticeably from more basic uses when it comes to productivity. DOC verb classes with low type frequency such as 'verbs of blocked transfer' (*deny, refuse*; 25a), attitudinal verbs (*forgive, envy, be-grudge*), or dispossession verbs (*cost, fine, charge,...?*; 25b), are markedly less productive than verb classes more closely associated with the basic sense of transfer (or are indeed unproductive).[40] This in line with Goldberg's (1995: 136) claim that a subclass that has a very low number of members (verb types) will be unproductive because there are too few instances to form a 'similarity class' (further Barðdal 2008, 2009 on the role of type frequency for productivity).

(25) a. Sally *refused/denied/*prevented/*disallowed/*forbade* **him** a kiss (Goldberg 1995: 130)
b. Sally *cost/ fined/ charged/ ?lost/ *robbed/ *stole/ *cheated/ *stripped/ *deprived* **him** £5

A clear example of a highly productive class, by contrast, is the DOC sub-class of 'communicated transfer' or 'verbs of communication'. New lexical items emerging e.g. due to technological advances such as *to fax, e-mail, text, skype, whatsapp* or *snapchat* readily assume DOC syntax (26a-c; also De Clerck et al. 2011; De Clerck, Delorge, and Simon-Vandenbergen 2011).[41]

(26) a. I *WhatsApped* **him** the wee 'no phones' image (twitter.com; via Googlesearch)
b. she had *Snapchatted* **him** the naked selfie (viraltalktime.com; via Googlesearch)

39 Interestingly enough, privative *cost* is among the ten verbs most strongly attracted to the DOC in Stefanowitsch' (2006) analysis, with approximately 35% of a total of 65 tokens of the verb in the corpus (ICE-GB) appearing in the DOC. Even though this might be taken to point to a more central status of *cost* than expected, its frequency in the DOC is still significantly lower than that of other verbs, though (e.g. *give*: 560 DOC tokens vs. *cost*: 23 DOC tokens, Stefanowitsch 2006: 64).

40 According to Barðdal's (2008) approach to productivity, DOC uses of verbs of refusal should in fact be semi-productive, since they show low type frequency but high semantic coherence (= low schematicity). However, this does not seem to apply in this case.

41 A much-discussed issue in this context is a number of dis-preferences of the DOC concerning a range of verbs such as *donate*. These verbs, despite being semantically compatible with the construction, and part of productive sub-classes, are prevented from entering it. Typically, they are at the same time restricted to the prepositional paraphrase with *to*; therefore, the issue is dealt with in the subsequent section (2.2).

c. She *tweeted/instagrammed* **me** the photo
(mypretty-art.livejournal.com; via Googlesearch)

Furthermore, more marginal uses are typically subject to regional and social variation concerning acceptability; they face greater (syntactic) constraints than other verb classes. The so-called 'derring-do' construction (*cry me a river*) is, for instance, more felicitous when used as a command, and with pronominal 'recipient'-arguments (Goldberg 1995: 150–151; Oehrle 1976). Last, a number of marginal verbs are frequently found only in fixed phrases, or show a clear predilection for light-verb, lexicalised strings, such as *do so. a favour* (cf. also Mukherjee 2005). Such strings, which are also often referred to as 'complex verbs' or 'complex predicates' typically have "a tripartite structure consisting of a verb of general actional meaning, most commonly *do*, *give*, *have*, *make*, and *take*, the indefinite article, and a deverbative noun" (Brinton and Akimoto 1999b: 2). Although many of these idiomatic combinations are transitives (*take a shower*, *make a decision*), a range of ditransitive verbs of this type can also be found.

An interesting case of high productivity plus constrained usage is the class of benefactive verbs or 'verbs of creation/preparation' (*bake, make, build, cook, sew, knit*, etc.). This sub-sense is sometimes treated as a separate category due to its paraphraseability by *for* rather than *to* (e.g. Kay 1996, 2005). However, it is in fact perfectly compatible with the basic sense of transfer posited for the DOC (e.g. Goldberg 1995).[42] Geeraerts (1998: 196) suggests that the benefactive DOC in fact evokes two sub-events, one of preparation or creation, and second, the transfer event of the outcome to a recipient (Colleman 2010a: 205–206; also Fillmore 2007; Colleman 2010b). While these events can be extended to metaphorical preparation and transfer as in the case of other transfer-senses, the benefaction events denoted by the DOC are importantly restricted to recipient-benefaction. The construction thus excludes deputatitve/substitutive benefaction, i.e. events in which a participant benefits but without receiving anything (Van Valin and La Polla 1997; Kittilä 2005; Colleman 2010b). Verbs associated with such acts of 'pure' or 'plain' benefaction, where no transfer (whether actual or virtual) is involved, are prohibited from entering the DOC – consider the ungrammaticality of the examples in (27).

42 Its rather central place in the semantic network of the construction is also signalled by a number of verbs of creation/obtainment figuring prominently among the verbs most strongly associated to it in Stefanowitsch and Gries's (2003) analysis.

(27) a. **Can* you *hold* **me** the door, please

b. *Sue *fixed* **Bill** the radiator

(Colleman 2010b: 225)

This limitation of the benefactive DOC to certain verbs or events, namely those where the beneficiary is projected to receive the theme, is commonly referred to as the 'intended reception constraint' in the literature (Colleman 2010a: 194).[43] [44] Although this constraint seems to hold generally, it is to some extent fuzzy: As Colleman (2010b: 195) shows, "whether a given event can be construed as involving intended causation of reception is a matter of degree rather than kind". The blurry boundaries between recipient benefaction and substitutive benefaction are nicely illustrated by the abovementioned case of an idiosyncratic subtype of benefactives often labelled 'derring-do' constructions. In sentences such as (28), the agent clearly does not transfer an entity, but instead acts in a courageous or in some way remarkable way, with the aim to impress and please another person observing the action or its outcome (Colleman 2010a: 226; also Van Valin and La Polla 1997: 383–384; Takami 2003: 211–212, among others). Goldberg (1995: 150–151) attempts to explain these uses by positing a metaphorical extension of the central sense of transfer along the lines of 'actions performed for the benefit of a person are objects transferred to the person' (but see Takami [2003: 208–209] for a critique of this proposal).

(28) a. *Crush* **me** a mountain

(Goldberg 1995: 150)

b. They're going to *kill* **Reagan** a hippie

(Green 1974: 95)

---

43 See also Allerton (1978); Wierzbicka (1988); Jackendoff (1990); Langacker (1991); Wechsler (1995); Goldberg (2002); Nisbet (2005).

44 It should be mentioned, however, that there is again great variation (both regional and stylistic) concerning the strictness of this constraint. This means that we can observe a continuum of acceptability of benefactives, with the cut-off point varying between individual speakers and varieties (Colleman 2010b: 240). For example, instances such as *Open me the door* are reportedly perfectly acceptable in Yorkshire English (Petyt 1985: 236; referred to in Colleman 2010b). In contrast, uses like the example below, which serve to stress the agentivity of the referent of the subject, are common in southern American vernacular speech (Webelhuth and Dannenberg 2006: 36; Colleman 2010b: 227).

Ima *drink* **me** some beers (twitter.com; via Googlesearch)

For an overview and detailed discussion of benefactives in PDE and other languages see Colleman (2010a, 2010b); for a recent investigation into the diachrony of benefactives, see Zehentner and Traugott (forthc.).

The important message to take away from this discussion is that there is clearly a great deal of variability in the semantics of the DOC; this concerns both the definition of the categories themselves, as well as inter-/intra-speaker acceptability judgements. At the same time, however, the construction is consistently and intimately associated with a meaning of transfer. Verb classes denoting events of physical or metaphorical 'giving' display distinctly more prototypical features than other, more marginal and decidedly less frequent uses. Less clearly connected senses such as the 'derring-do' construction, although present, are located at the periphery of the network, and are typically highly marked in some way, either regionally, syntactically, or else (Goldsmith 1980; Gropen et al. 1989; Goldberg 1995). The centrality of giving senses is also confirmed by acquisition studies as well as experimental evidence (Gries and Wulff 2005; Goldberg 2006; de Marneffe et al. 2012).[45] To investigate the diachronic distribution of different verbs and verb groups in the DOC is one of the main objectives of this book; this enables us to explain and account for (at least some of) the PDE features of the construction.

Disregarding the question of how many and which sub-senses should be assumed for the PDE DOC, there is broad agreement on viewing narrowly defined sub-senses and verb classes as an integral part of studying the construction. A distinction between various senses moreover seems to be warranted considering empirical evidence such as Hay and Bresnan's (2006). They find that the vowel of the verb *give* is more centralised when used in a DOC expressing abstract, metaphorical transfer (as in *give a chance*) than with concrete giving events (*give a pen*); further Bybee (2013: 57).

As to the issue of how to analyse or model these distinct sub-senses in a constructionist framework, I adopt Croft's (2003) lexicality-schematicity model, which represents a counter to Goldberg's (1995) polysemy model. As already mentioned above, Goldberg (1995: 38) treats the DOC as a prime example of constructional polysemy and assumes a formally rather schematic construction radially linked to various senses. One of these senses is the prototype meaning of transfer; other senses included are e.g. verbs of refusal, which clearly differ in their degree of centrality in meaning. That is, in Goldberg's approach the same form [SUBJ V OBJ1 OBJ2] is paired with different sub-senses, which are related through polysemy links. Croft (2003: 53–65), and also e.g. Kay (2005), vehemently argues against this approach. As Croft lays out, the variation that can be observed in the semantics of the construction is very different from polysemy as

45 See also e.g. Branigan et al. (2006); Hartsuiker et al. (2004); Dodson and Tomasello (1998); Campbell and Tomasello (2001).

in the case of lexical items. This is because the sub-senses are systematically and clearly associated with (or indeed determined by) specific, mutually exclusive verb classes (Croft 2003: 56):[46]

> If the ditransitive construction were truly polysemous, one might expect that the verb *bring*, for example, would be found with ditransitive sense F [i.e. intended transfer], resulting in a meaning like 'X brings Z with the intention of causing Y to receive Z', or *kick* could also occur with ditransitive sense C [blocked transfer], resulting in a meaning like 'X kicks Z causing Y not to receive Z'. But we do not. Instead, it seems that the different 'senses' of the ditransitive construction are very closely tied to the verb classes that each 'sense' occurs with.

Instead of Goldberg's 'one abstract form - many meanings' representation, Croft therefore proposes a multi-level account with 'verb-class-specific constructions'. These sub-constructions include schematic slots for the arguments of the construction; yet they delimit the range of verbs to those compatible with the meaning of the sub-construction. The subsidiary, lower-level generalisations involve particular semantic constraints concerning the verb slot, which emerge from and parallel the specific verb classes that are associated with them. This results in a modulated version of the basic transfer-meaning of the DOC (Perek 2015: 113). The difference between Goldberg and Croft is illustrated in the representation of the two sub-senses given in (29a-b) and (30a-b), respectively (Croft 2003: 56–57).

(29) a. [[SUBJ VERB OBJ1 OBJ2] / [actual transfer of possession]]
b. [[SUBJ VERB OBJ1 OBJ2] / [enabling transfer of possession]]

(30) a. [[SUBJ GIVING.VERB OBJ1 OBJ2] / [actual transfer of possession]]
b. [[SUBJ PERMIT.VERB OBJ1 OBJ2] / [enabling transfer of possession]]

In addition to these verb-class-specific generalisations, Croft (2003: 58–60) posits even lower levels of verb-subclass-specific constructions and verb-specific constructions, on which irregularities such as the infelicitous use of *prevent* and *forbid* in the DOC (in contrast to *refuse* and *deny*) are stored. However, lower-level verb(-class-)specific constructions do not exclude the possibility of a highly general, superordinate DOC, which specifies the common denominators of all sub-constructions (Croft and Cruse 2004: 274; also Croft 2003: 59–60). The DOC then represents a collection of constructions at various levels of schematicity, from verb-specific to schematic, via possible verb-subclass-

46 A similar discussion surrounds Goldberg's 'metaphorical extension' links (e.g. Boas 2003: 94–97, 2013: 250, n11; Kay 2005).

specific and verb-class-specific constructions. This multi-layered, hierarchical network is depicted in Fig. 4 (cf. Croft 2003; Barðdal, Kristoffersen, and Sveen 2011; Barðdal and Gildea 2015).

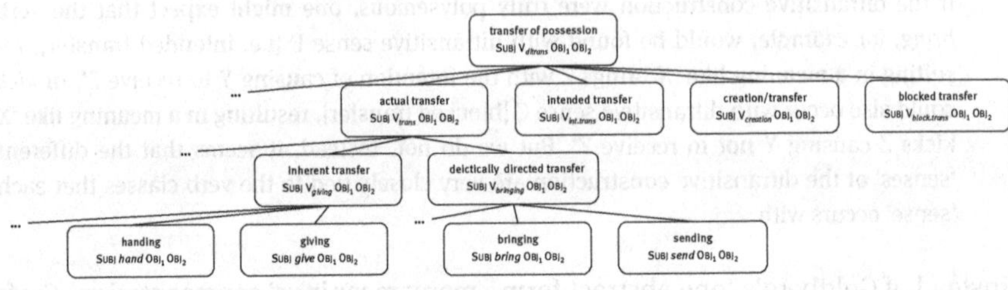

Fig. 4: Constructional network of the DOC and its sub-constructions (following Croft 2003; Barðdal, Kristoffersen, and Sveen 2011)

As can be seen, at the top of the network there is the abstract DOC, unspecified in regard to type of verb, and expressing a general meaning of 'transfer'. Below this, there are verb-class-specific constructions such as 'actual transfer', 'blocked transfer' or 'intended transfer'. In contrast to the more general DOC schema, these sub-constructions specify the range of verbs able to appear with them. One level further down, we find verb-subclass-specific constructions; for instance, actual transfer can be divided into 'inherent giving' and 'deictically directed transfer', among other things. The specific verbs associated with these sub-sub-constructions then constitute a limited sub-set of those in the more abstract construction. Finally, verb-specific constructions are located at the bottom of the network; these constructions are item-specific and have a very narrow meaning, directly linked to the verb instantiating them (e.g. *give*/ *hand* or *bring*/ *send*). Although Croft does not explicitly integrate prototypicality into his account, the various sub-constructions can be assumed to differ in terms of entrenchment, frequency, productivity and prototypicality, along the lines discussed above.

To sum up, this section has discussed that the PDE double object construction is reliably associated with a meaning of transfer. This is reflected in, or indeed results from the fact that the verbs which are most frequently found in the construction and which are acquired earliest, are verbs evoking events of transfer. The verb most prominently associated with the construction is *give*, indicating (concrete, physical) successful transfer from a volitional agent to a willing recipient. Apart from this core sense of giving, a number of other senses can be found, including transfer-related meanings such as creation (*build*, *bake*) or verbs of intended transfer (*offer*, *promise*). Furthermore, the DOC is used with more peripheral senses such as refusal (*deny*) or mentality/attitude (e.g. *forgive*, *envy*) – these can be viewed as metaphorical extensions along different dimensions. Although the DOC is therefore not limited to transfer, but also comprises senses quite removed from it, it is clear that these senses are less productive, and less central to the construction.

I therefore essentially view the PDE double object construction as a schematic category associated with a core meaning of 'transfer'. The different subsenses, extensions of the basic transfer sense, constitute more specific, lower-level, sub-constructions; they are associated and hierarchically related to this abstract schema. On an even lower level, verb-sub-class-specific constructions and additional verb-specific constructions can be posited. This allows us to account for several idiosyncrasies and non-semantically motivated restrictions, while at the same time acknowledging that more specific uses are likely to be abstracted over. In general, I take the network of constructions such as the DOC to be organised in a bottom-up way, with the meaning of higher-level schemas resulting from abstractions over specific verbs (and verb-classes, etc.) found with the same form in actual usage. The main reason for taking such an approach is that the empirical focus of the present project is on textual attestations, meaning patterns which we can identify on the surface. If we take usage to fundamentally shape and determine cognitive representations in a bottom-up approach and assume that frequency of linguistic constituents in usage plays a crucial role in representation and change, this enables us to draw conclusions about the competence level based on actually attested data. That is, in the following I work on the assumption that the range of verbs found in the constructions at hand as well as their relative frequency in the historical corpus used in my study directly reflects how the constructions (and its components) are cognitively represented.

The following section deals with the issue of alternations in construction grammar. This matter is clearly highly relevant for the present book, which focuses on the dative alternation in the history of English. The main point of debate in this regard is the status ascribed to the alternation: As is shown, I subscribe to the view of Perek (2015) and others, in emphasising alternations as independent categories rather than superficial phenomena resulting from partial semantic overlap.

2.2 Argument structure alternations (and the dative alternation)

(Re)turning now to the main phenomenon at hand, in the following I briefly discuss constructionist approaches to syntactic alternations, and specifically the dative alternation. Most notably, Goldberg's (1995, 2002) account is compared to Cappelle (2006) and Perek's (2012, 2015) usage-based construction grammar view on alternating argument structures. Overviews of the dative alternation in various other theoretical frameworks can be found e.g. in Levin and Rappaport Hovav (2005: Ch.7), Mukherjee (2005: Ch.1), Ozón (2009: especially Ch.2), as well as Gerwin (2014: Ch.2). The wide range of (mostly) functionalist studies carried out on the semantic and discourse-pragmatic factors influencing the choice of one construction over the other are only dealt with in passing here. Instead, they are discussed in the subsequent section on the choice between order of objects and correspondingly, choice of construction in the history of English (3.2.2). The present section loosely follows Perek (2015) in starting with an introduction to alternations in (Goldbergian) construction grammar (2.2.1) before moving on to a more usage-based model which sees alternations as an integral part of the constructional network (2.2.2). I also comment on the question of additional paraphrases, and their potential differences to alternations as envisaged in such a model. Last, some observable distributional (and other) biases as well as possible explanations for these phenomena are presented.

2.2.1 Constructionist views contra alternations (contra the 'dative alternation')

Mainly as a reaction to earlier transformational and projectionist accounts, which tended to place a strong focus on alternating structures and their relationship to each other, many constructionist accounts have argued against 'overplaying' the relevance of paraphrase relations. Some have downright denied or at least largely passed over any possibility of generalisations over formally distinct constructions. This is evident in the following quotes by Goldberg, the second of which is a formulation of her so-called 'surface generalization hypothesis':

> The question that arises, on the account presented here, is not whether verbs are allowed to undergo a lexical or syntactic rule that alters their semantic structure or subcategorization frame, as it is typically taken to be. Rather, the question becomes: How are the se-

> mantics of the independent constructions related such that the classes of verbs associated with one overlap with the classes of verbs associated with another? (Goldberg 1995: 89)

> There are typically broader syntactic and semantic generalizations associated with a surface argument structure form than exist between the same surface form and a distinct form that it is hypothesized to be syntactically or semantically derived from. (Goldberg 2002: 329)

On such an account, the alternation is seen as merely an epiphenomenon of the fact that verbs associated with the respective constructions evoke similar semantic frames.[47] Despite this (seeming) semantic overlap, however, both argument structure constructions are considered to be independent of each other, and a largely separate analysis of the constructions is thought to be preferable. Rather than conceding a central role to alternations, the advice is thus not to make too much out of the possible paraphrase relationship between them (cf. Goldberg 2002: 329; also Michaelis and Ruppenhofer 2001: Ch.3). As Perek (2015: 149) points out, Goldberg's account accordingly privileges 'vertical' relations between a construction and its instantiations, in that different tokens of a construction (involving different verbs) are taken to be more alike than instances of the same verb in different argument structure constructions, related through 'horizontal' links. The relevance of the latter relations is in general greatly downplayed or does not feature explicitly.

A similar point of criticism is found in Glynn's claim that the focus of current cognitive linguistic approaches on alternations "is the result of theoretical heritage from generative syntax and a matter of methodological convenience" (Arppe et al. 2010: 12). Note that his critique reflects a different motivation, though, as it aims at the fact that most speaker choices are not binary, but more complex. On his view, to emphasise alternation relationships in this way is 'simplistic' as well as 'reductionistic' (Arppe et al. 2010: 12). We will come back to this point later in this book, as it is relevant for the present investigation; although I am sympathetic to a more inclusive approach, as is clear from the methodological scope, the dative alternation is nevertheless regarded as special here.

Before doing so, let us go back to specifically constructionist views on the alternation, and particularly to the representation of the DOC paraphrases (re-

47 One consequence of this approach is also that it views the DOC as one unified constructions regardless of the possible paraphrases. This goes against accounts such as Kay (1996), who distinguishes between those DOC uses paraphrased by *for* (the benefactive DOC) and those paraphrased by *to* (the recipient DOCs).

gardless of their relationship). In Goldberg, among others, the *to*-PRC is analysed as a daughter of the 'caused-motion'-construction, which expresses a central meaning of 'X causes Y to move Z' and also licenses instances such as those in (31).

(31) a. Joe *kicked* the bottle **into the yard**
b. They *sprayed* the paint **onto the wall**
c. Frank *sneezed* the tissue **off the table**
(Colleman and De Clerck 2009: 11)

In distinguishing between a 'caused-motion' analysis of the *to*-PRC and a 'caused-possession' meaning of the DOC, Goldberg is in line with a wide range of other approaches stressing semantic differences between the constructions. In the *to*-PRC, the trajectory of a path is profiled, while the DOC emphasises the possessive relationship (Langacker 1991: 13–14; also e.g. Pinker 1989; Harley 2002; Krifka 2004).

Goldberg's precise account is, however, slightly more complex, because some uses of the *to*-PRC are claimed to represent a metaphorical extension ('transfer of ownership as physical transfer') of the larger caused-motion construction. The relationship between the caused-motion construction and the paraphrase, labelled 'Transfer-Caused-Motion Construction', is illustrated in Fig. 5 (Goldberg 1995: 90). Crucially, this metaphorical extension does not account for *to*-PRCs denoting a scene of actual, physical transfer, but only applies to more abstract transfer events (cf. Goldberg 1995: 89–97; Colleman and De Clerck 2009: 16). In other words, examples such as *John gave an apple to Mary* constitute simple instantiations of the caused-motion construction, while *John showed an apple to Mary* or *Joe gave his house to the Moonies* expresses a metaphorically extended caused-possession sense ('Transfer-Caused-Motion'). Only the latter construction is semantically similar to the DOC (indicated by the modified meaning of CAUSE-RECEIVE rather than CAUSE-MOVE in the box on the bottom of Fig. 5. Consequently, it is also only these metaphorical transfer events which are linked to the DOC by a synonymy-link; cf. Goldberg (1995: 91): "The semantic extension (via metaphor) is S(emantically) synonymous with the ditransitive construction [i.e. the DOC]".

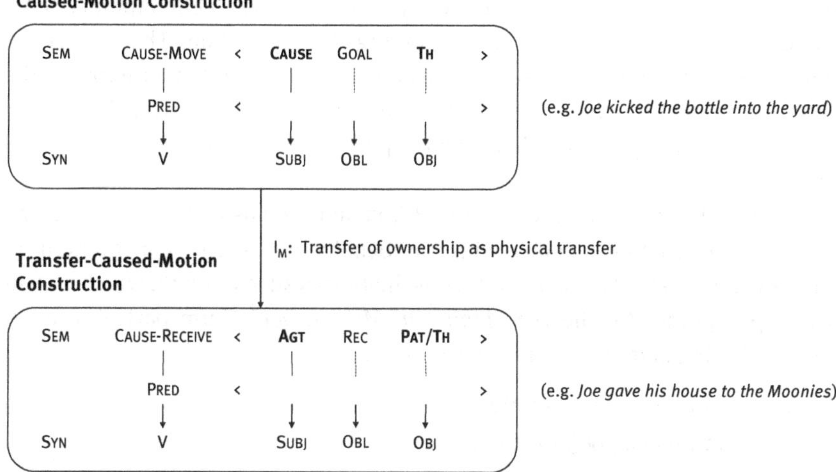

Fig. 5: Representation of the Caused-Motion Construction and its metaphorical extension Transfer-Caused-Motion (Goldberg 1995: 90)

What follows from this two-fold analysis is that pairs such as those in (32) are semantically non-synonymous, with the first example (a) denoting 'caused possession' in contrast to (b) expressing 'caused motion'. The sentences in (33), on the other hand, share the same meaning, since metaphorical transfer rather than concrete transfer is evoked. – As discussed in section (2.2.2) below, I reject this division, as I consider both concrete and metaphorical *to*-patterns to be synonymous to the DOC.

(32) a. John *gave* **Mary** an apple
b. John *gave* an apple **to Mary**

(33) a. John *gave* **Mary** his house
b. John *gave* his house **to Mary**

In general, synonymy between constructions is taken to be strongly dispreferred on Goldberg's account; see the principle of 'no synonymy', which states that syntactically distinct constructions need to be semantically or pragmatically distinct. Accordingly, it is assumed that the constructions (the DOC and *to*-PRC instantiating abstract transfer) differ in aspects pertaining to information structure, stylistics, or the like (Goldberg 1995: 67, 91; also Goldberg

2002: 347).[48] This assumption is perfectly consistent with contemporary functionalist investigations of the factors guiding the alternation. That is, several studies have shown that the two constructions typically differ in terms of the discourse-pragmatic status of the object arguments: While the DOC usually involves a given, topical recipient, the recipient in *to*-PRCs is mostly discourse-new.

The *for*-PRC, in contrast to the *to*-PRC, is analysed as a combination of the transitive construction together with the 'benefactive adjunct construction' in Goldberg (2002: 333–336, 344–347). Thus, instances such as (34a), which constitutes a paraphrase for the DOC ***John sent Mary a book***, form part of a larger group including patterns like those in (34b-c).

(34) a. John *sent* a book **for Mary**
 b. John *sent* a book **for the library**
 c. John *sent* a book **for her mother's sake**

Although this issue is not dealt with in more detail, the *for*-PRC is furthermore implied to differ from both the DOC and the *to*-PRC. This is because it involves a traditional adjunct rather than an argument (cf. e.g. *John bought a book yesterday for Mary* vs. ?*John sent a book yesterday to Mary* vs. **John bought/sent Mary yesterday a book*; Goldberg 2002: 331, 345).

The conclusion Goldberg finally draws in regard to the *to*- and *for*-PRC is that "the only thing that the respective paraphrases share with the ditransitives [i.e. the DOC] is the quite rough paraphrase relations themselves" (2002: 333). This is not to say that alternations are entirely ignored in Goldberg's account. As stated, S-links are posited to hold between the constructions, and "[p]araphrase relations [are also taken] to be relevant to online choices made in production" (Goldberg 2006: 44). Nevertheless, these relations are clearly not the focus of the investigation. The disregard for systematic and regular correspondences between formally distinct patterns has been challenged by numerous constructionist or construction grammar-sympathetic accounts, including Mukherjee (2005: 53). It has also sparked the emergence of alternative constructionist approaches lending more importance to alternations (e.g. Iwata 2005, 2008; Cappelle 2006; Boas 2010, 2011; García Velasco 2011; Perek 2015). These accounts attempt to meet the constructionist tenet of doing justice to languages in their entirety – assuming of course that alternations are in some way or the other part of the linguistic system (Kay and Fillmore 1999: 1). This is also reflected in

48 Goldberg (2002) also comprises a discussion of the paraphrase relations in terms of profiling differences.

Gilquin's reply to Glynn's assessment (see above): "There are good reasons to design research questions around binary response variables [...]; [f]inding and documenting such principles of linguistic organisation as they manifest themselves in frequency data is precisely what cognitive corpus linguistics should strive to do, and linguistic alternations provide a means to this end" (Arppe et al. 2010: 13–14).

The most elaborate proposal for integrating alternations into a constructionist framework so far, namely Cappelle's (2006) 'allostructions model', extended and substantiated by empirical evidence in Perek (2012, 2015), is introduced in the following section. The allostructions model is highly relevant for this book, as it places a strong focus on the dative alternation by itself and aims to investigate its emergence in the history of English. I also demonstrate that the establishment of the alternation had an effect on its members. That is, this book adduces historical evidence to support the cognitive reality of the 'alternation'.

2.2.2 Constructionist views in favour of alternations

2.2.2.1 The 'allostructions' model and the dative alternation

The Goldbergian account of ditransitive constructions as well as other linguistic alternations has frequently been found too restrictive and counter-intuitive, or rather, ignoring data which suggest that generalisations over formally different yet semantically similar structures are indeed present in the minds of speakers. Furthermore, alternations can provide a window into the cognitive configuration of language, even if other options exist.

Cappelle reviews different treatments of one case of alternation in PDE, namely particle verbs and the two alternative orderings available to them (*pull up one's socks* and *pull one's socks up*). He argues that considering such alternating idioms as two independently stored constructions "without there being a level of representation at which the two versions are perceived to be semantically identical lacks psychological plausibility" (Cappelle 2006: 13). The solution the author presents for accounting for such correspondence links between constructions is an 'allostructions' model, with allostructions referring to formally different variants of a partly underspecified construction (Cappelle 2006: 18). Structurally distinct yet semantically (near-)synonymous patterns are linked to a more schematic generalisation which only comprises the shared elements of the constructions. As Perek (2015: 153) points out, the postulation of such allostructions together with an alternation-based abstracted super-category or 'constructeme'[49] is superior to other representations because:

> [t]he constructeme and the inheritance links to each allostruction capture the fact that the constructions are similar and indicate at which level, and the allostructions themselves may include further syntactic and semantic/pragmatic details as to how they differ from one another.

Furthermore, according to Cappelle's discussion (2006: 21–25), allostructions and constructemes as part of constructional networks are 'fully expected' and in many ways related to Langacker's (1987) 'categorising relations' (cf. also Tuggy 1981). They are moreover easily combined with assumptions about horizontal links between constructions at all levels, as mentioned in e.g. Traugott and Trousdale (2013), Diessel (2015), and developed in more detail in van de Velde (2014), Traugott (forthc.), Zehentner & Traugott (forthc.).[50]

Applying this model to the dative alternation, whose members constitute distinct formal realisations of a specific meaning, i.e. encode the same event type, Perek (2015: 156) proposes an under-specified schematic construction with a meaning of 'X causes Y to have Z'. This abstract category is linked to the two allostructions of DOC and *to*-PRC (ditransitive and *to*-dative in Perek's notation) in Fig. 6.[51]

Despite the allostructions expressing more or less the same meaning, they nevertheless differ in syntagmatic order of the objects. Furthermore, they show substantial differences in respect to various discourse-pragmatic features such as givenness and discourse accessibility of the objects, as well as length, among others (De Cuypere 2015a: 227; Bresnan 2007; Bresnan et al. 2007; Theijssen et al. 2013, *inter alia*). These factors restrict the scope of usage of the respective constructions, meaning that they determine the choice of one variant over the other (Perek 2015: 158). As suggested in Perek (2015: 158), it appears that in addition to these object-related properties, we can observe certain verb-specific biases. For example, *sell* shows a preference for the *to*-PRC, while *teach* is more

49 The term is introduced in Perek (2012: 629) but was reportedly coined by Cappelle.

50 Van de Velde (2014) links his hypotheses to the biological concept of 'degeneracy', indicating a many-to-many mapping between different strategies for expressing semantic relations. Arguments in favour of an allostructional model (over horizontal, construction-to-construction links) are given in Perek (2015: 153). It is, however, unclear whether Perek includes lower-level horizontal links, or restricts such relations to higher-level schemas.

51 The assumption that the constructions' semantics are near-synonymous is also supported by Stefanowitsch and Gries' (2004) collexeme analysis of the *to*-PRC, in which *give* (and related verbs) figures prominently among those verbs strongly attracted to the construction.

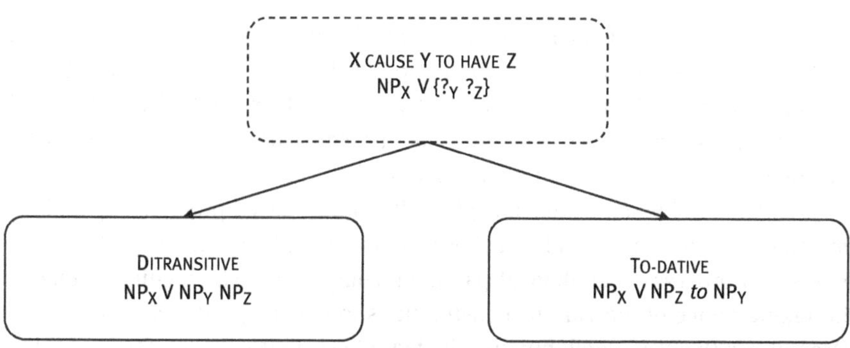

Fig. 6: The dative constructeme and its allostructions (following Perek 2015: 156)

prone to DOC use. These biases could be accounted for by verb-specific allostructions (alongside more schematic allostructions and constructemes), which vary in salience of the above-mentioned contextual factors (Perek 2015: 158). That such biases should exist is in fact not unexpected (or problematic): Allo-relations on other linguistic levels are typically also characterised by complementary, biased distributions. The allostructions concept in sum thus provides us with a possibility to integrate and account for both abstract generalisations as well as specific features of the individual constructions (including distinct verb preferences) within one model. In this book, I adopt this model and the various assumptions following from it and explore its applicability to the history of the English dative alternation.

The allostructions model is well supported by a number of general phenomena as well as experimental studies (see Perek 2015: 163–167 for an overview). First, there is clear evidence of verbs being coerced into the alternation. This largely ties in with Perek's (2015) proposal of 'alternation-based productivity': He focuses on the question whether the occurrence of a verb in one member of an alternation has an impact on the productivity of the other member, and argues that such productivity effects exist in addition to construction-based productivity. The latter is influenced by the semantic compatibility of a novel verb with the constructional meaning, which is in turn determined by the verbs used in the construction. That is, new verbs are added to a construction based on analogical extension from previous experiences of that construction (Perek 2015: 169; cf. also Bybee 1995; Barðdal 2008; Suttle and Goldberg 2011; Wonnacott et al. 2012; Zeschel 2012; among others). Alternation-based productivity, by contrast, acts on the basis of "*a paradigmatic analogy* between an existing use of a verb in a given allostruction and a productive use of that verb in another allostruction" [original italics] (Perek 2015: 169). The occurrence of an infelicitous overgeneralisation such as *Don't say me that* would accordingly be due to a child having encountered this verb in a *to*-PRC before, as well as several other communication verbs (or other ditransitives) in both the *to*-PRC and the DOC. From this, the child may conclude that the constructions express the same meaning, and that the default option is for verbs to alternate.

As Perek points out, the concept of alternation-based productivity finds its match in accounts such as Pinker (1989) or Marcotte (2006), the second of which refers to a process of 'analogical paradigm completion' which children engage in, taking notice of the various constructions in which specific verbs can occur (Marcotte 2005: 219). Perek pursues the hypothesis that productivity is positively influenced by alternation relationships by conducting an experiment on the dative and locative alternation with adult native speakers, following an experimental study by Conwell and Demuth (2007) on alternation-based productivity effects in child speech (further Wonnacott, Newport, and Tanenhaus 2008; Perek and Goldberg 2015).[52] His results indeed support these hypotheses; the findings of the study are reported in more detail in the next section (2.2.2.2).

Examples of recent changes in complementation patterns of verbs, illustrating coercion effects or alternation-based productivity, include the following. Here, the occurrence of a verb in one pattern enables the occurrence in the other pattern, even if this construction was unavailable to the verb before or is in fact in opposition with the semantics of the construction. For instance, *provide*, which is typically found in prepositional patterns (most frequently with a *for*-recipient, or a *with*-theme, followed by a *to*-PRC), is at least marginally attested in a DOC in American English now (35; Quirk et al. 1985: 1210; Mukherjee 2005: 13; De Clerck, Delorge, and Simon-Vandenbergen 2011).

(35) we'*re* also immediately *providing* **them** <u>food and shelter and clothing</u> (COCA; 2004; *NBC Today*)

The presence of *provide*-DOCs, despite the verb's clear general dis-preference for this construction, is likely caused by analogy to other alternating verbs, along the lines of 'if you can use a verb in one of the patterns, you can use it in the other, too'. It is of course clear that these DOC uses could also be triggered by the great semantic similarity of *provide* with other verbs of giving, meaning that the DOC tokens of *provide* could be formed in analogy to other transfer verbs

52 The 'locative alternation', also often labelled the '*spray/load* alternation' refers to the relation between the caused-motion construction (*John loaded hay onto the truck/ John sprayed paint onto the wall*) and the *with*-applicative (*John loaded the truck with hay/ John sprayed the wall with paint*); cf. Perek (2015: 158–163).

rather than indicating coercion into the alternation. Nevertheless, both options are at least equally plausible, and in fact, both processes might be at play at the same time.

An even more interesting phenomenon is the coerced use of verbs such as *deny* and *refuse* as well as *cost* in the *to*-PRC, which is somewhat unexpected considering the spatial/allative connotations that the preposition presumably still carries. Accordingly, the *to*-PRC for such uses is clearly marked, and DOC uses are certainly predominant. This is suggested by Colleman and De Clerck (2009: 24), who find that only about a fifth of *refuse* and *deny* tokens are found in the prepositional pattern in the *BNC* (see [36a-b] for examples from the *COCA*; also Goldberg 1992: 69; Panther 1997; Krifka 2004).[53] With *cost*, the *to*-PRC is decidedly 'awkward', as Colleman and De Clerck (2009: 36) put it; their query for combinations of *cost* and *to* in the *BNC* only yielded two tokens. Still, a quick google search for strings like 'costs billions to the' (on US sites) produces a considerable number of hits, including the example given in (37). These correspondences are highly conspicuous (see further section 2.2.2.2).[54]

(36) a. *denying* <u>marriage</u> **to gay couples** is unconstitutional
(COCA; 2014; St Louis Post Dispatch)

b. Management reserves the right to *refuse* <u>beverages</u> **to any patron**
(COCA; 2011; R. Bowen: *Man enough for me*)

(37) Graffiti taggers *cost* <u>millions</u> **to the @CityofSeattle**
(twitter.com)

Apart from noting cases of coercion/productivity, the question of alternation relationships has also been tested in other systematic ways, offering empirical and experimental support for the existence of allostructions and constructemes in the speaker minds (Perek 2015: 163). The studies involved include priming as well as sorting task experiments (Goldwater et al. 2011; Vasilyeva and Waterfall 2011; Perek 2012). As to the first, it has been shown that processing a (linguistic) stimulus influences or facilitates response to a later stimulus. A structure that has been heard or produced before has a high likelihood of being processed (or repeated) more readily afterwards (Chang, Bock, and Goldberg 2003; Gries and Wulff 2005, 2009; Eddington and Ruiz de Mendoza Ibáñez 2010, *inter alia*). Most

53 Colleman and De Clerck's (2009) study was carried out on a random sample of 3,000 instances of the verbs in question in the *BNC*.

54 It is clear that this argumentation is slightly problematic in that it runs the risk of circularity/illogicalness if the occurrence of verbs of blocked transfer in the *to*-PRC is taken as evidence for the high degree of grammaticalisation of the construction (3.2.3.2).

typically, priming effects are found with similar syntactic structures. Cases in point are e.g. the passive in (38a) priming a locative as in (38b), or the prepositional locative in (39a) priming the *to*-PRC in (39b), but not the DOC in (39c).

(38) a. the construction worker *was hit* **by the bulldozer**
b. the construction worker *was digging* **by the bulldozer**
(Traugott and Trousdale 2013: 54)

(39) a. The wealthy widow *drove* an old Mercedes **to the church**
b. The wealthy widow *gave* an old Mercedes **to the church**
c. The wealthy widow *gave* **the church** an old Mercedes
(Chang, Dell, and Bock 2006: 249)

Structural (or syntactic) priming of this kind therefore usually involves constructions overlapping in formal structure, but not encoding the same events or semantic relations and indicates that these patterns are perceived as related in some way. In contrast, a relation between the non-priming constructions, i.e. between constructions which are formally distinct but share a semantic relation through the third pattern (e.g. between the *to*-goal pattern and the DOC), is not confirmed. What this means, then, is that syntactic priming crucially results from competition between variant sequences of semantic roles, i.e. variant constructions. Consequently, the priming of one construction happens at the cost of the other (cf. Bock and Loebell 1990; Chang, Dell, and Bock 2006; Goldwater et al. 2011). In the case of the DOC, the *to*-PRC and the *to*-goal pattern, for instance, the latter prime each other at the expense of the DOC; the likelihood of using a *to*-PRC instead of a DOC increases when the speaker was confronted with a *to*-goal pattern before.

However, and highly relevant for this study, Goldwater et al. (2011) find that priming can also take place between semantically related but formally distinct constructions. Based on experimental evidence, they show that the two members of the dative alternation indeed prime each other. More specifically, they provide evidence that the probability of both ditransitive allostructions, the DOC and the *to*-PRC, to be used in subsequent discourse increased equally if the participants were primed with one of the alternants before (Goldwater et al. 2011: 166). With semantic-structure-priming, the use of both of the alternating constructions therefore increases. Both allostructions benefit from the use of the other, and benefit from being associated with each other (Goldwater et al. 2011: 159; cf. also Kaschak 2007; Kaschak, Kutta, and Jones 2011, 2014). Similar influences are found in Vasilyeva and Waterfall's (2011) study on transitive active and transitive passive in Russian. In line with Perek (2015: 167), this qualifies as support for the assumption that higher-level generalisations over alternating constructions with shared meaning components (constructemes) exist. Furthermore, I take this as corroboration that there is some 'profit' for the constructions in being linked to each other.

Additional evidence for the independent existence of alternations comes from a sorting task experiment conducted by Perek (2012). Here, participants were presented with a range of sentences instantiating three constructions, including the DOC, the *to*-PRC, and a *with*-applicative. The subjects were then asked to arrange the sentences into two classes according to their meaning. The expectation was that they would classify *to*-PRCs with verbs that are ambiguous between a locative and a recipient meaning (such as *throw*) as either (a) part of a larger caused-motion group (together with *with*-patterns), or (b) part of a dative alternation group (together with the DOC). As it turns out, the majority of participants tended to sort according to the latter option (b) rather than the former; this indicates that the semantic similarity between different occurrences of the caused-motion construction is perceived as less salient than the semantic similarity of alternating constructions. The results of the experiment thus again support the idea that the two constructions are strongly associated, and (I take it) the postulation of a constructeme (cf. Perek 2015: 164; also Bencini and Goldberg 2000).[55]

In sum, there is convincing evidence that structurally different constructions which encode similar event types are abstracted over, and that these generalisations are stored as well (Perek 2012: 609). More importantly, there is clear backing for the assumption that the members of the dative alternation (or ditransitive 'allostructions') are closely connected and are identified as encoding the same type of events. That this is the case is substantiated by priming experiments, but also by cases of coercion, where the use of a verb with one ditransitive allostruction enables it to be used with the other allostruction as well. The following section investigates this concept of 'alternation-based productivity' in some more detail, and also comments on observable distributional asymmetries.

2.2.2.2 Distributional and productivity asymmetries

It has often been noted that despite being closely associated, the members of the dative alternation display certain "puzzling lexical (dis)preferences" (Gries

55 Perek (2015: 165) adds the disclaimer that these results do not yet count as evidence that the generalisations are in fact stored, since they could also represent 'ad hoc'-categories formed in the experimental context. While there are good arguments to assume that the latter is not the case, additional support is certainly needed.

2009: 4). In other words, not all verbs readily alternate between the two variants. Some exhibit slight distributional biases, while others are near-categorical in their preferences towards one or the other (see e.g. Levin 1993 for an overview).[56] This is, however, hardly surprising – in fact, a complementary distribution is to be expected considering other allo-relationships, e.g. in phonology or morphology. For instance, the allomorphs of the past-tense morpheme clearly do not appear in random variation, but are instead complementarily distributed, depending on their phonological environment. In a similar way, we would predict that the ditransitive allostructions also show certain complementary verb-specific (or verb-class-specific) preferences.

Examples of constructional (or allostructional) biases include the following: Gries and Stefanowitsch's (2004) distinctive collexeme analysis of the dative alternation in the ICE-GB suggests that verbs of continuous motion like *bring*, *take* or *pass*, as well as verbs expressing commercial transactions such as *sell*, *supply* and *pay* have a high predilection for the *to*-PRC. Verbs traditionally taken to denote concrete or metaphorical caused reception (*give, offer, tell, show*), by contrast, are more clearly associated with the DOC. A number of other verbs including *lend, send, write* and *get*, show an approximately equal distribution. Verbs that are typically mentioned as examples of very strong biases towards the DOC are *deny* and *refuse*, as well as *cost*. Although 'counter-examples' can be found, these verbs nevertheless mostly tend to avoid the *to*-PRC. Furthermore, near-idioms involving complex predicates (e.g. *give so. a kick, give so. a headache, ask so. a favour/ the time, do so. a favour/harm*) are almost never found in a *to*-PRC – see Goldberg (1995: 92) and also Colleman and De Clerck (2009: 37), whose google search for 'asked a favor/favour to you' did not yield any hits. On the other hand, there are several verbs which are judged as inacceptable or highly marked if used in the DOC and are largely restricted to the *to*-PRC. Among these are verbs of communication such as *say* (40a-b), as well as verbs of manner of communication like *whisper, mutter* or *yell* (41a-b).[57]

56 Claims that these (dis)preferences are absolute are quite pervasive (cf. e.g. Goldberg's [1992: 69] assertion that *deny* and *refuse* "cannot occur with prepositional paraphrases"). However, it can be shown that they are not so much strict constraints but rather statistical tendencies which can be overridden by information structure requirements, among other things (Gries 2009: 4; also Stefanowitsch 2006, 2011).

57 This constraint is again not absolute – DOC uses of verbs such as *whisper* are e.g. notably more acceptable with pronouns (John *whispered* **her** goodnight); see Ford and Bresnan (2013) for more detail, and Bresnan and Nikitina (2009: 164–165) for exceptions.

(40) a. John *said* goodnight **to Mary**
b. *John *said* **Mary** goodnight
(Stefanowitsch 2011: 110)

(41) a. John *whispered* goodnight **to Mary**
b. *John *whispered* **Mary** goodnight

The DOC-incompatibility of a relatively large group of verbs including *donate, announce, provide, supply, confess, reveal, explain* (and others), has frequently been ascribed to the words' origins, as all of them were borrowed into English from Latin or French. Accordingly, the dis-preference is often labelled the 'Latinate restriction' (cf. e.g. Green 1974: 77–79; Oehrle 1976: 121–125; Pinker 1989: 118–119).[58] While the assumption that speakers actually possess etymological knowledge about verbs has by now largely been discarded, the constraint is commonly attributed to certain exceptional morphophonological features of these verbs such as their stress patterns. However, it is difficult to maintain this claim considering that other verbs excluded from the DOC, such as *say*, do not exhibit such properties. On the other hand, many verbs sharing a Latinate origin and stress pattern with this group in fact do allow for and are frequently found in the DOC (e.g. *assign*).

Therefore, various proposals have been put forward to account for the asymmetries observed in the dative alternation in a different way. For instance, Goldberg (1992: 69, 1995: 92) gives a semantic explanation, stating that verbs of blocked transfer are incompatible with the *to*-PRC due to their lack of 'caused motion'-semantics. The restriction of light verb constructions (*give a kick*) to the DOC, on the contrary, may be due to the focus lying on the action expressed by the theme (*to kick*) rather than on the recipient. In general, many biases have been explained by profiling differences as well as other semantic-pragmatic factors (e.g. Wierzbicka 1986; Gropen et al. 1989, 1991; Ambridge et al. 2009). Still, these explanations can hardly account for all idiosyncratic verb preferences, and sometimes seem to be formulated rather ad-hoc in order to account for problematic cases. Furthermore, they do not provide clear indications on how these idiosyncrasies are acquired (cf. also Boyd and Goldberg 2011: 58).

The issue of learnability and entrenchment in this context has been addressed in many studies, an overview of which, together with a discussion of challenging issues, is provided in Boyd and Goldberg (2011). Although there is evidence that higher token frequency and thus a higher degree of entrenchment of a verb with one construction has an impact on the usage of these verbs, this

58 See furthermore Harley (2007); Coppock (2009).

would also predict that high frequency verbs cannot be used creatively in new contexts – a prediction which is certainly not born out. By contrast, there is some indication that negative entrenchment, or statistical pre-emption, plays a role in language acquisition. This can possibly account for the non-availability of a construction to certain verbs (Foraker et al. 2007; Stefanowitsch 2008, 2011; Goldberg 2011; among many others). In brief, the concept of statistical pre-emption refers to blocking effects in language learning; in Stefanowitsch' (2011: 115) words, it is:

> a simple but powerful mechanism based on the idea that children assume that exact synonyms do not exist and therefore take the existence of a particular form in the input as evidence against the existence of a particular form in the input as evidence against the existence of synonymous forms that could be derived by a particular rule or set of rules.

For example, when confronted with a wide range of regular past forms of the type *walked* or *danced*, a child might acquire a general past tense construction 'V-*ed*/PAST'; they will assume that this applies to verbs such as *go* as well. However, input containing the form *went* might then lead to this construction/rule being blocked (cf. Stefanowitsch 2011: 115; also Clark 1995, *inter alia*).

As discussed in Stefanowitsch (2011), as well as Boyd and Goldberg (2011), pre-emption in the acquisition of larger syntactic constructions might work slightly differently, though, as most verbs typically appear in more than one construction (in contrast to inflectional patterns). On the basis of Pinker (1984: 400), as well as Goldberg (1995: 124), Stefanowitsch therefore argues for 'pre-emption by contextual mismatch' rather than the standard notion of pre-emption as just presented. He proposes that if a construction is used in a context that is typically associated with the other variant, this alternative is pre-empted/blocked (Stefanowitsch 2011: 117). This can be illustrated by the following examples: The large majority of ditransitive verbs would disfavour a structure such as (42a) due to discourse-pragmatic reasons (pronominal recipients strongly tending to appear in the DOC). The fact that *explain* is nevertheless used in this context (42b) might therefore be interpreted as evidence that the alternative option is unavailable with this precise verb.

(42) a. #John *told* the problem **to me**
b. John *explained* the problem **to me**

Although the role of statistical pre-emption in acquiring constructional restrictions seems to be supported by several studies, others notably argue that there is little clear substantiation (Boyd and Goldberg 2011; Goldberg 2011 vs.

Stefanowitsch 2011, and others). Further research is thus certainly needed to validate either assumption.

Incidentally, as discussed by Hoffmann and Trousdale, pre-emption is also supposed to play a role in the diachronic development of constructions:

> [I]f on a particular occasion one construction is used instead of a possible alternative, then the hearer will assume that this choice reflects a functional difference between the two structures. Ultimately, this will lead to the functional differentiation of the two alternatives (that is, the minimisation of constructional synonymy). (2011: 6; 2013: 10–11)

> [I]f preemption leads to the functional diversification of two (or more) variants, then each single usage event can trigger or reinforce contextual associations, which in the long run will affect the statistical probabilities of each variant in particular social and linguistic contexts. In other words, preemption encourages originally synonymous constructions to be interpreted as contextually-determined variants. Preemption, then, is inherent in socially and linguistically governed variation, which in the long run can result in diachronic change. (2011: 6)

This is interesting for the history of the dative alternation in English. I argue that such slight distributional tendencies and pre-emption effects are precisely what led to an increasingly stronger (complementary) differentiation between the variant constructions.

The phenomenon that a greater number of verbs appears to be restricted to the *to*-PRC than the other way round, i.e. the type frequency of non-alternating *to*-PRC verbs being significantly higher than the number of non-alternating DOC verbs, figures prominently in Perek's usage-based account of alternation-based productivity introduced in the preceding section (2.2.2.1).[59] His experiment shows that concerning the dative alternation, there is a clear asymmetry in the productivity of the DOC and the *to*-PRC, respectively.[60] That is, both with verbs of physical transfer and communication verbs, subjects presented with a DOC model consistently and frequently produced a *to*-PRC in the sentence completion tasks, while those trained on a *to*-PRC mainly stuck to this construction. This suggests that there is an impact on the productivity of the *to*-PRC by previous encounters with the DOC, but not necessarily vice versa.[61] The explanation

---

59 This conclusion can impressionistically be gathered from the literature and has been empirically tested on the ICE-GB by Perek (2015: 199–205).

60 The study included verb recall tasks, meaning decision tasks, and sentence completion tasks based on short stories with selected novel ditransitive as well as locative verbs in 'model' and priming conditions (viz. the respective constructions involved in the alternation).

61 As Perek (2015: 189–193, *inter alia*) demonstrates, a number of factors potentially influencing the asymmetry (such as the constructions' semantics, discourse-pragmatic factors, or

Perek (2015: 197–206) puts forward for the observed productivity asymmetry relies on differences in type frequency between the two constructions. Relating the issue to the 'allostruction model' of alternations, it is argued that in the case of such correspondences, productivity is determined by the type frequency of the super-ordinate constructeme in addition to the type frequency of the variants themselves. The higher the number of alternating verbs in a language is, the higher the likelihood is that newly encountered verbs are used with both alternants as well. A great number of non-alternating verbs, on the other hand, should lead to conservative use of novel verbs in either one or the other construction (Perek 2015: 198; cf. also Wonnacott, Newport, and Tanenhaus 2008; Perek and Goldberg 2015).

Both issues appear to apply to the dative alternation. On the one hand, there is a reasonably large group of verbs that do alternate, which determines the alternation-based productivity effects seen with the DOC. Perek and Goldberg (2015: 125) demonstrate that this group of verbs occurring in both constructions merely needs to reach a certain threshold of type frequency. A 'minority' of verbs witnessed to be alternating suffices to trigger the extension of verbs to the other allostruction, even if they have previously been observed in one construction only (also Wonnacott, Newport, and Tanenhaus 2008). On the other hand, the dative alternation also shows that this relation is not symmetrical, as the higher type-frequency of non-alternating *to*-PRC verbs, also including many more hapax legomena than the (non-alternating) DOC, leads to a productivity bias towards the former. In the present study, this question can unfortunately not be pursued in more detail, since the methodological approach is skewed towards the DOC, or rather, is restricted to alternating verbs. Any asymmetries in type frequency or the like can therefore not be detected in the data. Nevertheless, this issue is touched upon at least to some extent in the discussion part of the book.

2.3 Conclusion: The PDE dative alternation as an allostructional network

To conclude this chapter, it seems fair to say that the dative alternation is a highly "multifaceted phenomenon", which has unsurprisingly occupied many

---

priming) cannot be held responsible for the phenomenon as such, although they possibly exert a reinforcing impact. Perek's findings are overall in line with results by Conwell and Demuth (2007), who find a similar bias in the use of the dative alternation with children.

linguists for quite some time now (Colleman 2009: 602). I have here attempted to provide some basic information on how the members of the dative alternation, as well as the alternation itself, have been treated in constructionist accounts, and specifically in usage-based constructionist approaches.

The main assumptions the rest of this book works with are the following: Both constructions involved in the alternation express a basic meaning of 'successful transfer'. This includes events of concrete, physical transfer as well as abstract, metaphorical transfer events, regardless of the range of irregularities and semantically peripheral uses that are still found. Following a usage-based approach to the relation between verbs and constructions, I presume that the meaning of constructions develops in a bottom-up manner. This means that the semantics of the more abstract construction (e.g. the DOC) represent a generalisation over verbs and verb meanings that are frequently used in the construction. In the case of the DOC (as well as the *to*-PRC), the most prototypical verb is *give*, a fact which determines the basic transfer-semantics of the schematic DOC. In line with Croft (2003) and others, the verb-specific constructions (e.g. [SUBJ *give* OBJ OBJ]; [SUBJ *refuse* OBJ OBJ]) are taken to be vertically linked to constructions at higher levels of schematicity, ranging from verb-class specific subschemas ([SUBJ $V_{actual\ transfer}$ OBJ OBJ], [SUBJ $V_{refusal}$ OBJ OBJ]) to the most abstract, schematic DOC [SUBJ V OBJ OBJ], and further potential intermediate levels. In this constructional network, the lower-level constructions shape and determine the semantics of the more general constructions above them.

As to the relationship between the DOC and the *to*-PRC, I argue that there is a clear and intimate connection between them, and that the constructions are perceived as essentially synonymous. Even more so, the DOC and the *to*-PRC represent 'allostructions' of each other and are connected to each other horizontally as well as link to an overarching ditransitive constructeme, rather than being merely superficially related by the fact that their verbal instantiations largely overlap. This constructeme is taken to be independently stored in the minds of speakers; the alternation therefore receives an independent theoretical status. That this should be the case, i.e. that the two constructions should be strongly linked in an alternation-relationship, is supported by priming experiments, showing that the use of one allostruction increases the likelihood of the other being expressed in subsequent discourse. Furthermore, there is good evidence that the patterns are perceived as more systematically and more closely related to each other than other constructions (cf. Perek's sorting task experiment). It can also be shown that the alternation is productive, in that novel verbs found in one construction can typically also be used in the other. The effects of such alternation-based productivity have been confirmed empirically

(Perek 2015). This corresponds to instances of constructional (or alternation-based) coercion: Verbs that have previously been used in only one of the allostructions, have come to occur in the other construction, too, over time. Finally, I have argued that distributional asymmetries in the dative alternation, with certain verbs showing (more or less strong) preferences for either one or the other allostruction, are expected (rather than problematic) in an allostruction relationship. If two constructions show a complementary distribution concerning discourse-pragmatic features (such as topicality of the objects), a complementary distribution concerning verbal semantics can be seen as a further indication of a close relationship between the patterns.

The next chapter approaches the dative alternation and its members from a historical viewpoint, providing some background information on the DOC and the prepositional patterns in earlier stages of English, and thereby tracking their diachronic development from Old to Present Day English. These changes are moreover related to more general developments that took place in the history of English and which were of great consequence to the whole linguistic system.

3 Ditransitives in the history of English

This book starts from the assumption that a diachronic perspective can be of great help in explaining synchronic phenomena. It aims to provide a historical answer to the question why the dative alternation is there in PDE in its present form. In order to be able to so, this chapter first gives an overview of previous research on the diachronic development of the alternation (and, as far as possible, that of other alternative patterns, e.g. prepositional theme patterns as in *John told Mary about the news*). This discussion informs the basic research agenda of the corpus study which constitutes the empirical core of this project; its data and methodology as well as results are presented in (4).

In the next sections, I outline history of the English dative alternation and discuss the changes that resulted in its establishment. I do so in two steps. First, I present and review previous work on the emergence of the alternation itself (3.1). This involves assessing the availability of prepositional alternatives in earlier periods of English as well as their relation to the double object construction across time. Arguably, this particular change is the most important one for the present book, since it fundamentally shaped the PDE dative alternation in bringing about its second member. Section (3.2) is concerned with developments which influenced both nominal and prepositional constructions equally. They can therefore be regarded as changes to the factors influencing the choice of one or the other option rather than the constructions themselves. While the question of case marking in ditransitive patterns is considered here (3.2.1), this is kept comparatively brief, since the impact of its loss is only superficially investigated in the book's quantitative study. In Section (3.2.2), I talk about changes in the word order specifications of the constructions, primarily to account for the differences in object ordering between the members of the PDE dative alternation. Afterwards (3.2.3), I explore the semantic history of the patterns at greater length and find that the semantics of the PP-structures have widened, with collocational restrictions being lost. By contrast, the DOC has undergone a process of semantic narrowing. In the final chapter (3.3), various hypotheses that causally link these different changes are examined. Whenever possible, I focus specifically on constructionist approaches to the issues at hand.

https://doi.org/10.1515/9783110633856-003

3.1 Emergence of the dative alternation

3.1.1 Prepositional ditransitives (and other variants) in Old English

It is a well-known assumption that English moved (or rather, is still moving) from a predominantly synthetic language, which relied mostly on morphological structures to express grammatical relations, to a system dependent more on analytic, i.e. periphrastic, structures.[62]

Among other things, constructions with function words, above all prepositional paraphrases, greatly increased at the transition from Old to Middle English. This typically happened at the expense of the resident, more synthetic, case constructions (cf. Baugh and Cable 2002: 314; also Lundskær-Nielsen 1993; Iglesias-Rábade 2011; among others). In the case of ditransitives, there is no doubt that the DOC was the default option in earlier times. When and how its alternatives emerged, is a question we will address in this section. This will serve as the basis for discussion in the later chapters (especially section 7.1) – one of the crucial arguments of this book is that the emergent (prepositional) variants entered competition with the DOC, which was resolved in different ways.

What is clear from the extant literature on Old English syntax is that even though their use might have risen in later periods, prepositions and PPs were an integral part of the system already in Old English (e.g. Lundskær-Nielsen 1993: 17–19). Among other things, they frequently fulfilled the same or similar functions as synthetic case-marked NP constructions. For example, as Traugott (1992: 207) points out, they very often expressed adverbials, which could also be encoded by a noun phrase. The availability of both constructional means is illustrated in the following pairs of sentences, with the NP/PP denoting an adverbial of time in (43) and accompaniment in(44).

(43) a. **þam þryddan dæge**$_{NP}$ he *arist*
the third day he arose
'on the third day he [Christ] arose [from the dead]'
(West Saxon Gospels: Matt. (Corpus Cambr.) xx. 19; OED, s.v. *day*)

62 See Szmrecsanyi (2012) for a critical assessment of this issue; also Schwegler (1990); Vincent (1997) and Barðdal (2009) on the issue of syntheticity versus analyticity in the history of English and other languages.

b. *Com* **on wanre** niht$_{PP}$ *scriðan* sceadugenga
came on gloomy night striding shadowgoer
'There came in a gloomy night striding the shadowgoer'
(Beo. Th. 1410; B. 703; Bosworth-Toller, s.v. *niht*)

(44) a. he **lytle werede**$_{NP}$ æfter wudum *for*
he small troop after woods travelled
'he travelled with a small troop through woods'
(ChronA 74.28 (878); Sato 2009: 32)

b. Hi *habbað* **mid him**$_{PP}$ awyriedne engel
they have with them corrupt angel
'They have with them a corrupt angel'
(JECHom II, 38 283.113; Traugott 1992: 171)

Most importantly for our purposes, PPs also encoded semantic roles in various argument structure constructions. For example, nouns expressing agents or instruments in passive sentences were not only optionally, but almost always introduced by a preposition, most frequently by *from* or *through* (45); cf. Traugott (1992: 207–208).

(45) a. Hu *wurdon* L monna *ofslagen* **from**
how were 50 men slain from
hiora agnum sunum$_{PP}$
their own sons
'How fifty men were slain by their own sons'
(OrHead 64.8; Traugott 1992: 207)

b. **þurh eow**$_{PP}$ me *bið* *gehalgod* manegra
through you me is hallowed of many
oþre clennysse
other purity
'the purity of many is hallowed for me by you'
(ÆLS (Julien and Balissa),6; Traugott 1992: 208)

Examples of transitive clauses with PP arguments, contrasted with NP-patterns, are given in (46)-(47). In many cases, it is in fact only the prepositional construction that has survived into PDE (e.g. **rejoice*+NP vs. *rejoice in*). PPs were reportedly especially frequently used to 'replace' genitive NP-arguments (Allen 1995: 217–219; 2005: 239–240).

(46) a. Ne *gefeah* he **þære fæhðe**NP
not rejoice he this feud
'He did not rejoice in this feud'
(Beowulf i, 109; Glossary Old English Aerobics, s.v. *gefēon*)

b. Ðonne motan we **in ðære engellican blisse** *gefeon*
then must we in this angelic bliss rejoice
'then may we in this angelic bliss rejoice'
(Blickl. Homl. 83, 3; Bosworth-Toller, s.v. *ge-feón*)

(47) a. se þe **þæs**NP his wylles *gyrnð*
who this his will yearns
'who yearns for this with his will'
(cochdrul, ChrodR_1:67.1.885; De Cuypere 2015a: 233)

b. þa *gierndon* eac **æfter þæm onwalde**PP
when yearned also after the power
'when they also yearned after the power'
(tr. Orosius *Hist.* (BL Add.) VI. xxviii. 146; OED, s.v. *yearn*)

PPs as an optional alternative to nominal means of expression were thus firmly established before Middle English. Nevertheless, it does not appear as if they saw a more general increase within the Old English period (Mitchell 1985: 517–523; Lundskær-Nielsen 1993: 28–32, 184).[63] In addition, the use of the paraphrases was in most cases not entirely unrestricted, but they were instead often confined to specific semantic relations. This is strongly evident in the case of ditransitives, as shown in the next paragraphs.

Focussing first on the *to*-prepositional recipient pattern, as research on the dative alternation has traditionally done, we find the following: It has commonly been assumed that the *to*-PRC (as the periphrastic version of the DOC) was completely absent from OE, and only came into being in Middle English (e.g. Visser 1963: 637; McFadden 2002: 110). However, several studies have since revealed that the construction was in fact used from early OE onwards (cf. Cassidy 1938; Ogura 1980: 60; Mitchell 1985: 512; Allen 2006: 214; Sówka-Pietraszewska 2012; De Cuypere 2013, 2015c: 3–7). More precisely, it occurred with two specific verb classes. On the one hand, these were verbs of caused motion, e.g. *beran* 'bear', *bringan* 'bring', *(a)sendan* 'send' or *feccan* 'fetch' (48),

63 For opposing views on this issue see e.g. Traugott (1972: 110); Schibsbye (1977: 30); Kniesza (1991) versus Sato (2009: 184).

and on the other hand, verbs of communication such as *cweðan*, *tellan*, or *secgan* 'tell, speak, say' (49).

(48) *sende* þis ærendgewrit$_{TH}$ **him** **to**$_{REC}$
sent this letter him to
'sent this letter to him'
(coaelive, ÆLS_[Abdon_and_Sennes]:86.4777; De Cuypere 2015c: 8)

(49) God *cwæð* **to** **Moysen**$_{REC}$ ðæt he wolde cumin$_{TH}$
God said to Moses that he would come
'God said to Moses that he would come'
(cocathom2.o3: 196, 16; De Cuypere 2015c: 18)

As is evident from these examples, the construction was not constrained to locative goals, but also frequently involved human recipients/goals with verbs of sending. In the case of communication verbs, the theme was typically instantiated by a reported clause (Koopman and van der Wurff 2000: 262). What is more, De Cuypere (2015c: 3–7), based on a quantitative survey of the *York-Toronto-Helsinki Parsed Corpus of Old English Prose* (YCOE), shows that with these verbs the *to*-PRC even surpassed the DOC. They account for a significantly larger fraction of tokens.[64]

Despite the *to*-PRC therefore evidently having been better established in OE than often assumed, the construction was crucially very much lexically limited to these two specific verb classes, i.e. communication and 'bringing/sending'. Most importantly, prepositional uses of verbs of caused possession with a human or animate recipient ('giving'-verbs) are not attested in this period. This strongly suggests that the *to*-PRC was not yet established to the same extent and with the same range that was developed later on (Mitchell 1985: 513; Allen 2006: 214). This is clear even if we acknowledge De Cuypere's proposal that the use of the *to*-PP for recipients was embryonically present already in OE as well (De Cuypere 2013: 126–127; De Cuypere 2015c: 19–21).[65] His assumption is based on examples such as the following (50a-c):

64 More detailed results and the statistical analysis are found in De Cuypere (2015c: 3–7).

65 De Cuypere contemplates whether the addressee *to*-PP with verbs of communication could be considered a (metaphorical) recipient function as well, which would suggest an advanced grammaticalisation path (*to*GOAL > *to*REC > *to*ADDR). He concludes, however, "that the distinction between Addressee and Recipient is here warranted" (De Cuypere 2015c: 18), meaning that the reanalysis presumably took place directly between goals and addressees of communicative events, while *to* only came to mark prototypical recipients of concrete transfer-events at a later stage.

(50) a. Ic oswulf ond Beornðryð min gemecca *sellað*
I Oswulf and Beornthryth my wife give
to cantuarabyrg **to cristes cirican**$_{\text{REC?}}$ <u>ðæt land</u>$_{\text{TH}}$
to Canterbury to Christ's church the land
'I, Oswulf and my wife Beornthryth give to Christ's church at Canterbury the land'
(codocu1.o1: charter 37.2; De Cuypere 2015c: 20; also Visser 1963: 624)

b. Denewulf bisceop *leton* **to Beornulfa**$_{\text{REC?}}$
Denewulf bishop let to Beornwulf
<u>xv hiora hida landes</u>$_{\text{TH}}$
15 their hides of land
'Bishop Denewulf let to Beornwulf fifteen hides of their land'
(S1285, dated: c.AD 902; De Cuypere 2015c: 20)

c. and we <u>ðe</u>$_{\text{TH}}$ eft *genimað* **to us**$_{\text{REC?}}$
and we you again take to us
'and we will take you again to us'
(cocathom2,ÆCHom_II,_22:197.241.4383; De Cuypere 2015c: 21)

While the *to*-PP in (50a) is ambiguous between a goal and a recipient (the church as a social community, metonymically referred to through the place name), examples (50b-c) undoubtedly involve human recipients and abstract transfer rather than concrete movement of the theme. The latter therefore qualify as *to*-recipient constructions proper. Even so, De Cuypere (2015c: 21) also concedes that these uses are exceedingly rare in the OE data, serving as further evidence that the full establishment of the *to*-PRC as a viable alternative to the DOC was yet to come.[66] A gradual increase of the new recipient uses instead of a saltational shift from one meaning to the other at the transition from Old to Middle English is in any case expected in usage-based, cognitive/functional theories of language change (De Cuypere 2015c: 22).

Importantly, *to* was not the only preposition used with Old English ditransitive verbs. Quite the contrary, a range of prepositional constructions were available for speakers as alternatives to the DOC, ample attestations of which can readily be found. For example, verbs of privation or dispossession such as *ætbregdan* 'take away', *biniman* 'steal' or *afyran* 'remove, take away' (51) regularly occurred with a prepositional deprivee-REC, mainly introduced by *from* or

66 De Cuypere's explanation for the absence of 'real' *to*-PRCs, namely that this use "was syntactically blocked by the ACC+DAT DOC" (2015c: 21), will be discussed at greater length below.

of (De Cuypere 2015a: 233; cf. also Visser 1963: 633; McLaughlin 1983; Mitchell 1985; Molencki 1991).

(51) a.

afyrde	**fram**	**hire**$_{\text{REC}}$	þa	leohtnesse$_{\text{TH}}$
took away	from	her	the	brightness

'took the brightness away from her'
(Wærferth Dial. Greg. 288, I; Visser 1963: 633)

b.

Ðu	*afyrdest*	**of**	**Jacobe**$_{\text{REC}}$	ða	hæftned$_{\text{TH}}$
you	took away	of	Jacob	the	captivity

'you took the captivity away from Jacob'
(Ps. Th. 84, 1.; Bosworth-Toller, s.v. *a-fyrran*)

c.

him	ageafe	þæt$_{\text{TH}}$	he	ær	**on**	**him**$_{\text{REC}}$	*bereafode*
him	restored	that	he	before	on	him	robbed

'restored him what he had before stolen from him'
(Ors. 3, 11; S. 146, 30.; Bosworth-Toller, s.v. *be-reafian*)

It can also be assumed that the verb classes found in *to*-PRCs in Old English could occur with other goal-prepositions such as *towards* or *till.* Unfortunately, these PRC paraphrases including prepositions other than *to* have not received much attention so far, and an in-depth analysis (especially of quantitative data) of the constructions in Old English is still lacking. How frequent such other prepositional REC-patterns really were in comparison to the DOC uses in OE thus remains to be seen. What is nevertheless certain is that they were present and by no means rare in OE already.

A similar issue arises with prepositional theme patterns. Reference works and dictionaries of Old English suggest that "prepositional constructions of this kind were already widely current in Old English" (Visser 1963: 613). This is manifest in instances of verbs of dispossession as in (52), where the deprivee is expressed by a NP, but the theme is marked by a preposition. These examples stand in direct variation with the PRC-occurrences in (51) above, as well as with DOC uses of the same verbs (see e.g. 53).

(52) a.

Gif	hwylc	man	*reafige*	**oðerne**$_{\text{REC}}$	æt	his	dehter$_{\text{TH}}$
if	any	man	robs	other	at	his	daughter

'if any man robs another of his daughter'
(Ll. Th. ii. 208, 7.; Bosworth-Toller, s.v. *reafian*)

b. Hi *bereafodon* **Loth**$_{REC}$ æt his æhton$_{TH}$
they robbed Lot at his possessions
'they robbed Lot of his possessions'
(Prud. 2 b : Chr. 1043; P. 163, 34; Bosworth-Toller, s.v. *be-reafian*)

(53) Heo **hit**$_{REC}$ ne *mæg* his gewittes$_{TH}$ *bereafian*
she it not may its faculty rob
'she cannot rob it of its faculty'
(Bt. 5, 3; Fox 12, 25.; Bosworth-Toller, s.v. *be-reafian*)

Finally, there is some evidence that malefactive verbs like *to break* could be used in different NP-constructions; this is illustrated in the sentences in (54), which include a direct object (head) as well as a second argument specifying the affected entity (dragon/ men). However, it is unclear whether these should be analysed as DOCs, possessive patterns, or neither. This is due to the fact that in Old English, different cases were available for the objects of ditransitive verbs, including genitives (and that the cases were often formally indistinguishable). For example, the REC-argument in (54a) is most likely an accusative, whereas (54b) involves an affectee in the genitive and is accordingly ambiguous between a 'proper' DOC and a possessive construction. I table this issue for the moment but take it up again later (section 3.2.1).

(54) a. Ðu *gebræce* **ðæt** **dracan**$_{ACC?}$ heafod$_{ACC}$
you broke the dragon('s) head
'you broke the dragon's head'
(Ps. Th. 73, 13; Bosworth-Toller, s.v. *ge-brecan*)

b. Heafod$_{ACC}$ he *gebteceþ* **hæleða** **mæniges**$_{GEN?}$
head(s) he breaks men many
'he breaks the heads of many men (warriors)'
(Ps. Th. 109, 7. Bosworth-Toller, s.v. *ge-brecan*)

The essential conclusion to take away from this chapter is that at the end of Old English, several alternative patterns were used with specific ditransitive verb classes on top of the DOC. Nevertheless, these (prepositional) patterns did not extend to all verb classes; most strikingly, verbs of possessional transfer such as *give* could not occur in any of the variants, neither PRCs nor PTCs. I therefore argue that no abstract link between the DOC and the PRC, and specifically the *to*-PRC, had formed at this point. Instead, only lower level connections between (some) individual verb classes and individual PP-types existed. The emergence of the dative alternation proper – as a more schematic generalisation – is then essentially a Middle English phenomenon. This change is the main subject of the following section. Preceding this discussion, a brief comment on the general development of prepositional alternatives in Middle English is given.

3.1.2 The dative alternation in Middle English

Common wisdom holds that PP-patterns saw an overall substantial increase in the course of the Middle English period, possibly starting already in late Old English (e.g. Mustanoja 1960: 348; Lundskær-Nielsen 1993: 113–115; Fischer and van der Wurff 2006: 166; *inter alia*). This development is typically thought to reflect three sub-changes, namely the following:

First, the type frequency of prepositions rose from late OE onwards, with a number of new prepositions being added to the inventory. Overviews of this development are given in Mustanoja (1960: 345–346) as well as Strang (1970: 274–275) and Lundskær-Nielsen (1993: 113); a constructionist approach to the emergence of complex prepositions such as *by means of* in Late Middle English is presented in S. Hoffmann (2005).

Second, individual prepositions saw an expansion of their range of uses during Middle English, with many of them acquiring more procedural functions in addition to their originally basic spatial meaning (Lundskær-Nielsen 1993: 114; also Traugott 1972: 127). For instance, Iglesias-Rábade (2011) shows that figurative uses of PP-adverbials increased over time. This indicates that the prepositions became considerably bleached and extended to new contexts in this period.

Third, PP-patterns that had already existed as optional variants of more nominal constructions in Old English grew in proportional frequency during Middle English. A good case in point is the increase of the periphrastic *of*-genitive, which came to 'replace' the morphological genitive in most functions during the course of the period.[67] Importantly, this change also affected genitive case-marked NP-arguments of transitives: Verbs like *wundrian* 'wonder', for example, formerly construed with a genitive NP, are more and more frequently found with *of*-phrases in Middle English (55); cf. Fischer (1992: 233–234). This finds a correspondence in NP-arguments of transitive verbs taking other cases such as the dative or accusative, which were likewise increasingly often used in prepositional constructions. As seen in (56), the Middle English verb *hlysnan* 'listen' e.g. appears both with an originally accusative NP-object and in a prepo-

67 For more information on the *of*-genitive see Mustanoja (1960: 75); Fischer (1992: 225); Rosenbach (2002: 179); also Allen (2003, 2005, 2009).

sitional construction involving *to*; the former became progressively less frequent in favour of the latter over time.

(55) *Wundredenn* **off all þatt hemm . Wass Cwiddedd**PP
wondered of all that them . was told
'wondered about everything that they were told'
(Ormulum (Burchfield transcript) l. 7633; OED, s.v. *wonder*)

(56) a. *Listneð* nu **a wunder**NP
listen now a miracle
'Listen now to a miracle'
(Bestiary 398; OED, s.v. *listen*)

b. *Lustniez* nouþe **to mi speche**PP
listen now to my speech
'Listen now to my speech'
(S. Eng. Leg. I. 462/2; OED, s.v. *listen*)

Interestingly, these uses were often not limited to specific verb-preposition combinations. Rather, there was great variability, especially at the beginning of the period. For example, ME *wondren* 'wonder' collocates with a range of prepositions apart from *of*, including *on*, *upon*, *at* and *over*, while it is mostly restricted to *about* in PDE (OED, s.v. *wonder*; cf. also Fischer 1992: 233–234).[68] Traugott (1972: 127) alludes to such developments when she states that "in some instances they [i.e. PPs] were generalized considerably further than they are now and many prepositional uses that developed in ME and ENE [i.e. Early New English] dropped out again later". In the same vein, Strang (1970: 274–275) mentions that Middle English saw "a good deal of experimental exuberance" in PP-usage, which was re-limited in later periods (further Lundskær-Nielsen 1993: 113–114). Individual prepositions thus often 'crystallised' in their use with particular verbs over time, with stronger collocational preferences forming.

The same developments are seen with ditransitive patterns. This change is also much more systematic and more conspicuous than other examples, and

68 Fischer (1992: 234) suggests that the variability in preposition use was more restricted in the earlier texts but expanded later: "what we see developing is a system that at first shows a more or less one-to-one correspondence between the new prepositions and the old case forms; more prepositions enter into it at a later stage which could then be used to signal finer semantic role distinctions". However, Traugott's (1972) idea of an 'experimentation' phase seems to be closer to the actual data situation. Fischer's observation may be the result of a smaller sample set for the earlier stage or could point to a more complex development of expansion in a first step, and reduction only in a second step.

therefore deserves closer attention: In Middle English, the *to*-PRC expands in scope, i.e. becomes less lexically restricted, and comes to be used with other verb classes (importantly including verbs of transfer/ giving). Possibly as a reflection of this extension, the fraction of ditransitive verbs in *to*-PRCs rose substantially from early Middle English onwards. In late Middle English, it was reportedly used roughly with the same frequency as in PDE (Mustanoja 1960: 96; also Fischer 1992: 379–380; Sówka-Pietraszweska 2012). The *to*-pattern thereby establishes itself as a fully viable and productive alternative option to the DOC. Ultimately, it becomes the main, almost exclusive variant (as compared to PRCs including prepositions other than *to*). I consequently view the emergence of the dative alternation – as an increasingly strong link between one specific PRC-pattern and the DOC – as an essentially Middle English change. How this emergent connection can be modelled has to my knowledge not been addressed in more detail anywhere in the literature so far (with the exception of McFadden's generative account of 2002). In the following, I briefly outline previous accounts of the dative alternation in Middle English; all of the existing research centres on the *to*-PRC. Information on other possible alternatives in this period is again scarce. Visser (1963: 313), among others, remarks that they increased in Middle English as well, corresponding to the general move to more analytic structures.

Tab. 1: Frequency distribution of DOC vs. *to*-PRC as given in the studies of McFadden (2002: 113, top) and Polo (2002: 141, bottom)

	DOC	*to*-PRC	TOTAL	% *to*-PRC
M1	166	10	176	5.68
M2	22	52	74	70.27
M3	85	180	265	67.93
M4	60	44	104	42.31
PCI[69]	9	1	10	10
PCII	2	2	4	50
AW	24	22	46	47.83

69 PCI/PCII = First/Second Continuation of the *Peterborough Chronicle*; AW = *Ancrene Wisse*; St. Iul. = *St. Iuliene*; Rolle = Richard Rolle's *The Form of Living*. Note that Polo's results may also suggest dialectal variation, as the text with the highest proportion of *to*-PRCs (Rolle) is distinctly Northern.

	DOC	*to*-PRC	TOTAL	% *to*-PRC
St. Iul.	2	7	9	77.78
Rolle	0	52	52	100

Quantitative evidence on the frequency distribution of the dominant variants (DOC and *to*-PRC) is presented in McFadden (2002) and Polo (2002), whose results are reproduced in a condensed way in Tab. 1.[70] The validity of Polo's results can, however, be questioned, since her study is based on very few texts and a limited number of verbs. Polo claims that due to the complete absence of some patterns in individual texts in her database, "numbers, no matter how small, start having statistical relevance to our purposes" (2002: 133). Since this non-attestation could, however, also be due to pure accident, and the token frequency of the other patterns is also highly limited, I would tend to disagree with this statement.

As shown in McFadden's study on the two constructions in the *Penn-Helsinki Parsed Corpus of Middle English*, the number of *to*-PRCs is still comparatively low in M1 – certain texts exhibit no instances at all – but rises significantly after this earliest period (2002: 111). The reasons for this somewhat sudden increase of the *to*-PRC in early Middle English are typically either sought in the loss of case marking, with PPs having to step in more often to disambiguate semantic roles (see section 3.2.1), or in language contact with French (e.g. Ingham subm.). When a growing number of French loan words entered the language, this supposedly also included ditransitives, marked with a preposition *à*. As Allen (2006: 215) remarks, the influx of loan verbs in prepositional constructions, which also frequently replaced native OE verbs, might then have boosted the use of the *to*-PRC with native verbs as well (also Visser 1963: 624; Gerwin 2014: 142). In this book, language contact is not considered as a factor, so the focus will be on the role played by loss of case marking as well as inherent features of PP-constructions in contrast to NP-patterns.

What is furthermore notable in McFadden's data is the significant drop in proportion of the *to*-PRC towards the end of the period (from almost 70% to roughly 40%). This downwards trend presumably stabilised after Middle English. The constructions' precise fate and distribution in subsequent periods is investigated in Wolk et al.'s (2013) study of *A Representative Corpus of Historical English Registers* (ARCHER; 1650-1989), which finds that the proportions of *to*-PRCs as compared to DOCs has remained remarkably constant over the last

70 A third, more extensive study is in progress (cf. De Cuypere 2015b).

centuries. The fraction taken up by the prepositional construction "modestly fluctuates" between 30 and 39 per cent; minor changes in the proportional distribution are non-significant (Wolk et al. 2013: 392–393). A slightly different situation is suggested by Gerwin's (2014: 144–145) results drawn from the same corpus: Her data show a statistically significant increase in *to*-PRCs between the 17th (approximately 20 per cent) and the 20th century (ca. 29 per cent). In Gerwin's analysis, the prepositional pattern thus increased until the 1900s, when the trend reversed, and DOCs gained ground again (moving from about 50 per cent in the early 20th ct. to about 70 per cent in the 1980s).[71] Nevertheless, both accounts are comparable to and compatible with studies of the dative alternation in PDE. Although there is some deviation between different varieties of English, these accounts point to a distribution of about 70 per cent DOC and 30 per cent *to*-PRC today (e.g. Röthlisberger subm.). Furthermore, the assumption of Middle English being the major locus of change concerning an increased use of the *to*-PRC and the emergence of the dative alternation is not challenged by either of the two studies.

The establishment of the benefactive alternation, i.e. the paraphrase-ability of ditransitive verbs of creation or preparation (like *bake, build, buy*) by a *for*-PRC, has to my knowledge also been largely neglected in the literature so far. While it is plausible to assume that such verbs were occasionally found with *for*-RECs in Middle English, it is therefore difficult to determine whether a relationship between the DOC and the *for*-PRC that was of a similar systematicity as the DOC/*to*-PRC link developed around the same time. The results of the present study (chapter 4) suggest that this was not the case, but that the emergence of the benefactive alternation was rather a feature of post-Middle English only. This means that the benefactive alternation must have been established at some point between Early Modern English and PDE; data from later periods should yield more insights on this issue (Zehentner and Traugott forthc.).

In the next section, I briefly discuss the most important formal and functional changes in the members of the dative alternation (as well as the other variants, as far as possible). This is relevant for this book in that it aims to pro-

71 It is not entirely clear to me how these differences in results came about, as Gerwin is somewhat vague in her description of the ARCHER ditransitive data: Although it can be assumed that the same 21 verbs that were investigated for the other corpora in her study were also drawn on in the case of ARCHER, this is not explicitly stated. Wolk et al.'s data is based on a greater number of verbs, and generally seems to be more inclusive. Their findings are also more in line with the account proposed in the present study; however, in order to draw a decisive conclusion, the respective datasets and methodologies would have to be considered in more detail.

vide an explanation not only for how the alternation came into being, but also for the precise features the variants exhibit today. I start with an overview of how the loss of case marking affected ditransitive patterns, before commenting on the fixation of word order both in the ditransitive clause and concerning the order of objects. Last, the semantics of the constructions involved are dealt with.

3.2 Formal and functional changes in the members of the dative alternation

3.2.1 Loss of case marking with ditransitives

The system-wide loss of case-marking distinctions can be considered one of the most influential changes in the history of English, figuring prominently in discussions of the differences between Old and Middle English (e.g. Sweet 1874 on the periodisation of Middle English). Although there is disagreement as to the precise dynamics between various changes at that time, it is generally taken to have had profound consequences for the entire language system; this also goes for the complementation patterns of ditransitive verbs. In the following, I first provide some very basic information on case marking in Old English, before moving on to its demise at the transition between the periods, and potential causes of this development.

3.2.1.1 Case marking in Old English ditransitives

In Old English, the nominal inflectional system inherited from Germanic was, at least in comparison to PDE, still largely intact. It featured four productive cases (nominative, accusative, dative, and genitive), two numbers (singular and plural), as well as three grammatical genders (masculine, feminine, and neuter). However, as Lass (1992: 103) points out, case syncretism was already relatively advanced at this point as well, and "it was virtually impossible for any single noun form to be uniquely marked for all three" of these dimensions. In fact, many inflectional classes did not distinguish formally between various categories; for instance, nominative-accusative syncretism was widespread especially in the plural. Although many inflectional suffixes were therefore highly ambiguous regarding their precise function, some endings still exclusively expressed a single category. In addition, much less overlap was present in the adjectival and pronominal paradigms. This leads Allen (1995: 163) to conclude that despite significant reductions in the case marking system, no category distinctions had been lost yet in OE.[72]

As to the function of case forms in the clause (especially concerning verbal arguments), it has been noted that the nominative most commonly marked subjects/agents, while accusative marking is most frequently found with direct objects of transitive verbs, i.e. NPs expressing patients or themes of an event. Certain regularities also seem to have held for the other cases, whose occurrence often correlated with particular semantic relations. Genitive case, for instance, was reportedly preferred for the source of an emotion or mental state such as neglect, care, or enjoyment, in contrast to the dative, which most commonly denoted experiencers as well as recipients (Traugott 1992: 203). As Allen (1995: 25) remarks, "the case-marking possibilities of a given verb [were thus apparently] to a large extent related to the semantics of that verb". Nevertheless, many idiosyncrasies existed, and there was considerable variation in the case frames in which individual verbs occurred. For example, the animate experiencer of verbs such as *lician* 'to cause or feel pleasure' or *ofhreowan* 'to cause or feel pity' was variably marked with dative, accusative or nominative, while the cause/stimulus could be nominative or genitive (57); cf. e.g. Mitchell (1985: 449–464); Allen (1995: 25, Ch.3); Barðdal (2009).[73]

(57) **him**DAT *ofhreow* þæs mannesGEN
him pitied this man
'the man caused him pity/ he pitied the man'
Ælc.Th.I. 192.16 (Allen 1995: 68)

Discrepancies can furthermore be noted in the marking of the NP complements of prepositions: The same preposition can be found with different cases in various dialects or even texts. At the same time, two prepositions with highly similar meaning could be used with different cases. The latter situation is e.g. observed in passive constructions, where the oblique agent was usually marked by dative if introduced by *fram* 'from', but accusative if used with *þurgh* 'through'

72 For a more detailed overview and discussion of the morphological case system of Old English, see Mitchell (1985); Lass (1992); Allen (1995); Campbell (2001); Hogg (2002); Baker (2003-2012) and Quinn (2005).

73 Barðdal (2009: 138) provides a list of case constructions in earlier Germanic. However, this list is based entirely on historical Icelandic; whether the same case frames were in fact present in Old English as well is not guaranteed. A tentative list of OE verbs and their 'rections' is given in Mitchell (1985: 455–464). His inventory does not specify the case marking options for agent or experiencer arguments, though, but focuses on themes/patients of transitive verbs.

(Traugott 1992: 202; also Mitchell 1985: 497–498; van Kemenade 1987: 81; Lundskær-Nielsen 1993: 19–24; Alcorn 2011: 143–151).

Importantly, this variability in case marking is also found with the DOC as well as the prepositional ditransitive patterns available at this point. In regard to the former, verbs were not restricted to one individual case frame for marking the two object arguments in OE but could occur in a total of five different patterns (Tab. 2).

Tab. 2: Case frames for ditransitives in Old English (adapted from Allen 1995: 29)

	Recipient	Theme	Example
1.	Dative	Accusative	*giefan* 'give'
2.	Dative	Genitive	*forwyrnan* 'forbid'
3.	Accusative	Genitive	*bereafian* 'deprive'
4.	Accusative	Accusative	*læran* 'teach'
5.	Accusative	Dative	*bereafian* 'deprive'

Of these patterns, [DAT$_{REC}$-ACC$_{TH}$], i.e. the one which included a recipient-like argument marked with dative alongside an accusative-bearing theme (58a), was clearly prevalent, and appeared with a wide range of different verbs (Allen 1995: 29, 2006: 205–208; De Cuypere 2015a: 232).[74] The less prominent combinations of genitive themes with dative or accusative REC-arguments are illustrated in (58b-c). The clause in (58d) provides an example of [ACC$_{REC}$-DAT$_{TH}$], with the accusative in this case denoting the deprivee of an action, whereas (58e) features two accusative-marked arguments. The latter combination of [ACC$_{REC}$-ACC$_{TH}$] appears to have been the least frequent, available only to a small number of verbs (De Cuypere 2015a: 232).[75]

74 Although this frame is repeatedly mentioned as the most 'common' pattern in OE, no detail is given on the specific distributions in the relevant literature (with the exception of Visser 1963); neither do the authors always specify whether this statement refers to type or token frequency. The former is implied in e.g. Allen (1995: 28), who states that "[t]he majority of ditransitive verbs in OE selected for a dative Recipient, Source, or Goal, and an accusative Theme" (also De Cuypere 2015a: 231).

75 More examples as well as information on the (in)frequency of different patterns can be found in Visser (1963: 607–637); Mitchell (1985: 455–464); Allen (1995: 28–29), as well as De Cuypere (2015a: 231–233).

(58) a. *dældon* heora æhta$_{\text{ACC-TH}}$ **ealle** **þearfum**$_{\text{DAT-REC}}$
distributed their belongings all poor
'distributed their belongings to all the poor'
(coaelive, ÆLS_[Basil]:54.479; De Cuypere 2015a: 231)

b. and **him**$_{\text{DAT-REC}}$ mancynnes$_{\text{GEN-TH}}$ *benæmde*
and him mankind took away
'and took mankind away from him'
((*COE*) ÆCHom I, 31 460.8; Allen 1995: 28)

c. *bereafode* **Godes** **templ**$_{\text{ACC-REC}}$ goldes and seolfres$_{\text{GEN-TH}}$
stole God's temple gold and silver
'stole gold and silver from God's temple'
(coaelive, ÆLS_[Maccabees]:6.4838; De Cuypere 2015a: 232)

d. **hine**$_{\text{ACC-REC}}$ wædum$_{\text{DAT-TH}}$ *bereafian*
him clothes deprive
'to deprive him of his clothes'
(ÆCHom I, 29 426.4; Allen 1995: 29)

e. Se Halga Gast **hie**$_{\text{ACC-REC}}$ æghwylc god$_{\text{ACC-TH}}$ *lærde*
the holy spirit them every good taught
'The holy spirit taught them every good thing'
(Blickl. Homl. 12: 13121.1613; De Cuypere 2015a: 233)

Other possible case combinations such as [DAT-DAT] or [GEN-GEN] expressing a ditransitive relation of some sort are not attested, according to De Cuypere's (2015a) investigation of the YCOE. Clauses which feature a double genitive or double dative have to be interpreted differently; for example, in (59) we are dealing with a 'split', discontinuous phrase (cf. De Cuypere 2015a: 233).

(59) Ne *scealt* **þu** þæs andgites$_{\text{GEN-1}}$ *bedæled*
not shall you this wisdom imparted
beon þisses eadigan mannes lifes$_{\text{GEN-2}}$ Equities
be this blessed man life Equity
'you shall not be imparted of the wisdom of the life of the blessed man Equity'
(cogregdC, GD_1_[C]:4.33.12.365; De Cuypere 2015a: 233)

As to the semantics of the different case frames, some do seem to have been common with specific verb classes. However, they were typically not completely restricted in their scope. Many verbs and verb classes furthermore readily changed between the frames. A good case in point are genitive combinations such as [DAT_{REC}-GEN_{TH}], which often occur with verbs of privation or 'taking away' like *bereafian* 'deprive' but are at same time also found with *(ge)unnan* 'grant' or *(ge)tiþian* 'allow', among others. On the other hand, verbs of privation did not necessarily involve a genitive, since the theme could also be marked by dative, i.e. the verbs regularly appeared in an [ACC$_{REC}$-DAT$_{TH}$] frame (Visser 1963: 621; Mitchell 1985: 453; De Cuypere 2015a: 232). This means that although certain tendencies can be discerned, the case frames were not clearly associated with individual verb classes or senses. Mitchell even claims that "anyone who tries to erect these tendencies into elaborate and rigid schemes of classification will not get far" (1985: 453; cf. also De Cuypere 2015a: 231).

The idiosyncratic preferences of verbs in Old English have been taken to reflect lexical case assignment rather than structural case assignment in much of the (generative) literature (e.g. van Kemenade 1987; Allen 1995; Quinn 2005). Structural case here refers to a dinstiction in marking between 'subject' (typically nominative) and 'object' (typically accusative), meaning that case is assigned based on a sentence's structure. In contrast, lexical case assignment indicates that individual verbs idiosyncratically select for case marking on their arguments. For example, the OE verb *(ge)helpan* 'help' takes a genitive or dative direct object rather than an accusative one (Allen 1995: 25). This view is challenged by Barðdal in her recent paper on 'Lexical vs. structural case: a false dichotomy' (2011), in which she presents a constructionist approach to case frames on the basis of Icelandic data. On this account, all case marking of verbal arguments in Icelandic is lexical, and the different case frames are captured by different argument structure constructions at various levels of schematicity (Barðdal 2011: 651). As taken up in section (7.2), I argue that such an analysis also suggests itself for the Old English situation: The OE double object case frames constitute different constructions which are linked to each other as well as to a more schematic DOC, which is formally underspecified in regard to case marking. The abstract DOC is on the other hand connected to various subsenses, instantiated by specific verb classes. These semantic sub-constructions do not fully correspond to the formal sub-constructions, even though some (stronger or weaker) links between them might be present.

The availability of different case constructions must also have been given with the Old English prepositional ditransitive patterns. For example, in the case of the Old English *to*-PRC, the most frequent case frame was [*to*DAT$_{REC}$-ACC$_{TH}$], while e.g. dispossessive PTCs typically involved a genitive or dative theme (Visser 1963: 313; De Cuypere 2015c). In general, as Mitchell (1985: 497–498) shows, many prepositions selected for dative marking on their NP-complements – a tendency which certainly also held for ditransitive PP-patterns. It can also be expected that the various case frames likewise overlapped in meaning, and that no systematic correspondence between frame and meaning held. However, the specific number of types of ditransitive prepositional case constructions in Old English and their frequency distribution as well as semantics remains to be established.

3.2.1.2 Case marking in Middle English ditransitives

From late Old English onwards, what had been left of the formal case marking system increasingly disappeared; this led to a largely non-inflectional state of the language by the end of the Middle English period. It is clear that this change was gradual rather than sudden in all aspects: First, it proceeded at different speeds in different dialects, with most changes being more advanced in the North, while Southern texts tended to be more conservative. This phenomenon has often been attributed to the greater impact of Scandinavian in the northern parts of England. Language contact may indeed have contributed to the faster spread of the change, but even so did not necessarily trigger it in the first place (Fischer 1992: 207–208; Lundskær-Nielsen 1993: 19–24; Allen 1995: 212). Second, the loss of case marking was not a unified process which affected all categories and forms simultaneously, but rather represents a conglomerate of individual changes taking place over an extended period of time. As mentioned in the preceding section, the distinction between nominative and accusative had already been lost in many classes in Old English times, even if it was maintained for others. Allen (1995: 165) shows that this specific instance of syncretism then further progressed during Middle English (cf. also Quinn 2005: 13).

From 1100 onwards, the English inflectional system was hit with a number of further changes, which greatly blurred the boundaries between the different case categories (Allen 2005: 230–231). Genitive-marked object arguments of transitive and ditransitive verbs were increasingly replaced by dative, accusative or prepositional objects (e.g. *yearn*+ GEN vs. *yearn+after*) from late OE onwards (Fischer 1992: 225–232; Allen 1995: 217–219; 2005: 227–242). Barðdal (2009: 17–18) ascribes this development to the fact that constructions with genitive arguments had a lower type frequency and accordingly lower productivity than other case-constructions with very similar semantic functions (cf. also Croft 2000: 121–124). Also, case agreement on modifiers (determiners, quantifiers, and adjectives) disappeared, and category distinctions between dative and accusative became fuzzier in both in the nominal and the pronominal system

(Lass 1992: 110).[76] With the completion of this change around 1300, the morphological system of the language became more or less what it is in PDE now (Allen 1995: 210). The only inflectional suffixes retained until today are possessive -s[77] and the plural marker -s, both of which derive from the most common masculine *a*-stems. A distinction between nominative and object case, or rather, between 'subjective' and 'objective' or oblique case is maintained only in the pronominal system (compare the maintenance of *he* vs. *him*, but at the same time the increasing unpopularity *whom*-interrogative).

What did these developments mean for the double object constructions and its prepositional paraphrases? As presented in greater detail in section (7.2.1.1.), I propose that already in the earliest Middle English texts, genitive objects of ditransitive verbs were infrequent or (in some classes) difficult to distinguish from dative and accusative forms. This added to the prevalence of the 'generic' [DAT$_{REC}$-ACC$_{TH}$] DOC and generally decreased the number of ditransitive case frames. Over the course of the period, the formal differences between dative and accusative were then further obscured. The (late) Middle English DOC is thus best described as involving two inflection-less, unmarked (or ambiguously marked) NPs which fulfilled the functions of recipient and theme. Identifying and distinguishing between the semantic roles of the two arguments accordingly became more and more reliant on context and animacy asymmetries instead of case marking (Fischer 1992: 379). The sentence in (60) illustrates this – contextual rather than formal evidence would have led ME speakers to conclude that it was Joseph who was being sold to the merchants and not the other way round.

(60)	*Wolle*	we	*sullen*	<u>Iosep</u>$_{OBJ/TH}$	**þis**	**chapmen**	?
	Will	we	sell	Joseph	these	merchants	?

'Shall we sell Joseph to these merchants that have come here?'
(JacobandJ. 118; Fischer et al. 2000: 74)

Similar processes took place in the case of the prepositional patterns: With the *to*-PRCs, for instance, the case frame of [*to*DAT$_{REC}$-ACC$_{TH}$] probably increased at the expense of others, before an unmarked [*to*REC-TH] emerged with the convergence of the two categories.

76 See also Pinsker (1959: 159); Lundskær-Nielsen (1993: 120–124); Allen (1995: 185–195, 2005: 233); Baugh and Cable (2002: 160); Haselow (2011: 252).

77 Presupposing, of course, that PDE possessive -s in fact is a morphological case marker, which is debated (e.g. Huddleston and Pullum 2002: 479–481).

Although determining the semantic relations in a sentence was not made impossible by the loss of morphological case marking, it nevertheless represented a major change for the English language. Among other things, the development is likely connected to the increase of more analytic means of expression as well as the growing fixation of word order during Middle English (see also section 3.3). The triggers of the demise of case are traditionally sought in phonological erosion due to stress shift to the first syllable, with unstressed final syllables becoming weakened and eventually lost (e.g. Fischer 1992: 222; Lass 1992: 105; Barðdal 2009: 123–125, 142). Even without stress shifts, however, the OE system of case marking would have been "ripe for analogical remodelling", as Lass points out (1992: 103).[78] That is, the great deal of formal ambiguity already present in Old English, and the (universal) trend towards eliminating or avoiding synonymy/semantic overlap between formally distinct case constructions, could have led to to the convergence and eventual disappearance of case distinctions (Barðdal 2009: 140–141; also Luraghi 1987; Croft 2000). Van Trijp (2013) furthermore shows that paradigmatic simplifications may be driven by the communicative needs and constraints of language users; he suggests that language systems tend to develop towards greater efficiency for processing, pronunciation and perception (for example by reducing case markers). This is beneficial for the speakers as long as disambiguation of utterances is still possible or enabled by other strategies (van Trijp 2013: 127–129). In any case, it is safe to assume that the change was the "result of a complex interplay of several mechanisms" rather than the product of one single process (Barðdal and Kulikov 2009: 474).

To conclude, it is undeniable that the case marking system saw an increasing and sweeping reduction at the transition from Old to Middle English and during Middle English period. The main consequence of the change for ditransitives was the emergence and eventual categorical use of an unmarked DOC with a form [V NP NP], and correspondingly, prepositional patterns of the type [V *prep*NP NP].

3.2.2 Fixation of word order in ditransitives

In the following sections, I introduce a second development which affected ditransitives in the history of English, namely the fixation of word order. This

78 See e.g. Allen (1995); Blake (2001); Quinn (2005); Harbert (2007); Barðdal and Kulikov (2009); Bertacca (2009); Boas (2009); Kulikov (2009) for more detail on these issues.

concerns both clause level order as well as the VP-internal order of objects in ditransitive patterns. As to the former, it is clear that the present discussion will not do justice to the immense amount of research that has been carried out on this more general issue. It is nevertheless relevant for the development of ditransitives, since the emergence of a clear subject versus object slot based on discourse-pragmatic and semantic features such as animacy and topicality is complicated by the presence of a second object argument in ditransitive clauses. Moreover, changes in the position of prepositional phrases of any kind in the clause are certainly of interest concerning the order of objects in PRCs and PTCs.

3.2.2.1 Word order in the (ditransitive) clause

An in-depth overview of various theoretical approaches to word order changes in the history of English can be found in Denison (1993), as well as other handbooks on historical English linguistics (cf. e.g. Fischer 1992; Fischer et al. 2000). The most extensive data-based accounts presented so far – to my knowledge – are Bech (2001) and Trips (2002). The latter, like most (or a large part of) the literature on diachronic English word order, was written in an explicitly generative framework.[79] Recent accounts have mostly focussed on the impact of information structure on word order variants. Cognitive-functional (in particular construction grammar) approaches to changes in the history of English word order are more or less non-existent; a constructionist perspective on word order changes in the history of Dutch is provided in van de Velde (2014).

Word order in Old English has generally been regarded as a thorny issue. Allen (1995: 32) e.g. points out that "OE constituent order was in fact so complex that analyses which assume a rigid positioning for the verb have not been successful in both accounting for all the observed possibilities and ruling out patterns not found in the texts". The issue is worsened by Old English often eluding a straightforward assessment in terms of subject, verb, object positioning: As discussed in Allen (1995), Barðdal (2009) or Möhlig-Falke (2012), among others, it is questionable whether a clear subject vs. object slot really existed in (early) Old English already. On the one hand, the presence of an explicit subject was not an absolute requirement at this point yet, which is why OE is sometimes mentioned as a pro-drop language. On the other hand, various constructions

79 See also Pintzuk and Kroch (1985), van Kemenade (1987, 1997, 1999, 2002), Koopman (1990), Pintzuk (1991, 1995, 1996), Kroch and Taylor (1994, 1997, 2000b), Roberts (1997, 2007), Koopman and van der Wurff (2000), van Kemenade and Los (2006); van Kemenade (2009, 2011, 2012); Westergaard (2010); Hinterhölzl and van Kemenade (2012); Taylor and Pintzuk (2012a, 2012b, 2014, 2015), and many others.

(usually called 'impersonals') existed where none of the involved arguments exhibited all features typically associated with a subject – such as nominative case marking or control of verbal agreement (cf. Harbert 2007, *inter alia*). This evidently makes it difficult to discuss clausal word order in a way that goes beyond analysing relative verb placement.

Even if we assume a clear distinction between the syntactic roles of subject and object in Old English, assessing word order in this period is highly problematic because of the great deal of variation that the system exhibited. For example, both OV and VO orders (61) are found, and despite a preference for V2, V3-position is not strictly excluded at any time (e.g. van Kemenade 1987; Pintzuk 1991; Denison 1993).

(61)

Se	mæsse-preost	*sceal*	**monnum**	*bodian*
the	mass-priest	shall	men	preach
SUBJ		V_{fin}	OBJ	$V_{non\text{-}fin}$

þone	soðan	ȝeleafan
the	true	faith
OBJ		

'the mass priest must preach the true faith to the people'
(Ælfric's letter to Wulfstan 1, 175; Gast 2007: 48)

Furthermore, word order crucially seems to have depended on a variety of factors including clause type (main or subordinate) or type of constituents (e.g. Bech 2001). While main clauses were e.g. generally associated with (S)VO/SVX order (62a), subordinate clauses tended to be verb-final (62b).[80] SOV/ SXV was also preferred in main clauses with an initial conjunction such as *ac* 'but' or *ond* 'and' (62c).[81] Pronominal forms moreover typically behaved differently to nominal forms in that they frequently occurred in pre-verbal position even if this violated the V2 constraint; see, for instance, the pronominal object in (62d). Initial adverbials (especially *þa* 'then') as well as initial negative particles or interrogative pronouns, on the other hand, usually resulted in 'subject-verb inversion', i.e. XV(X)S order, for both pronominal and nominal subjects (62e-f; Allen 1995: 36; Haeberli 2000).

80 Bech (2001) is in fact not concerned with the positioning of S, V, and O, but rather distinguishes between subject, verb, and a slot for 'X', which could be filled by either objects, subject or object complements, or adverbials of any kind (adverbs, adverbial clauses, PP-adverbials).

81 But see Bech (2001: 89), who shows that clauses with coordinative conjunction are in fact more frequent with SVX order in OE already – of all conjunct clauses, 27.9% are found in this pattern, whereas only 15.3% occur with verb-final, i.e. SXV order.

(62) a. Se *bið* eallenga blind
he is quite blind
SUBJ V X
'he is quite blind'
(CP, 65:6; Bech 2001: 51)

b. þa he þa wiþ þone here
when he then with that army
X SUBJ X X
þær wæst *abisgod* *wæs*
the west occupied was
X $V_{non\text{-}fin}$ V_{fin}
'when he then was occupied against that army in the west'
(ASC. 894; Lundskær-Nielsen 1993: 62)

c. ac hie nugiet *ricsiende* *sindon*
but they still reigning are
X SUBJ X $V_{non\text{-}fin}$ V_{fin}
'but they are still reigning'
(Or, 38:7; Bech 2001: 58)

d. God him *worhte* ða reaf of fellum
God him made then garments of skin
SUBJ OBJ V X OBJ
'God then made them garments of skin'
(Ælfric's Homilies I, 147–148; Gast 2007: 48)

e. hwi *sceole* we oþres mannes *niman*
why should we other man's take
X V_{fin} SUBJ OBJ $V_{non\text{-}fin}$
'why should we take those of another man?'
(ÆLS 24.188; Haeberli 2000: 110)

f. þa *genam* hine se awyrgda gast
then took him the accursed spirit
X V OBJ SUBJ
'then the accursed spirit took him'
(BlHom, 27:8; Bech 2001: 54)

Although these 'rules' can account for a large number of instances, they were by no means absolute and categorical. Rather, as Bech (2001) and others show, they constitute probabilistic tendencies, and exceptions are readily found. This has led some authors to conclude that there is no systematicity at all, but that word order in Old English was essentially free (e.g. Fries 1940). More recently, however, it has been proposed that

> there is in fact nothing coincidental about Old English word order at all [...] if the verb is placed in clause-final or clause-late position, there are very good reasons for doing so, and these reasons may be found in the interplay between syntax, pragmatics, semantics, and sometimes stylistic factors. (Bech 2001: 194)

That is, the variation in word order patterns is now typically attributed to differences in givenness/accessibility of the subject and other constituents: While discourse-new arguments tend to be clause-late and often follow the verb, discourse-old or given arguments appear early in the clause, in pre-verbal position (Allen 1995; Los 2009; Los and Dreschler 2012; among others). A further factor assumed to have played a role in word order is the relative length or 'heaviness' of arguments, with longer constituents tending to be placed later in the clause (e.g. Pintzuk and Taylor 2006: 254; also Taylor and Pintzuk 2014, 2015).

In the course to Middle English and beyond, we then see a clear move away from the OE heterogeneity in ordering towards greater homogeneity. The VP gradually comes to be fixed to a position to the right of the subject argument, until by late Middle English a large majority of clauses show SVO order (Bech 2001: 197; also Kroch and Taylor 2000b; *inter alia*).[82] As to the reasons for this change, they may lie in the strong impact of pragmatic factors on OE word order, which could have led to syntactic constraints (such as the V2 tendency) being overridden. For example, pre-verbal position could have been reanalysed as a categorical subject position if subjects occurred in this slot with sufficient frequency due to discourse-pragmatic factors (Bech 2001: 194–195; van Kemenade 1987; Lightfoot 1991). Furthermore, loss of case inflections as well as language contact with Scandinavian are often mentioned as potential causes of the fixation of SVO (e.g. Kroch and Taylor 2000b; Trips 2002).

Before moving on to word order changes in ditransitives, a quick comment on the general distribution of prepositional phrases in Old and Middle English clauses is in order, as this is particularly relevant for ditransitive constructions. First of all, it should be mentioned that word order within the PP was not entirely fixed in Old English: In some cases, the prepositions could vary between pre- or post-position in relation to their complements (e.g. Alcorn 2011: 8; Visser

82 Bech (2001: 198) points out that other orders "had become pragmatically motivated by late ME". For instance, XVS was increasingly restricted to existential clauses, where the order still persists to today (cf. PDE *There*$_X$ *was*$_V$ *a change in the distribution of XVS*$_S$).

1963: 394, 396; Mitchell 1985: 441–443). This variation is strikingly absent from Middle English texts. As Lundskær-Nielsen (1993: 44) reports, "[d]uring the 12th century, a rather sudden standardization appears to have taken place in the sequential order of prepositions with a personal pronoun complement, so that from then onwards the order was invariably preposition followed by personal pronoun".

Regarding the position of PPs in the clause, it has been pointed out repeatedly that they could appear virtually everywhere in the clause in Old English, even more so than in PDE. This is especially true for adverbial, adjunctive, PPs. In both main and subordinate clauses, these PPs could occur before subject and verb, either clause-initially (63a), or after an initial adverbial, clause-medially after S and V (63b), intervening between subject and verb (63c) or clause-finally (63d) (Lundskær-Nielsen 1993: 66; Sato 2009: 177).

(63) a. **On þy ylcan gere**$_{PP}$ *worhte* se here geweorc
on the same year made the army fortress
'in the same year the army made a fortress'
(ASC, 896; Lundskær-Nielsen 1993: 66)

b. *foron* he **mid þrim scipum**$_{PP}$ ut ongen hie
went they with three ships out against them
'they went out against them with three ships'
(ASC, 897; Lundskær-Nielsen 1993: 66)

c. ær Hæsten **to Beamfleote**$_{PP}$ *come*
before Hæsten to Benfleet came
'before Hæsten came to Benfleet'
(ASC, 894; Lundskær-Nielsen 1993: 66)

d. *wæs* Hæsten þa þær *cumen* **mid his herge**$_{PP}$
was Hæsten then there come with his army
'Hæsten had then come there with his army'
(ASC, 894; Lundskær-Nielsen 1993: 66)

Middle English PPs are described as similarly variable, with both pre- and post-verbal position being found. Nevertheless, PPs increasingly came to be preferred in clause-peripheral position, or rather, PPs in intermediate position between subject and verb came to be dis-preferred (cf. Fischer 1992; Lundskær-Nielsen 1993). This is corroborated in Bech's (2001) survey of word order in main clauses, which includes adverbial PPs. In her data, a clear trend away from medial position can be observed. While almost 40% of adverbial PPs are found between subject and verb (in any order) in early Old English, these figures significantly drop to less than 5% in late Middle English. At the same time, PP-adverbials in position before subject and verb (either clause-initially, or following another adverbial), which are already highly frequent in Old English (roughly 50%), represent a large majority of all adverbial PP tokens in late ME (Bech 2001: 119–143). The infrequency of clause-late PPs in Bech's data might be due to the exclusion of certain patterns; also, final or late position of PPs might have been more frequent in subordinate clauses. Finally, including other types of PPs which were already present in OE and most certainly quite frequent in Middle English, may have a considerable effect on the proportions. For example, as indicated in De Cuypere (2015c: 10), the large majority of *to*-phrases in combinations with accusative NP objects (expressing e.g. directional locations as in [64]) were strongly associated with clause-late position. They thus usually followed the object rather than preceding it.

(64) Florus hine$_{\text{NP-ACC}}$ *astrehte* **to Maures fotum**$_{\text{PP}}$
Florus him prostrated to Maures' feet
'Florus prostrated himself at the Maures' feet'
(coaelive, ÆLS_[Maur]:180.1601; De Cuypere 2015c: 7)

As shown in the following section, clause-late position was also definitely an option for prepositional Recs in ditransitive clauses, if not even the preferred order. The same goes for PTC patterns, which still show a clear tendency towards PP-late order in PDE. Unfortunately, however, the latter issue has not been dealt with in any detail so far; therefore, most of the discussion below is focussed on the DOC vs. (*to*-)PRC constructions only.

3.2.2.2 Object order in Old English ditransitives

The order of the two object (or object-like) arguments of ditransitive verbs in PDE as well as the factors determining the choice between the patterns have received considerable attention in the linguistic literature, much more so than the diachronic dimension of this issue. However, De Cuypere's studies on word order in Old English ditransitives (2010, 2015a, 2015c), with an investigation of Middle English ditransitives being in progress, have remedied the situation to some extent.

Starting with the Old English double object construction, it is evident from the sample sentences in (65) that the order of the objects (independent of the specific case-marking) was flexible at this point, as both [Rec-Th] (65a) and [Th-Rec] (65b) orders can be found.

(65) a. and þær *geoffrode* **Gode**$_{\text{REC}}$ menigfealde lac$_{\text{TH}}$
and there offered God manifold gifts
'and offered God manifold gifts there'
(Ælfric, AS Hom. 578; De Cuypere 2010: 340)

b. Ðu *cyðest* mildheortnysse$_{\text{TH}}$ **ðinum ðeowan**$_{\text{REC}}$
you show mercy your servant
'you show mercy to your servant'
(Ælfric, AS Hom. 146; De Cuypere 2010: 340)

A number of studies on the frame of [DAT$_{\text{REC}}$-ACC$_{\text{TH}}$] report that the orders are distributed rather evenly in the investigated datasets, which suggests that no order can conclusively be regarded as basic or underlying (Koopman 1990; Allen 1995: 48).[83] De Cuypere (2015a: 26), who in his mixed-effects logistic regression analysis of data from the YCOE takes into account nominal as well as pronominal objects of ditransitives, arrives at a total of 38% [ACC-DAT] vs. 62% [DAT-ACC] orders (N=1,832). His findings furthermore show that contrary to some claims, and irrespective of the later development of the patterns, both orders were perfectly viable and productive at the end of the Old English period (De Cuypere 2015a: 244; cf. further Koopman and van der Wurff 2000: 262; Fischer and van der Wurff 2006: 189).

As to the factors influencing which order is chosen over the other, various suggestions have been put forward: For instance, relative length has quite unsurprisingly been found to affect the order of objects, with longer elements typically following shorter ones. This means that the shorter DAT$_{\text{REC}}$ is in relation to ACC$_{\text{TH}}$, the higher the likelihood will be that it precedes ACC$_{\text{TH}}$, and vice versa (De Cuypere 2015a: 239–240, 244). Also, the general tendency for pronominal elements to come before nominal constituents holds for ditransitive objects as well (e.g. Allen 1995: 48; Koopman and van der Wurff 2000: 261).[84] This is corroborated by De Cuypere's (2015a) results, which indicate that the orders of [*pron*DAT$_{\text{REC}}$-ACC$_{\text{TH}}$] and [*pron*ACC$_{\text{TH}}$-DAT$_{\text{REC}}$], as illustrated in (66a) and (66b) respectively, were more likely than the reverse patterns.[85]

83 I am not aware of any studies of word order with other case frames, but the underlying assumption is that they behaved roughly the same as the most frequent [DAT$_{\text{REC}}$-ACC$_{\text{TH}}$] pattern.

84 See also e.g. Huchon (1923); Bacquet (1962); Shannon (1964); Brown (1970); Carlton (1970); Kohonen (1978); Mitchell (1985); Koopman (1990); Fischer (1992) or De Cuypere (2010) for comments on the influence of length and pronominality.

85 DOCs with two pronominal objects are something of a special case (see section 3.2.2.4).

(66) a. þæt hi **him**REC heora lacTH *offrian* *sceoldon*
that they him their offerings offer should
'that they should offer him their offerings'
(cocathom1, ÆCHom_I, 31:439.11.6079; De Cuypere 2015a: 237)

b. þæt heo hiTH *dælde* **þearfum and wædlum**REC
that she them distributed poor and needy
'that she distributed them to the poor and needy'
(coaelive, ÆLS_[Eugenia]:140.276; De Cuypere 2015a: 237)

Two further variables relating to the ACC-theme which emerge as influential in De Cuypere's analysis are definiteness or 'specificity' and concreteness vs. abstractness (2015a: 237–238, 243; also Koopman 1990: 196). Sentences (67a-b) present examples of a definite and indefinite theme, respectively, while (68a) shows a concrete ACCTH-object 'meat', in contrast to the physically non-perceivable abstract theme object in (68b). The former, i.e. definite and/or concrete themes are expected to precede the latter (indefinite and/or abstract themes).

(67) a. and he *æteowð* þa wundaTH gewislice **him**REC
and he showed the wounds truly him
'and he truly showed the wounds to him'
(coaelhom, ÆHom_11:290.1637; De Cuypere 2015a: 237)

b. he *sealde* sum þingTH **þearfendum mannum**REC
he gave some thing poor people
'he gave something to poor people'
(cowsgosp, Jn_[WSCp]:13.29.6924; De Cuypere 2015a: 238)

(68) a. hi *moston* **him**REC *beran* unforboden flæscTH
they must him bear unforbidden meat
'that they might bring him unforbidden meat'
(coaelive, ÆLS_[Maccabees]:90.4871; De Cuypere 2015a: 238)

b. and **him**REC *forgeaf* ingehid ealra gereordaTH
and him gave knowledge all languages
'and gave them knowledge of all the languages'
(cocathom1, ÆCHom_I,_22:358.109.4414; De Cuypere 2015a: 238)

The choice between different object orders in OE ditransitives therefore seems to have been largely driven by discourse-pragmatic factors. More specifically, the distribution can, with De Cuypere (2015a: 245) be taken to reflect the principle of topicality or 'harmonic alignment'. This is defined by Bresnan and Ford (2010: 183) as follows:

> linguistic elements that are more or less prominent on a scale (such as the animacy or nominal-expression type scales) [tend] to be disproportionately distributed in respectively more or less prominent syntactic positions (such as preceding in word order or occupying a superordinate syntactic position).

This overlaps with findings on the dative alternation in later stages of English (with some exceptions). Furthermore, the results closely correspond to those for the choice between *to*-PRCs orders in Old English (De Cuypere 2015c). These patterns with prepositional addressees of communication verbs or goals of verbs of sending/bringing, were flexible in regard to the order of the objects, just like the double object construction. Accordingly, both [ACC-*to*DAT] (69a) and [*to*DAT-ACC] (69b) are found. However, as De Cuypere (2015c: 10, 14) shows, the former is far more frequent than the latter. Nevertheless, PP-first orders were a more than viable option in Old English – this is in stark contrast to PDE, where this order is highly marked, and restricted to specific contexts (e.g. heavy constituent-shifts).

(69) a. *sende* <u>his</u> <u>gewrit</u>TH **to þam wælhreowan casere**REC
sent his letter to the cruel emperor
'and sent his letter to the cruel emperor'
(coaelive,ÆLS:249.1090; De Cuypere 2015c: 17)

b. God *cwæð* **to Moysen**REC <u>ðæt</u> <u>he</u> <u>wolde</u> <u>cumin</u>TH
God said to Moses that he would come
'God said to Moses that he would come'
(cocathom2.o3: 196, 16; De Cuypere 2015c: 18)

De Cuypere's findings also indicate that the distribution of the orders remained stable during Old English, meaning that there was no change concerning the relative frequency of the orders towards the end (2015c: 13). The factors which are influential in the choice of one order over the other were pronominality, definiteness, relative length, as well as number of the *to*DAT, with singulars showing a higher likelihood of appearing in second position. Furthermore, animate *to*-recipients are preferentially associated with [*to*REC-TH] ordering, while inanimate *to*-recipients almost categorically select for the reverse order [TH-*to*REC] (De Cuypere 2015c: 13). As in the case of OE DOCs, these findings lend support to the 'harmonic alignment' or topicality hypothesis mentioned before (De Cuypere 2015c: 15; also Bresnan and Ford 2010: 183).

In sum, De Cuypere (2015c: 13–15) confirms that although all possible orders of DOCs and *to*-PRCs occurred with considerable frequency, already in Old English the ordering was to a certain extent dependent on the construction used. While *to*-PRCs appear to have preferred a [TH-REC] order, DOCs were more inclined towards [REC-TH] order. These biases, as well as the general distribution of orders with both constructions were most certainly motivated by discourse-functional (and semantic) factors such as topicality.

3.2.2.3 Object order in ditransitives in Middle English and beyond

The tendency for specific orders with the individual constructions became more pronounced in the course of Middle English, until [REC-TH] established itself as the canonical order for the DOC, in contrast to [TH-REC] for the *to*-PRC (Fischer 1992: 379; Kroch and Taylor 2000b: 150). This presumption is supported by McFadden's (2002) investigation of the ordering of nominal objects in ditransitive constructions in the PPCME2, represented in Tab. 3. As can be seen, [REC-TH] was clearly the preferred order for DOCs already in early Middle English texts. Nevertheless, the reverse order still accounted for about a third of all tokens in the earliest period (M1), which is to be expected judging from the OE distribution. During the period, there is a significant decrease of [TH-REC] DOCs; no tokens at all are found in later Middle English (further Koopman and van der Wurff 2000: 265; Polo 2002: 130–135; Allen 2006: 210). In constructions with a pronominal theme, the order possibly survived until the 15th century (Allen 1995: 420).

Tab. 3: Ordering of full NP objects in ditransitive constructions (based on McFadden 2002: 113)

	DOC			***to*-PRC**		
	REC-TH	**TH-REC**	**% TH-REC**	**REC-TH**	**TH-REC**	**% TH-REC**
M1	109	57	34.3	3	7	70
M2	18	4	18.2	5	47	90.4
M3	85	0	0	33	147	81.7
M4	60	0	0	14	30	68.2

With the prepositional construction, [TH-*to*REC] orders appear to have been more frequent from the beginning onwards, accounting for around up to 90 per cent of *to*-PRC tokens in all sub-periods. What is interesting is that despite this predominance of [TH-*to*REC], it is far from categorical at the end of the period. This suggests that the emergence of a canonical order for the prepositional pattern only took place in later times.[86] It is commonly assumed that [*to*REC-TH] gradually disappeared after 1500, and only survived into PDE in restricted contexts (e.g. Rissanen 1999: 268). Possible reasons for the eventual demise of the pattern are the lack of a parallel pronominal construction or rhythm – cf. the clash of two unstressed syllables in *I gave to the man the book* (Fischer 1992: 381; Gerwin 2014: 145). McFadden (2002: 113–114) furthermore notes a slight correlation between the frequency of *to*-PRCs and the frequency of [TH-REC] in DOCs, in that in texts with a low frequency of the former, the number of the latter appears to be higher. This is in line with Allen, who postulates that "the spread of the *to*-dative would have led [...] to a reduction in DO IO order [...since] both these constructions serve a similar pragmatic function: to focus on the Recipient by putting it sentence-finally" (2006: 214; also Fischer and van der Wurff 2006: 190). De Cuypere (2015c: 16) assumes that it was in fact a combination of this rise of the *to*-PRC with its preferred [TH-REC] order and the 'the winner-takes-it-all behaviour' of the DOC's [REC-TH] order which caused the demise of [TH-REC] in the DOC: Both processes reinforced each other. A similar hypothesis will be put forward in the present book, since I assume that the now canonical order of the PRC reflects its historical origins in adverbial adjuncts and the discourse-pragmatic features corresponding to this. The fixation of the DOC to [REC-TH] order is taken to likewise reflect functional properties of the arguments involved; moreover, I assess the possibility that the increasingly close link between the patterns caused them to develop a complementary distribution.

As to factors influencing the ordering of the objects, McFadden (2002: 116–121) mentions the possibility of an impact of length/syntactic weight, and furthermore suggests differences between pronominal and nominal objects as well as objects with animate or inanimate referents. On the basis of the results of a preliminary study on variables determining the choice between the four sub-patterns ([REC-TH], [TH-REC], [*to*REC-TH], [TH-*to*REC]) in Middle English, which he presented at a workshop organised by the *Ghent research team on linguistic meaning and structure* (GLIMS) in February 2015, De Cuypere (2015b) tentatively concludes that the ME data largely reflect the same discourse-pragmatic tendencies that seem to account for the choice between the options for Old English and PDE ditransitives, with relative length as a strong factor.

86 McFadden (2002: 114–116) suggests that part of these marked orders might be due to heavy NP shift of long themes. Although this is borne out by his data to some extent, it cannot explain why the DOC (which was at this point strongly, or even categorically associated with [REC-TH] order) was not used in these cases instead. Gerwin (2014: 142) relates the consistent frequency of *to*REC-TH patterns to French influence.

While comparable studies on the early Modern period are lacking, Late Modern English is covered by Wolk et al.'s (2013) investigation of the dative alternation in ARCHER; they include data from 1650 to 1990. The findings more or less agree with those for the earlier periods (Wolk et al. 2013: 22–24; De Cuypere 2015a: 246; also Gries and Hilpert 2010). For the PDE ditransitive alternation, the following variables have been put forward and tested in the literature (the non-exhaustive list is taken from De Cuypere 2015a: 227).

- semantics of the verb (Levin 1993; Lapata 1999; Gries 2005; Bresnan et al. 2007)
- givenness/ newness, i.e. discourse status, of Rec and Th (Halliday 1970; Erteschik-Shir 1979; Smyth, Hogan, and Prideaux 1979; Givón 1984; Thompson and Koide 1987; Thompson 1995; Bresnan et al. 2007; Ozón 2009; Theijssen et al. 2010[87])
- pronominality/ definiteness of Rec and Th (Ransom 1979; Bresnan et al. 2007; Theijssen et al. 2010, 2011)
- animacy/ person of Rec (Bresnan 2007; Bresnan and Nikitina 2009; Bresnan and Ford 2010; Theijssen et al. 2011)
- weight of Rec and Th, i.e. length or syntactic complexity (Bock and Irwin 1980; Bock, Loebell, and Morey 1992; Hawkins 1994; Collins 1995; Arnold et al. 2000; Prat-Sala and Branigan 2000; Wasow 2002; Snyder 2003; Wasow and Arnold 2003; Ozón 2009; Theijssen et al. 2010, 2011)
- language-external factors, e.g. speaker variables such as age and gender (Bresnan and Ford 2010; Bresnan and Hay 2008; Theijssen et al. 2011) or geographic region (e.g. Bresnan and Hay 2008; De Cuypere and Verbeke 2013; Gast 2007; Gerwin 2014; Hughes and Trudgill 1996; Kendall, Bresnan, and Van Herk 2011; Mukherjee and Hoffman 2006; Schilk et al. 2013; Siewierska and Hollmann 2007; Szmrecsanyi et al. 2016; Tagliamonte 2014; Theijssen 2008; Wolk et al. 2013; Yáñez-Bouza and Denison 2015)
- style and modality (e.g. Bresnan et al. 2007)

Many of the variables postulated for PDE ditransitives, such as pronominality, animacy, as well as givenness, are again compatible with the principle of prominence, topicality, or 'harmonic alignment' as indicated above. This principle appears to have remained a stable predictor of object order choice over time. In spite of possible changes, and in spite of the slight differences between the

87 Theijssen et al. (2010) in fact deal with the 'benefactive alternation' rather than the dative alternation but find that the factors driving both alternations are approximately the same (see also Szmrecsanyi et al. forthc.).

specific factors that influence ordering in ditransitive constructions in the respective periods, it can therefore be assumed that the alternation(s) between the orders, and correspondingly between the two constructions in later times, has been roughly motivated or guided by the same semantic and discourse-pragmatic factors throughout the history of English (De Cuypere 2015a, 2015c).

3.2.2.4 Object order in ditransitives with two pronouns

A slightly different issue is posed by ditransitive constructions with two pronominal objects, which are quite special in PDE. They also followed a slightly different diachronic path than those with at least one NP object (Gast 2007; Gerwin 2013, 2014; Yáñez-Bouza and Denison 2015). For PDE, it has been claimed that "the prepositional construction (e.g., *give it to me*) is by far the most frequent" (Biber et al. 1999: 929; also Quirk et al. 1985: 1396n; Huddleston and Pullum 2002: 248, n23). However, this only seems to hold for Standard British and American English, as there is reportedly great dialectal variation especially in the British Isles. For example, [REC-TH] order (*give me it*) is said to be preferred or at least perfectly acceptable in the North and elsewhere (Hughes and Trudgill 1996: 16). By contrast, [*pron*TH-*pron*REC] (*give it me*) is frequent in the Midlands, according to Siewierska and Hollmann (2007).[88]

The last of the patterns, i.e. [*pron*TH-*pron*REC] has often been argued to be the historically preferred one, with the other orders only slowly creeping in (Allen 1995: 48; Fischer and van der Wurff 2006: 189). However, this has recently been challenged by De Cuypere (2015a: 246–247), who finds a comparatively even distribution of [DAT$_{\text{REC}}$-ACC$_{\text{TH}}$] and [ACC$_{\text{TH}}$-DAT$_{\text{REC}}$] also in cases with two pronouns. Although there might accordingly have been a preference for [TH-REC] in earlier times (70), the tendency was by no means universal. This is also line with Gast (2007), who presents evidence of both orders in Middle English (71a-d).

(70) *hæfde* <u>hit</u>$_{\text{TH}}$ **him**$_{\text{REC}}$ wel neh twelf monæð
had it him well almost twelve months
'kept it for himself for about twelve months'
(Anglo-Saxon Charters S 1467; Gast 2007: 49)

88 Cf. also Kirk (1985); Cheshire, Edwards, and Whittle (1993); Koopman and van der Wurff (2000); Gast (2007: 52); Hughes, Trudgill, and Watt (2012: 20).

(71) a. he *wule* hit$_{TH}$ **me**$_{REC}$ *for3euen*
he will it me forgive
'he will forgive me it'
(Lambeth Homilies; a1225; Gast 2007: 50)

b. 'Gossip' , quod þe wolf , *'for3ef* hit$_{TH}$ **me**$_{REC}$'
friend , said the wolf , forgive it me
'"Close friend", said the wolf, "forgive me it"'
(The Fox and the Wolf; a1300; Gast 2007: 50)

c. Gode faith **me**$_{REC}$ it$_{TH}$ *tau3te*
good faith me it taught
'good faith taught me it'
(Piers Plowman B; c1378; Gast 2007: 51)

d. A pure man prayed þaim to *giff* **hym**$_{REC}$ it$_{TH}$
a pure man prayed them to give him it
'a pure man prayed them to give him it'
(Alph. Tales; c1450; Gast 2007: 51)

These findings also cast considerable doubt on, or would seem to even downright disprove, the often-made assumption that [REC-TH] in British English constitutes a recent innovation, only to become frequent from the 19th century onwards (Gerwin 2013: 448). Similar claims can be found in Yáñez-Bouza and Denison (2015), who on the basis of a large-scale quantitative investigation of these patterns from the 15th ct. up until today, conclude that [REC-TH] only increased in frequency and became a productive alternative in the early 20th ct. (also Fischer and van der Wurff 2006: 190).

These positions are not necessarily incompatible, though, since as far as I see, the mere presence of [REC-TH] orders in ME is not enough to prove that the reverse order was not the preferred option. It might well have been the case that although both orders were equally frequent in OE, one pattern decreased in later periods, only to rise again in the 19th/20th century. Moreover, as De Cuypere (2015a: 247) shows, there are striking differences between the various types of pronouns: While OE *tat* 'that' and *tis* 'this', for instance, were closely associated with [REC-TH] order, *(h)it* 'it' strongly favoured [TH-REC]. The fact that both Gerwin (2014) and Yáñez-Bouza (2015), as well as many previous accounts, primarily focussed on the latter pronoun, which probably showed a preference for [TH-REC] (even if not categorical) throughout the periods, could then have easily brought about this apparent mismatch. Possible reasons for why *it* showed such a high predilection for this order are its phonological shape. Due to its greater 'weakness' (more phonological reduction, less stress) in comparison to other pronouns, it should tend to precede other elements in the clause (De Cuypere 2015a: 248; also Jespersen 1927: 288). Another possibility is influence of information structure, as *it* is typically used anaphorically (i.e. refers to given information), in contrast to the typically cataphoric pronouns *this* and *that*, introducing new information (De Cuypere 2015a: 248). Since given information is commonly assumed to precede new information, this would explain *it*'s preference for first position. Gast (2007), on the other hand, proposes that the dominant order of [TH-REC] reflects the 'principle of frequency-based serialization', meaning that the high token frequency of verb+*it* strings is able to override analogical pressures from other DOC patterns (cf. also Gerwin 2014: 187–188). Yáñez-Bouza and Denison (2015) take a similar approach: Making use of the concept of 'prefabs' (e.g. Bybee 2013), they assume that the great frequency of specific strings leads to a greater autonomy of these patterns through constructionalisation. Other, less frequent patterns are in contrast linked to a more schematic DOC/*to*-PRC construction with distinct ordering of the objects. This proposal is also taken up in the present study; that is, I put forward the hypothesis that non-canonical orders were able to survive as lower-level idiosyncrasies if they were (token-) frequent and therefore entrenched enough.

Finally, the prepositional [TH-*to*REC] pattern, which is supposed to be the prototypical choice for a large majority of English speakers when dealing with ditransitives with two pronominal objects, entered in Middle English. It then increased over time at the expense of the non-prepositional [TH-REC] in some or even most dialects (Gerwin 2014: 181–186). The history of the pronominal patterns hence partly diverges from the general development of ditransitive constructions, in that the DOC variant in this case did not become limited to [REC-TH] order to the same extent as nominal DOCs. On the other hand, the emergence and spread of the prepositional pronominal object-construction (*gave it to her*) corresponds to the rise of the general *to*-PRC, with the exception of e.g. Northern varieties of British English, where the PP-pattern is clearly more marginal than the DOC (with both orders).

3.2.2.5 Summary

To sum up, it has been shown in this chapter that significant changes were under way from late Old English onwards (or even before) in regard to word order, which had considerable consequences for the shape of the PDE dative alternation. As to the ordering of constituents in the entire clause, Old English exhibited a great deal of variation. Beginning in late Old English/ early Middle English, however, SVO orders increased and eventually became near-obligatory. This rise was most likely discourse-pragmatically motivated, with specific orders appearing more frequently due to information structure issues. Although this change is usually not addressed in discussions of Old and Middle English ditransitives, I argue that it is especially interesting in this case: First, the additional argument of ditransitive verbs – the recipient – can be analysed as intermediate between subject and object concerning its prototypical discourse-pragmatic/topicality status. What this means for the placement as well as case marking of this argument is discussed in detail in section (7.2.1.3). Second, prepositional phrases increasingly moved to clause-peripheral position, outside the core group of subject, verb and object. However, PPs marking core semantic roles might have been exempt from this rule to some extent; this is in fact precisely what happens in the case of the (*to*-)PRC.

Concerning the sequence of the two arguments of ditransitive verbs, both [REC-TH] and [TH-REC] orders were found with all patterns, i.e. DOC, (*to*-)PRC as well as PTCs, in Old English. This choice became increasingly associated and correlated with the choice between specific construction types over the course of the Middle English period, until the DOC came to canonically show [REC-TH] order, while the *to*-PRC was used almost exclusively with [TH-REC]. PTCs today pattern with the DOC in this regard: A preliminary look at characteristic verbs in the *Corpus of Contemporary American English* (COCA) and the *BNCweb* confirms the intuition they are strongly biased towards [REC-*prep*TH] order.

At least for the members of the PDE dative alternation, we find that the factors guiding the use of one order/construction over the other are roughly the same in all periods; only minor differences can be detected. Most strikingly, the choice seems to continuously have been driven by features linked to the principle of topicality/focus or harmonic alignment. I argue that this development of a complementary distribution of orders between the two constructions (according to discourse-pragmatic features) can be taken as a sign or indeed a consequence of the establishment of the dative alternation. In the next sections, I outline a further point of interest, namely changes in the semantic scope of the patterns involved. While the functional expansion of the PP-constructions has been mentioned already, the functional specialisation of the DOC is also conspicuous; this is especially so because the developments of the two variants seem to directly mirror each other.

3.2.3 Changes in the semantics of the constructions

3.2.3.1 Semantic narrowing of the DOC

The semantics of the DOC and the set of verb classes associated with the construction in Present Day English have received much attention in linguistic research (section 2.1.2). Despite some idiosyncrasies, the construction is taken to prototypically express a sense of transfer, and to be most frequently and commonly instantiated by giving-verbs. Such a 'transfer of possession'-sense is also highly salient with ditransitives cross-linguistically; in languages which feature some sort of double object construction, *give* is almost invariably included in the range of verbs used in the pattern. However, when compared to other (Germanic and Indo-European) languages, we find that the English construction is much narrower in this respect: Typically, DOCs have a wider scope of meaning than transfer (cf. Newman 1996; Kittilä 2006; Lambert 2010; and particularly Malchukov, Haspelmath, and Comrie 2010). The same held true for earlier stages of English, as shown in the following.

Malchukov, Haspelmath, and Comrie (2010) demonstrate that rather than expressing transfer in a very restricted sense, double object constructions often denote 'indirect affectedness'. That is, the pattern is used to depict individuals as affected in their personal sphere by an action that is instigated by an agent participant (Dąbrowska 1997: 17). This includes, as illustrated in the examples from Modern High German and Polish below, sub-senses such as 'dispossession' (72a), 'malefaction' (72b), and 'pure benefaction' (72c):[89]

(72) a. John *hat* **Mary**$_{\text{REC}}$ ein Buch$_{\text{TH}}$ *gestohlen*
'John stole a book from Mary'
b. John *hat* **Mary**$_{\text{REC}}$ die Schulter$_{\text{TH}}$ *gebrochen*
'John broke Mary's shoulder'
c. Krystyna *otworzyła* **Oli**$_{\text{REC}}$ drzwi$_{\text{TH}}$
Krystyna opened Ola door
'Krystyna opened the door for Ola'
(Dąbrowska 1997: 35; cf. also Colleman and De Clerck 2011: 194)

Zooming in on Germanic languages, and more precisely on North Germanic (Icelandic, Faroese, Norwegian), Barðdal, Kristoffersen, and Sveen (2011: 57) come to a similar conclusion. They assert that "there is much more to ditransi-

89 These relations are nicely illustrated in Malchukov, Haspelmath, and Comrie's (2010: 51-53) cross-linguistic semantic network maps.

tivity than only the concept of transfer" in this language family (also Barðdal 2007).[90] Among other things, the DOC in Icelandic, for instance, can express events of hindrance or constraining (73a), as well as 'possession' (73b).

(73) a.

hafi	hugsanlega	*byrgt*	**honum**$_{REC}$	sýn$_{TH}$
has	possibly	blocked	him	view

'may have blocked his view'
(Barðdal, Kristoffersen, and Sveen 2011: 63)

b.

Dýr	*áttu*	**sér**$_{REC}$	bústaði	og	fjölskyldur$_{TH}$
animals	had	themselves	homes	and	families

'animals had houses and families'
(Barðdal, Kristoffersen, and Sveen 2011: 62)

The authors also provide examples of dispossession verbs being used in the construction in Old Norse, i.e. the ancestor of the Modern Scandinavian languages (e.g. ON *stela* 'steal sth. from so.'). Most or indeed all of the sub-senses identified in their data are found in Old Norse as well as the younger Scandinavian languages, indicating that the lexical range of the construction in North Germanic has not changed much over the centuries (Barðdal, Kristoffersen, and Sveen 2011: 79). Based on this, Barðdal and colleagues posit a general meaning of 'indirect affectedness' for the contemporary West-Scandinavian DOC, but also for its historical predecessor. Moreover, they suggest that the semantic scope of the Scandinavian DOC is a direct continuation and reflection of the (Proto-)Germanic situation (Barðdal 2007: 25; Barðdal and Diáz-Vera forthc.).

Evidence from the history of English would seem to support this proposal: The DOC was reportedly once associated with a wide range of verb senses, including many of those identified for other Germanic languages and beyond (Rohdenburg 1995: 108). However, several of these common sub-senses are lacking from Present Day English (74a-b). This means that the language must have undergone some significant changes.

(74) a. *John stole **Mary** a book
b. *John *broke* **Mary** the shoulder

This issue is addressed in detail in Colleman and De Clerck (2011), following up on Rohdenburg (1995, 2007) and Mukherjee and Hoffmann (2006) as well as Hoffmann and Mukherjee's (2007), the latter of which attempt to relate 'odd' DOC uses in Indian English to superstrate retention of earlier British English

90 Barðdal (2007) furthermore includes data on Swedish and Norwegian dialects.

usage. Colleman and De Clerck present a survey of a sub-set of DOCs in parts of the *Corpus of Late Modern English Texts* (CLMET, cf. De Smet 2005). Their main intention is to compare the semantics of the 18th ct. DOC to that of the PDE construction, and to thereby detect any potential diachronic changes in its semantic range (Colleman and De Clerck 2011: 185).

The results of the study first of all show that individual verbs have changed regarding the complementation patterns they occur with. This is not surprising, considering that the members within a specific verb class might well change even if there are no changes in the construction's semantic scope as such (Colleman and De Clerck 2011: 191). For example, the innovative DOC uses of *issue* and *feed* mentioned by Rohdenburg (2009) in fact constitute additions to the class of transfer verbs; at the same time, this class has also experienced losses of individual members, with e.g. *deliver* having fallen out of use from the DOC. A highly conspicuous case of loss is the development of verbs of Latinate origin such as *donate* or the just mentioned *deliver*, which have become increasingly restricted to prepositional constructions (75a-b); see (2.1.2); also De Clerck and Colleman (2009) and Sówka-Pietraszewska (2013). To my knowledge, no conclusive explanation for this diachronic change exists.[91] In contrast, quite some research has gone into determining how the idiosyncratic behaviour of Latinate verbs in PDE, meaning their strong preference for the *to*-PRC, can be learnt. It is now assumed that pre-emption and priming effects are at play in such cases (see the discussion in section 2.1.2).

(75) a. *John *donated* **the foundation** <u>five pounds</u>
     b. John *donated* <u>five pounds</u> **to the foundation**

A further type of changes within verb classes is that of individual verbs becoming obsolete or changing meaning, which might result in their being ousted from the DOC or remaining only marginally associated with the construction. Colleman and De Clerck (2011: 192) illustrate this with *bespeak*: This verb has lost its older meaning of 'order' or 'arrange for', and is only infrequently used in PDE, where it means 'to be evidence of' (cf. also *reach, engage*).

In terms of verb classes, it seems that the DOC has not clearly extended its meaning in recent times, although differences can be found. Two classes have been added to the DOC, namely (i) the class of 'instruments of communication',

91 With the exception of Sówka-Pietraszewska's (2013) analysis of ditransitive Latinate verbs in Middle English and PDE in terms of Rappaport Hovav and Levin's (2008) verb-sensitive account, no explanation for this phenomenon has really been put forward so far.

namely verbs such as *to text, to e-mail* or *to skype* and *to whatsapp*, and (ii) verbs of ballistic motion (76).

(76) and *threw* **him** an old rug to cover himself
(BNCweb; 1983, M. Magorian: *Goodnight Mister Tom*)

Both uses are absent from Colleman and De Clerck's data and can also not be found in the Northern Germanic languages investigated by Barðdal (2007: 16–18) and Barðdal, Kristoffersen, and Sveen (2011: 60). However, their non-appearance in earlier times is easily explained. In case of the former, technological advances made since then are to blame; many of the instruments were simply not available yet at this point. Although verbs expressing an equivalent notion such as *to pigeon, to pen*, or *to post* are not attested in Colleman and De Clerck's corpus either, it can be assumed that this is rather due to an accidental gap in the data than caused by a grammatical constraint. Other compatible verbs of the larger group of 'sending' or communication verbs certainly did appear in the 18th century (Colleman and De Clerck 2011: 190–191; also De Clerck et al. 2011). In the case of the latter, it is plausible to assume that the semantic closeness between verbs of ballistic motion and verbs of transfer may have motivated the addition. While this development might be seen as an expansion in semantic range, it therefore nevertheless takes place within a very narrowly defined semantic field (further Visser 1963: 629).

More severe changes to the semantics of the construction are caused by the loss of certain verb classes. Colleman and De Clerck (2011: 193) observe five main differences between Late Modern and Present Day English: First, verbs of banishment such as *banish, dismiss, discharge, expel*, as well as *forbid* are amply attested in 18th century texts (77a-d), but are unavailable for DOC use in PDE (also Rohdenburg 1995: 109–113).

(77) a. I will put it entirely into your power to *discharge* **her**$_{\text{REC}}$ the house$_{\text{TH}}$
(Richardson 1740; Colleman and De Clerck 2011: 194)

b. I therefore for the present *dismiss'd* **him**$_{\text{REC}}$ the Quarter deck$_{\text{TH}}$
(Cook 1771; Colleman and De Clerck 2011: 194)

c. I should expect that **the eunuchs**$_{\text{REC}}$ were not *expelled* the palace$_{\text{TH}}$
(Gibbon 1776; Colleman and De Clerck 2011: 194)

d. therefore *forbade* **her**$_{\text{REC}}$ the court$_{\text{TH}}$
(Walpole 1744; Colleman and De Clerck 2011: 194)

Second, verbs of pure benefaction (78a-b) or malefaction (78c-d), commonly used in the DOC in other languages, were still felicitous members of this construction in the 18th and 19th century (Colleman and De Clerck 2011: 194–197).

(78) a. and the young Benedictine *holding* **him**$_{\text{REC}}$ <u>the torch</u>$_{\text{TH}}$ as he wrote
(Sterne 1767; Colleman and De Clerck 2011: 1965)

b. would expect his wife to *open* **him**$_{\text{REC}}$ <u>the door</u>$_{\text{TH}}$, to reach him a chair
(The Sporting Magazine 1819: 164; Colleman and De Clerck 2011: 196)

c. þe deofol **him**$_{\text{REC}}$ *scorteð* <u>his</u> <u>dazes</u>$_{\text{TH}}$
the devil him shortened his days
'the devil shortened him his days'
(Lambert Homilies, 1175; Colleman and De Clerck 2011: 196)

d. *spoiled* **me**$_{\text{REC}}$ <u>a complete set of blond lace triple ruffles</u>$_{\text{TH}}$
(Smollett 1751; Colleman and De Clerck 2011: 197)

Most basically, these verbs denote situations in which an action is performed to the disadvantage or advantage of the REC-participant, without any (metaphorical) reception being intended; this may include events of 'substitutive benefaction' as discussed in Van Valin and LaPolla (1997); Kittilä (2005) as well as Colleman (2010a, 2010b). In contrast to verbs of creation, or 'receptive benefaction' (*John baked Mary a cake*), these benefactive/malefactive verbs are not grammatical in the PDE DOC any more. English therefore seems to have developed an 'intended reception' constraint at some point in history. This means that the REC-argument encodes a participant that is necessarily both a beneficiary and an intended recipient (Colleman and De Clerck 2011: 194; also section 2.1.2 above). Since uses without intended transfer of possession were, however, still acceptable in the 19th century, and there is considerable regional variation in the strength of the intended reception constraint, the confinement of the benefactive DOC appears to be a fairly recent phenomenon (Colleman and De Clerck 2011: 194–197; Zehentner & Traugott forthc.).[92]

A further striking case of now obsolete DOC verb classes is the group of privative verbs. More specifically, agentive verbs of dispossession involving volitional subjects (79a-c) are attested in Rohdenburg's (1995) set of 16th to 17th century DOCs, but are rare already at the beginning of Late Modern English, and missing from Colleman and De Clerck's 18th century texts (2011: 200–201; also Hoffmann and Mukherjee 2007: 16).[93] Accordingly, the process of ousting these verbs must have started before the time span investigated by these authors.

92 Dutch shows an even more advanced state in this regard, since benefactives have fallen out of use of the DOC entirely at least in the standard variety (Colleman 2011: 403).

93 Colleman and De Clerck stress the agentivity of the subject in order to be able to account for the continuing use of *cost* in PDE DOCs (2011: 200–201; also Colleman and De Clerck 2009).

(79) a. did altogether *bereave* **him**$_{REC}$ his night's rest$_{TH}$
(Gascoigne 1575; Rohdenburg 1995: 108; Colleman and De Clerck 2011)
b. nor all the Gods aboue, Shall *rob* **me**$_{REC}$ this rich purchase$_{TH}$
(Heywood 1613: I; Visser 1963: 635; Colleman and De Clerck 2011)
c. All joy$_{TH}$ was *bereft* **me**$_{REC}$ the day that you left me
(Scott 1804; Colleman and De Clerck 2011: 200)

Verbs of manner of speaking constitute a smaller-scale and less complete case of change: While verbs such as *whisper*, *shout*, *scream*, or *yodel* have repeatedly been labelled exclusively 'non-ditransitive', Colleman and De Clerck show that the exclusion of this class from the DOC is a strong statistical tendency rather than a strict rule (2011: 197–198; cf. further Stefanowitsch 2006: 69). Attested in sufficient numbers in the 18th century (80a-b), examples of DOC uses of e.g. *whisper* can also be found in PDE data. This indicates that even though it seems like there is a ban on manner of speaking verbs from DOCs in PDE, it is not an absolute one, and only strengthened after the 18th century (Colleman and De Clerck 2011: 198).

(80) a. she took occasion to *whisper* **me**$_{REC}$ her opinion of the widow$_{TH}$
(Fielding 1751; Colleman and De Clerck 2011: 198)
b. all those who were able to *inform* **her**$_{REC}$ any thing concerning him$_{TH}$
(Haywood 1744; Colleman and De Clerck 2011: 198)

As demonstrated by example (80b), the 18th century DOC furthermore allowed for a wider variety of communication events, including verbs such as *state* or *command*; Rohdenburg mentions these as lost uses (1995: 108); see also Mukherjee and Hoffmann (2006).

Finally, Colleman and De Clerck (2011: 198–200) discern an interesting development regarding verbs expressing feelings or attitudes such as *envy*, *forgive*, *excuse* or *(not) begrudge* (also Hunston and Francis 2000: 88–89). Although these verbs are still associated with the DOC in PDE, they may instantiate a case of change in progress. Based on a quantitative survey of the CLMET and the imaginary writing component of the *BNC*, it is shown that DOC uses with both *envy* and *forgive* consistently and significantly dropped in relative frequency over the last centuries (Colleman and De Clerck 2008: 195–196). This is in line with Goldberg's (1995: 132) assumption that

> it seems reasonable that syntactic change should tend toward patterns that are more transparent to the speaker. If the construction with the semantics outlined here [i.e., the DOC with its basic sense of transfer] is psychologically real, then it would be natural for odd cases of ditransitives involving forgive and envy to drop out of use.

A slightly different type of verbs concerned with attitudes or feelings are *wish* or *intend*, which continue to be available for DOC use in PDE. While both appeared with a range of themes in the 18th century still, the latter is now restricted to collocating with *evil, harm* or *good*, though, and is limited to fossilised phrased (Colleman and De Clerck 2011: 199–200). *Wish*, on the other hand, continues to enjoy considerable freedom in choosing themes; nevertheless, it is frequently found in comparatively fixed phrases such as *wish so. luck/ success/ a nice day/* etc. as well (cf. further Stefanowitsch and Gries 2003).

The conclusion Colleman and De Clerck (2011: 201–203) finally draw based on their comparison of verb classes associated with the 18th century and the PDE DOC is that we can indeed observe a reduction in the semantic scope of the construction within the last centuries. This was most certainly in progress even before Late Modern English.[94] Since the construction's range of meanings has become narrower, i.e. "the semantic range of application of the DOC in the present-day language is a subset of its semantic range in earlier substages of Modern English, [this development] qualifies as an example of specialization in constructional semantics" (Colleman and De Clerck 2011: 188). In such specialisation processes, prototype effects typically determine which uses are lost. While central senses such as 'caused reception' in the case of the DOC are assumed to be relatively stable, less prototypicality and remoteness from the core meaning of a construction means greater vulnerability to change (Colleman and De Clerck 2011: 204; also Geeraerts 1997: 47–68; Grondelaers, Speelman, and Geeraerts 2007: 991).[95] This is precisely what we expect to see in the history of English: With the move of the DOC towards a more coherent 'transfer'-meaning, more peripheral, further removed uses such as verbs of dispossession should cease to be used in the construction.

94 See also Allen (1995: 28–29) and Visser (1963: 606–635), who comment on the DOC, or rather, the different ditransitive case frames in OE covering a broader range of semantic possibilities then than they do now. Incidentally, a similar reduction in the semantic domain of the DOC is also seen in Dutch, while other Germanic languages such as the North Germanic languages mentioned above, but also German, still permit for many sub-senses (furthermore Colleman 2010a, 2010b; Lambert 2010).

95 As Colleman (2011: 406) points out, the central position of giving verbs in the DOC's semantic network probably also played a role in their retention in the DOC "despite the availability of a good prepositional alternative". The assumption that the sense of received transfer is (and was already in the 18th ct.) dominant in the DOC semantics is furthermore supported by Colleman and De Clerck's (2011: 204) data, as 41% of the tokens in their dataset are taken up by the verb *give* alone (N=2,205). I develop this idea in more detail in the later chapters.

The loss of DOC usage typically goes hand in hand with an increased use in other constructions. For example, Colleman and De Clerck's (2008) study confirms that prepositional theme-constructions have been on the rise with attitudinal verbs (*envy/forgive NP for NP*). Verbs of dispossession, by contrast, usually occur in a *from-*/*of*-PRC or PTC in PDE (81a), whereas verbs of substitutive benefaction are now restricted to *for*-PRC patterns (81b) and malefactive verbs predominantly use possessive phrases to indicate the affected person (81c).

(81) a. They only *stole* sheep **from the Romans**
(BNCweb; 1989; M. Nabb: *Death in springtime*)
b. Do you think you could just *open* the door **for me**
(BNCweb; 1991; 'Ann', KB7 11271)
c. He *broke* **Sonny's** nose
(BNCweb; 1991; T. Hayden: *The killing frost*)

Importantly, as I demonstrate in my study (chapter 4), many of these developments can already be seen in Middle English. I furthermore later argue that these changes represent a specific type of competition resolution in that one of the competing constructions wins out in this case, while the other (DOC) is less successful (section 7.1.2).

Summing up, we have seen in this section that the English DOC has become associated with a significantly narrower range of meanings in the course of its history. While it once probably denoted an indirect effect on a participant, it has moved towards a more restricted meaning of (intended or concrete, successful) transfer. Uses peripheral to this prototypical transfer meaning, including e.g. the verb class of dispossession but also that of pure benefaction/ malefaction, have accordingly been lost. The potential causes of this change have received relatively little attention so far, although it has been tentatively linked to some of the changes introduced in the preceding sections, including case loss and the rise of prepositional competitors (e.g. Colleman and De Clerck 2011). The present book pursues this hypothesis. More specifically, the semantic narrowing of the DOC is connected to the emergence of the dative alternation, and I investigate whether the closer link between the DOC and the *to*-PRC might have promoted the loss of DOC uses not compatible with the semantic relations expressed by *to*, and vice versa. In the following section, I briefly look at the semantic development of the prepositional patterns, finding that they developed quite differently to the DOC.

3.2.3.2 Semantic widening of the prepositional patterns

Prepositional patterns in general have been subject to substantial change since their original emergence in pre-Old English times, as already shown above (3.1). Many of the functions they fulfil in Present Day English were not present in earlier stages, and only gradually developed over time. Most importantly for us, prepositional (more analytic) structures frequently extended into new domains previously covered by nominal expressions at the turn to Middle English. This process is typically addressed in terms of grammaticalisation – for quite obvious reasons (e.g. Hundt 2001; Heine and Kuteva 2002; Rostila 2007; *inter alia*). The development of prepositional ditransitives is a clear case in point: Originally encoding concrete, spatial relations, the prepositions involved have come to fulfil the more grammatical/ procedural functions of denoting core semantic roles such as (abstract) recipients, deprivees or affectees in ditransitive events. For instance, *from* originally introduced a locative source, but can now also refer to animate participants deprived of abstract entities (82). Thus, they have come to stand in variation with the older, more nominal construction, the DOC.

(82) temporarily *stealing* attention$_{TH}$ **from underachieving men's team**$_{REC}$ (COCA; 1999; Washington Post)

A number of publications deal with these types of developments, many zeroing in on specific prepositions in the history of English.[96] In the context of ditransitives, most explicit discussions of the semantic potential of prepositions focusses on *to* (perhaps unsurprisingly).

De Cuypere (2013, 2015c) shows that the spatial semantics of the preposition (83a) were considerably bleached already in Old English; a majority of tokens in his random sample of *to* instances in OE texts express a non-spatial meaning (83b). In addition to *to* indicating a state, quality, or condition to be attained (as illustrated in the example), it could also be used non-spatially to refer to a specific point in time, a price, an occasion to be attended, or as a source, comparison, or purpose marker (for representative examples see De Cuypere 2013: 127, 2015c: 18–19).

96 See e.g. Traugott (1972, 1982); Langacker (1992); Lundskær-Nielsen (1993); Taylor (1993); Newman (1996); van Gelderen (1996); Fischer (2000); Jarad (1997); Haspelmath (2003); Hopper and Traugott (2003); Luraghi (2003); Tyler and Evans (2003); Molencki (2005, 2007a, 2007b, 2008, 2011a, 2011b); Rice and Kabata (2007); Tungseth (2008); Sato (2009); Iglesias-Rábade (2011); Cziskek-Kiliszewska (2013, 2014a, 2014b, 2015); among many others.

(83) a. ðæt he *cumen* **to Galileum**
that he come to Galilee
'that they may come to Galilee'
(cocura.o2: 43, 20; De Cuypere 2013: 126)

b. Crist hi *gebrohte* **to ecere reste**
Christ her brought to eternal rest
'Christ has brought her to eternal rest'
(cocathom2.o3: 440, 28; De Cuypere 2013: 126)

Moreover, OE *to* frequently introduced the goal of a bringing/caused motion event, as well as the addressee of communicative events. The *to*-PRC was even more frequent than the DOC in these cases, and this was more pronounced with the latter verb class (De Cuypere 2015c: 5, based on Cassidy 1938; see also section 3.1). This serves as a further indication of the comparatively advanced semantic bleaching of *to* at this point already, since the concept of ADDRESSEE is arguably more abstract than the relatively concrete notion of GOAL (cf. allative > dative in Heine and Kuteva 2002: 38).

The bridging context for the development of the recipient function of *to* is typically sought in phrases with goals ambiguous between places and (human) institutions, as in (84). Here, a reanalysis of GOAL to RECIPIENT could easily have taken place. As Colleman and De Clerck (2009: 9) point out: "[A]s a prototypical act of giving involves a concrete object being passed from one person to the other, one can think of the recipient participant as the stationary entity at the end of the path traversed by the theme, i.e., as the goal of the theme's movement" (also McFadden 2002: 108).[97]

(84) Ic oswulf ond Beornðryð min gemecca *sellað*
I Oswulf and Beornthryth my wife give
to cantuarabyrg **to cristes cirican**$_{\text{REC?}}$ ðæt land$_{\text{TH}}$
to Canterbury to Christ' church the land
'I, Oswulf and my wife Beornthryth give to Christ's church at Canterbury the land'
(codocu1.o1: charter 37.2; De Cuypere 2015c: 20; Visser 1963: 624)

At first sight, the semantic development of the *to*-PRC seems to rather straightforwardly present itself as an instance of grammaticalisation, at least if gram-

97 Cf. also Newman (1996: 88), who claims that "there is a sufficient match of cognitive topologies involving goal and RECIPIENT to support categorizing the RECIPIENT as a goal".

maticalisation is defined predominantly as semantic extension, and features such as phonological reduction are not taken into account (Newman 1996: 88; Cuyckens and Verspoor 1998: 63; Hagège 2010: 277-278; Lambert 2010: 14; among others).[98] However, there has been considerable disagreement about the degree of bleaching of the construction's meaning and the specific semantic input of PDE *to*.[99] The debate furthermore very much relates to the question of semantic overlap between the DOC and the *to*-PRC, meaning the extent to which both constructions are taken to be semantically/ pragmatically synonymous, and their forming part of an alternation relationship.

An overview of the different opinions on the issue and their respective proponents can be found in Colleman and De Clerck (2009). Colleman and De Clerck themselves, after investigating the semantic range of PDE *to*-PRCs, conclude that while *to* has widened to a large extent, there are still some traces left of the preposition's basic semantics, which are "to mark the goal at the end of a spatio-temporal path" (2009: 17; cf. also Colleman, De Clerck, and Davos 2010). This is perfectly compatible with other accounts of semantic change in which the older meaning is gradually replaced by the newer meaning, with a potentially very long period of co-existence ('layering'). Colleman and De Clerck's precise line of argumentation is as follows: The meaning of the *to*-PRC originates in the spatial dimension but has been extended to cover a considerably wider range of 'caused possession' events. These include not only prototypical giving events, but also abstract, projected or verbal transfer, metaphorical transfer (e.g. *to lend credibility to so./sth.*), or acts of refusal/blocked transfer as in the case of *deny* or *refuse* (see also section 2.2.2). One the one hand, the construction therefore seems to have become extended to a large degree. On the other hand, the fact that the *to*-PRC is clearly marked with some verb classes (e.g. refusal), and extremely rare with others (e.g. *cost*), is taken to indicate that this development is still in progress.[100]

This study will largely follow Colleman and De Clerck's analysis, assuming that in the constructional network of ditransitives, the *to*-PRC constitutes a separate construction but still inherits from the more schematic caused motion-

98 See furthermore Jespersen (1927: 291); Heine and Kuteva (2002: 37–38); Lehmann (2002: 73); Haspelmath (2003); Rostila (2007: 52, fn45); Lambert (2010: 14).

99 For a discussion of the semantics of PDE *to* from a functional-cognitive perspective, see e.g. Tyler and Evans (2003); Evans and Tyler (2007) as well as De Cuypere (2013).

100 Note that the English preposition also differs from the otherwise comparable French *à*, as well as Dutch *aan*, in this regard, as these are compatible with an even wider range of meanings including source constructions (the latter possibly due to its locative rather than directional origins); cf. Colleman and De Clerck (2009: 37, n14; 33–37).

construction and thus maintains a (horizontal) link to purely locative *to*-constructions. At the same time, the construction and its preposition are sufficiently bleached to qualify as semantically (near-)synonymous to the DOC. This process of semantic widening is argued to have been essential in the establishment of the strong link between the two constructions, and the ensuing emergence of the ditransitive constructeme (Perek 2015: 155–156). The specifics of this scenario, and what it actually means to be 'widened' or 'bleached' on the present account, are discussed later (chapter 7).

What should be clear from this and the preceding sections is that variants involving a range of different prepositions for marking the REC-argument of ditransitive verbs greatly increased during Middle English and came to be used for all kinds of ditransitive verb classes. (This is presumably also true for PTC patterns, although possibly to a lesser extent). The most frequent and conspicuous among these prepositional patterns was the *to*-PRC. This construction saw a considerable semantic widening over time and thereby came to develop into a member of the dative alternation as known in PDE. I have also (implicitly and explicitly) demonstrated that the question how this alternation came about has not been adequately addressed in the literature so far. To close this gap and to propose a plausible scenario for this development is one of the major aims of the present book. The issue is reassessed based on the empirical data analysis that forms part of this study at a later point. Before doing so, however, I briefly comment on possible links between the different developments that affected the ditransitive variants in the history of English.

3.3 Correlations and causal effects between the main changes

The bottom line of the preceding sections is that several changes of great consequence took place in and around Middle English. The question of what triggered these changes, and whether, since they all occurred roughly around the same time, they correlated or had a causal effect on each other, has occupied historical linguists for quite some time now.

In general, it has been observed that (fixed) word order and the use of any sort of 'flagging', most saliently case marking or prepositions, are among the primary strategies of encoding arguments cross-linguistically (Malchukov, Haspelmath, and Comrie 2010: 6; cf. also Hagège 2010: 10). These means of role-marking are typically more or less functionally equivalent: As Zwicky notes, "[e]verything you can do with Adps [i.e. adpositions] you can do with case inflections, and vice versa" (1992: 370). It is furthermore assumed that an inherent relationship holds between the various strategies, with the presence of one often impeding the use of the other. For example, Haspelmath's typological study on ditransitive constructions in the world's languages suggests that word order tends to be more flexible in cases where at least one of the objects is flagged, while a more rigid object order is to be expected when flagging is lacking (2015: 31–32; also Allen 2006: 214). In the latter case, the order of the objects is predominantly [REC-TH] – a fact which Malchukov, Haspelmath and Comrie (2010: 12) explain by topicality effects such as REC generally being animate (remember also the principle of 'harmonic alignment). In contrast, in the former case REC is more likely to follow TH if it is flagged by an adposition, and the other way round if case affixes are involved; see Hawkins' (1994, 2014) 'Early Immediate Constituents principle' (further Givón 1984; Primus 1997; Heine and König 2010). Languages have also been shown to vary diachronically in regard to which strategies they use. If more strategies to mark clause constituents are available in a language, one strategy tends to be lost, or the competing means of coding tend to functionally diverge (Hagège 2010: 37).[101]

Present Day English argument encoding and the history that is reflected in it pretty obviously fit very well into this picture. With almost no traces of the original inflectional system left, its word order is rather inflexible, and prepositional paraphrases are abundantly used. In contrast, Old English featured a (comparatively) rich case morphology, employed prepositional phrases to a lesser degree, and showed less rigid constraints on word order.[102] Although the different strategies used at various points in English thus evidently seem to be correlated, this does not necessarily mean they are causally related, in that the loss of one strategy was the result (or cause) of another strategy rising. Moreover, alternative explanations without making recourse to the other changes can be found for all of the developments discussed. Nevertheless, several (often

101 These correlations are tendencies rather than hard rules. Within the Germanic languages, for example, both Icelandic and Dutch do not fit the pattern: The former has developed relatively fixed word order despite a largely intact case system, whereas the latter has lost most case morphology, but has nevertheless retained comparatively flexible word order (Barðdal 2009: 129–131).

102 Note that many languages closely related to English also show such a correlation. For example, a number of Germanic languages such as Dutch, which has similarly undergone a reduction of the case system, frequently use prepositions for semantic role marking. Recipients are furthermore also marked prepositionally in the comparatively inflection-poor Romance languages (cf. also Malchukov, Haspelmath, and Comrie 2010). While Standard German strikingly lacks a prepositional ditransitive construction, a PP-variant has reportedly formed in some regional varieties like Bavarian and Northern as well as Central Swiss Alemannic (Seiler 2006). At least in the first of these dialects, this development quite clearly seems to be linked to the absence of case distinctions, as Seiler remarks (2006: 174–176).

directly opposing) theories on cause and effect in the changes witnessed in the history of English have been put forward:

On the one hand, it has been argued that the breakdown of the morphological case marking system resulted in the rise of other means of encoding the function of the clause constituents. In our case, this concerns prepositional paraphrases and fixed word order (see Fischer and van der Wurff 2006: 166; Gast 2007: 50; among many others). On the other hand, push-chain scenarios, with an increasingly rigid word order and more frequent use of PPs rendering case inflections redundant and unnecessary, have also been suggested (e.g. Horn 1921: 131; Traugott 1972: 81; Mitchell 1985: 518). A compromise solution integrating both approaches is proposed in Samuels (1972: 80–84; also Lundskaer-Nielsen 1993: 25–27).

In regard to ditransitives, drag-chain hypotheses have been pursued by McFadden (2002) and Polo (2002); both attempt to relate the emergence of the *to*-PRC as well as the fixation of object order in the DOC to the demise of the morphological case marking system. More precisely, McFadden claims that once an overt distinction between dative and accusative case on the objects of ditransitive verbs had disappeared, disambiguating between the objects' semantic roles was complicated for speakers. This issue was made worse by the flexibility in ordering of the objects. At this point then, *to*-PRCs and fixed object order 'stepped in' to fill the functional gap (McFadden 2002: 108–112). Allen (2006: 209–214) challenges both accounts, stating that it was only when dative-fronted passives (as in **Him was given a book*) disappeared that category distinctions were finally lost. With this, [Th-Rec] order would also have been ousted. Although Allen's argumentation indicates a drag-chain analysis, she on the other side also remarks that loss of case marking is unlikely to be the only cause of the changes in question (2006: 202). Furthermore, she hints at one of the major arguments against such a scenario: Both prepositional paraphrases for the DOC as well as certain word order tendencies were already present in Old English, which was therefore arguably less reliant on case marking than often taken for granted (Allen 2005: 226). This would then count in favour of a push-chain scenario rather than the loss of case marking leading to a growing use of PPs and fixed word order.

The present book critically reviews the plausibility of both scenarios, and ultimately follow Lundskær-Nielsen (1993) as well as Allen (2005, 2006) in assuming that the interaction between the processes is mutual rather than one-sided. For example, Allen (2005: 246, 2006: 215) draws on the development of the DOC and asks whether if one order of objects becomes more frequent due to a reduction in reliability of inflections, speakers could associate position with a specific semantic role. This could lead to more careless use of case marking. If we then add an increasingly frequent use of prepositional paraphrases, case syncretism could become even greater, in turn causing the speakers to rely more heavily on word order to interpret and encode semantic relations.

If at all dealt with, the triggers of the semantic specialisation of the DOC are usually seen in the process of case loss and the concomitant rise of prepositional competitors. For instance, Colleman and De Clerck (2011: 201–202) point out that it appears entirely reasonable to link the semantic development of the DOC with the lack of explicit and unambiguous marking of semantic roles of the arguments involved. This is supported by the fact that languages with a limited morphological case marking system (such as Dutch or Swedish) also usually show a narrowing in the semantics of the DOC (cf. further Barðdal 2007; Colleman 2010b, 2011; Barðdal, Kristoffersen, and Sveen 2011). In contrast, languages such as German or Faroese, which have maintained a rather rich inflectional system, have also preserved many of the uses that are obsolete in English. Although the specialisation of the construction could therefore be regarded as a 'long-term effect' of the loss of morphological case marking, there is no clear one-to-one correspondence. Icelandic, for instance, shows certain semantic restrictions which cannot be explained by deflection, as case marking is still rather prominently present in this variety (Barðdal 2007; Barðdal, Kristoffersen, and Sveen 2011). Rather than linking the process to the loss of case marking, in this book I therefore test the plausibility of a causal link between the construction's semantic narrowing and its entering an alternation relationship with the *to*-PRC. That is, I discuss which role the establishment of a stronger link between the variants played in the fixation of object orders, the semantic narrowing of the DOC, and the semantic widening of the *to*-PRC.

4 Ditransitives in a corpus of Middle English

The main foundation of this project is a large-scale quantitative study of ditransitive instances in the *Penn-Helsinki Parsed Corpus of Middle English* (PPCME2). This dataset is used to investigate empirically a number of questions and hypotheses relating to the key research interests of this book, which most basically are to revisit the questions why the dative alternation is there in PDE, and why its members exhibit certain formal and functional features. On the basis of the overview of previous research on the dative alternation in Present Day English and its history given in the preceding chapters, several more specific hypotheses regarding the research questions can be formulated.

i. The prepositional variants (PRCs) increase in proportional frequency at the expense of the DOC in early Middle English. However, we do not expect the PRCs to completely overtake the DOC but hypothesise that both patterns persist.
ii. Additional alternatives such as the PTC and POSS are available and likewise increase in Middle English.
iii. Prepositional alternatives to the DOC include a wide range of prepositions, but specific PRC-types (particularly PRCs involving *to*) are more frequent than others. The earlier the texts, the greater the variability is.
iv. Both the types of prepositions involved, and the proportional distribution of PRCs in comparison to the DOC are highly dependent on verb classes: a) Verb classes are predicted to differ in the specific PRC-types they occur with; these differences become more pronounced over time, with the overall range of types being reduced, and the scope of individual prepositions becoming restricted. b) Verb class has a significant impact on choice of pattern in that with certain classes (most importantly transfer-related verbs), both patterns are retained, while with others (such as dispossession verbs or verbs of pure benefaction), DOC uses decrease in favour of PRC uses.
v. Corresponding to point (b) in (iv), the range of verb classes the DOC appears with is reduced over time.
vi. Object order becomes regularised within Middle English: I anticipate that in the earlier sub-periods, both REC-TH and TH-REC orders are attested with all patterns in a (roughly) equal distribution. For the DOC and PTC, we expect an increase of REC-first orders over time; for PRCs, TH-first orders significantly increase during Middle English.

https://doi.org/10.1515/9783110633856-004

vii. Changes also take place in clause-level constituent order of ditransitive patterns. (S)VO increases at the expense of other orders with all patterns; this represents a system-wide change and no impact of clausal word order on the choice of construction is expected.
viii. There is an increase in ambiguity of case marking (dative vs. accusative) on both objects of the DOC over time.
ix. The changes investigated all take place within the specified timeframe – the timeframe covered by the corpus – although slight differences in precise progression of change are expected.
x. The changes observed are causally related in a complex, multi-directional way.

Hypotheses (i) to (ix) are tested in the corpus study presented in the following, while (x) is addressed in terms of an Evolutionary Game theoretic model in section (5.2). In the next sections of this chapter, I briefly introduce the basic features of the corpus used (4.1.1), and discuss the methodology applied (4.1.2). Afterwards, the results of the study are presented. I start with basic frequency distributions (4.2.1), before showing the outcomes of a logistic regression model (4.2.2). This is followed by a brief comment on productivity (4.2.3) and findings based on distinctive collexeme analyses of the data (4.2.4). The main results are summarised in section (4.2.5).

4.1 Data and methodology

4.1.1 Corpus description

The *Penn-Helsinki Parsed Corpus of Middle English, 2nd edition* (Kroch and Taylor 2000a) was compiled by researchers at the University of Pennsylvania and University of Helsinki. It is part of the *Penn Corpora of Historical English* (PPCHE). I chose the PPCME2 for this project because of its ready availability, its acceptable representativeness (given the circumstances) and most notably its presentation: All texts are part-of-speech tagged as well as syntactically annotated, allowing researchers to approach questions of syntax rapidly and easily.

The corpus comprises a total of 1,155,965 words, distributed over 56 text samples dating from 1150 to 1500, and stemming from five dialects areas and fifteen different genres. The texts are divided into four main periods (M1–M4); each period covers roughly 100 years (Kroch and Taylor 2010). Aside from these core sub-periods, which contain the large majority of texts and approximately 80 per cent of the total number of words, there are five extra periods. These include texts for which the dates of the earliest manuscripts differ from the date of original composition (Mx1, M23, M24, M34, Mx4). Due to the unclear status of the additional sub-periods in the chronological development of Middle English, and since this study is crucially concerned with diachronic change, I decided to disregard these texts.

Information on the sizes of the respective periods (M1–M4), as well as the representation of different dialect areas and genres can be found on the corpus' website (Kroch and Taylor 2010). Unfortunately, the corpus is somewhat imbalanced and unrepresentative in that it is clearly biased towards certain periods (e.g. M3), dialects (especially the East Midlands) and genres (religious texts). While some insufficiencies could be remedied by including more data/ texts from so far underrepresented dialect areas etc., the possibilities for doing so are, however, naturally limited due to the generally limited availability of historical texts.[103] – This 'bad data' issue is of course nothing new to historical linguistics (Labov 1994; Nevalainen 1999). One possible way to improve on it is using different, inter-disciplinary methodologies to watch 'language change in the lab'. The present book illustrates this by means of evolutionary game theory in section (5.2). – In spite of its drawbacks, the PPCME2 is (to my knowledge) the largest and most elaborately prepared database for Middle English at this point. Furthermore, as Kytö and Rissanen (1992: 4) argue, it has proven to be "extensive enough to show fairly reliable and consistent trends of development in a large number of topics". We can be confident that the dative alternation as a comparatively frequent phenomenon is sufficiently well represented in it.

The files of the PPCME2 can be accessed in three different formats. Apart from plain text and POS-tagged files, parsed, syntactically annotated data allows the user to search for syntactic structure (Kroch and Taylor 2010). The corpus mark-up is in general carefully done and largely consistent, with only some discrepancies noted.[104] The next two sections explain how the mark-up was used to extract the relevant tokens of ditransitive constructions from the PPCME2, i.e. present the methods of data collection. Afterwards, the classification schemata applied to the resultant database are introduced.

---

103 The corpus of the *Middle English Grammar Project* (MEG-C; carried out at the University of Stavanger) might present an interesting addition to the PPCME2, also because it is reportedly biased towards Northern texts. However, the compilation of this database was still in progress at the time the present study was undertaken.

104 For example, the objects of privative verbs such as *robbing* are often marked differently (either as IO or DO) without any clear systematicity.

4.1.2 Methodology

4.1.2.1 Data collection/ extraction

Like other corpora, the PPCME2 was specifically designed to be compatible with the Java-program *CorpusSearch*, a DOS-based tool allowing the user to both construct and search syntactically annotated corpora (Randall 2009). The necessary ingredients for working with the program are on the one hand, the parsed files of the corpus (.psd) as input/source files, and on the other hand, a command file with a certain query, meaning details on the structures the user is interested in. Based on these elements, *CorpusSearch* then creates an output text file which contains clauses with the structure searched for as well as basic frequency counts (Randall 2009).

In this research project, I took the DOC as a point of departure for practical reasons, although this comes with several problems which I discuss below. The query was kept as broad as possible. While the command 'node: $ROOT' indicates that the entire tree should be regarded as the search domain, the queries '(NP-OB1 precedes NP-OB2)' / '(NP-OB2 precedes NP-OB1)' limit the output to only those sentences in which both a NP-OB1 (DO/TH) and a NP-OB2 (IO/REC) are present.[105] This search also yielded by-products such as passive DOCs (85) and DOCs with clausal TH-arguments (86a-b). However, these had to be excluded, since the search strategy did not guarantee that all such instances would be found. This study accordingly only covers active ditransitive patterns with two explicit and non-clausal object arguments. This restriction clearly limits the scope of the project, as important issues like passivisation in the history of English cannot be addressed.

(85) and hit$_{TH}$ *schal* *beo* *forȝeue* **þe**$_{REC}$
and it shall be forgiven you
'and you shall be forgiven for it'
(CMANCRIW-1,II.102.1233; PPCME2: M1)

105 Since word order variation (also concerning the whole clause) is one of the major foci of this study, the option of restricting the output to immediate sequences of the objects ('X iPrecedes Y') was deliberately not chosen.

(86) a.

no-man	may	be	so	bold	*to*	*aske*	**þe**$_{REC}$	:
no man	may	be	so	bold	to	ask	you	:
'Why	dust	þu	so	?'$_{TH}$				
Why	do	you	so	?				

'Nobody may be so bold as to ask you: 'Why do you do this?'
(CMAELR3,43.512; PPCME2: M3)

b.

grauntede	**hem**$_{REC}$	to	be	kyst	of	a	womman$_{TH}$
granted	them	to	be	kissed	of	a	woman

'he allowed them to be kissed by a woman'
(CMAELR3,43.502; PPCME2: M3)

After manually filtering through the obtained results, a total of N=2,542 instances of the DOC were retained. From this database of Middle English DOCs, a list of 205 ditransitive verbs used in the construction was compiled. Using the freeware program *AntConc* (Anthony 2014), and drawing on information about spelling variation in the *Electronic Middle English dictionary* (University of Michigan Regents 2013), I then searched for potential prepositional paraphrases of the DOC. This included, first and foremost, instances of these verbs selecting for a PP-'recipient' and a NP-theme (PRCs).[106]

For these patterns, the search resulted in a final total of N=2,886 observations. Importantly, these PRCs were not limited to *to* and *for*, but included a range of different prepositions such as *till, in, from, of, with, on* or *at* and others (cf. Herriman 1995; Mukherjee 2005). The potential periphrases were defined by exclusion, because starting with a fixed set of criteria to identify the competitors was considered difficult if not circular. The approach was thus rather exploratory in nature – nevertheless (or precisely because of this), operationalising the search represented some of the major challenges in the empirical part of this book. Among others, the following types were excluded from the database, since I consider them as not being near-equivalent to the DOC (also De Cuypere 2015c). Evidently, this puts further limits to the representativeness of the results and means we cannot address a number of issues empirically (such as the question of semantic extension of the preposition).

106 In fact, two different approaches were used in order to cross-check the results; the alternative method was to search for sequences of PPs and NP-OB1s in the corpus by means of *CorpusSearch*. Although this approach was probably the less complicated one, it was found to be equally time-consuming as the other procedure, since a great number of instances had to be weeded out manually. See Percillier (2018) for a potentially more systematic and elegant way of data extraction.

(87)

– locatives/ spatial uses

a. if eny man *sette* hande **oppon him**
if any man set hand upon him
'if any man lay hand on him'
(CMBRUT3,24.700; PPCME2: M3)

b. and *put* **in hym** the liknesse of the devel
and put in him the likeness of the devil
'and put the likeness of the devil into him'
(CMCTPARS,305.C2.710; PPCME2: M3)

c. and *sent* him **into Normandye**
and sent him into Normandy
'and sent him into Normandy'
(CMCAPCHR,101.2140; PPCME2: M4)

– 'resultatives'

d. And fynally *broughte* man **to reste and blysse**
and finally brought mankind to rest and Bliss
'and finally brought mankind to rest and bliss'
(CMFITZJA,B6V.225; PPCME2: M4)

– object complements

e. mine halend Criste , ðe ihc *cheas* **to lauerde**
my saviour Christ , that I chose to lord
'my saviour Christ, who I chose as my lord'
(CMVICES1,23.240; PPCME2: M1)

– accompaniment

f. And he *hadde* **with hym** Harry
and he had with him Harry
'and he had Harry with him'
(CMGREGOR,98.79; PPCME2: M4)

– comparison

g. *Make* we man **to oure ymage and liknesse**
make we man to our image and likeness
'let us make mankind in our own image and likeness'
(CMOTEST,I,20G.61; vM3)

– change/alteration

h. Icc *hafe* wennd **inntill** **Ennglissh** ||
I have turned into English ||
Goddspelles hall3he lare
gospel's holy teaching
'I have translated the gospel's holy teaching into English'
(CMORM,DED.1.4; PPCME2: M1)

– purpose marker

i. se ðe ne *3ifð* naht his eihte **te** **goule**
he that not gives not his money as rent
'he who does not lend his money at interest'
(CMVICES1,79.903; PPCME2: M1)

This method greatly overlaps with another option of restricting the data, namely excluding tokens involving inanimate recipients. Even though inanimate Recs are occasionally found in Middle English and PDE DOCs (e.g. *the flowers brought life to the party*), there is a clear tendency for animate Rec-arguments (Goldberg 1995: 146–147; De Cuypere 2015a: 236; De Cuypere 2015c: 3). Therefore, and because this study is not predominantly concerned with the factors influencing the choice between constructions and/or orders, imposing this constraint was deemed acceptable here.

The strategy of taking the DOC as a starting point for further investigations may appear to resemble Mukherjee's approach, who in his treatment of ditransitives in PDE asserts that he "ascribe[s] the label 'ditransitive' only to those verbs which are attested in the basic form of ditransitive complementation [i.e. in the DOC]" (2005: 12). However, this does not reflect my theoretical take on the status of the DOC, as I do not consider it as the more 'basic' construction in any way. Instead, the approach taken here is simply due to reasons of practicability and feasibility (cf. Szmrecsanyi 2007; Bresnan and Hay 2008; Gerwin 2014). As seen below, the data is also biased towards the DOC in that certain features such as case marking were only analysed for the DOC and not the (*to*-)PRC.

In addition to (i) DOCs and (ii) PRCs, the data was then furthermore searched for (iii) tokens of PTCs, i.e. combinations of PP-themes (any preposition) and NP-recipients. This was done using the same methodology as in the case of prepositional Rec-patterns; however, the search was limited to particular verb classes beforehand. This means that the data for this constructional type might not be entirely representative. It also explains, at least to some extent, the much lower total number of PTCs (N = 79). Similarly, in a last step I extracted (iv) instances of verbs of selected classes, specifically malefactives, in possessive structures (cases of the type 'VERB + possessive pronoun/ genitive NP + object NP'). Again, the small numbers (N=53) for this construction can be explained by the specific approach taken. The final frequency counts for the database of ditransitive structures are given in the following table.

Tab. 4: Raw token frequency of ditransitive constructions in the PPCME2

Construction	DOC	PRC	PTC	POSS	TOTAL
N	2,542	2,886	79	53	5,560

In sum, the main empirical focus of this study was clearly on the DOC and PRCs, and the database is not as encompassing as we would want it to be. Nevertheless, the project is more inclusive than previous work in taking into account not only one type of prepositional paraphrase, but both PRCs and PTCs and all potential sub-types of these patterns, as well as possessive structures. I expect that looking at this whole range of alternatives will provide us with relevant insights on the history of the dative alternation even if we acknowledge that certain methodological compromises had to be made.

4.1.2.2 Classification

For the classification of the Middle English ditransitive constructions, various different criteria were drawn on, reflecting the main research questions of the project. Most importantly, the tokens were classified according to type of construction (DOC, PRC, PTC or POSS); in the case of the prepositional patterns, the precise preposition involved was further specified. For example, (88) was classified as an instance of a PRC featuring *till.*

(88) þabbesse *offirs* <u>ani</u> <u>þing</u> **til ani of hir sisturs**
the abbess offers any thing till any of her sisters
'the abbess offers anything to any of her sisters'
(CMBENRUL,30.1009; PPCME2: M3)

In order to address developments in the formal and functional features of the constructions, I then proceeded in the following way. As to case marking in the DOC, we have seen in section (3.2.1) that formal case syncretism was already greatly advanced by early Middle English; the (pro-)noun paradigm preserved only very few and rather unreliable or ambiguous traces of the original inflectional suffixes at this point. For example, (89a) illustrates a clear [DAT$_{REC}$-ACC$_{TH}$] frame, since *hine* is unambiguously accusative, and the recipient NP features the characteristically dative *-e* suffix. By contrast, the theme pronoun *him* in (89b) could represent either an intended accusative, formally merged with the dative, or constitute a continuation of the less frequent Old English [ACC$_{\text{REC}}$-(*prep*)DAT$_{\text{TH}}$] frame. Similarly, the suffixed <-e> in (89c) either continues an OE dative or an OE accusative (since syncretism was even especially advanced with feminines at this stage already). At the same time, it could illustrate the new, Middle English generic (cross-declension and -gender) dative marker (Baker 2003-2012). Accordingly, it is difficult, if not impossible, to determine whether speakers would still have used case marking as a clear indication of semantic role in such examples.

(89) a. and *bitahte* hine$_{\text{ACC-TH}}$ **þan** **hors-horde**$_{\text{DAT-REC}}$
and gave him the horse-herdsman
'and gave him to the horse-herdsman'
(CMLAMB1,85.204; PPCME2: M1)

b. *haffde* *gifenn* himm$_{\text{DAT-TH}}$ **to** **manne**$_{\text{DAT?-REC}}$
had given him to mankind
'had given him to mankind'
(CMORM,II,256.2557; PPCME2: M1)

c. ealle **hine**$_{\text{ACC-REC}}$ *iæfen* micele gife and mære$_{\text{DAT/ACC?-TH}}$
all him gave much gifts and splendid
'all of them gave him many splendid gifts'
(CMPETERB,47.166; PPCME2: M1)

In the present study, the issue was approached from a rather hypothetical and abstract level. That is, I marked the data in a two-fold way: On the one hand, the objects were analysed from an Old English viewpoint. I checked which cases the marking on the respective nouns would have represented taking into account their inflectional classes. This was done based on the Old English nominal and pronominal paradigms as given by Baker (2003-2012), as well as the digital edition of the *Bosworth-Toller Anglo-Saxon Dictionary* (Bosworth 2010).[107] For example, the theme in (90a) is classified by Baker (2003-2012, s.v. *help*) as a strong feminine. In this class, both the dative and accusative, as well as the genitive, were marked by an *-e*-suffix, the noun was thus classified as 'ambiguous'. Concerning the REC-argument *god* 'god', both sources agree that it varied between a strong masculine and strong neuter inflection; in both cases, the suffix-less

107 The analysis was furthermore supplemented by information on word forms gained from the LAEME corpus (*A Linguistic Atlas of Early Middle English 1150 to 1325*; Laing 2013).

form in the example would have represented accusative rather than the dative (Baker 2003-2012; Bosworth-Toller, s.v. *God*). In contrast, the pronoun in (90b) would have unambiguously signalled dative (singular or plural) in Old English, while the theme does not seem to be clearly associated with one single class (Bosworth-Toller, s.v. *drinc, drync*). Although the form probably constituted accusative rather than anything else, it therefore received the tag '?', indicating that there was some uncertainty concerning its classification.

(90) a. and innwarrdlike *badd* 3ho **Godd** Hiss hellpe
and intensely bid she God his help
'she intensely bid God for his help'
(CMORM,I,81.712; PPCME2: M1)

b. to his þurst *3ef* **him** drunh
to his thirst give him drink
'give him something to drink for his thirst'
(CMANCRIW-2,II.297.864; PPCME2: M1)

On the other hand, the objects were approached from a late Middle English perspective on the basis of the nominal and pronominal paradigms given in Smith and Horobin (2002: 104, 109–110). It was then determined to what extent the forms might have been ambiguous between dative and accusative for late Middle English speakers.[108] Ambiguity would have been especially high if case marking was absent, as datives were not systematically but only occasionally marked by a final *-e* in the singular, and not differentiated at all in the plural. Similarly, personal pronouns were only marginally distinguished in the singular, specifically only if the old masculine accusative form *hine* was used. The objects *Godd*, *him* and *drunh* in the above examples (90a-b) were accordingly tagged as 'ambiguous' in this second analysis.[109] The form *hellpe*, by contrast, though ambiguous between dative and accusative in Old English, was classified as 'non-ambiguous, dative'. It should be noted, however, that this entire procedure is relatively risky, since Middle English *-e*-spellings are not reliable. With schwa-loss being quite advanced especially in the later periods, the suffix might represent stylistic/ orthographic convention instead of the actual pronunciation. Rather than disregarding the endeavour altogether because of the concep-

108 Ambiguity with the genitive was, however, probably very rare at this point (i.e. assuming a late Middle English to PDE perspective). This is because the genitive *-s*-ending was already highly widespread or indeed almost categorical then (Baker 2003-2012).

109 ME *hine*, in contrast, would have been classified as 'non-ambiguous, accusative', since the accusative form was never or only very rarely used in 'dative' contexts.

tual and methodological issues involved, the results are kept in the final analysis. It is, however, clear that the results are only tentative and coarse approximations and the focus of the project is certainly on the other questions involved.

The set of tags used for the 'Old English' and 'Middle English' analysis is presented in Tab. 5. Based on these two different schemata for Old and late Middle English, a joint value of ambiguity ranging from 0 (low probability of ambiguity) to 3 (high probability of ambiguity) was finally calculated for all REC- and TH-arguments in the dataset (Tab. 6).

Tab. 5: Set of tags for REC- and TH-arguments (OE, ME)

Old English			
<d>	unambiguously dative	<d/a/g>	ambiguous between various cases
<a>	unambiguously accusative	<?>	unclear (suffix not consistent with inflectional class/ unknown suffix)
<g>	unambiguously genitive	<F>	French origin
<d/a>	ambiguous between dative and accusative	<RPd>	relative pronoun, dative
<d/g>	ambiguous between dative and genitive	<RPa>	relative pronoun, accusative
<a/g>	ambiguous between accusative and genitive		
Middle English			
<amb>	ambiguous (Ø-suffix on R/TH; originally dative forms of pronouns)		
<n-amb>	non-ambiguous (-*e*-suffix on R, -*s*-suffix on R/TH, originally accusative form of pronouns)		
<na-d>	dative -*e*-suffix for TH-argument		

Tab. 6: Probability scores for case marking ambiguity

Old English	**Middle English**	**'Case-syncretism'-score**
<d>, <a>, <g>, <RPd>, <RPa>	<n-amb>	0 (low)
<d/a>, <d/g>, <a/g>, <d/a/g>, <?>, <F>	<n-amb>	1 (mid-low)
<d>, <a>, <g>, <RPd>, <RPa>	<amb>, <na-d>	2 (mid-high)
<d/a>, <d/g>, <a/g>, <d/a/g>, <?>, <F>	<amb>	3 (high)

Fortunately, other features of interest could be addressed and operationalised more convincingly. Concerning syntactic properties, I marked the tokens in terms of word order of the clause constituents. The classification scheme used in this regard was rather straightforward and did not present any major challenges; an example is presented in (91). As can be seen, the objects were not analysed regarding discourse-pragmatic features such pronominality or givenness, since this is outside the scope of the study.[110]

(91) Drihhtin **me**$_{\text{REC}}$ *3ifeþ* witt and mihht$_{\text{TH}}$
lord me gives skill and power S-IO-V-DO[111]
'the lord gives me skill and power'
(CMORM,I,101.867; PPCME2: M1)

Intervening material, meaning clause constituents that did not denote either the verb or the core roles of subject or objects, for example vocatives (92a), adverbs (92b) or whole (subordinate) clauses (92c), were subsumed under 'x'. They were not analysed any further, however, as the specific distribution of these elements was not of immediate interest to the present study.

(92) a. *3yf* **us**$_{\text{REC}}$ helpe of tribulacioun$_{\text{TH}}$
give us help of sorrow V-IO-x-DO
'Give us help against our sorrows'
(CMEARLPS,71.3114; PPCME2: M2)

b. *pay* **hem**$_{\text{REC}}$ 3erly x þousand pound$_{\text{TH}}$
pay them yearly 10 thousand pounds V-IO-x-DO
'pay them ten thousand pounds a year'
(CMCAPCHR,96.1960; PPCME2: M4)

110 A study on this aspect of the history of ditransitives in English is in progress (De Cuypere 2015c).

111 Since the focus here was only on word order, and no passives were included in any case, the labels 'IO' (indirect object), 'PO' (prepositional indirect object) and 'DO' (direct object) were used; the former two always correspond to REC, while the latter is equal to TH.

c.

hauest	**ham**$_{REC}$	*bihaten*	ȝef	ha
have	them	promised	if	they

mahen	on	me	þe	herre
may	on	me	the	upper

hont	habben	kinewurðe	meden$_{TH}$	aux-IO-V-x-DO
hand	have	royal	rewards	

'and [you] have promised them, if they were able to get the upper hand on me, royal rewards'
(CMKATHE,31.189; PPCME2: M1)

Example (92c) shows that combinations of finite and non-finite verb forms were labelled as 'aux-V', disregarding the question to what extent such finites had acquired auxiliary status at that time. Further issues that had to be dealt with in the classification were e.g. the absence of explicit subjects in a large number of cases (predictable in imperatives and non-finites as in [92a-b] above, but also found in main clauses, [92c, 93a]). Furthermore, we find frequent detachment of auxiliaries/modal verbs in relation to the main verb (93b), as well as special features pertaining to the objects such as 'extracted/anaphoric' objects (93c), split objects (93d) and stranded prepositions (93e). All these non-canonical orders and patterns were kept in the dataset but were classified accordingly.

(93) a.

him$_{REC}$	*be-nimþ*	þane	mete	/	and	þane	drinke$_{TH}$
him	steals	the	food	/	and	the	drink

'at other times SUBJ steals from him food and drink'
(CMAYENBI,29.475; PPCME2: M2)

b.

him$_{R}$	ich	*habbe*	meiden	mi	meiðhad$_{TH}$	*iȝettet*
him	I	have	young girl	my	virginity	gotten

'I have given him my virginity as a young girl'
(CMMARGA,58.63; PPCME2: M1)

c.

alle	þe	delites	þat$_{TH}$	þu	*myȝt*	*schewen*	**hym**$_{REC}$
all	the	delights	that	you	might	show	him

'all the delights that you might show him'
(CMAELR4,31.150; PPCME2: M4)

d.

he	*gate*	**hem**$_{REC1}$	lyf$_{TH}$	**that**	**slowe**	**him**$_{REC2}$
he	got	them	life	that	slew	him

'he gave them who slew him life'
(CMAELR4,21.635; PPCME2: M4)

e. alle **þat**$_{REC1}$ sche *schewed* <u>hyr</u> <u>secretys</u>$_{TH}$ **vn-to**$_{REC2}$
all that she showed her secrets unto
'all those that she showed her secrets to'
(CMKEMPE,3.29; PPCME2: M4)

The last point in the classification scheme concerns semantic information about the ditransitive verbs/constructions involved. Here, the individual verb tokens were categorised into ten (to twelve) fairly broad verb classes based on their semantics in the specific contexts.[112] The set of verb classes proposed is heavily influenced by comparable studies by Barðdal (2007), Barðdal, Kristoffersen, and Sveen (2011: 65), Colleman (2011: 404), Colleman and De Clerck (2011: 191–197) as well as the models in Goldberg (1995: 38, 75–76) and Pinker (1989: 110–118), among others.[113] Tab. 7 illustrates the individual classes together with selected example verbs.

Tab. 7: Classification scheme for verb classes (with sample verbs)

#	Verb class	Example verbs
i)	ACTUAL TRANSFER	
	concrete transfer	giving/delivering, lending, paying, sending, bringing, obtaining
	abstract transfer	paying so. a visit, giving so. a kiss
ii)	INTENTION: verbs of future transfer	offering, promising, guaranteeing
iii)	COMMUNICATION: verbs of communicated message	telling, asking, showing
iv)	DISPOSSESSION: hindrance, constraining	stealing, robbing, taking away
v)	REFUSAL: blocked transfer	denying, refusing, withholding
vi)	'reverse transfer'	asking so. mercy/ one's name
vii)	MENTAL/ATTITUDINAL: mental activity, emotion	envying

112 As discussed in more detail in section (2.1.2), these lexical-semantic verb classes are taken to instantiate and determine the meaning of the various sub-constructions of the ditransitive construction (Barðdal and Gildea 2015: 27; cf. also Croft 2003; Perek 2015).

113 See also Gropen et al. (1989), Levin (1993), and Croft (2003), as well as Vázquez-González & Barðdal (subm.).

#	Verb class	Example verbs
viii)	BEN/MAL: benefactive, malefactive	
	'pure' benefaction/malefaction	opening so. the door
	creation	creating, building
ix)	**LV:** light verbs/ complex multi-word predicates[114]	doing so. harm
x)	other (possession, comparison, signifying)	

There are two basic problems involved in this kind of classification. First, there is the polysemous nature of many verbs, which often allows them to fluctuate between two or more different verb classes depending on the context. While in some cases, the appropriate interpretation is rather obvious (94a: 'actual transfer' vs. 94b: 'intended/future transfer'), other instances unfortunately escape a clear-cut analysis.

(94) a. *Offre* **me**$_{\text{REC}}$ þine sune Ysaac$_{\text{TH}}$
offer me your son Isaac
'offer me your son Isaac/ sacrifice your son Isaac for me'
(CMVICES1,111.1342; PPCME2: M1)

b. *offirs* ani þing$_{\text{TH}}$ **til ani of hir sisturs**$_{\text{REC}}$
offers any thing till any of her sisters
'offers anything to any of her sisters'
(CMBENRUL,30.1009; PPCME2: M3)

Related to this (but even more demanding) is the blurriness of the categories themselves. There is a large degree of overlap between the classes, and very frequently, a verb could easily be subsumed in two or more different classes at the same time. The class of verbs of 'intended/future transfer', for example, overlaps with the 'benefactive/malefactive' class to a certain extent – while (potential) transfer is definitely implied, the action is at the same time carried out for the benefit of REC (95a-b). This issue is furthered by the prepositional

114 Class (ix) is somewhat special as it does not constitute a separate 'sister'-class to the other verb classes but is more of a meta-class instead. Verbs classified as light verbs or idioms are at the same time always members of another class as well. For example, *do so. harm* could be classified as both 'BEN/MAL (pure)' and 'LV', whereas *give so. a kiss* represents both 'abstract transfer' and 'LV'. I mainly comment on benefactive/malefactive light verb patterns below; these are labelled 'bmLV'.

paraphrases available for individual classes typically not being restricted to one single preposition (cf. *to* vs. *for*, 95c-d). As shown elsewhere (section 2.1), in PDE ditransitives are commonly distinguished from benefactives based on their being paraphrased by a *to-* vs. a *for*-pattern, respectively. Such a clear-cut distinction is not there in Middle English (and is also fuzzy in PDE). Furthermore, this strategy is slightly circular in itself.

(95) a wið þe wurð of heouene *buð* **hire**$_{REC}$ helle$_{TH}$
wit the price of heaven buys her hell
'buys herself hell with the price of heaven'
(CMANCRIW-1,II.120.1508; PPCME2: M1)

b. *breideð* **þe**$_{REC}$ crune of blisse$_{TH}$
weaves you crown of bliss
'he weaves you a crown of bliss'
(CMANCRIW-1,II.174.2423; PPCME2: M1)

c. Salamon *bildide* a noble hous$_{TH}$ **to** **himself**$_{REC}$
Salomon built a noble house to himself
'Salomon built a noble house to himself'
(CMPURVEY,I,12.477; PPCME2: M3)

d. *haþ wrou3t* **for** **him**$_{REC}$ meny a faire miracle$_{TH}$
has worked for him many a fair miracle
'has often worked great miracles for him'
(CMBRUT3,101.3058; PPCME2: M3)

Cases where a decision was difficult to make were either resolved in favour of one or the other verb class (often following the example of previous studies as cited above), or, if in doubt, an ambiguous instance was counted for both verb classes (as 0.5 and 0.5 tokens, respectively). While far from ideal, this method was chosen due to the overall number of tokens not allowing me to discard ambiguous instances altogether. The rather low frequency of certain verb classes (such as 'refusal') in the corpus generally represents a clear challenge, as it makes it difficult to generalise and restricts any clear conclusions to the more predominant verb classes such as 'actual transfer'. Despite these limitations, the database is still sufficiently large to yield significant results on the behaviour of most verb classes; we just cannot overstate the representativeness of some of the findings.

A more overarching methodological problem of this kind of manual semantic annotation is, as Perek (2016: 14) points out, that it is based on "the semantic intuitions of a single individual, which renders it potentially subjective". Some of this conundrum could be solved by involving more than one annotator, or even a group of non-academic similarity raters as done in e.g. Bybee and Eddington's (2006) semantic norming study. However, such methods are often difficult to employ for practical reasons, as was the case in the present study. A very interesting solution to remedy this situation is proposed in Perek (2016), who uses distributional semantics and vector-space models to come up with a method to measure the semantic similarity between lexical items based on their co-occurrence/ collocation patterns in corpora (cf. also Gries and Hilpert 2008; Perek 2014; Perek and Hilpert 2017; Percillier subm.). Applying this methodology to the present data will be the focus of a follow-up study to this book, and I expect the findings to confirm the trends observed here.

To sum up, the instances of ditransitive patterns extracted from the corpus were analysed in regard to type of construction, type of preposition (where applicable), ambiguity of case marking (only DOC), order of constituents (relative placement of subject, indirect object, direct object, and verb), and semantics, that is, verb class involved. Furthermore, extralinguistic variables such as period, dialect and genre were indicated for each token. The dataset thus compiled was then subjected to statistical analysis in various ways. Some basic information on this is given in the following section.

4.1.2.3 Analysis

All statistical analysis and visualisation of the data was carried out by means of *R*, "a free software environment for statistical computing and graphics" (R Development Core Team 2014). For graphic representation, I mainly used the R-package 'ggplots2' (Wickham 2016).

In a first step, the basic frequency distribution and development of the variables was investigated, providing the main descriptive and some analytic statistics. Most statistical testing here involved pairwise comparisons of proportions. When dealing with the diachronic development of relative frequencies of a variable, I plainly compared two periods with each other at a time (e.g. typically M1–M2, M2–M3, M3–M4, as well as M1–M4 as an indicator of change over the whole period). For these comparisons, 2-by-2 chi-square tests of independence were calculated. This method of testing of course does not indicate directionality of change (but only whether one distribution is significantly different from another). The very low number of data points (N=4; M1–M4) obtained in the study unfortunately impeded the use of other measures popular in historical linguistics such as *Kendall's tau*, which allows to evaluate distributional data by testing the strength of a correlation between two variables, e.g. time and relative frequencies (Hilpert and Gries 2009: 390; Gries 2010: 279–280; among others).

For comparisons of two (or more) values within one sub-period, for example to assess whether the proportional frequencies of DOC and PRC in a given period differ significantly from each other and are not equally distributed, chi-square goodness-of-fit tests were performed. In the latter case, Cramer's V was calculated as a measure of effect size. In the case of 2x2 contingency tables (tests of independence), Cohen's ϕ-coefficient was determined for each test, assuming the conventional classification 0.1=small effect size, 0.3=medium effect size, and 0.5=large effect size.

To address some of the problematic issues with this approach, the data was then further analysed with mixed effects modelling and other statistical techniques. Specifically, I used logistic regression to model "the relationships between a categorical response variable with two or more possible values and one or more explanatory variables, or predictors" (Levshina 2015: 253). The dependent variable in the study is the choice between the members of the dative alternation, or more generally, the alternation between DOC and alternative, prepositional, patterns. The largest part of the project deals with two synonyms (DOC vs. PRC); this analysis was therefore carried out by means of binary/binomial regression modelling (Gries 2009: Ch. 3–5; Levshina 2015: Ch. 12). Independent variables included above all time, but also dialect, different word order features (clausal word order, object order), verb (class), as well as preposition type. The outcome of the model thus gives the chances of construction A (e.g. the DOC) "to be chosen in a particular context (compared with chances of B to be used in same type of context)" (Levshina 2015: 253). The chances are dependent on the predictors, entailing also that they can increase or decrease with changes in the value of one of the independent variables. For example, we expect time to have a significant impact on the likelihood of the PRC to be used instead of the DOC. To fit the model then involves determining values for all coefficients, the estimated effects of the predictors on the outcome. Furthermore, we can test for interactions between the effects, e.g. assess whether time and verb class have a joint impact on the odds of the DOC to be chosen at the expense of the PRC. The specific R-functions used were lrm() (Harrell 2018) and glm() (R Core Team).

In addition to examining these issues, I provide results on the productivity of the different patterns as well as changes in productivity. This concerns, on the one hand, type frequency, and on the other hand, a measurement referred to as 'potential productivity' (Baayen 2009; also Hilpert 2011). This assessment "operationalizes the productivity of a schema as the number of its hapax legomena (i.e. the types that occur only once in a corpus) divided by its overall text frequency (i.e. all of its tokens in a corpus)" (Hilpert 2011: 442). Following previous studies, type frequency and potential productivity can be joined in a plot to show 'global productivity' (Baayen and Lieber 1991: 819; Hilpert 2011: 442). This can be useful in detecting correspondences and/or differences between the two measurements of productivity and is more valuable than relying on one aspect of productivity only.

Finally, I carried out (multiple) distinctive collexeme analyses on the data, using Gries' R script for collostructional analysis (Gries 2014). This is a procedure which is "specifically geared to investigating pairs of semantically similar grammatical constructions and the lexemes that occur in them" (Gries and Stefanowitsch 2004: 97; cf. also Hilpert 2006; Wulff 2006; Wulff et. al. 2007). The tool detects distributional differences between competing constructions and allows the user to test whether certain lexemes show preferences for one option or the other, indicating at the same time the strength of such biases (Gries and Stefanowitsch 2004: 97). For binary distinctions, it does so by determining, on a lexeme-to-lexeme basis, four values: the frequency of the form in question in the respective constructions (A and B), as well as the frequency of other verbs in the constructions (i.e. frequency of construction A/B - the frequency of the lexeme in A/B). A Fisher exact test is then performed on the 2x2-table created with these values, and the sizes of resulting p-values specify how distinctive a given lexeme is for any of the two constructions. Which of the two options this is, is determined by comparing the observed frequencies to the expected frequencies, assuming a random distribution. The method can also be applied to variation between more than two patterns. In the present study, this is used to examine preferences between the DOC, PRC, PTC and POSS constructions. The main difference between the two versions is that in multiple distinctive collexeme analyses, each of the variant constructions is compared against all of the others (Levshina 2015: 248). Instead of a Fisher-Yates exact test, a one-tailed exact binomial test is performed. – For further information see Gries and Stefanowitsch (2004) as well as Gries (2012) as a response to the critical view on association measures voiced in Bybee (2010: Ch.5).

4.2 Results

The following sections present the main findings of the corpus study just outlined, starting with the (proportional) frequency distribution of the patterns investigated (4.2.1). This section loosely follows the issues dealt with in the literature review above, in that I start by providing data on the emergence of the alternation, more precisely the general distribution of DOC vs. (*to*-)PRC. This is followed by a more detailed examination of verb classes and their constructional preferences (and concomitantly, developments in the semantics of the DOC).

Afterwards, I comment on word order changes in ditransitives, before briefly discussing the loss of case marking. In section (4.2.1.4) the results of the logistic regression model(s) are given; section (4.2.3) is on productivity measures. Last, section (4.2.4) shows the outcome of the distinctive collexeme analyses performed on the data.

4.2.1 Frequency distribution

4.2.1.1 Emergence of the dative alternation

When investigating the establishment of the dative alternation, the first thing to do is to compare the fractions of the total of ditransitive tokens taken up by DOC and PRC in the four sub-periods of the PPCME2 (Fig. 7). What is immediately evident here is that the DOC significantly decreased in proportional frequency at the beginning of the period (M1–M2: $p < 0.001$, $\phi \approx 0.3$). This points to early Middle English as the main locus of change. Although a decrease is also confirmed for the overall period (M1–M4: $p < 0.001$, $\phi \approx 0.3$), the development levels off after this initial point of change (in spite of the still significant difference between M2 and M3, the effect size is considerably smaller at approximately 0.1). Even more interestingly, the trend appears to reverse towards the end of

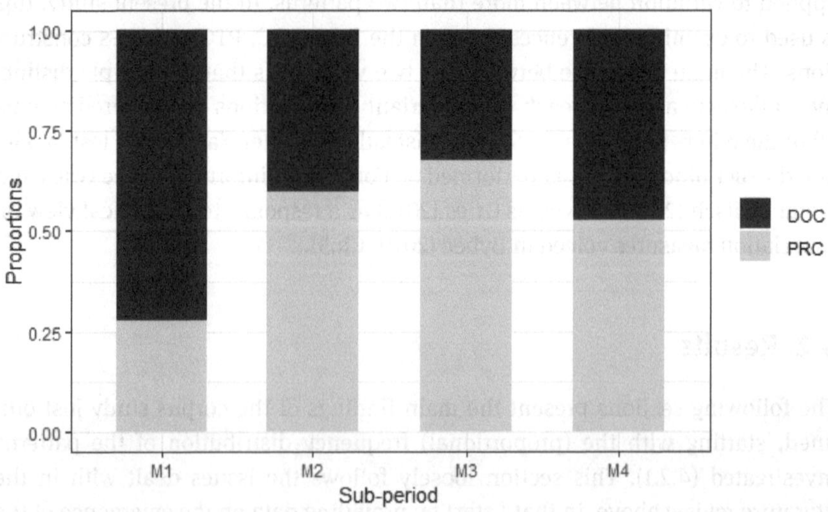

Fig. 7: Proportional distribution of DOC (vs. PRC) tokens, M1–M4

the period (M3–M4: $p < 0.001$, $\phi \approx 0.2$). The difference in fractions taken up by DOCs and PRCs, respectively, is significant in the earlier periods. This is, however, not the case in M4, where the two patterns rather come to 'share the workload' on equal terms, with both constructions accounting for about 50 per cent of the tokens (DOC: 47 per cent vs. PRC: 53 per cent).[115] Importantly, the (relative) frequency of the DOC is here compared against PRCs involving a range of different prepositions, including e.g. constructions with *from*, *of* or *on*.

Shifting the focus to one specific type of PRC, namely the *to*-PRC (and, correspondingly, only those DOCs that alternate with a *to*-PRC), a similar distribution is seen. Tab. 8 presents a comparison of the two sets of constructions, meaning the DOC vs. all PRCs, and the DOC(alt) vs. the *to*-PRC only (with absolute and relative numbers of tokens).[116]

Tab. 8: Raw/proportional figures for the distribution of DOC/PRC and DOC(alt)/*to*-PRC

	DOC(all)	PRC(all)	TOTAL	% DOC
M1	905	346	1251	72.3
M2	246	366	612	40.2
M3	645	1352	1997	32.3
M4	739	822	1561	47.3
	DOC(alt)	***to*-PRC**	**TOTAL**	**%DOC(alt)**
M1	701	125	826	84.9
M2	214	241	455	47
M3	577	849	1426	40.5
M4	688	487	1175	58.6

Nevertheless, there are also striking differences. The divergence in the distribution of the competing patterns is much larger in early Middle English (M1), with over 80 per cent of tokens found in the DOC. Furthermore, as also shown in Fig. 8, the drop in frequency of the DOC between M1–M2 is sharper than in the former case (M1–M2: $p < 0.001$, $\phi \approx 0.4$; M2–M3: $p < 0.05$, $\phi < 0.1$; M3–M4: $p < 0.001$, $\phi \approx 0.2$; M1–M4: $p < 0.001$, $\phi \approx 0.2$).

115 M1: $p < 0.001$, $V \approx 0.2$; M2: $p < 0.001$, $V \approx 0.1$; M3: $p < 0.001$, $V \approx 0.2$; M4: $p > 0.05$.

116 DOC(alt) here refers to a sub-set of DOC tokens, including only occurrences of verbs that alternate with the *to*-PRC.

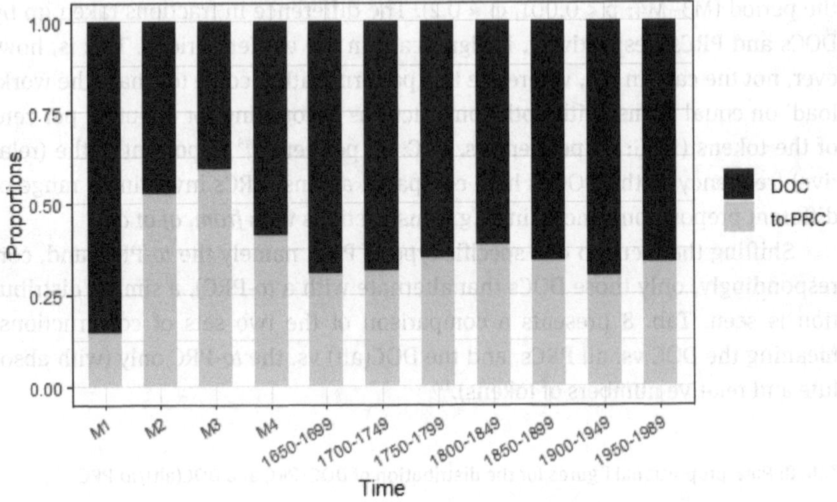

Fig. 8: Proportional distribution of DOC (vs. *to*-PRC) 1150–1989 (e/lModE data: ARCHER; Wolk et al. 2013)

The trend reversal towards the end of the period found above is even more pronounced if only *to*-PRCs are taken into account – while in M3, the DOC is still significantly less frequent than the to-*PRC*, and only accounts for about 40 per cent of the tokens, this number rises to about 60 per cent in the last sub-period (M1: $p < 0.001$, $V > 0.5$; M2: $p > 0.05$; M3: $p < 0.001$, $V \approx 0.2$; M4: $p < 0.001$, $V \approx 0.3$). This clear turnaround in the distribution of the constructions is surprising, even though we know from PDE evidence that the *to*-prepositional paraphrase did not completely replace the DOC, but instead has entered into a close relationship with its alternative. In this alternation, the DOC today constitutes the dominant (more frequent) partner. As mentioned above (3.1.2), the u-turn development observed in the development of the *to*-PRC can also be seen in McFadden's (2002) analysis of Middle English ditransitives (although McFadden does not in fact comment on this particular aspect). The precise figures of his study deviate from those found in my data in that the changes are slightly less sharp in our case (e.g. the *to*-PRC does not move less than 10 per cent in M1 to a peak of 70 per cent in this study but from about 12 to 50 per cent, meaning that the construction does not increase tenfold, but only quadruples). Nevertheless, the fact that both McFadden's work and my own arrive at the same overall picture regarding the behaviour of *to*-PRCs in relation to DOCs is positive.

Interestingly enough, the establishment of a stronger DOC/ weaker *to*-PRC distribution is thus not a later, more recent change in the history of the constructions, but happened rather quickly, within the comparatively short time span of about 400 years covered by the corpus. That Middle English (to Early Modern English) should be the period of most pronounced change is also confirmed by findings on the subsequent development of the constructions as presented in Fig. 8 (data for Early/Late Modern English – 1650 to 1989 – taken from Wolk et al. 2013's study of ARCHER). From the early 18th century onwards, there is little or in fact no change in the relative frequencies of the two constructions; the DOC takes up about 65-70 per cent of the tokens, whereas the *to*-PRC constitutes around 30-35 per cent in all periods.[117] It is conspicuous to see that when looking at the fraction of DOCs and PRCs in the individual texts included in the PPCME2 and map these distributions according to the texts' date of composition, a slightly more complex picture presents itself (Fig. 9). In the figure, each text is represented by a data point; the size of the respective dots indicates the raw frequency of tokens of (all) ditransitive patterns found in the individual texts. Fitting a curve giving the smoothed conditional means (method=loess, with the grey area indicating the confidence bands for the regression line), we see that texts at the beginning of the period quite consistently exhibit a higher frequency of the DOC. They are much more interspersed in the 15th century,

117 It should be noted again, however, that Wolk et al.'s findings do not fit with Gerwin's (2014: 143–145) analysis of the same corpus of Late Modern English (ARCHER). In her analysis, the *to*-PRC makes up only about 20 per cent of ditransitive tokens in the 17th century and slightly rises in frequency towards the 1900s, only to again drop in usage in the course of the 20th century. This development is explained as a typical s-curve pattern in Gerwin (2014: 143). That is to say, the construction is assumed to exhibit "a slow increase in late Old English and early Middle English followed by a rapid rise of the construction and an extension to other syntactic contexts in the 14th and 15th century [as well as a] tailing-off phase of the increase [in later centuries]" (Gerwin 2014: 143). However, the present data do not entirely fit this narrative (which is in any case based on relatively outdated sources). In fact, we see a sharp increase of *to*-PRCs in earlier Middle English rather than later in the period, at which point the use of the construction falls again. If Gerwin's analysis of the later centuries was followed, the construction would have shown an up-and-down behaviour throughout the periods, first increasing and then decreasing within Middle English, rising again in Late Modern English, and dropping once more in the 20th century. While a development like this is not entirely inconceivable as such, Gerwin's explanation is somewhat difficult to combine with the results of the present study. The proposal that is put forward in this book is also generally more compatible with Wolk et al.'s (2013) findings. In order to arrive at a more definitive answer on the subsequent development of the alternation, a more detailed investigation of the two studies and their methodologies, and possibly further research on the constructions in the relevant periods, would of course nevertheless be needed.

though, and the trend does not entirely correspond to the figures presented above. This is not necessarily problematic or contradict the more general trend outlined on the basis of Fig. 7 and Fig. 8, since the selection of texts represented in the corpus is generally considerably skewed towards certain dialects and genres. Also, a number of texts are not clearly datable. I therefore proceed on the basic assumption that there is a resurgence of the DOC towards the end of the Middle English period, which essentially lays the ground for the PDE dative alternation.

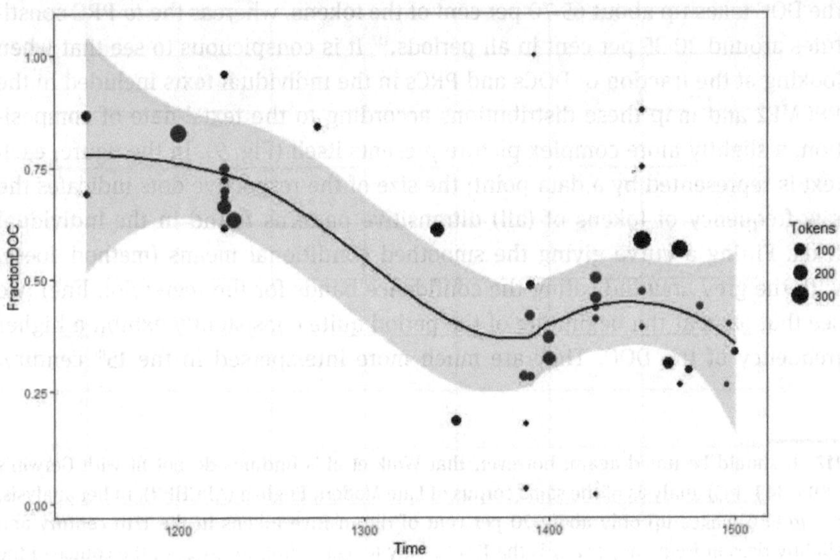

Fig. 9: Proportional distribution of DOC (vs. PRC) over individual texts, 1150–1500

Apart from developments in the distribution of (*to-*)PRCs in relation to the DOC, it is also worth taking a separate look at the prepositional competitors, or more specifically, at the role individual PRC-types play within this broader category. The main focus in this regard is quite obviously the distribution of *to*-PRCs as compared to patterns involving other prepositions, e.g. *from*-PRCs, or *till*-PRCs, etc. As the data indicate, PRCs with *to* take up a large fraction of tokens in all sub-periods, and account for a maximum of around 60 per cent in M2 and M3. This is shown in Fig. 10, which presents the proportional distribution of *to*-patterns within the total of PRCs, i.e. *to*-PRCs as compared to all other PRC-patterns. – For reasons given in the following paragraphs, the figure also includes results on the distribution of *unto* and *onto* against the rest of PRCs. What this suggests is that *to* was prevalent already at the beginning of the period and continued to be so at all further stages. As regards the development of the proportions over the course of the period, there is a rapid initial growth in *to*-patterns as compared to other PRCs, followed, however, by a significant drop in the later sub-periods (M1–M2: $p < 0.001$, $\phi \approx 0.3$; M2–M3: $p > 0.05$; M3–M4: $p < 0.001$, $\phi \approx 0.1$). Nevertheless, the overall change during the period is significant (M1–M4: $p < 0.01$, $\phi \approx 0.1$), and *to*-PRCs still make up a very large part of PRCs in M4 (approx. 45 per cent).

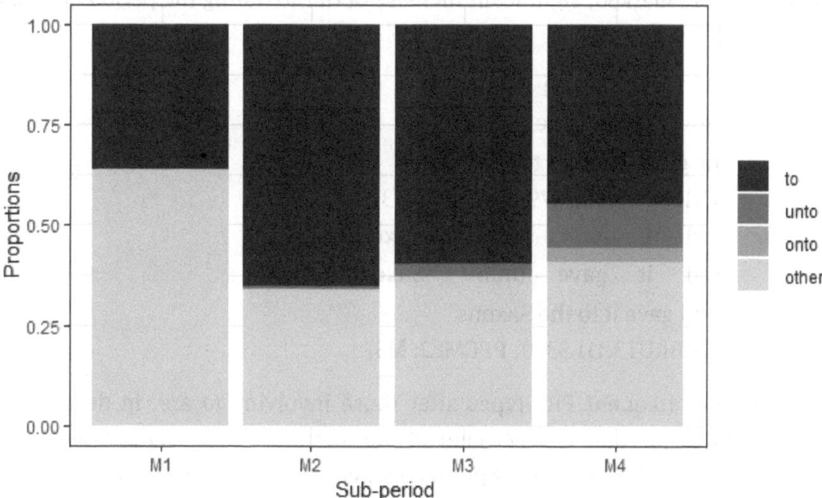

Fig. 10: Proportional distribution of *to/onto/unto*-PRCs as compared to PRCs involving all other prepositions, M1–M4

Despite the fact that we can observe some change concerning the role of *to*, the intuitive expectation would be that this change was much more pronounced (note also that the effect size concerning the change from M1–M4 is small at 0.1). There are three possible explanations for why this is not the case:

First, certain verb classes in the DOC were never paraphrased by *to* (e.g. dispossession verbs). These increasingly switched to prepositional patterns when they were marginalised from the DOC, thereby increasing the token frequency of other PRCs. Second, variation concerning the specific prepositions a verb occurred with was relatively high in the earlier sub-periods. That is, even those verbs that could be paraphrased with a *to*-PRC, could also be used with other prepositions such as *towards* or *till*, and others (and vice versa). As also supported by the results of the distinctive collexeme analysis below, this changed towards the end of the period. Thus, it seems that a regularisation of the system took place, and specific verbs became increasingly restricted to individual prepositions (cf. Strang 1970: 274–275; Traugott 1972: 127; Lundskær-Nielsen 1993: 113–114). Last, note that from M3 onwards, the preposition-combinations *un-to* and *on-to* came into existence (Mustanoja 1960: 415). These can be assumed to correspond closely to *to* since they appear in the same texts as well as contexts, and with the same verbs as the simple preposition (96a-b). Combing the figures for these complex prepositions with those for simple *to*, there is a more marked, significant increase of *(un)to* during the period (M1–M4: $p < 0.001$, $\phi \approx 0.2$).[118]

(96) a.

he	*ȝaf*	<u>þe</u>	<u>londe</u>	**to**	**þe**	**Saxones**
he	gave	the	land	to	the	Saxons

'he gave the land to the Saxons'
(CMBRUT3,95.2879; PPCME2: M3)

b.

and	<u>it</u>	*ȝaf*	**vnto**	**Saxonus**
and	it	gave	unto	Saxons

'and gave it to the Saxons'
(CMBRUT3,111.3350; PPCME2: M3)

The five most frequent PRC-types after those involving *to* are, in descending order, *of*-PRCs (around 12.5 per cent of the total), *on*-PRCs (5.5 per cent), *for*-PRCs (3.6 per cent), *from*-PRCs (approx. 3.4 per cent) as well as *upon*-PRCs (3 per cent). Additional information on the frequency and distribution of individual prepositions will be presented where relevant in later sections.

As a final note, let us briefly look at the frequency of ditransitive patterns in the entire corpus. Fig. 11 indicates that the overall number of investigated tokens does not change significantly over time, only falling slightly from approximately 65 instances per 10,000 words in M1 to about 60 in M4 (DOC/*to*-PRC/*unto*-PRC/*other*-PRC, M1 vs. M4: $p > 0.5$). However, the combined normalised frequency of DOC and *to*-PRCs does experience a significant decrease (DOC/*to*-PRC, M1 vs. M4: $p < 0.00001$, $\varphi \approx 0.3$). The change is less drastic, but still present, if *unto* and *onto* are taken into account again (DOC/*(un)to*-PRC, M1

118 As Rostila (2007: 216, fn107) claims, *onto* and *unto* constitute independent lexemes in PDE, suggesting that the meanings of the prepositions diverged from *to* (and each other) at some point after Middle English.

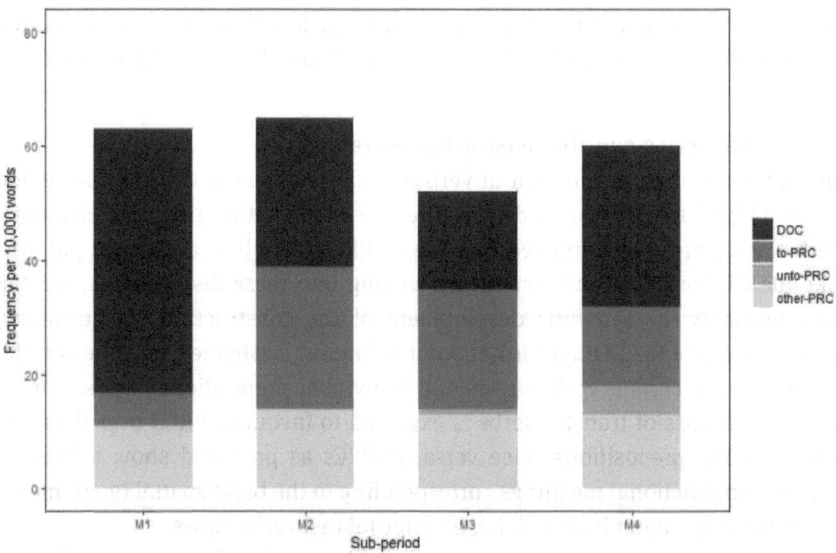

Fig. 11: Normalised frequency (per 10,000 words) of DOC, *to*-PRC, *unto/onto*-PRC, and PRCs involving all other prepositions, M1–M4

vs. M4: $p < 0.01$, $\varphi < 0.1$). This corresponds to Wolk et al.'s (2013: 393) findings, which show that the total number of instances of dative alternation members drops further in Late Modern English (in contrast to the genitive alternation, which increases in this period). It follows that we cannot straightforwardly equate mutual benefit in cooperation between alternating constructions – as discussed in chapters (6) and (7) – with overall growth, or at least stability, in frequency. Since these developments may be influenced by a range of factors not investigated in this study, I leave this for future consideration.

In sum, the results shown in this chapter corroborate that the prepositional alternatives greatly increased during Middle English. Crucially, however, the PRCs did not straightforwardly oust the DOC, but instead peaked in the middle of the period and afterwards fell again in relative frequency. At the end of the period, we therefore see a relatively balanced 50/50 distribution of DOC and PRCs. Within the group of PRCs, the type involving *to* is the most frequent one. This special status becomes even more visible over time, indicating that *to*-PRCs played a special role among the prepositional paraphrases. Comparing the proportions of *to*-PRCs and DOCs, the u-turn development seen with all PRCs is still more evident: DOCs again take on a stronger position towards the end of the period and surpass the *to*-PRCs in frequency again. That this distribution more or less corresponds to that in Late Modern English and also PDE confirms that the ground for the PDE dative alternation was essentially set in Middle English.

4.2.1.2 Verb class-specific constructional preferences

In contrast to the examination of verb-specific preferences which is presented below (4.2.4), this section addresses the question whether particular semantic verb classes are more attracted to DOCs or PRCs as well as additional patterns like the PTC or POSS-construction. By looking into these distributions, we can also re-assess the semantic development of the constructions in questions, above all that of the DOC. A further point of interest is whether there are correlations between certain verb classes and individual prepositional types. For instance, the class of transfer verbs is expected to favour *to*-PRCS over those involving other prepositions. Vice versa, *to*-PRCs as predicted show a bias for certain constructional meanings corresponding to the basic spatial (goal) meaning of the preposition involved, i.e. transfer-related verb classes.

A first observation that can be made in this regard is that as seen in Fig. 12, the general increase in prepositional patterns at the expense of DOCs is mirrored by the data for a group of verb classes with a meaning related to transfer. That is, all verbs of transfer, more precisely, the sub-sets concrete and abstract transfer (concrTrans and abstrTrans) as well as intended transfer (intTrans) and communication (comm), show an initial decrease in the proportional frequency of the PRC, followed by a levelling off or even a reversal of the trend towards the end of the period. Transfer (and transfer-related) verbs are generally most frequently paraphrased by a *to*-PRC already at the beginning of the period; over 50 per cent of the relevant verb tokens (transfer-related verbs in PRCs) in M1 select for *to*-patterns rather than PRCs involving any other preposition. Like in the entire dataset, there is no significant overall change throughout the period if only *to* is taken into account, but the increase is significant when *to* is considered together with its complex variants *unto* and *onto*. This indicates that there is a considerable attraction between transfer (and transfer-related) verbs and *(un)to* from the beginning of the period onwards. That this tendency should become even stronger during the period is a welcome detail. It also supports the idea that the foundations of the PDE dative alternation, as a very close association between DOC and *to*-PRC with a prototypical meaning of transfer, was formed within Middle English. The reverse figures, i.e. figures for the distribution of *to* with the various verb classes, are not explicitly reproduced here, but further corroborate the point made in this section – *to*-PRCs clearly occur more frequently with transfer-related verbs. Again, this suggests that there is a strong relation between the two patterns of DOCs and *to*-PRCs with transfer verbs, which became only more intimate in the course of the period.

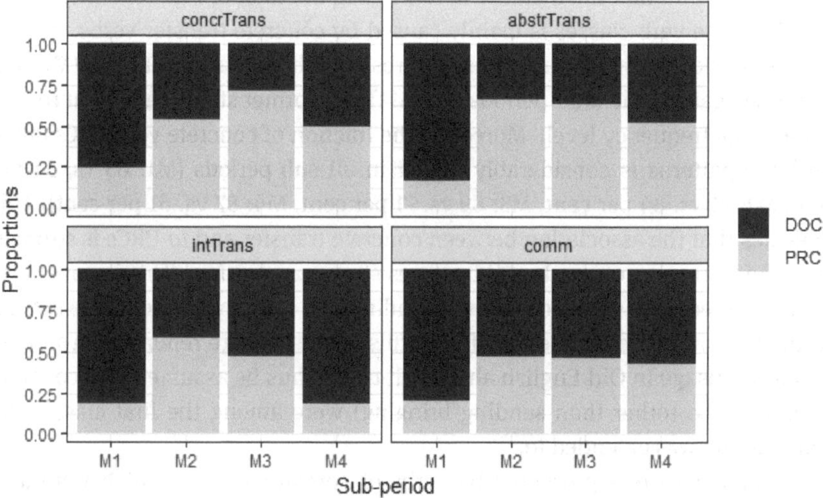

Fig. 12: Proportional distribution of DOC (vs. PRC) with transfer and communication verbs (concrTrans=concrete transfer, N=1,094; abstrTrans=abstract transfer, N=1,271; comm=communication, N=1,035; intTrans=intended transfer, N=276), M1–M4

If we consider the broad classes of transfer and transfer-related verbs in more detail, we see that as expected, there is a significant decrease in the proportional frequency of DOCs in favour of PRCs with verbs of physically concrete successful transfer. A similar drop in relative frequency can be observed with verbs denoting abstract events/ metaphorical transfer such as *pay so. a visit*. While the DOC accounts for approximately 75 (85) per cent of concrete (abstract) transfer tokens respectively in M1, these figures fall below 40 per cent until M3, before re-rising up to 50 per cent towards M4 in both cases. This development likewise reflects the turnaround already mentioned; the constructions seem to enter into a balanced distribution towards the end of the period. Although the trend is thus the same with both concrete and abstract transfer verbs, the specific pathways are remarkably different: In the former case, the DOC decreases rapidly and steadily from M1 to M3, and only increases towards the end (M3–M4). By contrast, in the latter there is an initial sharp fall in frequency (M1–M2), after which the development stagnates to a certain extent, and the later resurgence of the DOC is slower (M2–M4). It is furthermore interesting that the percentage of concrete transfer verbs in DOCs is lower than that of verbs of abstract transfer in M1 (75 per cent vs. 85 per cent).

As to the specific PRC-types associated with verbs of concrete and abstract transfer, we find that the increase in *to*-PRCs in the total of PRC tokens instantiated by these verb classes is mainly caused by concrete transfer verbs. In contrast to *to*-PRCs with abstract transfer verbs, which after an initial rise (M1–M2) decrease again in the later periods (M2–M4), the former stably remain at roughly the same frequency level. Moreover, the fraction of concrete verb PRCs taken up by *to*-patterns is considerably higher in all sub-periods (M1: 63 vs. 54 per cent, M2: 91 vs. 84 per cent, M3: 89 vs. 71 per cent, M4: 87 vs. 61 per cent). This indicates that the association between concrete transfer and *to*-PRCs is stronger from the beginning onwards and becomes stronger over time. This is not entirely unexpected, though, since verbs of sending and bringing, which were included in the group of 'concrete transfer' in this analysis, were reportedly available for *to*-PRC usage in Old English already. It could thus be assumed that concrete transfer verbs (other than sending/bringing) were among the first classes the construction was extended to.

A similar case is presented by verbs of communication, which were also present in *to*-PRCs in OE: The *to*-PRC is likewise comparatively frequent with these verbs in M1 already. It is in this context that the seemingly less close association between verbs of abstract transfer and the *to*-PRC especially in M1 might be seen as surprising – due to their semantic affinity to other verbs of metaphorical giving such as communication verbs, abstract transfer verbs could be predicted to occur in the pattern at an early stage as well. However, the figures are compatible with and lend support to De Cuypere's assessment that the grammaticalisation path was not one of GOAL > concrete RECIPIENT > abstract RECIPIENT/ ADDRESSEE, but that we should instead assume two separate developments (GOAL > ADDRESSEE and GOAL > concrete RECIPIENT > abstract RECIPIENT) with potential additional steps in between (see also section 3.2.3.2).

Moving on to the remaining transfer-related verb classes, namely verbs of intended transfer such as *promise* and communication verbs (*tell, teach*), and their preferences for either one or the other of the two variants (DOC vs. PRC), a slightly different picture presents itself. Unfortunately, the results on intended transfer-verbs are somewhat difficult to interpret due to the very low numbers of tokens for this particular verb class (N=83 for the whole period). It seems to be the case that the DOC falls in proportional frequency between M1 and M3, after which there is an increase (M3–M4), which re-establishes the point of departure (M1: 81.5 per cent DOC - M4: 81.9 per cent DOC). Nevertheless, the representativeness of the results is to some extent questionable.

Quite in contrast, communication verbs show that the DOC in this case was more frequent (although only significantly so in M1, $p < 0.001$; $V > 0.5$) than the PRC at all times. The initial drop in relative frequency of the DOC (M1–M2) therefore did not result in a temporary surpassing of the PRC over the DOC, but only in co-existence. It is unclear how these data relate to De Cuypere's (2015c) findings on Old English communication verbs showing a higher proportional frequency of *to*-PRCs over DOC tokens; in fact, the Middle English distribution would indicate a weaker association of these verbs and the prepositional patterns. It is possible that this divergence is a result of clausal objects being excluded in the present study, as these are especially frequent with verbs of saying or speaking. Without further investigation, however, this remains speculation. It is furthermore notable that in Middle English, verbs of instrument of communication and verbs like *whisper* are still found in the DOC; any constraints in this regard were probably introduced at a later point. Finally, among the PRCs used to paraphrase verbs of communication, *(un)to*-PRCs account for about half of all tokens in M1; this number rises to over 80 per cent in M3 and M4 (M1 vs. M4: $p < 0.001$, $\phi \approx 0.3$).

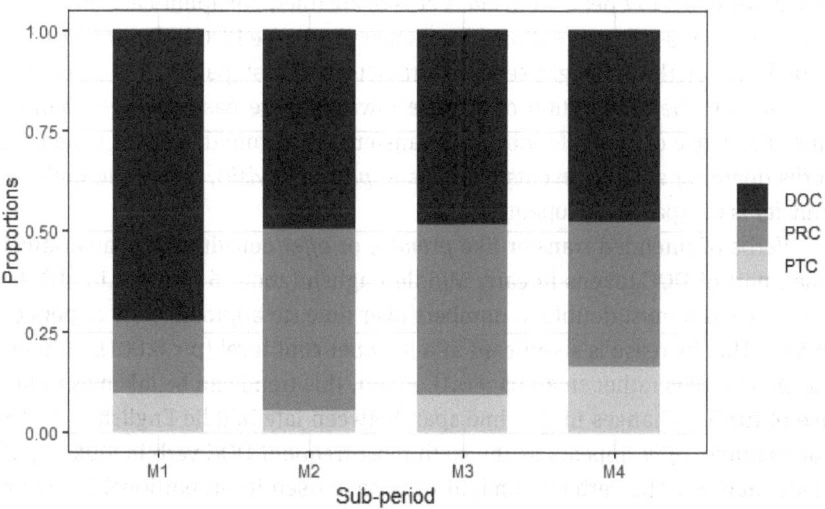

Fig. 13: Proportional distribution of DOC vs. PRC vs. PTC with verbs of communication (N=1,146), M1–M4

Communication verbs are also one of the verb classes where prepositional theme patterns are popular in PDE: Assessing this question in Middle English, we can observe that PTC-uses of verbs like *tell* (*John told him about the issue*) are not excessively frequent in this period (Fig. 13). Still, they account for a considerable number of tokens (approx. 10 per cent in M1). Over time, this figure rises to over 20% of all occurrences; this change is significant at the 0.5 level (PTC vs. DOC+PRC, M1 vs. M4: $p \approx 0.1$, $\phi \approx 0.3$). What we can take away from this that PTC-patterns constituted a stable alternative option at all times.

In terms of the semantics of the DOC, meaning the range of verb classes associated with the construction, it is evident that transfer and transfer-related verbs are highly predominant in M1 already. Taken together, verbs of concrete or abstract transfer, intended transfer and communication account for more than 70 per cent of the total of DOC tokens in the beginning of the period. This fraction of transfer-related verbs within the DOC significantly increases between M1 and M4 (although only at a small effect size). I take the late Middle English situation as suggestive of later developments in that transfer-senses are assumed to be further foregrounded in the construction's semantics up until today.

Among the different transfer verb classes, verbs of concrete transfer show a significant increase over time, almost doubling in figures from around 14 per cent in M1 to over 27 per cent in M4. Verbs of abstract, metaphorical transfer, by contrast, decrease in proportional frequency within the DOC in the course of the period. Although this might seem contradictory at first glance, it is taken to in fact support the assumption of a move towards more basic giving-semantics, since the sense of concrete, physical transfer is foregrounded at the expense of verbs denoting abstract events (such as to *pay so. a visit*), where the notion of transfer is comparatively opaque.

Verbs of intended transfer like *promise* or *offer* constitute a comparatively small part of DOC tokens in early Middle English (about 6 per cent in M1), but nevertheless almost double in numbers over time (to approximately 12 per cent in M4). This increase is significant at a 99.9 per cent level ($p < 0.001$), although the effect size is rather small ($\phi \approx 0.1$). Again, this trend can be taken as indicative of further changes in the time span between late Middle English and PDE: For example, *offer* appears as the sixth most frequent DOC verb in Mukherjee's (2005) dataset. The verb class might thus have risen in proportional frequency after Middle English (cf. also Stefanowitsch and Gries 2003; Gries and Stefanowitsch 2004).

The results on communication verbs are somewhat surprising in that they do not increase in frequency within the DOC within the period. Nevertheless, they steadily account for about 23 to 29 per cent of all DOC-tokens in the respective sub-periods. They therefore rank among the three most prominent verb classes associated with the DOC, alongside concrete and abstract transfer verbs. This finding is in line with accounts of PDE ditransitives, in which verbs like *tell* or *ask* are mentioned as prototypical members of the DOC (Gries and Stefanowitsch 2004).

Dispossession verbs can count as representative of verb classes that display an opposite development to transfer(-related) verbs over the course of the period. This verb class is lost from the DOC; the DOC does not maintain or regain its strength with such verbs during the period but loses out against PRCs. As seen in Fig. 14, there is a steady decrease of DOC uses in favour of PRCs towards late Middle English. While only around 26 per cent of all dispossession verb tokens are found in the PRC in M1, it is 86 per cent in M4. The DOC is significantly more frequent than the PRC in the earliest sub-period, whereas the opposite situations holds for the latest period. Among the PRC-types available for dispossession verbs are *from*, *of*, and *at* (in the sense of 'from'); the first one is prevalent above all in the later periods.

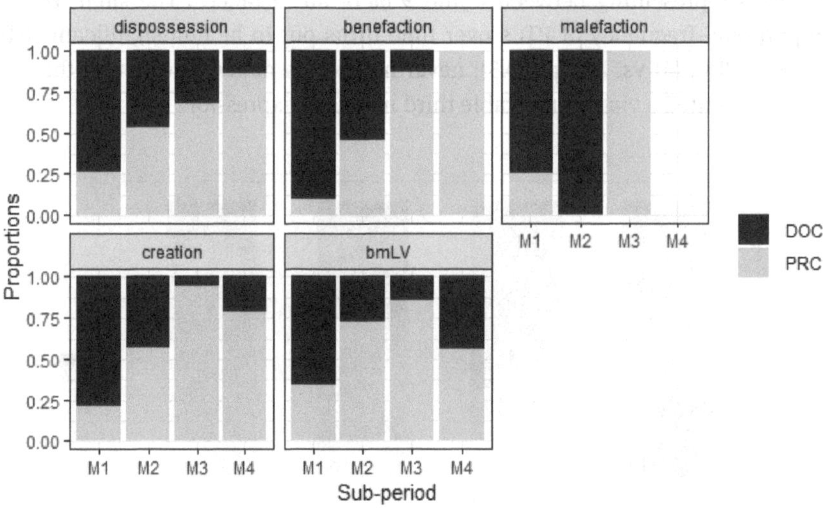

Fig. 14: Proportional distribution of DOC (vs. PRC) with dispossession (N=251), benefaction (N=44), malefaction (N=10), creation (N=138) and benefaction/malefaction light verbs (bmLV; N=511), M1–M4

Within the total of DOC uses, dispossession verbs are highly infrequent already in the earliest period – they account for only approximately 5 per cent of all DOC tokens in M1. These verbs furthermore show a significant decrease between M1 and M4 ($p < 0.001$; small effect size: $\phi \approx 0.1$), with only 8 DOC tokens remaining in M4. This change is again taken to be indicative of later developments, more precisely the complete ousting of privative verbs from the DOC. The results on dispossession verbs therefore confirm the proposal that the sub-sense of 'X CAUSES Y to lose Z' is increasingly dropped in the course to PDE (cf. Rohdenburg 1995; Colleman and De Clerck 2011). As just shown, they 'compensate' for this dropping out of use from the DOC by occurring more frequently in PRCs. This development is accordingly in direct contrast to that of other, more central verb classes such as transfer verbs, which after an initial rise in frequency of prepositional competitors reach a stable equilibrium between DOCs and PRCs. I assume that this difference in development is crucial in explaining the changes visible in the history of ditransitives in English.

What I take to be an additional important factor is the availability of PTC-patterns for dispossession verbs (Fig. 15). Although less frequent than in the case of communication verbs, verbs of stealing and robbing have the option of being used in a prepositional theme-construction throughout the period, with PTC uses representing between 4 and 9 % of all instances. The slight rise in proportional frequency of PTCs over time turns out to be non-significant (PTC vs. DOC+PRC, M1 vs. M4: $p > 0.5$); nevertheless, the data suggests that the pattern represented a viable and stable third means of expression.

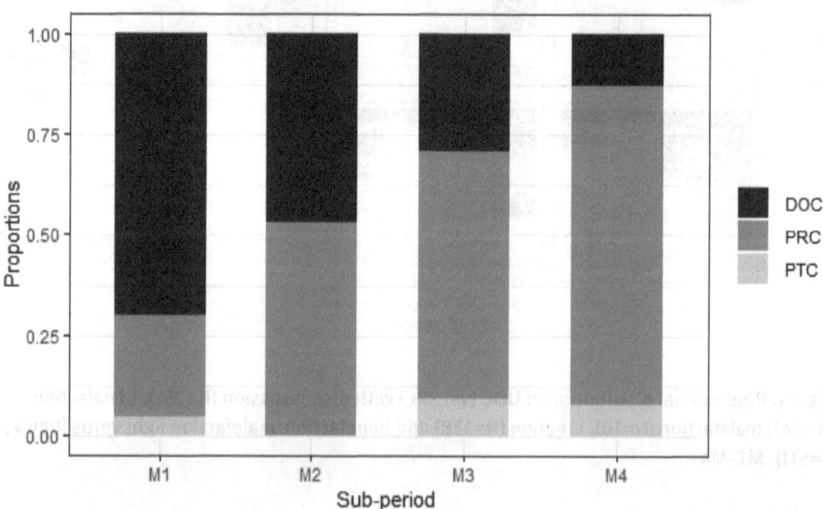

Fig. 15: Proportional distribution of DOC vs. PRC vs. PTC with verbs of dispossession (N=269), M1–M4

Within the larger class of benefactive/ malefactive verbs, whose development is also shown in Fig. 14 above, four main groups need to be distinguished: First, verbs of 'pure' benefaction; second, verbs of malefaction, and third, verbs of creation (e.g. *John built Mary a house/ John baked Mary a cake*). A fourth subset includes benefactive/ malefactive light verb or complex predicate constructions such as illustrated in (97a-b). Importantly, the DOC is still acceptable with such complex combinations in PDE, at least with pronominal REC-arguments. This is reflected in their behaviour in Middle English, as can be seen in the figure. Rather than falling out of use, these patterns show a similar u-turn behaviour as transfer-related classes, although the drop in DOC usage between M1 and M3 is greater than in the other cases. In terms of proportional frequency within the DOC, there is no significant change with this group between M1 and M4. Instead, expressions of this type take up about 4 to 9 per cent of all DOC tokens in all sub-periods.

(97) a. **his** **louerd** he *dede* michel harm
his lord he did much harm
'he did much harm to his lord'
(CMVICES1,115.1415; PPCME2: M1)

b. *doþ* / **to** **þe** **poure** **men** / greate harmes
does / to the poor men / great harms
'[he] does great harms to the poor men'
(CMAYENBI,40.678; PPCME2: M2)

In the case of the first group of 'pure benefaction' (98) the figure shows a substantial and steady decrease of DOC uses during Middle English: While DOCs account for a fraction of almost 90 per cent in M1, this number steadily falls throughout the period (M1–M4: $p < 0.001$; $\phi \approx 0.6$). This is perfectly in line with accounts on the semantic history of the DOC, as such uses have reportedly been lost.

(98) a. *mihht* *oppnenn* **hemm** þe ʒate off heoffness blisse
might open them the gate of heaven's bliss
'might open the gate of heaven's bliss for them'
(CMORM,I,142.1171; PPCME2: M1)

b. sche *openyd* hir hert **to** **hym**
she opened her heart to him
'she opened her heart to him'
(CMKEMPE,224.3623; PPCME2: M4)

The same holds for verbs of malefaction (**John broke Mary the shoulder*); despite a conspicuous peak in M2, such verbs rapidly disappear from the DOC and are not attested in the construction at all in M4. Simple verbs of pure benefaction/malefaction thus pattern together with dispossession verbs rather than transfer verbs in that DOC uses are superseded by PRC uses in the course of the period. They are therefore also in stark contrast to complex predicative benefactives/malefactives; a further difference between the sets is that the latter are predominantly paraphrased by a *to*-PRC (ca. 65 per cent of the total) in Middle English, whereas there is no clear association to one PRC-type in the case of the simple benefactives/malefactives in this period.

Finally, malefactive verbs are interesting because of their use in additional alternative patterns, like communication and dispossession verbs. However, we are not dealing with prepositional theme patterns here, but a possessive or genitive construction of the type *Mary broke John's nose* (POSS). As seen in Fig. 16, such uses are not only marginal variants, but make up a good part of the malefactive tokens in early Middle English (M1: 55%); by the end of the period, they are more or less categorical at 95% (POSS vs. DOC+PRC, M1 vs. M4: $p < 0.005$). Instead of resorting to PRCs (and to a lesser extent, PTCs) as dispossessive verbs, verbs of malefaction thus clearly opt for non-prepositional uses when lost from the DOC.

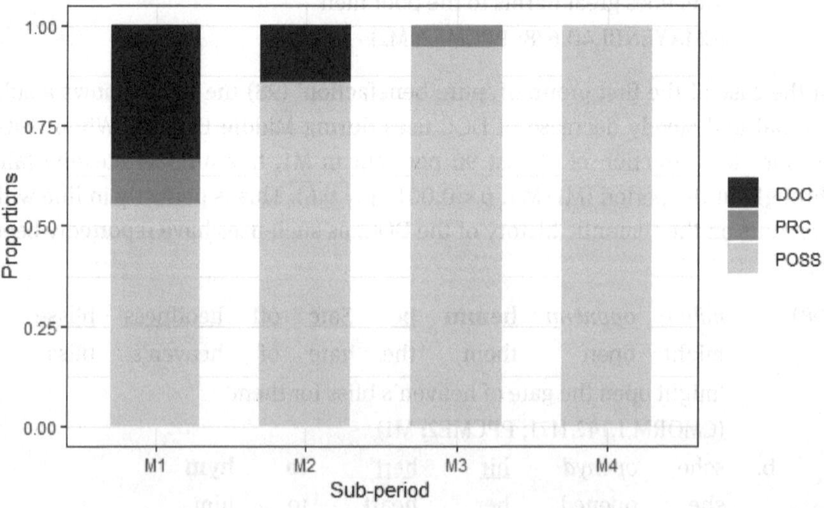

Fig. 16: Proportional distribution of DOC vs. PRC vs. Poss with malefactive verbs (N=60), M1–M4

The final sub-class of benefactive verbs of creation is of special interest, since as pointed out above, verbs of this type are assumed to participate in a second alternation (the benefactive alternation) with a *for*-PRC in PDE. This phenomenon is undoubtedly present in PDE; however, it seems to be strikingly absent from Middle English. Although DOC uses similarly seem to bounce back in M4 (after not being attested in mid-Middle English at all), there is no clear association with *for*-PRCs at this point. Instead, prepositional uses of verbs of creation oscillate between a range of prepositional patterns. This holds true even in the later sub-periods of M3 and M4, meaning at a time when *to* was already well established as the periphrasis for verbs of transfer. Both *for*-PRCs and *to*-PRCs are strongly present with this class (above all the latter), as is shown in (99) below. Examples (99b-c) indicate that even single verbs tend to vary concerning the PP-construction they appear in. Also, other PRCs are found as well – an evident systematicity or association is thus missing in the case of this verb class.

(99) a. Salamon *bildide* a noble hous **to himself**
Salomon built a noble house to himself
'Salomon built a noble house for himself'
(CMPURVEY,I,12.477; PPCME2: M3)

b. God *haþ wrou3t* **for him** meny a faire miracle
God has worked for him many a fair miracle
'God has often caused great miracles for him'
(CMBRUT3,101.3058; PPCME2: M3)

c. so mych sorow *wrought* **to þ=e= Britouns**
so much sorrow worked to the Bretons
'he caused so much sorrow to the Bretons'
(CMBRUT3,45.1365; PPCME2: M3)

What these data then suggest is that the establishment of the benefactive alternation only occurred at a later stage in the history of English and cannot be assessed based on the present results. I still briefly touch upon the issue again in the discussion (7.1), but the arguments made are only tentative (see Zehentner and Traugott forthc. for a more in-depth investigation of the question). It should finally be pointed out that verbs of creating in ditransitive patterns are overall very rare in all sub-periods (e.g. 3.5 per cent of DOC tokens in M1) and decrease towards M4 (0.8 per cent). This phenomenon is to some extent expected since verbs of creation such as *bake* or *build* are in fact not very frequent in such constructions in PDE either.

Refusal verbs are unfortunately highly infrequent throughout the whole period (N=30, between 1 and 11 tokens per sub-period). This is also reflected in their errant behaviour in terms of pattern choice as depicted in Fig. 17. No conclusions on the verbs' development can therefore confidently be drawn. Incidentally, also within the PRCs, there is no clear systematicity, but verbs of refusal select for various different prepositions in Middle English (e.g. 100a-b).

(100) a. But Crist *denyeþ* þis **to hem**
but Christ denies this to them
'but Christ denies this to them'
(CMWYCSER,I, 374.2660; PPCME2: M3)

b. he *wil* not / *denye* his feet **fro the**
he will not / deny his feet from you
'he will not deny you his feet'
(CMAELR4, 19.544; PPCME2: M4)

This might indicate that the members of this verb class were rather ambiguous concerning their precise semantics (in comparison to the more prototypical members of the DOC), meaning that the category of refusal verbs was not as semantically coherent as other verb classes. There is also no significant change in the proportion refusal verbs take up in the total of DOC tokens over time (M1–M4/M1–M2/M2–M3/M3–M4: $p > 0.05$). The maximum that refusal verbs amount to is about 1 per cent of DOCs in M4.

Further examples of infrequent verb classes with no noteworthy or indeterminate development over time are the classes of verbs of reversed transfer (*take so. leave*) and verbs of reversed communicated transfer (*ask someone a favour/the way*). These classes, which are labelled 'revTrans' and 'comm.revTrans' in Fig. 17, each account for less than five per cent of DOC tokens in all periods. Similarly, the frequency of mental/attitudinal verbs oscillates between three and six per cent but does not change significantly over time (M1–M4/M1–M2/M2–M3/M3–M4: $p > 0.05$).

In terms of the choice between DOC and PRC, complex predicate combinations encoding reversed transfer (such as *take one's leave*) show a distinct preference for the latter, typically patterns formed with *of*. As seen in the figure, the PRC accounts for over 80 per cent of reverse transfer verb tokens in M1 and is near categorical in M4 (94 per cent), i.e. the prepositional pattern is significantly more frequent in all periods (?*take so. leave* vs. *take leave of so.*). Reverse communication verbs, on the other hand, are clearly associated with the nominal member of the alternation pair, the DOC, in the beginning. These uses decrease during the period until both constructions take up about half of the occurrences. This 50/50-situation is still present in PDE, where *ask so. a favour* co-exists alongside *ask a favour of someone.*

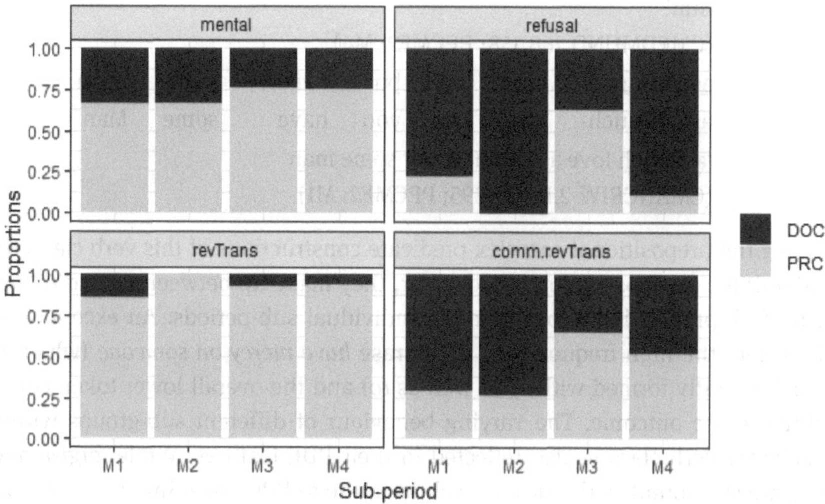

Fig. 17: Proportional distribution of DOC (vs. PRC) with mental (N=341), refusal (N=30) and reverse transfer verbs (revTrans=reverse transfer, N=260; comm.revTrans=reverse communicated transfer, N=120), M1–M4

Like with reverse transfer verbs, the PRC is also stronger in the case of mental/attitudinal verbs. The DOC is restricted to about 35 to 25 per cent of tokens per sub-period, and there is again no significant change in proportional frequency. It should be noted, however, that the contrary is true if only simple mental/attitudinal verbs such as *forgive* are included – in this case, the DOC is clearly dominant (80-89 per cent). The large majority of PRC-instances of mental/attitudinal verbs is taken up by light verb, complex multi-word combinations as in (101), which show a clear bias for the prepositional patterns. An example for one of the very rare DOC-occurrences of complex predicate verbs of mentality/ attitude is given in (102).

(101) a. he *hade* pite **of ham**
he had pity of them
'he had pity on them/ he pitied them'
(CMBRUT3,28.808; PPCME2: M3)

b. the feende that *had* gret envy **to** **hym**
the fiend that had great envy to him
'the fiend that had great envy to him/ the fiend that greatly envied him'
(CMEDMUND,168.158; PPCME2: M4)

(102) ase muche luue as þu *hauest* **sum** **mon**
as much love as you have some Man
'as much love as you have for some man'
(CMANCRIW-2,II.299.895; PPCME2: M1)

Among the prepositional complex predicate constructions of this verb class, *of-* and *to*-PRCs are most common. Together, they make up between 65 and 89 per cent of all prepositional tokens in the individual sub-periods. An exception is M2, where the high frequency of the phrase *have mercy on someone* (which is also frequently formed with *of* as well as *to*) and the overall lower token count influence the outcome. The varying behaviour of different sub-groups within this larger verb class is also reflected in their PDE features: While *forgive* and *envy* are still found in the DOC as well as in the *to*-PRC, meaning that they participate in the dative alternation, light verb constructions as illustrated above are typically restricted to PRCs, and among those, PRCs that include prepositions other than *to* (**have so. love/ *have love to so.* vs. *have love for so.*). Importantly, these constructions are not limited to individual prepositions even in PDE. Rather, there is still great variability in the verb combinations' subcategorisation for preposition types (cf. e.g. *feel envy towards* vs. *have love for* vs. *feel hatred against*, etc.). Furthermore, PRC uses are of course in direct competition with monotransitive uses (*love so.* > *have love for so.*). These were, however, not included in the present study.

Summing up, the results presented in this section demonstrate that there are striking differences in the distribution of DOC vs. PRC as well as additional patterns between the individual verb classes. Nevertheless, certain tendencies can be observed. More specifically, the classes can be divided into three larger groups according to their development:

The first group sees an initial rise in frequency of (mainly *to-*)PRCs, followed by a later (less drastic) decrease and resurgence of the DOC. This ultimately leads to a 'division of workload' situation. This relationship is still present in PDE, and crucially characterises the dative alternation today. The development of this group therefore represents the emergence of the dative alternation as such. The set most prominently includes transfer and transfer-related verbs (concrete, abstract, and intended transfer, as well as communication verbs).

The same behaviour is furthermore shown by verbs of mental activity such as *forgive* and *envy* as well as verbs of refusal (to some extent). Importantly, these classes are also still part of the DOC in PDE, and also participate in the dative alternation today (even if their *to*-PRC uses are marked). Benefactive/ malefactive complex predicates (*intend harm, do good*) are similarly still found to alternate in today's English. In these cases, it is the DOC that is marked, however, and the class is not productive in PDE, but restricted to fixed expressions.

Second, classes such as verbs of dispossession and simple benefactives/malefactives clearly indicate a 'victory' of PRCs during the period. DOC occurrences become increasingly infrequent in the later stages and are even absent entirely in some cases. Accordingly, these verb classes are also not acceptable in the DOC anymore in PDE but are limited to PRCs (typically involving prepositions other than *to*) or other means of expression such as PTCs and POSS-patterns.

Third, there is a group of verb classes with heterogeneous behaviour, which subsume a number of smaller sets. On the one side, we here find classes such as verbs of reversed communicated transfer (as in *ask so. a favour*) and verbs of creation, which are still used in the DOC in PDE, but do not take part in the dative alternation. Instead, they are associated with different PRCs (*from/of* in the case of the former, and *for* in the case of the latter). On the other side, verbs of reversed transfer and complex predicates of emotion or mentality (*have love/ envy*) are strongly biased towards PRCs at all times. Although some DOC tokens can be found, these became even rarer towards the end. In contrast to the first two groups, in which the PRCs tend to become limited to one specific preposition, the third group still fluctuates between various prepositional constructions at the end of the period; there is no reduction in variability in this last set of verb classes.

This section has thus also confirmed that the semantic scope of the double object construction was reduced over the course of Middle English. Certain senses, most importantly those related to transfer, seem to have been foregrounded. Even within the larger group of transfer-related verbs, a move towards more concrete, basic situations of giving took place. Senses which are clearly far removed from the concept of transfer, such as dispossession or pure benefaction/ malefaction, were in contrast increasingly marginalised or even ousted entirely from the DOC. These two developments corroborate that the DOC saw a substantial semantic narrowing over time and support the assumption of a semantic specialisation of the construction in line with Colleman and De Clerck (2011). Also, the data suggest that the crucial changes were under way in Middle English. Nevertheless, it has also been seen that transfer-related verb classes were highly frequent at the beginning of the period, whereas classes peripheral to the core meaning of transfer were relatively rare at this stage. It can therefore be presumed that the trends observed in Middle English were present to some extent also before.

Moreover, it is interesting that a third group of verb classes (including mental/attitudinal verbs and verbs of refusal, among others) were retained in the construction throughout the period and have been until today. Even though these verb classes are comparatively low in proportional frequency in Middle English, and do not show any increases, they are nevertheless stably attested. Semantically, this group takes up an intermediate position on a cline between transfer and non-transfer, since they can be conceptualised as metaphorical extensions of the core meaning but are clearly not prototypical categories of this sense. Accordingly, they seem to have escaped the fate of more peripheral classes in Middle English; nonetheless, they still have a higher probability of being lost than more central senses (cf. also Goldberg 1995; Colleman and De Clerck 2008 on the marginalisation of *forgive* and *envy* in PDE).

To conclude and come back to the larger research questions of this book, the findings shown in this and the preceding section suggest that the emergence of the dative alternation indeed took place within Middle English and was the result of the predominance of *to*-PRCs within the prepositional paraphrases, triggered by its high semantic compatibility with the very frequent transfer-verbs. Concomitantly, the DOC moved towards an ever more dominant association with a transfer-meaning and uses not fitting to these semantics were increasingly ousted from the construction. In the following, a further change in the particular features of the patterns at hand is examined.

4.2.1.3 Fixation of word order

In this section, potential changes in the constituent order in ditransitive clauses as well as in the ordering of objects in the DOC and PRCs (as well as PTCs) are investigated. Based on the literature on this topic, what we expect to see in this regard is an increasing fixation of word order in the course of the period: Both patterns should move towards strict (S)VO sequences, i.e. post-verbal object positions. As for object order, the DOC and PTCs are predicted to invariantly show REC-TH order at the end of the period, whereas the PRCs are assumed to move towards stricter TH-REC order.

As discussed at greater length in section (3.2.2), the fact that the English language experienced a fixation of SVO order at some point in its history can hardly be doubted, and a large body of previous literature has dealt with the issue in detail. This section does not aim to contribute to this more general discussion as such but presents findings on the regularisation of word order in ditransitive clauses only, in order to find out whether there are any differences between the DOC and prepositional patterns in this context.

Since non-finite clauses as well as subject-less (pro-drop) clauses were included in the study, the following graph distinguishes between SVOO orders and VOO orders. 'VOO' here means that the verb (directly) precedes both of the objects. The order of the objects themselves is not taken into account; what matters is only that both objects occur in post-verbal position and in direct sequence. Likewise, 'SVOO' exclusively refers to those tokens in which the subject immediately precedes the verb, which immediately precedes both objects.

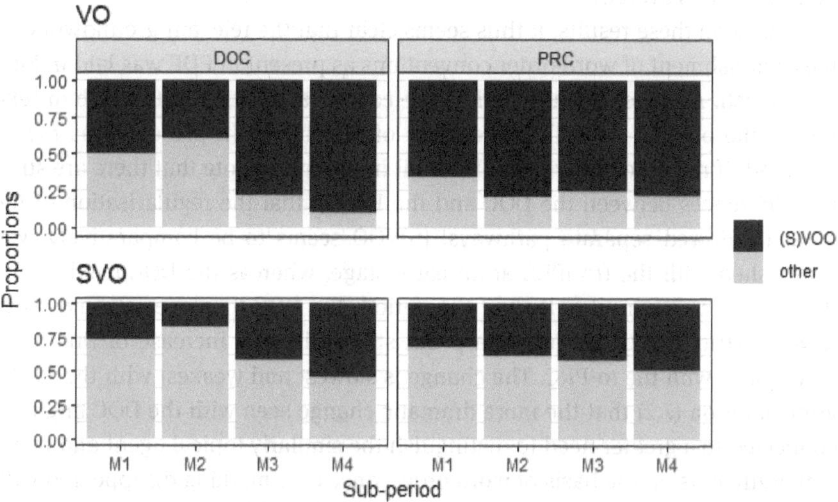

Fig. 18: Proportional distribution of clausal word orders (VOO/ SVOO) in DOC and PRC, M1–M4

Focussing first on the DOC, Fig. 18 indicates that with this construction, the canonical orders rocket between M1 and M4, almost doubling in percentages. The main locus of change is between M2 and M4; before this, there is little development.[119] As expected, the change is less striking when the subject is included: VOO orders are almost twice as frequent (proportionally) than SVOO orders in all sub-periods. However, as already mentioned, this does not suggest

---

119 DOC: *VO:* M1-M4: $p < 0.001$, $\phi \approx 0.4$; *SVO:* M1-M4: $p < 0.001$, $\phi \approx 0.3$.

that SVO orders were in general less frequent than VOO orders, but only reflects the fact that not all clauses included in the dataset featured an overt subject.

In contrast to the DOC, which sees an increase of SVOO in the later periods, the change concerning SVOO in the PRC is concentrated in the earlier stages of Middle English. The increase is furthermore slower, or rather, less sharp than in the case of the DOC. While VO orders do not significantly rise in (relative) frequency between M2 and M4, SVOO does see a significant increase in the very last stage. Nevertheless, the effect size is very low ($\phi < 0.1$).[120] If only *(un)to*-PRCs are taken into account, the developments seen in PRCs in general are paralleled, except that they appear to be more marked in the beginning. Moreover, the fractions of canonical VOO and SVOO orders are higher in M4 with *(un)to*-PRCs than with PRCs overall.

Based on these results, it thus seems clear that the relevant groundwork for the establishment of word order conventions as present in PDE was laid in Middle English. At the end of the period, the canonical position of the verb in relation to the objects, as well as the place of the subject (if present) was highly favoured, if not essentially fixed. It is still important to note that there are striking differences between the DOC and the PRC in that the regularisation of the system followed separate pathways. (S)VOO seems to be comparatively well established with the (*to*-)PRC at an early stage, whereas the DOC is still more flexible at the beginning. During the period, the DOC then sees a rapid move towards strict (S)VOO; a less sharp but still noticeable increase of this order takes place with the *to*-PRC. The change is slowest and weakest with the PRC. I argue later on (7.2) that the more dramatic change seen with the DOC might be connected to a greater need to distinguish the similarly topical agent and recipient arguments on the basis of word order, once case marking disappeared with this construction. That is, I propose that while disambiguating between recipient and theme may in fact have been comparatively easy even without case marking, on the basis of contextual and semantic biases. By contrast, agents and recipients prototypically being animate and topical may have caused more issues, resolved by fixing their positions to pre- and postverbal slots, respectively. The differences between *to*-PRCs and PRCs might in turn result from the increasingly close association between this precise PRC-type and the DOC in later times. That is, I below assess the hypothesis that the establishment of the dative alternation drove its members to align to each other also in terms of clausal word order.

120 PRC: *VO:* M1-M4: $p < 0.001$, $\phi \approx 0.2$; *SVO:* M1-M4: $p < 0.001$, $\phi \approx 0.2$.

Let us then move on to changes in object ordering, starting with 'broad' sequences of the objects and taking a general look at which of the arguments comes first in the clause, regardless of whether the objects immediately follow each other, or where they stand in relation to the subject and verb (top part of Fig. 19). DOCs with an object order that is highly marked from a PDE perspective, that is, those DOCs where the theme precedes the recipient (labelled TH-REC), are still comparatively frequent in early Middle English (around 20%), but become increasingly rarer towards the end of the period. This overall change is significant (M1–M4: $p < 0.001$, $\phi \approx 0.1$). REC-TH orders, on the other hand, increase steadily during the period: Accounting for about 6 out of 10 DOC tokens in M1, they make up over 85 per cent of the data in M4.

The sharp growth in proportional frequency of canonical DOC object orders is also seen when only DOCs with directly adjacent, post-verbal objects are taken into account ('narrow' object order; bottom part of Fig. 19). REC-TH orders rise from about 40 to over 80 per cent in the course of the period (M1 to M4); the main developments here take place from M2 onwards. The apparent drop between M1 and M2 is non-significant (M1–M4: $p < 0.001$, $\phi \approx 0.4$; M1–M2: $p > 0.05$; M2–M3: $p < 0.001$, $\phi \approx 0.3$; M3–M4: $p < 0.001$, $\phi \approx 0.2$). Generally, REC-TH orders are significantly more frequent than the opposite order in all periods (M1/M2/M3/M4: $p < 0.001$; $V > 0.5$). This discrepancy furthermore becomes even larger during the period (M1–M4: $p < 0.001$, $\phi \approx 0.2$; M1–M2: $p > 0.05$; M2–M3: $p < 0.05$, $\phi \approx 0.1$; M3–M4: $p > 0.05$). The results gained here more or less overlap with McFadden's results as presented above (section 3.2). While the proportions in the individual periods diverge slightly, both accounts conclude that in DOCs with directly adjacent objects, REC-TH order was close to categorical in the later periods. At this point, only rare examples of the reverse order (TH-REC) are found (cf. McFadden 2002: 113).

Interestingly, the same strong (and increasing) predilection for REC-TH orders is seen with prepositional theme constructions in the right-most plots of Fig. 19. The only difference here is that in this construction, REC-TH sequences are greatly favoured in early Middle English already, and are near-categorical at the end of the period. That is, by contrast to the DOC, which retains some flexibility in ordering in late Middle English, the PTC is very straightforwardly and strongly associated with this order throughout the whole period. This also holds true for object ordering in the narrow sense. The seemingly stark increase of 'other' orders – precisely PTC patterns with non-directly adjacent objects – in the earlier periods is insignificant and likely an artefact of the overall very low token frequency of this construction in M2.

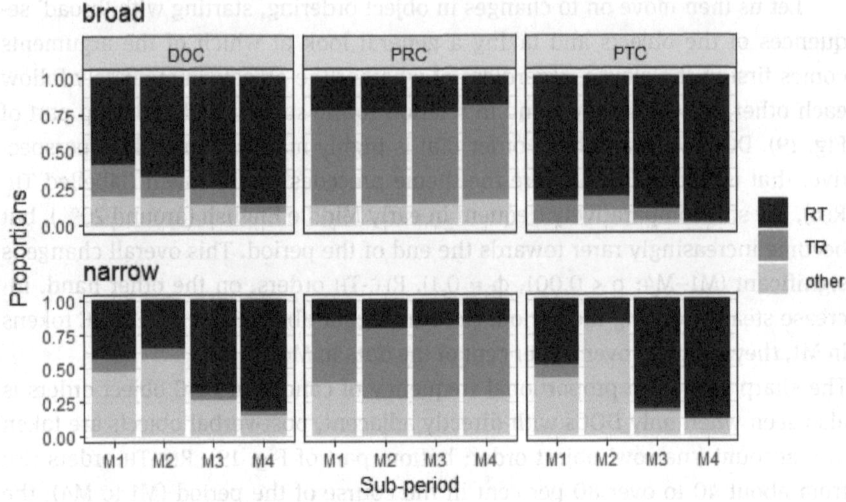

Fig. 19: Proportional distribution of object orders (broad/ narrow) in DOC, PRC, and PTC; M1–M4

Comparing these figures to the proportional distribution of the different object orders in the PRC, a very distinct picture presents itself, both in the broad and the narrow condition (mid-parts of Fig. 19). In the former, PRCs with 'canonical' (TH-REC) order start out as more frequent than 'standard' DOCs of this kind in M1. In the latter, they account for about half of the tokens and accordingly show an identical behaviour to both DOC and PTC. However, instead of experiencing a significant rise like in the case of these patterns, the preferred order with PRCs remains at roughly the same level throughout the whole period: Although there is a significant increase of TH-REC, this change is much weaker (with a very small effect size < 0.1). It is also only present if the whole period is taken into account (meaning there are no significant changes between the individual periods). Similarly, the reverse order, REC-TH, is less frequent than TH-REC in all periods, but there is no significant development over time (M1–M4/M1–M2/M2–M3/M3–M4: $p > 0.05$). The same distribution is seen if the results are restricted to only those PRCs where the objects are in direct sequence.

Furthermore, the absence of change as observed in PRCs is also evident in the sub-type of *to*-PRCs. In fact, it is even more striking with this subset. In contrast to the PRC, where we at least see some change in the proportional distribution of the canonical order, this does not happen with the *to*-PRC. The fraction of TH-REC stably remains higher than that of the opposite order (REC-TH); but neither decreases nor increases over time. Again, this lack of change is also observed if we investigate the distribution of orders within the narrower set of *to*-PRCs with directly adjacent objects. As in the case of the DOC, these results are roughly in line with McFadden (2002: 113), although the deviations between figures in the individual periods are somewhat larger in his data. Even so, both McFadden's and my results indicate that the canonical TH-REC order was notably more frequent than the opposite sequence in Middle English, and no major drops or upsurges in the respective frequencies occurred in the period.

The implications of the remarkable differences in behaviour between the constructions (DOC/ PTC and PRC) as well as between PRC and *to*-PRC are taken up in more detail in section (7.2). I there argue that the strong preference of the prepositional patterns for clause-late position, translating into TH-*prep*REC or REC-*prep*TH order, drove the DOC to resort to the complementary order. Specifically, I claim that with the association between the DOC and the *to*-PRC becoming stronger, and the dative alternation coming into full bloom towards the end of the period, the PRC-variant would eventually have fully committed to its preferred order.

In this context, a further interesting issue arises: This concerns both clause constituent and object order, and furthermore also relates to the debate about the degree of grammaticalisation of the prepositional constructions. We might ask whether these patterns are syntactically more restricted than other clauses involving PPs, that is, whether the position of PP-RECs (and/or PP-THs) is fixed to a greater extent than other prepositional phrases which might not express core semantic roles. In order to investigate such differences, I compared PRCs to all other clauses featuring a verb, a NP object and a PP (where neither constituent is governed by the other) that could be found in the PPCME2. Such clauses include, for example, constructions with *to* (*from*) denoting a locative, inanimate GOAL (ORIGIN/SOURCE) rather than a recipient-like argument, but also other adverbials, e.g. of location (103a), time (103b) or manner.

(103) a. ne schal neauer *leaden* richt lif$_{NP\text{-}TH}$ **on eorðe**$_{PP}$
not shall never lead right life on earth
'shall never lead a good life on earth'
(CMANCRIW-1,II.63.652; PPCME2: M1)

b. *seggen* hit$_{NP\text{-}TH}$ **biforen ant efter vchtsong**$_{PP}$
say it before and after Matins
'to say it before and after matins'
(CMANCRIW-1,I.58.171; PPCME2: M1)

All PP-clauses were categorised into three groups according to the position of the PP, namely 'initial' (PP-NP-V/ PP-V-NP), 'medial' (V-PP-NP/NP-PP-V) or 'final' (V-NP-PP/ NP-V-PP). Regarding non-PRC ('PP') clauses, the results presented in Fig. 20 (right hand side) suggest that there is an increase of final PPs over time. This change occurs most notably between M1 and M2, after which there is a slight decrease again. Nevertheless, the overall change (M1–M4) is significant (final vs. initial+medial, M1 vs. M4: $p < 0.0001$, $\phi \approx 0.6$) Both medial and initial PPs decrease over time. While the former account for about 15 per cent of tokens in M1, this number drops to below ten per cent in the course to M4. The latter is slightly more frequent at all times, taking up a fraction of between 20 (M1) and 15 per cent (M4). The data accordingly suggest a significant trend away from intermediate ('medial') position towards clause-peripheral, and especially final position with NP-PP non-ditransitives (medial vs. initial +final, M1 vs. M4: $p < 0.0001$, $\phi > 0.6$). While the position of the subject was not taken into account in the present investigation, the findings still support a movement of the PP to the margins of the clause, as subject, verb, and object form an increasingly tight association. This is in line with the results gained by Bech's (2001) study on word order in Old and Middle English.

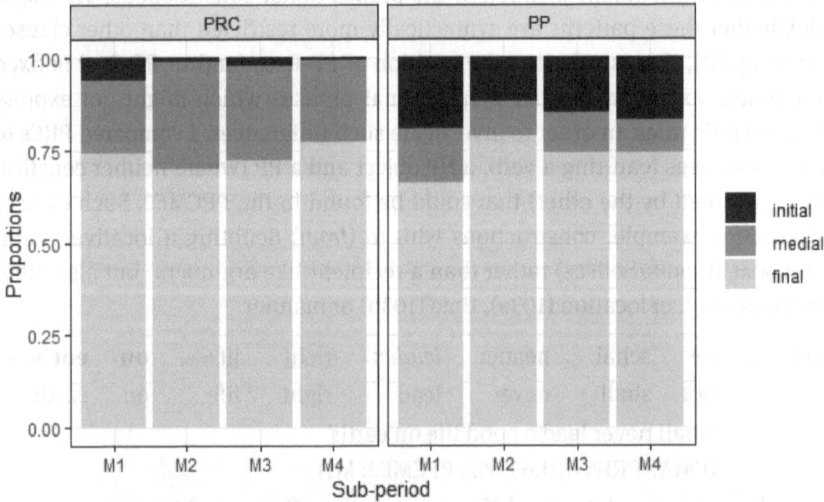

Fig. 20: Proportional distribution of PP-positions in PRC and other V-NP-PP combinations, M1–M4

PRCs (meaning patterns in which the PP expresses the REC-argument) are clearly most frequent in final position as well. This type accounts for 70 to 80 per cent of all tokens in each period. It is interesting to note that final position is even more frequent with PRCs than with PP-patterns in general. Changes between the individual periods as well as between M1 and M4 are non-significant ($p > 0.05$). Initial PP-RECs see a decrease over time: While they still constitute approximately six per cent of tokens in M1, their number is reduced to almost zero in the later periods. Most interestingly, however, is that contrary to non-ditransitive PP-patterns, medial position PP-RECs make up about a fifth to a third of the tokens throughout Middle English. (Importantly, 'medial' in this case is very much restricted to [V-PP-NP] patterns, meaning that verb-final clauses are exceedingly rare in all sub-stages. Medial position with PRCs thus corresponds to *prep*REC-TH order). These results correspond to what has been observed before, namely PRCs not settling on a categorical TH-REC order in this period but keeping the possibility of the alternative order. In that, they are clearly distinct from PPs in non-ditransitive complementation patterns, which increasingly favour positions at the margins of the clause: In M1, there is no significant correlation between position of the PP (medial vs. initial/final) and construction (PRC vs. PP), whereas in M4, there is a strong effect of pattern on position ($p < 0.0001$, $\phi \approx 0.2$).

The findings indicate that on the one hand, PP-RECs seem to strongly prefer a specific pattern, namely clause-final (or post-NP position) position, from early onwards. They also appear to be more restricted in this regard than other, more adjunct-like PP patterns. On the other hand, however, PP-RECs do not follow the overall trend towards clause-peripheral position in that they retain the option of occurring medially between the verb and the NP-theme. The prepositional RECs can accordingly be assumed to maintain a certain flexibility in their ordering in relation to the nominal theme argument, which might have had a positive influence on their success against the DOCs.

4.2.1.4 Loss of case marking

It is commonly assumed that case syncretism was already pretty advanced at the transition from Old to Middle English, although the question when case distinctions ceased to be perceived as functional or stopped to be present in the minds of speakers is notoriously difficult to answer. Investigating the DOC tokens in terms of ambiguity of case marking on the objects in the way outlined above, the results are as follows. Fig. 21 shows the proportions of REC- as well as TH-arguments with different degrees of ambiguity (high – mid-high – mid-low – low). In the case of the former, we find that recipients with overt marking that was very probably associated with one particular case, i.e. REC with a very low estimated ambiguity, was already highly infrequent at the beginning of the period. While score 0 recipients (lowest estimated ambiguity) account for approximately 1.3 per cent of tokens in M1, score 1 recipients (medium-low) take up a marginally higher fraction (2.8 per cent). However, there is no significant change in the course of the period in both cases. More striking developments can be seen in RECs with higher estimated ambiguity (scores 2-3/ mid-high to high). Interestingly enough, highly ambiguous recipients are slightly more frequent in M1 than score 2 recipients (49.3 per cent vs. 46.6 per cent) but decrease over time in favour of the somewhat less ambiguous variants. The difference between the two variants, which are the only remaining categories from M2 onwards, is significant in the later stages of the language (ca. 40 per cent vs. 60 per cent in both M3 and M4; $p < 0.001$, small-medium effect size: $V \approx 0.2$).

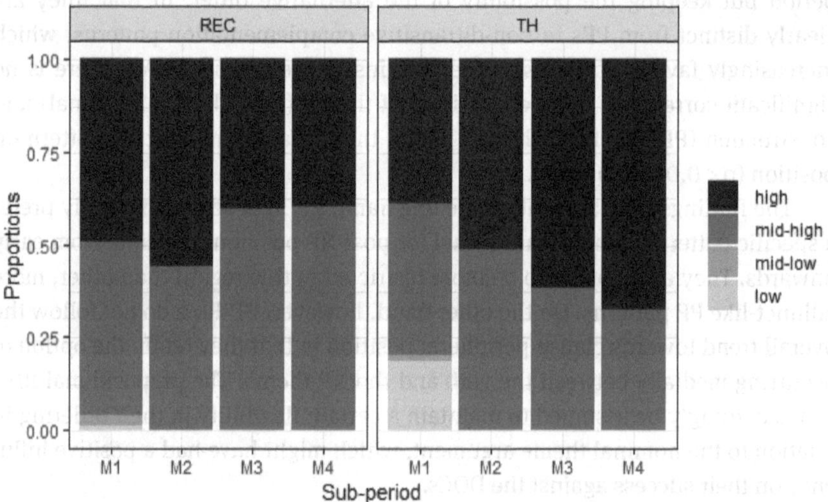

Fig. 21: Proportional distribution of case marking ambiguity scores with REC and TH, M1–M4

These results might seem unexpected at first glance since we would predict a straightforward increase in ambiguity, but there is a relatively simple explanation for the behaviour of score 2 and 3 recipients. This relates to the fact that a large majority of recipients (up to 99 per cent of the total of RECs in the DOC) in the database are pronominal. As is well known, case syncretism in pronouns typically worked in favour of the originally dative form (e.g. OE dat. *him*/ acc. *hine* > PDE *him*; OE dat. *hire*/ acc. *hīe* > PDE *her*). Following the classification scheme used in the present approach, REC in example (104) would have been categorised as OE <d> 'unambiguous, dative' and ME <amb> 'ambiguous', resulting in an ambiguity score of 2.

(104) The fyrste *gaffe* **hym**REC Scyence_{TH}
the first gave him science
'the first gave him science'
(CMGREGOR,173.1061; PPCME2: M4)

The prevalence of score 2 recipients in later periods is therefore most probably caused by the general predominance of pronominal recipients and shows that the decision to attribute pan-chronic ambiguity scores to each token is problematic, or at least not very helpful in this regard.

As illustrated on the right-hand side of the figure, the development of the THEME argument conforms more clearly to what is expected. While (more likely) non-ambiguous variants – score 0/low themes – still take up over 20 per cent in M1, they see a significant sudden drop right afterwards ($p < 0.001$; small-medium effect size: $\phi \approx 0.2$). Although the higher frequency of non-ambiguous themes could be taken as mirroring the pronoun effect found in recipients, this is only indirectly the case, since the percentage of themes represented by pronouns is rather small (8 per cent). The issue nevertheless does concern pronouns, in that the figures are probably influenced by the relatively large fraction of 'extracted/anaphoric' themes included in the dataset (almost 20 per cent of themes in M1). The majority of demonstrative pronouns involved in these anaphoric theme-constructions in the earliest period were classified as non-ambiguous, and thus received a 0 score.

Both themes with mid-high and high estimated ambiguity account for approximately 40 per cent in M1. However, in contrast to highly ambiguous themes (score 3), which increase significantly over the course of the period ($p < 0.001$; medium effect size: $\phi \approx 0.3$), mid-high themes drop in relative frequency ($p < 0.001$; small effect size: $\phi \approx 0.1$). The most likely explanation for the difference in behaviour of recipients and themes in this regard is the increasing influx of French vocabulary during the period – although French items were classified in the same way for both REC and TH, the issue affected themes much more severely than predominantly pronominal (and therefore native or Scandinavian) recipients.

The method applied here unfortunately does not allow us to investigate the possibility of a mutual impact of the degree of salience of case marking on REC on the degree of salience of case marking on TH and vice versa. Accordingly, the question whether the forms' development was interrelated to some extent (which seems likely) cannot be addressed on the basis of these results. Nevertheless, what we can take away from this is that ambiguity in case marking of the arguments of ditransitive verbs was high from early on and increased over time; this is relevant for the discussion presented later in the book (chapter 7.2.1).

4.2.2 Multiple logistic regression analysis

This section presents the results of a binomial logistic regression model fitted to the ditransitives data, more precisely the choice between DOC and PRC. The predictors taken to influence the Middle English dative alternation are as follows:

- Time: M1–M4
- Dialect: South, East Midlands (EM), West Midlands (WM), Kent, North
- Verb class: abstract transfer (abstrTrans), concrete transfer (concrTrans), intended transfer (intTrans), communication (comm), dispossession, pure benefaction, creation, malefaction, benefactive/malefactive light verb constructions (bmLV), mental/attitudinal, refusal, reversed transfer (revTrans), reversed communicated transfer (comm.revTrans), other
- Object order (narrow) - directly adjacent objects: REC-TH, TH-REC, other
- Object order (broad) - non-directly adjacent objects: REC-TH, TH-REC, other
- Clausal order (VO) – excluding subject: VOO, other
- Clausal order (SVO) – including subject: SVOO, other

Case marking was not included as an independent variable in this analysis, since I only coded the DOC data for it. In the following sections we then test whether these linguistic and extra-linguistic factors impact the odds of one of the constructions to be used at the expense of the other(s), and whether these effects interact with each other. Most relevantly, we are interested in the interaction of time with the other factors: For example, one hypothesis is that verb class significantly correlates with choice of construction and time. The reference levels were manually set to 'DOC', 'M1', 'South', 'abstrTrans', 'REC-TH' for object orders, and 'other' for clausal word order; that is, the results have to be interpreted against these base levels. The main R functions applied are lrm() and glm(). The analysis very closely follows the steps taken in Levshina (2015: 257–276; 277–289).

Tab. 9 and Tab. 10 below provide the outcome of fitting a logistic regression model with 'construction' as the response and the seven predictors outlined above by means of lrm() and glm(). In the former, a first observation to be made is that the model in significant in general (Pr(>chi2) < 0.05), meaning that "at least one predictor significantly deviates from zero" (Levshina 2015: 258). The C statistic of 0.864 suggests an excellent discrimination of our model (following the scale by Hosmer and Lemeshow 2000: 162). The coefficients present the log odds ratios of the predictors, i.e. the odds of DOC vs. PRC in specific contexts, compared to the default, reference level. Coefficient values of above zero indicate that the particular level increases the probability of the PRC to be used, while decreasing the odds of DOC. Negative values, by contrast, boost the chances of DOC at the expense of the PRC. The results are visualised by means of visreg() (Breheny and Burchett 2018).

Tab. 9: Logistic regression of factors influencing choice of DOC vs. PRC (lrm)

		Model Likelihood Ratio Test		**Discrimination Indexes**		**Rank Discrimination Indexes**	
Obs	5421	LR chi2	2599.32	R2	0.509	C	0.864
DOC	2535	d.f.	24	G	2.205	Dxy	0.727
PRC	2886	Pr(> chi2)	<0.0001	gr	9.074	gamma	0.729
max|deriv|	8e-12	gp	0.366	tau-a	0.362	Brier	0.146
			Coef		**S.E.**	**Wald Z**	**Pr(>|Z|)**
Intercept			-1.7046		0.1963	-8.68	<0.0001
Period			0.4594		0.0356	12.9	<0.0001
Dialect=EM			-1.1731		0.1423	-8.24	<0.0001
Dialect=Kent			-1.7325		0.2023	-8.57	<0.0001
Dialect=North			-1.6866		0.2465	-6.84	<0.0001
Dialect=WM			-1.3045		0.1506	-8.66	<0.0001
ObjectOrder.narrow=other			0.7923		0.1309	6.06	<0.0001
ObjectOrder.narrow=Th-Rec			2.1132		0.1884	11.21	<0.0001
ObjectOrder.broad=other			0.8515		0.1404	6.06	<0.0001
ObjectOrder.broad=Th-Rec			1.4169		0.1569	9.03	<0.0001
ClauseOrder.VO=VOO			0.3283		0.0946	3.47	0.0005
ClauseOrder.SVO=SVOO			-0.0894		0.0857	-1.04	0.2964
VerbClass=benefaction			0.1543		0.398	0.39	0.6983
VerbClass=creation			0.7262		0.2434	2.98	0.0028

	Coef	S.E.	Wald Z	Pr(>|Z|)
VerbClass=bmLV	0.5874	0.1356	4.33	<0.0001
VerbClass=malefaction	-0.1283	0.8481	-0.15	0.8797
VerbClass=comm	-0.3957	0.1076	-3.68	0.0002
VerbClass=dispossession	0.5791	0.1823	3.18	0.0015
VerbClass=mental	0.7315	0.1705	4.29	<0.0001
VerbClass=other	0.6834	0.4223	1.62	0.1056
VerbClass=refusal	-1.5428	0.4832	-3.19	0.0014
VerbClass=comm.revTrans	0.5625	0.2309	2.44	0.0149
VerbClass=revTrans	2.9014	0.2615	11.1	<0.0001
VerbClass=concrTrans	0.0007	0.1073	0.01	0.9945
VerbClass=intTrans	-1.0832	0.1775	-6.1	<0.0001

Tab. 10: Logistic regression of factors influencing choice of DOC vs. PRC (glm)

Min	1Q	Median	3Q	Max	AIC
-2.8731	-0.7351	0.1893	0.6067	2.8667	4943

	Estimate	Std. Error	z value	Pr(>|z|)	
(Intercept)	-1.70464	0.196342	-8.682	< 2e-16	***
Period	0.459406	0.035609	12.901	< 2e-16	***
DialectEM	-1.17311	0.142289	-8.245	< 2e-16	***
DialectKent	-1.73254	0.202278	-8.565	< 2e-16	***
DialectNorth	-1.68661	0.246531	-6.841	7.84E-12	***
DialectWM	-1.30446	0.150603	-8.662	< 2e-16	***
ObjectOrder.narrowother	0.792342	0.130856	6.055	1.40E-09	***
ObjectOrder.narrowTH-REC	2.113159	0.188428	11.215	< 2e-16	***
ObjectOrder.broadother	0.851472	0.140408	6.064	1.33E-09	***
ObjectOrder.broadTH-REC	1.416918	0.156876	9.032	< 2e-16	***
ClauseOrder.VOVOO	0.328303	0.094624	3.47	0.000521	***
ClauseOrder.SVOSVOO	-0.08945	0.085659	-1.044	0.296367	
VerbClassbenefaction	0.154277	0.398017	0.388	0.698301	
VerbClasscreation	0.726215	0.243409	2.984	0.00285	**
VerbClassbmLV	0.58745	0.135595	4.332	1.47E-05	***
VerbClassmalefaction	-0.12835	0.848117	-0.151	0.879714	

	Estimate	Std. Error	z value	Pr(>|z|)	
VerbClasscomm	-0.39567	0.107642	-3.676	0.000237	***
VerbClassdispossession	0.579072	0.182322	3.176	0.001493	**
VerbClassmental	0.731507	0.170523	4.29	1.79E-05	***
VerbClassother	0.683362	0.422282	1.618	0.105607	
VerbClassrefusal	-1.54282	0.483202	-3.193	0.001408	**
VerbClasscomm.revTrans	0.562487	0.230916	2.436	0.014855	*
VerbClassrevTrans	2.901401	0.261437	11.098	< 2e-16	***
VerbClassconcrTrans	0.000744	0.107255	0.007	0.994466	
VerbClassintTrans	-1.08316	0.177484	-6.103	1.04E-09	***

As can be seen, the value of the intercept, which is "the estimated log odds of the outcome when all predictors are at their reference levels" (Levshina 2015: 259), is negative. This shows that in early Middle English (M1) Southern dialects contexts with abstract transfer verbs and REC-TH object order as well as non-(S)VO clause order, the odds of the DOC are higher than those of the PRC. The predictor 'Period' has a highly significant impact on the alternation, in that it increases the odds of the PRC over the DOC. That is, the chances of encountering a PRC grow over time. This is also shown in Fig. 22, which demonstrates that time has a clear positive association with the likelihood of PRC to be chosen.

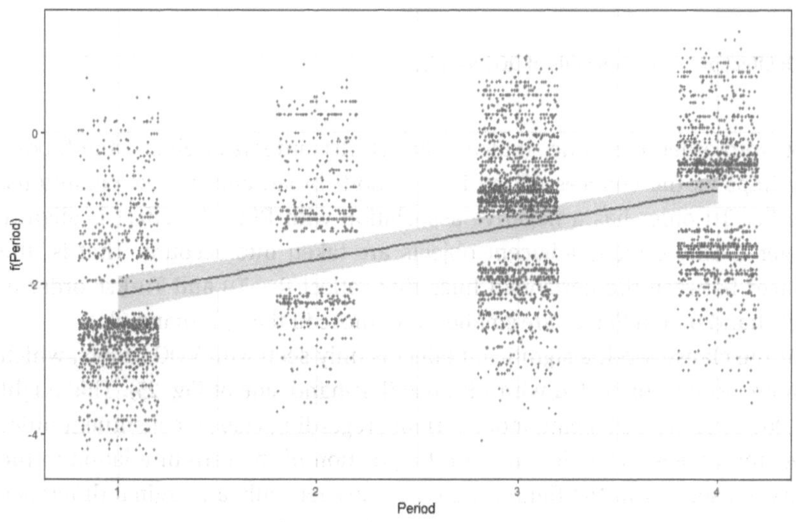

Fig. 22: Effect of 'Period' on odds of DOC vs. PRC

By contrast, compared to the South, all dialects positively affect the odds of the DOC, possibly suggesting that the PRC originated in Southern dialects. The horizontal bars in Fig. 23 depict this difference: The South clearly stands out from the other dialect as having a higher chance for the PRC to be expressed, while all others, especially Kent and the North, feature an increased probability of the DOC.

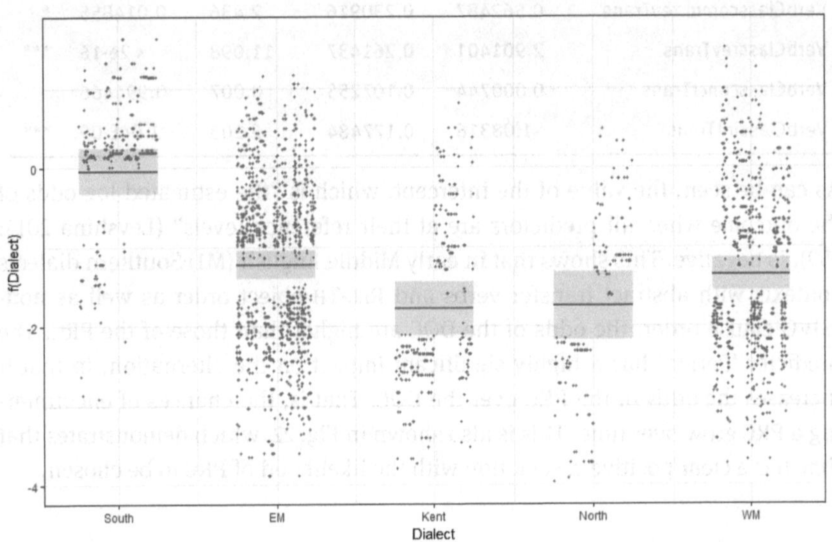

Fig. 23: Effect of 'Dialect' on odds of DOC vs. PRC

As for word order, the values indicate that TH-REC order (as well as 'other') positively impacts the chances of the PRC in both broad and narrow conditions, while REC-TH order has a negative association with PRC; the effect is slightly stronger if only directly adjacent objects are taken into account. That is, the distances between the horizontal lines that reflect REC-TH and TH-REC order in the left-hand plot in Fig. 24 are smaller than those in the right-hand plot.

At the clause level, a significant effect is only seen with VOO-orders, which are more closely connected with PRC use (left-hand side of Fig. 25). This might point towards the DOC being more variable regarding clausal constituent order in general, at least when it comes to the position of the verb in relation to the objects. As seen in in the figure, there is, however, only a marginal difference between the two conditions (between the effect of VOO order compared to that of all other orders). Furthermore, the rightward plot in Fig. 25 indicates that when the position of the subject is considered, the effect becomes non-significant.

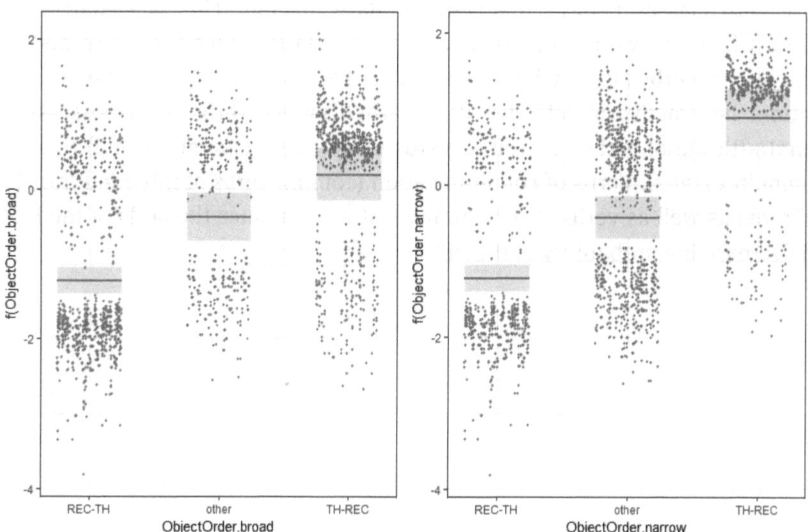

Fig. 24: Effect of 'Object order (broad/narrow)' on odds of DOC vs. PRC

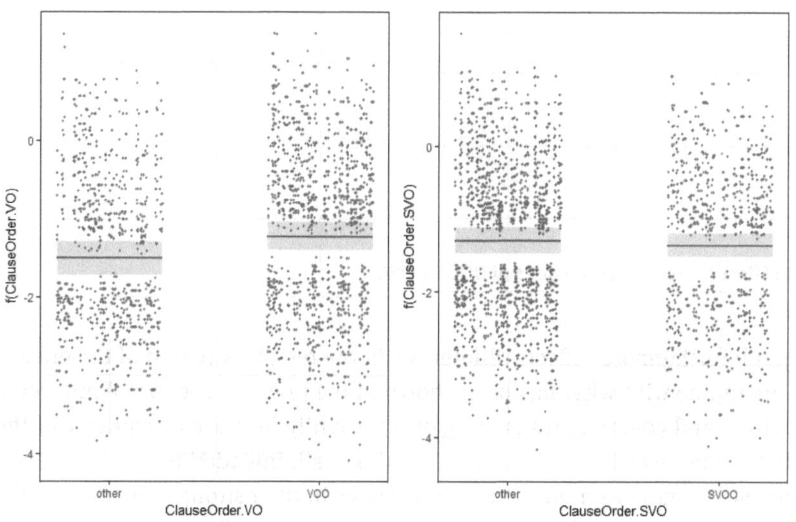

Fig. 25: Effect of 'Clausal word order (VO/ SVO)' on odds of DOC vs. PRC

Finally, in terms of verbs class, what is first interesting to note is that verbs of concrete transfer (concrTrans) as well as verbs of benefaction (and malefaction) do not significantly influence the choice compared to abstract transfer verbs. These verb classes behave relatively similarly overall. This is visualised in Fig. 26, which shows no notable distance between the lines for the respective verb classes. Verb classes which boost the chances of the PRC include verbs of creation, benefactive/malefactive light verbs (bmLV), verbs of dispossession, mental/attitudinal verbs, as well as verbs of reversed (communicated) transfer ([comm.]revTrans). Verbs of communication (comm), verbs of intended transfer (intTrans) as well as verbs of refusal, by contrast, enhance the odds of the DOC and decrease the probability of the PRC.

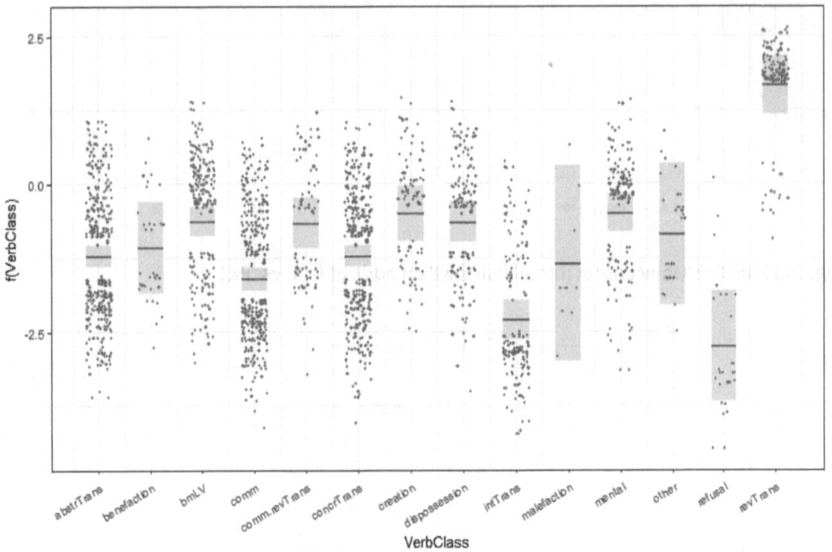

Fig. 26: Effect of 'Verb class' on odds of DOC vs. PRC

The graph furthermore reflects differences in the relative strength of the effects. They are in line with what has been shown in the previous section: While verbs of (abstract and concrete) transfer display a slightly increased frequency of the PRC but are more or less evenly distributed overall, intended transfer verbs are deviate most clearly from the other verb classes in their strong bias towards the DOC. Within the group of verb classes increasing the likelihood of prepositional uses, verbs of reversed transfer show the greatest divergence from the reference level. These findings are further supported by the distinctive collexeme analyses shown below. I take them to (a) suggest differences in prototypicality of 'ditransitivity', in that e.g. verb classes like reversed transfer are clearly marked members of this group in exhibiting very strong preferences. On the other hand (b), they may tell us about the prototypicality of the (emerging) alternation relationship: Those classes which are most robustly associated with the dative alternation in PDE, namely transfer verbs (abstract and concrete) also show the least effect in either direction in Middle English.

Tab. 11 provides the results of testing for possible interactions between the predictors, meaning that we determine whether the effect of one variable depends on that of another factor. Specifically, the figures presented here show the interaction between time and the other predictors, as we are mostly interested in changes in the impact of certain features over time. While I also checked for interactions between the other factors, these outcomes are more difficult to interpret, and I therefore do not comment on them in more detail. The results are again visualised with the help of visreg().

Tab. 11: Logistic regression of factors influencing choice between DOC vs. PRC (glm, with interaction)

Min	**1Q**	**Median**	**3Q**	**Max**	**AIC**
-3.0611	-0.7022	0.1379	0.5550	2.4574	4711.5
	Estimate	**Std. Error**	**z value**	**Pr(>|z|)**	
(Intercept)	1.504428	1.144655	1.314	0.188743	
DialectEM:Period	1.020179	0.348747	2.925	0.003442	**
DialectKent:Period	1.932499	0.80784	2.392	0.016749	*
DialectNorth:Period	NA	NA	NA	NA	
DialectWM:Period	0.929102	0.349787	2.656	0.007903	**
ObjectOrder.narrowother:Period	0.710136	0.12309	5.769	7.96E-09	***
ObjectOrder.narrowTH-REC:Period	0.950295	0.182266	5.214	1.85E-07	***
ObjectOrder.broadother:Period	0.003772	0.136377	0.028	0.977937	
ObjectOrder.broadTH-REC:Period	-0.11354	0.151714	-0.748	0.454227	
ClauseOrder.VOVOO:Period	-0.61744	0.07604	-8.12	4.66E-16	***
VerbClassbenefaction:Period	1.40528	0.676234	2.078	0.0377	*
VerbClasscreation:Period	0.504774	0.236857	2.131	0.033078	*
VerbClassbmLV:Period	-0.09311	0.120312	-0.774	0.438976	
VerbClassmalefaction:Period	-0.31047	1.4727	-0.211	0.833029	
VerbClasscomm:Period	-0.21205	0.099541	-2.13	0.03315	*

	Estimate	Std. Error	z value	Pr(>|z|)	
VerbClassdispossession:Period	0.29949	0.178423	1.679	0.093241	.
VerbClassmental:Period	-0.53298	0.153347	-3.476	0.00051	***
VerbClassother:Period	11.71627	225.0383	0.052	0.958478	
VerbClassrefusal:Period	-1.13041	0.413083	-2.737	0.006209	**
VerbClasscomm.revTrans:Period	0.059878	0.223774	0.268	0.789022	
VerbClassrevTrans:Period	-0.17897	0.233062	-0.768	0.442539	
VerbClassconcrTrans:Period	-0.14839	0.100654	-1.474	0.140411	
VerbClassintTrans:Period	-0.53702	0.157323	-3.413	0.000641	***

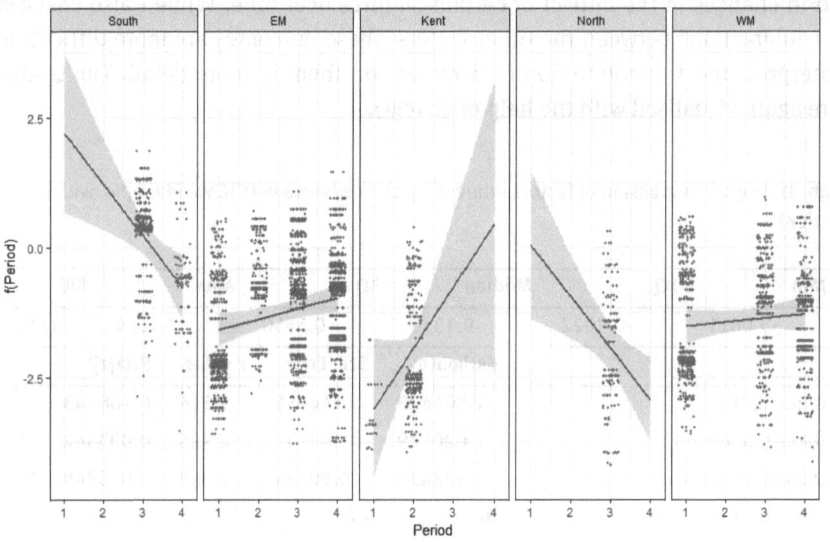

Fig. 27: Interaction between effects of 'Period' and 'Dialect' on odds of DOC vs. PRC/ predicted probabilities

Focussing first on the interaction between time and dialect as presented in Tab. 11 and depicted in Fig. 27, we find that the differences between the dialects (in terms of DOC vs. PRC usage) become weaker over time. While the South starts out with a high predilection for the PRC, this declines over time, whereas most of the other dialects become more accepting of the PRC between M1 and M4. Vice versa, this means that time shows a positive association with the DOC in the South while it has a slightly negative effect on the DOC in the East and West Midlands, as well as Kent. However, it should be noted (as also visible in the figures) that not all of the dialects are equally well represented in all periods (cf. especially the figures for Northern dialects). The results can thus only be taken at face value to some extent.

Second, we expect to see an interaction between time and object order in that the effect of the latter should become stronger over time. This is borne out by the data, albeit only for object orders in the narrow condition, that is, only counting object orders as REC-TH/TH-REC when the objects are in direct sequence. If taking into account clauses where the objects are separated by intervening material, no significant effect is seen. Consequently, Fig. 28 only shows the results for the narrow set. What can be observed in the plots is that the effect of TH-REC-object order clearly depends on time in that in comparison to REC-TH orders, the chances of PRC with this order increase over time (see the right-most part of the graph). This also means that the gap between REC-TH and TH-REC preferences widens; overall, the effect of object order thus becomes stronger over time. The results support our hypotheses based on the frequency data presented above. Middle English sees the development of a complementary object order distribution. I furthermore take the differences in significance of effect between the two sets (broad/ narrow) to be indicative of construction-status: There is a move towards immediate sequences of ditransitive objects, and it is only in this 'chunked' condition that there is a clear interaction between the patterns.

Similarly, in comparison to all other orders, VOO orders are increasingly associated with the DOC. While both free and VOO clausal word order have a positive effect on the odds of the DOC to be expressed in early Middle English, this impact is weaker for VOO in the beginning. In late Middle English, by contrast, orders other than VOO increase the chances of the PRC; VOO increases the chances of the DOC. These results are largely in line with the conclusions from the preceding sections – the PRC seems to retain some flexibility in clause-level ordering, whereas the DOC moves towards fixed word order more rapidly (Fig. 29).

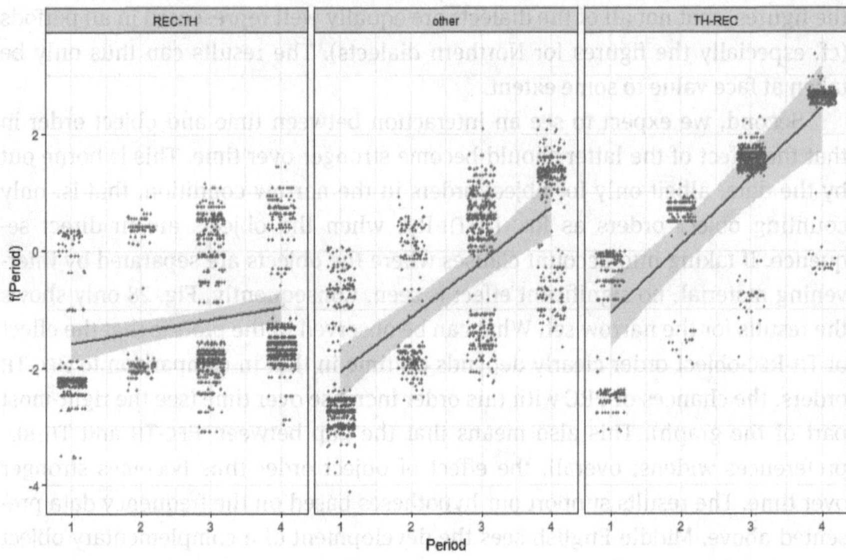

Fig. 28: Interaction between effect of 'Period' and 'Object order (narrow)' on odds of DOC vs. PRC/ predicted probabilities

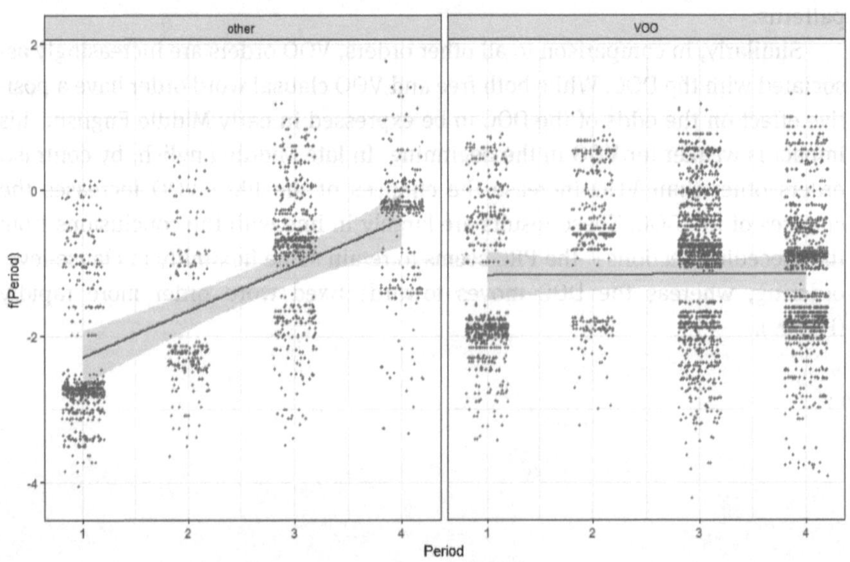

Fig. 29: Interaction between effect of 'Period' and 'Clausal word order (VO)' on odds of DOC vs. PRC/ predicted probabilities

There is some dependency between the effects of time and verb class, as demonstrated in the results above (Tab. 11). As can be observed, the combined effect of time and verb class is higher with some categories than with others: Verbs of reversed transfer and mental verbs increase the likelihood of PRC both in early and late Middle English. This is not dependent on time, meaning that the impact does not significantly change throughout the period. Most other verb classes, including transfer verbs, see an increase in the odds of the PRC; however, this impact is much stronger in the cases of dispossession verbs, as well as with verbs of benefaction and malefaction. With these groups, the odds of the PRC are significantly higher at the end of the period. Conversely, verbs of communication and verbs of intended transfer are less likely to appear with the PRC compared to other transfer verbs and display a more modest increase in predicted probability of this pattern. Refusal verbs are problematic due to their low overall frequency but seem to exhibit a greater affinity for the DOC without major changes.

Last, testing for interactions between the other factors yielded some interesting but knotty results. Possibly the most robust outcome is that the fixation of clausal word order seems to go hand in hand with fixation of object orders: VO and the canonical object sequences increase the likelihood for both constructions. This suggests that there was a general regularisation of the system in terms of word order which affected all constituents. Furthermore, there is certain evidence for dialects interactions: The effect of (VOO) word order is slightly more pronounced in the Northern dialects in increasing the chances of the DOC there. Since loss of case marking presumably proceeded from the North, this provides very tentative support for the assumption that the demise of case morphology might have had greater consequences for the DOC, resulting in stricter VOO. Furthermore, we find some indication that there are differences between the dialects in terms of their acceptability for TH-REC orders with the DOC (and the other way round). For example, this order seems to positively affect the DOC rates in West Midlands (and Northern) dialects. This is potentially interesting in view of the reported higher frequency of TH-REC orders with pronominal objects in these regions. However, little can be concluded from the present data, especially because it included nominal objects as well as pronominal ones. Interactions between verb class and other variables remain highly elusive and are too marginal or difficult to be interpreted to be reported here.

A final note to be made is that I also fitted a polytomous/ multinomial logistic regression model to the dataset of DOC, PRC and PTCs. Since these results essentially confirm the assumptions made based on the frequency distributions above and add little information to this, they are not represented separately.

4.2.3 Productivity measures

One of the main upshots of the developments discussed so far is that the DOC saw a reduction in the range of verb classes associated with it over time, even though there were substantial differences between individual verb classes and groups of verb classes. The decrease in verb class types is mirrored by a decrease in verb types found in the DOC between M1 and M4 (Tab. 12).

Tab. 12: Type/token distribution of verbs in the DOC

DOC	M1	M2	M3	M4
Types	134	50	74	70
Tokens	905	246	645	739
Type-Token-Ratio	0.148	0.2	0.12	0.1

In line with Barðdal (2008, 2009), who assumes that type frequency is inversely correlated with semantic coherence, this narrowing indicates an increase in semantic transparency of the construction over time. This in turn upholds the construction's productivity: With the construction becoming more coherent, it remains equally productive as before.

As for PRCs, and in particular the *to*-PRC, we assume that they experienced an opposing development to the DOC in the history of English, namely a considerable semantic widening. The originally spatial prepositional patterns extended into new contexts, and came to acquire more grammatical functions, including those of encoding ditransitive events. This should translate into an increased type frequency. There are again different ways to assess this question: First, changes in the range of larger verb classes associated with the construction were investigated to establish whether the (*to*-)PRC as a construction expanded in meanings, and thus became more productive. While a comparable analysis of the DOC yields at least some noteworthy results (the ousting of e.g. verbs of dispossession from the DOC), this was, however, not the case for (*to*-)PRCs. In fact, the number of verb classes associated with the construction(s) remains remarkably stable over time, with no classes being added or lost between the periods. This finding is on the one side quite unexpected, as it seems to contradict the hypothesis of a semantic widening of PRCs. On the other hand, it has to be kept in mind that this process in all likelihood started well before Middle English (Visser 1963; cf. also De Cuypere's [2015c] argument that the *to*-PRC with transfer verbs was already embryonically present in Old English). Even if the initial extension to new verb class-types might therefore have taken place in Old English, an increase in the individual verb types associated with the construction, as well as a rise in type frequency within the individual innovative classes, should still be seen in the Middle English data.

Establishing the frequency of individual verb types that occur with the (*to*-)PRC in the dataset, Tab. 13 indicates that the raw number of verb types in both constructions indeed increases over time. Types move from 62 (37) in M1 to 80 (59) in M4. This would suggest an extension in contexts (and thus a sign of a pre-constructionalisation constructional change on Traugott and Trousdale's 2013 approach).

Tab. 13: Type/token distribution of verbs in the (*to*)-PRC

PRC	M1	M2	M3	M4	*to*-PRC	M1	M2	M3	M4
Types	62	52	89	80	Types	37	44	68	59
Tokens	346	366	1352	822	Tokens	125	241	849	487
TTR	0.2	0.14	0.07	0.097	TTR	0.296	0.18	0.08	0.12

Still, it is important to note that the ratio of types and tokens in the relevant periods actually decreases rather than increases. However, since the tokens taken into account for the (*to*-)PRC were restricted in a number of ways a priori, the results presented here are not entirely representative in any case.

Let us then compare verb type frequency of the individual constructions with their potential productivity, i.e. the number of hapax legomena divided by the number of tokens in each sub-period. Fig. 30 shows these combined measurements and demonstrates that the two productivity values do not necessarily coincide. In the case of the DOC, the steady decrease in type frequency is accompanied by a slighter but still notable decrease in potential productivity (disregarding M2 as a generally problematic period). By contrast, the rising type frequency of the PRC and *to*-PRC conflicts with a clear overall decrease in potential productivity, even though the ratio rises again towards the end of the period (M3–M4). Note, however, that caution is in order with these figures: Since the data for the prepositional patterns was pre-selected on the basis of verbs occurring in the DOC, the actual range of PP-ditransitives might be quite different.

Last, changes in productivity of the constructions as such do not preclude the possibility that individual verb classes experience increases or decreases in type frequency/ productivity within themselves. For example, the reduction in the semantic scope of the DOC does not impact the productivity of the verb classes still found in it: New verbs of transfer or communication (e.g. *instagram* or *whatsapp*, cf. above) are readily added to the construction. This aspect was also

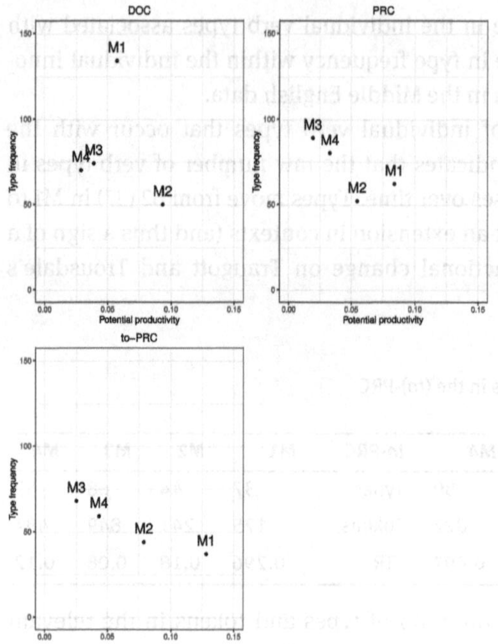

Fig. 30: Global productivity of DOC, PRC and *to*-PRC, M1–M4

investigated here. With the DOC, most verb classes did, however, not show clear signs of diachronic change; these results will therefore not be presented in more detail here. The same goes for the (*to*-)PRC. This is mainly due to the very low counts of tokens as well as types in some of the verb classes (such as verbs of refusal), which makes it difficult to generalise. What can nevertheless be gleaned from the data is that the most type frequent verb classes in the *to*-PRC are those of verbs of communication as well as verbs of concrete and abstract transfer. The former two are more prominent in M1 than verbs of abstract transfer. The raw number of types increases over the course of the period for all three verb classes. This might indicate a decrease in semantic coherence of the individual categories, following Barðdal (2008, 2009).

In sum, we can observe a reduction in productivity of the DOC in terms of verb classes and verb types, suggesting that the construction became more coherent over time, moving towards a more transparent basic transfer meaning. It is also safe to assume that a semantic widening of the PRCs involved, and specifically the *to*-PRC, did take place between Old and Middle English, and during the Middle English period. The final part of this section comments on changes in the associations between the constructions and individual verbs; this survey supplements our assumptions on the semantic scope of the patterns.

4.2.4 Distinctive collexeme analysis

It is a well-known claim in the literature on PDE ditransitives that there are significant differences between verbs regarding their frequency of occurrence in either one or the other variant of the dative alternation. Gries and Stefanowitsch (2004: 106–107), for example, by carrying out a distinctive collexeme analysis, find that verbs such as *give, tell, teach, show* or *offer* most frequently select for the DOC, while the verbs most clearly associated with the *to*-PRC include *bring, take, pass,* as well as *sell, supply* and *pay*. Following Gries and Stefanowitsch (2004) and Hilpert (2008), I also applied this method to the Middle English data in this project. As already pointed out, distinctive collexeme analysis "identifies lexemes that exhibit a strong preference for one member of the pair as opposed to the other, and thus makes it possible to identify subtle distributional differences between the members of such a pair" (Gries and Stefanowitsch 2004: 97). Performing this analysis thus allows us to detect any verb-specific preferences in the individual sub-periods, and whether these tendencies were subject to change within the entire period. The outcomes of the analyses moreover serve as further back-up for verb-class-specific trends or biases. This assumption is based on the expectation that constructional preferences of individual verbs match those of verbs with similar meanings, which means they can be grouped together into larger semantic verb classes. Investigating the types of verb classes found in a construction, as well as their token frequency distribution in relation to each other, in turn enables us to determine the meaning of the construction as a whole. In addition to testing association trends of verbs in the choice between DOC and (*to*-)PRC, I furthermore used multiple distinctive collexeme analysis to check for correlations between individual verbs and individual prepositional types and tried to identify any systematic patterns or clusters in these data. Last, I applied the tool to verb preferences between DOC, PRC, prepositional theme patterns (PTC) and possessive constructions (POSS).

The results of the first analysis on DOC vs. PRC are presented in Tab. 14. By contrast, Tab. 15 below shows the outcome of the same analysis on the sub-set of verbs alternating between DOC and *to*-PRC. The relevant columns in the tables are those labelled 'Verb' on the very left, the column 'preferred occurrence (pref.occur)', which specifies whether the verb is most distinctly used in the DOC or (*to*-)PRC, in the middle, as well as 'collocational strength (coll.str)' at the very right, which specifies how strong the collocation is. Note that values of above 3 for collocational strength correspond to a high significance level ($p < 0.001$), coll.strength>2 indicates a medium significance level ($p < 0.01$), and scores of over 1.30103 are significant at a $p < 0.05$ level. The remaining columns give the observed and expected frequencies of the two constructions. The tables do not include all the information provided by the analysis but have been condensed. They also do not show all values (columns), and not all verbs are covered: Those verbs which are not significantly associated with either pattern have been excluded.

Tab. 14: Distinctive collexeme analysis for verb-specific preferences (DOC vs. PRC), M1–M4 (obs.=observed frequencies, exp.=expected frequencies, pref.occur=preferred occurrence, coll.str=collocational strength)

Period	Verb	obs.1	obs.2	exp.1	exp.2	pref.occur	coll.str
M1	yeven	207	14	163.48	57.52	DOC	17.28
	bihoten	18	1	14.05	4.95	DOC	1.63
	nimen	4	29	24.41	8.59	PRC	13.49
	taken	3	18	15.53	5.47	PRC	8
	evenen	1	10	8.14	2.86	PRC	4.99
	setten	1	10	8.14	2.86	PRC	4.99
	willen	2	4	4.44	1.56	PRC	1.37
M2	binimen	14	1	7.27	7.73	DOC	3.6
	bringen	1	7	3.88	4.12	PRC	1.39
M3	tellen	56	13	28.83	40.17	DOC	11.1
	techen	40	5	18.8	26.2	DOC	10.5
	foryeven	30	7	15.46	21.54	DOC	6.06
	graunten	24	9	13.79	19.21	DOC	3.57
	bireven	11	2	5.43	7.57	DOC	2.71
	geten	12	3	6.27	8.73	DOC	2.54
	binimen	9	2	4.6	6.4	DOC	2.09
	chesen	7	1	3.34	4.66	DOC	1.96
	crien	7	1	3.34	4.66	DOC	1.96
	leren	5	1	2.51	3.49	DOC	1.31
	taken	11	152	68.1	94.9	PRC	25.56
	senden	11	61	30.08	41.92	PRC	6.14

Period	Verb	obs.1	obs.2	exp.1	exp.2	pref.occur	coll.str
	yelden	4	31	14.62	20.38	PRC	4.07
	bitaken	4	23	11.28	15.72	PRC	2.6
	speken	1	14	6.27	8.73	PRC	2.47
	seien	11	35	19.22	26.78	PRC	2.09
	leven	1	12	5.43	7.57	PRC	2.05
	bringen	7	26	13.79	19.21	PRC	1.98
	asken	11	30	17.13	23.87	PRC	1.48
M4	yeven	197	75	152.77	119.23	DOC	9.66
	graunten	47	5	29.21	22.79	DOC	7.35
	tellen	66	13	44.37	34.63	DOC	7.04
	foryeven	18	1	10.67	8.33	DOC	3.6
	geten	20	4	13.48	10.52	DOC	2.34
	lenen	10	1	6.18	4.82	DOC	1.78
	techen	11	2	7.3	5.7	DOC	1.5
	taken	12	125	76.95	60.05	PRC	34.78
	yelden	3	23	14.6	11.4	PRC	5.64
	seien	7	23	16.85	13.15	PRC	3.65
	paien	3	12	8.43	6.57	PRC	2.33
	deliveren	6	14	11.23	8.77	PRC	1.8

What is striking in Tab. 14 is first, that *yeven* 'give' (and to some extent, *taken* 'take') is unrivalled in terms of frequency at all stages, stably accounting for about a fifth of all hits. This means that this verb essentially carries the alternation. As to the verbs' preferences, there is considerable variation within and between the sub-periods and among semantically related verbs. For example, 'give' is clearly associated with the DOC in M1 and M4 but does not seem to have any preference in the time span in between (M2–M3). Its close synonyms *graunten* 'grant, give' and *geten* 'get, give' are likewise found most often in the DOC in the later periods, while *yelden* 'yield, give', also very close in meaning, favours the PRC (M3–M4). Similarly, there is no clear systematicity in the preferences of verbs of communication such as *tellen* 'tell', *techen* 'teach', *seien* 'say', *speken* 'speak' and *asken* 'ask' – the first two of these most frequently opt for the DOC, whereas the latter three more often occur in the PRC in M3 and M4. Interestingly, privative verbs such as *binimen* 'steal, take away' (M2–M3) and *bireven* 'rob, steal, take away' (M3) select for the DOC rather than the PRC. In the latest period, however, the verbs are not featured in the list any more, meaning they are unbiased in choice of construction. This is unexpected in that we would anticipate that these verbs show a noticeable inclination towards PRC uses in later stages, based on the findings presented above. Still, this result does not necessarily present a challenge or contradiction to claims about the behaviour of the entire verb class. For example, *taken* 'take', which is most commonly used in privative sense, are biased towards the prepositional pattern from early on. The most distinct lexemes for the PRC are consistent with those identified as distinctive for the *to*-PRC in PDE by Gries and Stefanowitsch (2004). They include verbs such as *bringen* 'bring', *senden* 'send', *(bi)taken* 'take', *nimen* 'take (away)' and *paien* 'pay'; many of these express meanings of concrete transfer and motion, and their predilection for the prepositional patterns thus supports the assumption that this sense is foregrounded in this construction.

The results for the alternation between DOC and *to*-PRC as shown in Tab. 15 largely correspond to those just described for the broader DOC - PRC alternation. What is interesting to observe, however, is that *yeven* 'give' shows even more variation in behaviour in the restricted alternation in that it oscillates between the DOC and the *to*-PRC in the earlier periods (M1: DOC, M2: *to*-PRC), shows no preference for either construction in M3 (and is therefore not included in the table), and returns to the DOC towards the end of the period (M4). This shifting behaviour of the most prototypical ditransitive verb is reminiscent of the reversing trend observed in the relative frequencies of DOC vs. (*to*-)PRC above. Verbs which are significantly biased towards the DOC in later periods are other transfer verbs like *graunten* 'grant, give', *geten* 'get' or *lenen* 'lend', as well as communication verbs such as *tellen* 'tell' or *techen* 'teach'. At the same time, other communication verbs strongly favour the *to*-PRC (e.g. *seien* 'say', *speken* 'speak'), and verbs of transfer like *yelden* 'yield' or *deliveren* 'deliver' are similarly clearly attracted to the prepositional pattern. Verbs of caused motion (*bring*, *send*), as expected based on the PDE distribution and the data presented above, are likewise mostly found in prepositional patterns. What the analysis thus corroborates is that there is an obvious intimate link between the *to*-pattern and verbs related to transfer meanings, especially in later stages of Middle English.

Tab. 15: Distinctive collexeme analysis for verb-specific preferences (DOC vs. *to*-PRC), M1–M4 ((obs.=observed frequencies, exp.=expected frequencies, pref.occur=preferred occurrence, coll.str=collocational strength)

Period	Verb	obs.1	obs.2	exp.1	exp.2	pref.occur	coll.str
M1	yeven	207	10	181.83	35.17	DOC	9.5
	evenen	1	9	8.38	1.62	to-PRC	6.32
	nimen	4	7	9.22	1.78	to-PRC	3.34
	taken	3	5	6.7	1.3	*to*-PRC	2.42
	willen	2	3	4.19	0.81	*to*-PRC	1.49
M2	techen	21	4	12.73	12.27	DOC	3.39
	yeven	58	75	67.73	65.27	*to*-PRC	1.73
	bringen	1	7	4.07	3.93	*to*-PRC	1.53
M3	tellen	56	12	32	36	DOC	9.16
	techen	40	5	21.17	23.83	DOC	8.61
	foryeven	30	7	17.41	19.59	DOC	4.77
	graunten	24	9	15.53	17.47	DOC	2.66
	geten	12	2	6.59	7.41	DOC	2.48
	chesen	7	1	3.76	4.24	DOC	1.63
	crien	7	1	3.76	4.24	DOC	1.63
	senden	11	55	31.06	34.94	*to*-PRC	6.97
	yelden	4	26	14.12	15.88	*to*-PRC	4.05
	taken	11	37	22.59	25.41	*to*-PRC	3.41
	bitaken	4	23	12.7	14.3	*to*-PRC	3.39
	bringen	7	26	15.53	17.47	*to*-PRC	2.76
	leven	1	12	6.12	6.88	*to*-PRC	2.51
	seien	11	27	17.88	20.12	*to*-PRC	1.79
	speken	1	9	4.71	5.29	*to*-PRC	1.78
M4	graunten	47	5	33.1	18.9	DOC	5.12
	tellen	66	13	50.29	28.71	DOC	4.34
	yeven	197	73	171.87	98.13	DOC	4.05

Period	Verb	obs.1	obs.2	exp.1	exp.2	pref.occur	coll.str
	foryeven	18	1	12.09	6.91	DOC	2.69
	geten	20	3	14.64	8.36	DOC	1.91
	lenen	10	1	7	4	DOC	1.3
	yelden	3	23	16.55	9.45	*to*-PRC	7.44
	seien	7	19	16.55	9.45	*to*-PRC	3.91
	writen	2	10	7.64	4.36	*to*-PRC	2.95
	paien	3	11	8.91	5.09	*to*-PRC	2.83
	taken	12	20	20.37	11.63	*to*-PRC	2.7
	deliveren	6	14	12.73	7.27	*to*-PRC	2.68
	senden	56	52	68.75	39.25	*to*-PRC	2.3

For example, we see that transfer-related verbs like *give*, *lend*, *get*, *yield* or *bitechen* 'give, grant' largely co-occur with the DOC in the beginning (M1–M2). In later Middle English, however, these verbs diversify in preferences. While some show a clear attraction towards the DOC, and are repulsed by the PRC (e.g. *give*, *grant*, *lend*, *let*), others exhibit the exact opposite behaviour (e.g. *get*, *send*, *beget*, *yield*, *betaken* 'give, grant'). Yet others which belong to this group are indeterminate between those two constructions. I take this to support the assumption that the patterns were (perceived as) quasi-synonymous and were used with a relatively balanced frequency. Within the larger set of transfer-verbs, it is interesting to note that verbs of intended or future transfer such as *offer* or *promise* (ME *offren*, *profren*, *promisen*) are strongly distinctive for DOC use at all stages, while verbs of concrete transfer are seemingly not significantly associated with either pattern at any time: This is in line with the frequency distributions shown above. I assume that the fact that verbs of abstract transfer were still more prone to the DOC in earlier stages and only slowly took on alternating uses reflects the increasing grammaticalisation of the PRC-patterns. Finally, what is interesting to note is that overall, the large majority of verbs are in fact not biased towards one or the other pattern; however, this fraction decreases over time. While in the first half of the period, about 85 per cent of all verbs are not significantly associated with one of the constructions, this drops to about 65 per cent in the latter periods. This may be interpreted as corroboration for a functional diversification of the patterns, with each construction becoming more clearly linked to a particular construal, even though they share a basic, more abstract meaning.

The notion that specific verbs and verb-classes cluster with particular preposition types is manifest in the results of the multiple distinctive collexeme analysis presented in Tab. 16. This table shows how distinctive the verbs are for specific prepositional patterns (PRC-types), and whether this co-occurrence is statistically significant. The distinctiveness values (typically labelled pbin, here shown in the columns headed by individual prepositions) provide the log-transformed probabilities of the observed frequencies, given the expected frequencies. The same ranges as before apply also in this case (pbin > 1.3 *, pbin > 2 **, pbin > 3 ***). While positive scores indicate a strong attraction, negative values mean that a verb is repelled by the pattern. 'S.A.D.' gives the sum of all absolute deviations: A higher number points to a greater deviation from the expected frequency. The final column ('Larg.D') tells which preposition a verb is most distinctive for, in case it is attracted or repelled by more than one. Note that the table only includes significant outcomes and excludes all verbs which are indeterminate in their behaviour. The relevant cells are marked in bold. Furthermore, prepositions which only strongly collocated with one single verb were also discarded, since we are interested in potential broader generalisations.

Starting in M1, what is conspicuous about the results is that there seem to be no larger clusters or general patterns. While some correspondences are present – e.g. *kithen* 'say, tell, show' frequently selecting for *till*, or *biseken* 'beg, pray' occurring together with *at* 'from' – many verbs do not appear to be significantly associated with one specific prepositional type. Some of the most distinctive collocations furthermore involve light verbs like *do*, *have* and *set* which are difficult to classify due to their underspecified meaning. Interestingly, no clear attraction between transfer-verbs, specifically 'give' and *to* shows up in the data. Clearer trends begin to emerge in M2, where we find *yeven* very strongly favouring *to*, while being repelled by numerous other prepositions. By contrast, privative *taken* clearly disfavours *to*, pointing to a growing regularisation or divergence among the verbs and verb classes. Other dispossession verbs such as *stelen* 'steal' and *nimen* 'take (away)' are highly distinctive for *of*, confirming our predictions. Similarly, the PDE collocation preferences for 'ask' in a sense of what was above labelled 'reverse communicated transfer' (*ask a favour of someone*) are already seen in early Middle English. Finally, *haven* 'have' commonly patterns with prepositions like *of* and *on*. As discussed above, this is likely due to their frequent appearance in complex predicates of the type 'have FEELING *prep*REC' (e.g. *have pity on/of someone, have love of someone*, etc.).

In the later periods (M3–M4), we can observe a hardening of fronts of some sorts: While a range of transfer-verbs (including typical ditransitive verbs like *give, bring, send, leave* but also *deal, yield* or *bitaken* 'give, grant' and *gaderen* 'gather') are greatly drawn to *to* (as well as, in M4, *unto/onto*), they are at the same time strongly resistant to being used with *of* or *from*. The exact opposite holds true for a number of dispossession verbs like *(bi)reven* 'rob, steal', *stelen* 'steal', *binimen* 'take away, rob, steal' or *withdrauen* 'withdraw'. Several verbs of communication (*moustren* 'show' and *kennen* 'tell, teach, show', *seien* 'say') are similarly drawn towards goal-prepositions (*to, till, unto, onto*). Notably, there is a set of transfer-verbs which shows a clear predilection for *on/upon* and an aversion to *to*; this group mainly includes variants of 'get'. The aberrant behaviour of these verbs can be explained by the fact that they occur mainly in (semi-)fixed expressions referring to the impregnation of women (105).

(105) he *bigate* **on** **her**$_{REC}$ a dou3ter
he begot on her a daughter
'he begot on her a daughter'
(CMBRUT3,122.3705; PPCME2: M3)

In addition to being closely connected to verbs of stealing and robbing, *of* is also typically used with verbs of reversed (communicated) transfer (e.g. *buy/ purchase sth. of somone, ask/ beg sth. of someone*); these verbs are furthermore often found with *at*. The latter preposition is somewhat promiscuous in Middle English in that it denotes both a source- as well as a goal-meaning. A last interesting point is that three of the verbs distinctive for *for*, namely *maken* 'make' (106), *werken* 'create' and *dighten* 'prepare', are verbs of (benefactive) creation. Although it is highly difficult to find evidence for the existence of the clear, systematic association between such verbs and *for* which characterises the PDE benefactive alternation, this correlation might indicate at least an incipient closer relationship.

(106) *made* þat hous$_{TH}$ **for** **his** **children** **Ismaelites**$_{REC}$
made that house for his children Ishmaelites
'made that house for his children, the Ishmaelites'
(CMPOLYCH,VI,31.201; PPCME2: M3)

In sum, the results of the multiple distinctive collexeme analysis of verbs-specific preferences for PRC-types confirm that after an initial period of 'experimentation' with a great deal of variation and lack of clear allegiances, the system of prepositional ditransitives moved towards higher regularity. That is, in late Middle English, verbs associated with particular meanings usually select for specific prepositional types and are increasingly restricted to only those. This is, however, not the case with a set of verbs pertaining to the third group identified

Tab. 16: Multiple distinctive collexeme analysis for verb-specific preferences for individual prepositions, M1–M4

Period	Verb	again	at	before	by	for	from	of	till	upon	S.A.D.	Larg.D
M1	yarken	**2.03**	-0.09	1.08	-0.05	-0.04	-0.04	-0.68	-0.04	-0.04	4.51	agains
	biseken	-0.13	**5.9**	-0.06	-0.08	-0.06	-0.06	-1.13	-0.06	-0.06	8.23	at
	seien	-0.13	-0.15	-0.06	**1.88**	-0.06	-0.06	-1.13	-0.06	-0.06	5.05	by
	forleten	-0.03	-0.03	-0.01	-0.02	-0.01	**1.55**	-0.23	-0.01	-0.01	2.04	from
	haven	-1.04	-1.22	-0.51	-0.27	-0.51	-0.51	**5.26**	-0.51	-0.51	11.35	of
	don	0.97	-0.3	**1.51**	0.5	**1.51**	0.6	**-2.26**	-0.12	-0.12	8.53	of
	kithen	-0.1	-0.12	-0.05	-0.07	-0.05	-0.05	-0.33	**2.33**	-0.05	4.07	till
	setten	-0.18	-0.21	-0.09	-0.12	0.74	-0.09	**-1.58**	-0.09	**1.82**	7.29	upon

Period	Verb	against	before	for	from	in	into	of	on	to	unto	upon	S.A.D.	Larg.D
M2	yelden	-0.22	**1.61**	-0.15	-0.26	-0.49	-0.06	0.2	-0.46	1.09	-0.06	-0.28	5.11	before
	leten	-0.06	-0.03	**4.16**	-0.07	-0.13	-0.02	-0.12	-0.13	-1.28	**1.39**	-0.08	7.55	for
	don	-0.27	**1.36**	0.52	**4.02**	0.89	0.43	**-1.4**	**-1.47**	-1.23	-0.2	-0.9	14.98	from
	putten	-0.01	-0.01	-0.01	**1.48**	-0.03	0	-0.02	-0.03	-0.46	0	-0.02	2.08	from
	setten	0.89	-0.14	-0.19	-0.33	**2.7**	-0.08	-0.56	-0.59	-1.18	-0.08	**1.33**	9.56	in
	maken	-0.28	-0.14	0.44	0.27	**1.97**	-0.08	-0.19	-0.59	**-1.57**	-0.08	**1.33**	8.76	in
	holden	-0.02	-0.01	-0.02	-0.03	-0.05	**1.79**	-0.05	-0.05	-0.24	-0.01	-0.03	2.31	into
	asken	-0.02	-0.01	-0.02	-0.03	-0.05	-0.01	**2.52**	-0.05	-0.92	-0.01	-0.03	3.68	of
	stelen	-0.02	-0.01	-0.02	-0.03	-0.05	-0.01	**2.52**	-0.05	-0.92	-0.01	-0.03	3.68	of
	nimen	-0.04	-0.02	-0.03	-0.04	-0.08	-0.01	**2.06**	-0.08	-0.55	-0.01	-0.05	3	of
	haven	-0.45	-0.22	0.29	-0.54	0.41	-0.13	**3.87**	**16.3**	**-12.2**	-0.13	-0.58	35.66	on
	yeven	-0.89	-0.44	-0.62	-1.07	**-2**	0.34	**-1.81**	**-1.9**	**12.1**	-0.27	-1.17	23.63	to
	speken	**2.82**	-0.05	-0.08	-0.13	-0.24	-0.03	-0.22	-0.23	**-2.87**	1.15	**2.49**	11.22	to
	taken	0.7	-0.05	-0.07	0.63	1.1	-0.03	0.44	-0.21	**-1.61**	-0.03	0.6	5.58	to
	strenen	-0.01	-0.01	-0.01	-0.01	-0.03	0	-0.02	-0.03	-0.46	0	**1.45**	2.04	upon

Period	Verb	against	at	for	from	in	into	of	on	till	to	upon	S.A.D.	Larg.D
M3	holden	**4.14**	-0.04	-0.15	-0.14	-0.13	0	1.17	-0.32	**1.39**	**-2.05**	-0.16	10.12	against
	areren	**1.73**	0	-0.01	-0.01	-0.01	0	-0.06	-0.02	-0.01	-0.39	-0.01	2.29	against
	bien	-0.02	**1.66**	-0.04	-0.03	-0.03	0	**1.37**	-0.07	-0.03	-1.17	-0.04	4.56	at
	leren	-0.01	**2.13**	-0.01	-0.01	-0.01	0	-0.06	-0.02	-0.01	-0.39	-0.01	2.7	at
	bidden	-0.02	**1.83**	-0.02	-0.02	-0.02	0	-0.12	-0.05	-0.02	-0.19	-0.02	2.36	at
	ordeinen	-0.12	-0.05	**2.17**	-0.16	-0.15	0	-0.86	-0.37	-0.17	0.42	-0.18	7.94	for
	offren	-0.16	-0.06	**2.76**	-0.21	-0.2	-0.01	-1.15	-0.49	1.05	0.64	-0.24	7.64	for
	dighten	-0.01	0	**1.58**	-0.01	-0.01	0	-0.06	-0.02	-0.01	-0.39	-0.01	2.14	for
	reven	-0.03	-0.01	-0.05	**6.45**	-0.04	0	-0.23	-0.1	-0.04	**-1.56**	-0.05	8.68	from
	withdrauen	-0.04	-0.02	-0.06	**5.76**	-0.05	0	0.31	-0.12	-0.06	**-1.95**	-0.06	8.59	from
	stelen	-0.03	-0.01	-0.05	**2.46**	-0.04	0	1.11	-0.1	-0.04	**-1.56**	-0.05	5.57	from
	bireven	-0.02	-0.01	-0.02	**3.23**	-0.02	0	-0.12	-0.05	-0.02	-0.78	-0.02	4.34	from
	binimen	-0.02	-0.01	-0.02	**1.32**	-0.02	0	0.63	-0.05	-0.02	-0.78	-0.02	2.94	from
	helen	-0.01	0	-0.01	**1.61**	-0.01	0	-0.06	-0.02	-0.01	-0.39	-0.01	2.17	from
	piken	-0.01	0	-0.01	**1.61**	-0.01	0	-0.06	-0.02	-0.01	-0.39	-0.01	2.17	from
	taken	-0.01	0	-0.01	**1.61**	-0.01	0	-0.06	-0.02	-0.01	-0.39	-0.01	2.17	from
	putten	-0.16	-0.06	**1.82**	0.41	**4.14**	-0.01	-1.15	-0.15	-0.22	-1.19	0.37	10.34	in
	confermen	-0.02	-0.01	-0.02	-0.02	**1.34**	0	-0.12	-0.05	-0.02	-0.19	-0.02	1.86	in
	restoren	-0.03	-0.01	-0.05	-0.04	-0.04	**2.53**	-0.23	-0.1	-0.04	0.33	-0.05	3.57	into
	taken	-1	0.22	-0.44	**4.29**	-0.65	-0.04	**24.62**	-0.31	**-1.36**	**-19.5**	**3.23**	58.4	of

Period	Verb	against	at	for	from	in	into	of	on	till	to	upon	S.A.D.	Larg.D
M3	asken	-0.23	0.71	-0.34	-0.31	-0.29	-0.01	**23.97**	-0.71	-0.32	**-11.3**	-0.35	39.53	of
	maken	0.71	-0.26	**3.47**	-0.88	**2.55**	-0.03	**-3.62**	-0.78	-0.41	0.37	-0.99	19.32	of
	seien	0.87	1.56	0.21	-0.38	-0.35	-0.01	**-2.01**	-0.85	0.66	1.01	-0.42	10.5	of
	geten	-0.19	-0.08	-0.28	-0.26	-0.24	-0.01	-0.38	**13.02**	-0.27	**-7.82**	**3.38**	26.61	on
	yeten	-0.17	-0.07	0.36	-0.23	-0.21	-0.01	-1.21	**12.77**	-0.23	**-6.7**	**2.64**	25.26	on
	biyeten	-0.15	-0.06	-0.21	-0.19	0.47	-0.01	-1.04	**8.16**	-0.2	**-7.03**	**6.56**	24.68	on
	moustren	-0.04	-0.02	-0.06	-0.05	-0.05	0	-0.29	-0.12	**5.71**	-1.03	-0.06	7.59	till
	kennen	-0.01	0	-0.01	-0.01	-0.01	0	-0.06	-0.02	**1.6**	-0.39	-0.01	2.16	till
	yeven	**-1.88**	-0.75	**-1.85**	**-2.49**	**-2.33**	-0.07	**-13.4**	**-5.66**	0.64	**26.45**	**-2.79**	62.4	to
	haven	0.4	1.19	-0.24	-0.72	**6.72**	-0.04	**17.15**	2.1	**-1.37**	**-23.2**	0.6	55.31	to
	senden	-0.49	-0.2	-0.29	-0.65	-0.61	-0.02	**-3.51**	-0.46	0.7	**3.86**	-0.73	13.82	to
	sheuen	-0.33	-0.13	-0.48	-0.44	-0.41	-0.01	**-2.36**	-1	-0.45	**4.88**	-0.49	12.98	to
	bitaken	-0.19	0.07	-0.27	-0.25	-0.23	-0.01	**-1.32**	-0.56	-0.25	**5.22**	-0.28	9.4	to
	yelden	-0.26	-0.1	-0.37	-0.34	-0.32	-0.01	-1.1	-0.78	**2.09**	**2.13**	0.23	8.79	to
	bringen	-0.4	-0.1	-0.35	-0.32	-0.3	-0.01	**-1.73**	-0.3	-0.33	**1.85**	-0.36	8.31	to
	leven	-0.1	-0.04	-0.14	-0.13	-0.12	0	-0.69	-0.29	-0.13	**2.72**	-0.14	4.88	to
	paien	-0.07	-0.03	-0.11	-0.1	-0.09	0	-0.52	-0.22	-0.1	**2.04**	-0.11	3.7	to
	ouen	-0.06	-0.03	-0.09	-0.09	-0.08	0	-0.46	-0.2	-0.09	**1.82**	-0.1	3.29	to
	bilden	-0.06	-0.02	-0.08	-0.08	-0.07	0	-0.4	-0.17	-0.08	**1.59**	-0.08	2.85	to
	delen	-0.05	-0.02	-0.07	-0.06	-0.06	0	-0.35	-0.15	-0.07	**1.36**	-0.07	2.45	to
	don	**1.99**	-0.62	-0.61	-0.51	-1.2	-0.06	**-5.94**	-0.78	0.27	1.04	-1	28.25	of

Period	Verb	against	at	before	for	from	in	of	on	onto	to	unto	upon	S.A.D.	Larg. D
M4	holden	**6.7**	-0.04	-0.06	0.43	-0.2	-0.06	-0.43	-0.16	-0.12	-0.65	-0.41	-0.13	9.5	against
	imaginen	**1.68**	0	-0.01	-0.03	-0.02	-0.01	-0.05	-0.02	-0.02	-0.26	-0.05	-0.02	2.18	against
	wagen	**1.39**	-0.01	-0.01	-0.05	-0.05	-0.01	-0.11	-0.04	-0.03	-0.51	-0.1	-0.03	3.73	against
	striken	-0.02	**3.92**	-0.01	-0.05	-0.05	-0.01	-0.11	-0.04	-0.03	-0.51	-0.1	-0.03	4.9	at
	bringen	-0.2	-0.11	**3.44**	-0.55	-0.54	-0.16	-1.19	-0.44	0.26	-0.35	**2.77**	-0.37	10.7	before
	reden	-0.07	-0.04	**3.68**	-0.2	-0.2	-0.06	-0.43	-0.16	-0.12	-0.31	-0.41	-0.13	9.09	before
	beren	-0.07	-0.04	**2.18**	-0.2	-0.2	-0.06	-0.43	-0.16	-0.12	1.07	-0.41	-0.13	5.18	before
	ordeinen	-0.13	-0.07	-0.1	**15.1**	-0.34	-0.1	-0.76	-0.28	-0.22	**-2.51**	-0.71	-0.23	20.81	for
	werken	-0.02	-0.01	-0.01	**2.55**	-0.05	-0.01	-0.11	-0.04	-0.03	-0.51	-0.1	-0.03	3.44	for
	taken	-0.14	-0.07	-0.1	-0.38	**9.25**	-0.11	0.6	-0.3	-0.23	**-1.94**	-0.76	-0.25	14.35	from
	withdrauen	-0.04	-0.03	-0.03	-0.1	**5.05**	-0.03	-0.22	-0.08	-0.06	-1.03	-0.2	-0.07	6.99	from
	setten	0.87	-0.02	-0.05	-0.18	-0.17	**5.55**	-0.38	**1.44**	-0.11	-1.8	-0.36	-0.12	11.14	in
	asken	-0.19	0.69	-0.15	-0.17	-0.17	-0.16	**13.8**	-0.42	-0.33	**-5.39**	-1.07	-0.35	23.2	of
	don	-0.33	-0.41	-0.21	**2.11**	**-2.08**	-0.63	**-4.582**	-0.59	-0.38	**1.3**	0.64	-0.43	17.13	of
	bien	-0.09	-0.05	-0.07	0.98	-0.24	-0.07	**5.9**	-0.2	-0.16	**-2.57**	-0.51	-0.17	11.16	of
	maken	0.51	-0.26	0.24	-0.19	**-1.32**	0.22	**-2**	-0.53	-0.37	**1.96**	0.41	0.48	8.93	of
	enqueren	-0.03	-0.01	-0.02	-0.08	-0.07	-0.02	**2.8**	-0.06	-0.05	-0.77	-0.15	-0.05	4.16	of
	purchasen	-0.03	-0.01	-0.02	0.8	-0.07	-0.02	**1.42**	-0.06	-0.05	-0.77	-0.15	-0.05	3.5	of
	haven	-0.03	-0.01	-0.02	-0.08	-0.07	-0.02	**1.42**	-0.06	-0.05	-0.77	0.53	-0.05	3.16	of
	geten	-0.1	-0.05	-0.08	0.33	-0.27	-0.08	-0.59	**6.98**	-0.17	-1.17	-0.19	-0.18	10.35	on

Period	Verb	against	at	before	for	from	in	of	on	onto	to	unto	upon	S.A.D.	Larg. D
M4	yeten	-0.08	-0.04	-0.06	0.39	-0.22	-0.07	-0.49	**6.21**	-0.14	**-1.39**	0.19	-0.15	9.55	on
	biyeten	-0.05	-0.02	-0.03	-0.13	-0.12	-0.04	-0.27	**3.07**	-0.08	**-1.28**	-0.25	**1.88**	7.29	on
	crien	-0.01	0	-0.01	-0.03	-0.02	-0.01	-0.05	**1.35**	-0.02	-0.26	-0.05	-0.02	1.84	on
	senden	-0.48	-0.25	-0.37	-0.71	**-1.3**	-0.4	**-2.86**	-1.06	**3.29**	**2.48**	1.2	-0.88	16.04	onto
	seien	**1.84**	-0.12	-0.17	-0.23	-0.61	-0.19	**-1.35**	-0.16	**1.97**	1.05	-1.27	-0.42	10.62	onto
	writen	-0.09	-0.05	-0.07	-0.25	-0.24	-0.07	-0.54	-0.2	**3.56**	0.59	-0.51	-0.17	6.49	onto
	rehersen	-0.02	-0.01	-0.01	-0.05	-0.05	-0.01	-0.11	-0.04	**2.9**	-0.51	-0.1	-0.03	3.86	onto
	gaderen	-0.01	0	-0.01	-0.03	-0.02	-0.01	-0.05	-0.02	**1.45**	-0.26	-0.05	-0.02	1.94	onto
	taken	-0.43	0.51	-0.71	**-2.58**	**9.62**	-0.77	**10.48**	-0.3	**-1.61**	**-11.6**	**-3.27**	**5.78**	50.15	to
	haven	-0.7	**1.99**	-0.18	-0.25	-0.7	**2.69**	**3.83**	**1.65**	-1.2	**-4.98**	-1.21	0.25	23.66	to
	yeven	-0.24	-0.33	-0.48	**-1.73**	**-1.69**	-0.51	**-3.72**	**-1.38**	-0.53	**9.28**	0.86	-1.15	22.91	to
	tellen	-0.12	-0.06	-0.09	-0.33	-0.32	-0.1	-0.7	-0.26	-0.2	**4.55**	-0.66	-0.22	7.81	to
	deliveren	-0.14	-0.07	-0.1	-0.38	-0.37	-0.11	-0.81	-0.3	-0.23	**3**	0.3	-0.25	6.28	to
	paien	-0.11	-0.06	-0.08	0.3	-0.29	-0.09	-0.65	-0.24	-0.19	**3**	-0.61	-0.2	6.01	to
	ouen	-0.05	-0.03	-0.04	-0.15	-0.15	-0.04	-0.32	-0.12	-0.09	**2.1**	-0.31	-0.1	3.57	to
	yelden	-0.2	-0.11	-0.15	-0.55	-0.54	-0.16	-1.19	-0.44	-0.34	0.42	**5.17**	-0.37	9.96	unto
	sheuen	-0.26	-0.14	-0.2	0.31	-0.71	-0.22	**-1.56**	-0.21	-0.45	**1.35**	**1.94**	-0.48	8.25	unto
	bitechen	-0.04	-0.02	-0.03	-0.1	-0.1	-0.03	-0.22	-0.08	-0.06	-0.4	**2.3**	-0.07	3.51	unto
	putten	-0.12	-0.06	0.73	-0.33	-0.32	0.7	-0.7	0.35	-0.2	**-1.55**	**1.33**	**1.94**	9.71	upon
	preven	-0.02	-0.01	-0.01	-0.05	-0.05	-0.01	-0.11	-0.04	-0.03	-0.51	-0.1	**2.85**	3.81	upon

above: Especially light verbs like *have* (in combinations with feeling-NPs) still show some variability in terms of preposition usage in PDE.

The same analysis as with different prepositional recipient patterns was in a last step also performed on the choice between DOC, PRC (*John told the news to Mary*), prepositional theme patterns (*John told Mary about the news*), and POSS (*John broke Mary's arm*). The outcomes are presented in Tab. 17. Again, cells with significant results are marked in bold, meaning that the respective verbs are significantly distinctive for certain constructions (either positively or negatively). The higher the value of 'S.A.D. (sum of absolute deviations)', the greater the distinctiveness of the verb; 'Larg.D' again indicates the construction which the verb is most distinctive for (if there is more than one).

Tab. 17: Multiple distinctive collexeme analysis for verb-specific preferences (DOC, PRC, PTC, POSS), M1–M4

Period	Verb	DOC	Poss	PRC	PTC	S.A.D.	Larg.D
M1	yeven	**17.38**	-0.74	**-14.08**	**-2.32**	34.52	DOC
	bitoknen	**3.39**	-0.07	**-2.97**	-0.23	6.66	DOC
	foryeven	**3.09**	-0.07	**-2.7**	-0.21	6.07	DOC
	toknen	**3.09**	-0.07	**-2.7**	-0.21	6.07	DOC
	binimen	**2.93**	-0.06	**-2.57**	-0.2	5.76	DOC
	lenen	**2.31**	-0.05	**-2.03**	-0.16	4.55	DOC
	yeten	**2.01**	-0.04	**-1.76**	-0.14	3.95	DOC
	bihoten	**1.97**	-0.06	**-1.67**	-0.2	3.9	DOC
	bitechen	**1.97**	-0.06	**-1.67**	-0.2	3.9	DOC
	offren	**1.79**	-0.08	**-1.47**	-0.24	3.58	DOC
	yelden	**1.56**	-0.07	-1.27	-0.22	3.12	DOC
M2	techen	**5.26**	-0.1	**-4.72**	-0.19	10.27	DOC
	binimen	**4.72**	-0.06	**-4.33**	-0.12	9.23	DOC
	foryeven	**3.66**	-0.04	**-3.4**	-0.07	7.17	DOC
	lenen	**2.85**	-0.03	**-2.65**	-0.05	5.58	DOC
	seien	**1.76**	-0.08	**-1.5**	-0.15	3.49	DOC
	sheuen	**1.58**	-0.12	-1.29	-0.22	3.21	DOC
	biseken	**1.63**	-0.02	**-1.51**	-0.03	3.19	DOC
	willen	**1.43**	-0.03	**-1.3**	-0.05	2.81	DOC
	breken	**-1.3**	**12.12**	**-2.27**	-0.05	15.74	Poss
	haven	**-7.99**	-0.15	**8.72**	-0.28	17.14	PRC

Period	Verb	DOC	Poss	PRC	PTC	S.A.D.	Larg.D
	setten	**-4.97**	-0.1	**5.42**	-0.18	10.67	PRC
	don	**-2.87**	-0.3	**3.56**	-0.56	7.29	PRC
	maken	**-1.86**	-0.12	**2.18**	-0.21	4.37	PRC
	speken	**-1.94**	-0.04	**2.12**	-0.07	4.17	PRC
	taken	**-1.73**	-0.03	**1.89**	-0.06	3.71	PRC
	thanken	-0.86	-0.02	**-1.51**	**7.03**	9.42	PTC
	bithinken	-0.65	-0.01	-1.13	**5.27**	7.06	PTC
	reprochen	0.2	-0.01	-0.76	**1.46**	2.43	PTC
	berwen	-0.22	0	-0.38	**1.76**	2.36	PTC
	bidden	-0.22	0	-0.38	**1.76**	2.36	PTC
	undon	-0.22	0	-0.38	**1.76**	2.36	PTC
M3	techen	**14.92**	-0.17	**-13.32**	-0.46	28.87	DOC
	yeven	**8.85**	**-1.61**	**-5.48**	**-4.32**	20.26	DOC
	foryeven	**9.24**	-0.14	**-8.11**	-0.38	17.87	DOC
	graunten	**5.93**	-0.13	**-5.09**	-0.34	11.49	DOC
	taken	**4.63**	-0.05	**-4.18**	-0.12	8.98	DOC
	binimen	**3.09**	-0.04	**-2.75**	-0.11	5.99	DOC
	chesen	**2.77**	-0.03	**-2.49**	-0.08	5.37	DOC
	crien	**2.77**	-0.03	**-2.49**	-0.08	5.37	DOC
	counseilen	**2.53**	-0.02	**-2.32**	-0.05	4.92	DOC
	beren	**2.07**	-0.07	**-1.73**	-0.18	4.05	DOC
	leren	**1.88**	-0.02	**-1.68**	-0.06	3.64	DOC
	ouen	**1.84**	-0.07	**-1.51**	-0.19	3.61	DOC
	enjoinen	**1.52**	-0.01	**-1.39**	-0.03	2.95	DOC
	lenen	**1.52**	-0.01	**-1.39**	-0.03	2.95	DOC
	leten	**1.46**	-0.03	-1.28	-0.07	2.84	DOC
	forbeden	**1.45**	-0.02	-1.29	-0.05	2.81	DOC
	commaunden	**1.32**	-0.05	-1.11	-0.12	2.6	DOC
	breken	**-2.76**	**31.73**	**-6.35**	-0.17	41.01	Poss
	blenden	-0.16	**2.06**	-0.46	-0.01	2.69	Poss
	confermen	-0.49	**1.59**	0.14	-0.03	2.25	Poss
	haven	**-20.17**	-0.47	**22.73**	-1.27	44.64	PRC
	taken	**-20**	-0.47	**22.55**	-1.26	44.28	PRC
	tellen	**11.21**	-0.31	**-19.64**	**7.24**	38.4	PRC
	don	**-11.23**	-0.83	**14.18**	**-2.23**	28.47	PRC

Period	Verb	DOC	Poss	PRC	PTC	S.A.D.	Larg.D
	maken	**-7.56**	-0.33	**9.01**	-0.9	17.8	PRC
	bireven	**3.44**	-0.05	**-3.93**	0.55	7.97	PRC
	yeten	**-3.42**	-0.08	**3.85**	-0.21	7.56	PRC
	senden	**-2.8**	-0.27	**3.63**	-0.74	7.44	PRC
	offren	**-3.25**	-0.08	**3.67**	-0.2	7.2	PRC
	putten	**-3.25**	-0.08	**3.67**	-0.2	7.2	PRC
	biyeten	**-2.93**	-0.07	**3.3**	-0.18	6.48	PRC
	yelden	**-2.33**	-0.14	**2.84**	-0.37	5.68	PRC
	holden	**-2.11**	-0.05	**2.38**	-0.13	4.67	PRC
	devisen	1.03	-0.02	**-1.85**	1.05	3.95	PRC
	bitaken	**-1.35**	-0.1	**1.68**	-0.28	3.41	PRC
	bringen	-1.15	-0.14	**1.51**	-0.38	3.18	PRC
	leven	-1.28	-0.05	**1.49**	-0.13	2.95	PRC
	setten	**-1.3**	-0.03	**1.47**	-0.08	2.88	PRC
	speken	-1.14	-0.05	**1.34**	-0.12	2.65	PRC
	thanken	-1.14	-0.03	**-3.24**	**11.44**	15.85	PTC
	chargen	-0.81	-0.02	**-2.32**	**8.17**	11.32	PTC
	letten	-0.65	-0.02	**-1.85**	**6.53**	9.05	PTC
	answeren	-0.81	-0.02	-0.65	**3.92**	5.4	PTC
	withdrauen	**-1.3**	-0.03	-0.25	**3.19**	4.77	PTC
	bithinken	-0.33	-0.01	-0.93	**3.27**	4.54	PTC
	warnen	-0.33	-0.01	-0.93	**3.27**	4.54	PTC
	enfourmen	0.28	-0.01	-0.93	1.34	2.56	PTC
	robben	0.28	-0.01	-0.93	1.34	2.56	PTC
	avisen	-0.16	0	-0.46	1.63	2.25	PTC
	biseken	-0.16	0	-0.46	1.63	2.25	PTC
	demen	-0.33	-0.01	-0.24	1.34	1.92	PTC
M4	yeven	**21.24**	-1.27	**-15.05**	**-4.59**	42.15	DOC
	graunten	**11.15**	-0.25	**-9.2**	-0.9	21.5	DOC
	foryeven	**5.21**	-0.09	**-4.42**	-0.33	10.05	DOC
	lenen	**2.66**	-0.05	**-2.23**	-0.19	5.13	DOC
	sheuen	**1.93**	-0.36	**-1.5**	-0.36	4.15	DOC
	profren	**2.04**	-0.04	**-1.71**	-0.16	3.95	DOC
	geten	**1.65**	-0.15	-1.13	-0.53	3.46	DOC
	promisen	**1.74**	-0.04	**-1.46**	-0.14	3.38	DOC

Period	Verb	DOC	Poss	PRC	PTC	S.A.D.	Larg.D
	forbeden	**1.73**	-0.02	**-1.51**	-0.09	3.35	DOC
	breken	**-4.41**	**33.33**	**-5.12**	-0.29	43.15	Poss
	taken	**-26.73**	-0.49	**30.98**	**-1.78**	59.98	PRC
	haven	**-19.98**	-0.37	**23.16**	**-1.33**	44.84	PRC
	tellen	**6.17**	-0.45	**-12.76**	**5.44**	24.82	PRC
	don	**-3.18**	-0.58	**5.07**	**-2.11**	10.94	PRC
	yelden	**-3.32**	-0.12	**4.1**	-0.43	7.97	PRC
	putten	**-3.37**	-0.06	**3.91**	-0.22	7.56	PRC
	seien	**-2.23**	-0.15	**2.97**	-0.55	5.9	PRC
	yeten	**-2.34**	-0.04	**2.71**	-0.16	5.25	PRC
	holden	**-2.08**	-0.04	**2.41**	-0.14	4.67	PRC
	maken	-0.95	-0.42	**1.8**	**-1.5**	4.67	PRC
	speken	**-2.08**	-0.04	**2.41**	-0.14	4.67	PRC
	techen	**1.94**	-0.07	**-2.19**	0.37	4.57	PRC
	setten	**-1.82**	-0.03	**2.11**	-0.12	4.08	PRC
	paien	**-1.37**	-0.07	**1.75**	-0.26	3.45	PRC
	writen	**-1.37**	-0.06	**1.71**	-0.21	3.35	PRC
	reden	**-1.41**	-0.04	**1.71**	-0.16	3.32	PRC
	biyeten	**-1.3**	-0.02	**1.5**	-0.09	2.91	PRC
	deliveren	-1.01	-0.1	**1.4**	-0.36	2.87	PRC
	bien	-1.03	-0.06	**1.33**	-0.22	2.64	PRC
	thanken	**-5.71**	-0.11	**-6.63**	**31.01**	43.46	PTC
	enfourmen	**-1.82**	-0.03	**-2.11**	**9.87**	13.83	PTC
	biseken	-0.78	-0.01	-0.9	**4.23**	5.92	PTC
	warnen	-0.78	-0.01	-0.9	**4.23**	5.92	PTC
	preven	**-1.3**	-0.02	-0.3	**3.25**	4.87	PTC
	letten	-0.52	-0.01	-0.6	**2.82**	3.95	PTC
	robben	-0.52	-0.01	-0.6	**2.82**	3.95	PTC
	senden	0.97	-0.52	-0.38	**-1.88**	3.75	PTC
	answeren	-0.26	0	-0.3	**1.41**	1.97	PTC
	chargen	-0.26	0	-0.3	**1.41**	1.97	PTC

Much of this analysis evidently overlaps with the results on DOC vs. PRC presented above, for example prototypical transfer-verbs showing a relatively balanced predilection for the two patterns. What is interesting about these figures is that communication verbs correspond to other sub-sets of transfer-related verbs in always being strongly attracted to the DOC. At the same time, however, verbs like *thanken* 'thank', *enfourmen* 'inform', *avisen* 'advise' or *warnen* 'warn', are greatly drawn to prepositional theme constructions from M2 onwards (107).

(107) *informyd* **hym**$_{REC}$ of the gydynge of Kyng Harry$_{TH}$
informed him of the behav- of King Harry
'informed him of the behaviour of King Harry'
(CMGREGOR,215.2022; PPCME2: M4)

I argue that it is this dual association that has kept communication verbs from being ousted from the DOC, or rather, I assume that despite the availability of another alternative pattern (the PTC), this verb class remained in the DOC (and was thus also coerced into the dative alternation) due to its very close ties with the DOC, and its semantic overlap with prototypical transfer-verbs. It is furthermore relevant to note that verbs of communication are repelled by the PRC throughout the period – this is somewhat unexpected considering the common presence of PRC-communication patterns in Old English (cf. De Cuypere 2015c). One explanation for this might be that such verbs often occur with a clausal theme (108), instances of which were excluded from the present study.

(108) Y *seid* **to our Lord**$_{REC}$, þou art my God$_{TH}$
I said to our Lord , you are my God
'I said to our Lord: "You are my God"'
(CMEARLPS,169.7469; PPCME2: M2)

Several dispossession verbs such *binimen* are conspicuously distinctive for DOC use in early Middle English but develop a clear repulsion (or at least uncertain behaviour) towards this construction in course to the end of period. From M3 onwards, a number of them significantly more often choose prepositional patterns. This concerns both PRCs and PTCs; specifically, *robben* 'rob' is closely associated with prepositional theme patterns by late Middle English, while others (such as *take*) are mostly found in a PRC with *from* or *of*. These verb-specific preferences in the choice between PRC and PTC is still found in PDE. As a quick query in both the *BNCweb* and the *COCA* demonstrates, *rob* is almost categorically restricted to prepositional (*of*-) themes, whereas e.g. *steal* shows a nearly absolute preference for *from*-PRCs (109a-b).

(109) a. That war *robbed* **him**$_{REC}$ of the prime of his career$_{TH}$
(*BNCweb*; 1992; AHU 1126)

b. He'll have been *stealing* the food$_{TH}$ **from her**$_{REC}$
(*BNCweb*; 1975-1984; CJX 521)

Importantly, dispossession verbs thus seem to have lost their strong connection to the DOC within Middle English. Even though PTCs were not available or favoured by all of the privative verbs, I claim that the mere option of an additional pattern, and the semantic clash of this class with the more prototypical ditransitive verbs crucially impacted the history of the dative alternation.

A similar issue presents itself with malefactive verbs. As can be seen, verbs like *breken* 'break' or *blenden* 'blind', which express actions that have negative consequences for their recipient, are intimately connected with the Poss-construction from early on (110a), despite occasional DOC uses (110b). These verbs are generally strongly repelled by both the DOC and the PRC. It is therefore evident that the class must have been at the periphery of the DOC (and the alternation) in earliest Middle English already and that it was prone to being lost from these constructions.

(110) a.

Y	*shal*	*breken*	alle	þe	heuedes$_{TH}$	**of**	**sinȜers**$_{REC}$
I	shall	break	all	the	heads	of	sinners

'I shall break all the heads of the sinners'
(CMEARLPS,91.3970; PPCME2: M2)

b.

Ich	*habbe*	*ibroken*	**ham**$_{REC}$	þe	schuldren
I	have	broken	them	the	shoulders
and	te	schonken$_{TH}$			
and	the	legs			

'I have broken their shoulders and legs'
(CMJULIA,114.303; PPCME2: M1)

Further observations which can be made based on this analysis are as follows: Light verbs like *do*, *make*, *have*, *set*, *put* (as well as non-privative *take*) display an obvious bias towards PRCs and against the DOC. The same holds for verbs of reversed transfer. Verbs of reversed communicated transfer as well as verbs of pure benefaction/ benefactive creation, by contrast, do not significantly co-occur with any of the patterns involved in Middle English, or at least do not show any discernible trends.

4.2.5 Summary of results

Summing up the results of the corpus study of ditransitives in Middle English as presented in the preceding sections, there are several basic conclusions we can draw:

i. The prepositional variants (PRCs) increase in proportional frequency at the expense of the DOC in early Middle English. However, we do not expect the PRCs to completely overtake the DOC but hypothesise that both patterns persist.
ii. Additional alternatives such as the PTC and Poss are available and likewise increase in Middle English.
iii. Prepositional alternatives to the DOC include a wide range of prepositions, but specific PRC-types (particularly PRCs involving *to*) are more frequent than others. The earlier the texts, the greater the variability is.
iv. Both the types of prepositions involved, and the proportional distribution of PRCs in comparison to the DOC are highly dependent on verb classes: a) Verb classes are predicted to differ in the specific PRC-types they occur with; these differences become more pronounced over time, with the overall range of types being reduced, and the scope of individual prepositions becoming restricted. b) Verb class has a significant impact on choice of pattern in that with certain classes (most importantly transfer-related verbs), both patterns are retained, while with others (such as dispossession verbs or verbs of pure benefaction), DOC uses decrease in favour of PRC uses.
v. Corresponding to point (b) in (iv), the range of verb classes the DOC appears with is reduced over time.
vi. Object order becomes regularised within Middle English: I anticipate that in the earlier sub-periods, both Rec-Th and Th-Rec orders are attested with all patterns in a (roughly) equal distribution. For the DOC and PTC, we expect an increase of Rec-first orders over time; for PRCs, Th-first orders significantly increase during Middle English.
vii. Changes also take place in clause-level constituent order of ditransitive patterns. (S)VO increases at the expense of other orders with all patterns; this represents a system-wide change and no impact of clausal word order on the choice of construction is expected.
viii. There is an increase in ambiguity of case marking (dative vs. accusative) on both objects of the DOC over time.

ix. The changes investigated all take place within the specified timeframe – the timeframe covered by the corpus – although slight differences in precise progression of change are expected.
x. The changes observed are causally related in a complex, multi-directional way.

First, and most importantly, the establishment of the dative alternation mainly takes place within the period of Middle English; later changes are only minor adjustments. That is, in Middle English we see a significant rise of prepositional competitors. The main locus of change in this case appears to be the transition from M1 to M2. Very importantly, though, this increase of PRCs does not lead to an overall ousting of the DOC, but the trend is reserved towards the end of the period. By M4, a situation of roughly equal distribution has emerged. Even more remarkable is the fact that if we restrict the prepositional paraphrases to those including *to*, the DOC overtakes its alternative construction again after some time, which results in a stable distribution with the DOC as the strong variant and the to-PRC as the weaker variant of the alternation. This distribution remains relatively stable after Middle English and is still found in the dative alternation today. An investigation of the productivity of the two constructions has revealed that the DOC clearly decreases in both type frequency and potential productivity. The results on the PRC, however, are less clear: The hypothesised increase is visible to some extent but drawing more convincing conclusions are impeded by the research design. I take these findings to largely confirm hypotheses (i)-(iii) as introduced at the beginning of this chapter.

Partially corroborating hypotheses (iv) and (v) but also indicating the need for further refinement, the broader results can be broken down to the level of individual verbs and verb classes, which vary in their behaviour regarding their preferences for either one or the other construction (DOC vs. PRC as well as other alternatives). These verb classes essentially fall into three groups. On the one hand, there are verb classes such as transfer and transfer-related verbs, which more or less directly reflect the more general development just described – while in the beginning, the DOC is clearly more frequent, it decreases in proportional frequency at the expense of the PRC in the course of the period. In the end, however, the DOC gains in strength again, and the tokens are approximately equally distributed between the two constructions. On the other hand, verb classes such as dispossession verbs or verbs of malefaction show a very distinct behaviour. Despite the DOC similarly being the more frequent construction in the earliest period, and the PRC rising from M1–M2 onwards, the DOC does not recover. Instead, it concedes to the PRC, which is the only option available to the verbs by M4, i.e. becomes almost categorical. These uses are generally on the semantic periphery of the construction, which may have impacted their development. Furthermore, and importantly, the verb classes typically have an additional construction at their disposal. In the case of dispossession verbs, prepositional theme patterns are also frequent, and present a stable alternative. With malefactive verbs, genitive patterns in which the REC-argument is expressed as a possessive NP are predominant from the beginning of the period onwards, and their use in the dative alternation is certainly not the norm. It is not entirely unexpected that these verbs should be lost from the construction(s). Nevertheless, it should be noted that communication verbs, which can also be found in a third (prepositional theme) pattern, are not ousted from the DOC. This is likely due to their great semantic connection with transfer-verbs and the fact that they are highly frequent in the pattern in general.

While the developments of the second group thus evidence a reduction in the range of verb classes associated with the DOC (a narrowing of the construction's semantics), there is a further, third class which is markedly different from the former ones. With this group, the PRC is the preferred variant in all subperiods; furthermore, there is typically little to no change during the period. Among the verb classes included here are mental/attitudinal verbs as well as verbs of reversed transfer. Verb classes of the mixed type accordingly also only account for a relatively low fraction of DOC tokens. However, they always remain present in this construction.

Concerning the specific PRC-types involved, the three groups differ in behaviour as well: While the first two groups have or develop clear associations with individual prepositions (e.g. *to* in the case of transfer verbs, and *from* in the case of verbs of dispossession) during Middle English, the latter group is not systematic, but the verbs and verb classes select for various PRC-types without clear systematicity and development.

Apart from the establishment of the alternation as such and developments in the semantics of the constructions, other changes in the formal and functional features, namely word order and case marking, have been assessed as well. Regarding the development of object orders, and the establishment of canonical orders for DOC and PTC (REC-TH) as well as *(to)*-PRC (TH-REC), it can be noted that the constructions follow remarkably different pathways – while DOC and PTC develop as hypothesised in point (vi) at the outset of this chapter, object order in the PRC is not as straightforward. That is, in the DOC, tokens with the regular order greatly increase from M2 onwards, while those with the reverse order (which are significantly less frequent already in the beginning) decrease over time. In the PRC, by contrast, the now near-obligatory order (TH-REC) starts out at a higher level than in the case of the DOCs, but only slightly grows over the course of the period. Even less change, or in fact no change at all, is seen in the *to*-PRC. Here, the prevailing order is TH-REC in all periods. Last, the PTC most frequently exhibits REC-TH throughout the period and is almost invariant in late Middle English. The prepositional patterns accordingly both display a general and early bias for PP-late position, whereas the DOC is more flexible in the beginning. At the end of the 14th century, however, the DOC as well as the PTC are very rigid in their behaviour and thus stand in contrast to the PRC, which preserves some variability.

As to word order in the ditransitive clause, the data indicate that in correspondence to hypothesis (vii), there is a clear increase of (S)VOO orders during the period. This means that both concerning the order of the objects, and the order of clause constituents, the system is greatly regularised within Middle English. Nevertheless, and counter our expectations, the constructions again differ quite substantially in this context – first, they diverge with respect to the fraction of (S)VOO orders in the beginning of the period, with the figures being higher with the PRC and significantly lower with the DOC. Second, between M1 and M4 (S)VOO orders only slowly rise in the case of the PRC, whereas there is a greater increase with the *to*-PRC, and an even more rapid and sharp rise with the DOC. In M4, the fraction of (S)VOO in the total of PRCs is therefore slightly lower than in the two members of the dative alternation. What these findings again suggest is that the (*to*-)PRC is more fixed at first but alternative constituent orders are still available even at the latest stage. Word order in the DOC is less rigid in early Middle English still, but the fixation of the clause constituents to certain positions, as well as the fixation of the canonical order (REC-TH), proceeds rapidly from M2 onwards, until the standard orders are nearly categorical in M4.

Finally, the corpus investigation has shown that the reduction of case marking was highly advanced already by early Middle English already, essentially supporting hypothesis (viii) as outlined before. Ambiguity concerning the semantic roles in the case of ditransitives was accordingly likely resolved based on context and animacy asymmetries rather than morphological clues. This ambiguity furthermore increased within the period and inflection-less DOCs became more frequent.

As discussed above (3.3), the different changes investigated in the preceding sections have frequently been claimed to be correlated and also causally related in various ways. Evaluating possible connections between the different changes at play (see hypothesis [ix]), it is then clear that they correlate in that the rise of prepositional patterns, the semantic narrowing of the DOC and semantic extension of the PRC, the fixation of word order, and the loss of case marking all took place in Middle English (at least to a large extent). At the same time, there seem to have been slight differences in timing of the individual changes. Ambiguity of case marking was already very high at the beginning of the period, suggesting that the demise of the morphological case system was comparatively advanced at this point. The rise of prepositional alternatives and the establishment of the dative alternation, in contrast, is clearly a Middle English development, meaning that the main changes took place within this period. This holds true for the dative alternation proper, with the distribution of the *to*-PRC in relation to the DOC changing significantly throughout the period, until in late Middle English a stable state which persists to this day is reached. However, also in other cases such as the ousting of the DOC in favour of the PRC with verbs of dispossession or malefaction, the crucial changes occurred within Middle English. This change is strongly correlated with the semantic specialisation of the DOC: Those verb classes which show an increasing preference for prepositional patterns are the same that are progressively ousted from the DOC. Again, this change seems to take place mostly within the confines of the time span covered by the Middle English corpus. Finally, word order fixation is a quite complex phenomenon. In general, this change can be located at a slightly later point in time than the other developments. Although certain tendencies are clearly already seen at earlier stages, some variability persists in late Middle English, especially with the PRC.

The specific chain of events that the data suggest is as follows: First, case-marking is reduced; second, prepositions increase and extend to new contexts, and the dative alternation emerges. This is followed by the semantic specialisation of the DOC, which in turn precedes the decrease of word order flexibility. It is nevertheless evident that this proposal is simplified to a great extent. I furthermore do not take this correlation to always suggest a straightforward causal impact of one change on the following one(s). Instead, I argue for a co- evolutionary scenario, in which the various constructions and sub-constructions (most importantly the DOC and the *to*-PRC) gradually and continuously adapted to each other. A micro-change in one construction could then trigger a micro-change in the other, which would in turn cause the first construction to respond, and so on.

This proposal, and the broader implications of the results just presented, are discussed at length in chapter (7). Before doing so, however, the second framework this book works in is introduced, including also the results of a second method applied, namely Evolutionary Game Theory. The inclusion of an evolutionary linguistic perspective, and the application of innovative methodologies to problems in historical linguistics and language change, is one of the major assets of the book.

5 Evolutionary linguistics and Evolutionary Game Theory

This chapter introduces the second main framework this book is grounded in, which is evolutionary linguistics. It also presents the second methodological approach taken in the book, namely evolutionary game theory (Hofbauer and Sigmund 1998, 2003; Nowak 2006; Jäger 2008; Deo 2015, among others). The application of this method to specific issues in historical linguistics builds on the assumption that language is an evolutionary system and involves replicating units. These replicators, which in our case are constituted by constructions like the DOC or strategies like 'CASE', compete against variant constructions and strategies, e.g. the *to*-PRC or 'PP'. Their respective success is determined by a range of cognitive, social or systemic factors. While competition may lead to the ousting of a less successful variant, the replicators can also form alliances, and enter mutualistic relationships in which they cooperate and benefit from each other's expression. In the specific evolutionary game presented in this chapter, I aim to investigate whether such a mixed strategy or construction cooperation plausibly emerged in the history of English recipient marking. That is, I investigate whether under universal pragmatic constraints such as the focus-last principle (focus elements like discourse-new, non-topical recipients typically being placed late in the clause), changes in the system-internal constraints of a language (e.g. case loss or increasing word order rigidity) can trigger the establishment of constructional/strategic mutualism.

The main reason for taking an evolutionary perspective in this book is that it provides us with a good explanatory basis for addressing questions concerning language change in general as well as particular changes in the history of a language. Applying an evolutionary approach means taking a more analytic instead of hermeneutic approach and allows us to investigate possible motivations for historical changes in a principled and more enlightening way. This chapter thus lays the ground for a discussion of the diachronicity of the dative alternation from an evolutionary constructionist point of view, presented in chapter (7).

The chapter is structured as follows: First, I outline the framework of evolutionary linguistics in some more detail (5.1). Starting with a brief introduction to the field and its history (5.1.1), I then comment on the main implications of viewing language as a cultural evolutionary system, and language change as reflecting natural selection of linguistic replicators (5.1.2). This includes thoughts on the precise nature of linguistic replicators and their material basis,

https://doi.org/10.1515/9783110633856-005

the specifics of the replicating mechanism, as well as an overview of (the emergence of) variation, competition and selection in language. All of these issues are to some extent debated; therefore, the chapter takes care to spell out the specific assumptions this book follows.

5.1 Evolutionary linguistics

5.1.1 Introduction and history of the field

Most basically, evolutionary linguistics, as the term already suggests, aims to investigate correspondences between evolution in the biological world and language. Although seemingly a rather recent field, the idea of a relationship or at least a similarity between biological and cultural/linguistic systems has been around for quite some time already. Specifically, it can be traced to the 19th century, when evolutionary biology emerged as a theory of life – above all with Darwin's highly influential publication *On the origin of species* (1859) – and modern (historical) linguistics as an academic discipline was established (cf. Rosenbach 2008: 24–25; Croft 2013a: 1). A clear example of analogies being drawn between biological and linguistic evolution can be found in Schleicher's (1863) discussion of 'family trees' of languages, which highlights similarities between languages and organisms, and between linguistic diversification and biological speciation. Representing language families as branching trees, that is, grouping languages together based on shared, common inherited features, is still very much standard practice in historical linguistics. However, these early endeavours to integrate linguistics and evolutionary theory were largely misleading and rather problematic (for a more detailed analysis, see e.g. Lass 1990; McMahon 1994; Ritt 1995, 2004). For this and other reasons, evolutionary approaches did not play a major role in the development of linguistics in much of the past century. Quite on the contrary, evolution, as McMahon (1994: 314) claims, "ha[d] become a 'dirty word' in modern linguistic theory".

Things appear to have turned within the last decades, though, with evolutionary models being more frequently applied both in the social sciences in general, and in linguistics in particular (Croft 2006b: 91). Interest in the idea of connecting evolutionary (biological) theory and linguistics as well as other disciplines has increased considerably since the 1980s. Ritt (2004: 57) identifies two main causes behind this development: First, writings by evolutionary biologists such as Richard Dawkins (1989[2006], 1982, 1986, and others) or Stephen J. Gould (e.g. 1983, 1989) have made evolutionary theory accessible to a larger audience. Second, and possibly resulting from this, the 'argumentative core' of evolutionary biology came to be transferred to a range of different areas such as philosophy, mathematics, medicine, economy, sociology, history of science, as well as cognitive science (Ritt 2004: 57). In many works going in that direction, explicit attempts to extend evolutionary ideas beyond the domain of biology and especially to language can be found; see, for example, Cavalli-Sforza and Feldman's (1973) or Lumsden and Wilson's (1981) discussion of the role of cultural evolution besides biological evolution.[121] Further crucial developments within the last thirty years include the establishment of research programs into complexity and complex adaptive systems such as the Santa Fe Institute (http://www.santafe.edu/), founded in the 1980s. There, researchers like Gell-Mann continue to investigate the fundamental principles of evolutionary systems of all kinds and on all levels (e.g. Hawkins and Gell-Mann 1992). This includes molecular systems, tissues, animal and human individuals, and systems of technology as well as economy and culture (Santa Fe Institute 2015). Some ten years after the foundation of the Santa Fe Institute, in 1996, the *Evolution of language conference* (EVOLANG) was brought to life, a very influential and inter-disciplinary biennial meeting which brings together a large number of researchers working on aspects of evolutionary theory in connection to language. The same year also saw the first publication of the *Journal of Memetics*, an important research outlet for evolutionary accounts of cultural information transfer for some time (also Ritt 1995, 2004).[122] More recently, evolutionary approaches have gained more widespread interest and are frequently found at mainstream linguistic conferences and other research outlets; this is also visible in the 2016 introduction of a new journal specifically geared towards evolutionary linguistic issues (*Journal of Language Evolution*, OUP).

The research area of evolutionary linguistics is highly diverse and subsumes a range of sub-disciplines. These are tied together by a shared interest in language and evolution, but are typically concerned with different ontological domains as well as different timescales, levels of analysis, and accordingly methods and tools (cf. Ritt 2013a; also Deacon 1997; Christiansen and Chater 2008; Kirby 2012). There are three key fields of investigation in evolutionary linguistics. First, and very prominently so, the origin of language itself, i.e. the

---

121 See also Hull (1988); Dawkins (1989[2006]); Dennett (1990, 1993, 1995); Plotkin (1994); Cziko (1995).

122 Hurford (2012b: 473) adds another reason for the growing popularity of research into the evolution of language, namely the "impressive empirical advances in relevant fields such as genetics, psychology of language, ethology (especially primatology), computer modelling, linguistics (especially language typology and some formal modelling) and neuroscience" that were made within the last decades.

evolution of the human linguistic capacity or language faculty, has been subject to discussion (cf. e.g. Pinker and Bloom 1990; Hauser, Chomsky and Fitch 2002; Jackendoff and Pinker 2005; Hurford 2007, 2012a, 2012b, 2014; Fitch 2010; McMahon and McMahon 2013, among many others).[123] A second way in which evolutionary ideas have been introduced to language concerns the diversification of language and the descent and spread of specific language families, issues which have recently begun to be approached with phylogenetic methods. These methods, as Dunn (2014: 190) points out, allow us "to test hypotheses about human dispersals, processes of cultural change, and the evolution of other linguistic subsystems" (see also Croft 2000: Ch.8).[124] While these two areas of evolutionary linguistics are not of immediate relevance to the present investigation, the third domain, namely historical language change or cultural evolution, clearly is. This subject evidently differs markedly especially from the first one, since the modifications observed in the history of individual languages occur within a comparatively short time span, and were therefore most certainly not caused by genetic, biological, changes (Rosenbach 2008: 23; also McMahon 2000: 154; Ritt 2004: 26).

Within the field of historical language change approached from an evolutionary viewpoint, we again see two major strands: On the one hand, there have been attempts to transfer concepts from evolutionary biology to linguistics, acknowledging certain parallels between the evolving systems, yet treating these correspondences as little more than superficial analogies or metaphors (cf. Croft 2013a: 2; Kaźmierski 2015: 67–68). Examples of such metaphorical approaches include Blevins (2004), but also Lass (1980) and Mufwene (2001, 2008). Considering that there are considerable risks and problems involved in employing the 'biological metaphor' in this way, it is questionable whether there is any real use in doing so. A strictly Darwinian, generalised evolutionary approach to language change, by contrast, is of greater explanatory value, and therefore certainly desirable. What such an approach entails is discussed in more detail in the sections following this one.

The enterprise of expanding ideas of evolutionary (biological) theory to other domains, including cultural systems, was taken up more rigourously from the late 1980s onwards. Influential researchers in this context include Dawkins

123 For further references see e.g. relevant contributions in *The Oxford handbook of language evolution* (Tallerman and Gibson 2012).

124 Examples of such approaches are e.g. Dixon (1997), Nettle (1999), Atkinson and Gray (2005), as well as publications by Dunn (e.g. 2014), and others. For a short introduction to the issue, see Croft (2008: 224–230).

(1989[2006]) and Hull (1988), as well as Dennett (1993, 1995, 1999), Plotkin (1994) and Cziko (1995). These and ensuing approaches, now typically subsumed under the cover-term of 'Generalised Darwinism' or 'Universal Darwinism', more specifically suggest that language is not subject to mechanisms of biological evolution. Instead, language systems, biological systems and many others, constitute manifestations of a more general, domain-unspecific phenomenon (Lass 1990: 96; Ritt 2004: Ch.5; Rosenbach 2008: 25; Croft 2013a: 3; among others).[125] In order for systems to be capable of evolution, or to qualify as evolutionary systems, the following crucial properties have to be present:

> there must be 'replicators', items 'heritable' in some medium (biological, cultural, whatever); variation, i.e. imperfect replication, must be possible; and there must be a selection process (what particular kind is unimportant) that biases survival in favour of some particular variant(s). (Lass 1997: 316)[126]

Although biological evolution is the most extensively studied and probably best understood example of a replicator system, it is therefore thought to be only one instance of evolutionary processes next to many others, including also e.g. vertebrate immune systems, economies, and human cognition. What follows from this is furthermore that the details of genetic, biological evolution might not be met by each and every evolutionary system; rather, we are concerned with those features that are shared by all of them (Cziko 2000: 287).[127]

In order to avoid the bias towards biological evolution inherent in labels such as 'Generalised Darwinism', evolutionary systems are now frequently approached in terms of complex adaptive systems theory, commonly abbreviated as CAS (e.g. Hawkins and Gell-Mann 1992; Gell-Mann 1994; Lansing 2003; Solé et al. 2010; and any publications from researchers associated with the Santa Fe Institute). Most basically, complex adaptive systems are self-organising, and control is not concentrated in one point, but is distributed through the systems. The properties of CAS emerge through multiple and complex interactions be-

125 A historical overview of literature on the correspondences between linguistic and biological evolution (among others), can be found in Atkinson and Gray (2005).

126 See also Dennett (1995: 343); Cziko (2000: 287); Ritt (2004: 91).

127 It is precisely due to this argument that commonly discussed issues such as what corresponds to the biological phenotype, organism or species, etc. in language do not get too much attention in this book. Although this debate has certainly been fruitful in some regards and has led to more refined ideas about how language and language change can be approached from an evolutionary perspective, I believe it may also at times have caused people to digress from other, equally or possibly more relevant questions. See also McCrohon's (2012: 158–161) discussion of the relevance of the 'phenotype' concept to language.

tween constituents (cf. Ritt 2004: 99–109; Frank and Gontier 2010: 37–39; Beckner et al. 2009: 15). Even though only some evolutionary accounts of language and language change explicitly adopt a CAS approach (see e.g. Beckner et al. 2009; Steels 2000, 2011b; Frank and Gontier 2010), the framework is easily compatible with most Generalised Darwinism accounts as well (Ritt 2004; Rosenbach 2008). In the present book, no difference is therefore made between the two approaches, but language is taken to represent an evolutionary, Darwinian, complex adaptive system. In the next sections, the main characteristics of language as such a system are presented. Focussing first on general properties of language as an evolutionary system, I then point out some of the main areas of debate that arise in this context and specify which positions this book takes.

5.1.2 Language as a cultural evolutionary system

Among the linguists that have in some way or the other discussed an evolutionary approach to language and language change are Lass (e.g. 1980), McMahon (1994), Rosenbach (2008), Beckner et al. (2009), McCrohon (2012), Petré (2014), as well as the research group around Luc Steels working in Fluid Construction Grammar (cf. e.g. Steels 2011a; van Trijp 2013; Wellens et al. 2013).[128] Researchers such as Smith (e.g. Smith et al. 2017) and Kirby (e.g. Kirby et al. 2015; Kirby 2017) have greatly contributed to the spread of evolutionary linguistics in the community, above all concerning iterated learning experiments. The following discussion is based mainly on Croft (2000, 2013a) and Ritt (2004), who to date provide two of the most extensive treatments of what it means to take an evolutionary approach to language change.[129] While the former is basically an elaborated application of Hull's (1988) *Generalised analysis of selection* (GAS) model to linguistic evolution, the latter builds on Dawkins' (1989[2006]) concepts of cultural replicators. As is shown, the accounts differ quite substantially in regard to many fundamental issues, including the question which ontological domain linguistic constituents should be ascribed to (Ritt 2013a). Before diving

128 See further Lass (1990, 1996, 1997, 2000, 2003), Keller (1990[1994]), Ritt (1995, 1996), Haspelmath (1999), Croft (2000, 2006a, 2006b, 2008, 2010); also Seiler (2006), Wedel (2006), Frank and Gontier (2010) and other contributions in Winters, Tissari, and Allan (2010), and van de Velde (2014). Note that this list is of course by no means exhaustive and represents a relatively subjective selection.

129 Croft (2013a) is in fact the revised version of the second chapter of Croft (2000), available as a draft online from http://www.unm.edu/~wcroft/Papers/ELC2-Chap02.pdf, and due to be published as part of the second edition of Croft (2000) by the Oxford University Press.

into these issues, however, a quick assessment of whether language fulfils the basic requirements of evolutionary systems in the first place is given.

5.1.2.1 General features of language as an evolutionary system

The crucial conditions necessary for systems to qualify as 'evolutionary' are that they exhibit the following features:

1) variation: there is continuing abundance of different elements
2) heredity or replication: the elements have the capacity to create copies or replicas of themselves
3) differential 'fitness': the number of copies of an element that are created in a given time varies, depending on interactions between the features of that element and features of the environment in which it persists. (Dennett 1995: 343)

In a nutshell, the central ingredient of any theory of evolution, including biological change, but not restricted to it, is therefore the process of replication. By this process, an element is copied, or rather produces an as close as possible copy of itself. Since replication does not occur once, but is iterative and cumulative, lineages of replicators are established. Change then takes place in two steps: (i) variation is constantly generated by mutation, or 'altered replication'. That is, variation presupposes replication. (ii) Variants are selected for via particular mechanisms, meaning that natural selection causes 'differential fitness' and 'differential replication' of variants. Those variants (replicators) that are more adaptive in view of certain environmental constraints or pressures will be more successful in replication, and thus possibly oust competing variants (Ritt 1995: 54; Croft 2000: 23, 2006b: 94, 2008: 221; Rosenbach 2008: 26).

Approaching language from this perspective, it quite obviously seems to fulfil the necessary conditions for an evolutionary system. Language is passed on, i.e. transmitted, from generation to generation in child language acquisition (a position that is typically held by generativists, e.g. Lightfoot 1999). In addition, however, language constituents also get transmitted through imitation in communication, that is, in language use among adult speakers (cf. e.g. Croft 2000; Ritt 2004; Rosenbach 2008).[130] By being transmitted, linguistic replicators

130 Rosenbach (2008: 51) points out that is in this regard also "interesting to see how the old controversy between formal and functional approaches to language change on the question of where to assume the locus of change [...] may become more 'relaxed' when taking an evolutionary approach to language (and change) [...] all [such approaches] acknowledge change

form lineages (Croft 2013a: 5). Every time an instantiation of a DOC is used (e.g. a person uttering the request of *can you pass me the salt* at the dinner table), this precise construction is transmitted, and thereby establishes a lineage.

Furthermore, variation is abundant in language, manifest on three different levels: First-order variation, according to Croft (2006b: 98, 2012: 4–5), concerns intra-systemic variation. For example, individual phonemes can have different phonetic realisations in actual language use, and different words or constructions can express the same meaning (without any social values attached to them). Second-order variation, in contrast, is socially-significant variation. Typically, this is dealt with in sociolinguistic research, which investigates social values of specific variants, e.g. formal vs. informal pronunciations of a sound. Last, there is third-order, or cross-linguistic variation. This type of variation is a result of variation within a community of speakers together with the divergence of languages over an extended period of time (Croft 2012: 4).

This book is clearly concerned mainly with first-order, intra-systemic, variation, since it investigates different constructions which are 'two ways of saying the same thing' (Labov 1972: 271). More specifically, the main and fundamental focus of this book is on the functionally near-equivalent members of the dative alternation, the double object construction and the *to*-PRC, in Middle English. The two constructions therefore constitute replicator variants of each other. Other instances of variation that this book is concerned with include the availability of more than one case frame for the DOC in Old English as seen above: These case constructions, e.g. [DAT-ACC], [ACC-ACC] or [DAT-GEN] fulfil a very similar function and are accordingly variants. Furthermore, the fact that verb classes occur with a range of different but (near-)synonymous prepositional paraphrases counts as variation in the system. For example, the *from*-PRC and *of*-PRC found with verbs of dispossession (*John stole a book from Mary/ John stole a book of Mary*) qualify as variants of each other. Second- and third-order variation, in contrast, are only dealt with in passing here – see e.g. the social dimension involved in the retention of pronominal [TH-REC] DOCs in certain regional dialects of British English, or the differences between Modern German and Present Day English regarding the semantic scope of the DOC.

Crucially, variants do not just exist, but compete against each other for territory, which equals 'being expressed' or more generally 'being activated' (Ritt 1995: 54; Mesoudi, Whiten, and Laland 2004: 4; Croft 2012: 6; also Hilpert 2013: 3). What this really means is that constituents that exist through being transmit-

---

taking place within adult speakers in language usage as well as in the process of first language acquisition".

ted/replicated are critically dependent on the frequency with which they are instantiated. For them to count as existent or stable, this frequency needs to be above zero. It also implies that they need to be transmitted at least once before disappearing. In competition, what variant types then really compete for is the relative frequency of their instantiations among all instantiations of the superordinate type. Although it might be interesting to measure that frequency on the competence level, this is unfortunately not possible. What we therefore do instead is measure the relative frequency of textual attestations and either assume that it reflects representation on the competence level or remain agnostic about this issue and describe evolution on the textual level. This book, in taking a usage-based perspective on language use and representation, clearly opts for the former approach. The important thing here is that every constituent is at any time instantiated as a population of copies (tokens) – what changes in time is the size of the population. In the case of emergence, this size moves from zero to above zero, while in the case of loss, it changes from >0 to zero.

Drawing again on the example of the DOC and *to*-PRC, the emergence of the latter in the history of English means that its population size grows above zero. The loss of the DOC with some verb classes, by contrast, means that the size of the DOC (dispossession) population falls to zero. Being variants of each other, the population size of one construction fundamentally depends on that of the other: The DOC and the *to*-PRC compete against each other for relative frequency of instantiation (among all instantiations of the superordinate type, i.e. among all instantiations of ditransitive constructions). Ways to establish or measure the relative frequency of the respective constructions, and to thereby also find out about ways of competition resolution, are to investigate their frequency in text corpora. This is precisely what has been done in chapter (4) above.

Once variation and, consequently, competition in the system has been produced, the variants are subjected to selection; the differential replication of the variants is caused by various selectional ('environmental') pressures (Rosenbach 2008: 32). The fitness or success of the individual variant is dependent on or regulated by these factors: They may bias replication in favour of one competitor over the other. If this is the case, a variant may be lost entirely, while the more successful and thus more frequent one thrives. This development can e.g. be observed in the ousting of the DOC in favour of PRCs in the case of dispossession verbs (**John stole Mary a book* vs. *John stole a book from Mary*), as just mentioned. A further case in point is the move towards a single case construction of [DAT-ACC] at the expense of other constructions, or the loss of the dispossessive *of*-PRC compared to the success of the dispossessive *from*-PRC (**John stole a book of Mary* vs. *John stole a book from Mary*).

This book adds another layer to the question of linguistic competition by assuming that antagonistic competition cannot only result in the ousting of one variant. Instead, the possibility of competition leading to mutually beneficial relationships, which has been implied in various places in the literature is sketched out and applied to the English dative alternation (Ritt 2004: 221–229; Petré 2014: 19; among others). I propose that linguistic alternations – in the sense of highly systematic correspondences between functionally near-identical patterns – generally represent instances of constructional cooperations.

In sum, the necessary conditions for language to qualify as an evolutionary system are clearly given, and an evolutionary approach to language and language change therefore appears to be more than justified. It is nevertheless evident on closer investigation that such an approach raises of number of essential questions, which are neither easy to answer nor agreed upon in the literature. Apart from the question of what ontological domain linguistic replicators are attributed to, or which units we assume as replicators in language, the most striking, and most debated problems that have come up in previous research are the following (cf. also Ritt 2004: Ch.6; Rosenbach 2008: 27).

- What is the material basis of the replicators?
- What precisely are the mechanisms of linguistic replication?
- What precisely is the role of the speaker in this scenario?
- How does variation arise?
- How does selection proceed? What factors determine replicative success?

A discussion of these key issues, as well as the ways this book deals with them are presented in the next sections.

5.1.2.2 Linguistic replicators and the replication process

The first of the questions mentioned in the previous section, namely what entities can be identified as linguistic replicators, is – although very basic – arguably also the most important one in approaching language from an evolutionary perspective. This is because it crucially determines whether an 'integrated evolutionary model of language and language change' is possible (Ritt 2004: 122). One of the first (and possibly most influential) contributions to this issue is Dawkins' monograph on 'selfish genes', in which the author famously coins the name of 'memes' for cultural replicators, an analogical formation to the biological 'gene' (1989[2006]: 192). These lineage-forming units of cultural transmission, as Dawkins specifies, necessarily exhibit the same general features as biological, and any other replicating entity: longevity, fecundity, and copying fidelity (1989[2006]: 194; further Ritt 2004: 123; Croft 2013a: 8). However, Dawkins' original (1976) conception of memes is rather vague.[131] Instead of a rigorous definition, he offers a list of potential candidates for memes, such as "tunes, ideas, catch-phrases, clothes fashions, ways of making pots or of building arches" (Dawkins 1989[2006]: 192), as well as "[p]opular songs and stiletto heels [...] Jewish religious laws" (Dawkins 1989[2006]: 194). Similarly, Dennett (1991: 201) argues that memes are "the smallest units that replicate themselves with reliability and fecundity", providing examples like wheels, wearing clothes, or calculus. The inherent ambiguity of such (quasi-)definitions lies in the fact that they comprise replicators of different ontological domains. That is, they involve *concepts*, i.e. mental, internal knowledge, such as 'ideas' or 'laws', *artifacts* (heels, wheels), as well as *behaviours* like building an arch or wearing clothes. The latter two constitute different types of physical, external manifestations of replicators (cf. McCrohon 2012: 153; Croft 2013a: 9).[132] On the other side, elements of culture are typically not restricted to one such domain – compare language, which is both a behaviour in that it is spoken, and an artifact (acoustic signals, written texts, etc.). However, it also involves concepts in some way or the other, as speakers can be presumed to have some abstract linguistic knowledge in their minds. Therefore, theories of cultural evolution building on Dawkins' suggestions have diverged quite substantially on this issue (Croft 2013a: 9–10). Basically, there are three strands of approaches to cultural replicators in general, and linguistic replicators in particular:

First, Dawkins himself in a later publication clarifies that memes should be considered as "unit[s] of information residing in a brain" (1982: 109).[133] Accordingly, replicators would be competence constituents (Ritt 2004: 157). Similar

131 Admittedly, providing a clear definition of memes, upon which a theory of cultural evolution could be built, was not the primary aim of Dawkins. They were rather used "to illustrate the replicator centric theory of biological evolution he was arguing for at the time" (McCrohon 2012: 153; referring to Dawkins 1999: xvi).

132 The ambiguity of Dawkins' initial definition, and the diverging (and often incompatible) theories of memetic/cultural evolution resulting from it, have incidentally also led to a drop in popularity of the field of *memetics*, inspired by Dawkins' writings (McCrohon 2012: 52; Kaźmierski 2015: 64). Generalised Darwinian accounts of cultural change, avoiding an explicit association with memetics, are gaining in acceptance. While I believe that there is still high value in the early as well as later memeticist accounts, I will similarly refrain from using this particular label, since I feel that the terminology of generalised and CAS accounts is more encompassing, and less culture-centric.

133 Dawkins here draws a comparison of memes to Cloak's (1975) i-culture instructions (cf. also McCrohon 2012).

views are presented in e.g. Blackmore (1999, 2000) and Aunger (2002), typically associating themselves with the framework of memetics. Arguments for linguistic replicators as "neuronally implemented instructions" (Ritt 2013a) rather than 'external' products include the fact that (knowledge of) abstract (or structural) linguistic patterns such as constructions or syntactic categories, as well as meaning itself, appear to be represented in speakers' minds. This means that these properties must have been and can be transmitted even though they do not have an articulatory expression (Ritt 2004: 153–157, 197, n39; Rosenbach 2008: 49). Furthermore, as McCrohon (2012: 154) asserts, brain-internal replicators are able to exert a direct impact on their hosts' behaviours and can therefore be seen as more active.

On this account, the specific units of linguistic replication correspond to the commonly agreed upon building blocks of linguistic structure, both formal and functional, meaning phonemes, morphemes, syntactic patterns as well as semantic concepts. Furthermore, combinations of these (clusters of phonemes, 'constructions' in the sense of form-meaning pairs, etc.) might function as replicator associations, also called 'memeplexes' (Ritt 2004: 132, 134; Rosenbach 2008: 52). The physical manifestations of these replicators in the environment – artifacts and behaviours – are treated as merely the effects, or products of the mental replicators (also Croft 2013a: 10). Languages are accordingly populations of competence constituents, and thus constitute replicator/complex adaptive systems.

As regards the concrete physical substrate of cognitive memes/ replicators, Dawkins (1999: xiii) does not commit himself to anything, but states that "[m]emes have not yet found their Watson and Crick; they even lack their Mendel" (Lass 1996: 5). Ritt (2004: 122, n1, 157–169) agrees that current neurolinguistics (or neurophysiological) research is not yet empirically and theoretically sufficiently advanced in order to be able to corroborate any assumptions in this respect, and that any account will therefore have to remain speculative to a certain degree for the time being.[134] Nevertheless, he fervently supports the as-

134 As Blackmore (1999: 54) rightly asserts, methodological or technical limitations in physically identifying replicators have not prevented biologists such as Darwin from hypothesising about them: "[the] intrinsic uncertainty about just what to count as a gene has not impeded progress in genetics and biology. It has not made people say, 'We cannot decide what the unti of the gene is so let's abandon genetics, biology and evolution'" (also Ritt 2004: 122, n1). It is, however, plausible that progress in theoretical and empirical neurolinguistics research will provide a sounder basis for ideas about the physical implementation of replicators in the not-too-distant future; Rosenbach (2008: 53), for example, refers to Pulvermüller (2002) "for a first step towards a neurobiologically realistic model of language".

sumption of replicators as real entities in the mind (Ritt 2004: 157). Presenting an elaborate sketch of how these cognitive units might be materially instantiated, the author finally proposes that a replicator might conceivably constitute a cluster of nodes within a network that consists of neutrally implemented constituents. This assembly of nodes is taken to have a distinct internal structure as well as a definite position in the network (Ritt 2004: 169). Language use is then the activation of these neural structures under specific circumstances (Rosenbach 2008: 50). By defining linguistic replicators as neuronal, associative activation patterns, Ritt (2004: 161, 169, n27) also links his account to Donald Hebb's (1949) cell assembly theory, as well as contemporary connectionist models to cognition and learning which build on this view, without, however, restricting himself to one particular connectionist approach (see also Rosenbach 2008: 53, n36, n37, and the references mentioned there). Despite the uncertainty thus surrounding the material basis of memes, it is generally contended that neuronal processes are involved in cultural replication (Hull 2001: 58). This is (evidently) also acknowledged by advocates of 'brain-external' replicators.

A connected, yet slightly different issue is posed by the question of discreteness versus gradience of linguistic replicators (or rather, of linguistic competence in general). While e.g. Ritt (2004: 159, 196–204), following Dawkins, argues for replication to be digital, involving non-gradient, categorical entities, Wedel (2006: 249), who takes an exemplar model to language, claims that "reproductive 'units' have no discernable boundaries" and that we are rather dealing with a continuum from non- to fully discrete (also Rosenbach 2008: 49–51). The question of discreteness is taken up in more detail in section (6.2).

The assumption of brain-external replicators, which indicates an almost diametrically opposed approach to the memetic, replicators as cognitive units-view, is followed by a number of researchers most prominently including Croft (e.g. 2013a; further Baxter et al. 2006, 2009; Blythe and Croft 2009, 2012), following Hull (1988, 2001), among others. Here, the focus is on the empirically observable behaviours and/or artifacts, i.e. on the acoustic or written manifestations of linguistic constituents. The replicating entities involved in language are termed 'linguemes' (Croft 2000: 28).[135] These linguemes have linguistic structure, and make up an utterance, that is to say, "a particular, actual occurrence of the product of human behaviour in communicative interaction (i.e. a string of sounds), as it is pronounced, grammatically structured, and semantically and pragmatically interpreted in its context" (Croft 2013a: 34, 36). An utterance is thus defined as a spatiotemporally bounded and observable entity, whereas a

135 Croft (2013a: 36) states that the creation of this term is attributed to Martin Haspelmath.

language is a population of linguemes, and consequently of utterances (Croft 2013a: 35).

Such a brain-external account has the clear advantage of dealing with more easily observable constituents. As argued by Ritt (2004: 158–159), however, its main and fundamental disadvantage – which also casts doubt on its more empirical foundation – is that due to the great variability of actual utterances it is difficult to see how they should be identified as copies of each other. In a similar vein, Mufwene (2002: 47) criticises that what speakers acquire is not in fact the ability to reproduce the utterances of others. Rather, they acquire 'instructions' for how to produce such utterances. The essential problem that opponents of Croft's approach thus take issue with is his failure to clarify where utterances 'get their structure from', although he repeatedly makes mention of structure being passed on in the lingueme replication process (Croft 2013a: 13–14, 37; among others).[136] Croft himself recognises the problem, and in the revised version of his (2000) work concurs that the question of how meaning, which constitutes the conceptual, internal part of a linguistic symbol can be integrated into his definition of linguistic replicators, cannot be answered at this point (2013a: 19). A further challenge for Croft's external replicator-account is the emergence of variation: If changes to linguistic constituents occur in the perception or production processes, they arguably affect or are caused by mind-/body-internal processes rather than external ones. For example, sound waves or written utterances typically do not change once produced (apart from fading). What is subject to change is instead the cognitive representations. This is also predicted by usage-based constructionist accounts, even if usage is an essential factor in language change in such approaches.

In sum, the Dawkinsian/Rittian assumptions about the units of replication might suffer from a certain vagueness, or rather, still await empirical confirmation. Nevertheless, they are better warranted than the lingueme-account proposed by Croft. Therefore, the present book follows the former in assuming replicators to constitute cognitive representations, and more precisely, constructions as mental form-meaning pairings. The external effects of such cognitive replicators are incorporated via McCrohon's (2012) i-/e-meme model as presented below.

Regarding the mechanism of replication, or the means by which linguistic constituents self-replicate and produce copies of themselves, this is typically taken to be *imitation* (cf. Dawkins 1989[2006]: 192; Blackmore 2000: 66; Ritt

136 See also e.g. Hull (1988: 409): "In order to function as a replicator, an entity must have structure".

2004: 196). How this process of imitation is supposed to work specifically is, however, usually not discussed in greater length. Ritt (2004: 160–169), as well as Lass (2003: 59), argue that imitation is ultimately a neuronal mechanism, in that certain synaptic connections are strengthened by activation or perception. This presumption, which logically follows from the Dawkinsian definition of replicators as neuronal units is very plausible. Still, it has the same drawback of remaining rather speculative at this point: As Rosenbach (2008: 54) points out, "[i]n general, evolutionary approaches to language change (as to cultural change in general) still face the problem of relating linguistic replication to more specific cognitive mechanisms or even a physical (i.e. neurophysiological) basis". A promising, but not yet fully explored possibility to account for cultural replication is the so-called 'mirror system hypothesis' by Michael Arbib and colleagues (Arbib 2012: 207). Furthermore, 'priming' has been proposed as a driving mechanism behind replication (Rosenbach 2008: 56; see further Jäger 2007; Jäger and Rosenbach 2008).

Apart from the issue of what imitiation actually boils down to, a shortcoming that both the memetic and the 'lingueme' approaches ultimately have in common, although arriving at it from opposite directions, is a problem of linkage (Kirby 1999: 20). Both accounts need to assume indirect replication of some sort. They neglect to clarify how the fact that replication necessarily occurs in actual language use can be united with the fact that it at the same time evidently involves structure and mental representation (also Lass 1996: 7; Hull 2001: 58–61; Croft 2013a: 10). This issue is captured nicely in Ritt's programmatic question-headline 'How can one copy what one cannot see?' (2004: 196). Very simply put, in order for an internal replicator to get transmitted, it needs to be physically realised in the environment in some way (e.g. via sound waves). This will in turn activate the cognitive unit the external manifestation corresponds to in another brain. Vice versa, if we assume the replicator to be external, it is dependent on some mental representation being activated to be replicated again (McCrohon 2012: 159). It is worth noting that in Ritt (2004), the issue of indirect replication is not as prominent as in other accounts, since the author never denies the relevance of external manifestations for the replication process. Quite on the contrary, the cognitive replicators crucially depend on being 'activated', meaning on being expressed or perceived.

A rather elegant and, I believe, plausible solution to the linkage problem is put forward in McCrohon (2012), who follows the path of Dennett (1991, 1995), Durham (1991), and Blackmore (1999) in considering replicators to be combinations of brain-internal and brain-external entities. Assuming an intermediary position between the 'replicators as concepts' and 'replicators as utterances' approaches, or rather, combining the two alternatives, McCrohon proposes a two-stage model of cultural replication. In this model, which is illustrated in Fig. 31, replicators appear in different forms (or stages): They are either stored in the brain – in which state they are called 'i-meme' – or appear in the external environment as e-memes (McCrohon 2012: 162).[137]

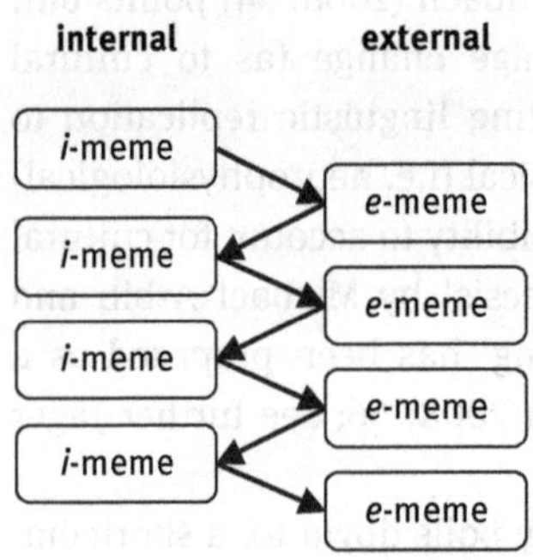

Fig. 31: Cultural replicator heredity (adapted from McCrohon 2012: 159)

Both internal and external replicator-manifestations are incapable of direct self-replication, but depend on intervening, or mediating instances of the opposite stage (McCrohon 2012: 158–161).[138] Replication is furthermore incremental and iterative, meaning that both i-memes and e-memes can potentially produce a multitude of copies of each other. While i-memes can create and therefore trigger the expression of e-memes, the latter act as models for the learning, recalling and (re-) activation of i-memes (McCrohon 2012: 161–169). As McCrohon (2012: 170) points out, a clear advantage of this two-stage model then is that it,

> by not committing a priori to a brain-internal or brain-external perspective, allows either to be adopted interchangeably as is necessary to explain the phenomena under consideration. This adds considerable flexibility to the model and allows a wider variety of explanations than was possible working under earlier definitions.

Furthermore, by clearly differentiating the two phases, the model allows us to analyse mechanisms of selection and variation on both levels separately, which

---

137 The labels 'i-meme' and 'e-meme' are evidently reminiscent of Chomsky's (1986) as well as Cloak's (1975) terminology; however, the author explicitly denies any deeper meaning behind this choice (McCrohon 2012: 158).

138 Compare Blackmore's (1999: 66) description of memetic evolution as a "zigzag" process.

might lead to a better understanding of how they really work. However, variation is arguably more difficult to emerge in external replicators. Hence, even though this book supports a two-stage cycle model of replication in linguistic evolution, the level of cognitive representations is still clearly emphasised, and will receive most attention.

Note that a further (final) difference between Ritt's and Croft's approach concerns the role of the speaker in linguistic replication (e.g. Rosenbach 2008: 49–50, n33). Ritt (2004), as already alluded to in the title of his book *Selfish sounds and linguistic evolution*, again adopts and extends Dawkins' (1976) notion of 'selfish genes' in this context. He and other memeticists follow Dawkins' idea that memes actively replicate. This proposed inherently active nature of replicators should, however, not be taken to imply that they constitute rational agents in any way. Rather, they proceed "stupidly and mechanically", as Ritt clarifies (1996: 36). By contrast, the organism's (i.e. the speaker's) role is simply that of a passive host or 'vehicle', instead of that of the primary agent driving the copying/replication process (Ritt 1996: 37).[139] Importantly, this does not mean that the speaker, as well as social factors and physiological and other properties pertaining to the speaker, play no role at all in the replication process. In fact, speakers are highly relevant in this account: Although they do not represent replicators themselves and are not focussed on as a single irreducible source of rational agentivity, they are treated as a fundamental part of the environment of the linguistic replicators. More specifically, features of the speaker (and 'speaker needs') are taken to crucially determine the success or failure of replicators (cf. also Dawkins 1982: 60; Keller 1990[1994]; Schendl 1996; Deumert 2003).[140] [141]

139 Dawkins, in the preface to his seminal work *Selfish genes*, programmatically states that "[w]e are survival machines – robot vehicles blindly programmed to preserve the selfish molecules known as genes" (1989[2006]: xxi). Genes (as well as memes) are here compared to parasites or viruses, who 'possess' their hosts (Dawkins 1989[2006]: e.g. 182). The idea is summed up in a somewhat provocative manner by Dennett (1995: 346): "A scholar is just a library's way of making another library" (also Deumert 2003: 23).

140 That the thought of humans as a means of reproduction for language constituents, rather than language as a tool used by humans for communication, is somewhat disturbing or at least difficult and unsatisfactory for us, who like to conceive (and are used to conceiving) ourselves as free-willed and agentive subjects, is evident. In the end, the matter in any case appears to pertain more to the domain of philosophy and the question of rationality and free will. Nevertheless, the sole exercise of changing one's perspective from time to time certainly can be beneficial in trying to explain any kind of issue (see also Ritt 2004: 230–233).

141 Critical accounts of the Dawkinsian approach have tended to misinterpret its stance on this particular issue and have often overstated its 'neglect' of the speaker. Parly due to these

To sum up, this book views replicators as cognitive, neuronally implemented patterns, which get transmitted via imitation in language use. This process can be conceptualised as a zig-zag process of competence constituents such as constructions (i-replicators) generating external manifestations of themselves (e-replicators), which in turn activate brain-internal replicators in others (etc.).

5.1.2.3 Variation and selection in linguistic replication

Having determined the nature of replicators and the replicating process and thereby having addressed the first essential question 'what is the replicating unit?' and issues connected to this, let us move on to the two remaining big questions of 'how does variation arise?' and 'how does selection proceed?'. There is some disagreement about these issues, for example on the locus or timescale of change (Croft 2006b: 108–110). Connected to this, the specifics of the process of change have been subject to debate. While some linguists assume a one-step model (e.g. Keller 1990[1994]), others such as Croft (2000, 2006b) argue for a two-step model of 'innovation' (or actuation), i.e. the creation of new elements, and the subsequent 'propagation' of the innovated forms. The latter process, frequently also referred to as 'transmission', 'spread', or 'diffusion', would then correspond to selection in evolutionary approaches. The former, on the other hand, is altered replication, which produces variation in the system (Lass 1997: 315; Croft 2000: 3, 2006b: 104–112; for a proposed three-step model see Rosenbach 2008: 34). A two-step model of altered replication/innovation and selection/spread is also supported in this book. While altered replication always concerns individual language users, selection takes place both on the level of individuals and of speaker populations.

Variation as such is generally considered an integral part of language and language use, meaning that language is intrinsically characterised by diversity on various levels (Beckner et al. 2009: 15; Croft 2013a: 4–6). Concerning poten-

points of critique, more speaker-based accounts have been put forward, which stress the role of the speaker as an 'interactor' (cf. Hull's generalised theory of selection [1988, 2001], embraced by Croft [2000, 2013a]). On this view, speakers have a direct agentive and causal, and thus more active, role in the process of linguistic replication in that they interact with whatever needs to be communicated, their interlocutors, as well as the social context the conversation is situated in (Croft 2013a: 16, 36, 49; also Hull 1988: 408; Beckner et al. 2009). The main difference between this account and the Dawkinsian approach is that the former includes the speaker as a third unit besides replicators and the environment, while in the latter, they (and their needs) are treated as environmental conditions. This book supports Dawkins' approach as the more appropriate and convincing account.

tial sources of such innovations, most accounts focus on innovation by means of using or changing already existing material (Lass 1997: 305). The processes typically included here are the well-known mechanisms of analogical extension/ analogy and reanalysis (Rosenbach 2008: 28; also Croft 2000: Ch.5). A further process sometimes mentioned is that of 'exaptation'. Exaptation is a concept originally used in biology to describe "features of organisms [which are] are non-adapted, but available for useful cooptation in descendants" (Gould and Vrba 1982: 12). A prime example of such a phenomenon is feathers of birds, which most certainly represent adaptations for thermoregulation rather than flying, for which function they were exapted (Gould and Vrba 1982: 12; Kaźmierski 2015: 80). Lass, in his 1990 paper 'How to do things with junk', introduced the term into linguistics, referring to the acquisition of new functions by old, 'useless' linguistic material. Since then, the notion of linguistic exaptation has been applied in various publications. Lass later extended the label to processes of perfectly functional material acquiring another function, thus connecting the issue to grammaticalisation (1997: 318; cf. also e.g. Croft 2000; Traugott 2004, as well as the contributions in Norde and van de Velde 2016). All three of these processes can evidently be drawn on in describing the expansion of prepositions into new contexts: The emergence of a new, prepositional construction for encoding ditransitive events is triggered by the reanalysis of a spatial preposition to recipient role marking (*to*: GOAL → *to*: RECIPIENT). Since this new construction does not appear out of the blue but represents a functional extension of an already existing pattern, it also qualifies as a process of exaptation. Analogy is then involved (among other things) in that the process started with high-frequency tokens such as *give*, from which the pattern was analogically extended to other, less frequent verbs, as well as connected verb classes.

A problematic, but unresolved issue in this regard is the question of when a deviation, or speaker-hearer mismatch counts as an innovation proper. That is, the question arises how different a copy of a replicator needs to be in order to qualify as 'altered', since every linguistic interaction is likely to involve some degree of alteration. Furthermore, there is disagreement on whether variation, or rather, innovation is entirely random, or instead guided by certain principles.[142] The latter view is supported by Croft, who argues that innovation is driven by functional mechanisms, and restricts any impact of functional (processing-related) factors such as economy to the emergence of variation (Croft

142 In some accounts, such as Blevins (2004), the 'randomness' of replication is used in order to signal 'non-teleology' rather than blind, random mutation proper (cf. also Rosenbach 2008: 39–40).

2000: 8; 2006b: 124). Haspelmath (1999: 192), in contrast, proposes that only some innovation is guided by functional factors, while other variants are functionally unmotivated, and occur randomly. Complete randomness of variation, as in biological evolution, is postulated in works such as McMahon (1994: 337) or Ritt (2004), the latter of which states that "[s]ince innovations come about through 'copying mistakes', evolution proceeds blindly, that is, by trial and error, merely preserving 'adaptive' mutations once they have occurred and discarding those that turn out not to be viable" (Ritt 2004: 84). The emergence of a new variant might be motivated by the functions it serves in the context of its emergence, meanings its first use. However, this does not mean that it will be functionally directed towards establishing the variant as historically stable in the population of replicating constituents. That is, it can be a random variation from the evolutionary point of view, even though its emergence might be strongly conditioned, perhaps functionally. – Note that also genetic mutation is not random in the strongest sense of the word, but is, for example, clearly constrained by bio-chemical factors. Therefore, not all mutations are equally likely. Nevertheless, from the evolutionary perspective it is random, as it is not constrained to produce fit variants (Ritt 2004; cf. also Cziko 1995: 288; Rosenbach 2008: 39–40).

Regardless of its source, variation is an essential precondition for selection, since selection needs to act on something, namely variants, in order to result in evolution (Croft 2013a: 8). Which forms count as variants of each other is of course dependent to a large extent on one's definition of a replicator. Most typically, however, they are taken to be structures that count as alternative expressions of the same function or meaning, e.g. two constructions or words used to express more or less the same meaning, morphemes fulfilling the same function, or also different phonetic realisations of a phoneme (Croft 2013a: 6, 37). A prime example of such variants are the constructions that constitute the focus of this book: The DOC and the *to*-PRC qualify as variants of each other because they are essentially synonymous, i.e. are used for a highly similar function. Although formally distinct, they are used with an overlapping set of verbs, and both express a meaning of caused reception or caused transfer. That this is more than a mere coincidental semantic overlap, but that the constructions are perceived as different ways of encoding the same meaning is strongly supported by experimental evidence (e.g. Goldwater et al. 2011; Perek 2015). Similarly, the different case frames of the DOC in Old English, as well as the different prepositional patterns found with individual verb classes constitute variants in the sense advocated here.

Once a variant of a resident form has arisen, the replicator variants then compete for expression, or rather, for activation (which translates into relative textual frequency). Since the variants typically differ in their fitness concerning environmental constraints, they are replicated differentially. Differential replication always means changes in the frequency distribution of variants. In contrast to the emergence of variation, this differential replication of variants – the operating of selectional forces – is clearly not random but shaped by specific factors. The nature of these factors is, however, again argued over; the most conspicuous differences lie in the inclusion or exclusion of functional pressures in the selection process. An example of an account explicitly denying any influence of functional factors in selection is Croft. On his account, propagation, that is, the (non-)successful replication of a variant, is instead determined exclusively by social factors (Croft 2000: 32, 38–39, 54–56, 178). This means that selection operates only on the basis of socio-linguistic principles such as accommodation or prestige (also Seiler 2006: 167–169; Rosenbach 2008: 42).[143]

The more broadly accepted view is to give functional factors a prominent role in linguistic selection, with e.g. Haspelmath suggesting that "frequency of use is determined primarily by the usefulness (or 'user optimality') of linguistic structures" (1999: 190; also Kirby 1999; Givón 2002; Jäger 2007). Evidence for either account can, as Rosenbach (2008: 42) maintains, only be gained by investigating the precise locus of functional pressures in language change. The mere presence of functional factors in variation is insufficient. Most recently, Seiler (2006) has set out to explore this issue: Based on a study of dialect variation in German-speaking areas concerning the competition between double object constructions and prepositional patterns, he finds that while comparable variants start out with the same arbitrary distribution in different dialects, they eventually take on very different functions (such as avoidance of stress clashes or marking differential information structure). This phenomenon is then taken to indicate that functional factors are at play in selection rather than in the emergence of variation as such (further Mondorf 2009). Nevertheless, social factors are not denied any part in these accounts. In general, it seems plausible that a number of different factors are at play in linguistic selection, including functional and social ones.

---

143 Interestingly enough, Croft's model is often presented as highly compatible with work by the LEC research unit at Edinburgh, despite the fact that many of the projects there are concerned precisely with investigating the role of functional factors in language evolution and change.

The precise model adopted in this book is that of Ritt (2004), which distinguishes between three types of factors: genetic, memetic, and social pressures (2004: 221–229). As regards the first set of selectional pressures, Ritt (2004: 222) here subsumes physiological and cognitive, processing-related factors, stating that greater ease of expression of a replicator will increase the likelihood of this replicator to be expressed/replicated. Similarly, ease of perception can positively influence probability of replication. In the case of the dative alternation, it could for instance be expected that the DOC is more successful, since it is shorter and more economical than the *to*-PRC, meaning it is easier to express. On the other hand, the *to*-PRC is arguably easier to perceive, because it is more expressive and more clearly indicates the semantic roles involved.

In addition to these "body-friendly" aspects (Ritt 2004: 235), the replicative success of variants is dependent on intra-systemic factors. Replicators are extremely rarely expressed on their own, but typically occur in 'replicator-plexes', and are thus crucially linked to other replicators at all levels in the replicator network. The activation and success of specific replicators is to a large degree dependent on the success of these other replicators (Ritt 2004: 223). A good case in point is the success rate of prepositional constructions. In a language where case marking is abundant, they are probably not too successful; the strategy of case marking selects against the strategy of PP-marking. However, under changed conditions such as a decrease in case marking salience and the ambiguity resulting from it, prepositional constructions possibly do much better. In this book, it is physiological-cognitive and intra-systemic factors, and above all the latter, that are focussed on.

The last type of factors indicated by Ritt is social ones. On the one hand, it can be assumed that the social environment of a speaker is highly variable, and replicators might therefore be able to resist being influenced by it. On the other hand, changes in the social environment proceed at a relatively slow pace; it is therefore stable enough to still affect the replicators' success. Among the social variables Ritt (2004: 236) mentions are prestige, in that replicators that are associated with powerful or high-status speakers (or groups of speakers) will have a greater fitness than those associated with non-prestigious individuals. Furthermore, the degree to which a given variant signals group-membership (conformity to in-group convention) or particularity (non-conformity to in-group convention) likely plays a role. In general, the frequency of a variant within a particular group will be of relevance (Ritt 2004: 225–227, 236). Regional preferences such as the continuing availability of [Th-Rec] order in DOCs with two pronominal objects in certain dialects in Britain can be subsumed here: Variant tokens such as *Give it me!* have presumably remained stable in these areas due to social factors.[144]

The result of these different selectional pressures is, as already pointed out, differential replication, and the resolution of competition. There are two typical scenarios of such competition resolution. The first option is that one variant declines, while the other variant wins out, managing to become the only expression. This is likely what happened with the case constructions of the DOC in Old English: The frame of [DAT-ACC] ousted the other available, but less successful frames. Similarly, with verbs of dispossession, the prepositional construction is supposed to have driven out the DOC uses. The second pathway is for both variants to survive, but to come to diverge functionally and to be relegated to their own complementary 'niches' (Traugott and Trousdale 2013: 18). In this case, variation is maintained rather than eliminated, but the competing forms typically become restricted to and are systematically used in specific functions (social or systemic). In addition to divergence, variants can also align to each other and become more similar to each other (cf. De Smet et al. 2018). I argue that both scenarios can reflect the emergence of a cooperative, mutualistic relationship (instead of ongoing competition). However, although the distribution of the variants in such cooperation is often quite stable, proportional frequencies might still vary over time even here (Rosenbach 2008: 40).[145] Constructional cooperation can be illustrated by the members of the dative alternation: As has been repeatedly shown, the DOC is typically used when the recipient is unfocused (discourse-given, pronominal, etc.), the *to*-PRC is the preferred choice with discourse-new, focal recipients. The constructions therefore seem to have developed a complementary distribution according to discourse-pragmatic factors, reflected in word order. It should be noted that neither maintenance nor reduction of variation is clearly more profitable than the other for the system and the replicators involved. Although a bi-unique system might be beneficial in some respects, (continued) variation could itself be advantageous since it allows for an expanded range of options to express meanings (see Smith, Tamariz, and Kirby 2013, among others, on the evolutionary trade-off between learnability and expressivity).

144 The sets of factors assumed to be at play in linguistic selection clearly "interact and feed into one another" (Beckner et al. 2009: 16). This can result in a 'tug-of-wars' between different factors (Ritt 2004: 229; also e.g. Zipf 1949; Du Bois 1985; Lindblom 1990; Cooper 1999; Steels 2006; Christiansen and Chater 2008).

145 Selection ceases to play a role once a variant has been ousted, or a stable equilibrium has been reached (also Rosenbach 2008: 40).

In conclusion, in regard to the emergence of variation and selection of variants, I assume here that the former is random in that variation is produced by copying mistakes in the replication process. The latter, by contrast, is fundamentally driven by three kinds of factors, namely cognitive-physiological (functional) and social ones as well as intra-systemic, network-related pressures. These factors crucially determine the success of the competing variants, with differential replication leading either to the ousting of one variant in favour of the other, or the development of a cooperative relationship in which the variants come to take over complementary functions.

5.1.3 An evolutionary approach to language: Summary

Summing up, the basic assumptions that this book works on are the following: Languages are replicator systems, meaning that they constitute populations of linguistic replicators. These replicating units are competence constituents such as constructions, and likely represent neuronally implemented patterns. Copies of these competence constituents are distributed (i.e. shared) in a population of speakers, which means they have been transmitted and imitated. The process of replication involves both i-replicators (competence constituents) and e(xternal)-replicators; these types constitute the two stages of the life cycle of cultural/ linguistic replicators. On a diachronic dimension, this suggests that constituents may emerge or disappear, and that constituent tokens establish lineages (each constituent token owes its existence to one or more previously existing ones and may cause new constituent tokens to exist). Importantly, constituent transmission is rarely, or indeed never, completely faithful. Therefore, variation among constituent types is constantly produced by altered replication (copying mistakes). In this, the emergence of variation is random, meaning that it is not goal-directed in any way, and is not influenced by functional or other factors. The variants so generated then compete against each other for expression, manifest in relative textual frequency. Whether a replicator variant is successful or not is determined by selectional pressures – these come in three types, namely cognitive-physiological factors such as economy or expressivity, intra-systemic factors, and social factors such as prestige. Differential replication caused by differences in performance of variants on these factors can, on the one side, result in the disappearance of one variant, and the 'victory' of the other. On the other side, the variants can come to form their own (functional) niches and coexist alongside each other in a cooperative instead of competitive relationship. Crucially, differential replication and accordingly linguistic change in this approach is always frequency change: If construction A changes into, or is overtaken by construction B, this means that tokens of variant B become more frequent in the population than tokens of variant A. If construction A and B develop a cooperative relationship, their relative frequency distribution is stable, with tokens of both variants being around. This implies that an evolutionary perspective is highly compatible with, or indeed suggests itself as the most appropriate framework for a frequency-based empirical approach as taken in this study.

5.2 Evolutionary Game Theory

Building on the assumptions outlined in the preceding sections, the present book employs methods developed within the general mathematic framework of Evolutionary Game Theory (EGT), in addition to the corpus study. As pointed out by Deo (2015: 30), "[e]volutionary game dynamics have been used to describe and understand the behavior of large populations over time as an evolving game, and in particular, changes in the frequencies of different strategies in a population over time" (cf. further Hofbauer and Sigmund 1998, 2003; Nowak 2000, 2006; Jäger 2004, 2007, 2008; among others). In sight of the sometimes comparatively scarce and certainly very limited amount of data available for historical stages of a language, such methods of modelling language change are considered highly valuable in testing and potentially providing further support for hypotheses about specific changes in language. In the following sections, I first introduce the basics of game theory and evolutionary game theory (5.2.1). I then go on to discuss one way in which EGT modelling could be used to address questions in historical linguistics and the development of ditransitives in Middle English (5.2.2). The main goal of the section is to outline and test a theory of why – under paradigmatic constraints that are assumed to be universal – changing environmental conditions such as the loss of inflections might bring about a stabilisation of the mixed strategy that characterises the PDE dative alternation. That is, I aim to demonstrate that strategies for recipient marking (like expression as NP or PP), and correspondingly, constructional variants (DOC and *to*-PRC) can be driven into cooperation through changes in the systemic environment.

5.2.1 Introduction to EGT

Most basically, game theory can be defined as "a branch of applied mathematics that models situations of strategic interaction between several [typically two] agents" (Jäger 2008: 406; cf. also von Neumann and Morgenstern 1944). The framework has been applied in and extended to various disciplines such as economics, biology, political science, and more recently, also linguistics (Nowak 2006: 45–46; Jäger 2008: 406–407). The key claims in game theory are the following: The interacting agents, usually referred to as 'players' can choose from a set of different strategies that are at their disposal. Whether the choice of one behaviour over the other will be beneficial or costly to the player is dependent on the behaviour of the other player, as well as (possibly) on the circumstances of the interaction. The results of the interaction are determined in terms of payoffs or 'utilities' for the respective player-strategy pairs.

An example of a simple game involving two players is 'rock-paper-scissors'. Here, the participants simultaneously select for one out of three strategies without being able to predict the outcome, since the utility of one behaviour depends entirely on the actions of the other player (Jäger 2008: 408; Benz, Jäger, and van Rooij 2006). This game also illustrates a symmetric game in that all strategies are available to all players, who are not restricted to one specific position. Furthermore, the payoffs do not depend on the position of the player (Hofbauer and Sigmund 1998: 114). In asymmetric games, on the other hand, players can assume different roles, possibly disposing of a different set of strategies. In contrast to symmetric games, in asymmetric games the payoffs do depend on position, and the players get different utilities. A typical case of an asymmetric game is the so-called 'battle of the sexes' as discussed in Maynard Smith (1982: 130–131) or Hofbauer and Sigmund (1998: 114–116). This game concerns courting and parental investment, specifically the costs and benefits involved in raising offspring for females and males. For both females and males, two different strategies are available: Females can be either 'coy' (insisting on a long courtship period) or 'fast' (short engagement period). Males, in contrast, can be 'philanderers', in which case they are not willing to engage in a long courtship, and are not prepared to take care of their offspring – or, they are 'faithful', meaning they conduct courtship and stay with the female to help in upbringing. Both females and males profit from successfully bringing up their children (e.g. +15 points each). However, there is also substantial costs in terms of time and energy (e.g. -20); these can be either shared by both parents or met by only one of them. A long courtship is costly to both players (e.g. -3). The results of this game turn out to be cyclical, with the payoffs differing according to position. In a population of coy females, males profit from being faithful, since moving on to other partners would mean another costly courtship. If males are faithful, however, it pays for females to be fast: If they will stay on and help in any case, the expenses involved in courtship are unnecessary. With fast females, philandering men profit, since they can avoid both the costs of courtship and of bringing up the offspring. If males are predominantly philanderers, there is greater benefits for females in being coy (Maynard Smith 1982: 130).

A further characteristic of games in the classical game theoretic set-up is, as Jäger (2008: 408) points out, that they are rationalistic. This means that the involved players are presumed to be perfectly rational, seeking to maximise their payoffs (Nowak 2006: 46; Jäger 2007: 84). Evolutionary Game Theory (EGT), in contrast, "studies the general problem of strategy selection and its propagation across a population, attributing a non-central role to rationalistic reasoning in this process" (Deo 2015: 23; also Nowak 2006: 46). This framework was developed above all by John Maynard Smith and George Price (Maynard Smith and Price 1973; Maynard Smith 1982) as well as by Josef Hofbauer and Karl Sigmund (Hofbauer and Sigmund 1998, 2003) and Peter Taylor (e.g. Taylor and Jonker 1978), who linked game theoretic assumptions to biology and also population thinking. As indicated in Deo's quote, EGT is not concerned with analysing one single game and its players, but rather investigates larger populations of potential participants. These players, each of which invariably plays the same strategy, randomly interact with each other in a pairwise sequence of games. The payoffs gained in each of these encounters are then added up in order to establish what a strategy's average utility is. More precisely, the payoffs are averaged across all the encounters involving all different strategies, taking into account their proportional distribution in the population (Deo 2015: 30). 'Utility/payoff' can here be translated into fitness, and accordingly, into replicative success. That is, a strategy whose average payoff is higher than that of other strategies will reproduce more rapidly, thereby outperforming less successful strategies and influencing the composition of the population. Importantly, it is the differential reproductive success of strategies rather than that of a single player that EGT is concerned with, i.e. we are dealing with natural selection acting on the strategies present in a population (Nowak 2006: 46; cf. also Jäger 2008: 408–409; Deo 2015: 30). Last, it is worth noting that strategies can also be non-deterministic, meaning that there can be mixed strategies in addition to pure strategies. Playing mixed strategies in EGT can, with Jäger (2007: 91), either be understood as a population being mixed, with different strategies being around, or it can be interpreted in a way that each player in the population chooses one strategy or the other with a certain probability.[146]

The payoffs of symmetric 2x2 (two players - two strategies) games such as the one that will be proposed in the next section are typically represented in matrices like the one in (111), indicating that playing strategy *A* against *A* yields a payoff *a*, *A* against *B* will result in a payoff of *b*, and so on.

(111)

$$\begin{array}{c c} & \begin{array}{cc} \text{A} & \text{B} \end{array} \\ \begin{array}{c} \text{A} \\ \text{B} \end{array} & \begin{pmatrix} a & b \\ c & d \end{pmatrix} \end{array}$$

Equating payoff with fitness and presuming x_A and x_B to be the frequency of strategy *A* and *B* in a population (with 'frequency' corresponding to the probability of interacting with an *A* or *B* player), the expected fitness of the two strategies is given by $f_A = ax_A + bx_B$ and $f_B = cx_B + dx_B$, respectively (Nowak 2006: 49; Deo 2015: 32). If we furthermore take selection to be frequency-dependent rather than constant, we arrive at five possible dynamics between the two strategies, as illustrated in Fig. 32 (Nowak 2006: 50).[147]

On the basis of these assumptions, it is then also possible to determine which situation would be optimal for both players. In such a setting, usually referred to as 'Nash equilibrium' (NE), unilaterally changing strategy is not beneficial to any of the player. In a Nash equilibrium, it is therefore impossible to improve one's payoff by switching to another strategy (Nash 1950; Jäger 2007: 87; also Nowak 2006: 51–53, among others). In other words, a Nash equilibrium describes a strategy pair whose members are the best responses to one another. If the strategies are furthermore the unique best responses to each other, we

146 The second interpretation is of course slightly at odds with the claim of each player in a population being programmed for a specific strategy. The contradiction could, however, be resolved by assuming that the programme assigning strategies is itself non-deterministic (Jäger 2007: 91).

147 The difference between constant and frequency-dependent selection (dynamics) is dealt with at length in Nowak (2006: 46–49), *inter alia*.

speak of a 'strict Nash equilibrium' (SNE). The criteria for identifying (strict) Nash equilibria established by Nowak (2006: 52) are the following:[148]

(i) A is a strict Nash equilibrium if $a > c$.
(ii) A is a Nash equilibrium if $a \geq c$.
(iii) B is a strict Nash equilibrium if $d > b$.
(iv) B is a Nash equilibrium if $d \geq b$.

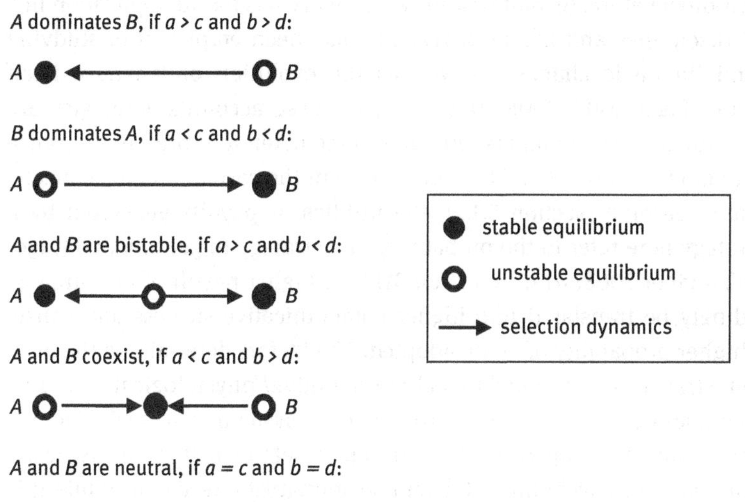

Fig. 32: Five possibilities for (frequency-dependent) selection dynamics between two strategies (adapted from Nowak 2006: 50)

A further concept, of particular importance in evolutionary game theory, is that of *evolutionarily stable strategies* (ESS). As Hofbauer and Sigmund (1998: 59) state, "[a] type of behaviour is said to be *evolutionarily stable* if, whenever all members of the population adopt it, no dissident behaviour could invade the population under the influence of natural selection" [original emphasis]. An ESS can thus be said to have an **"invasion barrier"** [original emphasis] protecting it against mutant strategies (Jäger 2007: 91). The notion of evolutionary

148 See e.g. Hofbauer and Sigmund (1998: Part 2), Jäger (2007: 87) and Nowak (2006: 51–53) for a more detailed discussion of the concepts and other criteria/ formulae used to calculate the optimal (possibly mixed) strategy pairs.

stability is related to the concept of Nash equilibria in that it can also be defined as '$a > c$, or $a = c$ and $b > d$' (drawing again on the general payoff matrix as presented above; this formula applies to scenarios [i] and [ii], types [iii] and [iv] work analogously). Each strategy that represents a strict Nash equilibrium is thus also an ESS (Jäger 2004: 5; Nowak 2006: 53–54). In asymmetric games, it is strategy combinations or pairs rather than one single strategy that turn out to be evolutionarily stable (Hofbauer and Sigmund 1998: 113–114).

As mentioned before, (evolutionary) game theory has found application in a number of disciplines and has most recently also been employed in studying cultural and linguistic change, as well as the evolution of language itself (Nowak 2006; Jäger 2007, 2008; Deo 2015). In these accounts, strategies are typically identified with grammars, and games are taken to represent utterance situations (e.g. Jäger 2007: 92). Since replication in the case of language means imitation and learning (section 5.1.2), the utilities or payoffs generated by a specific strategy here refer to the probability of a strategy to get imitated (Jäger 2004: 21; also Jäger 2008: 419; Deo 2015: 31).[149] A higher payoff of one strategy can accordingly be translated into higher communicative success and consequently a higher probability of being adopted. The factors determining the utility of a given strategy are assumed to include cognitive/ physiological and functional (discourse-pragmatic) issues, as well as intra-systemic and social factors. Assumptions about the impact of these different sets of factors are typically made on the basis of psycholinguistic and sociolinguistic research. While it is clear that further investigations are certainly needed in this regard, it is expected that, as Jäger also comments, "[a] combination of game theoretic and experimental methods is a very promising route for future research" (2008: 419).

The key benefits of employing the analytic tool of EGT for projects like the present one is that corpus data, and especially limited amounts of historical corpus data, can elucidate only some aspects of highly multifaceted developments. For example, while corpus data may allow us to detect temporal and contextual correlations, it is difficult if not impossible to deduce causality from these in the absence of further evidence. Mathematical modelling is immensely useful to test the soundness of a specific hypothesis in such cases, especially where different approaches predict the same or very similar empirical phenomena, or where the interactions between different phenomena are too complex to be conclusively answered.

149 A few pages earlier in Jäger's EGT primer, utility is interestingly equated with "social impact" (2004: 21) rather than imitation likelihood, which is taken to be based on various factors including, but not restricted to, social ones.

Of course, EGT models cannot predict or explain diachronic change as such, i.e. they do not provide explanations for the changes themselves (Jäger 2007: 93). EGT can, for instance, not be used to address the question why and how a new strategy (a mutation) entered the stage, or why the fitness landscape changed. What evolutionary game theory can do, however, is explain the success or non-success of the innovative strategy in comparison to the established strategy/strategies after it becomes available to the players. Linguists can therefore profit from investigating the consequences of particular changes within this framework; the approach enables us to test whether specific assumptions about driving factors of change actually predict its progression in the way we think. Introducing EGT (or any type of mathematical modelling or simulation) to linguistics and language change adds an explanatory layer to our investigation and helps to expand the inherent boundaries imposed by textual analysis. It clearly "enrich[es] [...] the study of cultural language transmission and [...] increase[s] our understanding of the historical development of specific languages" (Ritt and Baumann 2014). The fact that it combines methods originating in the natural sciences with more traditional corpus analysis is one of the main strengths of this book.

In the following section, I outline how EGT could be applied to the history of the English dative alternation. I test which strategy out of two (or strategy combination out of four behavioural types) emerges as most beneficial under differing conditions, dependent on a fixed set of functional factors.

5.2.2 Application of EGT to the history of English dative alternation

This section reports on an attempt to integrate and transfer evolutionary game theory (in)to the domain of historical linguistics. In particular, I use EGT to study one aspect of the history of English ditransitives, namely the competition between (case-marked) NPs and prepositional phrases as strategies for expressing the recipient of a ditransitive event. It should be mentioned beforehand, however, that the application presented below is necessarily (in order for things to remain mathematically feasible) highly simplified and radically abstracted. That is, this game evidently cannot reproduce the linguistic situation in its entirety and excludes several factors and issues which are certainly relevant. This is not a drawback: "The purpose of a scientific model [...] is not to approximate reality as closely as possible, but to explore the consequences of theoretical assumptions and to generate empirically testable hypotheses" (Jäger 2007: 102). Although the specific games played here are supposed to reflect the state of the

English language in different stages in time, the main objective of including EGT in this study therefore is not to provide a conclusive and detailed answer to the range of different issues involved in the development of the dative alternation. Instead, we assess whether this approach can be used to find support or refute specific assumptions that are difficult to test otherwise (for example due to a lack of psycholinguistic, experimental data).

In our case, the central question is whether optimal strategies for recipient marking could change in a certain way depending on a fixed set of factors and changing environmental settings. By addressing this problem in an EGT setting, I show that applying mathematical modelling to linguistic problems can yield interesting and also plausible and valuable results. While these results might not be the ultimate answer to open questions in historical linguistics, they are still able to make predictions from assumptions based on more traditional methods. That this is indeed true has been demonstrated in various relatively recent studies modelling specific changes and trajectories of changes in the framework of evolutionary game theory, such as e.g. Benz, Jäger and van Rooij (2005), Jäger (2004, 2007, 2008) or Deo (2015).[150] These, and other studies also indicate that the great complexity of language systems does not necessarily preclude the possibility of approaching them by means of mathematical modelling (Ritt and Baumann 2012: 220).

In line with the general approach to language taken in this book, the game here views competence constituents as cultural replicators, and does not put focus on the speakers as agents as such (see section 5.1.2). That is, the role played by the speaker as an individual who uses language with a particular communicative intention in particular contexts is disregarded to a certain extent, although their part is of course not denied (Ritt and Baumann 2014). This is due to the fact that, as explained below, the 'players' of the game are defined as (populations of) variants of a specific meaning/function instead of (populations of) speakers and listeners, i.e. the users of such meanings. Similarly to Jäger (2007: 92), the study is therefore concerned with replicator-based games, and takes (populations of) player/strategy pairs to represent (populations of) constructions. Since the cognitive-physiological properties of speakers as well as social factors are still taken to crucially influence the success of the replicators in concrete communicative events, I argue that this view does not stand in contradiction to a usage-based view on language (see also chapter 6).

150 Most of these studies are primarily concerned with pragmatics and highlight the roles of the speaker/hearer in communication games. They thus take a slightly different approach than the one presented here.

5.2.2.1 Set-up of the recipient game

The model to be presented, which we will call the 'recipient game', is a two-player two-strategy game, and can be either symmetric or asymmetric. The central issue dealt with in the game is the development of recipient marking in the history of English: As we know from the discussion in chapter (3), this changed considerably between Old English and PDE, shifting from predominantly case-affixes in noun patterns to zero-marked NPs (in the DOC) or PPs (in the PRC). The players or 'agents' I assume in the game are two discourse-pragmatic variants of this 'recipient' meaning. On the one hand, we have REC in focus, i.e. a discourse-prominent recipient argument (REC as rheme or comment); on the other hand, there is an unfocused recipient argument (REC as theme or topic). The variants are labelled 'REC [+focus]' (focused, non-topical REC) and 'REC [-focus]' (unfocused, topical REC), respectively, in the remainder of this section.

The choice of these two particular functions as players is motivated by the fact that there seems to be a near-universal tendency for placing non-focus-elements early in the clause, while focus constituents tend to come in clause-late position. This a well-known phenomenon and is variedly referred to in the literature as the 'principle of harmonic alignment', the 'given-before-new'-principle, the principle of end-focus, and others (e.g. Quirk et al. 1985: Ch.18). How this constraint is implemented and what consequences it has, however, differs between individual cases (and also between languages). The present game explores what bearing it had on the history of ditransitives in English: In PDE, the two members of the PDE dative alternation differ in discourse-pragmatic features, correlated with preferred order of objects. The DOC today is prototypically used when the recipient argument is unfocused, specifically animate, pronominal, discourse-given, definite, concrete, etc., and favours a [REC-TH] order. By contrast, the *to*-PRC is the preferred choice with focused recipients, i.e. non-topical, inanimate, nominal, discourse-new, indefinite, abstract, etc. participants, and is predominantly found with the opposite order (TH-REC). Similar distributions were also present in earlier periods, as has been shown in previous research. In Old English, for example, the different object orders in the DOC (REC-TH or TH-REC) were driven by factors like animacy, givenness or pronominality (De Cuypere 2015a); the same trends can be observed in the Old English *to*-PRC, with topical recipients being biased towards [*to*REC-TH] order, and non-topical, focal recipients favouring [TH-*to*REC] patterns (De Cuypere 2015c). Over time, the NP-pattern and PP-pattern accordingly appear to have settled on a complementary distribution. The specific assumptions I then test in the game are that given the seemingly universal end-focus constraint and given certain changes in the environmental conditions for their replication, the optimal outcome of competition between the two means of expression (NP or PP) is precisely the mixed strategy we find today.

The set of strategies among which both players (REC [+focus] and REC [-focus]) can choose comprises first, the option of being expressed as a NP, and second, expression as a PP. The available options amount to four behavioural types in total, namely G1 (both players choose NP), G2 ([-focus]: NP, [+focus]: PP), G3 (both players select for PP), and G4 ([-focus]: PP, [+focus]: NP). In each round of the game, that is, whenever one of the variants is used (and perceived) in an utterance, the players receive a payoff which reflects the quality and appropriateness of the selected strategy concerning several (functional) factors and other issues. – The two variants do not actually meet in language use in the sense of being expressed at the same time (a produced recipient is either in focus or not, but not both). Nevertheless, there is interaction in that the expression of one variant also activates the other. This is also the case if the utterance is perceived. All considerations are based on claims made in previous research, as well as the findings from the corpus investigation that is part of this project.

More specifically, the strategies are evaluated on the basis of the following criteria, which mainly reflect processing requirements (see Hawkins 1992, 1994; Rohdenburg 1996; Jäger 2004, 2007; Croft 2006b; Steels 2007, 2012c; Bisang 2009; Leino 2013; among others):[151]

- First, the degree of explicitness or distinctiveness of a strategy is determined, meaning that a given player will receive a higher payoff the higher the information value or cue reliability of the given strategy is; see e.g. Haspelmath's (2006: 3) principle that "utterances should contain the information necessary for understanding what is meant". A higher score concerning the disambiguation potential of an expression is therefore beneficial for a player (cf. also Lightfoot 1991: 160, 171; Heine 1994: 259; Harris and Campbell 1995: 54, 73).
- Second, the criterion of economy or parsimony is taken into account – as famously stated by Zipf's (1949) 'principle of least effort', and as generally proposed, speakers tend to favour shorter, unmarked expressions over longer and marked ones, striving to minimise their effort (Haspelmath 2006: 3; Jäger 2007: 78). Consequently, strategies that are less complex and

151 As Jäger (2007: 75) points out, "[i]t seems plausible to assume that functional, cognitive, and social factors interact in linguistic selection". My focus in this game is, however, only on functional (and systemic) factors, since these can be operationalised most easily (and since social factors are generally not at the centre of the present investigation).

involve fewer linguistic elements will receive a higher payoff in the game (also e.g. Goldberg 1995: 67–68; Clark 1996: 69; Croft 2000: 75).[152]

In addition, the individual player-strategy combinations are evaluated regarding their compatibility with word order preferences. While this issue might not be cross-linguistically or psycho-linguistically salient in the same way as the preceding factors, it can be argued to have been relevant in the history of the English language. This is especially so in light of the increasing fixation of word order in the period under investigation. The details of how this issue was implemented and translated into payoffs are presented below; essentially, the decisions were based on the results from the corpus study.

A final, yet equally crucial factor in determining the utility of a linguistic item or strategy was 'cooperation (coordination)' vs. 'defection' or 'anti- cooperation (anti-coordination)'. In our case, this means that there is a benefit or disadvantage for the players in either arriving at the same decision or, vice versa, in opting for opposite strategies. For instance, it could be argued that the players profit from choosing the same strategy since, according to the principle of bi-uniqueness (one meaning – one form), their common meaning (RECIPIENT) might be recognised more easily if it is always expressed in the same way, precisely either as a NP for both [+focus] and [-focus] recipients, or as a PP in both cases, respectively. However, the potential advantages of bi-uniquely indicating the overarching meaning may be weaker than the gains to be had for the variants from becoming differentiated from the other and associated with formal niches that correspond to their (even though subtle) meaning differences. As discussed in the following, I presume that this aspect was subject to change over time just like the other factors investigated.

In order to address the issue of diachronic development, three different games were devised. Although all games start with the same basic principles and the payoffs are calculated on the basis of the same factors laid out in the previous paragraphs, they differ in terms of several changing parameters. This means that the utility functions of the individual player/strategy pairs change from game to game due to a changing fitness landscape (Jäger 2007: 93). The

152 The combination of these factors is evidently highly reminiscent of the well-known 'minimax principle' (Carroll and Tanenhaus 1975), stating that language users attempt to minimise complexity (and effort) while at the same time striving to maximise the information value of an expression; further Du Bois (2014: 266): "[I]ncreased argument structure complexity calls for care in managing limited cognitive resources". For a much more elaborate agent-based modelling approach to such issues see van Trijp (2013).

changes posited are, on the one side, changes concerning the salience of case marking. More specifically, the degree of case marking salience is taken to decrease from game to game. On the other side, the degree of indicativeness or fixation of word order increasingly grows between the first and the third game, as preferences in word order become stronger and more dominant over time. Finally, I posit that the rewards of 'same strategy' are higher in the earlier games than in the later games; in an environment where both nominal and prepositional frequently co-occur, strategy combinations can strive.

The three games reflect different stages in the history of English: The first game represents a simplified Old English language situation, where case marking is still highly salient, while word order is flexible. At this point, strategy coordination – opting for the same strategy – is a safer bet, considering that despite some variation in the system, specific functions are typically almost exclusively associated with one formal means of expression. The second game, in contrast, models early Middle English, a 'mixed' state with reduced yet still present case marking that carries some content (even if only marginally). Word order is similarly in transition – while not yet entirely fixed, tendencies can already be observed, and constituents are more restricted in their movement within the clause. Nothing is gained from either choosing the same or complementary strategies, as the system is not inclined towards either option. Finally, a hypothetical 'late Middle English and beyond' situation is modelled in the third game. At this stage, case marking is largely absent and therefore not indicative at all, whereas word order is fixated in a way that NP-recipients predominantly appear in first position after the verb. PP-recipients are more prone to the last (second) position, following the THEME-argument, although this inclination is weaker than in the case of the DOC (as shown in section 4.2). Strategy combinations or overlapping strategies are frequent in the language system, and accordingly receive a higher payoff than bi-unique (same strategy) behaviour.

Concerning the utilities (or payoffs) calculated for the individual meaning-strategy pairs, I argue, with Jäger (2004: 27), that they "represent the difference in the absolute abundance of a certain strategy at a given point in time and at a later point. A negative utility thus simply means that the number of utterances generated by a certain strategy is absolutely declining". As can be seen in the tables in the following section, the payoffs are represented by real numbers in the individual games. Importantly, it is the relative ordering of respective payoffs that matters rather than the size of the numbers as such.[153] In the present game, payoffs range from -3 to +3.

5.2.2.2 Results of the recipient game

Moving on to the details of the games and their results, it can first be seen that regarding explicitness, NPs receive a score of 1 in Old English. This is due to case marking still being fairly prominent, and semantic distinctions thus still being expressed rather faithfully by means of morphology (Tab. 18). Even at this stage, however, PPs can be assumed to have a slight advantage over NPs since, as Kittilä, Västi, and Ylikoski (2011: 4) point out, it generally "holds that adpositions [in this case prepositions] are semantically more specific, whereas cases are more abstract in nature (especially if a language has both [...])". In addition to their inherently more explicit nature, the use of prepositional phrases furthermore allows speakers to make finer distinctions in the meaning to be expressed. For instance, the dative case in Old English was considerably bleached and was ambiguous between various different semantic roles. The specific semantic role, and even possible sub-senses within this category, could be expressed in a much more explicit way by the (comparatively) wide range of prepositions available. This is illustrated in the following examples (112a-b), where the same verb is used with two separate, even though related, prepositional phrases (*to* vs. *toward*). Although difficult to assess based on out-of-context examples, assuming that there is no absolute synonymy – or rather, functional equivalence – between formally distinct constructions means that these differences reflect at least minor differences in function. In the particular case of (112), object weight may be the decisive factor.

(112) a. to *quyte* **to the sones of Bersellay**$_{\text{REC}}$ the trewthe$_{\text{TH}}$ and kyndnesse of her fadir$_{\text{TH}}$
to repay to the sons of Bersellay the truth and kindness of their father
'to repay their father's truth and kindness to the sons of Bersellay'
(CMPURVEY,I,12.452; PPCME2: M3)

153 Cf. e.g. scenario (i) as referred to above (strategy A is NE if $a > c$). If $a > c$, then also $x \bullet a + y > x \bullet c + y$.

b. *schule* *quiten* <u>ure</u> <u>dettes</u>$_{TH}$ **toward** **ure** **lauerd**$_{REC}$
shall repay our debts toward our lord
'shall repay our debts to our lord'
(CMANCRIW-1,II.102.1229; PPCME2: M1)

PPs accordingly receive a payoff of 2 in the first game and remain stable in explicitness for the earlier stages/games concerning explicitness (Tab. 18). However, their scores are reduced to 1 in the final stage: Arguably, PPs in ditransitives lose explicitness as a consequence of their increasing semantic widening over time (2 → 1). The scores of NPs are similarly lowered, due to the growing case syncretism and eventual complete loss of case markers. Following from the results gained from the corpus study (section 4.2.1.4), I posit that this reduction process is quite advanced in early Middle English already, for which reason NPs get a neutral score of 0 in both the second and third game.

Tab. 18: Scores for NP/PP based on explicitness and economy, OE to lME games

		explicitness	economy	TOTAL
OE	NP	1	1	2
	PP	2	-1	1
eME	NP	0	2	2
	PP	2	0	2
lME	NP	0	2	2
	PP	1	0	1

As regards economy, it has been reported that prepositions are cross-linguistically longer than case affixes and vice versa – this general distributional fact predictably also holds true for English (Hagège 2010: 29). PPs are hence consistently ranked lower than NPs on the payoff scale for this criterion. Nevertheless, they see a slight increase between the first and second game, since with the reduction of case marking on the nominal complements of prepositions, they are shortened at least to some extent. The NP strategy is affected in the same way. While NPs start out with a rather low score of 1 since they still contain more phonological material and are thus not yet entirely economic, this score is raised to 2 after the initial stage, reflecting the loss of inflectional suffixes. Adding these numbers up, the total scores of the two strategies based on these criteria are given in the right-most column of Tab. 18.

In a next step, the payoffs of individual player/strategy pairs in the respective games are evaluated in terms of word order biases. What this criterion is about is in effect the following: I argue, with e.g. Quirk et al. (1985: Ch.18) and as already outlined above, that the principle of end-focus as a discourse-functional constraint on recipient expression is present in all hypothetical (and actual) language stages we are dealing with here. This means that while REC [-focus] is always (or at least typically) found in first position in the clause (in relation to the theme), REC [+focus] categorically appears in second/clause-late place (again in relation to the theme). This is a fixed parameter; however, the flexibility of the strategies as to which positions they can fill gets increasingly restricted over time, or rather, the strategies show different degrees of preferences over time. In the first (OE) game, both NPs and PPs are equally likely to serve as input for the first and second position. They are equally compatible with both [-focus] and [+focus] meanings. Nevertheless, the strategies differ to some extent in their preferences. Studies on the order of objects in the Old English DOC have shown a fairly balanced distribution, with the NP-recipients (whether case-marked or not) occurring in either position with a 50/50 chance, approximately (e.g. De Cuypere 2015a). PPs are often – at least implicitly – assumed to exhibit greater flexibility than other constituents in moving around the clause. For example, Lundskær-Nielsen (1993: 66) asserts that "PPs in OE can be found in virtually any position in the clause". They would therefore be expected to show a similar indifference concerning favoured position. However, the results of the corpus study (section 4.2.1.3) suggest that they are in fact slightly biased towards last position from early on, which is taken to reflect their adjunctival origins. Accordingly, as seen in Tab. 19, strategy 'PP' for [+focus] is scored slightly higher than PP [-focus] in both the first and the second game (1 vs. 0). NPs, in contrast, are set at a payoff of 1 for both players in the first two games, since there is no clear distributional preference yet.

Tab. 19: Word order preferences of NP/PP, OE to lME games

	[-focus]		[+focus]	
OE	NP	1	NP	1
	PP	0	PP	1
eME	NP	1	NP	1
	PP	0	PP	1

	[-focus]		[+focus]	
lME	NP	2	NP	0
	PP	0	PP	1

The situation in the last game is quite different: As also observed in the corpus data, order in the DOC is rapidly fixed during the period, as the pattern becomes clearly associated with REC-early position. PPs still tend to occupy the later slot in the clause; however, this strategy remains flexible to some extent even towards the end of the period, meaning that the constraint remains preferential rather than categorical. This translates into a small benefit for the [+focus] player to choose PPs, and small costs for choosing NPs. The opposite, but to a greater extent, goes for the [-focus] player. That is, the preferred strategies are scored better than the dis-preferred strategies (2/1 vs. 0). Choosing strategy 'NP' results in a higher positive payoff for the [-focus] player (+2) than choosing strategy either 'NP' or 'PP' for the [+focus] player.[154]

Last, strategy coordination or non-coordination has to be taken in to account. The payoffs for one player-strategy pair do not only depend on environmental factors as just outlined, but also on the choices made by the other player. I posit that in the first, OE game, there is a greater advantage for the players in opting for the same strategy. Both NP/NP and PP/PP combinations therefore receive an additional score of +1. In the second game, by contrast, there are no clear gains for either coordinated or complementary pairings, and the payoffs are not changed. Finally, we assume that in the late Middle English system, strategy combinations or mixed strategies are frequent, and that NP/PP pairings are consequently more successful. They are scored at +1.

By calculating the joint payoffs for each player-strategy combination, we then arrive at the following more comprehensive payoff matrices (Tab. 20 to Tab. 22). In each cell of the tables, the first number gives the utility of the row player (REC [-focus]), whereas the second number represents the payoff of the column player, in our case REC [+focus].

154 Although not explicitly dealt with here, the parameters taken into account here are also assumed to be interrelated to some degree. For instance, as Jäger (2007: 85) points out, "[c]ase marking will [...] be more useful in languages with free word order [...] than in languages with strict word order" (Jäger 2007: 85). The factors of explicitness and economy can accordingly be taken to be inversely related to the word order-factor.

Tab. 20: Payoff-matrix for OE recipient game

OE		**[+focus]**	
		NP	PP
[-focus]	NP	4,4	3,2
	PP	1,3	2,3

Tab. 21: Payoff-matrix for eME recipient game

eME		**[+focus]**	
		NP	PP
[-focus]	NP	**3,3**	**3,3**
	PP	2,3	2,3

Tab. 22: Payoff-matrix for lME recipient game

lME		**[+focus]**	
		NP	PP
[-focus]	NP	4,2	4,3
	PP	2,3	1,3

A first glance at the tables suggests that behavioural type G1 (NP for both meanings) wins out in the Old English game, while G2, i.e. [-focus]: NP/ [+focus]: PP, is most successful in the third game (lME). The intermediate, early Middle English game, on the other hand, appears to represent a transient stage where both G1 and G2 receive an equally high payoff. – This is indicated by the bold print of the numbers in the respective tables. Before drawing any conclusions, however, let us look at the games in a bit more detail, and calculate the (strict) Nash equilibria and ESS of the games. As pointed out in section (5.2.1), for a cell to constitute a strict Nash equilibrium, the first number in the cell needs to be the unique maximum of its column, at the same time as the second number is the unique maximum in its row (shown by the underlined numbers in the tables; Jäger 2004: 17). This corresponds directly to Nowak's (2006: 52) method of calculation reproduced as (113) here:

(113) (i) A is a strict Nash equilibrium if $a > c$.
(ii) A is a Nash equilibrium if $a \geq c$.

(iii) *B* is a strict Nash equilibrium if $d > b$.
(iv) *B* is a Nash equilibrium if $d \geq b$.

Assessing the three games in turn, we first consider the payoff matrices for both players in the first stage, illustrating a hypothetical Old English (114):[155]

(114)

OE: $$Player\ I\ [-focus] = \begin{bmatrix} 4^a & 3^b \\ 1^c & 2^d \end{bmatrix} \qquad Player\ II\ [+focus] = \begin{bmatrix} 4^a & 3^b \\ 2^c & 3^d \end{bmatrix}$$

In the matrix for both player I [-focus] and player II [+focus], *a* is greater than *c*, and *b* is greater than (or equal to) *d*; accordingly, strategy 'NP' is strict Nash for both players. Furthermore, the NP-strategy also constitutes an ESS since the condition of 'either (i) $a > c$ or (ii) $a = c$ and $b > d$' is fulfilled (Nowak 2006: 53). Strategy 'PP' is in contrast not a (strict) Nash equilibrium ($c < a$ and $d \leq b$) in either case, which means that ultimately, A = 'NP' dominates B = 'PP' at this stage (Nowak 2006: 50).

The same results are obtained following Hofbauer and Sigmund's (1998: Ch.6) approach, which furthermore determines which strategies chosen by the respective players are the optimal responses to each other. The exact steps in the formulae for deriving Nash equilibria/ evolutionarily stable strategy pairs are described in detail in their work as well as in many other handbooks of evolutionary game theory; here, the calculations will only be presented in a condensed form.

Assuming *p* and *q* to indicate the probability distributions of both strategies for the [-focus] and [+focus]-player, respectively (115a), and the pair $(\hat{p}, \hat{q})$ as the estimated strategy combination (115b), we can test the hypothesis that the most promising candidate for Old English is a distribution of 100 per cent 'NP' for both players. This is reflected in (116a-b).

(115) a. $$p = \begin{bmatrix} p_1 \\ p_2 \end{bmatrix}, q = \begin{bmatrix} q_1 \\ q_2 \end{bmatrix}$$ b. $$(\hat{p}, \hat{q}) = \left[\begin{bmatrix} p_1 \\ p_2 \end{bmatrix}, \begin{bmatrix} q_1 \\ q_2 \end{bmatrix}\right]$$

(116) a. $$p = \begin{bmatrix} 1 \\ 0 \end{bmatrix}, q = \begin{bmatrix} 1 \\ 0 \end{bmatrix}$$ b. $$(\hat{p}, \hat{q}) = \left[\begin{bmatrix} 1 \\ 0 \end{bmatrix}, \begin{bmatrix} 1 \\ 0 \end{bmatrix}\right]$$

155 Lower case letters in the matrices refer to the payoff constants as seen in the equations in (113).

We assess this by checking (i) whether '$\hat{\mathbf{p}}$ is a best reply to $\hat{\mathbf{q}}$' and (ii) whether '$\hat{\mathbf{q}}$ is a best reply to $\hat{\mathbf{p}}$', i.e. whether $p \times A\hat{q} \leq \hat{p} \times A\hat{q}$ (for all $p \in S_n$) and $q \times B\hat{p} \leq \hat{q} \times B\hat{p}$ (for all $q \in S_m$) (Hofbauer and Sigmund 1998: 113–114).[156] If this is the case, then the pair $(\hat{p}, \hat{q}) \in S_n \times S_m$ is a Nash equilibrium. For a strict Nash equilibrium, both equations need to involve 'strict inequalities', meaning that '$p \neq \hat{p}$' and '$q \neq \hat{q}$' (Hofbauer and Sigmund 1998: 114). As shown in the operation process in (117), this is indeed what we find for the OE game.

(117)

$$\hat{p} \times A\hat{q} = \begin{bmatrix}1\\0\end{bmatrix} \times \begin{bmatrix}4 & 3\\1 & 2\end{bmatrix} \cdot \begin{bmatrix}1\\0\end{bmatrix} = \begin{bmatrix}1\\0\end{bmatrix} \times \begin{bmatrix}4\\1\end{bmatrix} = 1 \times 4 + 0 \times 1 = 4$$

$$\hat{q} \times A\hat{p} = \begin{bmatrix}1\\0\end{bmatrix} \times \begin{bmatrix}4 & 3\\2 & 3\end{bmatrix} \cdot \begin{bmatrix}1\\0\end{bmatrix} = \begin{bmatrix}1\\0\end{bmatrix} \times \begin{bmatrix}4\\2\end{bmatrix} = 1 \times 4 + 0 \times 2 = 4$$

$$p \times A\hat{q} = \begin{bmatrix}p_1\\p_2\end{bmatrix} \times \begin{bmatrix}4 & 3\\1 & 2\end{bmatrix} \cdot \begin{bmatrix}1\\0\end{bmatrix} = \begin{bmatrix}p_1\\p_2\end{bmatrix} \times \begin{bmatrix}4\\1\end{bmatrix} = p_1 \times 4 + p_2 \times 1 = 4p_1 + p_2$$

$$q \times A\hat{p} = \begin{bmatrix}q_1\\q_2\end{bmatrix} \times \begin{bmatrix}4 & 3\\2 & 3\end{bmatrix} \cdot \begin{bmatrix}1\\0\end{bmatrix} = \begin{bmatrix}q_1\\q_2\end{bmatrix} \times \begin{bmatrix}4\\2\end{bmatrix} = q_1 \times 4 + q_2 \times 2 = 4q_1 + 2q_2$$

$$\rightarrow 4 \geq 4p_1 + p_2; 4 \geq 4q_1 + 2q_2 \quad \text{for all } p = \begin{bmatrix}1p_1\\0p_2\end{bmatrix}; q = \begin{bmatrix}1q_1\\0q_2\end{bmatrix}$$

What this essentially means is that no other probability distribution (such as e.g. 'NP in 60 per cent of cases, PP in 40 per cent of cases', or '100% PP') for either player is as effective as the pair we set out to test (e.g. $p_1=0.6$, $p_2=0.4 \rightarrow 4\times0.6+0.4<4$; $p_1=0$, $p_2=1 \rightarrow 4\times0+1<4$). No alternative best replies exist, and the strategy pair 'NP/NP' thus emerges as the best choice for the interaction between the players.

Applying the same procedures to the other two games, we arrive at the following picture: The payoff matrices in (118) indicate that strategy 'NP' present as a strict Nash equilibrium/ ESS for player I [-focus] in the intermediate stage (eME), since a > c (and b > d). For player II, however, there is no clear one optimal strategy; both A (NP) and B (PP) may be Nash (a = c; d = b).

---

156 $\boldsymbol{p \in S_n}$ denotes the mixed strategies for player 1 [-focus], $\boldsymbol{q \in S_m}$ those for player 2 [+focus]. $\mathbf{p} \bullet \boldsymbol{Aq}$ and $\mathbf{q} \bullet \boldsymbol{Bp}$ give the corresponding payoffs (Hofbauer and Sigmund 1998: 113).

(118)
eME: $Player\ I\ [-focus] = \begin{bmatrix} 3^a & 3^b \\ 2^c & 2^d \end{bmatrix} \quad Player\ II\ [+focus] = \begin{bmatrix} 3^a & 3^b \\ 3^c & 3^d \end{bmatrix}$

Let us then determine the evolutionary stable pairs ($\hat{p}$, $\hat{q}$) in this game, and posit a best reply of 100% 'NP' for [-focus], and a 50/50 distribution of 'NP' and 'PP' for [+focus]. In other words, we test whether it is most beneficial for player I to opt for 'NP' in all encounters when paired with a player II who varies between the two strategies, choosing 'NP' or 'PP', respectively, half of the time (and vice versa). Repeating the same steps as above leads to the results given in (119).

(119)

$$p = \begin{bmatrix} 1 \\ 0 \end{bmatrix}, q = \begin{bmatrix} 0.5 \\ 0.5 \end{bmatrix} \qquad (\hat{p}, \hat{q}) = \left[\begin{bmatrix} 1 \\ 0 \end{bmatrix}, \begin{bmatrix} 0.5 \\ 0.5 \end{bmatrix}\right]$$

$$\hat{p} \times A\hat{q} = \begin{bmatrix} 1 \\ 0 \end{bmatrix} \times \begin{bmatrix} 3 & 3 \\ 2 & 2 \end{bmatrix} \cdot \begin{bmatrix} 0.5 \\ 0.5 \end{bmatrix} = \begin{bmatrix} 1 \\ 0 \end{bmatrix} \times \begin{bmatrix} 3 \\ 2 \end{bmatrix} = 1 \times 3 + 0 \times 2 = 3$$

$$\hat{q} \times A\hat{p} = \begin{bmatrix} 0.5 \\ 0.5 \end{bmatrix} \times \begin{bmatrix} 3 & 3 \\ 3 & 3 \end{bmatrix} \cdot \begin{bmatrix} 1 \\ 0 \end{bmatrix} = \begin{bmatrix} 0.5 \\ 0.5 \end{bmatrix} \times \begin{bmatrix} 3 \\ 3 \end{bmatrix} = 0.5 \times 3 + 0.5 \times 3 = 3$$

$$p \times A\hat{q} = \begin{bmatrix} p_1 \\ p_2 \end{bmatrix} \times \begin{bmatrix} 3 & 3 \\ 2 & 2 \end{bmatrix} \cdot \begin{bmatrix} 0.5 \\ 0.5 \end{bmatrix} = \begin{bmatrix} p_1 \\ p_2 \end{bmatrix} \times \begin{bmatrix} 3 \\ 2 \end{bmatrix} = p_1 \times 3 + p_2 \times 2 = 3p_1 + 2p_2$$

$$q \times A\hat{p} = \begin{bmatrix} q_1 \\ q_2 \end{bmatrix} \times \begin{bmatrix} 3 & 3 \\ 3 & 3 \end{bmatrix} \cdot \begin{bmatrix} 1 \\ 0 \end{bmatrix} = \begin{bmatrix} q_1 \\ q_2 \end{bmatrix} \times \begin{bmatrix} 3 \\ 3 \end{bmatrix} = q_1 \times 3 + q_2 \times 3 = 3q_1 + 3q_2$$

$$\rightarrow 3 \geq 3p_1 + 2p_2; 3 \geq 3q_1 + 3q_2 \quad \text{for all } p = \begin{bmatrix} 0.5p_1 \\ 0.5p_2 \end{bmatrix}; q = \begin{bmatrix} 0q_1 \\ 1q_2 \end{bmatrix}$$

In contrast to the OE game, however, it appears that other distribution pairs yield the same results. In combination with a player I who constantly opts for 'NP', there are a number of other best replies by player II. For example, a 60/40 distribution (q_1=0.6, q_2 = 0.4) also gives 3 (3×0.6+3×0.4=3), and the same holds for a 25/75 or 0/100 distribution (q_1=0.25, q_2=0.75→3×0.25+3×0.75=3; q_1=0, q_2=1→3×0+3×1=3), i.e. ultimately any combination of q_1, q_2, with $0 \leq q_1$, $q_2 \leq 1$; $q_1 + q_2 = 1$. The existence of such alternative best replies demonstrates that there is no single evolutionarily stable pair ($\hat{p}$, $\hat{q}$) at this stage.

In the final game, 'NP' emerges as a strict Nash/ ESS for player I [-focus], because A strictly dominates B (a > c and b > d), while B = 'PP' is a Nash equilibrium/ ESS for player II [+focus]: d = b and c > a (120).

(120)

IME: $$Player\ I\ [-focus] = \begin{bmatrix} 4^a & 4^b \\ 2^c & 1^d \end{bmatrix} \qquad Player\ II\ [+focus] = \begin{bmatrix} 2^a & 3^b \\ 3^c & 3^d \end{bmatrix}$$

Based on this, we presume the pair of 'player I: 100% NP and player II: 100% PP' to be evolutionarily stable and the distributions to be the best replies to each other (121).

(121)

$$p = \begin{bmatrix} 1 \\ 0 \end{bmatrix}, \ = \begin{bmatrix} 0 \\ 1 \end{bmatrix} \qquad (\hat{p}, \hat{q}) = \left[\begin{bmatrix} 1 \\ 0 \end{bmatrix}, \begin{bmatrix} 0 \\ 1 \end{bmatrix} \right]$$

$$\hat{p} \times A\hat{q} = \begin{bmatrix} 1 \\ 0 \end{bmatrix} \times \begin{bmatrix} 4 & 4 \\ 2 & 1 \end{bmatrix} \cdot \begin{bmatrix} 0 \\ 1 \end{bmatrix} = \begin{bmatrix} 1 \\ 0 \end{bmatrix} \times \begin{bmatrix} 4 \\ 2 \end{bmatrix} = 1 \times 4 + 0 \times 2 = 4$$

$$\hat{q} \times A\hat{p} = \begin{bmatrix} 0 \\ 1 \end{bmatrix} \times \begin{bmatrix} 2 & 3 \\ 3 & 3 \end{bmatrix} \cdot \begin{bmatrix} 1 \\ 0 \end{bmatrix} = \begin{bmatrix} 0 \\ 1 \end{bmatrix} \times \begin{bmatrix} 2 \\ 3 \end{bmatrix} = 0 \times 2 + 1 \times 3 = 3$$

$$p \times A\hat{q} = \begin{bmatrix} p_1 \\ p_2 \end{bmatrix} \times \begin{bmatrix} 4 & 4 \\ 2 & 1 \end{bmatrix} \cdot \begin{bmatrix} 0 \\ 1 \end{bmatrix} = \begin{bmatrix} p_1 \\ p_2 \end{bmatrix} \times \begin{bmatrix} 4 \\ 2 \end{bmatrix} = p_1 \times 4 + p_2 \times 2 = 4p_1 + 2p_2$$

$$q \times A\hat{p} = \begin{bmatrix} q_1 \\ q_2 \end{bmatrix} \times \begin{bmatrix} 2 & 3 \\ 3 & 3 \end{bmatrix} \cdot \begin{bmatrix} 1 \\ 0 \end{bmatrix} = \begin{bmatrix} q_1 \\ q_2 \end{bmatrix} \times \begin{bmatrix} 2 \\ 3 \end{bmatrix} = q_1 \times 2 + q_2 \times 3 = 2q_1 + 3q_2$$

$$\rightarrow 4 \geq 4p_1 + 2p_2; 3 \geq 2q_1 + 3q_2 \quad \text{for all } p = \begin{bmatrix} 1p_1 \\ 0p_2 \end{bmatrix}; q = \begin{bmatrix} 0q_1 \\ 1q_2 \end{bmatrix}$$

As can be seen, this pair proves to be the optimal combination. Alternative distribution pairs such as 100% 'NP', 100% 'PP' for both players, or any variable distribution for one of the players, receive a lower payoff. They thus have a lower fitness ($q1 = 1, q2 = 0 \rightarrow 2 \times 1 + 3 \times 0 < 3$; $p1 = 0, p2 = 1 \rightarrow 4 \times 0 + 2 \times 1 < 4$; $p1 = 0.9, p2 = 0.1 \rightarrow 4 \times 0.9 + 2 \times 0.1 < 4$; etc.).

Summing up, the three games outlined here are taken to represent different stages in the history of English and in the development of the English dative alternation (evidently constituting a great simplification of the actual historical situation). The fitness environment for the players and strategies changes from game to game, as case marking is increasingly lost, and word order preferences become more salient. Furthermore, the benefits or costs incurred by the players opting for either the same or opposing strategies differ between the stages. Testing different assumptions about the most successful strategy combinations in an EGT model, we then find a move from NPs being the preferred and most beneficial option for both players (OE) to a situation in which the highest payoff is achieved if both players select for different strategies (lME). More specifically, in the latter case it is behavioural type G2, i.e. [-focus]: NP/ [+focus]: PP, which is fittest. Early Middle English in this scenario reflects a less clear-cut, in-between state in which more than one behavioural type (G1 and G2), or rather, any pair of '[-focus]: NP' and a variable distribution of 'NP'/'PP' for [+focus] are acceptable.

The results of the game theoretic approach can, in conclusion, be seen as corroboration for the general hypothesis that the emergence of the dative alternation is causally connected to the changes of loss of case marking and fixation of word order (see hypothesis [ix] put forward in the beginning of chapter 4). More precisely, I take the findings to support the postulation that under universal pragmatic constraints relating to the principle of end-focus, changes to the system-internal environmental conditions for the replication of strategies (and constructional systems corresponding to them) can lead to symbiotic cooperation between different strategies. For the specific case of the history of the dative alternation in English, this means that a decrease in case marking salience/indicativeness concomitant to an increasing rigidity in constituent ordering could have triggered a change away from a single strategy for recipient marking in ditransitives (and core semantic role marking in general) and the development of a mixed strategy involving both synthetic and analytic means of expression (NP vs. PP). As discussed in more detail in chapter (7), these developments can be interpreted as adaptations of the two constructions to selective pressures derived from changes in the fitness landscape. In a constructional network featuring less and less case-marking and more and more predictable variation in constituent order as well as strategy variation in general, a cooperative, complementary association between two constructions such as the dative alternation will be most successful. The findings therefore not only provide support for assumptions made on the basis of the more traditional empirical data analysis presented above. They also further add to our understanding of the emergence of the dative alternation in allowing us to draw conclusions about causal relationships not observable in or testable with corpus data. Moreover, the approach taken here confirms that integrating mathematical modelling into linguistic research is valuable and can lead to interesting insights, not least because it enables us "to re-approach [an issue] from an entirely new perspective" (Ritt and Baumann 2012: 236).

6 Evolutionary construction grammar

The preceding parts of this book have introduced the two main theoretical approaches this study builds on and have presented the results of two different methodological approaches linked to them. In the following, I discuss what the benefits of merging these frameworks are, and how they can be integrated into a paradigm of what I call 'evolutionary construction grammar'. I start by outlining previous perspectives on this issue (6.1), before zooming in on the main questions a fused account needs to address (6.2). These concerns are also related to Steel's model of language evolution by linguistic selection, which distinguishes between selection on the level of language strategies and on the level of paradigmatic choices in language systems, i.e. constructional variants (e.g. 2011b, 2012b, 2012c).[157] Section (6.3) introduces the core conceptual basis of much of the later analysis of the diachronicity of the English dative alternation: The section explores the specifics of constructional innovation, competition, cooperation as well as co-evolution. Last, the main principles of the integrated evolutionary constructionist framework are assessed and summarised (6.4).

6.1 Compatibility of the approaches and benefits in merging

Opinions on the degree to which cognitive linguistic approaches in general and construction grammar are consistent with taking an evolutionary linguistic perspective on language structure and language change are largely very affirmative. For instance, Hurford (2012b: 176) mentions that constructionist approaches are "more compatible with evolutionary considerations" than nativist or generativist theories. Similarly, Arbib (2012: x) claims that such approaches "may provide a more suitable framework for studying the evolution, historical change and acquisition of language", while Croft points towards points of agreement between the frameworks in several places (e.g. 2013a: 40). The connections are implicitly also visible in the fact that Croft, as one of the major proponents of integrating evolutionary thinking into linguistics, works within a particular strand of construction grammar (developed by himself), namely Radical Construction Grammar (e.g. 2001, 2013b). Petré (2014) both explicitly and implicitly elaborates on what unites (radical) construction grammar and 'language as a complex adaptive system' approaches. He focuses on the corre-

157 See also e.g. Bleys and Steels (2011), van Trijp (2012), and others.

https://doi.org/10.1515/9783110633856-006

spondences between biological ecosystems and language, labelling this framework as 'environmental linguistics'. Similarly, Steels and colleagues, who assume a fundamentally evolutionary perspective in their work, use the formalism of Fluid Construction Grammar for operationalising their agent-based modelling experiments (see e.g. Steels 2011a, and the contributions therein; Wellens et al. 2013). Further explicitly fusional accounts include Wedel (2006), who outlines possible ways to integrate evolutionary ideas with exemplar-based models of language and tackles specific issues such as phoneme mergers or splits by applying such considerations. From his point of view, combining exemplar models with evolutionary linguistics is particularly appropriate, since variation is an intrinsic part of exemplar-based categories, with the language system as a whole representing a population of exemplars/ variants (Wedel 2006: 248). Frank and Gontier (2010), as well as Pleyer (2014), Pleyer and Lindner (2014), and Pleyer and Winters (2015) address the potential benefits in merging concepts from cognitive linguistics (including construction grammar) with evolutionary accounts. More specifically, they propose that incorporating findings from cognitive linguistics can be useful in identifying and specifying cognitive processes and mechanisms that might qualify as selective pressures in linguistic evolution (Pleyer and Winters 2015: 19). That is, evolutionary linguistics is thought to provide a meta-framework for approaching language change, language acquisition, and the evolution of the language faculty, whereas cognitive linguistic approaches deal with the more fine-grained details of the mechanisms influencing the replication and selection process. This concerns above all domain-general cognitive mechanisms such as statistical learning, categorisation, generalisation and schematisation, analogy, entrenchment, chunking, or automatisation, as well as sociocognitive motivations and skills like mutual coordination and cooperation, joint attention, shared intentionality, and perspective-taking (e.g. Croft 2009; Hurford 2012b; Bybee and Beckner 2014).[158]

A good example of a negative evaluation of the compatibility of the frameworks is Rostila (2007). Drawing on Croft's (2000) notion of linguemes in his discussion of construction grammar, he concludes that "die Memtheorie erscheint zumindest aus meiner KxG-Perspektive vollkommen verfehlt [the meme theory seems to be entirely misguided, at least from my construction grammar perspective]" (Rostila 2007: 97). The author's main reasons for this rebuttal lie in the nature of the replication/spreading mechanism and the role of the speaker in this process; he vigourously rejects the assumption of imitation proceeding

158 Cf. further Clark (1996); Christiansen and Chater (2008); Tomasello 2008; Beckner et al. (2009); Bybee (2013); Goldberg (2013); among others.

'mechanically'. Instead, he proposes that constructions are used and propagated due to speakers' rational considerations about their social values. However, Rostila's argument is problematic in two important ways. First, he seems to confuse or conflate two different processes: While it is true that imitation is assumed to operate 'automatically', this does not mean that communication is completely unconstrained and random (Lass 1980; Ritt 2004). Quite the contrary, the question which variants will successfully propagate in the community is heavily determined by various factors such as social convention and prestige, physiological and cognitive factors pertaining to speaker bodies and brains, as well as systemic features, i.e. properties of the system of replicators itself. Replication/imitation may proceed blindly and mechanically, but selection is not random at all; rather, it responds to various influences (see also section 5.1.2). That is, linguistic variants are acted on by selectional pressures including social values (Beckner et al. 2009).

Second, Rostila (2007: 93–95, 96–97) in my view clearly overstates the role of the rational speaker in language acquisition and use, claiming that the fact that speakers have and act according to their intentions, desires, and beliefs are entirely ignored by evolutionary linguists. However, this is clearly not the case. While rational decision-making on the part of the speakers is denied, the speakers' feelings and intentions (however rational or conscious they may be) are certainly taken into account. More specifically, speakers' cognitive states of any kind are considered as one type of selectional pressures, meaning that the variant which most successfully aids my communicative (or other) intentions will have a higher fitness, and will thus likely be used again in future discourse. Moreover, restraining the role of the rational language user in this way does not negate the fact that humans have developed a very 'powerful cognitive system' which allows us to make predictions about the intentions, beliefs, knowledge status (and so on) of our interactants (Steels 2012c: 16). Rostila's (2007: 97) demand that evolutionary linguistics need to familiarise themselves with findings from functional linguistics and sociolinguistic research consequently seems to be more than unwarranted. Interestingly enough, the account Rostila's critique of the memetic/evolutionary enterprise mainly draws on is Croft (2000, 2001), who highlights the role of the interactor in the replication and selection process more than many other authors. It is therefore somewhat surprising that the approach is so forcefully rejected on these grounds. Although Rostila's take represents the extreme end of the spectrum of views on the role of the rational speaker in language use, the claim of an active, rational and consciously decisive speaker is implicitly or explicitly found in other constructionist accounts as well (e.g. Beckner et al. 2009: 6; Pleyer and Lindner 2014: 246). Nevertheless, construction grammar is not dependent on this conception. Taking a constructionist approach to language without speakers as rational agents, and without language viewed primarily as a tool or instrument used by speakers, is entirely possible (cf. also Bybee 2013: 50–51; Ritt 2013b). This is also reflected in the evolutionary game theoretic model presented in section (5.2), where constructions rather than language users feature as players (or more specifically, player/strategy pairs).

Coming back to more positive views on the compatibility of the accounts, we find that in general, there are some relatively obvious and basic correlations between the form of evolutionary linguistics advocated in this book and usage-based, cognitive construction grammar. Among these are the principled view of language as a non-static, dynamic system in constant flux, the rejection of an ideal speaker and ideal system in favour of ubiquitous presence of variation, as well as the assumption that language change occurs both in adult communication and child acquisition, rather than only in the latter – cf. e.g. Bybee's conclusion that "representations are dynamic and change with usage events, not just across generations but within the individual as usage patterns change" (2013: 68). Moreover, both approaches see language as influenced by domain-general cognitive processes instead of being a separate, uniquely human capacity. Accordingly, the processes at play in language use are taken to correspond to more general mechanisms involved in other forms of human (and animal) behaviour as well (e.g. Steels 2012c: 16–17).[159]

More particularly pertaining to this book, I argue that an approach joining construction grammar with evolutionary thinking is appropriate and useful for the research topic at hand for many reasons. Most basically, an evolutionary construction grammar framework presents itself as the best choice for the operationalisation, analysis, and explanation of the phenomena in question, since I primarily deal with syntactically complex patterns (namely the argument structure constructions of DOC and PRC/PTC) and since the history of these constructions involves competition between variants on many levels. More detailed reasons include the following:

In the present book the framework of construction grammar is mainly employed as a heuristic. If we want to assess the development and use of specific patterns (such as the members of the dative alternation) in a language, it certainly pays off to have a very clear conception of what constitutes a linguistic sign, how the various parts making up a sign are connected, and what the indi-

159 As Steels (2012c: 16) nicely puts it: "Biological evolution gets physics and chemistry 'for free'. Linguistic evolution also gets something for free, namely cognition".

vidual elements contribute. All of these criteria are fulfilled in construction grammar. As discussed in section (1.2.1), the definition of linguistic units in this framework is very straightforward: Constructions represent pairings of form/structure and meaning/function. Formal features of a sign are stored together with its functional properties and a symbolic correspondence link between these components. A construction such as the DOC, for example, relates a structure of [NP_X V NP_Y NP_Z] to a meaning of 'X causes Y to successfully receive Z', further specifying discourse-pragmatic aspects like 'Y is (prototypically) given', and 'Z is (prototypically) new'. By contrast, the *to*-PRC pairs a form of [NP_X V NP_Z *to* NP_Y] with a sense of 'X causes Z to move to Y, who thereby receives Z'. In this case, Y is typically new, while Z refers to a discourse-given entity (e.g. Goldberg 1995). The strong emphasis on distinctive (syntactic) units that characterises construction grammar clearly matches the central importance of replicating units in evolutionary linguistics.

Usage-based construction grammar as a paradigm in which the actual usage of such constructions plays a fundamental role is especially practical due to the empirical focus of this book lying on patterns that are identifiable on the surface, i.e. in texts. That is, this approach lends itself better to the investigation of changes in usage than a framework whose main agenda is the identification of universal constraints on grammar design. The great interest in frequency within usage-based construction grammar is a further clear advantage in this regard; it combines well with an evolutionary approach that attempts to account for the stability of patterns and requires measuring or estimating their frequency in populations.

Finally, a compelling argument for using construction grammar is that it conceptualises patterns as being integrated in a network whose constituents interact with each other. This is highly interesting for the present book in its focus on the emergence of the dative alternation, which is taken to constitute a constructional network involving the allostructions DOC and *to*-PRC as well as a more schematic ditransitive constructeme (Cappelle 2006; Perek 2015). Furthermore, I view the dative alternation as part of a larger network, including PTCs as well as a range of other connected constructions. The network structure posited in this approach also facilitates the conceptualisation of co-evolutionary interactions between constructions. For instance, I below lay out the claim that the members of the dative alternation co-evolve and adapt to each other (section 7.2.2).

It is also clear that a great amount of work has been carried out within construction grammar on the issue of how constructions are acquired, used and change throughout time. Often-employed relevant concepts such as reanalysis and analogy, entrenchment and productivity, priming, or construal and perspective, have been incorporated in the framework and have thereby received firmer theoretical as well as empirical grounding. These notions are also central to any discussion of ditransitives in Present Day English and in the history of English: For example, the development of prepositional patterns to include recipient marking in their function certainly involved reanalysis processes (e.g. from spatial goal to recipient). Analogy presumably aided and furthered the spread of the innovative meanings, in that the prepositional patterns may have been extended from verbs of sending/bringing to other verbs of concrete transfer. The higher type and token frequency of transfer verbs, and accordingly the higher entrenchment of this particular sub-sense of the DOC, on the other hand, was probably responsible for the transfer-meaning to persist, while sub-senses more peripheral to this meaning were lost. This move to a more basic transfer-meaning also had a clear effect on the productivity of verb-classes associated with the DOC – while the more central sub-constructions are highly productive (e.g. communication verbs), more removed sub-constructions have become unproductive (e.g. verbs of refusal such as *deny*). Working with well-developed definitions of such concepts, based in a specific theoretical approach in which they play an important role, is therefore certainly valuable for analysing ditransitives in (the history of) English.

Evolutionary linguistics, on the other hand, is used here as an explanatory rather than as a descriptive tool. Starting from the assumption that linguistic elements such as the DOC are present in PDE because they have managed to successfully produce copies of themselves at a higher rate than old copies fade, and have moreover successfully competed against other variants, the question why this should be the case can then be tackled in a systematic way. For instance, this can be done by looking at a clearly defined range of factors that determine the success of linguistic replicators. These pressures can be divided into different types, namely cognitive-physiological, social, and intra-systemic ones. The first two of these allow us to capture the often-mentioned but highly variable 'speaker needs'. While cognitive-physiological factors include human cognitive biases or preferences such as the tendency towards ease of articulation or perception (economy vs. explicitness), social pressures relate to social values of certain variants, group conformity, and the like. Both types of factors can be drawn on to explain the success of certain replicators over others. Investigating intra-systemic factors, by contrast, means that the fate of individual constructions can be analysed and explained in the context of other, connected constructions in the network. An evident benefit of this practice is that instead of being overwhelmed by the complexity of the linguistic system and changes to it, related constructions can simply be regarded as environmental pressures, similar to cognitive factors.[160] Taken together, we arrive at a still highly intricate and complex, yet more systematic and transparent model of language change, which in my view also provides a sounder basis for modelling and explaining specific linguistic changes.

Generally, the application of evolutionary concepts (such as competition between replicator variants, the resolution of which can also lead to mutualistic cooperation between variants) to issues in linguistics can add to our understanding of mechanisms and developments observed in language change. Although e.g. the notion of 'competition' is already often drawn on in all kinds of linguistic frameworks including construction grammar (e.g. Traugott and Trousdale 2013), evolutionary linguistics as understood in this book takes things a step further. Rather than using such terms metaphorically, and treating correspondences between biology and language as mere analogies, competition between linguistic variants is thought to be fundamentally subject to the same general evolutionary mechanisms as biological ones (see also Rosenbach 2008; Petré 2014; among others). A further advantage of connecting language and language change to other domains in this way is that we can gain from progress made in these other fields and can adopt methodologies developed in other disciplines into linguistics, exemplified in this book by the EGT approach in section (5.2).

In sum, I argue that combining the two approaches is not only possible, but also of advantage to the present research project and to (historical) linguistic investigations in general. A joint approach is beneficial for both sides in providing a new, and possibly more enlightening, perspective on often long-debated issues. The decision to study language in evolutionary terms does not remove the necessity of an analytic framework by which linguistic constituents or units can be identified, distinguished, categorised and related to one another. On the contrary, since evolutionary changes always involve changes in the number of 'tokens' representing (potentially competing) 'types', it is crucial for any evolutionary approach to language to employ a framework that allows one to identify constituent types, and to decide when a specific token represents an instantiation of it. Construction grammar represents a highly suitable framework for that purpose, because 'constructions', which play a central role in its conception of grammar, represent cohesive, yet at the same time internally structured units.

---

160 There is, of course, a certain risk involved in taking this approach: If we assume all patterns to be related in a network structure and to impact each other without any clear boundaries, the model loses in explanatory power.

Their internal structure allows them to be distinguished from one another and to be categorised into different types, and their instantiations in texts can be counted. Thus, an evolutionary approach to language combines well with a framework such as construction grammar. Conversely, construction grammar clearly profits from being applied in evolutionary accounts of linguistic change, since evolutionary theory represents the most coherent and best-understood framework for studying the diachrony of 'units' that are instantiated in terms of populations of copies and that are transmitted under environmental constraints.

6.2 Main questions in evolutionary construction grammar

A joint framework is useful because it supplies evolutionary linguistics with a highly developed analytic framework and provides construction grammar with an explanatory framework for diachronic investigations. Nevertheless, and although the frameworks seem to be compatible in many ways, the attempt to merge them naturally also raises some problematic issues. I tackle these concerns in the following sections. Specifically, the next sections address the following, very basic questions:

- What do we assume as linguistic replicators/the unit of replication in language?
- How does variation arise?
- How does selection proceed? What factors determine replicative success?

Decisions need to be made concerning whether it is constructions or parts of constructions that constitute replicators, whether constructions at all degrees of schematicity replicate, and whether replicators are actual constructions in usage (rather than their mental representations). As to the second point, the notion of constructionalisation is drawn on, and I determine to what extent this concept is compatible with the concept of emerging variation in evolutionary linguistics. Finally, the types of factors influencing the success of variants over others are discussed.

6.2.1 Constructional replication

Arguably the most essential question in trying to integrate evolutionary linguistics and construction grammar is the question of how to define and identify plausible units of transmission and selection, i.e. constituents that emerge, are transmitted, give rise to variants, and are sometimes lost in linguistic evolution. In short, the nature of linguistic 'replicators' needs to be pinned down. This necessity is also pointed to in Hruschka et al. (2009: 467, Box5), who ask: "What is actually changing? Forms, functions, form-function mapping, rules, and/or exemplars?".

Excluding rules as replicators from the start, we are still left with options on three (interrelated) dimensions: (i) First, we have to determine whether it is parts of a construction (form or function, or even components of these) that are replicating, or whether it is the construction as a whole (form and function, and the link between). (ii) The debate about the nature of a replicator discussed in section (5.1.2) needs to be re-addressed. Replicators may either be constituted by the external behaviour (the utterance) or the internal cognitive representation, meaning neuronal patterns in the brains of speakers. Framed in constructionist terminology and conceptual inventory, the choice here is between constructs (concrete actual tokens in usage) and constructions. If we assume that the latter is the case, a further problem then raises itself: (iii) It may be lowest-level constructions only that replicate (micro-constructions, which roughly correspond to exemplars, or stored categorised token memories).[161] On the other hand, abstract, higher-level constructions may qualify as replicators as well. In relation to the last point, we briefly also have to review the question of replicators as discrete, or potentially non-discrete, entities.

Regarding the first of the dimensions involved, the most straightforward option is to consider the entire construction – as a form-meaning pairing, however complex – as the replicator. The main reason for this is that both form-only and function-only replication are difficult to conceive of if the choice is not taken to correspond to the question between external and internal replication. Form-only replication is, for example, doubtful considering idiomatic expressions which are formally equivalent to less idiosyncratic, more compositional constructions (cf. *kick the bucket* 'die' vs. *kick the bucket* 'hit a round open container with your foot'). The idea of function-only replication, on the other hand, seems hard to maintain when taking into account highly atomic constructions such as individual phonemes, which arguably have a very abstract meaning only, or rather only have the function of differentiating meaning (cf. also the discussion in Ritt 2004: Ch.6.1). I therefore argue that form-meaning pairings of various sizes and degrees of complexity represent the most appropriate and most acces-

161 There is of course no full correspondence between these concepts; however, the definitions of both terms also vary between accounts and are generally relatively vague. I therefore use the terms interchangeably.

sible pick for linguistic replicators. This selection evidently also does most justice to the focus on constructions as independent items which is inherent to construction grammar approaches.

The idea of constructions as replicators is in fact the route taken by Croft (2013a: 42), who states that "they [i.e. constructions] are independent linguistic replicators that specify properties of their component parts". Interestingly enough, however, this assumption is highly problematic for Croft's own account, which he also acknowledges (at least to a certain extent). Seeing grammar as symbolic, with constructions as symbolic signs combining form and meaning, and taking such constructions to be linguistic replicators is essentially incompatible with Croft's concept of linguemes, which defines replicators as utterances (2013a: 42). That is, drawing on the second dimension mentioned above, if Croft assumes replicators to be acoustic signals rather than mental representations, this necessarily entails that it is constructs rather than constructions that are replicating. A less ambiguous definition of what we are actually dealing with is certainly desirable.

In general, the notion of replicators as utterances is rejected in this book, since as explicated in section (5.1.2), it can hardly account for the structured nature of linguistic elements (Ritt 2004). However, following the tenets of usage-basedness as viewed in this book, namely that linguistic structure is crucially influenced and shaped by usage, it is similarly problematic to argue for replication to involve mental, 'brain-internal' elements only. The basis for a compromise solution in this respect is provided by McCrohon's (2012) distinction between i-replicators and e-replicators introduced in section (5.1.2). Recapping, and applying this proposal to language as viewed in usage-based construction grammar, e-replicators then correspond to constructs, meaning actual tokens in single usage events (Traugott and Trousdale 2013). I-replicators, on the other hand, correspond to cognitive patterns, and accordingly to constructions.[162] It is at this point where the third dimension on which decisions have to be taken comes into play: I-replicators can be thought of as either micro-constructions only, or as encompassing constructions at all levels of schematici-

---

162 Compare also Börjars, Vincent, and Walkden (2015: 365), who comment on precisely this issue in their review of Traugott and Trousdale (2013):

> A construct, as they define it, is an empirically attested utterance or utterance-part – a token, rather than a type [...] But tokens are by definition unique, restricted to a single point in time, and not replicable, especially not across populations of speakers. What is replicable is the abstract type that the token instantiates: in other words, the construction, in T&T's approach, and the frequency associated with it.

ty. In the latter option, any member of the constructional network, whether substantive or abstract, would constitute a replicator and would therefore be able to compete against other constructions.

Arguments for both possibilities can easily be found. On the one hand, the former option seems to be intuitively more appropriate, since replication essentially takes place at the intersection of micro-constructions and constructs. Precisely, replication involves the memorisation and storage of an encountered acoustic sign (e- to i-replication) or the (re-)production of a stored memory (i- to e-replication). Abstract generalisations over individual usage events (subschemas and schemas at various 'heights' in the constructional network/ exemplar clouds) can on this account hardly replicate on their own but are always dependent on expression 'via' lower-level, completely filled micro-constructions; their formation and storage is a secondary process only. Furthermore, individual tokens are discrete rather than fuzzy, whereas categories or constructions are assumed to be gradient at least to a certain degree. Since discreteness is an important defining feature of replicators in the Dawkinsian tradition, this factor would clearly speak in favour of micro-constructions as replicators. On the other side, limiting replicators to the lowest level is very restrictive. What is more, it entails that it is only micro-constructional tokens that are able to compete against others. This assumption, even if not necessarily theoretically problematic, seems practically inconvenient for linguistic investigations of many kinds. Also, it calls into question the relevance of higher-order constructions, and the part played by them in language use.

A possible solution to this predicament is to follow an essentially 'micro-construction as i-replicator' account, but at the same time consider the possibility that higher-order constructions are nevertheless activated in any encoding/production or decoding/perception event. I suggest that the replication process proper only concerns the level of exemplars as such. Once abstractions have formed, however, each replication event involves the activation of whole parts of the constructional network. Replication on the brain-internal level therefore almost always means replication of what could be called 'i-replicator-plexes'. Importantly, higher-order constructions in this scenario cannot replicate on their own but are always dependent on lower-level instantiations. To illustrate this proposal, we can draw on the example of the DOC: The abstract double object construction [[NP_X V NP_Y NP_Z] / ['X causes Y to receive Z']] as well as the lower-level (verb-class-specific) 'intended transfer'-construction [[NP_X V_{int} NP_Y NP_Z] / ['X intends to cause Y to receive Z']] and the verb-specific construction [[NP_X *promise* NP_Y NP_Z] / ['X promises to cause Y to receive Z']] do not replicate independently. They are nevertheless activated as soon as they are instantiated by a construct such as *John promised me a chocolate cake* in usage. While only this particular clause is in fact replicated, its production and perception involve a range of other constructions at all levels of schematicity (like those exemplified). These constructions can therefore be said to replicate 'through' their concrete instantiation; together, they form replicator-plexes. In the following I nonetheless often take a shortcut and refer to e.g. the replicative success of the schematic DOC. It should be understood that this still refers to the fitness of the specific micro-construction the higher-level pattern is replicated through, and which is instantiated in use by a construct.

Note that these assumptions are possibly at odds with Wedel's (2006: 249) notion of evolutionary exemplar theory. On Wedel's account, non-discrete, gradient categories constitute replicators. We are dealing with "a system that has no real independent replicators, but simply consists of a distribution that replicates each point along the distribution in each generation by interpolating gradiently between all nearby points" (Wedel 2006: 249). In the present approach, by contrast, discreteness of replicators is retained as it is individual exemplars composing a category that are involved in replication proper. This account still allows for a certain 'fuzziness' of categories in the sense that abstract constructions can relate to a range of different lower (as well as horizontally near) constructions (and vice versa). The strength of these links varies in degree, which gives the impression of gradience. Furthermore, gradience of categories is always present at the population level, since individual speakers will never completely overlap in their precise representations of specific labels. That is, fuzziness emerges in a speech community as a result of variation in the distribution of exemplars across different speakers.

The process of replication itself, following McCrohon (2012), as well as Wedel (2006), involves both production and perception. In the former, i-replicators (micro-constructions) are drawn on to create e-replicators (constructs), whereas the latter process involves e-replicators activating i-replicators in the listener's brain. Repeated activation leads to increased entrenchment of the respective i-replicators. This positively impacts the probability of the construction to be activated again in the near future, and thus the likelihood of the corresponding e-replicators to be produced as well (e.g. Croft 2000: 236; Hoffmann 2013; Frank and Gontier 2010). Furthermore, frequently activated patterns will more likely be extended to other contexts, meaning they have an increased productivity. For instance, the sub-sense of 'communication' with the DOC is frequently expressed in usage, and this sub-construction is consequently taken to be highly entrenched. This in turn positively influences the future activation rate of this specific construction, and also its productivity, as new verbs can easily be added to the construction in analogy to its resident members (e.g. the use of new communication verbs such as *whatsapp* or *instagram* in the DOC).

A further idea that is interesting for the present book and in this context is Steels and colleagues' *selectionist theory of language evolution*, also referred to as *recruitment theory of language origins* (Steels 2012c; Bleys and Steels 2011; van Trijp 2012; among many others). In a nutshell, this theory proposes that:

> [H]uman brains are capable to dynamically recruit various cognitive mechanisms and configure them into strategies for handling the challenges of communication in particular environments. The configurations are retained if they increase communicative success and expressive power while minimising the effort involved (processing time, memory resources, etc.). (Steels 2007: 145)

Specifically, Steels distinguishes between two different levels at which language evolution takes place, namely language systems on the one hand, and language strategies on the other hand (2012c: 4). The former correspond to the more traditional notion of paradigms. Language systems are sets of linguistic choices – (parts of) networks of horizontally related constructions. Typically, a construction does not form part of one subsystem only, but instead incorporates parts of various distinct language systems. This can be illustrated by case marking systems such as the German or Old English one – in a German sentence that includes case markers, other systems such as argument structure systems or tense systems are typically drawn on as well. Further examples of linguistic systems are colour systems in different languages, or (tense-)aspect systems such as that of Russian. Language strategies, in contrast, constitute 'instructions' to form, extend, and also adapt constructions so that a specific communicative goal can be reached (Bleys and Steels 2011: 152). That is, language strategies comprise components for dealing with the formation, learning and alignment of language systems (Steels 2010: 5–6; 2011b: 345). As discussed in van Trijp (2012), for instance, German speakers are assumed to have a 'case strategy' for handling the concrete instantiations of participant roles that form the case system of German. Importantly, languages can vary in the strategies that they employ, with e.g. Japanese using a particle system to express participant roles instead of a case system. Even if they apply the same strategy, however, the systems that are formed by means of the strategy may differ substantially (compare the differences between the German and the Old English case system). Finally, languages frequently use more than one strategy for a particular domain: Present Day English employs word order in combination with prepositional phrases to express core semantic roles, while at the same time retaining some minor traces of the Old English case system (Steels 2012c: 5–6).[163]

As to the ontology of these language strategies, in the experiments conducted on the basis of these assumptions they are operationalised as objects in the memories of the language users. Precisely, constructions learnt and used by the agents are tagged, specifying which strategy was used to acquire (or develop) them (Bleys and Steels 2011: 254). Steels (2010: 5–10) draws on the distinction between genotypes and phenotypes in biological evolution, taking strategies to correspond to the former, and systems to the latter, but does not comment on the material or non-material basis of either. Elsewhere, however, it is specified that communal language strategies, which are shared by a majority of the members of a speech community, "emerge out of the collective activity of all individuals and is [sic] not explicitly accessible nor represented" (Bleys and Steels 2011: 152). This implies that strategies are fundamentally distinct to the choices within systems, which on our account constitute concrete neuronal activation patterns in individual brains. Rather than being physically real entities, language strategies are comparable to e.g. food foraging patterns arising from the collective behaviour of ant colonies without having a material basis in the mind of a single ant. Nevertheless, such a definition of strategies does not preclude the possibility that some speakers might form highly abstract 'strategy-like' constructions such as [[core semantic roles] / [CASE]], translatable as 'use case for marking core semantic roles'.

In conclusion, what constructional replication in this book thus amounts to is the following: Linguistic replicators are form-meaning pairings which replicate through imitation in language use. More specifically, we are essentially dealing with two types of linguistic replicators: 'external' constructs and 'internal' micro-constructions. While replication accordingly really only takes place at the lowest, most substantial level of the constructional network, abstract constructions are activated in every usage event as well and can thus be said to replicate via their concrete instantiations. Types of replicator network structures can be assessed as language systems. Furthermore, language strategies emerge in populations of speakers and are assumed to replicate as well, despite having no ontological basis in the minds of speakers.

---

163 As Steels (2012c: 6) points out, and as is well-known, the term 'strategy' as used in this regard is common in typological studies.

6.2.2 Constructional variation

Moving on to the emergence of variation from an evolutionary constructionist perspective, we find that depending on the precise definition of constructionalisation, this question presents less or more of an issue. Generally, considering the interface of the construct and micro-constructional level (and accordingly the individual language user) as the initial locus of altered replication/ innovation is perfectly compatible with what has been outlined so far. The relation between variation through altered replication and constructional change versus constructionalisation as distinguished by Traugott and Trousdale (2013), however, is decidedly more difficult to specify. By contrast, integrating Smirnova's conceptualisation of constructionalisation – followed in this book for this and other reasons – is comparatively straightforward (e.g. Smirnova 2015).

To briefly elaborate, Traugott and Trousdale's (2013) differentiation between 'constructional change' as changes affecting only one side of a construction, and 'constructionalisation' as the creation of a new node when both form and meaning of a construction change, has been criticised as difficult to uphold (see section 1.2.1 above for an introduction to these concepts, and Börjars, Vincent, and Walkden 2015 as well as Hilpert 2018 for critical comments on the issue).[164] From an evolutionary linguistic viewpoint, the main problem in this regard is that if we consider whole constructions to be replicators, any change to any aspect of the construction necessarily generates a variant replicator, which competes against the original unit. Whereas a listener's interpretation of a *to*-PP as a 'recipient' instead of a 'goal' would, for example, count as the emergence of a new variant on the present account, it would not constitute

164 There are two broader issues which are also discussed in Börjars, Vincent, and Walkden (2015) and are also problematic for the conceptualisation of constructionalisation as proposed in Traugott and Trousdale, as well as constructionist approaches in general: First, the question of change in the individual language user on the one hand, and change on the population level on the other hand, as well as the connection between these, is to some extent glossed over, or muddled in various places. Second, the notions of synonymy and polysemy in construction grammar are often employed in a rather vague way. As to the former, 'the principle of synonymy', if taken as a synchronic restriction, would a priori rule out the possibility of formal differences without meaning distinctions. This is of course less issue if we take the principle as a diachronic tendency in that we expect formal changes to be accompanied or followed by meaning differentiation. The idea of change leading to an encountered form being linked to a different meaning than before ($\text{SYN}_1\text{-SEM}_1 \leftrightarrow \text{SYN}_1\text{-SEM}_2$), by contrast, is difficult to uphold in an account that disallows (or argues against) constructional polysemy but instead posits schematicity hierarchies on the basis of collocational, i.e. formal, distinctions (cf. Croft 2003; Barðdal and Gildea 2015).

constructionalisation yet on Traugott and Trousdale's approach. There are three possible ways to deal with this mismatch: (a) we assume that parts of the construction, but not whole constructions, constitute replicators. Acquisition of replicator (variant) status is then not equal to developing construction status. Since this goes counter to what has been discussed in the previous section, where constructions have been identified as the most likely candidates for replicators, we disregard this option. Another possibility (b) is to say that variation is really only generated once innovation on both levels has occurred. Constructional changes may represent steps in the emergence of new variants, but do not yet produce them. This is similarly unsatisfactory, since it is unclear how these constructional changes can be accounted for in an evolutionary approach. Last, we can follow earlier critical reviews of Traugott and Trousdale's proposal, and dismiss the clear distinction between constructional changes and constructionalisation, and instead opt for a model which argues for constructionalisation as the gradual accumulation of very subtle changes, more specifically the accumulation of contextual restrictions. As discussed in section (1.2.1), this is precisely what Smirnova (2015), among others, suggests. Her approach is congruent with evolutionary thinking in that evolution in other domains such as biology proceeds exactly in this way. New variants are constantly produced through imperfect replication, but we may only come to see a 'visible' effect of such modifications after generations. What this essentially boils down to is the following: I work under the assumption that changes to any aspect of a replicator-construction always lead to the addition of a new variant, which enters competition with the resident one. However, these changes proceed in a crucially bottom-up and cumulative way, meaning that the 'constructionalisation' of a more abstract schema is inevitably preceeded by a potentially very large number of tiny modifications on lower, more substantive (micro-constructional) levels of the network.

As to the triggers of emergence of variation, there is no real conclusion to be drawn on the basis of constructionist accounts. Both considering innovation as random and taking it to be driven by functional motivations – as proposed by Croft (2000, 2013a) – seems to be readily compatible with constructionist ideas. As detailed in section (5.1.2.3), I thus continue to view innovation as proceeding 'blindly' and randomly, since the likelihood of mutations to occur is not causally related to their ensuing fitness (Rosenbach 2008: 39). Despite acknowledging the possibility of entirely random innovations to occur, altered replication is, however, thought to be influenced by the main mechanisms identified in constructionist accounts, including analogical thinking, priming, as well as spreading activation, among others.[165]

Finally, variation can not only be seen in constructional replicators, but can also be considered in terms of language systems versus language strategies, as introduced in the preceding section. That is, change can affect both systems and strategies. Regarding the former, these basically correspond to changes in the constructional network (e.g. Traugott and Trousdale 2013; Torrent 2015). For example, the complexity or range of choices that are adopted may increase or decrease, in that constructions can be added or lost to the paradigmatic network. On the other hand, existing constructions may change in their semantics or form, meaning that the 'semantic territory' covered by a certain choice may grow or shrink. Yet another possibility is that the formal marking of a feature changes (Steels 2012c: 7–8; also Steels 2010, 2011b). Importantly, however, such changes do not affect the underlying system and the strategy building it, but only the specific make-up of the system of (schematic) constructions. The weakening of formal and functional distinctions between the dative and accusative case in Old/Middle English, for instance, did not yet mean the complete loss of the case system as such, but merely changed its structure. Nevertheless, "changes in a language system can be very significant and may lead to a ripple effect destabilizing other language systems and eventually requiring the introduction of new strategies" (Steels 2011b: 346). That is, if many micro-changes accumulate into more systematic, larger-scale changes, this can trigger changes on the level of strategies that are used to maintain different subsystems, with individual strategies emerging or disappearing. A particularly apt example in this regard is the expression of core semantic roles in the history of English: As a result of great changes within the case system, the case strategy which predominantly characterised Old English (and early Middle English) has been mostly lost, while additional strategies such as prepositional phrases and fixed word order have emerged (see chapter 3). Further examples of this kind are abundant in the development of the world's languages – compare Van de Velde's (2014) discussion of verbal syntax and semantics in the history of Dutch, which can also be read in terms of strategy competition.

If more than one strategy is present in a population, these strategies frequently cooperate and coexist side by side. The individual strategies are typically more successful in certain contexts than in others. Another outcome of competition between strategies is dominance of one and loss of the other, due to the

165 The role of priming as a cognitive mechanism in both faithful and altered replication is discussed in detail in Rosenbach (2008: 55–62).

benefits for speaker populations that lie in sharing a default strategy for the same type of problem (Bleys and Steels 2011: 153–154).[166] Even if a strategy comes to be dominant in part of a speaker population, though, it is not necessary for a whole community to 'agree' on the same strategy. For instance, we see in dialect variation that multiple solutions can remain available in a larger population, with some parts converging on a distinct strategy (or combination of strategies) than others. In general, Steel's approach thus coincides with the main tenets of standard sociolinguistic accounts but also (diachronic) usage-based construction grammar in that change is assumed to be gradual. This holds both in the sense of smaller-scale changes incrementally leading to larger-scale changes, as well as concerning the fact that innovations propagate through a community at different speeds (Steels 2012c: 8–9).

6.2.3 Constructional selection

Independently of how variation emerges, the successful propagation of specific innovations in a community is determined by selectional factors, defined by Wedel (2006: 252) as:

> Any factor[s] that influence[] the likelihood that a given exemplar will participate in production or that influence[...] the way a given percept is likely to be categorized will influence the direction in which the category system updates over time. Exemplars that are more 'fit' by these criteria will leave a greater trace in the future behavior of the category than exemplars that are less fit.

These various selective pressures 'implicitly intervene' in the production and perception of the replicator, meaning that in every communicative event those replicators are chosen which appear to be the best solution in the respective case (Steels 2012c: 14). The success of the selected variant is then monitored and registered in memory via self-enforcing causal loops, which can increase or decrease the likelihood of future use of the specific element within individual speakers as well as the speaker population as a whole. Success in replication corresponds to repeated and frequent activation and use, which leads to an increased entrenchment of the construction in question. As Steels points out,

166 Strategies of course do not compete directly with each other, but rather do so "through the use of the language systems that they enable their users to build" (Bleys and Steels 2011: 155). Although it is clear that by omitting these details, information and a certain clarity is lost, I continue to do so for the sake of economy and reading flow.

"there is [furthermore] a cumulative effect because solutions that have been successful are maintained in the population, enabling their further use as building blocks for tackling more challenging communicative goals in more demanding contexts" (2012c: 15). Note that the idea of an accumulative self-enforcing effect is also reflected in the concept of pre-emption resulting in language change as briefly referred to in section (1.2.1):

> [I]f preemption leads to the functional diversification of two (or more) variants, then each single usage event can trigger or reinforce contextual associations, which in the long run will affect the statistical probabilities of each variant in particular social and linguistic contexts. (Hoffmann and Trousdale 2011: 6)

With regard to the types of selectional pressures determining the success of variants, I take these to comprise physiological-cognitive aspects, systemic factors, as well as factors pertaining to the social dimension of communication, in line with what has been discussed in section (5.1.2.3). In this context, there are clear mutual benefits of integrating evolutionary linguistics and construction grammar. Cognitive and usage-based linguistics (and with that, most versions of construction grammar) provide insights on the specifics of domain-general cognitive as well as socio-cognitive factors and motivations at play in language use or acquisition. Furthermore, the network-character of linguistic knowledge is highlighted and specified in construction grammar, which allows for a ready and accessible assessment of intra-systemic factors determining the success of variants. Among the former, factors that may aid the propagation of individual replicators and thus increase communicative success are learnability and expressivity (or expressive power/adequacy), as well as the cognitive effort that is involved in producing or parsing a construction (Steels 2007, 2010, 2012c; Smith, Tamariz, and Kirby 2013). An assessment of the impact of such factors is presented in van Trijp's (2013) experimental investigation of the definite article paradigm in the history of German. Taking into account the specific factors of cue reliability, ease of articulation, auditory distinctiveness, and processing efficiency, he demonstrates that case syncretism has led to an 'improved', more economical system in respect to processing as well as perception and pronunciation, while at the same time retaining the language's power of disambiguation (van Trijp 2013: 105). Within the system of definite articles, some (such as Old High German *dër* or *diu*) were more successful than others (e.g. Old High German *dëro*), due to their better performance concerning e.g. ease of articulation. On the other hand, they still possessed enough expressive power to prevent the system from collapsing. Similar cognitive biases are mentioned in many (usage-based) constructionist accounts and play a very important role in functional and usage-based approaches compatible with constructionist thinking (e.g. Goldberg 2006, 2013; Bybee 2010, 2013; Hoffmann 2013; Bybee and Beckner 2014, *inter alia*; cf. also Hruschka et al. 2009).

For intra-systemic factors, it is assumed that "[t]he structure of a language itself can also bias the use of one variant over another" (Hruschka et al. 2009: 467, Box3; also Wellens et al. 2013). That is, constructions rarely (if ever) occur in isolation, but typically form part of larger patterns in discourse which may affect their replicative success. Furthermore, they are not mentally represented in isolation, but horizontally and vertically relate to other constructions in the network (cf. section 1.2.1). These patterns form part of the constructional environment of the replicating item, meaning they can also impact their fitness: Structures better adapted to the constructional landscape will be more successful than other variants (see Petré 2014: 11–19 for a similar approach). This presumption fits well with, for instance, the concept of alternation-based productivity as discussed in Perek (2015) and introduced in section (2.2.2). If the use of one member of the dative alternation positively influences the probability of the other variant to be used in succeeding discourse, systemic factors – in addition to more general physiological-cognitive ones – can be taken to be at play. Another example would be case affixes, which are dependent on other elements as well as larger argument structure constructions to be produced; they are consequently also shaped by the reproductive success of the latter (e.g. van Trijp 2012). Also, system-wide changes like the loss of case marking may proceed on the basis of systemic impact. In a system in which case-less patterns are generally becoming more frequent (e.g. due to reasons of economy), new case-less variants will be at an advantage. This way change can proceed incrementally through the network. Petré suggests that the impact of changes in such environmental conditions for constructional transmission may even be more influential than competition between variants, or rather, that "[i]n the loss of [a linguistic item], competition is often subordinate to environmental change" (2014: 21).

Last, construction grammar has often been criticised for not paying sufficient attention to the social values of constructions, and the social dimension of communication, despite generally stressing the communicative function of language (e.g. Schmid 2015).[167] As is well known, the use of particular linguistic features can signal group identity, or conversely function to distance a speaker from membership in a certain group. The degree of social conformity, as well as prestige and status of a replicator is therefore certainly a criterion to take ac-

167 Cf. e.g. Rostila (2007) for a comment on this issue.

count of (Steels 2010, 2012c). Moreover, the structure of the population of speakers usually plays a role in the propagation of a replicator. This factor, which roughly corresponds to the criterion of 'coherence' in van Trijp (2012: 189), is especially highlighted in social network accounts such as Beckner et al. (2009) as well as Hruschka et al. (2009) and Blythe and Croft (2012). The constructionist shortcoming of neglecting such issues is remedied by the inclusion of social factors and population structure as one type of selectional pressures influencing the fitness of an individual replicator.

Making use of the distinction between constructions, systems, and strategies again, we find that the latter's replicative success (and thus their maintenance in a population) is determined by the same selectional pressures as just outlined. That is, linguistic selection operates on variants on all levels, including paradigmatic choices as well as strategic variants. Selection is conceptualised in Steels (2012c) as a process of 'testing' variants according to their performance in regard to particular selective factors. A crucial point is furthermore that the result of selection and the frequency of a variant are connected via a self-enforcing causal loop, making the process cumulative (Steels 2012c: 12; also Garrod et al. 2007; Fay et al. 2010; Steels and Loetzsch 2012). As to selection on the level of systemic choices, those constructional variants – or rather, their concrete instantiations in production and comprehension – that result in higher communicative success due to having greater expressive adequacy, requiring less cognitive effort, or being more learnable and more conforming to social convention, will have a higher probability of being re-used in future communication events. Being more entrenched, they are likely to be activated again (e.g. Bleys and Steels 2011: 153–154).

Regarding competing strategies, those that maximise communicative success on the basis of the same criteria as just mentioned will again be retained and propagated even further, with self-enforcing causal loops via communicative success acting on the strategy (Steels 2012c: 14–17). This view directly corresponds to usage-based, bottom-up approaches like the version of construction grammar used in this book, which share the fundamental assumption that actual linguistic experiences affect the mental representation of language. Such feedback-loops in linguistic selection can be imagined as follows: The communicative success of specific systemic choices has a short-term effect on the system, and potentially alters its structure. The success of variants within a system generated and maintained by means of particular strategy can on a long-term basis then also influence the strategy itself, and thus possibly causes it to be overtaken by a different strategy. The precise predictions made by this approach or rather, questions such as 'how can strategies emerge and propagate' or 'how are systems built given a strategy' that arise in taking such an approach, have been addressed and tested in various experiments including agent-based modelling (cf. e.g. van Trijp 2010, 2012; Beuls and Steels 2013; Lestrade 2016). Of special interest to the present book is van Trijp (2012), who deals with the emergence of case systems and case strategies, specifying the constructional basis of these developments as well as the various factors determining the success (or non-success) of the system. Similarly, Steels (2007) comments on the emergence of strategies and systems for marking predicate-argument structure.

The relevance of the distinction between language systems and language strategies is considered in some more detail in section (7.3), where it is also applied to the history of the dative alternation in English. More precisely, what I suggest is that there are benefits in distinguishing between linguistic selection on the level of constructional choices on the one hand, and language strategies, as emergent collective behaviours, on the other hand. This distinction has already been alluded to in the evolutionary game theoretic model presented in section (5.2), where the viability of different strategies (NP vs. PP) under changing environmental conditions has been tested. The main argument to be proposed is that the constructional variants moved from competition to cooperation; in terms of strategies, we see a switch from a single optimal strategy to a strategy combination/ mixed strategy. In the following section, I discuss the notions of competition and cooperation as well as constructional innovation and co-evolution, which are to form the crucial conceptual background to the account presented in chapter (7).

6.3 Constructional innovation, competition, cooperation, and co-evolution

The main focus of this book is on explaining the history of the dative alternation based on the concepts of constructional innovation, competition, cooperation, and co-evolution. The first of these, i.e. innovation in the inventory of constructions of a language, has already been dealt with in previous sections on the emergence of variation in a system. I assume that imperfect replication leads to a new constructional variant being added. I argue here that new variants arise whenever changes occur on the form OR on the function/meaning side of an existing construction. On the present account it is thus not necessary for both sides of a sign to be altered in order for a new construction to come into existence. Whenever some aspect of a resident construction changes, a new node is created, which qualifies as a variant of the old one. Nevertheless, change is taken to proceed in an incremental, gradual way, with lower-level variation accumulating to changes to more abstract schemas over time (cf. Smirnova 2015). The new form is taken to be clearly (horizontally) linked to its source construction in the network; it maintains a strong connection to it and typically also preserves certain features from it. That is, aspects of new items can be explained by the 'backward pull' of the constructions' history, in that they "tend to be constrained in many cases by the constructions from which they derive" (Traugott 2008b: 34; cf. also Petré 2012; Hopper's 1991 concept of 'persistence' in grammaticalisation). To illustrate this with the case of the dative alternation, the reanalysis of the PP-argument in a construction [[NP_X V NP_Y PP_Z] / ['X causes Y to move to Z']] from GOAL to RECIPIENT results in a new construction [[NP_X V NP_Y PP_Z] / ['X causes Z to receive Y']]. Although this new pattern is independent from the old construction, it is crucially still connected to its source. Its peculiar features are a consequence of its origins and these relations: Such a backward pull can e.g. be seen in the PRC's preference for clause-late position, since PPs generally occurred more frequently in the periphery of the clause.

Newly emerged constructions are not only connected to their source patterns but may also enter competition with formally unrelated resident constructions and come to qualify as variants of them. For instance, the emergence of the PRC creates a variant form for expressing ditransitive events, in addition to the older DOC. Importantly, the emergence of competition is here conceptualised as the emergence of constructional connections in the network; more precisely, competition ensues as soon as horizontal, paradigmatic links between two constructions, such as the DOC and the *to*-PRC, develop (cf. Traugott and Trousdale 2013: 15; Van de Velde 2014: 147; also Diessel 2015).

Applying the concept of competition to language change, or more generally language use, is of course not new in linguistics, but is explicitly and implicitly found in many studies from early on. Wang (1969), for example, uses competition to explain historical sound change, while Kroch (1989a, 1989b, 1994) and Pintzuk (1991, 1999) investigate competition in diachronic syntax. More recent studies on competition (or 'rivalry') in the domain of morphology are e.g. Bauer (2006), Gries and Hilpert (2010) or Arndt-Lappe (2014). Competition is thus fairly omni-present as a linguistic concept. One of the most basic definitions of the term, which I also employ in this book, is competition as "the struggle among alternative forms" (Berg 2014: 342). Two linguistic elements "vie for being selected in instantiations [...] of a function which they both can adequately fulfill" (Petré 2014: 16). That is, competition arises when there are two or more forms which are similarly suitable for a specific goal (Berg 2014: 343). Particularly interesting for the present study, and prime examples of competition in language variation and change, are syntactic alternations: For instance, *to*-

infinitive, bare infinitive and gerund compete against each other in patterns with *help* and *try* (Kjellmer 2000; Lohmann 2011; Rohdenburg 2013), and *that*- and zero- constructions are in competition for complementation (e.g. Elsness 1984; Thompson and Mulac 1991; Ferreira and Dell 2000). Similarly, *of*- and *s*-genitive are said to compete (e.g. Altenberg 1982; Rosenbach 2002; Szmrecsanyi and Hinrichs 2008) and different positions are possible for particles of verbs like *to look up* (Chen 1986; Gries 1999; Lohse, Hawkins, and Wasow 2004; Cappelle 2006). Mondorf (2009), among others (e.g. Lindquist 2000; Hilpert 2008), looks at the competition between synthetic and analytic adjective comparison, while Denis and Tagliamonte (2017) investigate competition in the English future temporal reference system. The competitive relationship that characterises the PDE dative alternation is at the heart of numerous studies mentioned above.

Such instances of variation may reflect ongoing language change or eventually lead to language change. That is, once variation is generated, and the variants have entered competition against each other, selection takes place. Differential replication, and thus the fitness of the variants, is determined by a range of environmental pressures, including cognitive-physiological, social, and intra-systemic factors (Ritt 2004: 221–229; Rosenbach 2008: 32; also Beckner et al. 2009). Certain constructions may be fitter than others due to greater ease of effort or social prestige, but also because of their connections to other parts of the network, since replicators rarely appear in isolation (also Petré 2014). Depending on how well a variant fares in respect to these pressures, it will be replicated more successfully/frequently, or less successfully/frequently than its competitor. A higher activation rate of one variant can then result in the complete loss and 'substitution' of the other variant: "[T]he functional domain over which expressions compete comes to be occupied by a single expression at the expense of all others" (De Smet et al. 2018: 198). Examples for such developments are again widespread in the linguistic literature. As is well known, the interdental fricative third person singular present tense suffix (e.g. *give-th*) has, for instance, yielded to its competitor alveolar fricative suffix (*give-s*); cf. e.g. Gries and Hilpert (2010). In regard to ditransitives, the results in chapter (4) and the ensuing discussion in chapter (7) shows that the prepositional pattern e.g. ousted the DOC with dispossession and benefaction verbs (**John stole Mary a book* vs. *John stole a book from Mary*; **John opened Mary the door* vs. *John opened the door for Mary*). Nevertheless, there are also instances where both items survive, and continue to co-exist. While it is commonly assumed that co-existence of old and new form means continuing competition (cf. e.g. Berg 2014: 357), I argue below that this is not necessarily the case.

The specifics of how competition is conceptualised differ between accounts and frameworks – in generative studies, competition is mostly seen as 'grammar competition', i.e. children acquiring a different grammar than their parents, and the different grammars then competing on a population level (e.g. Kroch 1994; Pintzuk 1999; Yang 2001, 2002). In other works, it is the linguistic elements themselves that compete. However, this is often approached in a rather vague and non-committal way. In the present book, among others, I use the concept in a non-metaphoric way, since linguistic items qualify as replicators and can thus directly compete with each other. Berg (2014: 343–348) discusses competition from a psycholinguistic perspective, and seeks the underlying mechanism affecting language variation and change in language processing. He states that "[a]t its core, competition is a psycholinguistic effect which arises in the task of selecting an intended unit from among a number of elements concurrently activated in the processing network (Berg 2014: 338). Competition is accordingly defined as taking place in the retrieval process and builds on co-activation in the linguistic network in speaker minds. Small differences in activation values of the competing variants means strong competition, weak co-activation means weak competition (Slowiaczek and Pisoni 1986; Berg 2014: 343–344). Frequency affects co-activation and competition in the following way: Low frequency competitors will have less impact on their competitors than high frequency items, and the latter are also less likely to be influenced. Finally, the similarity (phonological and semantic similarity) between the competitors are indicative – greater similarity leads to greater competition (Berg 2014: 344; cf. also e.g. Fay and Cutler 1977; Shallice and McGill 1978; Stemberger and MacWhinney 1986; Vitevitch 1997). Psycholinguistic evidence for competition comes from disfluencies and experimental data on alternations (e.g. Chafe 1979, 1994; Clark and Fox Tree 2002 on the former), as well as studies on priming effects (e.g. Bock and Irwin 1980; Bock 1986; Bock and Griffin 2000, Branigan et al. 2006; Hartsuiker et al. 2004; Kaschak 2007; Goldwater et al. 2011; Kaschak, Kutta, and Jones 2011, 2014 on the dative alternation). Similarly, findings from language acquisition research can be used to support these assumptions (e.g. Dodson and Tomasello 1998; Campbell and Tomasello 2001, Gries and Wulff 2005; de Marneffe et al. 2012 on the dative alternation).

In addition to linguistic elements in all domains of language (phonological, morphological, syntactic competition, etc.), linguistic competition can also be approached in a range of different ways. Berg (2014) demonstrates this, and presents an intricate overview of competition in linguistics, approaching it as a "unifying concept in the study of language". That is, competition is also often viewed as taking place between linguistic levels, for instance between phonological and morphological forces (Berg 2014: 350-351). Berg illustrates this with the competition between compounds (*atom bomb*) and adjective-noun phrases (*atomic bomb*). Viewing this as competition between morphology and syntax, the success of one variant over the other would then depend on the relative strength of the impact of either domain (cf. also Schlücker and Hüning 2009; Ackema and Neeleman 2010). On the other hand, numerous studies have concerned themselves with competition between motivations or functional factors, such as explicitness or economy, or innovative vs. conservative forces (e.g. Du Bois 1985, 2014; Haiman 1983, 2011; Kirby 1994, 1997; Haspelmath 1999).[168]

Returning to competition in language change – here defined as the emergence of horizontal links between constructions –, it has already been mentioned that one outcome of competition resolution is typically loss of one variant. However, antagonistic competition between variants and ousting of one variant crucially is not the only option of interaction between variants (cf. Ritt 2004: 221–229; also Berg, 2014; De Smet et al. 2018). Rather, competition can also result in stable co-existence of variants, and can even lead to mutualistic relationships between them. Such cooperative, mutually beneficial associations are frequent in the biological world, where they represent "interaction[s] between organisms in which each participant experiences a gain in *fitness*" [original italics] (Moore and Cotner 2011: 277). That is, we frequently find "interactions between species which are beneficial for both" (Petré 2014: 19). For instance, yucca moths and yucca plants depend on each other for reproduction: On the one hand, the moths profit from the plants in that they lay their eggs in them, and the larvae can then feed from their seeds. On the other hand, the moths act as pollinators for the plants, meaning that there is reciprocal benefit in their relationship (e.g. Moore and Cotner 2011: 175). Another term used in this book to describe mutualistic, cooperative associations is 'symbiosis'. Note, however, that in biology this label generally refers to any interaction between organisms or species, be it antagonistic, parasitic, predatory or mutualistic (Moore and Cotner 2011: 281; among others).

Loosely transferring and adapting these concepts to the linguistic domain, I propose that competition between linguistic items indeed often yields to cooperation.[169] I thus suggest that competition between constructional variants can

168 See further Malkiel (1968); Bates and McWhinney (1987); Ronneberger-Sibold (1987); Werner (1987); Croft (1990); Kemmer (1992); Gaskell & Marslen-Wilson (2002); among many others.

169 This idea is again not entirely new: For example, Petré (2014) comments on the possibility of mutualistic interactions between constructions.

lead to mutualistic cooperations between them. These cooperations likewise enhance the fitness of both (or all) constructions involved, corroborating the claim that the success of variant patterns is not only determined by cognitive and social factors, but also by their systemic environment. Among the clearest examples of constructional cooperation are, I argue, grammatical alternations (cf. also Berg 2014: 352–356). Positive priming effects as witnessed in such alternations count among the evidence for cooperative instead of competitive relationships. The beneficial, symbiotic nature of linguistic cooperation relationships as seen in the English dative alternation is dealt with in more detail in chapter (7).

As abundantly discussed in previous literature, competition relationships are typically characterised by 'differentiation' of the variants, meaning that the variants specialise to specific, complementary grammatical, discourse-pragmatic or social functions (also e.g. Traugott and Trousdale 2013). In other words, "the functional domain competed over ends up being divided, with each expression filling a unique functional niche" (De Smet et al. 2018: 198). This process can also be regarded as reflecting general trends towards elimination of unpredictable variation in a system (Fehér, Wonnacott, and Smith 2016; Samara et al. 2017; Fehér, Ritt, and Smith 2017; *inter alia*). While differentiation with a reduction in functional overlap does seem to be a common outcome of competition, it nevertheless appears that it is not the only one: As recently claimed by De Smet et al. (2018), a further frequent reaction to functional overlap is what they dub 'attraction', with constructions becoming functionally more similar to each other. This is illustrated, among other things, by the fact that *-ing*-clauses and infinitives following *begin* have become increasingly alike in regard to the type of subjects (agentive/ non-agentive) they appear with (De Smet et al. 2018: 8–12; for other cases of attraction see e.g. Rosenbach 2007; Hilpert 2013). In this book, I assume that both differentiation and attraction processes should also be observed in cooperative relationships. Even more so, I suggest that especially the former is indicative of emerging mutualistic cooperation rather than competition.

Furthermore, I view both differentiation and attraction processes as signs of co-evolution of constructions. This means that competition and, more importantly, cooperation relationships between constructions should show co-evolutionary effects, in that the connected patterns are expected to continuously adapt to each other and react to changes in their respective counterparts (cf. e.g. Savit, Riolo, and Riolo 2013). Such co-evolutionary responses then come in the two different forms just outlined: On the one side, constructions typically develop complementary distributional niches, becoming restricted to certain functions (cf. Torres Cacoullos and Walker 2009; Traugott and Trousdale 2013).

This niche construction is taken to be guided by the history of the constructions involved; the division of the functional space by the patterns is informed by features present in their source constructions (cf. Traugott 2008b; Petré 2012). On the other side, functionally similar, cooperating constructions are also anticipated to align to each other, becoming increasingly alike over time.

In biology, co-evolution commonly refers to the phenomenon of reciprocal evolutionary relationships between two or more species, meaning that "individuals of two or more species exert selective pressures on each other" (Moore and Cotner 2011: 161; also Dercole and Rinaldi 2008: 13). Instead of one party changing and the other reacting, until the first entity changes again, and the process starts anew, co-evolutionary scenarios see a zig-zag succession of adaptive changes or 'stepwise evolutionary responses' of the interacting entities to a (therefore) constantly changing selective environment. A good case in point is the co-evolution of certain flowers and the insects pollinating them, with both species reciprocally influencing each other's adaptations (e.g. Ehrlich and Raven 1964 on co-evolutionary patterns with butterflies and plants).[170] Ecological relationships which typically lead to co-evolution are those between predator and prey or parasite and host as well as competitive or mutualistic/cooperative associations (Cox 2006). Co-evolution in the former three, especially in competition, is often described in terms of an 'evolutionary arms race', in which the species are pressured to continually 'improve' in order to still be able to compete against the other. This means that each innovation of the antagonist has to be counteracted with an adaptation of the competing entity (cf. Dawkins 1989[2006]: 248; also Dawkins and Krebs 1979). However, the concept of an 'arms race' is also applicable to relationships between mutualists, which will continue to co-evolve and adapt to each other until an equilibrium of minimal cost and maximal benefit for both is reached (also Cox 2006). The most interesting relationships for the present study are necessarily those of competition and symbiotic mutualism, i.e. the latter two of the relationships just mentioned. In the case of competition, the species (or organisms) typically interact in an antagonistic fashion, 'fighting' for resources. In contrast, mutualism usually indicates cooperation. While changes in both competitors and mutualists can accordingly be mutually adaptive, it is only in the latter case that co-evolution is beneficial for both parties involved.

170 Incidentally, the problematic issue of correlation vs. causation is reflected in evolution in that 'co-evolution' is often distinguished from 'co-adaptation' – the latter indicates that two (or more) elements fit together in their adaptations, which does not necessarily indicate co-evolution in the sense of 'changing together' (Marten 2008: Ch.5).

Although co-evolution is best-known from biological evolutionary systems, various studies have shown that it in fact pertains to evolutionary, complex adaptive systems in general (e.g. Savit, Riolo, and Riolo 2013). Therefore, the definition of the concept can be extended to refer to "the parallel feedback process by which agents continuously adapt to the changes induced by the adaptive actions of other agents" (Savit, Riolo, and Riolo 2013).[171] Since languages are assumed to be complex adaptive systems in this book, this suggests that co-evolutionary phenomena should be seen in the historical development of languages or linguistic constituents as well. This proposal is taken up in more detail in section (7.2). Specifically, I define co-evolution as the process of constructions reacting to changes to one of them once they have become part of each other's environment, i.e. have formed horizontal relations.

Approaching the history of the dative alternation, and historical changes in general, from such a co-adaptationist/evolutionary perspective is viewed as highly useful for many reasons: Assuming a mutual influence between changes to two distinct elements (or rather, presuming that elements can engage in a reciprocal feedback and adaptive loop that gradually leads to larger changes on both sides) saves us from the danger of oversimplification. It moreover reduces the risk of confusing cause and effect that is inherent to suggesting a one-directional impact from one discrete, unified change on another, as is often done in historical linguistics. The fact that correlation between two variables does not imply and necessarily entail causation is a well-known and frequently found point of criticism in statistical analyses. Committing this logical fallacy is also widespread in historical linguistics: The lack of opportunities to obtain further data or conduct additional tests invites taking cause and effect relationships as facts where the most we can really determine is temporal correlation. A change that follows another in time is frequently taken to be the result of the earlier one (*post hoc ergo propter hoc* 'after this, therefore because of this'). Similarly, events that occur together in an overlapping time span are often interpreted as standing in a causal relation to each other (*cum hoc ergo propter hoc* 'with this, therefore because of this'), e.g. Damer (2009: 180–183). Especially in the latter case, it is furthermore easy to confuse cause and effect, since the direction of causality (if there is any) is difficult to determine when there is temporal simultaneity. In general, inferring causality from empirically observed correlation in historical linguistic data is therefore part of the theory, although

171 For a recent exploration of language change in terms of co-adaptation see e.g. Soskuthy and Hay (2017), who investigate interactions between the domains of word usage and word duration.

the plausibility of certain changes and directionalities can be assessed based on e.g. psycho- or neurolinguistic findings as well as trajectories of change in other domains. However, the possibility of co-evolutionary scenarios does of course not impede the possibility (and plausibility) of changes impacting each other in one direction.

6.4 An evolutionary construction grammar approach to language: Summary

In sum, I have suggested in this chapter that constructionist accounts and evolutionary linguistics are overall highly compatible, although compromise solutions need to be developed as well. The specific principles on which the remainder of this book builds are as follows: The unit of replication is the construction as a form-meaning mapping. Examples are the members of the dative alternation – both the DOC and the *to*-PRC in Present Day English qualify as replicators in this account. Replicators are present in two stages in language use, as external (e-)replicators in utterances, and as internal (i-)replicators in speakers' minds. These types of replicators correspond to constructs, meaning concrete token instantiations in usage, on the one hand, and micro-constructions as the cognitive representations or stored memories of such constructs on the other hand. Replication proper takes place between the levels of micro-constructions and constructs. Still, higher-level abstractions over individual usage events (subschemas, schemas) are activated in most communicative situations as well, with frequent activation leading to a higher entrenchment of specific constructions. For instance, the abstract, underspecified DOC is replicated together with, or through, less schematic, lower-level constructions, such as verb-class-specific, verb-sub-class-specific and verb-specific constructions, and finally the fully filled micro-construction (e.g. *John gave me a book*). Linguistic replication is therefore essentially a bottom-up process.

The locus of innovation is also the level of micro-constructions (and constructs). As soon as some aspect of a construction changes, a new variant constructionalises, which is nevertheless still strongly linked to the resident source construction. Often, such changes are caused by repair mechanisms in language processing. Examples of resolved mismatches leading to variation in the history of the dative alternation include the reanalysis of prepositional adjuncts (e.g. *to* expressing a locative goal) to markers of core semantic roles (e.g. *to* marking a recipient in ditransitive events). Encountering a goal-preposition with an NP ambiguous between a location and a human recipient could, for instance, trigger a partial mismatch, and the formation of a new link from *to* to a meaning previously associated only with more nominal, synthetic markers. Again, change in this approach is essentially a bottom-up process – variation through altered replication gradually accumulates both in individual speaker minds and on the population level. Most importantly for the present account, newly emerged constructions can also enter competition with previously unrelated existing patterns: In the case of ditransitives, the new PRC-construction comes to qualify as a variant and competitor of the formally different DOC due to their overlap in meaning. Emerging competition is conceptualised as the establishment of (neuronal) links between constructions which were not connected before. One consequence of this is also that the constructions become parts of each other's environment and are expected to 'react' to changes in the other.

The replicative success of the variants is determined by cognitive-physiological, systemic and social factors. As to the former, the DOC can be argued to be more economical in being shorter, while the *to*-PRC is arguably more expressive and indicative of the precise semantic role involved. Thus, the history of the dative alternation may also illustrate competing motivations in the sense of Du Bois (1985, 2014), Haspelmath (1999), and many others. Van Trijp (2013) shows that such issues can also be quantified and tested, e.g. through experimental modelling. As to intra-systemic factors, a construction's success is always also determined by its constructional environment: Tokens of the *to*-PRC with PP-late ordering are fitter than PP-early instances because they correspond better to the positional preferences in other prepositional constructions; a DOC case frame of [DAT$_{REC}$-ACC$_{TH}$] is more successful than other frames in a system in which accusative is the prototypical case for themes in other constructions; case-less ditransitive patterns are at an advantage in a system that is generally moving towards loss of case marking; transfer-related sub-senses of the DOC thrive at the expense of others once the construction becomes more strongly associated with the *to*-PRC, which expresses a matching meaning of caused motion/ possession. Finally, social conformity and prestige (or more generally social factors) play a role in determining a construction's fitness. While [TH-REC] orders with the DOC are clearly non-successful in most regions, their use might signal group membership and therefore succeed in other areas (cf. *give it me* in Northern British English). Independently of which specific factors are at play, the communicative success of the competing constructions – how well they fare regarding the different factors – is assessed in cumulative feedback loops.

The outcome of constructional selection can vary: In this book, an important distinction is made between competition and cooperation between constructions. While competition may lead to the ousting of one variant, and there can also be long-term competition, patterns may in specific circumstances enter mutually beneficial, symbiotic relationships. In both competitive and cooperative situations, constructions adapt to each other, or co-evolve. This often involves differentiation processes, but it can also mean that the constructions align to each other in some respects. I demonstrate in chapter (7) that the history of the dative alternation is essentially one of co-evolution in a cooperative relationship.

In addition to the level of language systems, which comprises parts of the constructional network and thus concerns the choice between paradigmatic constructional variants (such as the DOC and the *to*-PRC), linguistic selection also affects language strategies. These 'instructions' emerge out of the collective behaviour of speakers in a population and are shaped by alignment between individual users. Importantly, changes within systems available in a particular language can accumulate to changes in strategies: New strategies may oust older ones, or different strategies for the same functions may develop a cooperative relationship (mixed strategies emerge). A clear example is the establishment of PPs as alternatives to more synthetic means of expressing semantic roles, meaning that the constructional sub-system of semantic role marking has been extended. This systemic change (and others conforming to it) can accrue to a change in language strategies, in this case the addition of 'PPs' to the strategy inventory. What has been presented in this chapter consequently constitutes an essentially bottom-up approach, with changes triggered by usage events influencing lower-level constructions, which can in turn lead to more abstract and schematic constructions being modified. This can even amount to large-scale system-wide changes such as the loss of case markers. Changes in the paradigmatic choices available in language systems can furthermore result in long-term changes on the level of strategies.

Finally, I have shown that there are clear benefits in integrating construction grammar (and other cognitive, usage-based approaches) and evolutionary linguistics. From the perspective of the latter, construction grammar provides the necessary specifications to deal with concrete linguistic phenomena and changes in individual languages. It e.g. lets us model the network of constructions/replicators and the links between these elements in a highly detailed manner. Moreover, a great deal of research within these frameworks has gone into investigating the cognitive and neural processes at play in language use; taking into account the neuro- and psycholinguistic literature is certain to yield significant insights and helps to pin down developments on a much more concrete level. For instance, the specific trajectory of changes such as those typically described as 'grammaticalisation' or 'lexicalisation' are dealt with at length in (diachronic) construction grammar, whereas discussions of such regularities and more detailed investigations are usually not part of evolutionary accounts.[172] Constructionist approaches can thus be seen as supplementing evolutionary linguistics in providing important, more specialised information.

In the opposite direction, adding evolutionary linguistic ideas to constructionist accounts is evidently advantageous since this discipline goes "beyond [more traditional linguistic] efforts by developing explanations of how and why certain linguistic phenomena could have evolved" (Steels 2010: 2). By relating language use and evolution to other domains, and through the integration of findings and knowledge about processes at work in these other areas, new perspectives can be taken. Furthermore, and highly importantly, evolutionary linguistics paves the way for the inclusion of methods developed in other disciplines, such as systematic experiments involving agent-based modelling, or evolutionary game theory. Specifically concerning construction grammar, evolutionary thinking can be beneficial in allowing for a more general approach to certain issues: For example, distinguishing between language strategies and language systems (or rather, the variants within systems, the population of constructions available) can be helpful in dealing with larger-scale changes stretching over long periods of time, such as the loss of case marking or the fixation of word order.

In the following, the joint framework of evolutionary construction grammar as outlined in this chapter is applied to the history of the dative alternation in English. The discussion is largely based on the results of the empirical data analysis as presented in chapter (4) as well as the evolutionary game theoretic account offered in section (5.2).

172 But see e.g. the attempts to link grammaticalisation to the concept of 'exaptation' (Norde and van de Velde 2016).

7 Competition and cooperation in the English dative alternation: An evolutionary construction grammar account

The main objective of this book is to provide an evolutionary construction grammar account of the development of the dative alternation in the history of English. That is, I aim to find a historical explanation for the synchronic phenomenon of ditransitive verbs typically appearing in two different constructions, namely the double object construction and a prepositional pattern involving *to*. This issue is tackled in the following chapter, which constitutes the main discussion part of the book. It models the history of ditransitives in English in evolutionary constructionist terms and devises a plausible scenario for the development of the constructions in question. On the one hand, this involves sketching the emergence of the alternation as such. On the other hand, we need to provide an analysis of how the specific formal and functional changes in the PDE members of the alternation came about, specifically how changes such as the loss of case marking, or the increasing fixation of word order affected the patterns over time. Methodologically, the account presented in this chapter draws on the results of both the corpus study as presented in chapter (4), as well as the outcome of the evolutionary game theoretic model shown in section (5.2).

The conceptual toolkit employed in the chapter most prominently incorporates the notions of constructional networks, constructionalisation, variation, competition and competition resolution, cooperation, niche construction, symbiosis, alternation-based productivity, mutual adaptiveness, and co-evolution, which have been laid out in detail in section (6.3). As the basic starting point, the underlying assumption here is that ditransitives constitute a network of argument structure constructions linked by the fact that they involve three argument roles: an agent, an entity that is acted upon (theme), and a third participant affected by this action ('recipient'). The individual constructions forming part of this network are the replicators whose success we are interested in. They include, for instance, an Old English schematic, underspecified DOC, a range of case constructions connected to it, as well as several sub-constructions instantiating different meanings. Further relevant replicators are the *to*-PRC and various other PRCs involving e.g. *from*, *of* or *towards* and *till*, as well as prepositional theme patterns (PTCs) and possessive structures (POSS). These constructions are in turn associated with variants differing in terms of constituent order: For

https://doi.org/10.1515/9783110633856-007

example, [REC-TH] and [TH-REC] but also [*prep*REC-TH] and [TH-*prep*REC], respectively, are taken to represent variants to each other.

Regarding diachronic change, both the make-up of this network and the formal and functional features of the participating patterns are subject to quite substantial change. Moreover, the network as such is altered as new links emerge or fade. Structural properties of the constructions may be affected in that the specific marking of the constituents involved or their relative position in the clause changes over time. On the functional side, both semantic narrowing and semantic widening of members of the network can be seen. Constructionalisation in this context refers to the emergence of new constructions, often taking on similar meanings to those of already existing constructions. If such an overlap is given, links form between the pairings, and they count as variations of each other in the constructional network. This can be illustrated by the extension of prepositional patterns to cover new and more grammatical functions, including that of encoding ditransitive events, by which variation is produced. Through this process, the prepositional patterns are linked to the resident, non-prepositional construction, i.e. the double object construction. Since the two constructions can be used to express similar types of events, they enter competition with each other.

Competition can be resolved in various ways, often by one variant falling out of use. The loss of case marking, for instance, can be modelled as the result of competing case frames as well as case suffixes, while competition between different object orders results in the ousting of one and the fixation of the other (e.g. [REC-TH] with the DOC). Similarly, the demise of DOC uses with verbs of dispossession reflects the greater success of the PRC. In other cases, however, competition does not lead to the defeat of one constructional variant, but to the emergence of a cooperative relation. This is crucially what happens in the English dative alternation: Instead of the DOC being lost in favour of the *to*-PRC (or vice versa), the two variants have come to form a symbiotic, mutually stabilising relationship. In this relationship, the variants constitute allostructions rather than competing synonymous constructions. They are paradigmatically connected to each other, and are linked to a more schematic generalisation, the 'ditransitive' constructeme. Sharing the workload, the allostructions have come to functionally diverge and have constructed their respective niches to complement each other. At the same time, the patterns exhibit signs of alignment, or attraction, becoming more similar in certain aspects. Both divergence and convergence are here interpreted as co-evolutionary effects or mutual adaptiveness between the constructions. That is, once they become associated with each other, a change to one construction typically triggers a response in its variant, which in turn reacts again. Such a co-evolutionary scenario is argued to have taken place, among other things, regarding the semantics of the constructions. With the semantic widening of the PRCs, the DOC became semantically narrower; the end-product of this is a closer semantic connection between the latter and the *to*-PRC. On the other side, the patterns have retained (or created) subtle semantic differences and are thereby better apt at stabilising each other. Changes in the linguistic system of English finally correspond and determine changes to the strategies available in the population. Developments in the inventory of strategies for ditransitive event encoding (or semantic role marking in general) have led to the formation of a mixed strategy/ strategy cooperation between the DOC (NPs) and the *to*-PRC (PPs).

The chapter starts with a discussion of the emergence of the dative alternation as a case of constructional innovation, competition, and cooperation in (7.1). This section sees an assessment of the change in the context of systemic, network-wide developments in Middle English, more specifically the rise of prepositional patterns beyond ditransitives. Importantly, changes in the larger network are considered as changes in the environmental conditions for the structures at hand. They play a major role in determining the success (or fitness) of the members of the alternation. In section (7.2), changes in the formal and functional features of the patterns are revisited and explained as instances of constructional co-evolution. Again, these alternation-specific developments are contextualised in terms of the constructional fitness landscape: For example, outlining the increase in word order constraints in ditransitives also means taking a look at word order in other clause types (or indeed the entire system). It should, however, be noted that since these surrounding constructions were not investigated empirically in this project, much of this discussion necessarily remains speculative. In the section, I furthermore address the question of causality between different changes in this scenario. Instead of assuming a monodirectional and simple effect of one change on another, I argue for a complex interplay of changes influencing each other in continuous feed-back feed-forwards loops. It seems plausible, for instance, to presume that the increasingly close association between the DOC and the *to*-PRC played a causal role in the narrowing of the former's semantics. At the same time, the increase in semantic coherence of the DOC to a meaning more compatible with the *to*-PRC could also be seen as triggering or enabling the establishment of a stronger link between the patterns in the first place. Conceptualising these developments as part of a co-evolutionary process in which the two constructions successively and gradually adapt to each other saves us from having to decide between the two options of a) the emergence of the dative alternation causing the semantic narrowing of the DOC or b) the semantic narrowing of the DOC causing the emergence of the dative alternation. It provides us with a more realistic scenario than that of one-directional effects between monolithic changes. Section (7.3) then comments on the gains to be had from viewing the changes as instances of competition between language strategies which emerge from the collective behaviour of speakers 'implemented with' different constructional systems. Finally, the main points of the chapter are summarised and restated (7.4).

7.1 The dative alternation as a case of innovation, competition, and cooperation

In the following sections, the rise of prepositional competitors to the double object construction is discussed. The key argument to be made here is that from Old English onwards, we can witness a process of continuous and incremental extension in contexts and meanings of the prepositional paraphrases, with individual PP-constructions forming very close associations to specific ditransitive verb classes. These developments can be interpreted as constructionalisation processes in the sense outlined in section (1.2.1) and (6.2.2). A change in meaning results in the addition of a new variant node. Since these new constructions express very similar meanings to the DOC, they start to compete with each other. In some cases, such as with dispossession verbs, the emerging competition finally leads to the marginalisation and eventual ousting of DOC uses, as the PRCs win out. The reasons why the prepositional variant is more successful in replicating with such verb classes are addressed in section (7.1.2.2). By contrast, with another group, importantly instantiated by the most prototypically ditransitive verbs of transfer (and transfer-related classes), a cooperation relationship forms between the DOC and the *to*-PRC. This link between the two constructions is argued to increase in strength over the course of Middle English, culminating in the establishment of a cross-constructional generalisation, the PDE 'ditransitive constructeme' (7.1.2.1). In yet a third group, the relationship between the DOC and the PRCs is not quite as straightforward and is therefore assessed on a case-to-case basis (7.1.2.3).

7.1.1 Emerging competition between PRCs and DOC through constructional innovation

Analytic paraphrases for double object constructions were, as De Cuypere (2015c) among others forcefully argues, far from absent from Old English. Quite the contrary, it appears that specific verb classes strongly associated with the DOC could also be used in various prepositional patterns at this point already (see also section 3.1.1). Most prominently, these verb classes included verbs of communication (e.g. *sprecan* 'speak, say, utter' or *cweðan* 'speak, say') as well as verbs of accompanied motion such as *bring*, *send*, or *lead*; these are frequently found with a recipient/goal argument marked by the preposition *to*. Although this has not been clearly addressed in the literature, since the main focus has typically been on the *to*-PRC (due to its prevalence in all stages, and the salient role it came to play later on), I assume that these verbs were, however, in fact not restricted to one particular preposition. Instead, they probably appeared with a range of preposition types marking the animate argument as a kind of directional goal (e.g. *towards* or *till*). The same issue presents itself with verbs of dispossession, which were occasionally expressed with a prepositional deprivee (the target or victim of a robbing/stealing event) in Old English. These PP-patterns then involved not only *from*, but also *of* or *æt* (e.g. Visser 1963: 633; Harbert 2007: 110). I anticipate that a more thorough investigation of Old English ditransitives would confirm that there was some variation concerning verb and verb class subcategorisation for prepositional types.

The emergence of such prepositional paraphrases can, as discussed in section (3.2.3.2), be addressed in terms of grammaticalisation and possibly (grammatical) constructionalisation as proposed by Smirnova (2015), among others. I illustrate this in the following by drawing on a number of cases of emerging PRCs, specifically those of *to* coming to be used with verbs of accompanied motion and animate goals, of *to*-PPs developing the innovative function of marking addressees of communication events, and finally the case of *from*, *of* and *æt*, which acquire the additional meaning of 'animate source ~ deprivee'. Furthermore, I briefly address the use of *to* and other prepositions with the semantically very heterogeneous group of complex predicate constructions. Although these patterns include the most striking examples of extended functions of prepositions (and prepositional constructions), I posit that a range of different prepositions underwent a similar process at roughly the same time and exerted an analogical impact on each other. That is, even if the commonly strong focus on *to* is also seen here, I emphasise that other PRCs – involving for example *to-gainst* – were available in OE as well (122). They possibly aided the emergence of similar patterns with other prepositions (e.g. *towards* + animate goal → *to* + ...). Moreover, as shown in (7.1.3), these newly emerging constructions were supposedly influenced by developments in other parts of the constructional network such as the increasing availability of prepositional objects for transitive verbs.

(122) þe *specaþ* yfelu$_{\text{TH}}$ **togeanes** **sawle** **mine**$_{\text{ADDR}}$
that speaks evil towards/against soul my
'who speaks evil things towards my soul'
(Lambeth Ps. cviii. 20; OED, s.v. *speak*)

Starting with the class of verbs of accompanied motion (bringing/sending verbs) and their *to*-paraphrase, we can assume that initially, *to* – in its primary function of indicating spatial directionality – was confined to collocating with inanimate spatial goals. However, in certain critical contexts like in (123a), the pragmatic inference could have been made that it was an animate person (or group of persons) situated at a location rather than the location itself that was on the receiving end of the directed action.[173] Eventually, this could lead to a reanalysis from [*to*: inanimate goal] to [*to*: animate goal], licensing unambiguously animate examples like (123b).

(123) a. *seonde* þa his gewrite$_{\text{TH}}$ **to** **Englalande**$_{\text{GOAL(inanim./anim.?)}}$
sent then his bull to England
'the pope then sent his bull to England'
(ASChron., an. 675.10.534; De Cuypere: PC)

b. *Sende* digellice arendgewritu$_{\text{TH}}$ **to** **þam** **kasere**$_{\text{GOAL(anim.)}}$
sent secretly letters to the emperor
'[he] secretly sent letters to the emperor'
(Boeth., 1.7.19.65; De Cuypere: PC)

From such initial instances of innovation, which were presumably pragmatically strongly marked, the new uses analogically extended to other types. The lexical elements able to fill the various slots of the construction then progressively and incrementally diversified and the new elements (in our case different types of objects as well as verbs) were more and more often used in this pattern. As a consequence, a new variant of the original construction is added, which in turn means a semantic generalisation of the overarching scheme. More specifically, I suggest that this process ultimately resulted in the emergence of a new (lower-level) construction of [*to*: animate goal] besides the resident [*to*: inanimate goal] construction, as well as the establishment of a semantically rather general and more schematic construction linking the two [*to*: underspecified directional entity]. Rather than competing against each other, however, the addition of new sub-types to the higher-level construction in this case is benefi-

173 See Rosenbach (2010) for a similar argument concerning classifier constructions.

cial for the more abstract schema in that the likelihood of its form being expressed increases with the extension to new contexts.[174] By acquiring new functions and therefore new sub-constructions (in a process of host-class expansion), the abstract scheme increases in generality and productivity, but at the same time decreases in compositionality (Barðdal 2008).[175] This process qualifies as an example of constructionalisation as proposed by Smirnova (2015) or grammaticalisation in the sense of Diewald and Smirnova (2012), among others. – It is nevertheless clear that in the case of caused-motion verbs, change only occurred at a relatively fine-grained level, as the overall meaning of 'concrete transfer towards a spatial goal' was not affected.

Verbs of communication present a slightly different issue, since an entirely new semantic role was acquired by the preposition. Potential bridging (or 'critical') contexts can here be found in instances of speech acts directed towards an entity ambiguous between a locational goal and an addressee, or group of addressees, as in (124a). Resulting from the frequent occurrence of such invited inferences, an addressee meaning of the *to*-PP is gradually conventionalised and semanticised; we see the establishment of a new *to*-construction, able to serve as an alternative to the DOC in expressing communication events (124b).

(124) a. þæt hit$_{TH}$ **to Rome**$_{GOAL/ADDR?}$ *gebodode*
that it to Rome told
'who told/proclaimed it to Rome'
(Orosius, 4:11.109.12.2282; De Cuypere: PC)

b. God *cwæð* **to Moysen**$_{ADDR}$ ðæt he wolde cumin$_{TH}$
God said to Moses that he would come
'God said to Moses that he would come'
(cocathom2.o3: 196, 16; De Cuypere 2015c: 18)

Addressees are often taken to constitute a metaphorical extension of recipients in PDE. However, the fact that speech verbs as a clearly delineated class are consistently found in prepositional patterns at a noticeably earlier time than the first appearances of *to*-PRCs with giving verbs, suggests that addressees and

174 Since *to* had already acquired a range of other functions, including e.g. that of marking comparison, an even more abstract construction linking the preposition's form to a highly general meaning could also be posited.

175 Also, the phenomenon of 'old' material being drawn on to fulfil new functions can be conceptualised as an instance of 'exaptation' (cf. Gould and Vrba 1982; for a discussion of grammaticalisation as exaptation see e.g. the relevant contributions in Norde and van de Velde 2016).

recipients indeed represent separate semantic roles (De Cuypere 2015c: 18; also Daniel 2014). Nevertheless, the roles clearly overlap semantically to a large extent. Subsuming both recipients and addressees under a head label of 'concrete/abstract recipients' thus seems to be warranted in less detailed analyses, especially concerning later periods.

Following from this, we can assume that *to* had acquired additional functions (sub-constructional types) in Old English already. These variants competed with some of the nominal verb-class-specific ditransitive constructions, meaning that tentative links between the patterns and the prepositional constructions formed. Even so, and crucially, the use of *to* was not yet fully extended to cover prototypical recipients at this point. Although occasional instances of 'embryonic' recipient uses can be found in OE data, this expansion to all types of direct and indirect, concrete and abstract giving events only took place at the turn to Middle English (De Cuypere 2015c).

The development of *from*-PRCs (as well as *of*- and *æt*-PRCs) proceeded along similar lines as with *to*: Again, the preposition incrementally came to be used in new contexts, here dispossession events involving animate sources. In this process, the arguments of the verbs were reanalysed as expressing the roles of deprivees rather than those of locational sources/origins (125a-b). As can be seen in e.g. (125c), this development corresponds to an extension of the constructional meaning to more abstract, indirect dispossession events where no physical movement of a concrete entity is involved, and indicates the emergence of a new type of *from/of/æt*-constructions alongside the resident ones. These types could then furthermore be abstracted over, through which schemas with comparatively generalised, underspecified meanings could emerge.

(125) a. þeah þe *numen sie* neodlice **of cocrum**$_{\text{SOURCE}}$
even if taken be forcefully of quivers
'even if they [the arrows] were forcefully taken out of the quivers'
(Aldhelm's Riddle 33; Glossary Old English Aerobics, s.v. *(ge)niman*)

b. mec$_{\text{TH}}$ sinca baldor **æt Minum fæder**$_{\text{SOURCE/DEPR}}$ *ʒenam*
me treasures' lord at My father took
'when the lord of treasures took me away from my father'
(Beowulf, 2428-2429; Glossary Old English Aerobics, s.v. *(ge)niman*)

c. Ne *afyr* þinne fultum$_{\text{TH}}$ **fram me**$_{\text{DEPR}}$
not take away your support from me
'do not take your support away from me'
(Bl. H. 105, 30; Bosworth-Toller, s.v. *a-firran*; cf. Visser 1963: 638)

Incidentally, with both communication verb and dispossession verbs, the alternative option of expressing the theme by a prepositional phrase, i.e. using a PTC instead of a DOC or PRC, was also present in Old English already. OE verbs of telling/saying are found in patterns of the type [ADDR – *prep*TH] in addition to their other uses; the specific preposition involved varies (126a-b). Dispossession verbs likewise occur in PRC-constructions as well as patterns of the type 'deprive someone of something'. This is illustrated in example (126c).

(126) a. **Þam** **cnihte**$_{REC}$ *cyðan* be his Scyppende$_{TH}$
the knight tell by his creator
'to tell the knight about his creator'
(Hml. S. 3,27, I; Bosworth-Toller, s.v. *cýþan*)

b. *Cyþ* **him**$_{REC}$ ymbe þe$_{TH}$
tell him with you
'tell him about yourself'
(Hml. S. 3, 561; Bosworth-Toller, s.v. *cýþan*)

c. Gif hwylc man *reafað* **oðerne**$_{REC}$ æt his dehter$_{TH}$
if any man robs other at his daughter
'if any man deprives another of his daughter'
(Poenitentiale Pseudo-Egberti (Laud) iv. ix. 51; OED, s.v. *reave*)

For communication verbs, it is difficult to say how salient these PTC uses were in Old English. By contrast, judging from Visser's catalogue of verbal complementation patterns (1963: 613) as well as Bosworth-Toller's dictionary entries, with a majority of dispossession verbs the prepositional theme pattern might even have been the favoured choice (at least among prepositional variants; also Schwyter 2012; Lacalle Palacios 2016). Whether there really was a clear preference for one of these options in Old English, or whether both options were equally valid would again have to be corroborated by means of a (sounder) corpus investigation of OE data. For the moment, I assume that both constructions (PRC and PTC) were available and were used as alternatives to the more nominal DOC, but possibly showed some subtle differences in terms of profiling of the respective participant roles.

Finally, two more marginal groups which differ in semantic input but pattern together syntactically (at least to a certain extent) are of interest: first, light verb constructions denoting emotive events, and second, verbs of reverse (communicated) transfer, many of which constitute complex predicate constructions as well (Brinton and Akimoto 1999a for an overview of such patterns in Old English). As to the former, complex predicate patterns such as 'have forgiveness/ envy/ love' were most probably strongly associated with prepositional patterns if the target of the emotion was overtly expressed (127a-b).

(127) a.

Began	þa	*niman*	swyðe	micle	lufe$_{\text{TH}}$	**to**	**hyre**$_{\text{REC}}$
began	then	take	so	much	love	to	her

'then he began to feel such great love for her'
(LS 35 [Vit Patr] 74-75; Akimoto and Brinton 1999: 38)

b.

genam	saul	micelne	nið$_{\text{TH}}$	**to**	**Ðam**	**gecorenan**	**dauide**$_{\text{REC}}$
took	Saul	much	envy	to	The	chosen	David

'Saul felt great envy towards the chosen David'
(ÆCHomII 4.35.194-195; Akimoto and Brinton 1999: 39)

Similarly, events of reversed transfer such as 'take example/ leave of so.' as well as of communicated reversed transfer ('ask a favour/ permission of so.') frequently occurred with a prepositional REC-argument marked by source-prepositions like *at*, *from* or *of*, among others (128a-b). Again, I presume that at some point in the history of English a reanalysis of the prepositional semantics from indicating a spatial, concrete relation to a more abstract notion of affectedness took place in these cases. As is discussed in section (7.1.3), this semantic change is supposed to have been accompanied or followed by a change in syntactic analysis, as the relations between the constituents involved became increasingly stronger through a process of chunking (e.g. Bybee 2010: 34–37).

(128) a.

Nime	heo	bysne$_{\text{TH}}$	**be**	**ðisre**	**wudewan**$_{\text{REC}}$
take	her	example	by	This	widow

'let her take example of this widow'
(Homl. Th. i. 148, 5.; Bosworth-Toller, s.v. *niman*)

b.

Hi	*bædon*	læfa$_{\text{TH}}$	**æt**	**me**$_{\text{REC}}$
they	asked	leave	at	Me

'they asked leave of me'
(Guthl. 14; Gdwin 62, 13; Bosworth-Toller, s.v. *leaf*)

It is unclear whether other verb classes such as e.g. verbs of refusal or verbs of benefaction/ malefaction were associated with a prepositional construction of any type, or any other alternative construction in Old English. Especially with verbs of malefaction, based on their distribution in early Middle English it seems more than plausible that POSS-uses were frequent in Old English already. At the same time, however, it can be assumed that no highly systematic, perceivable correspondences between entire classes and different, more abstract constructional types (except for the DOC) held at this point. That is, links may not necessarily have extended beyond the verb-specific level.

Focussing on the DOC vs. PRC, the constructional network of ditransitive verb classes in Old English can then in a simplified manner be sketched as in Fig. 33. The abstract schema of the DOC is taxonomically linked to a number of verb(-class)-specific constructions, associated with the meanings of transfer, communication, caused motion, dispossession, reverse transfer, among others. Selected types of these sub-schemas are in addition horizontally related to prepositional constructions. The dashed line here indicates that these links are only in the process of being established. While they are linked to patterns involving specific preposition types, however, they are not (yet) restricted to individual prepositions. For example, the sub-construction of dispossessive DOC is connected with not only one, but a range of SOURCE-type prepositions including *of*, *from* and *æt*. Verbs of caused/ accompanied motion, on the other hand, do not show exclusive relations with *to*-PRCs but are rather taken to subcategorise for any preposition originally denoting a directional goal. This pattern can be represented as [V_{cm} PP_{GOAL}-REC TH] in contrast to [V_{disp} PP_{SOURCE}-DEPR TH] in the case of privative verbs. The lack of an exclusive relationship to one particular preposition still does not preclude the possibility that individual PRC types are more entrenched and productive than others; especially with verbs of communication, the *to*-PRC was likely highly salient already at this point.[176]

The individual PRCs furthermore differed markedly in regard to their success in competing against the resident DOC uses. The (*to*-)PRC appears to have surpassed the DOC with speech verbs in Old English, taking up a much larger percentage of attested tokens in De Cuypere's dataset (2015c: 6). This is supported by the comparatively large fraction of PRCs with communication verbs in the Middle English data. By contrast, with verbs of bringing and sending, the relationship between DOC and PRC was more stable and balanced. Similarly to communication verbs, in the case of reversed (communicated) transfer verbs and verbs of attitude/emotion with complex predicate syntax, the PRC was in all likelihood the preferred variant in OE already (also Akimoto and Brinton 1999). Non-light verb 'simple' ditransitive constructions with comparable semantics probably lacked an associated PP-construction altogether. As demonstrated in section (4.2), mental/attitudinal verbs such as *forgive* or *envy*, for instance, clearly selected for the DOC rather than PRC types in early Middle English and are expected to have shown an even stricter distributional bias before.

176 In general, I posit that the addressee marking-function was more soundly established with the *to*-PRC than with other prepositional patterns at the end of Old English.

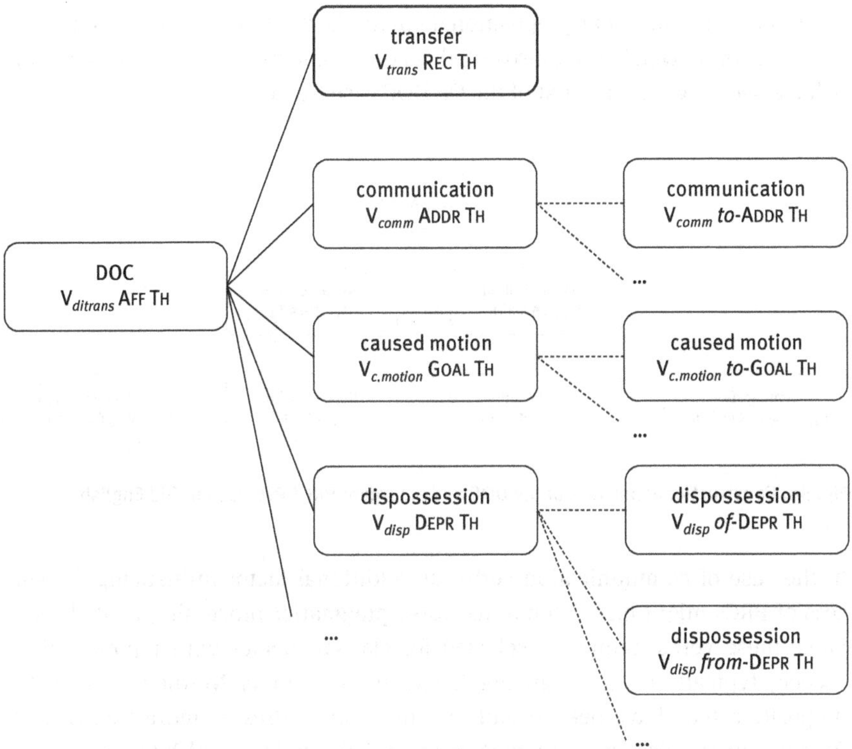

Fig. 33: Constructional network of the DOC and emergent PRC uses in Old English

As to dispossession verbs, the distribution of DOC vs. PRC is difficult to establish from a quick look at the data and literature. Even if the PRC uses turned out to be only marginally successful at this point, however, this may have been due to their standing in competition with yet another pattern, namely the prepositional theme-construction. The same counts for malefactive verbs. Fig. 34 illustrates the links of such additional patterns to the ditransitive verb(-class)-specific schemas as well as to the PRCs featuring the same verb types and prepositions. In the plot, a dispossessive DOC [V_{disp} DEPR TH] is connected 'horizontally' (vertically in the graph due to difficulties in representing complex relations in a two-dimensional model) to both an *of*-PRC [V_{disp} *of*-DEPR TH] and an *of*-PTC [V_{disp} DEPR *of*-TH], which are also associated to each other; a similar constellation is shown for communication verbs.

Overall, the fact that prepositional competitors should not only be present but doing quite well is not unexpected, as their expressive power would certainly have been higher than that of the OE DOC case frames.

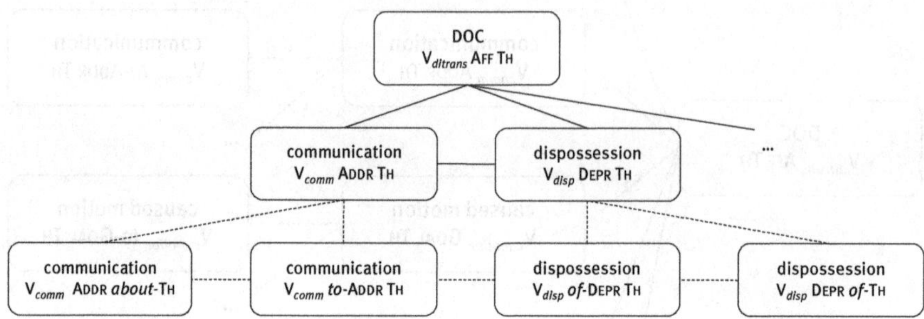

Fig. 34: Constructional network of the DOC and emergent PRC/ PTC uses in Old English

In the case of communication verbs, an additional factor influencing the success of PRCs might have been a discourse-pragmatic/ processing-related issue. Since these verbs frequently selected for clausal themes with reported direct speech, typically of much greater length than ordinary NP-themes (129), the preposition may have been useful in setting the addressee more clearly apart from the other object constituent (Koopman and van der Wurff 2000: 262).

(129) *cwæð* **to ðan scuccan**ADDR "Efne he is nu on
said to the devil indeed he is now on
ðinre handa swa ðeah hwæðere heald his sawle."TH
your hand nevertheless hold his soul
'The lord said to the devil: "Indeed he is now in your hand; nevertheless, preserve his soul."'
(Vsp.D.Hom. 125; Glossary Old English Aerobics, s.v. *(ge)cweðan*))

Nevertheless, as also suggested by the results of the evolutionary game presented above, the advantage PRCs would have had over the DOC concerning expressive power was not as great as at a later stage when case-marking was highly ambiguous or absent. That is, with the case marking system still being intact to some degree, the benefit of using the more explicit PRCs would have been cancelled out by the greater economy of the DOC, overall resulting in a tie-situation rather than an overtake of the prepositional competitors. With the changing environment at the transition from Old to Middle English, however, these conditions changed as well.

Before moving on to the various ways in which competition was resolved in the case of DOCs versus PRCs in subsequent periods, the further extension of the alternative patterns in the course to Middle English needs to be commented on. While only certain ditransitive verb classes were linked to a PP-pattern in Old English, this situation changed at the turn of the period, as successively more and more verb classes developed relations to prepositional constructions. Specifically, I argue that with time, prepositions such as *from* or *to* gradually but progressively extended to new contexts through analogy with already existing uses. Acquiring more and more functions put these new PRCs in relation to verb classes traditionally associated with the DOC only. For example, the use of *from* with ditransitive dispossession verbs could have motivated the use of *from* with verbs of refusal. Although this verb class did not express events of a participant losing an entity, being blocked from reception may have been perceived as semantically close enough to trigger analogical extension. Also, verbs ambiguous between different readings, i.e. verb class memberships, could have easily facilitated an expansion.

The most conspicuous case in point is of course *to* – but cf. also other goal-preposition types such as *till* or *towards* – which came to denote the recipient of a successful transfer event. As De Cuypere (2015c: 20) reveals, precursors to *to*-PRCs expressing a giving situation can be found in (late) Old English already. Both critical contexts of the type exemplified in (130a), where the REC-argument is ambiguous between an inanimate goal (the church as a physical location) and a recipient (the church as a social community, metonymically referred to by the place name), as well as uses with a relatively clear recipient function as in (130b), show up in the OE data.[177]

(130) a. Ic oswulf ond Beornðryð min gemecca *sellað*
I Oswulf and Beornthryth my wife give
to cantuarabyrg **to cristes cirican**$_{\text{REC?}}$ <u>ðæt landTH</u>
to Canterbury to Christ's church the land
'I, Oswulf and my wife Beornthryth give to Christ's church at Canterbury the land'
(codocu1.o1: charter 37.2; De Cuypere 2015c: 20; Visser 1963: 624)

177 Rostila (2007: 52, fn45), among many others, points out that a reanalysis of a directional goal-preposition to a more abstract, procedural function of 'recipient'-marking is neither unexpected – considering that the semantic roles of goal and recipient are very close – nor unusual, but can in fact be witnessed in many languages (cf. also Newman 1996: 88; Haspelmath 2000: 789; Heine and Kuteva 2002: 37–38; Lehmann 2002: 73; De Cuypere 2013, 2015c).

b. Denewulf bisceop and ða hiwan *leton*
Denewulf bishop and the community let
to Beornulfa$_{REC?}$ <u>xv</u> <u>hiora</u> <u>hida</u> <u>landes</u>$_{TH}$
to Beornwulf 15 their hides of land
'Bishop Denewulf and the community have let to Beornwulf fifteen hides of their land'
(S1285, dated: c.AD 902; De Cuypere 2015c: 20)

Incrementally, such innovative uses could become more frequent, and established themselves as legitimate competitors to the double object subconstruction of 'transfer-DOC'. We assume that this extension process started in a small corner of the network, most certainly with events of concrete physical transfer involving verbs such *giefan* 'give' or *sellan* 'give' and a tangible entity moved towards a recipient. From such instances, the new pattern spread to increasingly more abstract event descriptions, including situations of intended or future transfer (ME *offren, proffren* 'offer', *promisen* 'promise') as well as metaphorical transfer of the type 'pay so. a visit'. Goldberg (2006) argues that facilitating factors for extending an innovative schema to more contexts include its occurrence in a highly token frequent collocation pattern (here OE/ME *giefan/geven* 'give') as well as a certain amount of type variation. The latter is provided by the similarly frequent ME *yelden* or *yeten* 'give, yield, grant'; see also Rostila (2007: 151–158).

Comparable developments took place simultaneously with other prepositions as well as other verb classes. We then arrive at an early Middle English constructional network in which all verb-class specific constructions associated with a schematic DOC are individually linked to a number of different preposition-specific constructions (Fig. 35). As in Old English, some PRC-types are more successful in competing against the other PRC-patterns, occurring more frequently. With transfer (or communication) verbs, the *to*-PRC is e.g. clearly prevalent and more entrenched than the other variants, indicated by bold lining around the box in the figure. Dispossession verbs, on the other hand, are predominantly found in *from* or *of*-patterns, although further variants can still be observed, too.

It is possible that at this point abstractions over the various PRC-types formed in at least some speaker minds, leading to a highly schematic construction which linked a ditransitive verb to a prepositionally marked affected

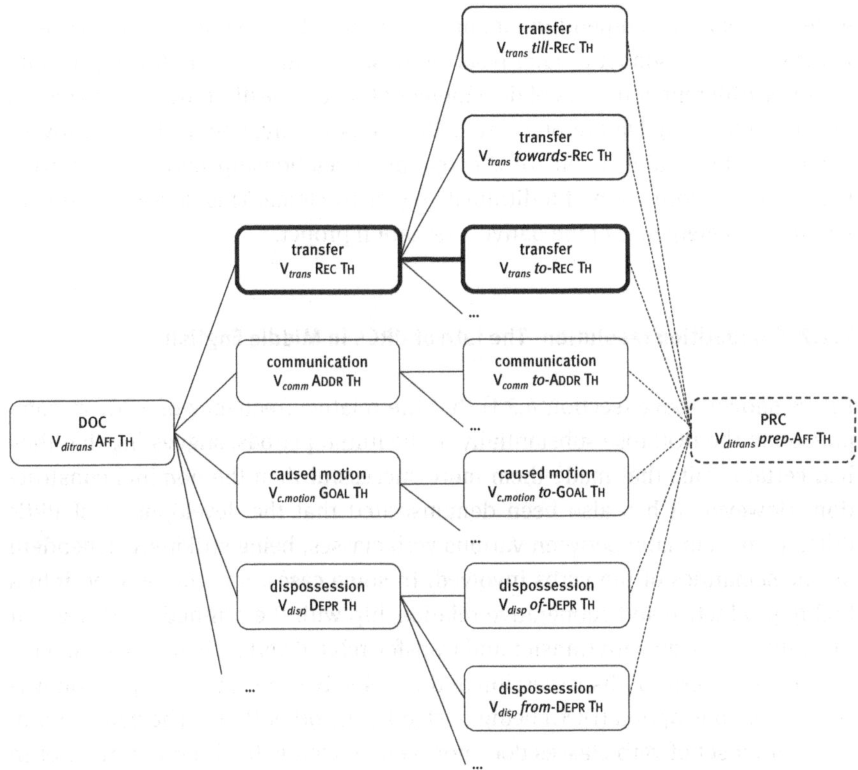

Fig. 35: Constructional network of the DOC in early Middle English

(typically animate) entity and a bare theme-argument [V$_{\text{ditrans}}$ *prep*AFF TH].[178] Again, the emergent, potential nature of such a schema is indicated by its dashed frame, and the dashed lines connecting to it. Although not shown in the plot, a tentative horizontal link developing from the PP-schema to the abstract DOC construction can in turn be envisaged. This would mark the beginning of an alternation relationship between the nominal and the prepositional means of expressing a ditransitive event. Still, a relatively complex system with a great deal of variation such as the one proposed here for early Middle English is bound to be subject to change since it is difficult to maintain. It is therefore

178 This construction would also be linked to, and inherit from, a more abstract caused motion construction, which also licenses instances such as *John loads hay onto the wagon* (Goldberg 1995).

expected that the competition among individual PRC-types as well as between DOCs vs. PRCs is sooner or later resolved in some way. In the following section, the three different pathways of development that can be discerned in this regard during Middle English are presented. Most importantly, one of these pathways results in the establishment of a cooperative relationship between allostructions, and the formation of a ditransitive constructeme. This development constitutes the emergence of the dative alternation proper.

7.1.2 Competition resolution: The fate of PRCs in Middle English

I have shown above (section 4.2.1) that the relative frequency of PRCs in comparison to the DOC rose substantially in the initial periods, suggesting that they had certain traits that made them more successful than the nominal construction. However, it has also been demonstrated that the development of PRCs differed substantially between various verb classes, being strikingly dependent on the semantics of the verbs involved. In some cases, the PRC entered into a highly productive and cooperative relationship with the synthetic and resident DOC; this was seen with transfer and transfer-related verbs. In other cases, most notably with verbs of dispossession and malefactive verbs, the competition was resolved by one option (DOC) being ousted by the other (PRC). The behaviour of yet another set of verb classes does not seem to clearly fit either pathway, or in fact did not show any change at all. Often, this meant continuity of Old English usage. A good case in point is the development of complex predicates of emotion/mentality, such as *have love*. The history of other examples like verbs of reverse communicated transfer (*ask so. a favour*), by contrast, is slightly more complex in that both DOC and PRC uses are retained, but the verb class does not participate in the PDE dative alternation. The next sections discuss each of these groups after one another, with a focus on changes in the relationship between DOC and PRC. The availability of additional patterns such as the PTC is taken up again where relevant. Although the issue is evidently strongly linked to the semantic development of the DOC as a whole, this matter is left for separate discussion in the subsequent chapter (7.2.1.2).

7.1.2.1 Cooperation: The ditransitive alternation emerges

The *to*-PRC and related prepositional constructions had extended their functions to cover events of successful transfer to a typically animate recipient by early Middle English. They had thereby entered a relationship of competition with the corresponding verb-class specific DOCs. (The more schematic DOC construction at this point subsumed a variety of different verb-class specific constructions and was probably still linked to some extent to a [Dat-Acc] case construction, although increasingly giving way to an unmarked pattern).

In the course of the Middle English period, the 'goal'-PRCs analogically expand to ever more contexts, and frequently come to denote abstract, intended transfer situations. This has been demonstrated with the data for verbs of abstract transfer (section 4.2.1.1). As a consequence of this generalisation in meaning, the prepositional competitors greatly increase in frequency. Their success is furthered by the (still) greater explicitness of the prepositions in comparison to the highly underspecified DOC, as finer distinctions can be expressed by using subtly distinct prepositions (e.g. *give towards* vs. *give to*). Cursory evidence for the presence of such semantic differences can be gained from a look at the collocational profiles of the prepositions; a precise delineation of the distinction would require further analysis.

For some time, the higher expressiveness that is made possible by this availability of a number of different prepositional construction types aids the fitness of the PRC-strategy as a whole. However, the different PRCs also compete against each other, and *to*-patterns soon take the lead, gradually ousting the other variants until the *to*-PRC establishes itself as the alternative to all transfer-related DOCs. This is indicated by the bold outline of the *to*-pattern in Fig. 36; the gradual disappearance of the other prepositional constructions is pointed to by the dashed outlines.[179] The greater success of the *to*-PRC can be explained by its greater frequency and entrenchment from early onwards, in turn determined by its being more economical than other PRC types (*to* vs. *towards*) as well as its greater semantic flexibility. As shown by De Cuypere (2013, 2015c), the preposition *to* had already acquired a number of non-spatial functions in other constructions by Old English. By contrast, other prepositions were still more limited at this point. This greater generality promotes the *to*-preposition's expansion to new contexts in other parts of the constructional network and constitutes an advantage of *to* over other prepositions like *till*, which were arguably less advanced in respect to semantic bleaching (meaning that the sub-sense of spatial direction was more salient in the case of *till* than with *to*). An exception to the broad restriction to *to*-PRCs is the case of *unto* and *onto*. Section (4.2.1.1) has demonstrated that these composite prepositions came into being and began to mark recipients from mid-/late-ME onwards. However, I take them to have cooperated with and to have constituted variants of *to* rather than contestants.

179 Note that dashed lines in the graphs presented in this chapter signpost a transitory state, which can be either emergence or loss.

Nevertheless, they appear to have been ousted later on, as their use in the PDE dative alternation is not grammatical anymore; this suggests that the complex prepositions diverged semantically from their 'parent' lexeme at some point after Middle English (Rostila 2007: 216, fn107).

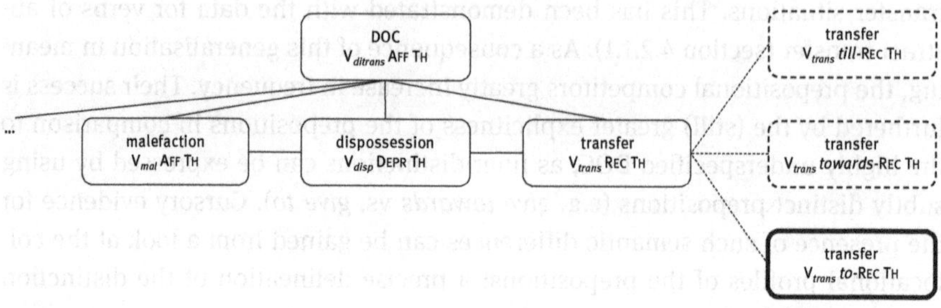

Fig. 36: Constructional network of DOC and variant transfer-PRCs in Middle English

While the semantic openness of *to* benefited this prepositional pattern compared to other PRC-patterns, it may at the same time have hindered its complete overthrow of the DOC: With the *to*-PRC becoming increasingly 'empty' in meaning, it also loses its plus in explicitness. In addition to other factors (such as the lack of additional alternatives), this may have helped the retention and later resurgence of the DOC, as well as the establishment of a cooperative relationship (cf. also section 5.2).

To recapitulate, I therefore propose that in the course of the period, *to* establishes itself as a potent competitor to the DOC, which concomitantly moves towards a more coherent meaning of 'transfer' (also section 7.2.1.2). After an initial period of high variation in prepositional complementation of (transfer-) DOC paraphrases, the system sees a certain degree of regularisation, with the *to*-PRC remaining as the only competition to a more narrowly defined DOC. Interestingly enough, though, this situation of [transfer: DOC] versus [transfer: *to*-PRC] does not result in the ousting of one of the variants in favour of the other. Although the prepositional pattern does take over for a certain period of time, there is a reversal of this trend towards the end of Middle English; the DOC gains in frequency again. This u-turn behaviour can be attributed at least in part to the increasing fixation of constituent order as well as the semantic development of the DOC. In general, it can be seen as the outcome of competing pressures which favour different constructional means. While the DOC is, for example, more successful in terms of economy (in being shorter than the *to*-PRC with its additional element), the *to*-PRC still retains at least some degree of greater expressivity and is thus equally successful. (This claim is of course radically simplified. Nevertheless, as also confirmed by the EGT account in 5.2, it is plausible that such factors did play a role in the establishment of the alternation). A further important factor in the maintenance of the DOC is the non-availability of other alternatives to express the same contrasts. With verbs of dispossession, for example, there is the additional option of using a PTC for events involving a given REC-like argument (*rob so. of sth.*). In the case of transfer verbs, such variants are absent – this may have facilitated the rise of a combined strategy, i.e. the alternation.

Rather than causing one construction to be lost, the increasingly close link between the two patterns thus results in the emergence of a symbiotic relationship, in which the constructions co-exist and cooperate with each other (Steels 2011b). Competition for the same function accordingly yields to cooperation; one consequence of this is that the semantically quasi-synonymous constructions begin to diverge in regard to discourse-pragmatic factors, with each of them constructing their own functional niche (also Traugott and Trousdale 2013). In this mutually beneficial relationship, the DOC comes to play the part of the strong variant (taking up about 70 per cent of all ditransitive tokens between Early Modern English and PDE; cf. Wolk et al. 2013; Gerwin 2014; Röthlisberger subm.). The relationship is taken to be advantageous for both constructions in that the expression of one also results in the activation of the other pattern, resulting in a higher degree of entrenchment of both constructions, and an increased likelihood to be activated in the future. This is still plausible even if we acknowledge that the constructions have decreased rather than increased in terms of overall frequency in usage since Middle English – positive priming effects between the two constructions do not necessarily positively impact their success against other means of expressing similar events. The association between the patterns clearly has been shown to affect their respective productivity: If a new verb comes to be used in one of the members of the alternation, it is typically available for use in the other variant as well (see Perek's notion of 'alternation-based productivity, section 2.2.2.2).[180]

The assumption of a cooperative, symbiotic relationship between the two constructions can be conceptualised in terms of Cappelle's (2006) and Perek's (2015) constructeme proposal: I here assume that at some point in this story, a schematic process takes place that gradually leads to the establishment (or

180 Despite slight asymmetries in the productivity of the constructions, with a considerable number of verbs being restricted to the *to*-PRC, this issue can be counted as a clear benefit in forming a constructional relationship.

constructionalisation) of a higher-level alternation-based generalisation over constructions which, although different in form, are used to encode similar categories of events. This development is illustrated in Fig. 37. As discussed in more detail in section (2.2.2.1), such a 'constructeme' has the following properties:

> (i) a constructional meaning abstracted from the meaning of the variants of the alternation, with (ii) an underspecified form which contains only the commonalities between variants, and thus leaves unspecified the syntactic type [...] and linear order [...] of the post-verbal complements (Perek 2012: 629–630; also Cappelle 2006)

The constructeme forms a network with its 'allostructions', in this case the DOC and *to*-PRC, which in contrast to its higher-level abstraction "fully specify their syntactic form and add semantic and pragmatic information to the meaning inherited from the constructeme" (Perek 2012: 630). The alternating constructions are accordingly considered to be independent yet strongly connected constructions (Perek 2012: 604). As demonstrated by the differences in lining in the figure (solid, bold line between the two constructions vs. dashed line between the constructions and the constructeme), I take horizontal links between allostructions to be a precondition to the development of a constructeme: Horizontal connections may hold between many constructions, but only very strong, systematic and pervasive links will lead to abstractions forming in the minds of at least large parts of the speaker population.

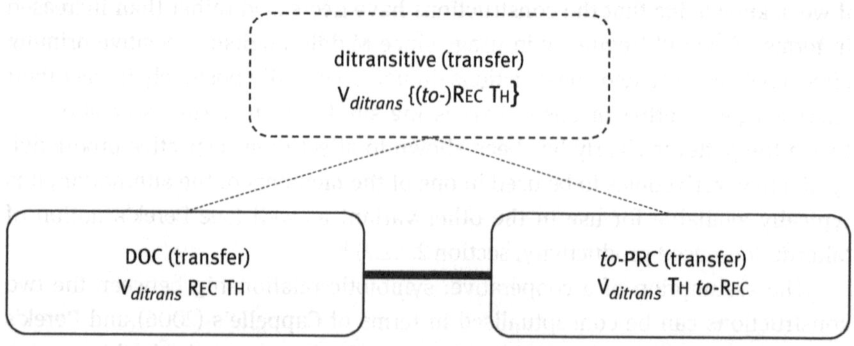

Fig. 37: The ditransitive constructeme and its allostructions (DOC and *to*-PRC) in PDE

Evidence for the presence of horizontal links and the resulting higher-level 'ditransitive' generalisation between the two patterns in PDE comes from sorting task experiments as well as priming experiments (e.g. Goldwater et al. 2011;

Perek 2015). It is furthermore reflected in the fact that certain (less prototypical) verb classes – which are still used in the DOC in PDE despite not clearly corresponding to a basic transfer-meaning – are frequently coerced into the alternation. For example, verbs of refusal occasionally (if not very often) occur in the *to*-PRC, and even a dispossessive DOC verb such as *cost*, if exceptionally used in a prepositional pattern, selects for a *to*-complement (Colleman and De Clerck 2009: 24, 36). Interestingly enough, as also shown in section (4.2) above, this constraint is still absent from Middle English, where even in the later subperiods, verbs such as *deny* or *refuse* vary concerning the PRC-type they appear in (131a-b).

(131) a. But Crist *denyeþ* þis$_{TH}$ **to** **hem**$_{REC}$
but Christ denies this to them
'but Christ denies this to them'
(CMWYCSER,I, 374.2660; PPCME2: M3)

b. he *wil* not / *denye* his feet$_{TH}$ **fro** **the**$_{REC}$
he will not / deny his feet from you
'he will not deny you his feet'
(CMAELR4, 19.544; PPCME2: M4)

What this variability tells us is that although the link between DOC and *to*-PRC was already fairly strong at the end of Middle English, and although the Middle English data clearly indicate that the large bulk of changes that led to today's situation took place within Middle English, the establishment of the dative alternation as we know it from PDE was still in progress then. In other words, while the constructions had entered a tight cooperative relationship with mutual benefits by the beginning of Early Modern English, the association only became (near-)exclusive and fully productive at a point beyond the period under investigation here.

Despite there being good arguments for assuming a strong relation between the DOC and *to*-PRC in PDE, there are certain verbs (and light verb combinations) which do not typically participate in the alternation. Examples for DOC-biased verbs include patterns such as 'give so. a headache/kick'. These complex predicates are near-categorically restricted to the DOC in PDE (Goldberg 1995: 94). Nevertheless, these constructions do not pose too much of a problem for the cooperation-approach taken in this book. I argue that the predominance of the DOC in this respect is caused by the strong focus on the action expressed by the theme, meaning that the *to*-PRC is considerably less well-suited for use in these cases on relatively straight-forward discourse-pragmatic grounds (Goldberg 1995). Verbs that are semantically and discourse-pragmatically compatible with the DOC but are confined to *to*-PRC use (e.g. *explain, donate*) are slightly more challenging. As discussed in section (2.2.2.2), the preference for the prepositional variant with such verbs needs to be explained by productivity asymmetries which work in favour of the *to*-PRC. Furthermore, pre-emption effects might play a role (Boyd and Goldberg 2011; Goldberg 2011; Stefanowitsch 2011; Perek 2015). In general, restrictions in one direction or the other are not necessarily problematic for the present account: In any allo-relationship, certain contexts (categorically or probabilistically) select for one variant over the other. I view these phenomena as perfectly expectable instances of shared labour.

Another challenging point is that for communication verbs, a (third) alternative pattern was available; this raises the question why the verb class did not resort to prepositional uses only (as seen with dispossession verbs). I return to this issue in more detail in section (7.1.2.1): The most plausible explanation for the continuing usage of the DOC with this verb class seems to lie in their great semantic overlap with transfer verbs. It is easily conceivable that communication events which involve two non-agentive entities (a message as well as a second animate participant) are indeed mostly conceptualised as events of metaphorical, abstract transfer, in which a piece of information is transferred to a recipient. Furthermore, the Middle English data (as well as introspective ideas about PDE usage) suggest that communication PTCs may be highly frequent but are nevertheless limited in the range of verbs they are used with: For example, verbs like *show, reveal, narrate* or *report* are arguably ungrammatical in prepositional theme patterns (**John reported Mary about the news*). That is, the association is likely more idiosyncratic than assumed at first glance. Coupled with the highly prototypical semantics of communication verbs, this may have been essential in the preservation of DOC uses.

Finally, we need to comment on the fate of the so-called 'benefactive alternation', referring to the phenomenon that in PDE, with benefactive verbs of creation there is a choice between the DOC (132a) and a prepositional variant involving *for* (132b) (Theijssen et al. 2010: 115; cf. also Kittilä 2005). As touched upon in Malchukov, Haspelmath, and Comrie (2010: 3) and elaborated on in Zehentner and Traugott (forthc.), however, the distinction between benefactive and ditransitive verbs in PDE is fuzzy. This is also true for the distinction between creation events and events of 'pure (or substitutive/ deputative) benefaction'; the category of the latter is in itself controversial.

(132) a. John *baked/bought* **Mary**$_{\text{BEN/REC}}$ a cake$_{\text{TH}}$

b. John *baked/bought* a cake$_{\text{TH}}$ **for Mary**$_{\text{BEN/REC}}$

Still, the second alternation is undoubtedly present in PDE. It is, however, strikingly absent from Middle English. Even in the later subperiods of M3 and M4 – i.e. at a time when *to* has clearly formed a near-exclusive paraphrase relationship with transfer-DOCs – prepositional uses of verbs of creation oscillate between *for*-PRCs and *to*-PRCs, with the latter tending to be the dominant pattern.[181] Examples for this phenomenon a given in (133) below, with (133b-c) indicating that even single verbs tend to vary concerning the construction they appear in.

(133) a. Salamon *bildide* a noble hous **to himself**
Salomon built a noble house to himself
'Salomon built a noble house for himself'
(CMPURVEY,I,12.477; PPCME2: M3)

b. God *haþ wrou3t* **for him** meny a faire miracle
God has worked for him many a fair miracle
'God has often caused great miracles for him'
(CMBRUT3,101.3058; PPCME2: M3)

c. so mych sorow *wrought* **to þ=e= Britouns**
so much sorrow worked to the Bretons
'he caused so much sorrow to the Bretons'
(CMBRUT3,45.1365; PPCME2: M3)

These results demonstrate that the recruitment of *for* as a definite marker of this function, and accordingly the establishment of the benefactive alternation proper, is a development that only occurred at a later stage in the history of English. Possibly, this was due to the semantics of *to* being perceived as too restrictive to include the aspect of benefaction after all, meaning that an innovative variant with *for* instead of *to* would have been able to propagate more successfully than the resident construction. Instead of loss of this verb class from the DOC due to its disuse in one member of the alternation, this development appears to have led to a division in the alternation, with two separate (but closely related) paraphrases having come to be available for ditransitive verbs (cf.

181 While the difference in proportions of *to*-PRCs and *for*-PRCs is significant for M3 ($p \approx 0.0001$; $\phi = 0.6$), this is not the case for M4. This can, however, not really be taken as an indication for a possible decreasing trend of *to*-PRCs with verbs of creation, since we need to add the disclaimer that this verb class is very low in numbers (*M3*: N=50; *M4*: N=22; cf. also section 4.2.1). The representativeness of the figures is thus questionable.

Zehentner and Traugott forthc. on benefactives in Early Modern English).[182] Nevertheless, the benefactive alternation in PDE seems to be less entrenched and less systematic than the dative alternation in PDE (Theijssen et al. 2010, though see Szmrecsanyi et al. 2017 for diverging results).

In conclusion, I have shown in this section that the PDE dative alternation can be seen as the outcome of competition resolution on two distinct levels. On the one hand, the *to*-PRC managed to successfully oust any other prepositional paraphrase types that were linked to the OE 'transfer'-verb-class specific double object construction. Once it had acquired this status, after a period of competition with the DOC the *to*-PRC formed a cooperative relationship with its nominal alternant. This ultimately suggests that the history of ditransitives in English and the relationship between DOC and PRCs followed a path of 'stable symbiosis' (OE) > 'competition' (ME) > 'stable symbiosis' (late ME). I argue that possible reasons for why competition should lead to cooperation instead of loss of once construction can be found in the interaction between the competing forces of 'economy' and 'explicitness' as well as the absence of other constructional alternatives for prototypical transfer verbs. Although still subject to changes (such as the introduction of the benefactive alternation), and still in progress to some extent, it is safe to assume that the alternation was relatively advanced and reliably established by the end of the Middle English period. In this paradigmatic relationship, the DOC then assumes the role of the 'stronger' variant, and the *to*-PRC that of the 'weak' variant, with the choice for one or the other pattern being determined by semantic and discourse-pragmatic factors. Crucially, the constructions have thereby come to constitute allostructions of each other rather than competing synonyms. That is, with the horizontal association between the constructions becoming closer and closer, a constructeme formed over the formally distinct allostructions. The dative alternation in PDE accordingly represents a network of tightly connected constructions at different levels of schematicity.

An entirely different pathway concerning the DOC-PRC relationship development is taken by the second group observable in the data; this group, which prominently includes verbs of dispossession, is discussed in the following section.

---

182 An ousting of this class from the DOC was probably again prevented by the semantic closeness to the core meaning of the construction, since although reception is not guaranteed with 'benefactive (creation)' verbs, the notion of transfer is still highly salient (see section 7.2.1.2).

7.1.2.2 Confinement: Prepositional pattern ousts DOC

By contrast to the scenario of both constructions surviving and constructing their niches seen with the first group of verb classes, the second group (exemplified here by verbs of dispossessions) follows a very straightforward path of one construction winning out at the expense of the other. The precise scenario I propose here is the following: In Old English, SOURCE-PP constructions are available as optional paraphrases for dispossession DOCs. Furthermore, another type of prepositional competitor, namely PP-theme (PTC) constructions, is present – these seem to have been similarly popular as the PRC-patterns at this stage. From early Middle English onwards, the prepositional constructions become increasingly frequent, or rather, dispossessive PRCs become more and more successful over time. As the data have shown, patterns of the type 'V_{disp} TH *from/of*-DEPR' rocket in the course of the period, until they become near-obligatory in late Middle English. While occasional DOC uses of privative verbs can still be found, they are clearly in demise, and are bound to disappear from the language entirely. (Rare examples of DOCs with privative verbs do occur in later periods; however, they are highly marked and archaic).[183] Interestingly, PTCs steadily account for about a tenth of all tokens but do not increase markedly over time. In addition to the general positive impact of the loss of inflectional markers on the frequency of prepositional patterns, the particular upsurge of PRCs in this case – as compared to the PTC – is likely fuelled by the growing success of other PRC paraphrases to the DOC such as the *to*-PRCs.

The development of this verb class can be modelled as involving an increasing entrenchment and growth in productivity of the prepositional REC- construction over time, which results in an incremental complementary weakening of the resident DOC sub-construction (Fig. 38). The fewer times the latter construction is activated, the more it fades, until it is eventually lost (almost) completely. This is again indicated by the dashed lining of the dispossession-DOC in the figure, here reflecting weakening in progress. The disappearance of the DOC uses is accompanied by a reduction in the range of individual PRC-types, meaning that the dispossession-PRC is increasingly restricted to *from* and *of*, while other prepositions such as *at* (in the meaning of 'from') slowly fall out of use.

Although not yet visible in the Middle English data, the further development of the dispossessive PRC is particularly interesting also in comparison to the other prepositional option, the PTC, in that the decrease of PP-types appears to have continued in later times for both types.

---

183 A slightly problematic issue is the continuing use of *cost* in PDE, addressed in more detail in (7.2.1.2.2).

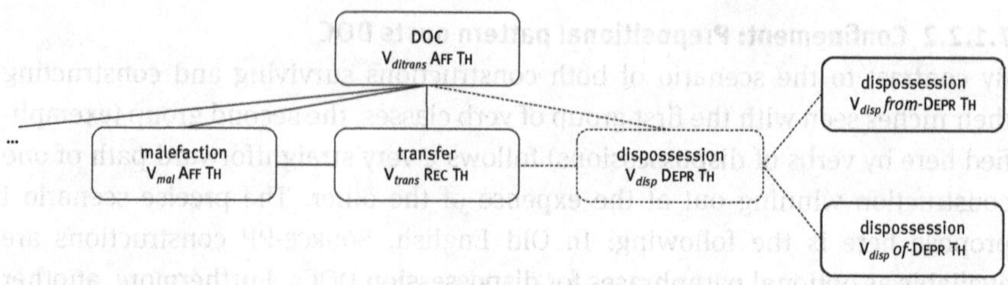

Fig. 38: Constructional network of DOC and variant dispossession-PRCs in Middle English

As manifest in (134a-d) and (135a-b), both *of* and *from* were readily available for both PRC and PTC dispossessives in the second half of Middle English. This variability has been reduced in the course to PDE, though, as the PRC-construction today is largely associated with *from* only, while *of* is ungrammatical in most varieties of English (*John stole money from Mary* vs. **John stole money of Mary*, cf. Goldberg 1995: 45). The exact opposite holds for the PTC, which is clearly associated with *of* and repels *from* today (*John robbed Mary of her money* vs. **John robbed Mary from her money*).[184]

(134) a. and *steleth* <u>hir</u> <u>soule</u>$_{TH}$ **fro** **Crist**$_{DEPR}$
and steals her soul from Christ
'and steals her soul from Christ'
(CMCTPARS,319.C1.1317; PPCME2: M3)

b. theves that *stelen* <u>the</u> <u>soules</u>$_{TH}$ **of** **Jhesu** **Crist**$_{DEPR}$
thieves that steal the souls of Jesus Christ
'thieves that steal the souls from Jesus Christ'
(CMCTPARS,315.C1.1156; PPCME2: M3)

c. þornes *reuen* **fro** **schep**$_{DEPR}$ <u>þer</u> <u>wolle</u>$_{TH}$
thornbushes rob from sheep their wool
'thornbushes rob sheep of their wool'
(CMWYCSER,254.535; PPCME2: M3)

184 These restrictions are supported by a preliminary survey of the relevant patterns in the *BNCweb* and the *COCA*. Note that there is some exception to this rule in that *steal* infrequently appears in PRCs with *off* (instead of *from* or *of*), e.g. *John stole* <u>*money*</u> <u>*off Mary*</u>.

d. þat$_{TH}$ þai *miȝt* *reue* *and* *robbe* **Of** **Sarraȝins**$_{DEPR}$
that they might rob and rob of Saracens
'what they might rob and plunder of the Turks'
(c1330(?a1300) Arth.and M.(Auch); MED, s.v. *robben*)

(135) a. thei *robbyn* **pore** **men**$_{DEPR}$ of her due porcoun$_{TH}$
they rob poor men of their due portion
'they rob poor men of their due portion'
(CMPURVEY,I,34.1635; PPCME2: M3)

b. ȝif hit *reueþ* **þe**$_{DEPR}$ fro þi slepe$_{TH}$ aniȝtes
if it robs you from your sleep at night
'if it robs you of your sleep at night'
(c1390 Hilton ML (Vrn) 290; MED, s.v. *reven*)

Similarly, the constructions seem to have developed some verb constraints. As clear from e.g. Visser (1963) and also visible in the corpus data (section 4.2.4), the majority of privative verbs in Old and later in Middle English fluctuated between the two prepositional variants. This is illustrated in the sample sentences of *reven/robben* 'rob' above: While (134c-d) represent PRC uses of these verbs, the instances in (135a-b) constitute PTCs (see further Roberts 2000 on the lexical field of robbing). By contrast, at least in standard PDE, most verbs are now found exclusively in one or the other. *Rob* and *steal* are prime examples of this phenomenon: The former is almost exclusively associated with a prepositional theme construction, whereas the latter is typically restricted to the PRC-variant today 136a-b). These differences in syntactic realisations of participant roles are taken to reflect profiling differences (as well as slight differences in the participant roles themselves) between the patterns or verbs. That is, *rob* specifies a semantic frame of <**robber victim** goods> in contrast to *steal* with a frame of <**stealer** source **goods**> (Goldberg 1995: 48). Both patterns are moreover associated with complementary object orders – [TH-REC] in the PRC versus [REC-TH] in the PTC – and, correspondingly, differ in discourse-pragmatic context.

(136) a. Jesse *robbed* **the rich**$_{DEPR}$ of their money$_{TH}$
*Jesse *robbed* money$_{TH}$ **from the rich**$_{DEPR}$

b. Jesse *stole* money$_{TH}$ **from the rich**$_{DEPR}$
*Jesse *stole* **the rich**$_{DEPR}$ of their money$_{TH}$[185]

185 All examples taken from Goldberg (1995: 45).

This development could of course be attributed to changes in the semantics of the individual verbs, as they specialised to one particular construal of the event. On the other hand, it can be argued that the constructions (that is, the PRC vs. the PTC) have themselves come to increasingly diversify in meaning. Reinforcing tendencies that were present in OE already, they have come to more clearly 'dividing up' the semantic and discourse-pragmatic space, thus cooperating rather than competing against each other. Combined with profiling differences between individual verbs, this has led to the restrictions on verb usage seen in PDE. The latter view is tentatively supported by the fact that corresponding developments can be observed with other dispossessive verbs such as *take* (**take so. of sth.*) or *deprive* (**deprive sth. from so.*).

I interpret this development as a similar process as the emergence of the dative alternation, even though it applies to a much narrower set of verbs: With dispossession verbs, the PRC and PTC have reached a cooperative relation, with each pattern becoming restricted to specific contexts in a complementary distribution. (Whether this association is pervasive enough to be abstracted over, as shown in Fig. 39, can be debated). I furthermore argue that it was precisely the fact that an alternative pattern – with comparable semantic and discourse-pragmatic preferences as the DOC – was available that essentially lay the groundwork for the demise of the DOC with the verb class. This is the case despite the proportional frequency of dispossessive PTCs not being excessively high, and not changing significantly over time. The mere stable presence of an additional option was sufficient.

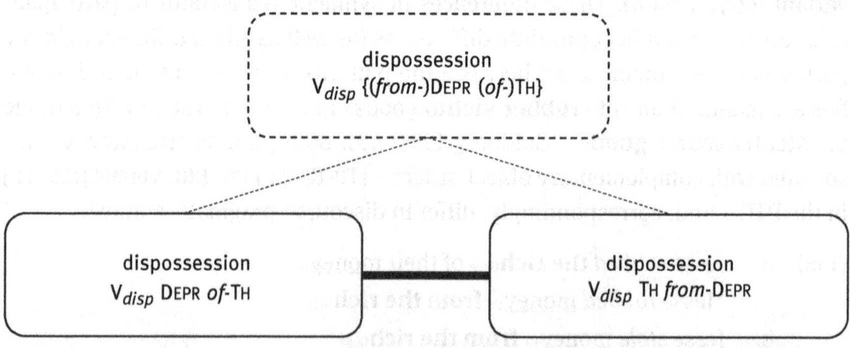

Fig. 39: The 'dispossessive' constructeme and its allostructions (*of*-PTC and *from*-PRC) in PDE

Incidentally, the 'dispossessive' alternation between PRC and PTC is reminiscent of another well-known constructional relationship often referred to as the '*spray/load-*' or 'locative alternation'. This is illustrated by the sentence pair below; (137a) represents an instance of a 'caused motion' construction, whereas (137b) is a '*with*-applicative' (Perek 2015: 158–163, also Goldberg 1995). The PDE prepositional deprivee-construction is likewise taken to be related to and inherit from the more abstract caused motion-construction. Through this (among other things), the dispossessive PRC retains a clear link to the *to*-PRC and other related paraphrases, as they also instantiate the caused-motion schema (alongside types like *put a plate on the table/ take a friend to Rome*). I assume that the emergence of the dispossessive alternation and of the locative alternation influenced each other in a process of analogical extension, although determining the direction of such an impact would require further investigation (cf. Iwata 2008, especially Ch.9 on the correspondences between verbs of removal like *clear* and *spray/load* verbs).

(137) a. John *loaded* hay **onto the wagon**
b. John *loaded* **the wagon** with hay

Returning to the competition between DOC and PRC, we have seen that another case of verb classes reportedly disappearing from the DOC is the group of verbs of pure benefaction. Unfortunately, the number of instances of such verbs that do not constitute complex predicate constructions in the present database is rather low, which makes it more difficult to test assumptions about their behaviour. Nevertheless, it does seem that as predicted, this (sub-)class increasingly drops out of DOC use in the course of the Middle English period, and more frequently appears in PRCs. The development of an exclusive association of benefactives with a *for*-pattern could, however, not be captured by the data investigated in this project: The relevant verbs typically vary between *to-* and *for*-PRCs similar to verbs of creation, suggesting that a clearer relation was established only later. Quite possibly, this development went hand in hand with the emergence of the benefactive alternation; the reason behind verbs of pure benefaction not being used in the DOC any more today must be sought in their incompatibility with the basic transfer meaning of the construction. It is still interesting to observe that in the case of these verbs, no alternative pattern is in fact available in PDE. That is, verbs of pure benefaction (when used with three overtly expressed participants) are almost categorically found in *for*-PRCs. Both PTC and POSS-patterns are impossible (at least according to introspective judgments). Examples (138a-c) illustrate this limitation.

(138) a. John *opened* the door$_{\text{TH}}$ **for Mary**$_{\text{REC}}$
b. *John *opened* **Mary**$_{\text{REC}}$ PREP? the door$_{\text{TH}}$
c. *John *opened* **Mary's**$_{\text{REC}}$ door$_{\text{TH}}$

Both the Middle English data and the PDE situation accordingly suggest that the different sub-types subsumed in the broad class of benefactives/malefactives diverged quite substantially in behaviour, continuing distributional differences that were likely present in earlier English. This is, on the one hand, seen in the deviating development of pure benefactives and verbs of (benefactive) creation, as just outlined. On the other hand, it has been demonstrated that malefactive verbs present a sub-class on their own in showing a clear preference for an alternative POSS-pattern from early on. This bias becomes increasingly stronger during Middle English, until DOC and PRC uses are lost entirely with this class. Malefactive verbs therefore did not resort to PRCs when ousted from the DOC, but instead came to use different means of expression, in which the affected person was marked by a genitive phrase (*John broke Mary's shoulder*). In this case, the impact of having an additional option is even more evident than with dispossession verbs – with POSS-patterns being predominant in early Middle English already, the verb class was always at the periphery of the DOC. The growing restriction to this construction and concomitant loss of the DOC uses is then not too surprising.

Considering that complex predicates with benefactive/malefactive semantics of the type 'do so. harm/good/a favour/ justice' took yet another trajectory, lumping these types together into one larger group of benefactives/malefactives seems little warranted. This last type, as discussed in section (4.2), participates in the prototypical dative alternation in PDE, although it has to be noted that these instances are comparatively infrequent. For example, 'do good' and 'do harm' both occur with a pmw frequency of around or below 5 in the *BNCweb* and *COCA*. They are moreover highly confined to a very small number of NP-complements, and their productivity is low. In the following section, the similarly thorny cases of the highly mixed group of marginal or unusual DOC uses is addressed, rounding off the discussion of the fate of different PRCs in Middle English and beyond.

7.1.2.3 Continuity: Stable distribution is maintained

The last group to be dealt with here does not constitute one coherent category with homogeneous development in respect to the relationship between DOCs and PRC uses. Instead, this group subsumes three smaller sets of verb classes (or indeed single verb classes, or even parts of semantic verb classes), which are joined together by the circumstance that their development differs from that of the groups presented so far. Furthermore, the classes in question are comparatively infrequent, rather heterogeneous within themselves, and also to some extent idiosyncratic in their behaviour in PDE. This means that a closer investigation of the patterns throughout the periods is definitely needed.

To begin with, a rather straightforward case is provided by verbs of emotion/attitudes (referred to as 'mental' verbs in 4.2) as well as verbs of reverse transfer of the type 'take one's leave of so./ take an example of so'. As to the former, it has to be remarked that the discussion here concerns only a sub-part of this broader verb class. More specifically, it is only complex predicate constructions involving mental verbs that are of interest in this case (139a-c). This set of verb constructions importantly differs strikingly from other, 'simple' verbs of emotion/attitude such as *forgive* or *envy*. These vary between DOC and *to*-PRC in Middle English, accordingly representing members of the first group (7.1.2.1).[186]

(139) a. John *had* pity$_{\text{TH}}$ **on (upon/of?/...) Mary**$_{\text{STIM}}$
b. John *had* love (feelings/...)$_{\text{TH}}$ **for Mary**$_{\text{STIM}}$
c. John *felt* envy (hatred/...)$_{\text{TH}}$ **at (towards/...) Mary**$_{\text{STIM}}$

Regarding verbs of reverse transfer, these evidently show a close affinity to dispossession verbs, as the REC-argument denotes an animate source of a typically abstract 'reception'-event. The main reason for keeping these groups apart is their affinity to light verb constructions. Due to this, they were expected to behave slightly differently, which was also borne out by the data (4.2.1).

What is striking about both of these classes, i.e. reversed transfer and (light verb) emotion, is that they were strongly associated with prepositional syntax in Old English already. Indeed, it is unclear whether DOC uses of these verbs were anything more than marginal in early English, if attested at all (Akimoto and Brinton 1999). In the Middle English dataset, occasional examples of the DOC with such verb classes can be found; nevertheless, the PRC is undoubtedly much more entrenched. Interestingly, the (in any case marginal) DOC variant seems to disappear again at some point after Middle English, as in PDE such light verb combinations are entirely confined to the PP-constructions. It is therefore plausible to presume that the state of (near-)total predominance of PRCs in Old English was replaced by a short period of competition against DOC uses.

186 As discussed in Goldberg (1995), Colleman and De Clerck (2008), and others, *forgive* and *envy* do not constitute prototypical members of the DOC in PDE, and appear to increasingly resort to prepositional constructions. In addition to PRCs, the verbs also frequently occur in a PTC today, as in *John envied Mary for her energy/ John forgave Mary for her digression*). Based on the Middle English data and a cursory investigation of Old English dictionary information, this was, however, likely a later development (see also section 7.2.1.2 below).

This emergence of DOC variants in Middle English was likely driven by the increasing ability of PRCs (involving the same prepositions used to express 'ditransitive' reversed transfer and emotion) to paraphrase DOCs. The DOC pattern could easily have been extended to reverse transfer V+NP combinations in analogy to dispossessive verbs (*steal sth. of so.*: *steal so. sth* → *take example of so.*: *take so. example*).

Similar processes of reanalysis/analogical thinking may have triggered the appearance of innovative DOC variants with mental complex predicates. Nevertheless, the competition was soon re-resolved in favour of the PRC. The DOC with these verb classes was not able to succeed against the fitter prepositional patterns for a number of reasons also responsible for the (brief) general decrease of the DOC. Moreover, the PRC may have been preferred in these cases due to the fact that its favoured syntactic form was more suitable for the discourse-functional properties of such events (by placing a focus on the stimulus of the emotion). Instead of the two constructions forming a quasi-cooperative relationship in which the DOC was able to survive as the weaker variant, we here see short-lived competition; the increasingly strong association of the construction with the *to*-PRC, among other things, must have led to the classes eventually 'resorting' to the PRC again.

Summing up, the Old English prepositional light verb combinations expressing reverse transfer and emotion were coerced into alternating with the DOC during Middle English. Once the ditransitive alternation was restricted to a specific PRC-type (namely the *to*-PRC), however, the prepositional patterns returned to being the only option (cf. also the contributions in Brinton and Akimoto 1999a).[187] A further curious difference between this group and the classes discussed so far is that in the latter case, we see a reduction in the range of verb classes at a more abstract level (e.g. the schematic category of dispossession verbs being associated with *from* only). By contrast, in spite of some reduction in preposition-type variation over the course of time, the verb classes in question (reverse transfer, emotion) are still used with a range of prepositions, as illustrated in the examples above (139). I therefore argue that we are dealing with a range of lower level (complex predicate-specific) constructions, each subcategorising for a particular (set of) PRC-type(s), rather than an abstract construction which specifies the preposition involved. These cases qualify as instances of lexicalisation: They show a decrease in schematicity, productivity

187 Of course, this does not mean that other means of expression of these semantic relations were not possible (e.g. *John felt envy towards Mary* vs. *John envied Mary*; *John took example of Mary* vs. *John took Mary as an example*/...).

and compositionality as they moved from unrestricted constituent combinations towards increasingly tighter relations between verb, noun and preposition, and eventually became reanalysed as one idiomatic chunk (Traugott and Trousdale 2013: 193; also Akimoto 1995; Brinton and Akimoto 1999a; Brinton and Traugott 2005).[188] Whether they also constitute instances of lexical constructionalisation may be debated, since this would involve the formation of new nodes.

A slightly different issue is presented by the case of reverse communicated transfer, meaning verbs/phrases "used to encode events where something is required of the indirect object referent" (Colleman and De Clerck 2009: 34). This can be illustrated by instances like *John asked Mary permission*, or *John asked Mary her name*. The class is special insofar as based on its semantics it may be expected to act like verbs of reversed transfer and dispossession verbs. Accordingly, it should either show a preference for PRCs throughout the history of English or come to be confined to prepositional uses from Middle English onwards. However, the group appears to pattern with neither. As demonstrated in the examples in (140) below, in Old English such inquiries could be expressed by a DOC (140a-b) as well as a PRC including *to* (140c) but also *from*, *of* and others (cf. Visser 1963: 612–613). Moreover, these combinations frequently occurred in prepositional theme constructions (e.g. *ask a person of/for mercy*). The state of affairs for this event description differs from reversed transfer uses in that there is no clear preference for PRCs in Middle English.

(140) a. Hig **hine**$_{SOURCE}$ *acsodon* ðæt bigspell$_{TH}$
they him asked the parable
'they asked him the parable'
(Mk. Th. 4, 10.; Bosworth-Toller, s.v. *acsian*)

b. Gif hit **hine**$_{SOURCE}$ hlafes$_{TH}$ *bitt*
if it him of bread asks
'if it [i.e. the child] asks him for bread'
(Homl. Th. i. 250, 8; Bosworth-Toller, s.v. *biddan*)

188 The same decrease of compositionality etc. is evidently also seen in other ditransitive complex predicates such as 'give so. a kiss/ headache'. As discussed in various places, these idiomatic combinations are typically prevented from entering the dative alternation in PDE (**John gave a headache to Mary*) – a sign of their rather idiosyncratic nature.

c. hy eaðmode **to** **eow**SOURCE <u>arna</u>TH *bædun*
they the humble to you compassion asked
'the humble-minded prayed to you for compassion'
(Exon. 27 b; Th. 83, 9; Cri. 1353; Bosworth-Toller, s.v. *biddan*)

The same situation continues in Middle English, where all possibilities are frequently attested – although PRCs rise in proportional frequency in the beginning of the period, there is a reversal of the trend towards the end, when the DOC gains in frequency again (section 4.2.1). Instead of a clear move towards PRCs as in the case of dispossession verbs, DOC uses remain available, and even thrive to some extent. In PDE, we accordingly find reverse communicated transfer events expressed in the DOC (141a), a prepositional REC-pattern typically involving *of* or *from* (141b), as well as a prepositional theme construction with *for* (141c); e.g. Goldberg (1995: 131); Geeraerts (1998); Colleman and De Clerck (2008: 204–205, 2009: 34–36).

(141) a. John *asked* **Mary**SOURCE a favour/the time/her name/her numberTH
b. John *asked* a favour/the time/her name/her numberTH **of/ from Mary**SOURCE
c. John *asked* **Mary**SOURCE for a favour/the time/her name/her numberTH

As a quick search of the *COCA/BNCweb* and on *Google* shows, the DOC constitutes the most frequent of these options, followed by the PP-theme construction with *for*, and finally the *of/from*-PRC as the least popular variant.

Although the overall constructional possibilities did not change over time, some changes did take place: First, there was a reduction in preposition types available, as the PRC in this case is now restricted to *of* and *from*, while the *to*-PRC is used to mark 'ordinary' communication events (*John asked a question to Mary* vs. **John asked a favour to Mary*).[189] Furthermore, the DOC seems to have become limited to a certain type of collocation. For example, concrete, physical themes are disallowed from the construction (**John asked Mary bread*). This means that this particular sub-construction has ceased to be productive in the history of English. The reason why the DOC should stay productive with a subset of these uses is briefly addressed in section (7.2.1.2) below. Most probably, the semantic closeness (and overlap in verbs involved) between this type of

189 Note that in the case of 'to cry a person mercy' in the sense of 'begging someone for pardon', the prepositional paraphrase still involves *to*, *on* or *upon* rather than *of* or *from* (cf. OED, s.v. *mercy*). However, this expression is highly idiomatic and archaic; it can therefore not be considered as representative.

communication verbs and the class of 'transfer of communicated message' exemplified by *John asked Mary a question* or *John told Mary a story* played a role in this development. In conclusion, this second set of miscellaneous verb classes is characterised by alliances between the DOC and the PRC on a relatively low level in the network. In contrast to the group of transfer verbs, where I have argued that a more abstract generalisation over the two patterns has formed in the history of English, such a more schematic link is likely lacking in the case of reverse communication verbs.

Finally, a last group that is of interest in the present discussion is verbs of ballistic instantaneous motion like PDE *throw* or *cast*. Although no DOC examples of such verbs are given in Visser (1963), an exploratory look at the AS dictionary (Bosworth 2010) suggests that the DOC was available with this verb class in Old English (142).[190] Nevertheless, it can be assumed that prepositional uses were prevalent at this point. In PDE, both the DOC and various PRCs (most prominently including *to*, but also *at* or *towards*) are used (*John threw the ball to/towards/at Mary*).

(142) *Weorpaþ* hit$_{\mathrm{TH}}$ **hundum**$_{\mathrm{GOAL/REC}}$
throw it dogs
'throw it [i.e. the meat] to the dogs'
(Ex. 22, 31.; Bosworth-Toller, s.v. *weorpan*)

Unfortunately, clear DOC instances of ballistic motion verbs are not attested in the database used for this book. This may simply be due to an accidental gap in the data, but makes it difficult to say whether this verb class followed a path similar to that of verbs of caused motion such as *bring* or *send* (which are semantically relatively close), or whether the increased use of the *to*-PRC with these verbs is a more recent development, caused by the increasingly close association between the members of the dative alternation. The latter scenario would seem to be supported by the fact that ballistic motion verbs are not present in Colleman and De Clerck's (2011) database of 18th ct. DOCs either. Furthermore, they are still found in PRCs involving prepositions other than *to* in PDE (cf. *John threw a ball at/towards Mary*; *John cast a glance at Mary*). A possible scenario is that this verb class showed a strong preference for the PRC (in several types) until recently, although sporadic DOC variants appeared from time to time. Since the *to*-PRC was, however, the most frequent of these para-

190 For a discussion of this verb class in various Germanic languages see Barðdal (2007: 25–27).

phrases, the verbs were more and more often coerced into the DOC due to the strong link between these two constructions. This development (the verb class being 'forced' to participate in the dative alternation) might then in turn cause a decrease of the other PRC-types. Whether this is indeed the case will have to be checked in more detail in the future (cf. also Mukherjee 2005).

To sum up, what has been dealt with in this section is a highly heterogeneous group of ditransitive verbs which are quite difficult to assess on the basis of the present data, and which seem to have followed relatively different pathways in the history of English. The competition between DOC uses and prepositional periphrases here was resolved in very distinct ways dependent on the semantics of the verbs involved. A number of issues that have been mentioned, such as the acceptance in the DOC of a semantically idiosyncratic group of verbs denoting reverse communicated transfer, comes up again in section (7.2.1.2) below. There, the matter is discussed in respect to the semantic development of the schematic double object construction. Before moving on to this question, however, the next section sees a brief outline of the development of PRCs in the context of a system-wide increase in prepositional competitors to nominal constructions.

7.1.3 Competition (resolution) in the network: The dative alternation in context

The development of PRCs from Old to Middle English and beyond necessarily hinges on changes in the rest of the constructional network. As already touched upon in section (3.1), prepositional constructions in general saw a substantial increase during Middle English; they more and more often took over functions that were previously encoded by case constructions. This applies both to verbal complementation as well as noun or adjective modification. Still, this process is supposed to have started long before Middle English, since a number of nominal, more synthetic patterns already faced considerable competition with PP-patterns in Old English. For instance, prepositional phrases were frequently employed instead of case-marked time, place or manner adjuncts at this point already. Furthermore, *of*-phrases more and more often came to 'replace' genitive NPs in all kinds of constructions in Old English, including genitive objects of transitive verbs and genitive noun modifiers as in partitives. Although most conspicuously seen with genitives, similar processes took place with other cases/ prepositions as well, cf. e.g. the OE dative competing against a preposition in linking two NPs in a relation of accompaniment ('the boy with the dog').

While in some cases, the PP-constructions won out against the resident, case-marked or (from late Old English onwards) zero-marked constructions, in other instances both the prepositional and the nominal variants were retained but diverged according to discourse-pragmatic or semantic function. Focussing on PPs in the verbal domain, in the following sections I first discuss the development of PPs in the history of English as a case of increasing chunking, and possibly grammaticalisation. Second, the various ways in which the competition between case-constructions and PP-constructions was resolved in English is briefly commented on, relating the issue also to the discussion on competition in the case of DOCs and PRCs.

7.1.3.1 Emerging competition between nominal and prepositional constructions

In Present Day English, PPs are traditionally divided binarily into complements versus adjuncts. Among other things, the latter assumedly have greater mobility, while the former are greatly restricted regarding their position in the clause (e.g. Huddleston and Pullum 2002: 224–228). However, as discussed most recently by Th. Hoffmann (2005, 2007, 2011), a strict complement-adjunct dichotomy of PDE prepositional phrases is not warranted, since it does not capture the wide range of different patterns PPs are used in today. Hoffmann shows that instead, and more appropriately so, PPs should be considered as constituting a network of several constructions with varying degrees of schematicity. These constructions differ with regard to factors such as optionality, semantic import/degree of semantic bleaching of the preposition, degree of syntactic freedom, and their performance in various syntactic operations such as preposition stranding (Hoffmann 2011: Ch.6; also Quirk et al. 1985: 1166; Biber et al. 1999: 403). The continuum from complement to adjunct as suggested by Hoffmann is shown in (143); the networks are illustrated in Fig. 40 and Fig. 41. It can be seen that the postulated sub-constructions range from prototypical adjuncts (sentence adjuncts with temporal or spatial meaning) to tight verb-preposition combinations (subcategorised prepositions).

(143) **optional PPs** (sentence adjuncts > mixed > complements)
obligatory PPs ((obligatory complement) > subcategorised PP-type > subcategorised P)

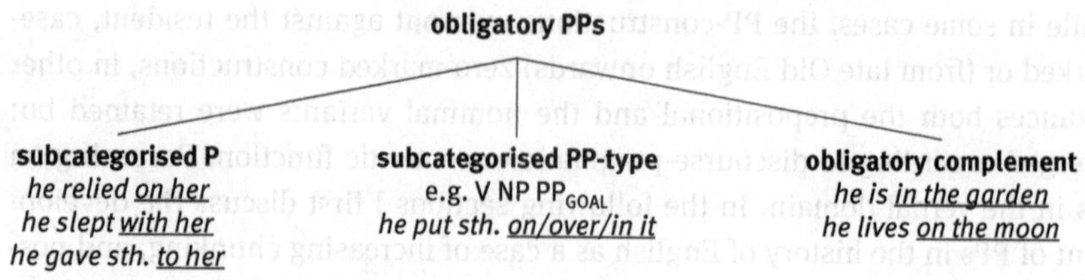

Fig. 40: Different types of V-PP obligatory relationships (adapted from Hoffmann 2005: 265)

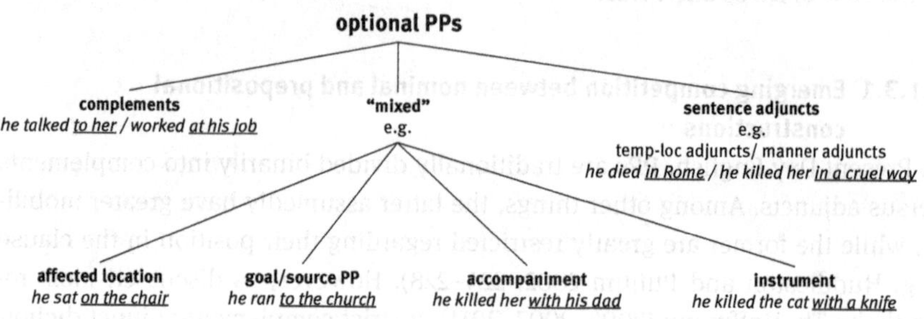

Fig. 41: Different types of V-PP optional relationships (adapted from Hoffmann 2005: 266)

Although this is not explicitly dealt with in Th. Hoffmann (2005, 2011), it could be argued that these different constructions in PDE are manifestations of different degrees of grammaticalisation, with a cline from sentence adjuncts (least/non-grammaticalised) to subcategorised prepositions (most grammaticalised). Following up on this assumption, the development of PP-constructions in the history of English is then proposed here to have proceeded along the following pathway:[191]

In pre-Old English times, prepositions emerged out of adverbs used in apposition to case-marked NPs in order to reinforce the meaning of the case morpheme (e.g. Beekes 1995: 218–222; Ringe 2006: 64–65; Harbert 2007: 110–111).[192]

191 The formalisation of the various constructions as well as the classification of types is largely taken from Th. Hoffmann (2005, 2007, 2011). Although the scenario as presented here seems possible from a PDE standpoint, a more convincing proposal of course needs to be based on empirical data from the relevant language stages. This is addressed in Hundt and Zehentner (2018).

192 See also Bruckmann (1911: 762); Hirt (1927: 15); Meillet (1934: 193); Lehmann (1974: 197); Friedrich (1975: 38); Hawkins (1983); Hock (1986); Lundskær-Nielsen (1993: Ch.1).

While these elements would have been optional at first, variant constructions including them may have been more successful compared to non-reinforced case constructions due to their greater explicitness. This would have led to a gradual obligatorification of the adverbial constituent, which developed an ever-closer association to the NP it occurred with, through a process of habituation and chunking (Bybee 2010). The precursors to prepositions probably occurred in post-position to the NP they came to govern instead of preceding them. With an increasingly close link developing between the constituents, this order was subject to change, though, resulting in the canonical preposition+NP order seen today. This change again proceeded incrementally; in fact, post-positional prepositions are still comparatively frequent in Old English (Alcorn 2011). The greater success of pre-positional prepositions can be attributed to their being better able to fulfil an 'introductory' function, i.e. their marking the relations between the sentence constituents earlier and more clearly. As to the function of these early PPs, they were initially restricted to expressing sentence adjuncts of time, location or manner, as also present in Old English and as illustrated in example (144).

(144) and ic **on ðam endenextan dæȝe of eorðan** *arise*
and I on the last day of earth arise
'and I shall arise on the last day of earth'
(Cath.Homilies Aelfric; Glossary OE Aerobics, s.v. *dæg*)

In this, the PPs were optional, and the constructions only very broadly subcategorised for type of preposition. This first phase of development can be formalised as follows:

(145) 'appositive adverb' $[\ ]_{VP}\ [\ ]_{NP}\ [\ ]_{AdvP}$
→ 'sentence adjunct': $[\ ]_{VP}\ [\ [\ ]_{P}\ [\ ]_{NP}\ ]_{PP\_TEMP/LOC/MANNER}$

In a second stage, slightly before or within Old English, PPs are extended to cover additional adverbial functions such as 'accompaniment' (*John cooked dinner with his dad*) or 'instrument' (*John killed the cat with a knife*). While the PP in these cases is still outside the VP, it nevertheless adds a participant role to the event, and thus differs from the more basic sentence adjuncts expressing spatial or temporal meaning (*John killed the cat in Rome/ on Monday*); cf. (146).[193]

193 See Th. Hoffmann (2005, 2007, 2011) for a discussion of the various syntactic tests that can be applied to determine these distinctions. Both 'extended adjuncts' and 'adjunct ~ comple-

(146) 'sentence adjunct': $[\ ]_{VP}\ [\ [\ ]_{P}\ [\ ]_{NP}\ ]_{PP\_TEMP/LOC/MANNER}$
→'extended adjunct': $[\ ]_{VP}\ [\ [\ ]_{P}\ [\ ]\ ]_{PP\_ACCOMP/INSTR/...}$

Still within the period of Old English, the relations between the elements in such constructions become tighter and tighter, with the PP moving inside the VP construction (147). Examples of such constructions given in Th. Hoffmann (2007: 99) include *John slept in a bed* ('affected location') or *John ran to the church* ('goal/sourcePP').

(147) 'adjunct': $[\ ]_{VP}\ [\ [\ ]_{P}\ [\ ]_{NP}\ ]_{PP}$
→'adjunct ~ complement': $[\ [\ ]_{V\_ACTION/MOVEMENT/...}\ [\ [\ ]_{P}\ [\ ]\ ]_{PP\_LOC/GOAL/SOURCE}]_{VP}$

Concomitantly to or influenced by this development, a similar process is supposed to take place with PPs linking two NPs (as well as in adjective constructions). I assume that such combinations also moved from an appositional relationship to an increasingly close association, meaning that the PP was integrated into the NP (e.g. *the student with the dog* > *the student with red hair* > *the student of physics*); see Harbert (2007: 110–111). Although a more careful analysis of such changes is outside the scope of the present study, it can be traced in the history of the *of*-genitive, which came to acquire progressively more functions both in the verbal and the nominal domain from late Old English onwards (Rosenbach 2002; Allen 2003, 2005, 2006, 2009).

In some cases, we see strong links forming between specific verb and preposition types. For example, *talk* is used exclusively with *to* in PDE. Other fixed combinations include *work at sth.* or *keep sth. in a place* (see the representations in [148a-c] below). Importantly, however, as indicated by the brackets around the PP constituents, these complement-types are optional, meaning they have not yet undergone obligatorification.[194]

(148) a. $[\ [\textit{talk}\ ]_{V}\ ([\ [\textit{to}]_{P}\ [\ ]\ ]_{PP})\ ]_{VP}$
b. $[\ [\textit{work}\ ]_{V}\ ([\ [\textit{at}]_{P}\ [\ ]\ ]_{PP})\ ]_{VP}$
c. $[\ [\textit{keep}]_{V}\ [\ ]_{NP}\ ([\ [\textit{in}]_{P}\ [\ ]\ ]_{PP})\ ]_{VP}$

This process constitutes the final big step in the development of PP-verb constructions in English and indicates that the elements in the clause have come to be perceived as a chunk rather than separate constituents to an even larger extent. As in the case of optional complements, we can here observe various

ments' are referred to as 'predicative adjuncts' in Quirk et al. (1985: 511–512); further Ernst (2002: 131).

194 Cf. also verbs of cognition such as *believe* (*in, on*) or *think* (*about, of*).

degrees of restriction in preposition type. Some verb classes, such as that of caused motion, subcategorise for a particular type of preposition (goal-prepositions like *in*, *on*, or *onto*; 149a), whereas other groups of verbs have come to be confined to one single specific preposition. The latter is the case with ditransitive verbs, which are used with a *to*-PRC only in PDE (149b). On a lower level, verb-specific preferences can develop into fixed associations, as e.g. with *rely+on* (149c).

(149) a. $[\,[\,]_{\text{V-CAUSED MOTION}}\,[\,]_{\text{NP}}\,[\,]_{\text{PP\_GOAL}}\,]_{\text{VP}}$

b. $[\,[\,]_{\text{V-DITRANS}}\,[\,]_{\text{NP}}\,[\,[\textit{to}\,]_{\text{P}}\,[\,]_{\text{NP}}\,]_{\text{PP}}\,]_{\text{VP}}$

c. $[\,[\textit{rely}]_{\text{V}}\,[\,[\textit{on}\,]_{\text{P}}\,[\,]_{\text{NP}}\,]_{\text{PP}}\,]_{\text{VP}}$

Tentative support for the assumption of such a cline of increasingly tighter relations between verbs and PPs comes e.g. from the fact that pied piping structures, which more adjunct-like constructions tend to favour (150a), were present and even obligatory in some contexts already in Old English.[195] By contrast, the phenomenon of preposition stranding (150b), which is strongly preferred by constructions from the other end of the cline, emerged and became frequent only during the Middle English period, once the more adjunct-like OE PPs had grammaticalised into constructions with a tighter association between preposition and verb (Johansson 2002: 152; Th. Hoffmann 2005, 2011; Yáñez-Bouza 2015).

(150) a. the ways **in which** the satire *is achieved*
<ICE-GB:S1B-014 #5:1:A> (Hoffmann 2011: 164)

b. the teacher **that** Jane *relied* **on** (Hoffmann 2011: 188)

In light of this discussion, the development of PRCs in the history of English presents a highly interesting case, since the different PRC-types specified above arguably represent different stages in the cline. All of the prepositions involved are supposed to have started out as marking sentence adjuncts. The PRCs in OE and early ME then constitute instances of the type 'adjunct ~ complement' – integrated into the VP and adding an (optional) participant role to the event, they subcategorise for PP-type (e.g. goal-prepositions in the case of transfer verbs, or source-prepositions for verbs of dispossession). The subsequent behaviour of the PRCs differs quite substantially, however, with some classes having moved further along the continuum over the course of the periods than

---

195 Manner adjuncts as in the example given in fact do not allow preposition stranding at all (Th. Hoffmann 2011: 262).

others. Verbs of ballistic motion, for instance, involve an optional 'adjunct ~ complement', and specify a PP-goal-type in PDE still, although they are potentially moving towards a more restricted usage. In contrast, verbs of dispossession, which were used with source-type PPs in Middle English, have become limited to *from*-PPs. They constitute a type of optional-complement construction in Hoffmann's (2007) classification. A slightly different issue is posed by the group of verbs of emotion/attitude and reverse transfer. In this case, lower-level associations between specific verb+NP-type combinations and prepositions have formed rather than a verb-class-specific subcategorisation frame for a PP-type (cf. *have love for so.* vs. *feel envy towards so.* vs. *have pity on so.*). While with these groups, the complements are optional, the two remaining classes have moved towards (near-)obligatory complement constructions. With verbs of reverse communicated transfer the PP-complement typically cannot be dropped (?*John asked a favour*). The same is true for PDE ditransitive (transfer) verbs, with some exception.[196] By contrast to the latter, which specify a particular preposition (*to*-PRC), the former only subcategorise for a PP-type (source PPs, including *of/from*).

Approaching the periphrastic competitors to Old and Middle English DOCs in the context of more general developments that appear to have been under way throughout the history of English can yield quite interesting results. More specifically, the PRCs and related constructions show increasingly tighter relationships with the verbs (and other constituents) they appeared with, a development which is thought to be still ongoing in PDE. From a replicator-based perspective, such a process is arguably highly beneficial for the constructions involved, since replicating as one chunk instead of forming replicator-collaborations may lead to greater ease in being expressed and higher activation rates. As to the PPs in question, I suggest that there is a great profit in managing to establish oneself as an obligatory part of a larger construction. In general, acquiring new functions of any kind is clearly of advantage, since more functions means a greater likelihood for being replicated. From the perspective of the functions involved (such as 'ditransitive event'), the benefits of becoming associated with more forms (e.g. case constructions as well as PRCs) can be questioned: On the one hand, this creates opportunities to be used in new and more contexts, on the other hand, too many forms could lead to instability in the system. The following section briefly comments on this issue, and again addresses the various pathways of resolution of competition between nominal

196 See Mukherjee (2005), among others.

and prepositional structures that can be seen in the history of PP-patterns in English.

7.1.3.2 Competition resolution with prepositional paraphrases

Once variation has been generated, there are various ways in which the competition between constructional alternatives can be resolved. Most typically, these include the loss of one of the variants or niche construction, with both patterns diverging to some extent in their function. In the case of competition between the PP-constructions and nominal means of expression (case constructions in Old English, and bare NP-constructions in later times), three basic developments can be discerned.

Loss of one variant is found in a large majority of cases. In most instances I am aware of, it is the nominal construction that is ousted in favour of the prepositional pattern.[197] Examples of this development are manifold: First of all, PP-constructions appear to have completely replaced NP-variants of adverbials of time, place and manner (151a-b, both of which are translated with a PP-adverbial). There is some exception to this rule in that in PDE, certain NPs can still be used adverbially (e.g. *This morning, John woke up early*). However, such uses are clearly special and do not contradict the assumption of a general trend towards PP-adverbials in the history of English.

(151) a. **þam þryddan dæge**$_{NP}$ he *arist*
the third day he arose
'on the third day he [i.e. Christ] arose [i.e. from the dead]'
(West Saxon Gospels: Matt. (Corpus Cambr.) xx. 19; OED, s.v. *day*)

b. ic **on ðam endenextan dæ3e of eorðan**$_{PP}$ *arise*
I on the last day of earth arise
'I shall arise on the last day of earth'
(Cath.Homilies Aelfric; Glossary OE Aerobics, s.v. *dæg*)

A similar picture presents itself in the case of accompaniment- as well as instrument-adjuncts. These functions can be expressed by PPs in Old English already, and presumably become restricted to these rapidly from late Old English/ early Middle English onwards (152a-b). In PDE, prepositional patterns have remained as the only option (*John killed his cat *[with] a knife*).

197 Counter-examples include e.g. congratulate, whose direct object could also be introduced by *with* in earlier times.

(152) a. he **lytle werede**$_{NP}$ unieþelice æfter wudum *for*
he little troop with difficulty after wood travelled
'he travelled with a small troop with difficulty through woods'
(ChronA 74.28 (878); Sato 2009: 32)

b. Hi *habbað* **mid him**$_{PP}$ awyriedne engel
they have with them corrupt angel
'They have with them a corrupt angel'
(JECHom II, 38 283.113; Traugott 1992: 171)

A further case of a rise of prepositional patterns at the expense of nominal constructions is the fate of a set of verbs which were construed with oblique case-marked objects in Old English, but soon started to compete with a variety of PPs. These verbs include e.g. *wonder* and *rejoice*, both of which are restricted to prepositional complements in PDE (*wonder about*, *rejoice in*; see 153a-b). Usually, we furthermore see a reduction in the range of prepositions associated with the verbs over time. For example, *rejoice* (or rather, its Germanic equivalent) could be used with a variety of different prepositions in Middle English, but is almost invariably found with *in* today.

(153) a. secg **weorce**$_{NP}$ *gefeh*
man deed rejoiced
'the man rejoiced [in] the deed'
(Beowulf xxiii, 1659; Glossary Old English Aerobics, s.v. *gefēon*)

b. Đonne *motan* we **in ðære engellican blisse**$_{PP}$ *gefeon*
then may we in the angelic bliss rejoice
'then may we in angelic bliss rejoice'
(Blickl. Homl. 83, 3; Bosworth-Toller, s.v. *ge-feon*)

Examples from ditransitives that behave in this way include verbs of dispossession, as well as benefactive/malefactive verbs, mental verbs and verbs of reversed transfer. With all of these, we have seen that the DOC has disappeared entirely from modern usage. Only PRC uses remain.

Apart from loss of one pattern, a second pathway that can be observed in this respect is the establishment of lower-level, relatively unsystematic associations between the verb-class-specific (and verb-specific) nominal and prepositional constructions. For instance, verbs of cognition such as *think* and *believe* are found with both prepositional and non-prepositional objects in earlier stages of English as well as in PDE; cf. (154) and (155). However, although these options might have been interchangeable at some point, they have come to diversify functionally. While PDE *believe in* for example has a meaning of 'have confidence, faith in', the transitive, nominal construction expresses a sense of 'to give intellectual assent to, accept the truth or accuracy of (a statement, doctrine, etc.), according to the OED (s.v. *believe*). Furthermore, putting them in contrast to the first group, the prepositional constructions in this set have not been confined to specific prepositions, but still show some variation. *Believe* is usually used with *on* in addition to *in*, whereas *think* can take both *of* and *about*, among others.

(154) a. he þat *bi-lefeþ* **hit**$_{NP}$ nauȝt
he that believes it not
'he that does not believe it'
(William of Shoreham Poems, 7; OED, s.v. *believe*)

b. Ge *gelefeð* **on God**$_{PP}$, belefeð eac on me$_{PP}$
you believe on god , believe also on me
'you believe in god, believe in me as well'
(*John* (Vesp. D.xiv) xiv. 1; OED, s.v. *believe*)

c. To *bileuen* **in god**$_{PP}$
to believe in God
'to believe in god'
(MS Trin. Cambr., 2nd Ser. 19; OED, s.v. *believe*)

(155) a. fals louers in herte cunne *thenke* **a thyng**$_{NP}$
false lovers in heart can think a thing
'false lovers can think one thing in their heart'
(Chaucer Romaunt Rose, l. 2541; OED, s.v. *think*)

b. *to thinc* **apon his care**$_{PP}$
to think upon his care
'to think about his care'
(Cursor Mundi, l. 15612; OED, s.v. *think*)

As to ditransitives, a corresponding development is seen in the case of verbs of reversed communicated transfer. As shown in the preceding section (7.1.2.3), these verbs do not participate in the dative alternation despite still occurring in the DOC, but are associated with various source-type prepositions instead.

Finally, a third possibility in development is the emergence of an abstract, relatively schematic generalisation over the nominal construction on the one hand, and the prepositional pattern on the other hand. These variants have entered a highly systematic constructional symbiosis in which both fulfil different discourse-pragmatic and/or semantic functions. An obvious case in point in this regard is the dative alternation, as well as to a lesser extent the benefactive alternation. Furthermore, a similar process of an emerging paradigmatic relationship can be seen in the history of the 'genitive alternation' in English (*my father's dog* vs. *the dog of my father*); e.g. Rosenbach (2002).

In conclusion, this section has aimed to show that the changes taking place with ditransitives have to be viewed in the context of corresponding changes in the larger network and surrounding constructions. It is plausible to assume that the relationship between DOC and PRCs was greatly influenced, for example, by the increasing tendency to replace dative NPs in transitive constructions with *to* or genitive NPs with *of*. In a system in which PP-patterns become more frequent overall, a ditransitive prepositional construction will also be more successful, as it is better adapted to its constructional environment. Where these changes ultimately originated or whether similar variants were produced simultaneously in the network and positively impacted the spread of other associated constructions is difficult to determine but is also not entirely relevant.[198] What is important is that the success of various types of PRCs in comparison to the DOC can be addressed in relation to comparable patterns.

7.1.4 Summary: Constructional innovation, competition, and cooperation

The main point of section (7.1) has been to show that the emergence of prepositional paraphrases to existing case- or later zero-marked constructions is by no means a straightforward case of replacement, but instead varies quite markedly in several respects. In the case of ditransitives, three main types of development can be observed, each associated with specific semantic verb classes:

First, with transfer- and transfer-related verbs, we see a cooperative, paradigmatic relationship being established between the DOC and a prepositional alternant involving *to*. Together, these patterns form the well-known dative alternation in PDE. I have proposed here that these constructions are strongly horizontally linked in the constructional network and have come to constitute allostructions of each other. The association between them may even have resulted in the emergence of a higher-level 'ditransitive' abstraction (a con-

198 We can here presume that once a case form was replaced by a prepositional phrase in one function (or one particular construct, micro-construction, etc.) it could be analogically extended to other, similar types, and from there to more and more contexts. That is, once the door was opened there was no way to stop the development – for example, using *to* for DAT in ditransitive communication events (or any other event) could have opened the gate for a 'rule' of 'use *to* for DAT everywhere' to be inferred.

structeme) over the formally distinct patterns. Rather than competing against one another, the DOC and the *to*-PRC are taken to cooperate with each other in that both patterns are connected to particular, complementary discourse-pragmatic functions. By contrast, with verbs of dispossession as well as verbs of malefaction the prepositional uses have come to succeed at the expense of the DOC, meaning that the DOC is not available to be used with these verbs anymore in PDE. I argue that the ousting of this construction here is greatly influenced by the availability of alternative patterns: prepositional theme patterns for dispossession verbs, and possessive constructions for malefactive verbs. A last group of verbs, which includes complex predicate constructions with emotion verbs, among others, is different in showing a clear preference for PRCs in Old English already. Although occasional instances of the nominal construction can be found in Middle English, the prepositional patterns soon take over again, and no such uses are found in PDE. In general, the development of the prepositional competitors for ditransitive verbs is mirrored and likely heavily influenced by developments going on in the system as a whole at the turn of Old to Middle English. Changes in other verbal constructions, such as transitives or locatives/applicatives, constitute changes in the fitness environment against which the ditransitive structures replicate. Patterns better adapted to the system will be more successful. We have seen this in the increasing success of PRCs at a time when PP-patterns generally became more frequent, among other things.

7.2 The dative alternation as a case of co-evolution

The preceding sections have explained the emergence of the dative alternation in English as the outcome of constructional innovation, competition, and cooperation. In this section, I review and discuss changes in the formal and functional features of the constructions involved. This includes, on the one hand, an outline of how the loss of case marking with ditransitives can be conceptualised from a constructionist-evolutionary viewpoint (7.2.1.1). On the other hand, we revisit changes in the semantic make-up of both the DOC and PRC (7.2.1.2), before having a more detailed look at changes in the word order options available for the constructions (7.2.1.3). All these developments ultimately yielded the specific properties the members of the dative alternation exhibit today. They are approached and explained as indicators of constructional co-evolution in section (7.2.2).

7.2.1 Formal and functional changes in the members of the dative alternation

7.2.1.1 Loss of case marking in ditransitives

As is well known, one of the major changes defining the history of English was the increasing reduction and eventual loss of morphological inflections both in the verbal and nominal domain (see section 3.2.1 for an overview). In the following, no attempt is made to account for this phenomenon in its entirety, but I specifically focus on the effect of this change on ditransitive patterns, and how we can interpret this sub-change. I start with a brief constructionist sketch of case with ditransitives in Old English; this is followed by a discussion of the changes seen in Middle English and beyond. Last, I tentatively comment on what it means to consider case marking in ditransitives in the context of the wider, systemic changes underhand in earlier English. Note that although these developments are assumed to have taken place with both the DOC and the prepositional patterns, I illustrate them on the basis of the DOC only. This is, on the one side, due to the empirical restriction to the DOC in the respective part of the corpus study (4.2.1.4). On the other side, I claim that the processes affecting the constructions were essentially the same. A two-fold discussion is thus redundant.

7.2.1.1.1 Ditransitive case constructions in Old English

Both nominal and prepositional ditransitive patterns featured a variety of different 'case frames' in Old English, meaning that different combinations of case marking on the objects of three-place predicates were possible. With the DOC, five argument structure constructions featuring specific case frames can be distinguished: To express ditransitive events, the NPs could be marked by [DAT-ACC], [DAT-GEN], [ACC-GEN], [ACC-DAT] or [ACC-ACC] (Allen 1995: 29, 2006: 205–208; Barðdal 2009: 10–11; De Cuypere 2015a: 230–233).[199] In contrast to the objects, the subject argument in ditransitive events is unchangeably associated with nominative case, and is therefore disregarded for the moment. As indicated in Fig. 42 by differences in strength and shape of lining around the respective boxes, the individual case constructions differed in type and token frequency and thus in degree of entrenchment: For instance, [DAT-ACC] is reported as the most type-frequent frame (and probably also the most token-frequent one), with Visser (1963: 621–634) listing over 320 verbs observed in this pattern. The sec-

199 If case frames are given in square brackets, the first element refers to the REC-argument, whereas the second specifies the case marking of the theme participant.

ond most type frequent frame, though at a considerable distance, was [ACC-GEN] with approximately 75 verb types, followed in descending order by [DAT-GEN] (ca. 60 verbs) and [ACC-DAT] with about 40 types. Finally, the case construction of [ACC-ACC] was instantiated by a very low number of verbs. More precisely, merely 10 verbs are mentioned as occurring in this construction in Visser's inventory (1963: 635–636).

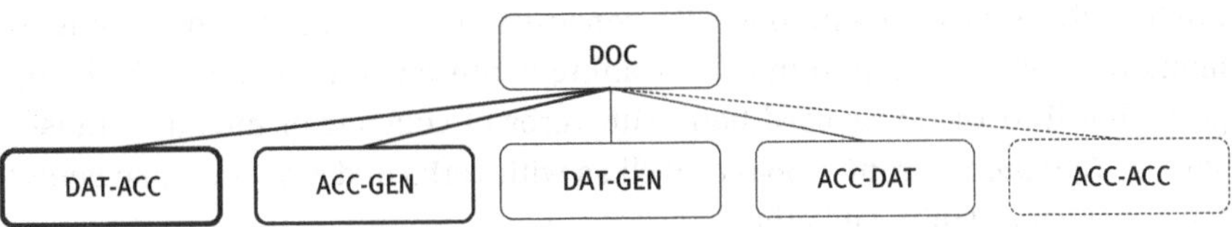

Fig. 42: Network of DOC case frame constructions in Old English

The figure also shows that I take these individual case frame constructions to be horizontally linked to each other in speakers' minds. They could furthermore be abstracted over, resulting in a higher order double object construction. This abstract DOC has a structure of [$V_{ditrans}$ NP-CASE NP-CASE], meaning that it is underspecified regarding the specific case marking on the objects. The schematic form is paired with a similarly underspecified meaning of 'X causes Y to be affected by acting upon Z'. As discussed in more detail in section (7.2.1.2), the schematic semantics of this higher-level construction represent a generalisation over the various senses associated with the pattern such as 'dispossession', 'transfer' or 'benefaction/malefaction', instantiated by different verb classes – the common denominator of which is that there is some sort of effect on the second, mostly animate, participant (cf. Goldberg 1995; Croft 2003). The postulation of a schematic DOC linking the case constructions in addition to the case frames as such is motivated mainly by the fact that they show a great amount of semantic overlap. Although they are therefore formally clearly distinct, this does not correspond to clear semantic boundaries. More precisely, the main characteristics of the OE system of DOC case frames are the following:

On the one hand, the choice of case frames with particular verbs or sets of semantic verb classes appears to have been semantically motivated to some extent. For instance, as Visser (1963: 621) points out, the pattern [ACC_{DEPR}-GEN_{TH}] is relatively reliably associated with events of dispossession or taking away. If such an event of dispossession is conceptualised as 'agent takes animate person away from an entity', the association between case frame and meaning in this instance seems to rather straightforwardly reflect the prototypical semantic functions of the two nominal cases involved. This is because in Old English, the accusative most commonly marked the patient/theme or affectee of an action, whereas genitive case characteristically indicated the source or “spatial reference point from which another participant originates or can be accessed” (Möhlig-Falke 2012: 38; also Croft 2000: 122). On the other hand, the system was far from featuring a bi-unique relationship between forms and functions. Neither was one frame consistently linked to one single meaning, nor was one meaning predictably associated with one case construction only. An example of one-to-many relations between form and meaning is presented in Fig. 43, which suggests that [DAT-GEN] was used both with verbs of concrete or intended transfer such as *(ge)unnan* ‘grant’ (156a) as well as with verbs of deprivation like *bereafian* or *beniman* (156b), and others.

(156) a. and **him**$_{\text{DAT-REC}}$ mancynnes$_{\text{GEN-TH}}$ *benæmde*
and him mankind took away
‘and took mankind away from him’
((*COE*) ÆCHom I, 31 460.8; Allen 1995: 28)

b. Se cyning *nolde* **him**$_{\text{DAT-REC}}$ his feores$_{\text{GEN-TH}}$ *geunnan*
the king would not him his life grant
‘the king would not grant him his life’
(Bt. 29, 2; Bosworth-Toller, s.v. *ge-unnan*)

The frame of [DAT-ACC], on the contrary, is found with a large range of different verb classes including transfer (*agyfan* ‘give’), caused motion (*asendan* ‘send’), intended transfer (*behatan* ‘promise’, *beodan* ‘offer’), refusal (*ofteon* ‘deny’) as well as communication (*cweþan* ‘say’) and dispossession (*ætbredan* ‘take away’); see Allen (1995: 28). This frame therefore appears to have been the semantically broadest or most versatile one, in addition to its being most type and probably token frequent. However, [DAT-ACC] nevertheless likely exhibited a strong affinity to ‘transfer’ semantics in Old English; this is also clear from Visser’s (1963) list of verbs found in this pattern. Accordingly, this frame was also the most prototypical pattern regarding the semantics of the more abstract DOC construction, for which a sense of transfer was most certainly salient.

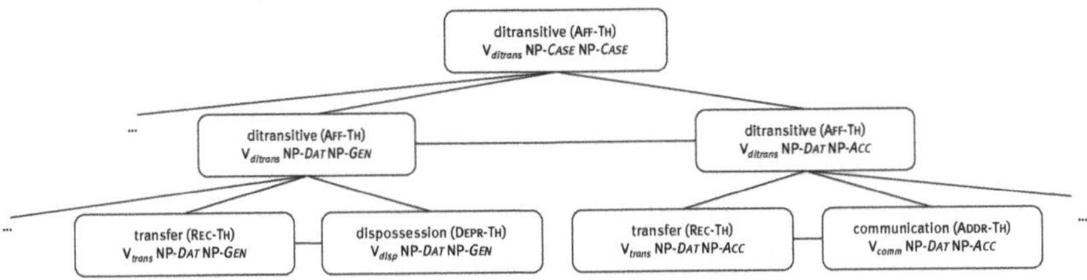

Fig. 43: Constructional network of DOC case frames and verb-class specific meanings in Old English

As for many-to-one relations between form and meaning, the same broader meaning was commonly linked to a variety of case frames. A clear example of this is the notion of dispossession, which was not limited to [ACC-GEN] but could also be expressed by [DAT-GEN], [ACC-DAT] as well as [DAT-ACC]. The former of these would seem to constitute quite basic combinations of the prototypical functions of the constituents involved. The latter two, by contrast, are unexpected considering that the most typical semantic role played by the dative was to mark a spatial goal referent rather than a source (Möhlig-Falke 2012: 38; also Mitchell 1985: 565–568; Traugott 1992: 204). The phenomenon of verbs of dispossession appearing in four different case constructions is illustrated in Fig. 44 and examples (157a-d).[200] The same variability in not being restricted to one particular pattern was also given with all other classes, including verbs of transfer.

Still, it is plausible to assume that the system was not entirely chaotic, but that more subtle differences in construal of the situation or the relationship between the participants involved were present. Tentative support for this assumption lies in the fact that as claimed by Allen (1995: 28), most individual verbs able to appear in genitive combinations showed a strong predilection for either dative or accusative marking on the REC-argument (often denoting a deprivee). They selected for either the frame of [DAT-GEN] or [ACC-GEN]. For example, *forwyrnan* 'to forbid, deny' is almost invariantly found with the former construction, while *bireafian* 'bereave, deprive' shows a distinct preference for accusative marking on the deprivee.

200 The two figures presented here are related in a multi-dimensional way. While Fig. 43 depicts the constructional network of case frames with a focus on form, Fig. 44 presents an approximation to the semantic network of different case frames.

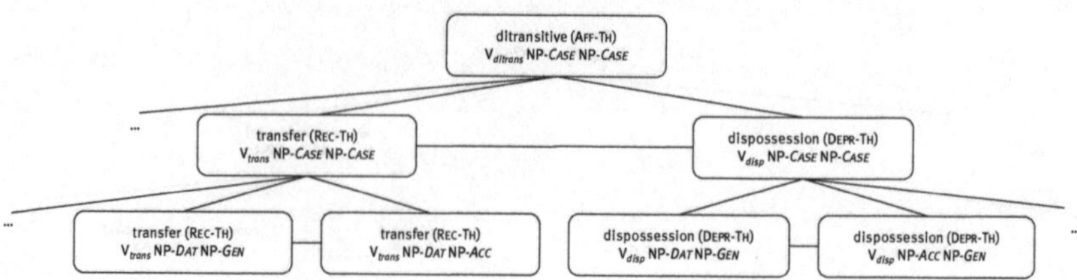

Fig. 44: Constructional network of DOC verb-class specific meanings and case frames in Old English

This distribution possibly points towards a slight contrast in specific meaning of the case frames, with the former denoting a more abstract effect on the dative-argument, in contrast to a more concrete, spatial separating impact on the accusative 'recipient' in the latter. Subtle differences like these would then also have been present in choice contexts, e.g. with *biniman* 'deprive, take away from', even if the distinction is not always entirely easy to detect (e.g. examples 157a vs. 157b).

(157) a. and **him**$_{\text{DAT-REC}}$ mancynnes$_{\text{GEN-TH}}$ *benæmde*
and him mankind took away
'and took mankind away from him'
(ÆCHom I, 31 460.8; taken from Allen 1995: 28)

b. and **hine**$_{\text{ACC-REC}}$ mankynnes$_{\text{GEN-TH}}$ *benæmde*
and him mankind took away
'and took mankind away from him'
(ÆGenEp I; taken from Allen 1995: 28)

c. **hine**$_{\text{ACC-REC}}$ yldo *benam* mæȝenes wynnum$_{\text{DAT-TH}}$
him age took away strength's joys
'age took away from him the joys of his strength'
(Beowulf 1885^{b}-1887; Glossary Old English Aerobics, s.v. *beniman*)

d.

Drihten	me	forȝeaf	ða	æhta	,	and
lord	me	gave	the	possessions	,	and

Drihten	hi$_{\text{ACC-TH}}$	**me**$_{\text{DAT-REC}}$	eft	*benam*
lord	them	me	again	took away

'the lord gave me the possessions, and the lord took them away from me again'

(Hom. II. 450. 24; Glossary Old English Aerobics, s.v. *beniman*)

Concerning the further case frames, Visser (1963: 618) notes that in [ACC-DAT] instances, the person affected is typically "represented as being separated from something that may be looked upon as being 'possessed' by him (head, life, power, etc.)". This frame may accordingly have been associated with situations of deprivation of entities closely connected to the deprivee, corresponding to the OE dative's core semantic function of marking inalienable possession (also Pasicki 1998: 118–119; Möhlig-Falke 2012: 37). This contrast in construal can also account for the differences in complementation between (157c) and the other examples in (157), as well as those between (158a) and (158b), since one's clothes are arguably more intimately attached to someone than alienable possessions like gold and silver.

(158) a.

hine$_{\text{ACC-REC}}$	wædum$_{\text{DAT-TH}}$	*bereafian*
him	clothes	to rob

'to deprive him of his clothes'

(ÆCHom I, 29 426.4; Allen 1995: 29)

b.

bereafode	Godes	**templ**$_{\text{ACC-REC}}$	goldes	and	seolfres$_{\text{GEN-TH}}$
robbed	God's	temple	gold	and	silver

'stole gold and silver from God's temple'

(coaelive, ÆLS_[Maccabees]:6.4838; De Cuypere 2015a: 232)

Likewise, fine contrasts can be posited in regard to the other case frames and verb classes. This leads us to an intricate and complex constructional network in which the combination of particular sets of verbs with particular case frames expresses a range of distinct meanings at various levels of specificity, sometimes only distinguished by very slight semantic differences in perspective (Langacker 1987: 117; also Traugott 1992: 211). An analogous account can also be put forward for prepositional paraphrases of the double object construction, suggesting that specific combinations of verbs, case-marked themes and prepositional recipients (including a case-marked NP complement, typically in the dative) were available to encode specific semantic relations or event construals (e.g. van Kemenade 1987: 81; Lundskær-Nielsen 1993: 19–24; Alcorn 2011: 143–151).

Although this account is appealing, there are a few problematic issues with it: First, the suggestions are highly tentative, and lack confirmation by empirical data. Second, multiple attempts at establishing clear correlations between the use of certain case frames and event construals have been made so far. Still, they have largely failed in creating conclusive models of classification, and the endeavour has therefore often been considered as essentially futile (Mitchell 1985: 453). Furthermore, postulating very fine-grained semantic distinctions which are often difficult to perceive is risky. Irregularities, i.e. instances in which the chosen case frame does not seem to match the proposed semantic motivation, can be explained away as cases of constructional coercion into a certain meaning. This, however, clearly runs the danger of circularity and ad-hoc explanations, especially without careful examination of actual usage data. An additional problem is posed by the question of how much of the semantic information is contributed by the verb and by the case construction, respectively (Croft 2000: 122). A thorough assessment of the frequency with which verbs in fact alternated between case frames in Old English would allow us to shed more light on the issue.

Even if subtle semantic distinctions between the case frames were present, the OE system of ditransitive case constructions was certainly characterised by a large degree of idiosyncrasy and very low-level subcategorisations (cf. also the concept of lexical case assignment; Allen 1995). Abstractions formed over instances of individual case constructions with particular verbs and verb classes would furthermore necessarily have been comparatively underspecified regarding their semantics. This in turn would have meant a great deal of semantic overlap between the (more schematic) case constructions. Accordingly, such a system must have been rather difficult to acquire and maintain. I claim below that it was therefore prone to change, inviting convergence of the case frames (also Croft 2000; Barðdal 2009).

In sum, in the remainder of this section I work on the basic assumption that the OE system of argument structure construction did not unambiguously link form and meaning in an isomorphic way. In such a situation, in which the individual case frames are not associated with clearly defined semantic niches but stand in competition for the same semantics, we can expect two possible pathways of developments: Either (i) the case frames cooperate and develop systematically distinct functions, or (ii) they continue to compete against each other, which may result in the ousting of certain patterns in favour of others. I demonstrate in the following that it was the latter scenario that took place in the history of English ditransitives, and ultimately also led to the loss of case distinctions in general (Traugott and Trousdale 2013: 18; Barðdal 2009).

7.2.1.1.2 Merging case constructions in late Old English to Middle English

A system exhibiting substantial semantic overlap between different constructions, such as that of ditransitive argument structure described in the preceding section, is presumably rather unstable. This lack of stability invites change, which is precisely what we observe with ditransitives at the transition from Old to Middle English. As demonstrated by the corpus data in section (4.2.1.4), and as confirmed in earlier studies, the various case frames of the DOC gradually merged, until we arrive at the 'bare', non-case marked double object construction still present today.

The development as witnessed with ditransitives finds its parallels in other parts of the network, including the so-called 'impersonal' or 'experiencer' constructions, dealt with in von Seefranz-Montag (1983), Allen (1995), Barðdal (2009) or Möhlig-Falke (2012), among others. Barðdal (2009: 13–14) shows that the semantic spaces taken up by the case constructions for one- and two-place predicates (including impersonals) intersect in various places within individual Germanic languages. Since constructional synonymy tends to be avoided, it is assumed that this state of semantic overlap is temporary only, and that 'therapeutic' measures to resolve the issue will be taken. The specific pathways of change suggested by Barðdal are a) the complete loss of case distinctions and subsequent convergence of case constructions, as case markers are perceived as redundant, or b) a movement towards more productive constructions, resulting in the gradual demise of low-type frequent constructions (Barðdal 2009: 14; also Luraghi 1987: 356). It is, however, clear from the ensuing discussion of individual Germanic languages that Barðdal in fact envisages these two options as being dependent on each other. The reduction of the case system as a whole is seen as the result of a step-wise gradual reduction in the range of case constructions.[201] Although not dealt with explicitly in her account, a question of interest would be whether those constructions that are productive and thus manage to

201 Another important factor in Barðdal's argument is language contact. It is assumed that loan-verbs "will be attracted by the high type frequency constructions, thereby lowering the type frequency of the low type frequency constructions, increasing the chances of them becoming extinct" (2009: 15).

survive have developed complementary (cooperative) relationships over time, i.e. whether synonymy has been decreased in this way.[202]

A similar, yet still slightly distinct approach is taken by Croft (2000: 121–123), who deals with object marking in non-impersonal transitives. Assuming that the marking of the non-agentive arguments of transitive verbs in general was highly conventionalised, and that there was a large degree of synonymy between patterns involving accusative, genitive or dative objects, he suggests that non-accusative objects were first 'recoded' as accusative, only later to be followed by case loss proper. Croft thus sees the primary effect of semantic overlap between case constructions in the ousting of certain patterns in favour of others, but attributes the whole-scale demise of morphological case marking to different (unspecified) causes.

The present book argues for a scenario for ditransitives which combines both proposals (see also section 3.2.1.2). In a first stage, the competition between the different case constructions for the same (or overlapping meanings) was settled in favour of the most type-frequent and most productive [DAT-ACC] frame. That is, the corpus data drawn from the PPCME2 shows little evidence of genitive-bearing frames at all. Where case marking is still comparatively unambiguous, dative recipients and accusative themes are predominant. Incidentally, as shown in the preceding section, the frame of [DAT-ACC] also constituted the most open construction in that it could express most or indeed all senses associated with the other frames. This included even verb classes such as verbs of privation, which were more commonly associated with genitive combinations. Furthermore, this frame can be considered as most successful in the context of the constructions surrounding and connected to ditransitives in the larger network. Accusative marking became increasingly closely associated with 'object' position by most frequently instantiating the semantic role of theme or patient. At this point, a ditransitive case construction corresponding to this trend would clearly have been most successful.[203] In this process of increasing movement towards the most productive frame, the least entrenched construction of [ACC-ACC] was lost earliest, followed by the remaining frames.

---

202 This is indeed what appears to have occurred in German (at least to some extent), as the individual cases and correspondingly, the individual case constructions are strongly correlated with particular functions.

203 In accordance with the ideas presented in (7.2.1.1.3), I assume this bias to have worked in both directions. Since the accusative in ditransitive events most frequently and most prototypically marked themes transferred to another participant in OE already, this predilection likely impacted the bias towards accusative (direct) object marking in other events.

As to the subtle meaning distinctions which were before associated with the individual case constructions, I claim that they could still be retrieved through context, the nature of the objects, as well as the verbal meaning itself. The convergence of case frames thus did not necessarily have a negative impact on the system but – quite on the contrary – made it easier, while retaining a similar degree of expressivity. This 'retrievability' may ultimately also have caused the loss of the last remaining case markers. Once [(NOM-)DAT-ACC] was the only frame available for three-place predicates, case marking on the participant arguments involved came to be perceived as redundant in speakers' minds, since in most cases the REC-argument was clearly distinguishable from the TH-argument on the basis of animacy asymmetries (and other features) anyway. In other words, with only one particular case frame left, variants involving unmarked, bare NP arguments, i.e. [NP-$Ø_{REC}$ + NP-$Ø_{TH}$] could easily emerge. These were able to replicate very successfully as they had a similar cue reliability as the case-marked pattern but were simultaneously more economical. Furthermore, this particular construction would have had greater replicative success considering its intra-systemic fitness environment, in that it reflected the general trend towards case reduction in the system of argument structure constructions and beyond.

While the account presented so far is largely in line with Barðdal's proposals on case in Germanic, it differs in one aspect. Contrary to most constructionist accounts, which typically downplay the role of phonetic erosion, I do take formal ambiguity in case markers as a contributing factor in the story of case loss in English (Blake 2001: 176–178). This is also reflected in the empirical analysis presented in section (4.2.1.4). As shown in the results, formal ambiguity between dative and accusative markers was high already in early Middle English and increased significantly over the course of the period. One motivation for including formal ambiguity as a separate process is that the arguments against including phonetic/phonological changes and the formal reduction of case affixes are, in my opinion, debatable, or do at least not exclude the possibility of phonetic reduction playing a minor part in the development. For example, Barðdal's (2009: 3) contention that the loss of case marking in Swedish did not affect the first person plural ending of verbs in the present tense (*-e*) is only remotely relevant. Morphological markers in verbs might have reacted differently to formal and systemic pressures as those in the nominal system, and this particular ending could have been preserved for a number of different reasons. Second, and more importantly, the loss of case frames other than [DAT-ACC] and the rise of a zero-marked DOC constitute two distinct processes. While the former is thought to have been driven by semantic overlap and differences in type frequencies between the case constructions, the latter may have been (partly) promoted by the fact that the formal instantiations of the category markers were often highly ambiguous in early Middle English already. If the markers of the participant arguments showed a high degree of formal overlap in addition to their being semantically redundant, this would only have aided their eventual reduction.

To conclude, the scenario suggested here is one of two-fold competition – in a first step, we find different case frames competing for expression with ditransitive verbs in a system that is characterised by semantic overlap between formal patterns and semantic irregularity. The same (broad) meanings, instantiated by specific verb classes, are associated with more than one form at the same time. This system involves competition on too many levels, making it vulnerable to changes. In the particular case of English ditransitives, change takes place in that the most entrenched and most general case construction of [DAT-ACC] successfully manages to attract members of other frames, and eventually ousts them altogether. This construction in time enters competition with a newly emerged, case-less DOC. The competition is ultimately resolved in favour of the latter variant due to the formal ambiguity of the phonetically reduced case affixes, as well as the little semantic contribution of the case markers once [DAT-ACC] is retained as the sole frame. The final outcome of these processes is that in early/mid Middle English, we find a schematic and relatively underspecified DOC construction which features two case-less NP-objects and expresses a comparatively wide range of meaning relations. This development is reflected in Fig. 45.

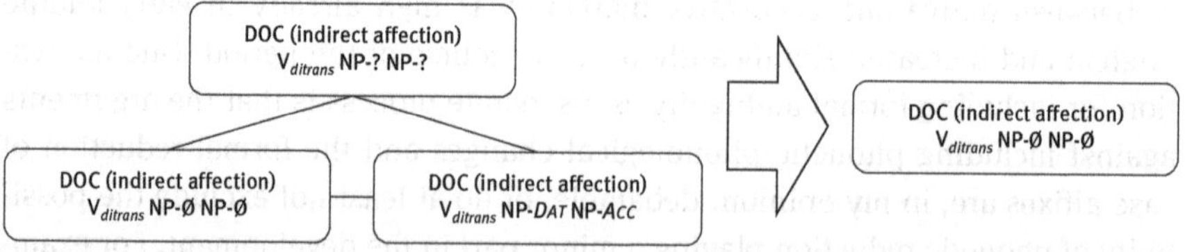

Fig. 45: Competition resolution between case construction [DAT-ACC] and a zero-marked construction

Although the focus has here largely been on the DOC and its case constructions, I argue that a comparable scenario holds for PRCs (and PTCs) between Old and Middle English. With case marking on the complements of prepositions being perceived as largely redundant and contributing little to the semantics of the constructions, a reduction of case frames towards the most frequent [*prep*DAT] in general, and in consequence, [*prep*DAT-ACC] for PRCs is expected. Eventual complete loss of case marking soon ensued. It is furthermore possible that with PRCs an unmarked construction established itself even more rapidly, since double-marking (preposition plus case) is arguably rather uneconomical.

7.2.1.1.3 Ditransitives in the context of a system-wide loss of case

The development of Old English case constructions cannot be adequately addressed without taking into account the larger network of constructions connected to them, as well as the smaller constructions which participate in their formation. That is, since one of the main foci of the present book is on the intra-systemic factors determining the success of a certain variant, it follows that constructions need to be investigated not in isolation, but in relation to their constructional environment (also Hoffmann and Trousdale 2011: 10).

Among other things, the Old English DOC (with its various case sub-constructions) was closely linked to other argument structure constructions, including intransitives and transitive patterns of all kinds. As with ditransitives, these constructions were typically not associated with one single case frame but connected to a variety of different case constructions (see section 3.2.1). Fig. 46 shows that semantically highly transitive, prototypical two-place predicates could for example appear with dative-, accusative- or genitive-marked 'object' arguments, meaning that even in patterns featuring an invariably nominative 'first' argument, there was room for variation.[204]

Möhlig-Falke (2012: 35, 48) points out that [SUBJ: NOM – OBJ: ACC] was clearly the most type frequent frame; this is also indicated in the figure. In the lists provided by Visser (1963: 607–637) and Mitchell (1985: 455–464), over 40 per cent of the OE transitive verbs are mentioned as being used in this construction. Therefore, it "may be considered to be the prototype of the OE transitive construction on the basis of being the most typical example" (Möhlig-Falke 2012: 35; also Lakoff 1987: 86–87).[205] What is important to note here is that again we find a system that is far from bi-unique but is instead characterised by many-to-many relationships. On the one side, the same meaning could be expressed by various forms. On the other side, one particular form could express a variety of

204 We of course know that not all sentences necessarily involved a nominative agent- argument – the focus on prototypical transitive clauses is therefore a simplification for practical purposes (cf. Barðdal 2009; Möhlig-Falke 2012; among others).

205 The relevance of these differences in type frequency for the emergence of a subject and object slot prototypically associated with nominative and accusative is dealt with in more detail in section (7.2.1.3).

meanings. For instance, as also hinted at in the figure, an agent-theme relation could be expressed both by [NOM–ACC] and [NOM–DAT] (and possibly others), while [NOM–DAT] could also be used to mark a possessive relation between two NPs.

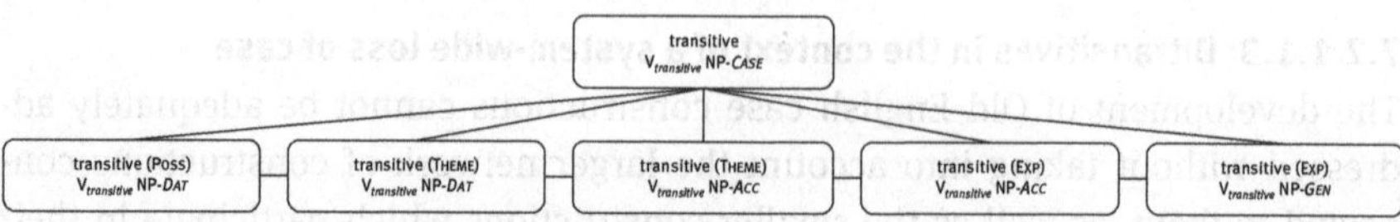

Fig. 46: Network of transitive case constructions in Old English

With Barðdal (2009) and Croft (2000), such semantic overlap is likely to lead to a reduction in case frames in favour of the most frequent one, and eventually even the complete loss of morphological case marking. Crucially, we can furthermore presume that changes affecting individual constructions (clause types) mutually influenced each other. The establishment of accusative as the prototypical object case in the transitive construction through the loss of less type-frequent patterns, or rather, the move towards a prototypical [NOM–ACC] frame for two-place verbs, certainly had some impact on the ditransitive case constructions and vice versa. The convergence on one specific case pattern in construction A would then have furthered the fixation of the same case pattern for a similar relation in construction B. This means that against the backdrop of similar constructions in the constructional environment, a frame of [(NOM–) DAT–ACC], in which the accusative marked a role comparable to that of the prototypical theme argument in transitive verb frames, had a clear benefit over other ditransitive case constructions. It was able to procreate even more successfully. In a comparable way, the fact that most prepositions showed a preference for dative marking on their complements, and that prepositional paraphrases for ditransitive verbs became increasingly frequent from late Old English onwards, possibly furthered the success of the [DAT–ACC] construction: The use of dative-marked REC-arguments in PRCs (and dative-marked PP-complements in general) may have had a positive or reinforcing impact on the fitness of dative-marked REC-arguments in the DOC. Moreover, as already said, the redundancy of 'double-marking' with PP-arguments may have aided the emergence of case-less prepositional constructions, which in turn had an effect on case-marking in nominal constructions, including the DOC.

The phenomenon of functional overlap between formally different constructions, in addition to analogical influence from other constructions, is therefore seen as the main trigger behind the loss of case frames in the history of English ditransitives. At the same time, however, I have suggested that competition and overlap on the level of individual affixes, i.e. more atomic case-suffix constructions, had a contributory effect on the demise of case marking. In such case-suffix constructions, a particular form (such as *-e*, *-an*, or *-as*) was paired with a particular, possibly relatively concrete participant role (Booij 2002b: 19). These affixes may also have been abstracted over, either labelled as part of a specific inflectional paradigm (e.g. strong masculines), or as part of a cross-paradigmatic case category (e.g. *-e*, *-an* and *-e* as instantiations of a more abstract 'dative singular' category). The more abstract category constructions presumably combined with more abstract meanings emerging from their use in context and fed into the larger case constructions just mentioned. For example, dative marking indicated that the NP bearing it expressed the semantic role of 'experiencer', 'theme', 'possessor', or 'recipient' in a ditransitive event among other things (Pasicki 1998: 118–119; Möhlig-Falke 2012: 36–37).

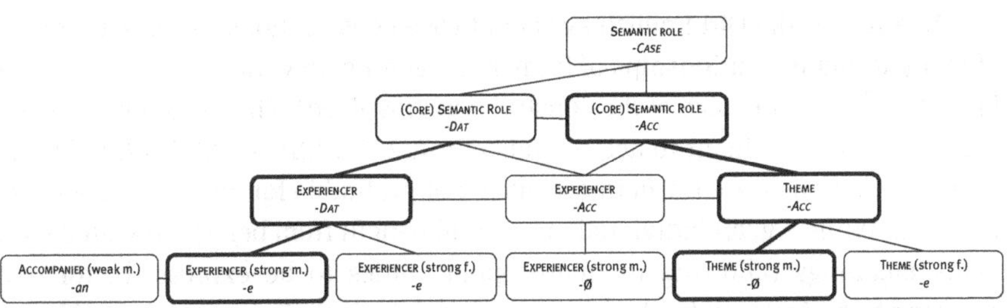

Fig. 47: Simplified constructional network of OE case affixes, categories, and higher-level abstractions

An illustration of such a network of 'case marking constructions' is presented in Fig. 47, which also shows additional, more schematic constructions such as [-DAT: semantic role]. Differences in lining are again used to indicate differing degrees of entrenchment of the constructions. For instance, the strong masculine inflectional class and the affixes associated with it were commonly more type frequent than other paradigms and thus represent more productive and prototypical members of the categories.[206] Also, some categories are more close-

206 Cf. also PDE possessive and plural -s, both of which have their origins in the OE strong masculine class.

ly linked to specific semantic roles than to others, meaning that some pairings are more entrenched than others (e.g. [-DAT: Experiencer]).

The Old English system, as known from comparative studies on (Proto-) Germanic, already represents a reduced version of earlier systems. – In pre-Old English times, competition between individual case marking suffixes (as well as categories) for the same function may have led to a reduction of the entire system, with both intra- and cross-paradigmatic levelling taking place (e.g. Luraghi 1987; Lass 1992; van Reenen and Schosler 2000; Harbert 2007; Barðdal and Kulikov 2009; Bertacca 2009). The Old English system accordingly featured a reduced inventory of affixes compared to Indo-European as well as Germanic. Only those markers remained that allowed the system to become more flexible and functionally efficient without, on the whole, diminishing too much in disambiguation power (cf. van Trijp 2012). However, this reduction did cause an even greater deal of functional overlap between the individual affixes and contributed to the functional overlap between certain categories and case constructions.

As a result, the Old English system of case constructions exhibited a range of many-to-many relationships of form and meaning on various levels (concerning schematicity and size of the constructions involved). This would have made it comparatively difficult to acquire (also Croft 2001: 122; Barðdal 2009). Many-to-many relations were furthermore likely not profitable for any of the elements involved. While e.g. an individual form could benefit from being associated with many meanings (allowing for more opportunities to be expressed), for one meaning to be instantiated by many forms (exclusively linked to it) would also be an advantage. However, non-exclusive association of one meaning with many forms also used for other functions, is disadvantageous. At the same time, if there are many different forms all expressing the same function, it is similarly bad for them, since they face heavy competition. Too much competition of this kind causes instability in the system, with regularising changes bound to occur in several places, on several levels and in several constructions at roughly the same time.

It could be argued that such a regularisation of relations between forms and meanings in the network is of advantage to the entire system because it becomes more transparent (in the sense of Kiparsky's 1995 optimisation account). Nonetheless, it is only beneficial as long as the language's expressive potential is not limited by these changes. It is difficult to address this issue on the basis of corpus data. – Still, the fitness of a reduced system with little or no case marking, as well as a random distribution of constituent order but a biased distribution of animate, topical etc. constituents, can easily be tested and be compared against a more elaborate but also less easily learnable system by means of e.g. an agent-based modelling experiment (van Trijp 2013).

In sum, I subscribe to the widely held view that the loss of case marking in the history of English was indeed not a sudden, unified change proceeding from the top of the hierarchical network to the bottom. Rather, it represents an accumulation of similar and interrelated changes in a number of different constructions, including the double object construction as well as its prepositional paraphrases. Moreover, the prime cause of these developments is taken to have been the partial (or considerable) synonymy between different sub-constructions, which was promoted by formal pressures on the system due to changes in the phonetic domain. Ultimately, this brought about the PDE situation. Today, instead of a variety of case paradigms and forms, we find an almost entirely caseless language, with only traces of the original system remaining in pronominal forms. With ditransitives, this meant the emergence of an unmarked DOC with two NP object arguments, and various prepositional competitors likewise involving two bare NP arguments, one of which functioned as the complement of a PP.

In the following, I provide some further discussion on the semantic development of the two constructional types. Since the semantic development of the prepositional patterns has already been looked at in detail in (7.1.2), the section is again concerned mostly with changes in the DOC.

7.2.1.2 Semantic changes in ditransitives

The story of PP-constructions in English and especially that of PRCs can confidently be described as one of semantic widening or functional extension, in that they appear to have acquired more and more procedural meanings over time. This amounts to a generalisation in meaning, and the constructions qualify as good examples of grammatical constructionalisation (at least in terms of semantic development). In contrast, the DOC has undergone the opposite change – rather than expanding in associated sub-senses, it has lost several types of verb classes. More precisely, as shown in section (4.2), the DOC has moved towards more coherent and more transparent semantics, now being strongly linked to a meaning of ‘transfer’ and transfer-related senses. The development of the DOC therefore constitutes one of semantic specialisation or narrowing. The construction exhibits some features often linked to lexical constructionalisation (in contrast to grammatical constructionalisation), although this proposal is problematic (or at least less than straightforward). In the following, I first re-address the issue of constructional specialisation in the history of the DOC, outlining also the potential benefits this change had for the construction(s) involved (7.2.1.2.1).

Afterwards, some aspects of the PDE DOC and its semantics that are still in need of explanation are discussed (7.2.1.2.2). Since many issues in this context have already been touched upon in various places before, this is kept as brief as possible.

7.2.1.2.1 Moving towards 'transfer' in the DOC

Most basically, what the data obtained in the present study show is that we indeed find a specialisation of the semantics of the DOC in the course of Middle English: Transfer- and transfer-related meanings such as communication (telling) or intended transfer (offering, promising) significantly grow in proportional frequency. They take up an increasingly large part of the semantic space of the DOC. Furthermore, within this larger group of giving-senses, concrete, spatial giving is foregrounded at the expense of metaphorical, abstract or indirect giving (as in e.g. *give so. a kiss* or *pay so. a visit*). In other words, the DOC moves towards a core meaning of denoting basic transfer situations, in whose most prototypical instantiations, a volitional agent successfully transfers a concrete entity to a willing animate recipient (Goldberg 1995: 141). Other senses, which do not involve a prototypical transfer-event visibly decrease over time in Middle English and are at best marginal at the end of the period. The latter group most prominently includes verbs of dispossession and verbs of pure benefaction/malefaction (with the exception of light verb constructions of the type 'do so. good/harm'). The results of this book essentially confirm the findings of Rohdenburg (1995, 2007), Barðdal (2007), Barðdal, Kristoffersen, and Sveen (2011) and Colleman and De Clerck (2011). They thereby lend further support to the hypothesis that the double object construction saw a considerable narrowing in its constructional semantics in the history of English.

The results have moreover indicated that this change did not take place before or within Old English times. Nor does it represent a very recent development which started in Late Modern English only (as could by hypothesis be assumed based on the investigations that were carried out on this issue so far). Instead, putting my findings in relation to those of previous studies suggests that even though the change towards a basic transfer-meaning was gradual and continuous, essential steps were taken in Middle English. For example, it is clear that the sub-schema of 'transfer' was highly entrenched (more so than others) already at the beginning of the period, accounting for a large percentage of DOC uses – both in respect to types and tokens. Non-transfer constructions were less productive at the outset of the period. On the other hand, verbs of pure benefaction are still attested in the construction in Colleman and De Clerck's (2011) dataset of 18th ct. English. This implies that notwithstanding the relative rareness of this sense at the turn from Middle English to Early Modern English, it still resisted its complete ousting for a certain time.[207] Furthermore, less prototypical uses such as the attitudinal/mental verbs *forgive* or *envy* have not been lost from the DOC until this day, despite indications that change might be in progress at this moment (see Goldberg 2006). Some processes pertaining to the development hay thus have been ongoing since Proto-Germanic (or are at least paralleled in other Germanic languages). Others are still in progress, and the changes continue to affect the construction to this day (also Goldberg 1995: 132). Nevertheless, a crucial part of it – such as the marked increase of transfer-meanings and the complete loss of dispossession verbs – can be observed within the comparatively short time frame of Middle English. I consequently argue that this period saw a more rapid progression of the changes involved. That the development as such should be gradual rather than saltational is generally perfectly in line with the principles of usage-based linguistics.

Approaching this development from an evolutionary constructionist perspective, and following Croft (2003), among others, in presuming 'polysemous' argument structure constructions to be organised in a lexicality-schematicity hierarchy, the DOC in Old and early Middle English can be conceptualised as a highly schematic construction. This construction has an underspecified meaning of 'X causes Y to be affected by acting on Z' and is linked to several lower-level verb class-specific constructions. The distinct senses that can be identified for the DOC at this stage constitute sub-constructions tied to (and indeed emerging from) specific sets of verbs instantiating them. The changes occurring during Middle English and beyond are visualised in Fig. 48.

On the left, a simplified and cut-down version of the network of the OE/ early ME DOC is depicted. The abstract DOC, which specifies little more than the presence of a three-place predicate and two object NPs as well as a very general meaning of 'indirect affectedness', is related vertically (rotated by 90 degrees in the figure for better use of space) to the more specific verb-class constructions.

207 The fact that malefactive uses apparently disappeared earlier than benefactive verbs can be taken as a further support for the account presented here, since DOCs of pure benefaction are arguably still closer to the core meaning of the PDE DOC ('successful and beneficial transfer to a willing recipient'). By contrast, malefactive events, in which a negative, non-beneficial effect is transferred onto the – most likely unwilling – person denoted by the REC-argument, are further removed from the prototype (cf. also Mukherjee 2005 on core and periphery in PDE ditransitives).

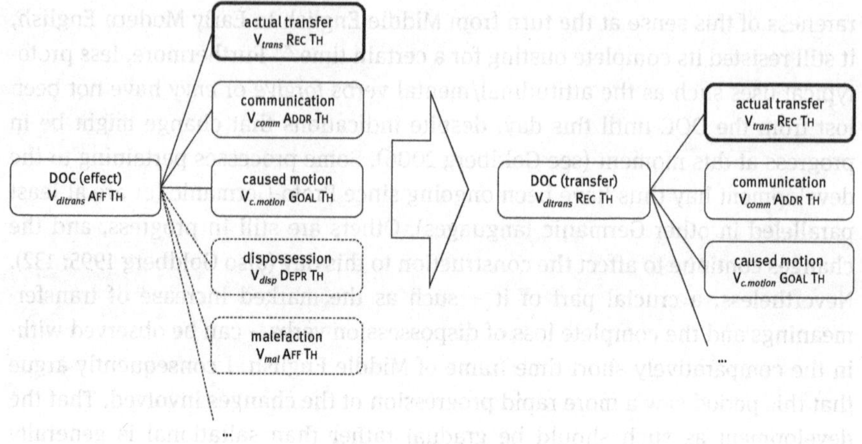

Fig. 48: Semantic narrowing (loss of sub-constructions) of the DOC in Middle English

These lower-level constructions include e.g. the senses of 'actual transfer' (instantiated by verbs of physical transfer such as ME *yeven* 'give') or communication (ME *cwethen* 'say', *tellen* 'tell') and caused motion (ME *bringen* 'bring', *senden* 'send'). These senses are stably associated with the DOC, with the sub-construction of actual transfer being the most entrenched of all (bold lines). By contrast, several other constructions are less entrenched and show weaker links to the DOC.[208] In the figure, this is illustrated by the examples of verbs of dispossession and malefaction. Their less prototypical status is indicated by broken lining around the boxes as well as in their relations to the DOC schema. The differences in strength of connection and degree of entrenchment can be viewed as the outcome of considerable competition at this point already. The various sub-constructions are taken to compete against each other for more exclusive association with the DOC's formal features (rather than competing for expression as such).

Competition starts to be resolved in Middle English, with those constructions that are more successful (for reasons that are dealt with below) forcing out the weaker variants, and thereby reducing the range of senses linked to the schematic DOC. More specifically, we observe a process in which the less productive and more peripheral uses are increasingly marginalised, and eventually

208 Incidentally, the group of transfer-related senses is also most reliably associated with the most frequent [DAT-ACC] case frame, which further increases the entrenchment of these constructions.

lost altogether. This means that the sub-schemas are activated less and less frequently, until they and their links to the DOC disappear (demonstrated on the right of the figure).[209] Importantly, this loss of constructional types of the DOC is not random, but highly motivated in that only certain, related senses are retained: I take the most successful construction (in our case that of actual transfer) to exert a positive influence on those senses that show a high degree of similarity to it. Forming a cooperative relationship instead of a competitive one, this association is beneficial for both sides. On the one hand, the less frequent, slightly less successful senses profit from being 'dragged with the older and more popular brother', so to say. This can be explained by the mechanism of spreading activation. Each time the fitter variant is activated, different yet closely related concepts are triggered as well, making them more stable than other, further removed variants (Traugott and Trousdale 2013). On the other hand, the transfer-construction evidently gains from a clearer one-to-one relationship between form (DOC syntax) and meaning. Collaborating with near relatives is also of advantage for the more successful construction, due to more or less the same reasons of stabilising and strengthening (competition equals less activation, cooperation equals more activation through association).

The opposite is the case with a number of other DOC senses such as verbs of dispossession or malefaction. Such events, where the agent causes someone to lose an entity rather than to receive one, or where transfer of possession is only involved on a rather indirect level, are arguably much more peripheral to 'giving' semantics. They therefore have a high probability of being ousted from the construction. As we have seen in section (4.2.1), these verb classes typically 'resort' to other means of expression such as the various PRCs, PTCs or Poss. Although this development might be considered a loss situation, from the perspective of the verb classes involved it can in fact be profitable to be released out of competition against fitter variants and to become associated with a more expressive construction instead.

As to the more abstract construction of the DOC, the loss of peripheral subsenses or semantic narrowing to a certain degree corresponds to a loss of schematicity. Although the construction's meaning becomes more specialised and less general, it still remains at a high and clearly still procedural level in the network. The 'status' of the construction correspondingly does not really

209 That occasional examples of such uses are still found at later points – for example in specific varieties of English – is not necessarily problematic for this account, since the loss of sub-constructions may only be partial in some speaker minds, and (very) faint ties may continue to exist.

change too much through this change. The development does result in a reduction in constructional polysemy. This makes the schema semantically more coherent as well as transparent, as it comes to be associated with a basic, unified meaning of transfer – including all kinds of metaphorical indirect transfer – instead of denoting the considerably vaguer notion of indirect affectedness (also Goldberg 1995: 132).[210] Greater semantic coherence is, as has been discussed in (1.2.1), conducive to the higher productivity of a construction, inversely related with type frequency (cf. e.g. Bybee 1995; Barðdal 2008; Barðdal and Gildea 2015, Perek 2015; among others). This can explain the construction's productivity regarding new members of associated semantic classes (such as *e-mail*, *text*, *skype* and *whatsapp* or *feed* and *issue*), even if the type frequency of entire associated classes of verbs has in fact decreased (De Clerck et al. 2011; De Clerck, Delorge, and Simon-Vandenbergen 2011). Furthermore, it provides an explanation for the survival of the construction as such. It has not only managed to successfully compete against its prepositional paraphrases, but has res-established itself and has maintained its position over time (e.g. Colleman and De Clerck 2011: 203; also Rohdenburg 2009).[211]

To conclude, a move towards a more isomorphic, coherent relationship between form and meaning can be highly beneficial for a construction; this is precisely what we see in the history of the English DOC. Moreover, specialising to a giving-sense is advantageous for the DOC as it enables or eases its association with the *to*-PRC, and thereby allows it to profit from the resulting alternation-based productivity.

7.2.1.2.2 Integrating idiosyncrasies and exceptions with the DOC

The account just presented is challenged by a few idiosyncrasies, as the situation indicated by the PDE data is not as straightforward as one would wish (as it probably never is). One of the problematic issues is posed by the verb *cost*, which is still regularly found in the DOC in Present-Day English (e.g. Colleman and De Clerck 2008: 204–205, 2009: 34–38; also Goldberg 2002; Pinker 1989). As Colleman and De Clerck (2009: 36) point out, *cost* in fact exhibits an almost

210 This holds true for PDE even if we acknowledge that there is clearly still some variability in the semantic range of the DOC in PDE, as discussed in the following section.

211 The development of the DOC is accordingly characterised by a decrease in schematicity, an increase in productivity (or a steady rate of productivity) and no major changes regarding compositionality. The construction's history nevertheless does not convincingly qualify as a case of lexical constructionalisation after Traugott and Trousdale's (2013) analysis. This is because no new node is created by the loss of the sub-senses.

absolute preference for the DOC, meaning the verb is virtually never paraphrased by a *to*-PRC. This restriction is only to be expected considering the verb semantics' incompatibility with the relations expressed by *to*. (Presuming, of course, that *to* has not completely bleached, but still retains some of its locational goal-meaning). Nevertheless, it is difficult to explain why the verb should appear in the DOC at all, since it can be classified as a verb of dispossession and should have dropped out of use from this construction in Middle English, or not long after. Not much can be gained by looking at the Middle English data, though, as *cost* occurs very rarely (N= 1), and no prepositional paraphrases of any kind are attested in the whole period. Interestingly, *cost* does not seem to have any prepositional competitors in PDE, either (at least none I am aware of), suggesting that the verb is special in its behaviour in any case. Following Colleman and De Clerck's argumentation, this peculiarity might be connected to *cost* being an atypical verb of dispossession in that "it is incompatible with an agentive subject, and [in that] there is no suggestion that the subject eventually possesses the direct object" (2008: 204, cf. also 2009: 34). While it is plausible that the verb escaped the fate of other, more prototypically privative verbs such as *steal* or *rob* due to its marginal status within this group, as well as its general infrequency, the issue would still need to be investigated in a corpus of Early/Late Modern English.

Similarly, the continued use of 'verbs of blocked transfer/ refusal' such as PDE *deny* and *refuse* in the DOC is surprising. According to my account, they too would have been hypothesised to be ousted from the construction due to their not corresponding to the basic transfer-semantics of the construction (Green 1974; Krifka 2004; Colleman and De Clerck 2008, 2009). One explanation for this persistence is again the scarcity of these particular verbs in ME (*deny:* N=4; *refuse:* N=0). Note that the slightly more frequent verb of refusal *forbid* (N= 17), as well as the later addition *prevent*, have indeed fallen out of use in the DOC (or are at least only attested very marginally; e.g. Goldberg 1995; Coppock 2009). As Goldberg (1995: 130) states, the class is also special in that it seems to be entirely unproductive in PDE. This, as well as the verbs' slight reluctance to partake in the dative alternation, constitute further indications of its odd standing within the DOC's verb classes, and suggest that it is indeed perceived as not-quite belonging there. Incidentally, in Middle English verbs of refusal selected for various different prepositions (see 4.2). This hints at their being rather ambiguous concerning their semantics (in comparison to the more prototypical members of the DOC). Nevertheless, it can be argued that on a cline from most prototypically transfer-related to least prototypically transfer-related, verbs of refusal or 'future not having' are still closer to the core meaning than verbs of pure benefaction/malefaction or verbs of dispossession (Colleman and De Clerck 2008: 205). Verbs which encode scenes of 'not-giving' are still more compatible with the idea of transfer than verbs which express the antonymic relation of giving, i.e. denote events in which the animate participant is caused to lose an entity.

A further, particularly conspicuous case of irregularity is that of mental/ attitudinal verbs. The corresponding, always marginal, light verb constructions of the type 'have so. love' have fallen out of use as predicted, since their semantics do not nicely fit the basic meaning of the construction. The simple verbs *envy* and *forgive*, however, have persisted in the DOC, despite the fact that their semantics are similarly difficult to account for in terms of transfer (Colleman and De Clerck 2008).[212] Nevertheless, the unproductive nature of this subclass in PDE, as well as their recent slow disappearance from the construction – as reported by e.g. Goldberg (1995: 131–132) – lends additional support for the assumption of a semantic narrowing, no matter how gradual it may be. The differences in acceptability in the DOC between the two verbs in PDE – with ditransitive uses of *envy* apparently being more prone to loss than *forgive* – possibly reflect a difference in position on the cline of prototypicality. The former can also be grouped with *cost* and other verbs of dispossession, while the latter can be subsumed in the class of 'verbs of future not having'. It should accordingly be more readily accepted (Pinker 1989: 111; Goldberg 1995: 131–132; Colleman and De Clerck 2008). Furthermore, *forgive* is presumably still more compatible with the DOC than *envy* in respect to willingness of the recipient of the emotion. While being on the receiving end of an act of forgiving can be considered beneficial for a participant, it is less clear how a recipient of an envious feeling would profit from this event.

The perseverance of 'verbs of reverse communicated transfer' such as *ask* in patterns like *John asked Mary the time/ a favour* presents another problem. This is because they plainly do not involve transfer of an entity, but rather a request to receive information (or help). As dealt with in (7.1.2), the typical prepositional paraphrases for these patterns include *of* or *from* (*John asked a favour of Mary*), while *to* is restricted to *ask* as a verb of communicated message (*John asked a question to Mary*). This suggests that the reverse transfer use of *ask* (and related verbs) is again closer to the use of dispossession verbs, making it necessary to

212 Even though the meaning of the complex predicate emotion patterns could be explained as metaphorical extensions of giving semantics, the event of loving someone clearly does not necessarily involve a volitional agent (or a willing recipient), and the indirect 'transfer' of emotion can be unsuccessful. These constructions were accordingly undoubtedly at the periphery of the DOC; their ousting is expected.

explain their permanence in the PDE DOC. Possible ways to do so include the tight connection of the verb class to the sub-construction of communication. More specifically, the verbs involved in such uses participate in another, closely linked sub-construction of the DOC. The strong association of verbs like *ask* with the DOC together with the large overlap (or similarity) in the events encoded by them is likely to trigger a generalisation of the kind 'use *ask* in the DOC no matter what the precise semantics of the pattern are'. This argument is to some extent backed by the fact that verbs of reverse transfer, which do not have the same ties to another, more prototypical DOC verb class, were marginalised from the construction very early on.

Finally, a note on pure benefactives is in order: As has been demonstrated in (4.2) and (7.1.2), a number of complex predicate patterns denoting malefaction or benefaction such as 'do/intend so. harm/good' have not followed the general trend of this verb class, in having survived into PDE rather than being lost (159a-b).

(159) a. there are people out there who mean to *do* **runners**$_{AFF}$ harm$_{TH}$ (COCA, 2013; Pittsburgh Post-Gazette)

b. a little competition from the fighting Irish may *do* **them**$_{AFF}$ good$_{TH}$ (COCA, 2013; American Spectator)

However, these uses are again almost entirely unproductive, and appear to constitute fixed, lexicalised expressions at a very low level in the network. The overall schema associated with the patterns – which would have been able to license more types – has disappeared, leaving the more or less fully filled micro-constructions behind. Example (159b) also illustrates that the patterns furthermore do not fulfil the criterion of volitionality of the agent in a majority of cases (especially in the case of 'do so. good'). Typically, it is inanimate action-NPs that encode the role of subject/agent in such sentences. This feature additionally points to their non-prototypical status, even if the events expressed could on some level be explained as the metaphorical transfer of a positive or negative effect.

To sum up, this section has shown that we can indeed witness a semantic specialisation of the double object construction in the history of English. Through a reduction of sub-constructional types associated with distinct verb classes, the construction has come to encode a core meaning of 'transfer'. Resulting in a more semantically coherent schema, this has furthered its productivity – a fact which is thought to be highly beneficial for the pattern. A number of remnants of older uses, as well as verb classes which may be predicted to have fallen out of use but are retained in the construction, have to be explained separately. Still, they do not call into doubt that a narrowing in the semantics of the DOC has taken place in the history of English, but rather indicate that this change is ongoing.

7.2.1.3 Constituent order in ditransitives

The following sections review the issue of fixation of word order in ditransitives both in respect to the ordering of the objects involved, i.e. the REC- and TH-argument, as well as concerning the increasing rigidity on constituent order on the clause level. The latter led to a strict SVO order in ditransitive constructions. The most striking point to be observed here is that the members of the dative alternation (DOC and *to*-PRC) behave conspicuously different to other PRCs and PP+NP combinations, indicating that their increasingly close association had some effect on their development. For example, all prepositional constructions show a distinct and progressively stronger preference for clause-peripheral position, typically meaning that they follow subject, verb, and (NP-)object. However, in the case of the *to*-PRC (as well as to a lesser extent other PRCs), the option of coming before the NP-object is maintained throughout the period. As to changes on the clause level, the DOC and *to*-PRC differ from other PRCs (as well as other PP-constructions) in that the latter maintain some flexibility in constituent ordering, while the former are strongly associated with canonical (S)VO at the end of the Middle English period.

Below, I first address the changes visible in the ordering of objects of ditransitives, before commenting on the establishment of a fixed SVO order in these patterns. Especially concerning the latter point, ditransitives cannot easily be dealt with in isolation, as the fixation of SVO represents a cross-constructional, system-wide change. The analysis is therefore again followed by a discussion of the changes in ditransitives in the context of this more general move in the network.

7.2.1.3.1 Object order in ditransitives: Towards a complementary distribution

Recapitulating the results on object ordering presented in section (4.2), we have seen that the DOC had a preference for [REC-TH] order in early Middle English already. This tendency is present both when the objects are in direct sequence and when they are separated by some intervening element. Although a slight preponderance of this order is also there in Old English – see De Cuypere (2015a), whose data show a distribution of about 60 per cent [REC-TH] vs. 40

percent [TH-REC] – there was accordingly a change towards the canonical order at the turn from Old to Middle English.[213] The slight overall dominance of [REC-TH] in Old English is explained by the fact that recipients tend to be animate, given, pronominal and definite, and are therefore predicted to favour REC-first orders. This is also reflected in the PDE relation between the strong REC-first DOC and the weak REC-late *to*-PRCs. The increase in [REC-TH] orders in the course to Middle English, however, needs to be explained differently. A possible way to do so, I argue, is to draw on the progressively close association between DOCs and PRCs in late Old English. Since the prepositional competitors strongly preferred PP-late, and therefore REC-late, order, the increase in DOC [REC-TH] orders may represent a first indication of competition resolution. The DOC was driven to become associated more exclusively with this other, more frequently used order. This account to some extent challenges De Cuypere's (2015c) proposal that the prepositional constructions with their partiality towards REC-late order 'stepped in' to compensate for the loss of DOC patterns of this type.[214] Rather than assuming a drag-chain process in this case, I posit a push-chain development. The distributional preferences of the PRCs drove out, or are responsible for, the disappearance of DOC [TH-REC]. Nevertheless, it is more than plausible that this development reinforced tendencies that were anyway already present in the DOC before, and that there was a bi-directional trade-off between the different processes.

The situation in early Middle English can be visualised as follows (Fig. 49). Both the DOC and the PRC, represented on the left and right of the figure, respectively, are associated with two lower-level constructions each, which in contrast to their parent constructions fully specify the order of objects involved. These schemas differ in terms of entrenchment of their daughter constructions. While in the case of the DOC, the [REC-TH] sub-construction is more frequent (and more entrenched), the opposite is true for the PRCs, which show an even more pronounced preference for one of the constructional types, namely that of [TH-*prep*REC]. It could even be questioned whether for PRCs the opposite order [*prep*REC-TH] had already acquired construction status in Old English, or wheth-

213 Remember also that De Cuypere's (2015a) data in fact demonstrated a slight increase in [ACC_{TH}-DAT_{REC}] patterns towards the end of the period. It is therefore evident that changes must have taken place at the transition from Old to Middle English which cannot be captured by the corpora used in the present study and by De Cuypere (2015a); cf. also Koopman (1990); Allen (1995: 48); Koopman and van der Wurff (2000: 262); Fischer and van der Wurff (2006: 189).

214 To be precise, De Cuypere (2015c) comments on [DAT–ACC]/[ACC–DAT] and the OE *to*-PRC only, while the present book takes into account all kinds of case frames and prepositional paraphrases. Nevertheless, the proposals are comparable.

er the occasional examples were rather an epiphenomenon of an in general freer system of word order, in which the basic order of REC-late could be overridden in certain circumstances.

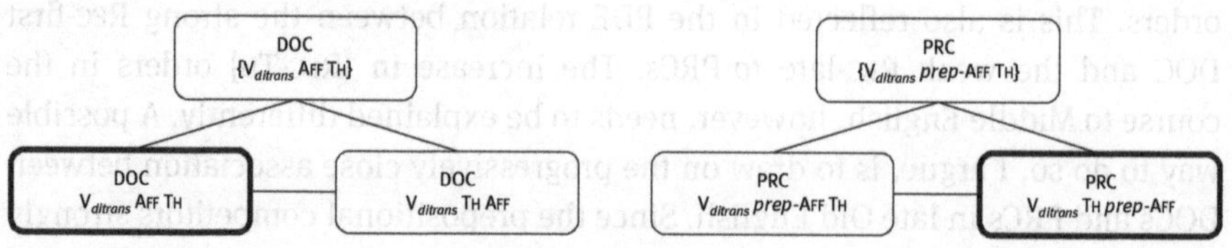

Fig. 49: Constructional network of DOC and PRC with associated object order subconstructions in late OE

As to the further development of the constructions in the course of Middle English, I have shown that the tendency towards [REC-TH] order in the DOC grew substantially from early/mid Middle English onwards, until it became near-categorical at the end of the period. PRCs, by contrast, seem to have had a distinct bias towards clause-peripheral position. This bias increases during Middle English, with [TH-*prep*REC] clearly constituting the most successful variant. This rise is, however, not too substantial. In this, the development of PRCs closely corresponds to that of PPs in general. In other words, the PRC preferences from Old to Middle English reflect the fact that PPs on the whole came to display an increasingly higher predilection for clause-peripheral slots between Old and Middle English (Lundskaer-Nielsen 1993; Bech 2001; among others). In many cases, this inclination towards peripheral position translated into clause-final occurrence, but PPs also frequently appeared clause-initially. Although they accordingly retained some flexibility for moving around in the clause, they were more and more often restricted to slots outside the 'core constituent group' of subject, verb, and object (in transitive constructions). It is in this respect that the PRCs begin to diverge from other PPs, or rather, other PP+NP patterns such as *John cooked dinner in the kitchen/ John loaded hay onto the truck*, during Middle English. As a consequence of POs becoming more tightly integrated into the VP, and of their acquiring core functions in becoming able to express more primary participant roles such as recipient or deprivee, they also maintain the option of occurring within this string of S-V-O constituents. By contrast to non-PRC PP-constructions, in which the variant of PP-NP order is progressively ousted in favour of PP-final sequences, the option [*prep*REC-TH] is still available for PRCs at the end of Middle English.

The same trend can be observed when only the *to*-PRC is investigated. But not only that, the tendency is stronger in this case: Even though the *to*-PRC is similarly strongly associated with REC-last order in all sub-periods, no real change takes place during the whole period, and the opposite order stably remains in the language. This means that there is a cline developing in Middle English concerning the acceptability of PPs intervening between verb and NP-object. While PP-adjuncts and other less grammaticalised PPs are increasingly restricted to external position, the variant featuring an 'internal' PP (V-PP-NP) is more felicitous with the more grammaticalised PRCs. The *to*-PRC finally retains the most flexibility in that both sub-constructional types of [*to*REC-TH] and [TH-*to*REC] are linked to the more schematic construction, even if the latter is nevertheless evidently the preferred variant. The *to*-PRC is therefore different to other PRCs and PP-patterns: It more often occurs with the PP in post-verbal position ([V-*to*REC-TH]) than comparable patterns. I argue in (7.2.2) that this is a direct consequence of the strong association of this construction with the DOC and the emergence of the dative alternation.

In sum, the distribution of orders in the *to*-PRC seems to be strongly influenced by its links to other, more 'ordinary' PP-constructions. These connections promote PP-late orders and add to their success. At the same time, PP-early orders manage to establish themselves as weaker variants. This is due to this formal pattern doing justice to the more integrated meaning of the PP in this construction, i.e. its more prominent contribution to the construction's semantics. Furthermore, the continuing availability of the anti-prototypical pattern can be related to the increasingly tighter alliance between the *to*-PRC and the DOC. Instances of [*to*-REC-TH] may form in analogy to DOC [REC-TH] tokens if the two constructions are perceived as linked. That this development should be asymmetric in that the *to*-PRC extends its syntactic contexts through association with the DOC (or at least maintains the situation despite the odds not being in favour of it), whereas the DOC sees an increasing narrowing in syntactic options is not entirely unexpected. Considering that the *to*-PRC constituted the more successful variant for a substantial part of the period, it is in fact predictable that it should parasitically profit from the relationship at the expense of the DOC. (See also Perek's 2015 discussion of asymmetrical productivity in the dative alternation; although the point of departure is slightly different in this case, there are still parallels). Once the competitive relationship turned into full co-operation, however, the asymmetry is sorted out. This is exactly what we find in the history of English. Although not captured by the Middle English data, we can assume that at some point after this period, the non-canonical order [*to*REC-TH] was lost almost entirely, to the point that it is only found in cases of heavy-

NP shift in PDE (Gast 2007: 33). As was also confirmed by the results of the evolutionary game presented in (5.2), the language eventually settles on a mixed strategy of DOC and *to*-PRC, in which the former is associated with [REC-TH] order, whereas the latter specifies a [TH-*to*REC] sequence (Fig. 50). The distinct orders, correlated with distinct constructions, stand in complementary distribution, each having constructed their own niche linked with specific discourse-pragmatic and semantic features. This functional diversification is beneficial for the constructions involved as well as for the entire system, since its result is a more transparent relationship between form and meaning.

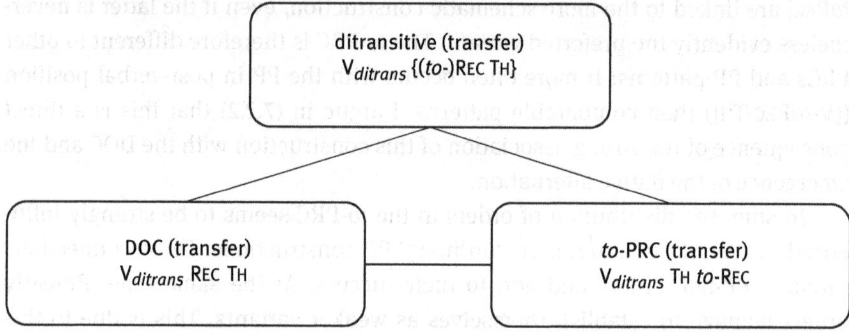

Fig. 50: Ditransitive constructeme and allostructions (specifying object order)

Note that in the case of dispossession verbs, and to some extent, with communication verbs, the third contender of PTC is in competition with both the DOC and the PRC. With the former, it shares preferred object order tendencies (both opting for [REC-TH]), with the latter, it agrees in terms of object marking. What this eventually leads to is the demise of the nominal construction, and the establishment of a similarly cooperative relation between PRC and PTC with the class of dispossession (as argued for in 7.1.2). The strong entrenchment of [REC-TH] orders with the PTC may in effect have been influential in the ousting of the DOC in this case, as it provided an equally or even more viable counterpart to the PRC, with the added advantage of corresponding to the general rise of prepositional patterns.

The scenario of object order development proposed in this section is as follows: In Old English, both orders are found with the DOC, and show a comparatively balanced distribution. This holds even though [REC-TH] is slightly more frequent due to discourse-pragmatic issues, such as REC frequently being more topical and therefore often in clause-early position. PP-constructions in general, and PRCs in particular, are on the contrary biased towards PP-late order, due to their adjectival origins as 'afterthoughts/ less central information'. In a second phase at the turn from Old to Middle English, DOCs and PRCs enter clearer competition, which results in a decrease in DOC [TH-REC] orders in favour of the corresponding prepositional variant. During Middle English, we see the DOC and the PRCs (especially the *to*-PRC) competing on a schematic level; the latter is more successful for some time. On a lower level, the greater success of the (*to*-)PRC is reflected in that the prepositional pattern competes against the DOC for REC-first orders (at least to some extent), in addition to REC-last orders being almost invariably expressed prepositionally already. However, with the (semantic) association between the constructions, the DOC and the *to*-PRC, becoming tighter and tighter, and with the establishment of the 'ditransitive constructeme', the patterns finally arrive at a shared-workload situation. Each discourse-pragmatic function instantiated by ditransitives – labelled [+focus REC] and [-focus REC] in a simplified manner in (5.2) above – becomes linked to one particular construction. The constructions form a symbiotic relationship. The main reasons for the DOC being the stronger type in PDE, while the *to*-PRC constitutes the weaker variant in this paradigmatic relation, can again be explained by the prototypical features of recipients corresponding better to the specific object order requirements of the DOC. The issue of non-canonical orders with pronouns in PDE (of the type *Give it me*!) is not problematic for this account either; I take these idiosyncratic variants to represent lower-level specifications which have managed to reproduce successfully despite not conforming to the more general pattern (Gast 2007; Gerwin 2013, 2014; De Cuypere 2015a; Yáñez-Bouza and Denison 2015). Reasons for this may include the phonological properties of the elements involved: For example, the most frequent theme-argument in these patterns is the exceedingly short pronoun *it*, which may trigger early position merely for its minimal length (cf. also De Cuypere 2015a: 247). On the other hand, related and highly frequent constructions in which the pronoun is typically found in immediate post-verbal position are likely to have an impact on ordering. If such effects are strong enough, they could well overtake the higher-level DOC specifications (see Gast's 2007 'principle of frequency-based serialisation').[215] That is, theme-first DOC uses can be more successful than theme-

215 A quick search of the *COCA* for verb+*it* combinations yields an excessively high number of types, the five most frequent of which amount to between 20,000 and 50,000 tokens. This alone can be taken as good support for Gast's assumption that *it* displays a distributional bias in transitives which also impacts its positional distribution in other constructions.

second DOCs if the theme involved (*it*) very often occurs in a different construction whose structure corresponds to these uses.

In the following, the development of the ditransitive constructions in regard to clause-level word order is discussed. The main focus here is on the differences in development of the patterns involved which can be observed in the data, as well as on possible ways to explain these.

7.2.1.3.2 Clausal word order in ditransitives: Towards fixed (S)VOO

As to the fixation of SVO order in ditransitive patterns, it is interesting to observe that the data show curious similarities as well as dissimilarities in behaviour of the various constructions involved (section 4.2.1.3, among others). I have demonstrated that what all patterns have in common is a general trend towards post-verbal object order: Both objects (in whatever order) increasingly occur immediately after the predicate. Furthermore, although no significant change was seen in this regard, direct sequences of SVO come to grow in proportional frequency during Middle English. The lower figures for SVO compared to VO orders are mainly due to negation particles (160a) and adverbs (160b) maintaining their ability to intervene between subject and object. The former issue is gradually resolved by the introduction of *do*-support in the history of English, with instances such as (160a) becoming markedly less frequent towards the end of Middle English. Adverbs, in contrast, are still highly flexible in terms of positioning in PDE in that they can appear in all kinds of slots, including the one intermediate between subject and verb (Quirk et al. 1985: 490–496).

(160) a. 3ho *ne* *se33de* <u>itt</u> **nani3** **mann**
you not said it no man
SUBJ NEG V DO IO
'you did not say it to any man'
(CMORM,I,83.739; PPCME2: M1)

b. the kynge fulle humbely *grauntyde* **hyr** <u>grace</u>
the king fully humbly granted her grace
SUBJ ADV V IO DO
'the king very humbly granted her grace'
(CMGREGOR,206.1794; PPCME2: M4)

Furthermore, it has to be kept in mind that non-finite patterns as well as pro-drop forms were included in the present dataset, which automatically leads to a smaller proportion of SVO compared to VO orders. Considering this, the smaller number and insignificant effects may be expected. All in all, the Middle English period evidently sees a move towards stricter word order in ditransitive patterns, both concerning the relative position of verb and objects, and in terms of sequences of subject, verb, and objects. That such a regularisation should take place is of course far from surprising and constitutes a well-known fact in English historical linguistics (e.g. Fischer et al. 2000; Harbert 2007; Los 2015, among many others). Nevertheless, confirmation that the more general processes are paralleled in ditransitive constructions provides support to the assumption that the change towards (S)VO really represented a system-wide, large-scale development. A piece of information that is more specifically relevant for investigations of ditransitives is that there is an increase in immediate sequences of the objects, meaning that both objects are progressively restricted to occurring together on the same side of the other constituents involved (specifically subject and verb).

Although the constructions accordingly to pattern with each other concerning the overall tendencies shown, there are also conspicuous differences between DOC, PRC and *to*-PRC. For example, the extent to which the canonical order was established in early Middle English with the different constructions varies. Also, the speed of progression of the change as well as the final outcome of the development in late Middle English are not the same across all patterns. As to the former issue, DOCs diverge from PP-constructions in that (S)VO variants are less frequently found with this construction than with the prepositional competitors in the very beginning. This means that while PRCs exhibit a preference for (S)VO order from early on, this predilection is weaker with DOCs. Quite possibly, this unequal distribution is again a manifestation, or rather a consequence, of the adjunctival origins of the PRCs. I assume that in the case of PRCs, the predominance of PP-late position combined with a bias towards [AGT-V-TH] sequences inherited from transitives and resulted in a preferred order of [AGT-V-TH-*prep*REC] in late Old English/ early Middle English already. In the more independent DOCs, on the other hand, no such predilection would have been given, but both non-agentive arguments, which both expressed tightly integrated core participant roles, could move around freely (in terms of their positional relation to each other as well as in the clause). Even if SVO order was the favoured option in the closely related transitives at this point already, fronting one object to initial position would still have been possible without either violating object-specific preferences (in contrast to the PP-late constraint of PRCs) or diverging from the emerging norm. In other words, the availability and potentially higher acceptability of patterns such as [TH-AGT-V-REC] or [REC-AGT-V-TH] than that of the corresponding PRC-variants could be taken as responsible for the higher frequency of (S)VO orders in PRCs at the beginning of the period. Evidently, this is highly speculative. Nevertheless, it is plausible that the greater independence of the DOC (as a highly conventionalised and entrenched construction in the network) allowed for more flexibility in constituent ordering. PRCs, by contrast, were strongly linked to other PP-patterns at this point, or indeed only in the process of emerging out of them and might therefore still have been more restricted in their internal structure.

A similar problem concerns the changes visible within the Middle English period: Here, we find a relatively rapid and steep increase of (S)VO in the DOC, whereas PRCs do not show too much change overall. They only slowly rise during the period. In the latest stage of Middle English, (S)VO is then fixed to a greater extent in DOCs than in PRCs. A considerably larger fraction of DOC tokens has adopted the canonical order at this stage, while the initially more progressive PRCs have stagnated in their development and maintain some flexibility. Crucially, however, the prepositional *to*-construction in this case behaves more like the DOC. The fixation of (S)VO order at the end of the period is similarly more advanced with this variant (i.e. the *to*-PRC) than with PRCs in general.

The sharp growth of rigid (S)VO orders in the DOC can be tentatively linked to the fact that once the morphological case system had more or less collapsed, it became increasingly important to distinguish between the agent and the recipient of the action by means other than case distinctions. More precisely, it is possible that distinguishing between participant roles of the arguments involved in ditransitives was more problematic without case marking than in other constructions. For instance, if transitive constructions were prototypically used to express interactions between animate agents and inanimate themes, identifying the respective participants would have been comparatively easy without any marking on the constituents on the basis of animacy asymmetries. Ditransitive events, however, prototypically involve two animate participants – an agent and a recipient – in addition to the usually inanimate theme. The animate participants furthermore typically overlap in terms of discourse-pragmatic status in that both tend to be topical (given and definite, among other things). Consequently, topicality asymmetries could likely not be exploited as readily as in other cases. In PRCs, this issue would not have been particularly pressing since the REC-argument was marked by the preposition. By contrast, case-less DOCs may have caused difficulties. In such a situation, variants with fixed, invariable positions for the arguments were able to spread quickly. In other words, in an unstable system as the DOC at this point represented, sticking to one specific order – in our case the already frequent and preferred SVO – was certainly beneficial.

Despite the fact that distinguishing between participant roles in PRCs would have been eased by the prepositional marking of one of the arguments, a slight increase in canonical clause patterns is still expected due to systemic pressures. If most related constructions move towards this option, PRCs will profit from adopting it more frequently as well. Nonetheless, this does not explain why one particular PRC-type, namely the *to*-PRC, should see a more substantial increase in fixed SVO orders. In this regard, the increasingly close association between the *to*-PRC and the DOC can be drawn on. I argue that the stronger this connection becomes, the more the structure of the DOC impacts that of the *to*-PRC. The growing success of SVO in the DOC in turn causes SVO variants of the *to*-construction to become more frequent: Having the same overall (clause-level) form, the functional link between them is more evident. Because formal and functional diversification is still possible through differences in object ordering, this development is in fact a rather clever one. The strategy allows the patterns to be as similar as necessary and at the same time as different as possible. This idea is taken up again in (7.2.2) below.

In sum, what I have suggested in this section is that first, there is a clear trend towards regularisation of the ditransitive argument structure system in Middle English, which corresponds to and is influenced by the overall tendency towards reduction of variation in the language system at that time. In the special case of ditransitive constructions, this development is visible in that the two object arguments more and more frequently appear in direct sequence in postverbal position. Furthermore, the position of the subject in relation to the verb and the objects is increasingly fixed to initial place. These regularisation processes are good for the system as a whole as long as the expressive potential of the language is maintained.

As to the individual constructions available to ditransitive verbs, I have demonstrated that the patterns differ in their development in Middle English (and possibly before that). DOCs are more variable in early Middle English but rapidly develop a fixed (S)VO order. This may be due to disambiguation issues between animate agents and recipients once case marking is lost; it encourages a consistent positional separation of the arguments. PRCs, by contrast, are more likely to exhibit stricter word order in the beginning, which has been explained by their adjunctival origins. However, they are not under the same pressures as the DOC for participant identification, meaning they can afford to keep some flexibility in ordering. Finally, the slightly distinct development of the *to*-PRC is interesting, as it seems to align increasingly with the DOC. I take this as a result of the emergence of the alternation.

It should still be clear that the account put forward in this section is quite simplified and speculative. Moreover, the distinctive developments of the patterns observed in the data are small enough that they could be accidental results of inappropriate or too coarse classification schemes. It is therefore certainly necessary to investigate word order in Middle English ditransitives in a much more detailed manner. Unfortunately, this is outside the scope of the present book, and must be left for future research.

7.2.1.3.3 Ditransitives in the context of a system-wide fixation of word order

As discussed in section (3.2.2), the notions of 'subject' and 'object' in Old English as well as the question of word order change on the clausal level represent a tricky issue. An encompassing analysis of the matter requires a lot more space than available within the limits of the present book (cf. Harbert 2007; Barðdal 2009; Möhlig-Falke 2012, among many others). Nevertheless, the matter is briefly touched upon in this section, since it ties in with the development of ditransitives in the history of English.

In general, the category of subject is defined based on a number of different dimensions, including syntactic, morphological, semantic as well as discourse-pragmatic properties of the constituents. Objects are typically defined negatively in relation to the subject. Concerning the former, subjects are usually associated with control of verbal agreement, control of coordinate subject deletion, the triggering of reflexivisation as well as sentence-initial position. Apart from verbal agreement, these features are all present in PDE subjects. As to morphological characteristics, nominative case marking, or unmarked case is commonly seen as a defining property of subjects, by contrast to objects, which prototypically receive oblique marking. As is well-known, in PDE case marking differences between subject and object only show with pronouns (*he* vs. *him*). Semantically, subjects of active clauses are linked to the role of 'agent'; the prototypical subject is highly agentive, while objects lack such agentivity. Although objects very often instantiate the role of 'patient' or 'theme', i.e. a participant that is maximally different or opposed to the agentive subject, they are far from restricted to this, but can take on a wide range of different parts (e.g. *John loves pears*, where the object expresses a stimulus or cause rather than a theme). Finally, subjects tend to be topical, meaning that they often refer to given, accessible, and backgrounded information, in contrast to objects frequently constituting the sentence focus and presenting new, unpredictable information (Möhlig-Falke 2012: 41–42, 44–45; also Keenan 1976; Lambrecht 1994; Allen 1995; Traugott 2006).

In PDE, most of these criteria are fulfilled, and in the majority of sentences identifying the subject and object does not present much of a challenge. Old English, however, is more problematic in this regard, since often, no constituent appears to match the definition of subjects as just presented. A prime case in point is the so-called 'impersonal' or 'experiencer' construction prominently discussed in von Seefranz-Montag (1983, 1984), Allen (1995), Barðdal (2009) as well as Möhlig-Falke (2012). These patterns, sometimes also labelled as 'non-canonical subject constructions' are conspicuous due to the constituents involved frequently not meeting the requirements for prototypical subjects. For example, in the first part of the sentence in (161a), the only nominal element present is a dative/accusative pronoun, marking a clearly non-agentive referent. Similarly, (161b) has two NPs, both of which do not express agents, but rather an animate experiencer and a likewise animate cause/stimulus. Furthermore, neither of the arguments is marked by nominative or accusative, but both receive oblique marking. In (161c), in contrast, a nominative NP (referring to the cause/stimulus of the emotion) is given, which displays agreement with the verb. It is not the nominative that is in first position, though, but the dative experiencer. In addition, the nominative here marks an inanimate, clearly non-agentive participant. The constituent accordingly only qualifies as a subject in some respect.

(161) a. Me$_{DAT/ACC}$ *hyngrede* , and ge me nawuht
me hungered , and you me not
ne sealdun etan
not gave to eat
'I was hungry, and you did not give me anything to eat'
(CP 1604 (44.327.24); Möhlig-Falke 2012: 6)

b. him$_{DAT}$ *ofhreow* þæs mannes$_{GEN}$
him pitied the man's
'he pitied the man'
(Ælc.Th.I. p.192.16; Allen 1995: 68)

c. Ðam wife$_{DAT}$ þa word$_{NOM}$ wel *licodon*
the woman these words well liked
'the woman was much pleased by these words'
(Beo. 0174 (639); Möhlig-Falke 2012: 12)

These and other issues lead Möhlig-Falke (2012: 47–48) to conclude that the oblique experiencer in such constructions represent grammatical hybrids between subjects and objects. The clear subject-object distinction we see in PDE was not as well-defined in OE yet. What is more, it appears that the presence of a distinctly definable subject was not entirely necessary in Old English still. Such a constraint seems to have emerged only at a later point, as is evident from the introduction of 'dummy' *it*-subjects with e.g. weather-verbs (**Ø snowed* vs. *It snowed*). More specifically concerning the structure of the clause, it has moreover been suggested that (early) OE was a topic-prominent rather than a subject-prominent language in that clause-initial position was associated with the sentence topic (von Seefranz-Montag 1984: 528; cf. also Möhlig-Falke 2012: 18, 44–48). Rather than necessarily featuring the subject, as is typical for PDE, the first slot in the clause could be filled by any topical element or be used for contrastive (marked) focus.

The development of a subject vs. object slot, and fixed SVO order in transitive clauses can be conceptualised as follows: In early Old English, we find a very salient information structure construction specifying a [topic-focus] order for transitive predicates. These transitive clauses, according to Möhlig-Falke (2012: 35), are prototypically "dynamic and involve an asymmetric relationship between two maximally opposed participants". The most prototypical construction type is one in which there is an animate agent that represents the topic of the sentence and is accordingly given and accessible. This agent asymmetrically interacts with an inanimate, new and inaccessible patient/theme (the focus of the sentence). Although less pronounced, animate experiencers can be expected to be topical in a greater number of cases than inanimate, possibly abstract causes or stimuli, which will often constitute the more relevant piece of information. In other words, a general tendency for sentences to be 'about' animate participants, and highlighting non-recoverable inanimate participants is predictable. This prevalence, or greater success of agent/experiencer-topic theme/cause-focus constructions is most likely caused by human cognitive biases, in that human, animate participants are *per default* more accessible to speakers. Furthermore, human experiencers might be perceived as still more agentive than clearly non-animate entities.

Together with the fact that the most prototypical case-marking pattern is one of agent-Nom theme/patient-Oblique (or indeed -Acc), these distributional preferences can eventually lead to the emergence of a clearly-defined subject (vs. object) slot. This means that a subject (and object) category forms which is associated with the above-mentioned properties. On the level of argument structure constructions such as the transitive, this corresponds to the formation of a construction in which the respective placement of subject and object in relation to each other is fixed. We can assume that this process of category establishment and the increasingly transparent differentiation between subjects and objects also had an impact on case marking (see further 7.2.2). More precisely, the increasing case syncretism between nominative and accusative on the one hand can be linked to the progressively clearer association of the respective cases with the opposed categories. On the other hand, the gradual ousting of genitive (and later dative) marked objects may have been triggered by the increasing entrenchment and greater success of an object category associated with accusative case. In this scenario, the loss of lexical case in favour of structural case (e.g. Allen 1995) constitutes an epiphenomenon of a move towards more prototypical subject vs. object slots, maximally differentiated from each other in consistent ways.

Ditransitives now pose an interesting challenge in this regard, since they typically involve not only one animate participant, but instead two, namely an agent and a recipient-like argument. The latter of these mainly patterns with typical objects in terms of case-marking, clause-position, absence of verbal agreement and the like, and is also clearly less agentive than the 'giver', 'depriver' or whatever participant role the first argument of ditransitives specifies. Nevertheless, it often overlaps in topicality with the agent argument (in addition to prototypically being animate as well). It consequently takes up an intermediate place between prototypical 'subject' and prototypical 'object'. In PRCs, this issue is readily resolved by the REC-argument being marked by a preposition. In DOCs, however, mismatches or ambiguities can arise, especially once case marking becomes less indicative. This difference may explain – as already discussed in the previous section – the more rapid adoption of fixed S-first, O-late orders in this case. While the generally growing fixation of subjects to clause-early position and objects to clause-late position can accordingly be accounted for by biases concerning discourse-pragmatic/ information-structure features of the arguments, the relative placement of the verb is a different issue. Here, Ferrer-i-Cancho's approach to verb positioning in terms of mathematical modelling can be drawn on: As he shows, "placing the verb at the center is optimal in terms of online memory minimization; placing it somewhere else is not" (Ferrer-i-Cancho 2015: 124). That is, movement towards either OVS or SVO is predicted by processing-related factors. Furthermore, verb-medial constructions tend to be very stable, with the order typically not being reversed once fixed (Ferrer-i-Cancho 2015: 114). Taken together, these preferences result in the rigid SVO order visible in PDE today.

Finally, the overall trend towards a closer connection and tighter positional integration of the core constituents of subject, verb and object (or objects in the case of ditransitives) can be interpreted as the result of chunking and habituation, in that elements which often appear together will tend to be perceived as one whole. This is furthered by the fact that these elements represent the core and most salient information in the clause. Variants in which these prominent constituents occur in direct sequence will be more successful – a development towards tighter formal links will be beneficial for the constructions because it reflects the close semantic relations between the components. One result of this is the increasing confinement of e.g. sentence adjunct-PPs to clause-peripheral position, and the greater difficulties of any non-core constituent intervening in this strict SVO string during Middle English. As I have shown in this section (7.2.1.3), the continuing ability of PP-RECs to appear before themes even in late Middle English is a clear indication of its advanced state in marking core participant roles.

To conclude, this section has demonstrated that the system of ditransitives in Middle English was subject to a number of changes ultimately leading to a very regular situation, in which both members of the PDE dative alternation are associated with rigid SVO order. In that, they correspond to other constructions in the network. As concerns the order of objects, the DOC and the *to*-PRC have each come to resort to one particular order, [REC-TH] in the case of the former and [TH-*to*REC] in the case of the latter. In doing so, the patterns have diverged functionally, with the DOC being used in one type of discourse-pragmatic context, and the *to*-PRC in the complementary functions. The development of the dative alternation thus represents a story of emerging symbiosis and 'sharing the discourse-functional workload'. In the next section, the changes discussed in the previous sections are approached as instances of constructional co-evolution in the sense outlined in section (6.3): Both diverging developments and alignment between the members of the dative alternation are interpreted as signs of the constructions adapting to each other.

7.2.2 Formal and functional changes in ditransitives as co-evolution

The history of ditransitive constructions in English evidently entails changes on various levels, not only constructional emergence and loss, but also formal and functional changes in the individual constructions. In the preceding sections, we have seen that these included the loss of morphological case marking and the fixation of word order syntax. Furthermore, semantic (and pragmatic) changes can be observed with all structures. It is often difficult to treat these different developments separately, since they seem to correlate in time of occurrence. Some of these correlations between the changes and their outcomes also seem to hold cross-linguistically. For example, the absence or presence of case marking frequently corresponds to increased or decreased rigidity in word order or the presence or absence of more analytic means of expression (e.g. Hagège 2010: 10; Malchukov, Haspelmath, and Comrie 2010: 6; Haspelmath 2015: 31–32). Since correlation is often taken to imply causation (although not always justly so), it is not surprising that causal relationships between the sets of changes have often been suggested (cf. section 3.3). One point of debate concerning these proposals is the question of directionality of causality. This is usually seen as an either-or situation, where we have to decide between change A causally influencing change B or vice versa. In the following, I contest this notion, or rather, supplement it by arguing that in many cases, a co-evolutionary account might be more appropriate. In such a scenario, linguistic replicators adapt to their environment; meaning that certain variants are more successful in regard to particular environmental factors, and accordingly survive and thrive at the expense of others. One type of such 'environmental factors' are competing or cooperating variants: Once links have formed between constructions, they form part of their respective environment. They may then adapt to each other and/or respond to changes in the other, which may set in motion further changes. In other words, competing (or cooperating) constructions can come to co-evolve and mutually adapt to each other, in addition to adapting to other types of environmental pressures. Incrementally, accumulations of such smaller changes can also amount to larger developments on both sides. This may give the impression of one-sided, discrete causal effects even where this was not the case. Such an argument is perfectly in line with, or indeed follows from, taking a usage-based constructionist approach. It is also appealing from an evolutionary linguistic perspective, since co-adaptation and co-evolution are highly common phenomena in the biological domain. In this section, I first address how the dative alternation can be viewed as an adaptation to changes in the linguistic network (7.2.2.1). Afterwards, I quickly sketch which changes can be interpreted as adaptations of the members of the alternation to each other; I approach this issue with a focus on diversification versus alignment (7.2.2.2).

7.2.2.1 The dative alternation as an adaptation to changes in the network

In what follows, I review the correlations observed in the data on Middle English ditransitives, and approach the question of directionality in causal effect scenarios from a co-evolutionary (and/or co-adaptationist) perspective. Doing so is highly useful for a number of reasons. Among them is that assuming a mutual influence between changes to two distinct elements (or rather, presuming that elements can engage in a reciprocal feedback and adaptive loop that gradually leads to larger changes on both sides) saves us from the danger of oversimplification. It furthermore weakens the risk of confusing cause and effect that is inherent to suggesting a one-directional impact from one discrete, unified change on another. Still, the possibility of co-evolutionary scenarios does of course not impede the possibility (and plausibility) of changes impacting each other in one direction only. The main argument to be put forward here is that the history of ditransitives is characterised by adaptations of two constructions, namely the DOC and the (*to*-)PRC, to changes to the environment, i.e. changes to parameters such as the salience of case marking, and the degree of fixation of word order. Furthermore, the constructions are driven into a co-evolutionary (first competitive, then cooperative) relationship, in which they adapt to each other in addition to adapting to 'external' systemic changes.

The loss of case marking in the history of English has frequently been related to the increasing use of prepositional paraphrases, typically assuming either a push-chain or a drag-chain (see 3.3 above). In the former, it is suggested that prepositional constructions came to 'rescue' the system in helping to disambiguate semantic roles once morphological case marking had been lost. By contrast, the latter set-up sees case being lost due to the increasing availability of analytic periphrases making it redundant. Moreover, combined approaches have also been put forward, positing that it was neither only the one nor only the other, but rather a sequence of push-chain processes first, and drag-chain developments later (e.g. Samuels 1972: 80–84). This book supports the idea of a bi-directional influence between the changes, but moreover takes up Lundskær-Nielsen's (1993: 26–27) proposal of a stepwise impact instead of a clear one-time progression from push-chain to drag-chain. Focussing on the changes in question (as manifest in ditransitives), I also argue that it is necessary to consider the developments leading up to the early Middle English situation. For example, the availability of PRCs in Old English, meaning at a time when case was still rather prominent, is often taken to refute push-chain scenarios (cf. Allen 2006: 214; De Cuypere 2015c). However, these accounts seem to neglect the fact that case syncretism was highly advanced in Old English already, even if case marking as such persisted. Considering that PRCs did not appear as alternatives to the nominal construction overnight, this bit of information is therefore not really of explanatory value – and is admittedly also not presented as such in Allen (2006) – but only pushes the question back to early or pre-Old English. The initial emergence of PRCs may still have been triggered by the increasing loss of case distinctions between Germanic and Old English. At the same time, the emergence of PPs and their expansion into new domains from Proto-Indo-European onwards may have been involved in the reduction in the case marking system of

Old English, as they were equally or even more apt to express similar functions as the resident NP-case frames due to their greater expressivity.

While it is difficult if not impossible to determine which of the changes came first, it is then nevertheless plausible to assume that the developments reciprocally influenced each other. A gradual decrease in case marking salience in nominal patterns likely caused adaptations in the prepositional patterns available, furthering their use in new contexts, and thereby increasing their success. This in turn could have triggered further reductions in the case marking system, and so on. In addition, it is plausible that the presence of twofold participant marking (once through the preposition, and once through case-marking on the NP-complement of the PP in PRCs) negatively impacted the relative importance of case-marking. Competition between nominal and prepositional means would therefore have prompted co-adaptation and co-evolution of the constructions involved. Following this line of argumentation, the history of the English DOC and PRC (as well as other argument structure constructions and still other parts of the network) can be conceptualised as a gradual co-evolution of structures over an extended stretch of time, with case marking incrementally becoming superfluous, and PPs in turn growing in frequency and acquiring increasingly more functions. Although this assumption seems probable and can plausibly account for the developments up to Old English, the decidedly more rapid changes seen between late Old English and early Middle English are slightly problematic for this account. That is, explaining why the gradualness of changes in the beginning should be replaced by a much quicker progress in development is challenging. Even though the pathway does resemble the typical s-curve of linguistic changes, the initial period of slow growth would seem to be excessively long in this case.[216]

What I suggest here is that by Old English, a relatively stable equilibrium between case marking and prepositional constructions had been reached, which was, however, subsequently disrupted by other developments, leading to further changes in the system. This is supported by the fact that the DOC and its case constructions were stable within Old English, and a reduction in case frame types only took place at a relatively late point. PRCs also did not enter large-scale competition with the DOC in Old English, but only reached local

216 Note that the evolutionary notion of 'punctuated equilibrium' may be of use in this context. This concept refers to the fact that in biological evolution (among other things), long periods of stasis or equilibrium, in which changes take place very slowly, are interrupted by short periods of punctuation, i.e. very rapid changes (e.g. Eldredge and Gould 1972; Dawkins 1986; Bowern 2006).

peaks with some verb classes. Furthermore, even though there was some reduction in case frames in Old English, this did not correlate with the availability of prepositional paraphrases concerning verb classes. Case marking was not lost more rapidly or earlier with those verbs (and verb classes) for which periphrases were present. Based on these points, I argue that the emergence of PRCs did not constitute the main trigger of the reduction in the range of DOC case frames seen towards the end of the Old English period (e.g. the move towards [DAT-ACC]). Instead, the ousting of less productive types and the eventual loss of case marking in the DOC resulted from the unpredictable variation in (formal) case frames for expressing particular semantic functions which characterised the construction in earlier English. This tendency was promoted by the substantial amount of variation in the morphological marking of the individual case categories (see section 7.2.1.1). Ambiguity between the dative and accusative suffixes was very high already in early Middle English, and greatly increased over time. I accordingly take the initial move towards the most productive [DAT-ACC] frame as well as the beginning loss of case in the DOC to have been first and foremost caused by the semantic overlap between the constructions, as postulated in Barðdal (2009). That such a process is plausible is backed by studies on reduction in cases of unpredictable variation (cf. e.g. Smith, Fehér, and Ritt 2014, who show that the mechanism of accommodation/ alignment during interaction can account for such tendencies; also van Trijp 2013). Similar processes are assumed to have occurred in other constructions around the same time (e.g. in transitives), which mutually influenced in each other. This way, the loss of case marking in individual constructions could incrementally amount to a system-wide change and the demise of the morphological case marking system in general.

The further development of the DOC and the PRCs is one of further co-evolution: The increasing reduction of case frames and case markers, which also reduces the cue reliability of the system, encourages the use of the more explicit PPs. This in turn influences the loss of case, which again adds to the relative fitness of PRCs (and so on). The outcome of these accumulative processes in early/mid Middle English is the final merging of case frames (or the loss of case marking in the remaining case construction), and the emergence of a (nearly) case-less DOC with a form [V NP-Ø NP-Ø]. This variant is clearly less successful than the PRCs at this point since it is little indicative of the semantic roles involved. In this context, we can address the question whether the different pathways of competition resolution seen with different verb class types can be related to the reduction in case frames at the turn to Middle English. On the one hand, these differences may simply result from differences in type and token frequency and semantic features of the verb-class-specific constructions. On the other hand, it is conspicuous to note that the verb class of transfer was most often and most prototypically associated with the most frequent and most salient case frame of [DAT-ACC] in Old English already. Verbs of dispossession, on the other hand, were more reliably associated with the less productive case frames of [DAT-GEN] or [ACC-GEN]. That these case frames were lost relatively early (in favour of the more productive [DAT-ACC] frame, which did not match the semantics of verbs of dispossession too well) may explain the greater success of PRCs with this verb class. By contrast, the fact that the frame of [DAT-ACC] was retained longest, and was closely associated with a meaning of transfer, may have aided the DOC's chances of survival alongside the PRC. This would eventually have led to the establishment of the dative alternation. In sum, such distributional differences (even if they were only subtle) might have had an impact on the fate of the DOC versus PRCs with individual verb classes.

A comparable situation as with PPs presents itself regarding potential correlations and causal effects between the process of deflection and the increasing rigidity of object order in ditransitives (as well as the increasing frequency of SVO orders in these constructions). Again, influences in both directions have been proposed in this respect. As to word order fixation affecting case loss, it is plausible to presume that specific semantic roles were often associated with particular positions in the clause as a consequence of their prototypical discourse-pragmatic features; this could then advance case syncretism (Allen 2006; Möhlig-Falke 2012). For instance, it is plausible that the most prototypical transitive clauses involved a 'subject' which was maximally opposed to the 'object' in terms of agentivity and accordingly in degree of topicality, which influenced the placement typically associated with it. This tendency may have resulted in the case markers of these arguments being perceived as redundant. On the other side, increased ambiguity in morphological case marking may, with Allen (2006: 215), cause "speakers to rely more heavily on word order to interpret and encode semantic relations". Rather than presuming this connection to be a 'one-way street', a bi-directional, co-evolutionary account suggests itself here (cf. Allen 2006: 215). Instead of the loss of word order flexibility either triggering the demise of morphological case marking or resulting from it, both processes probably interacted with each other in a reciprocal way. The intensification of one change – such as case frames being reduced due to semantic overlap – would have led to the other following suit, and so on. We can conceptualise this as an evolutionary arms race between further reduction in case marking and greater rigidity in ordering. The ultimate outcome was strict SVO order, and the minimal traces of case marking that are visible in Present Day English. A stable situation of no further changes (or only very little) has accordingly been reached by now.

As to links between case marking and the fixation of word order in ditransitives, I have suggested above (section 7.2.1.3) that the loss of the former might have triggered the very rapid increase of SVO order in the DOC observed in the Middle English data. Specifically, I propose that the syncretism between nominative and oblique case was comparatively unproblematic for prototypical transitives (and was incidentally possibly even furthered by this). For the DOC, however, this change plausibly presented a much higher challenge as it involved two arguments with relatively similar semantics (two animates), and similar degrees of topicality (two discourse-given, accessible entities). These were only distinguished in terms of (non-)agentivity and usual case-marking.[217] In the PRC, this ambiguity was unproblematic, since the recipient was additionally marked and therefore clearly identified by a preposition. I have argued that these asymmetries may explain the differences between the constructions.

Contrary to clause-level word order in ditransitives, the fixation of object orders with ditransitives and the differences displayed by the constructions involved proceeded independently of the loss of case marking. That is, I contradict Allen's claim that the loss of [TH-REC] is a direct outcome of the loss of the category distinction between accusative and dative (cf. Allen 2006; also Fischer 1992). The main reason for arguing against this account is that animacy and topicality asymmetries together with contextual clues in a large majority of cases would have prevented ambiguity even if both object arguments were unmarked. Furthermore, the data presented in this book indicates that the DOC only moved towards the canonical object order once its association with PP-constructions, which strongly favoured clause-late position, became stronger. Hence, rather than presuming case loss to have been causally involved in the fixation of [REC-TH] order in the DOC, I take word order preferences of PPs that were present already in Old English, and the emergence of the dative alternation, to have played a key role in this development.

In sum, I argue that the broad demise of case marking in early Middle English was motivated by reasons unrelated to changes in word order constraints or the rise of prepositional means, namely little semantic distinctiveness of various case constructions, and phonetic erosion/ increased formal ambiguity. Howev-

217 Note that this assumption is to some extent dependent on the REC-argument being prototypically marked by dative, since syncretism between e.g. nominative and accusative was already highly advanced by Old English. This is unproblematic if we assume that by Middle English, the only remaining case frame was [DAT-ACC].

er, the loss of case distinctions itself did affect clause level word ordering, which was stronger in the DOC, and can therefore explain differences between the constructions. On a more general level, what we can conclude here is the emergence of the dative alternation and its specific features can be interpreted as adaptations to a changing constructional environment.

7.2.2.2 Mutual adaptation within the dative alternation: Divergence vs. alignment

In this section, the establishment of PP-constructions as competitors to the DOC, and in particular the emergence of the dative alternation as a cooperative relation, are reassessed. On the one hand, we expect to see diversification processes, with the constructions developing complementary distributions. On the other hand, we should also see alignment between the constructions, meaning that they become more similar in certain aspects. Both types of changes can be conceptualised as instances of constructional co-evolution: Changes in one construction trigger changes in the other pattern. Furthermore, both types can be seen as beneficial for the constructions as well as the alternation. While the development of a division of labour situation is profitable for the patterns, it is also of advantage for them to share specific features. A balance between 'similar enough to be recognised as essentially the same' and 'different enough so as to not encroach upon each other' is optimal for both structures. In the following, changes in word order and semantic-pragmatic features of the members of the dative alternation are briefly discussed from this perspective.

First, in respect to the rise of SVO order in ditransitive patterns, I have shown in section (7.2.1.3) that the DOC and the *to*-PRC are more frequently found with SVO order in late Middle English than PRCs in general. I now argue that it was the increasing rigidity in SVO sequences in the DOC from mid-Middle English onwards, which was itself affected by the loss of case marking, that prompted the move towards stricter clause level word order in the *to*-PRC once the patterns became more intimately connected. When SVO orders rapidly became more frequent with the DOC, the *to*-PRC responded by an increase in SVO orders, too. Such a mutually adaptive formal alignment between the constructions is generally possible both in situations of competition and cooperation. However, seeing that the *to*-PRC is more advanced in this regard than the other PRCs, I assume that structural similarity was especially useful for the constructions once they had come to form a cooperative relationship. In a system which was not yet characterised by strict SVO order everywhere, and strict SVO would therefore not necessarily have been successful in general, it is questionable whether following the DOC in this change would have been beneficial for the *to*-

PRC, i.e. increased its success rates in competition. In a cooperative relationship, by contrast, changing one's shape to be more alike to one's associate is arguably more profitable, since their connection is made visible. As demonstrated in (4.2.1), the other PRCs in the corpus data, by contrast, retained some flexibility in clause-level ordering. This observation is also in line with e.g. Haspelmath's (2015: 31–32) observation that the presence of 'flagging', such as prepositional marking of arguments, typologically correlates with fewer restrictions on word order. Nevertheless, SVO is eventually also fixed in PRCs and PP-constructions in general, since they are necessarily affected by system-wide changes. The tighter connections between the core elements of subject, verb, object(s) in all parts of the system increasingly forced any other elements to more peripheral position.

The development of object orders in the different ditransitive constructions is argued to represent another case of mutual adaptation between the DOC and the *to*-PRC (but also the PRC, at least to some extent). The distributional phenomena outlined in (4.2) are explained as follows: I take the preference of PRCs for clause-late, or clause-peripheral position to have had a causal effect on the loss of [TH-REC] order in the DOC. That is, when the patterns became more strongly associated with each other, the strong bias of the PRCs for one order drove the DOC to settle for the complementary order. At the same time, however, I argue that the fact that [REC-TH] order was available and highly frequent with the DOC had an effect on the prepositional ditransitive patterns, which thereby diverged from other PP-constructions. More precisely, I claim that the extension of PPs to cover core semantic roles such as those of recipients, deprivees, and the like, and consequently their association with the DOC, enabled them to retain a [*prep*TH-REC] order even at a time when PPs progressively moved to the periphery of the clause. With the ousting of the DOC – the loss of this association and the resolution of competition – the flexibility finally decreased after all, and the more prototypical order [TH-*prep*REC] became canonical. The persistence of [REC-TH] orders is, as already mentioned, even more conspicuous in the case of the *to*-PRC, in that both orders are equally available during Middle English (although [TH-*to*REC] is more frequent at all times). This phenomenon again reflects the greater degree of integration into the VP of the PP in this case; since the *to*-PRC has come to mark the core semantic role of recipients of ditransitive events, it shows the same distributional features as other means of encoding this role. That the *to*-PRC differs from other PRCs in this regard is furthermore due to its stronger association with the DOC.

At the end of Middle English, the members of this dative alternation are characterised by the following word order features: The DOC is almost categorically associated with [REC-TH] order, whereas the *to*-PRC favours [TH-*to*REC] but is not limited to it. With the association between the patterns becoming stronger and stronger beyond Middle English, the constructions then develop an ever-increasing tendency towards sharing the workload more clearly. – In the course to PDE, the *to*-PRC gives up its flexibility in ordering and becomes increasingly limited to the complementary order of the DOC, namely [TH-REC]. This clearer formal, and correspondingly also functional, differentiation then adds to the stabilisation of the alternation relationship, which in turn positively influences the complementary distribution of orders. Both the constructions themselves, as well as the underspecified 'ditransitive' constructeme, which emerges at some point, profit from this development. Functional differentiation correlated with formal differentiation enhances the learnability of the system while maintaining its expressiveness. Despite a fixation in word order, syntactic freedom is not lost entirely, or rather, discourse-pragmatic differences such as topic and focus can still be expressed. In fact, this development constitutes a move from unpredictable variation towards predictable variation, which may be beneficial for a system (also Smith, Fehér, and Ritt 2014). What we thus see here is an initial alignment of the patterns, which is eventually replaced by complementary divergence. Incidentally, a similar diversification in syntactic choice to enable discourse-pragmatic differentiation has also taken place with verbs lost from the DOC: For example, verbs of dispossession in PDE are now found in two distinct prepositional patterns, PRCs and PTCs, each of which is associated with a different information structural and semantic profile (see 7.1.2.2).

As a final side remark, I assume that the distinct discourse-pragmatic features associated with each order (and correspondingly, with construction type) can also account for the circumstance that some verb classes (or sub-sets of verb classes, or even individual verbs) are restricted to one of the members of the dative alternation. Complex predicates of abstract transfer such as *give a kick* have e.g. been argued to place a particular focus on the action expressed by the theme argument. For this reason, the DOC appears to be pragmatically much better motivated in this case than the *to*-PRC (Goldberg 1995: 94–97). On the other side, complex predicates of mental activity or emotion such as *have love* or *feel envy* arguably give greater relevance to the cause or stimulus of the feeling. This greater compatibility with REC-late ordering then explains their strong bias towards prepositional constructions.

A comparable mixture between differentiation and alignment adaptations to those seen in word order are presented in the semantic development of the constructions. Specifically, I suggest that the increasing functional extension of the PP-patterns, and the ensuing increasingly strong association between the

DOC and the *to*-PRC is closely connected the semantic specialisation of the DOC. Linking the reduction in range of verb class types of the DOC to the rise of more explicit PP-constructions is not an entirely new idea. However, it is usually not made explicit whether the processes are thought to be causally connected or are only mentioned together since both are taken to have been triggered by the same change, namely deflection (Colleman and De Clerck 2011: 201–202; also Barðdal 2007; Colleman 2010b, 2011; Barðdal, Kristoffersen, and Sveen 2011). This book argues in favour of the former option, in that it posits a clear cause and effect development between the changes involved, even if these processes were gradual and stepwise.

Let us then outline the specific co-evolutionary scenario proposed for the semantic development of DOC and PRCs in the history of English. Despite the fact that in Old English, we find different case frames associated with different (overlapping) semantic relations for ditransitive verbs, the most common of these case frames already at this point is [DAT-ACC], i.e. a combination of a dative object denoting the REC-argument and a theme marked with accusative case (Visser 1963: 606–646, De Cuypere 2015a: 7). This pattern in turn most frequently (concerning both types and tokens) and as a consequence most prototypically expresses transfer situations, which are instantiated by 'giving'-verbs. The increasing loss of less prototypical and less productive case constructions in late OE adds to the token frequency of the [DAT-ACC] frame. Furthermore, it results in an increase in type frequency, since even those verbs (and possibly verb classes) that were exclusively associated with other case frames before, are now found with [DAT-ACC] marking. The semantic distinctions present before (although merely tendencies) are blurred to a considerable degree, with all kinds of semantic relations coming to be expressed by this frame. This is clearly supported by the Middle English data: A large range of different verb types and verb class types is found in the construction in the earliest sub-period. The assumption moreover appears plausible even if we acknowledge that some verbs may have increasingly resorted to available PRC-patterns once these changes took place – before Middle English.

With the final loss of case marking, an inflection-less, formally underspecified and rather general DOC pattern emerges at the turn to Middle English. At this point, the DOC can encode a rather wide range of meaning relations, meaning that it is associated with a number of sub-constructions with varying degrees of productivity and prototypicality. As shown by the corpus results, the most entrenched of these is the sub-sense of transfer, which suggests that the tendencies present in the OE DOC case constructions are carried over to the schematic Middle English DOC. Concomitant to the establishment of a schematic DOC is the steady increase in the use of the more explicit (and more flexible) prepositional competitors (Mustanoja 1960; Fischer 1992; Allen 1995; McFadden 2002; De Cuypere 2010, 2015b). Among the most prominent (and most frequent) of these PRCs are those involving GOAL-prepositions such as *towards*, *till* or *to* since their spatial/allative meaning corresponds most adequately to the 'trans-fer'-semantics of the large majority of ditransitive verbs (the verbs most frequently used in the DOC). Within this group, the *to*-PRC is most successful, due to its best performance concerning semantic as well as articulatory/perceptory factors. It is sufficiently expressive and maximally economic, accordingly representing the best match concerning benefits and costs.

During Middle English, an increasingly stronger link between the *to*-PRC and the DOC develops because of the former's prevalence and high frequency. The patterns thus enter into a closer and closer associative relationship, until the *to*-PRC is perceived as *the* analytic alternative to the DOC. The two constructions are then interpreted as two ways of expressing approximately the same meaning, and a preferential association between two linked patterns develops into a (near-)categorical association.[218] Subsequently, in later Middle English and beyond Middle English, 'the rich get richer, the poor get poorer': With the tighter association between DOC and *to*-PRC, verbs with corresponding paraphrases that include prepositions other than *to* (e.g. *from* or *of*), that is to say, verb classes that do not fit the semantic relations expressed by *to* (GOAL/ ADDRESSEE/ RECIPIENT) are increasingly marginalised from the DOC. They are eventually ousted completely. Not compatible anymore with the DOC, whose meaning is increasingly narrowed to encoding 'transfer'-events, these verbs (e.g. verbs of dispossession) become restricted to the prepositional patterns, or other means of expression (e.g. possessive phrases).

The emergence of the *to*-PRC variant is accordingly taken to have stood in a cause and effect relationship with the changes to the function of the DOC. These changes indicate that the patterns functionally approximated each other, and that stronger horizontal links between them formed, eventually resulting in the establishment of the ditransitive-constructeme. More specifically, I propose that the narrowing of the DOC's meaning to transfer-related senses correlates with the emergence of the *to*-PRC in that those are the senses that are compatible

218 It is clear from PDE data that the association is in fact not categorical but involves a range of irregularities and exceptions; nevertheless, there are good reasons to assume that the relationship between the patterns constitutes a more systematic and conspicuous phenomenon than mere partial semantic overlap. In other words, the constructions constitute 'allonyms' instead of only partial synonyms in PDE.

with the relations expressed by this particular preposition. Verbs not expressing such senses, and thus not licensed to participate in the alternation, are increasingly also prevented from being used in the DOC. As discussed in the preceding section, this development is not thought to be one-directional, but to constitute a series of reciprocal evolutionary responses in the constructions. The relation works in both ways: On the one hand, the emergence of the *to*-PRC plausibly promotes the DOC's move towards narrower giving-semantics. On the other hand, the prototypicality of transfer-senses in the Old and Middle English DOC could itself lead to a reduction in non-transfer verb-classes, and in turn trigger changes to the *to*-PRC, driving it to further expand in contexts. Although changes in this regard are visible in Middle English, it is clear that this process of mutual adaptation between the DOC and the *to*-PRC, with changes in the semantics of the one triggering changes in the other and vice versa, was not complete by the end of Middle English, but is still ongoing today. More precisely, the relationship between the allostructions is continuously becoming tighter. At the same time, uses that are further removed from the core meaning of transfer, but have for some reason survived until today, continue to become marginalised from the DOC. The latter is, for example, seen with the verbs of *forgive* and *envy*, whose use in the DOC has been decreasing recently.

To conclude, this book takes the semantic widening or extension in contexts seen in prepositional competitors in the history of English to have stood in a reciprocally causal relationship with the semantic narrowing of the DOC. This functional approximation of the patterns crucially serves as evidence for the assumption of a strong connection between them. I adduce the fact that the DOC saw a semantic specialisation over time as evidence of one of the central proposals of this book, which is that the DOC and the *to*-PRC have come to form a tight network, in which they are linked to each other and also to a more abstract constructeme. In this replicator-plex, the constructions express more or less the same meaning, and stabilise and adapt to each other rather than standing in competition. Importantly, this relationship does not constitute a mere coincidental overlap in the semantics of the constructions but represents the outcome of a development reflecting the psychological reality of an association in the minds of speakers. This made them first avoid the use of verbs in either of the two constructions unless they could also appear in the other. Later, however, it came to license the use of verbs that appeared in one of the two constructions also in the other (e.g. the use of *provide* in the DOC, or the rare, but attested use of verbs like *cost* or *refuse* in the *to*-PRC). Still, this development does not prevent semantic diversification processes on a lower level – distributional biases such as *sell* or *bring* showing a stronger preference for the *to*-PRC in PDE or *explain* being categorically associated with this construction only are to be expected in allo-relations. This means that while we see alignment in terms of the basic semantics of the constructions, they at the same time diverge regarding certain subtler semantic features. Subtle differences in event construal can also be explained in this way.

7.2.3 Summary: Co-evolutionary effects in the dative alternation

In a nutshell, the preceding sections have discussed the main changes that influenced the trajectory of ditransitives in the history of English, with a particular emphasis on the development of the constructions during the period of Middle English. More specifically, the following changes have been identified and investigated in more detail:

- Coalescence of ditransitive case frames: Potentially triggered by the large overlap in the semantics of the case constructions, the DOC first loses less productive types and moves towards the most prominent [DAT-ACC] frame; in a later stage, all case marking on the object arguments is lost due to perceived redundancy of the suffixes and increased formal syncretism.
- Semantic specialisation of the DOC: The DOC sees a reduction in verb-class-specific types, i.e. associated sub-constructions. Moving towards a prototypical basic meaning of 'transfer', uses peripheral to this sense (such as 'dispossession' or 'pure benefaction/malefaction') are increasingly marginalised, and eventually ousted entirely.
- Fixation of object order: The preference of PPs for clause-late placement translates into PRCs being strongly associated with [TH-*prep*REC] order. This causes the DOC to opt for the opposite order of [REC-TH]. As a consequence, a complementary formal distribution of the members of the dative alternation develops, which corresponds to distinctions in discourse-pragmatic functions.
- Fixation of word order in the clause: Parallel to a fixation of SVO order in the whole network, ditransitives move towards rigid clause-level word order as well. This change takes place more rapidly in the case of the DOC, possibly due to the greater need to distinguish the similarly typically animate and given agent and REC-argument from each other on the basis of position. The *to*-PRC also comes to show a stricter fixation of SVO than other PRCs, which I take to be the result of the emergence of the dative alternation.

In sum, what this chapter has so far proposed is essentially that the history of the dative alternation was characterised by a variety of adaptive responses of two types – on the one side, the emergence of the alternation as such can be seen as the evolutionary result of changes in the environment of the two constructions involved, namely the DOC and the *to*-PRC. The establishment of the dative alternation represents an adaptive response to the decreasing salience of morphological case marking (itself caused by the large semantic overlap between constructions) and the increasing tightness of word order constraints. The fact that the two constructions became associated and developed a relationship that was competitive at first and then became cooperative, however, also led to the constructions mutually adapting to each other in addition to adapting to their environment. (In fact, a link forming between the constructions means that they come to be part of their respective intra-systemic environments).

To illustrate this, consider the suggestion that the increasing ambiguity of case inflections and their eventual loss triggered the increasing use of prepositional patterns and their increasing functional extension. The DOC 'reacting' to this change by moving towards more specialised semantics (in turn causing the PRCs to extend even more, etc.) can be viewed as confirmation for an intimate relationship between the patterns, and accordingly for the existence of the dative alternation. In a similar way, I have posited that the loss of case marking and the ensuing need for disambiguation between the agent and recipient argument drove the DOC to a more rigid SVO order; this would then constitute an adaptation of the DOC to environmental changes. The increasing fixation of SVO in the *to*-PRC, in contrast, arguably constitutes an adaptive response of the prepositional pattern to the DOC, and therefore again corroborates the idea of a close and mutually adaptive relationship between the two. Finally, we have seen that word order changes which increasingly restricted PPs to clause-peripheral position could cause the PRCs to become associated with certain discourse-pragmatic functions (such as +focus). This bias in placement, which translates into [TH-REC] order in ditransitive constructions, could then force the DOC to resort to the opposite order, suggesting again that the constructions adapted to each other. In this case, the development is even more conspicuous, since the association between the patterns enabled the (*to*-)PRC to retain a certain flexibility in ordering. Rather than becoming limited to PP-late order like other PP+NP-patterns, the *to*-PRC maintained the option of having the PP in post-verbal position. I argue that this is again a sign of the close relationship between the patterns, and of their mutually adapting to each other. That the constructions eventually come to settle on a complementary distribution concerning object orders (and accordingly, discourse-pragmatic function) is further support for this assumption. A similar complementary distribution can also be seen in passives, where the *to*-PRC allows for the theme argument as the subject (*a book was given to Mary*), while the DOC is used with a recipient subject (*Mary was given a book*). The patterns furthermore seem to stand in a complementary relationship in regard to verb (and verb-class) preferences – while some verbs (e.g. *give, offer* or *tell*) are biased towards DOC uses, others such as *bring* or *sell* have been shown to favour the *to*-PRC in PDE (Gries and Stefanowitsch 2004).

In conclusion, I have demonstrated here that the dative alternation was the consequence of system-wide changes to specific morpho-syntactic parameters in the history of English. The establishment of the close relationship that is the alternation triggered its members to formally and functionally adapt to each other, with the patterns either approximating each other or developing a complementary 'division of labour'-distribution.

7.3 The dative alternation as an adaptation to changes in the constructional network

The preceding sections have focussed mainly on competition and cooperation between different (higher-order as well as lower-order) constructions. However, following Steels (2007, 2010, 2011b, 2012c) in distinguishing between linguistic selection on the level of (sub-)systems and selection of language strategies, we can also approach the history of English ditransitives and argument structure constructions in general from the viewpoint of competition and cooperation between different strategic means. These strategies are, as discussed in (6.3), taken to "emerge out of the collective activity of all individuals and [to be] not explicitly accessible nor represented" (Bleys and Steels 2011: 152). Nonetheless, they are subject to change via feedback loops on the communicative success of specific utterances instantiating language systems. For instance, drawing on the example of ditransitives in the diachrony of English, the selective fitness of the case-strategy changed when ambiguity between the individual case markers that formed the Old English/ Middle English system of case became too high to guarantee successful communication.[219] A tentative exploration of how the history of recipient marking in English could be modelled in terms of an evolution-

219 Or, following the line of argumentation presented in (7.2.1), the case-strategy weakened in fitness when the semantic overlap between various case constructions led to case being perceived as redundant.

ary game between the strategies of NP and PP has been presented in section (5.2). It has furthermore been shown that selection on the level of language strategies is guided by the same physiological-cognitive factors that also determine the success of constructions and sub-systems stored in the minds of speakers. Among such pressures are expressive adequacy or articulatory economy. Moreover, alignment between speakers plays an important role, meaning that changes in the grammar of individuals can spread through a population and eventually accumulate into innovations on the meta-level of emergent, collective linguistic strategies (or changes to existing strategies).

On this account, the diachronic development of argument structure strategies (and ditransitive strategies in particular) in the history of English can best be described as one of a change from a single strategy towards a cooperation of various strategies or a stably mixed strategy system. Starting out in pre-Old English, we find a population that is characterised by using a predominant case strategy both for core semantic role marking/ argument structure expression (e.g. themes, recipients, experiencers) as well as for non-core semantic roles such as temporal or location adjuncts.[220] In ditransitive events, the NP/CASE-strategy is furthermore used for all discourse-pragmatic functions. Both focused recipients and unfocused ones are maintained by this strategy. With the emergence of prepositions and PPs, which take over specific functions in the pre-OE language systems, a new strategy slowly establishes itself. This PP-strategy is first restricted to competing against the resident one for non-core role marking. However, the extension of PPs into more and more contexts previously fulfilled by case-NPs only (including argument-marking) finally results in full-fledged competition between the two strategies. At the same time, tendencies towards preferred word order choices are present in Old English, but this does not necessarily imply that a 'fixed word order' strategy has been introduced to the system yet. Rather, we can assume with Möhlig-Falke (2012), Los (2015), and others, that OE employed a 'topic-focus' strategy for sentence structuring, which to some extent aided argument structure identification, and could therefore develop into an innovative strategy at some point. Even if a word order strategy had been added to the inventory of argument structure strategies in Old English already, it seems that the competition between WORD ORDER, PPs and CASE in this

220 The distinction between core and non-core semantic roles corresponds largely to the distinction between complements and adjuncts often made in the literature (cf. Huddleston and Pullum 2002: 224–228; Th. Hoffmann 2005, 2011). Although such a strict binary division is unwarranted for PDE (as also argued in 7.1.3), it is likely still warranted for PPs in earlier periods, at least to a certain extent.

period was largely resolved in favour of the latter.[221] The greater success of CASE in Old English compared to the other strategies is reflected in the fact that a majority of semantic role types are exclusively associated with case constructions. It can be attributed to its better overall performance in respect to factors such as economy, expressivity as well as possibly flexibility. For example, case markers are typically shorter and thus more parsimonious than prepositions, similarly (although slightly less) semantically informative than PPs, and allow for more syntactic freedom than invariable word order (cf. section 5.2 on the 'recipient game'; also e.g. Haspelmath 2006: 3; Hagège 2010: 29; Kittilä, Västi, and Ylikoski 2011: 4).

A visual representation of Old English argument structure strategies is given in Fig. 51: It shows that the system of core semantic role marking (e.g. marking of recipients, themes or causes/stimuli) is most clearly sustained by a case-strategy, despite also being associated with PPs and a fixed word order strategy to some extent. Although these strategies can be considered to compete against each other for the functions in question, it could also be argued that they were in a state of stable, yet temporary, cooperation, with CASE constituting the dominant variant and PPs and WORD ORDER as the weak alternatives.

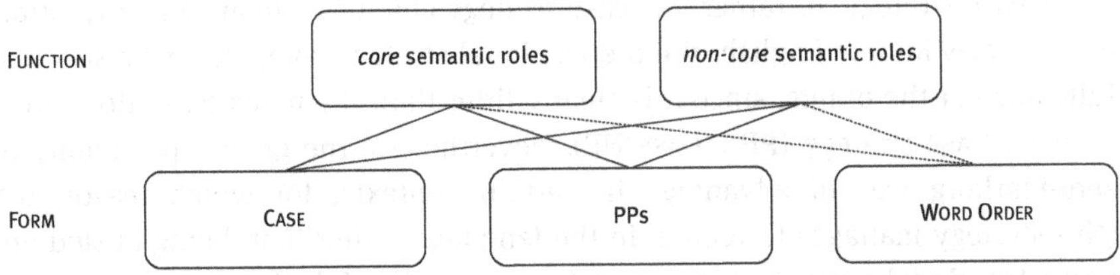

Fig. 51: System of semantic role marking strategies in Old English (with many-to-many relationships between form and function, cf. Van de Velde 2014)

As also indicated in the figure, in contrast to CASE being most successful in core semantic role marking (i.e. argument structure), with non-core semantic roles the prepositional strategy fares very well in Old English already. While case is still used to mark adverbials of time, among other things, the prepositional competitors have turned out to be equally or even more apt for these functions. Quite possibly, this is due to their greater distinctiveness and their allowing for

221 The strategy of WORD ORDER can also be treated as part of the strategy environment of CASE and PPs. The establishment of a mixed strategy of CASE/NP + PP could then again be viewed as an evolutionary effect to changes to the environment of these strategies.

finer distinctions (cf. *to* vs. *towards*), which is arguably more relevant in expressing spatial/temporal location or movement than in marking more abstract concepts. It should, however, be noted that the binary distinction between the functions of core and non-core semantic roles made in Fig. 51 is fairly arbitrary. Rather, what we could presume is a continuum of related functions (and systems) which are maintained by a range of strategies, with individual strategies performing more successfully in regard to some systems/functions than concerning others. This assumption would correspond to van de Velde's (2014) degenerate systems approach to language; the same semantic distinctions can be expressed through different strategies in a many-to-many relationship (also Edelman and Gally 2001; Whitacre 2010). In such systems, strategies can still be added and lost; however, even if the inventory of formal strategies remains the same, the links between function and form can change over time.

A move from one mixed strategy to another is precisely what we see in the history of English, as with the increasing weakening of the case strategy towards the end of Old English, the make-up of the strategic system of semantic role marking changes. The other strategies eventually come to form the stable equilibrium of cooperation that is still present in PDE. More specifically, the decreasing expressivity of case markers eventually leads to a decrease in fitness of the case strategy, or rather, the case strategy changes into an 'NP-only' strategy. In early Middle English, the prepositional strategy competes most successfully against the others, since it is clearly fitter than the much less informative reduced CASE strategy (PP > CASE/NP). Nevertheless, the greater parsimony of zero-marking was of advantage in certain contexts, for which reason the (NP-)strategy manages to remain in the language rather than being ousted entirely. PPs do take over in some cases (as with verbs of dispossession or reverse transfer, as well as verbs of cognition/emotion such as *wonder*, *yearn*). In other linguistic sub-systems, however, the strategies ultimately enter a mutualistic relationship, where they stabilise each other instead of competing. Often, this also includes cooperation with WORD ORDER. For instance, the greater economy of CASE/NP makes it a more suitable fit for certain discourse-pragmatic functions, such as marking REC [-focus] constituents. Together with the fact that PPs show a preference for clause-late position and are accordingly more appropriate for non-focal elements (REC [+focus]), this can result in functional diversification and division of labour between the strategies. Exposed to variable input produced by a mixed PP/NP strategy, some speakers/hearers might infer a rule/conditioning. If such "local disambiguation efforts undertaken by [variable] speakers [are then interpreted] as conventionalized", with larger and larger parts of the population aligning to each other in this respect, a mixed yet conditioned system can establish itself (Deo 2015: 34).[222]

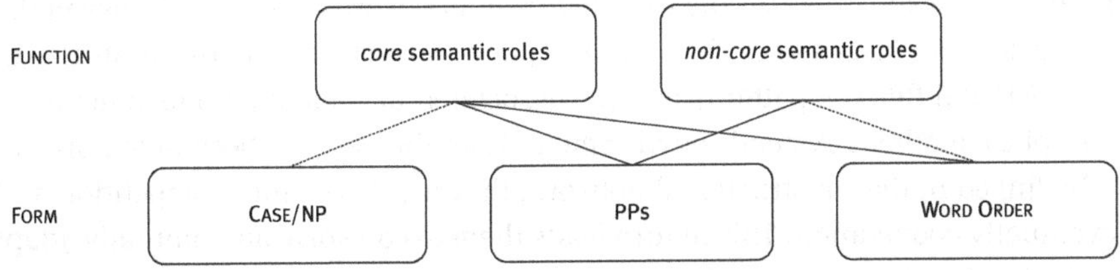

Fig. 52: Degenerate system of semantic role marking strategies in Present Day English (with many-to-many relationships between form and function, cf. Van de Velde 2014)

To sum up, as also indicated by a comparison of Fig. 51 and Fig. 52, the history of English argument structure marking is characterised by various changes on the level of language strategies, with strategies being both innovated (PP) and lost (or fading considerably, as with CASE). Furthermore, there are adjustments in the links between functions and strategies. In some cases, this means the emergence of new links or the loss of others (e.g. [core semantic roles - CASE]). In other cases, existing links are strengthened or weakened (e.g. [core semantic roles - PPs]). In the course to PDE, we see the establishment of a stable, mixed strategy. In this symbiotic, cooperative relationship the strategies typically fulfil different, yet complementary functions. With ditransitives, this translates into the emergence of a paradigmatic distribution of NP (DOC) and PP (*to*-PRC).

7.4 A proposed scenario: The rise of the English dative alternation

This section has attempted to develop a plausible scenario for the development of ditransitives in the history of English and has approached this issue with a focus on competition and cooperation on different levels, including that of language (sub-)systems – constructional networks – and that of language strategies. I have proposed that causal effects between the changes involved can be seen in various stages of this development, often leading to a co-evolutionary,

222 The question whether the strategy maintaining the DOC is one of Ø-marking (and would therefore have to be included in the figure), or whether the DOC reflects the absence of a strategy is not addressed here.

mutually adaptive relationship between the constructions concerned. More precisely, the dative alternation has been claimed to constitute an adaptive response to environmental changes: Changes to the constructional/ strategic fitness landscape triggered the establishment of a close connection between the constructional means of DOC and *to*-PRC, and in consequence, the strategies of CASE/NP and PP. The patterns become associated to each other and come to be part of each other's systemic environment. With the patterns becoming horizontally linked in the constructional network, they are driven into competition and eventually cooperation. This in turn leads them to co-evolve and mutually adapt to each other. This can, on the one hand, mean that the constructions align to each other formally and functionally; on the other hand, they develop a complementary distribution.

The more specific scenario I have postulated here is the following: In Old English, we find different case constructions which are available to ditransitive verbs. Among these, the frame [DAT-ACC] is the most frequent and most productive one. This sub-type of the DOC is also the most semantically open frame, in expressing a range of different senses including transfer, dispossession, and attitudinal verbs. In general, the choice of case constructions appears to be to some extent semantically motivated in that the frames are roughly associated with certain meanings. However, there is also large semantic overlap between the case constructions, with individual frames instantiating several senses, and individual meanings typically relating to more than one frame. The schematic, more abstract DOC representing a generalisation over all case constructions is accordingly semantically underspecified. It joins three case-marked NPs with a ditransitive predicate and denotes an event in which an agent causes another participant to be affected by acting on a third party. Nonetheless, despite being associated with different more or less productive senses, the meaning of transfer is presumably quite strongly present in the OE DOC.

Already in Old English, some of the verbs and verb classes connected with the DOC are also found in prepositional (case) constructions. Although there is some competition between the DOC and prepositional paraphrases at this point, it takes place on a lower level in the network, between more substantive constructions. It is furthermore clearly resolved in favour of the nominal construction. (On the level of strategies, CASE is therefore clearly the more successful one at this point). More precisely, the PRCs at this stage are still restricted in their use and are only found with certain verb classes such as dispossession (*take away*) or caused motion (*bring, send*). These PRCs constitute early reanalyses of spatial prepositions in utterances with participants that are ambiguous between inanimate goals or sources and animate recipients or deprivees (and the like).

Moreover, the paraphrase-able ditransitive verb classes are not limited to one particular prepositional type, but rather appear with a range of semantically related PRCs. For example, verbs of bringing and sending are associated with several GOAL-type prepositions including *to*, *towards* and *till*, among others. As to word order preferences, both the DOC and the PRCs in Old English are relatively flexible concerning clause-level order and the order of the two object arguments. Nevertheless, some tendencies can be assumed: In general, SVO order is quite frequent due to differences in topicality of prototypical 'subject' and 'object' arguments. Quite importantly, PPs exhibit a bias towards clause-late or clause-peripheral position, possibly due to their common adjunctival function of 'afterthoughts', providing additional, optional information. In the DOC, both object orders are frequently attested in an almost equal distribution. However, [REC-TH] orders are slightly more prominent due to animacy and topicality asymmetries between the objects, which influence relative placement.

In late Old English or at the turn to early Middle English, several processes take place. First, within the ditransitive case constructions there is a movement towards the most productive case frame of [DAT-ACC]. The other frames are increasingly lost. This move is paralleled in the prepositional competitors (*prep*-DAT-ACC). The development is mainly caused by the unpredictability in variation concerning form (case frame and ditransitive verb) and function (ditransitive sub-sense), which invites reduction. In addition, there is considerable formal as well as functional ambiguity between the individual case affixes, meaning that the system as a whole is unstable in involving competition on varying levels. It is prone to change. With only one case construction left, and little formal distinction between the affixes maintained, the case markers are increasingly perceived as redundant, and are reduced even more. In sum, this results in the loss of case marking in general. For the PRCs, this means the establishment of inflectionless patterns with a form [V NP-Ø *prep*NP-Ø]; for the DOC, this means the convergence of case frames into one larger double object construction involving two bare NP object arguments. This DOC expresses a comparatively wide range of meaning relations. Distinguishing between the semantic roles of the objects is not severely complicated by this change since they are prototypically located on the opposed ends of the topicality cline – REC-arguments tend to be animate, given, definite, among other features, whereas themes are more often inanimate, new, indefinite, etc. However, the change does result in heightened potential ambiguity of the two similarly topical constituents of agent/subject and REC/indirect object. This issue is resolved by a rapid increase in strict SVO ordering in the DOC in early Middle English, allowing the agent to be distinguished from the recipient on the basis of pre- versus post-verbal position. PRCs interestingly retain a certain amount of flexibility throughout the period, despite the fact that they tend to favour SVO order to a greater extent than the DOC in the beginning. This preference may reflect the adjunctival origin of the PP-objects, making the PRCs more dependent on changes in the transitive construction they inherit from. DOCs, by contrast, are possibly more independent in their behaviour.

A further change which interacts (reinforces and is influenced by at the same time) is the increasing use of PRCs in comparison to the bare DOC. In addition to increasing in frequency with those verb classes already paraphrased by PP-constructions in Old English, the prepositional patterns also extend analogically to new verbs and verb classes, which are more abstractly connected to spatial motion. This development represents a rather straightforward case of functional extension and possibly grammaticalisation, as the individual prepositions acquire more and more (and more abstract) functions over time. The prepositions' expansion in the context of ditransitive role marking can be seen as part of a larger development, with prepositional constructions progressively moving from their adjunct-beginnings along a cline towards more procedural function (such as expressing obligatory complements in tight verb-preposition combinations like *rely+on*).

The competition between the DOC and PRCs (corresponding to a weakened NP/CASE-marking strategy and a PP-strategy on a meta-level of emergent collective behaviour) is resolved in crucially different ways during Middle English: First, the most prototypical and most frequent verb-class specific constructions of transfer and transfer-related senses increasingly enter competition with GOAL-type prepositions. Within this group, the most productive and frequent one is *to*, which besides being the most economical, is also sufficiently expressive and thus constitutes the best 'maximal gain-minimal cost' variant. Although the *to*-PRC initially surpasses the DOC and although there is a temporary phase of competition which is settled in favour of the prepositional periphrasis, the constructions eventually develop a cooperative relationship. In this, they stabilise each other and mutually benefit from the replication of the other. The existence of such a symbiotic relationship in PDE is confirmed or at least strongly supported by evidence from cross-constructional priming and alternation-based productivity effects of the members of the dative alternation.

The establishment of a paradigmatic link between the DOC and the *to*-PRC, with the former as the stronger (more frequent) variant, and the latter as the weaker (less frequent) option in PDE, can be conceptualised as a strengthening of horizontal links between the two constructions in the network. Moreover, I have argued that it results in the emergence of a ditransitive constructeme in the sense of Cappelle (2006) and Perek (2015), in that the two formally distinct constructions are both associated with a formally underspecified generalisation. Rather than representing synonyms, the DOC and the *to*-PRC have therefore come to form allonyms, or better 'allostructions'. Instead of continuing to compete for the same function, they have diverged functionally, and have formed their respective complementary niches. The allostructions have developed differences in regard to discourse-pragmatic functions such as topicality of the recipient or theme. They furthermore show distributional differences in terms of semantic-pragmatic information, as they exhibit certain verb-specific preferences and evoke subtly distinct event construals. The history of the dative alternation thereby constitutes a prime case of constructional division of labour in a cooperative, mutualistic relationship. Importantly, this differentiation in contexts correlates with differences in object ordering. While the DOC early on develops a tendency for [REC-TH] order as a response to the [TH-REC] order preferred by PP-constructions already in Old English, the PRCs (and especially the *to*-PRC) again remain comparatively flexible. (This is due to the increasingly close connection with the DOC, which drives the constructions to formally align as well). Ultimately, however, with the establishment of the alternation, the *to*-PRC settles on the complementary order from the DOC. It develops a canonical order of [TH-REC] in contrast to the (near-)categorical [REC-TH] order of the DOC in PDE. On the clausal level, on the other hand, the constructions appear to move closer to each other, as the rapid increase in SVO orders in the synthetic pattern is followed by a more fixed SVO order in the *to*-PRC in comparison to other PRCs. This is taken as a clear indication of a co-evolutionary attraction behaviour of the constructions, with one aligning itself to changes in the other.

The increasingly stronger association of the DOC and the *to*-PRC can also be related to changes visible in the semantics of the DOC. I have here demonstrated that through the stronger and stronger link between the two patterns, uses that cannot be paraphrased by this particular PRC due to their unsuitable semantics are increasingly marginalised from the DOC; they are eventually lost altogether. For instance, verbs of dispossession, which instantiate a sense of 'taking away' and therefore involve a SOURCE-meaning, are almost diametrically opposed to the GOAL-semantics of *to*. Accordingly, they do not fit with the close relationship that is developing between the two constructions. They become more and more peripheral to the DOC. With the loss of sub-types that are only remotely connected to a movement towards a goal, the meaning of the DOC is increasingly narrowed to basic giving-semantics. This process of constructional semantic specialisation, in which the prototypical meaning of successful transfer to a willing recipient is progressively foregrounded at the expense of other senses is still ongoing in PDE. For example, marginal uses such as verbs of refusal or mental/attitudinal verbs such as *forgive* or *envy*, which are also markedly awkward in the *to*-PRC might fall out of use of the DOC at some point in the future.

As to the fate of the ousted verb classes, they usually become restricted to the prepositional competitors. Their pathway is therefore one of competition resolved in favour of one construction rather than emerging cooperation. This is precisely what is seen with verbs of dispossession: These verbs more and more frequently occur in PRCs with *from* or *of* rather than the DOC, until the prepositional uses become entirely categorical (after Middle English, but before the 18th century). I have further argued that the availability or non-availability of extra alternative patterns plays an important role in determining how competition is resolved. The fact that prepositional theme patterns presented an additional option for dispossession verbs was essential in allowing for the loss of DOC uses without losing expressive power. That is, with PTCs showing a similar distributional, discourse-pragmatic profile as the DOC, maintaining all constructions was costly and invited reduction. I suggest that ultimately, the PRC- construction has likewise entered a cooperative relationship with the PTC, enabling verbs of dispossession to choose between two syntactic structures according to event construal (cf. *John stole money from Mary* vs. *John robbed Mary of money*). A similar situation can be observed with verbs of malefaction, which had another nominal pattern, namely a possessive construction, at their disposal. As a consequence, they too fell out of use from the DOC, and are today only found in the alternative variant (*John broke Mary's nose*). Competition yielding to cooperation between DOC and PRCs in the case of transfer-verbs can be seen as reflecting the absence of such added choices; this lack forces the constructional types into collaboration.

A third pathway taken by some minor verb classes is continuity, or rather, reinforcement of OE tendencies. This is illustrated by the group of reversed transfer verbs as well as mental/attitudinal complex predicates (such as *have envy/love towards/for so.*). These verb classes have a strong bias towards PRCs in Old English already, or may even have been used exclusively in the prepositional patterns at this point. After a short-term expansion to DOC usage, they move back to categorical PRC-use. Contrary to the other two groups, the variation in prepositional types found in Old and Middle English is not reduced in this case, but different PRC types are still used today. While some verb-specific preferences are there, no generalisations over semantic sub-senses associated with specific prepositions can be assumed. Although the situation is thus a bit more complex than a simple straightforward move towards transfer within Middle English, changes are clearly underway. I interpret these as another reflection of co-evolutionary tendencies, with the members of the dative alternation becoming more alike in terms of their basic semantics.

In sum, the history of ditransitives in English presents a fascinating illustration of how competition can be resolved both on the level of systems or constructions as well as language strategies, where we see a move away from a single, pure strategy towards an intricate system of mixed strategies. Furthermore, the history of the dative alternation constitutes a compelling case of co-evolution of linguistic units, in that the emergence of the alternation as such can be regarded as an evolutionary effect of system-wide changes, which means changes to the environment of the constructions. Importantly, such adaptations to the changing fitness landscape also led to the constructions adapting to each other, indicating that they have come to be intimately connected. In this close relationship, changes to one of the members of the alternation inevitably produce an adaptive response in the other member.

8 Conclusion

8.1 The dative alternation in Middle English

The main question this book has attempted to answer is how the PDE dative alternation came about in the history of English, and how it can be modelled in an innovative framework of evolutionary construction grammar. The link between the nominal double object construction (DOC) and the prepositional pattern involving *to* (*to*-PRC) easily qualifies as "one of the most extensively studied alternations in the grammar of English" (Wolk et al. 2013: 385). Its PDE properties have been subject to quite some debate. However, the history of the alternation, although equally complex and intriguing, has received considerably less attention so far. One reason why the diachronicity of the alternation is so special is that it presents a case of stable long-term variation rather than the reduction of syntactic variation. In addition, its development reflects most of the major and most pervasive changes the English language went through between Old English and PDE, including the collapse of the morphological case marking system and the concomitant rise of prepositional paraphrases, as well as the fixation of word order. This means that dealing with ditransitive constructions in the history of English also means revisiting issues which have occupied linguists for a long time, and which are therefore certainly highly interesting. By investigating the effect of these broader changes on the constructions involved, I have aimed to provide a historical explanation for the synchronic phenomenon of the dative alternation and for its conspicuous features. That is, the basic questions this book has addressed are (i) the emergence and stability of the dative alternation in English and (ii) the development of the specific formal and functional properties its members exhibit today.

8.1.1 Synopsis of the book

In order to address the main research questions of this book and to conceptualise this development in a joint framework of evolutionary linguistics and construction grammar, the following steps have been taken:

First, some major issues in constructionist approaches to ditransitives in Present Day English have been introduced. More specifically, the question has been outlined of how the constructions in question, i.e. the DOC and the *to*-PRC (and, to a lesser extent, the *for*-PRC) as well as their formal and functional features are treated in this framework. Most importantly, this chapter has dis-

https://doi.org/10.1515/9783110633856-008

cussed argument structure alternations in usage-based construction grammar. The main conclusions to be drawn in this regard have been that the DOC and the *to*-PRC both encode a basic meaning of transfer and are thus roughly synonymous. This synonymy has led to their being perceived as closely related, meaning that they are strongly connected via horizontal links in the constructional network, and are even linked to a higher-order generalisation. This abstraction specifies only those features that are common to both constructions. Essentially, the dative alternation is accordingly viewed as more than a mere epiphenomenon of a partial overlap in verbs instantiating the constructions. Instead, it receives an independent theoretical standing, and is thought to be represented in the minds of speakers as such. This assumption is supported by observational and experimental evidence. Furthermore, the constructions can be shown to exhibit effects of 'alternation-based productivity' –the use of a verb in one construction typically increases the likelihood of it also being used in the other construction. The members of the dative alternation seem to stabilise each other rather than competing against each other.

In a second step, the history of the dative alternation has been reviewed (chapter 3). This included first, a discussion of the rise of prepositional patterns to contexts previously exclusively expressed by the DOC only; ultimately, this is what gave rise to the dative alternation. Afterwards, some of the major changes that took place in the history of English and affected the particular features of the constructions in question have been reported on: Among these are the demise of the morphological case marking system at the transition from Old to Middle English and the increase in word order rigidity around the same time. The latter issue concerns not only word order on the clausal level, but importantly also the order of objects of ditransitive verbs, which became progressively more fixed in the history of English. Moreover, changes in the semantics of the patterns have been dealt with. The DOC saw a considerable reduction in the range of verb classes associated with it over time. This is taken to represent a narrowing of the construction's semantics. Finally, I have briefly discussed previous suggestions on correlations and causal relationships between the individual changes, as they seem to be connected in various ways.

The hypotheses gleaned from this overview have been approached empirically in a two-fold way, by means of two different methodologies. On the one hand, a large-scale analysis of corpus data on the one hand was undertaken, on the other hand, an evolutionary game theoretic model was employed.

As to the first of these, the book is based on an extensive corpus study of Middle English texts, more precisely an investigation of the *Penn-Helsinki Parsed Corpus of Middle English* (PPCME2). This corpus study entailed the extraction, classification and analysis of all tokens of the DOC, i.e. sequences of two NP-objects, as well as all instances of prepositional alternatives. Crucially, the latter were not restricted to constructions with *to*, but included all kinds of prepositions able to paraphrase a double object construction. While *to*-PRCs did make up a large part of this prepositional database, periphrases involving e.g. *from*, *of* or *for* were therefore incorporated as well. The combined tokens were analysed according to their morphological properties (case marking salience), syntactic features (word order on the clause level and concerning object order), as well as semantic characteristics (verb classes such as transfer, dispossession, or mental/attitudinal, etc.). The inclusion of non-prototypical patterns, meaning that patterns other than the typically focussed on DOC case frames and *to*-prepositional patterns were investigated as well, constitutes a crucial difference of this book to previous studies on the history of ditransitives in the history of English, and counts as one of its major merits. Furthermore, I investigated a range of additional patterns for specific verb classes: For example, prepositional theme patterns were looked at for dispossession and communication verbs. With malefactive verbs, another option, namely possessive constructions, were examined. The study thus presents as much more extensive and less restricted to binary, proto-typical correspondences than what has been done so far, and has allowed us to reflect on the concept of 'syntactic alternations' in general. The results gained by the analysis have been used as the basis for discussing ditransitives in Middle English. Since the main aim of this book has been on devising a plausible scenario for the evolution of the constructions in question, and most importantly, the emergence of the dative alternation, particular emphasis has here been given to diachronic change within, but also beyond, the Middle English period.

The application of the second method of evolutionary game theory follows from the second main framework this study has used, that is, evolutionary linguistics. This framework has been introduced in the fifth chapter of the book, with a focus on the question how and why language should or can be considered an evolutionary system. I have concluded that language indeed must be viewed from an evolutionary perspective since it fulfils all of the necessary criteria for replicator systems. Language use involves units that replicate – they are transmitted and shared between minds of speakers. They involve variation, as new constructions are continuously generated by copying errors in the transmission process. Crucially, language use is also characterised by differential replication, meaning that some variants are able to replicate more successfully than others. The success of linguistic variants is determined by a variety of factors, most importantly cognitive-physiological ones, social pressures, and intra-systemic factors. Depending on how well individual variants fare regarding these factors, they will either oust their competitors, lose against them, or come to construct their respective niches, and form a cooperative relationship with other variants. I have argued that taking such an evolutionary perspective, in which competition between variants and frequency of occurrence (success in replication) play a key role, is particularly suitable for investigating the history of the dative alternation. While social and other factors are certainly of interest, I have concentrated on systemic issues in this book: The dative alternation is approached as part of a network of constructions which constitute its fitness environment and which it adapts to.

Evolutionary game theory has been used to model the development of competing strategies for argument marking, paralleling different stages in the development of the English language. The main aim in employing an evolutionary game theoretic model in this study has been to test the assumption that under universal pragmatic constraints such as the focus-last principle, changes in system-internal constraints (such as the decrease of case marking indicativeness and an increase in word order rigidity) competition between constructions (e.g. the members of the dative alternation) can lead to mutualistic cooperation. Furthermore, by including this tool, I hope to have demonstrated that methodologies from other disciplines can be used to assess hypotheses about historical language change. Taking an evolutionary game theoretic approach, and connected to this, working within an evolutionary linguistic framework, has enabled us to view the history of the English dative alternation from a new perspective.

The book accordingly combines two different methodologies and is grounded in two different theoretical frameworks. What fusing these viewpoints means, and which questions arise in doing so has been discussed in chapter (6). Based on this discussion and the findings of the two empirical analyses, the final part of the book has then put forward a scenario for the development of ditransitives in English which centres around the concepts of constructional innovation (the emergence of variation in the system), competition (and competition resolution), as well as cooperation and co-evolutionary effects. The main proposals and arguments offered are briefly summarised below.

8.1.2 Main results and proposed scenario for the rise of the dative alternation

In brief, the narrative that has been suggested for the development of the dative alternation in English on the basis of the empirical analyses is the following: In

Old English, there are different case constructions for ditransitive verbs, which eventually collapse into one main case frame due to their large semantic overlap. At the turn to Middle English, case marking is lost altogether, as a result of the redundancy of a single case pattern, as well as increasing phonetic erosion. The outcome of these developments is the Middle English DOC, a sequence of case-less noun phrase objects, which expresses a relatively abstract notion of indirect affectedness. Prepositional paraphrases, on the other hand, are also already available in Old English, but are not yet used with all verb classes at this point, and generally seem to be still restricted in a number of aspects. This changes in late Old English/ early Middle English, possibly instigated by the increasing demise of case marking – in an initial stage, PRCs extend to more and more functions (verb classes), see an overall increase, and even surpass the DOC for some time. The later development of the PRCs is, however, strikingly dependent on the verb classes (or rather, verb-class specific constructions) involved. With certain verbs, e.g. verbs of dispossession or verbs of benefaction/ malefaction, PRCs clearly win out over the course of the Middle English period, corresponding to their ousting from the DOC. While there is considerable variation in PP-types in these cases in the beginning, the verb classes eventually settle for a particular kind, meaning that variation is reduced. Importantly, the classes lost from the DOC typically also have a third constructional option at their disposal (e.g. prepositional theme patterns or possessive patterns). Since these often show similar discourse-pragmatic biases as the DOC, their availability may have significantly influenced the changes in argument structure of the respective verb sets.

A different development can be observed in the case of transfer- and transfer-related verb classes, such as communication or intended, future transfer. Here, we observe a reversal of the trend for more PRC use during Middle English, with DOCs in fact taking over again towards the end. Although there is a similar tendency for PRC-variation in the initial phase, with time the *to*-PRC emerges as *the* analytic equivalent to the transfer-DOC. This then lays the ground for the establishment of the dative alternation as we find it in PDE: With the range of verb classes associated with the DOC being reduced to those of transfer-like senses, the association between the two patterns becomes progressively tighter, and they come to constitute allostructions or paradigmatic variants of each other. This link can be conceptualised as a generalisation (constructeme) over formally distinct, yet semantically similar constructions.

Last, there is a group of somewhat miscellaneous uses which do not follow either the one or the other pathway in a clear manner: For instance, complex predicates of attitude/emotion or verbs of reverse transfer are more frequently found in PRCs in Old English already, and do not change significantly except for entirely ousting DOC uses eventually. In PDE, these verbs are then exclusively associated with prepositional constructions. What unites this group is their non-conformity to the behaviour of the other verb classes in PDE. This includes their not having becoming restricted to one particular preposition (at least not on a more systematic level).

As to word order changes in the diachrony of ditransitives, I have shown that the overall increase in SVO orders is paralleled in both patterns, but is slightly more advanced in the DOC, possibly due to ambiguity issues between agents and recipients after case loss. In respect to object ordering, PPs tend to prefer clause-late (i.e. recipient-second) position from early on, which 'forces' the DOC to more frequently choose recipient-first order. Although there is some competition for orders during the period, these are also the orders which become canonical for the respective constructions.

8.1.3 Main arguments: Constructional innovation, competition, cooperation, co-evolution

One of the main arguments that this book has put forward is that the history of ditransitives in English essentially constitutes a story of *constructional innovation*, *competition* and *cooperation* on various levels. As to the first of these, I have taken the emergence of new PP-patterns for ditransitive events out of more locational constructions to constitute the establishment of new nodes – and thus new variants – in the network. Competition is, among other things, seen between case constructions in Old English and between the DOC and PRCs in early Middle English, as well as between different PRC-types who 'fight' for the same function. Also, the various lower-level constructions specifying object order in the DOC and PRCs compete against each other. While in some cases, such competition has been resolved in favour of one of the variants, in other cases a cooperative relationship has formed. One of the most striking examples of the latter development is the emergence of the dative alternation. That is, the key point of this book has been to show that the members of the PDE dative alternation have come to form a cooperative, mutualistic relationship over the course of time. In this symbiotic, paradigmatic association, the patterns stabilise each other and positively impact their respective productivity rather than contesting against each other for expression.

Furthermore, the history of ditransitives in English can be described as a tale of competing selectional pressures, most importantly those of expressivity and economy. While the prepositional, analytic competitors would seem to be more successful in regard to the former, the more synthetic double object construction is preferred in respect to the latter. It is one of the main benefits of providing an evolutionary linguistic perspective on language that it allows us to assess the various types of factors influencing the replicative success of one variant over another in a more systematic and transparent way. Moreover, the influence of such factors can readily be tested by the innovative methodologies evolutionary linguistic approaches frequently draw on (cf. e.g. agent-based modelling investigations of reductions in case marking systems).

I have further argued that the diachronic development of the constructions involved is crucially characterised by *co-evolution*. This means that the ditransitive allostructions, the DOC and the *to*-PRC, have come to stand in a mutually adaptive relationship to each other, in which changes in one pattern will inevitably be followed by changes in the other. Such co-evolutionary effects can come in two forms: On the one hand, diversification processes are frequent, with the competing or cooperating patterns creating their respective complementary (discourse-pragmatic and/or semantic) niches. On the other hand, the constructions may also align to each other and become more similar. Such mutually adaptive developments can e.g. be observed in regard to the semantics of the DOC: Through its increasingly close association with the most frequent (and most suitable) of the prepositional paraphrases, namely the *to*-PRC, the construction undergoes a process of semantic specialisation. It changes to denote a basic meaning of transfer rather than indirect affectedness, losing a range of sub-senses such as 'dispossession'. At the same time, the narrowing of the semantics of the DOC can be seen as responsible for the stronger and stronger link between this pattern and the *to*-PRC in the first place, indicating that the two developments impacted each other. While the constructions have become more alike each other in terms of their general semantics, they have diverged to a complementary distribution on a lower level, in that construal differences and verb-specific preferences can be found. A similar development is shown with word order. With the increasingly intimate link between the constructions, they align to each other in clause-level word order, but formally and functionally diverge in respect to object order. The final outcome of this is the shared workload relation of DOC and *to*-PRC according to functional factors in PDE, reflected in their word order preferences (DOC: topical recipient followed by theme [REC-TH]; *to*-PRC: topical TH followed by *to*-REC). I have thus proposed that the particular formal and functional features of the members of the PDE alternation can be explained as co-evolutionary effects of their developing a close connection. What the idea of co-evolution also entails is that there is typically no simple one-directional causal influence of one discrete, large-scale change on another, but that causal effects are two-way, step-wise, and gradual developments, with many small adaptations on both sides.

Most interestingly, the emergence of the dative alternation as such can be argued to constitute an evolutionary effect of or adaptive response to system-wide, environmental changes: The loss of overall case marking, and the increasing move towards stricter word order triggered the closer and closer association between the constructions. Under certain conditions (such as universal principles like that of end-focus), two constructional means (or strategies) can enter an intimate relationship, in which they share the labour. Once such a link has been established, the patterns begin to co-evolve. Having come to be part of their respective systemic environments, they adapt to each other, and react to changes in the respective other.

8.2 Theoretical implications

A more theoretically focussed aim of this book has been to discuss the potential benefits of approaching language change in general, and the development of ditransitives in particular, from the joint viewpoint of construction grammar and evolutionary linguistics. Concerning construction grammar, the precise framework chosen here was usage-based, cognitive construction grammar, in which language is seen as crucially shaped by language use and frequency in use in a bottom-up way. In respect to evolutionary linguistics, the specific assumptions I have worked on are that linguistic replicators are competence constituents rather than utterances, that variation is generated in a random way rather than being guided by functional factors, and that selection is driven by cognitive-physiological, social and intra-systemic factors. Language change in this framework is always frequency change, meaning that the strong focus on frequency in use in usage-based construction grammar finds its parallel here.

Integrating the two approaches, a number of decisions had to be made – most importantly, evolutionary replicators are taken to correspond (or indeed be) constructions rather than either form or meaning. Furthermore, the book has mainly focussed on replicators as cognitive patterns (i-replicators) rather than concrete utterances, while at the same time acknowledging that replication inevitably involves actual expression, and that mental constituents are fundamentally influenced by the communicative success of their external manifestations. Regarding the different degrees of schematicity that define constructions in a network, I have assumed that replication essentially takes place only at the very lowest level. Nevertheless, more abstract constructions constitute replicators as well in that they are activated in a bottom-up fashion every time an associated construct/micro-construction is used. A potentially problematic issue is posed by the concept of constructionalisation as outlined in standard versions of diachronic construction grammar: There is a clash here in that a new construction is only claimed to emerge when both form and meaning of an older construction change. By contrast, in an evolutionary approach, any change to an existing replicator will result in a new variant which competes against the resident one. Since competition plays an integral part in the scenario proposed in this book, the latter assumption has been followed here, and a view of constructionalisation as the very gradual semanticisation of restrictions in linguistic contexts has been adopted.

As to the benefits gained by proposing a merged account of construction grammar and evolutionary linguistics, the former framework was thought to be especially useful in that it lets us describe language phenomena in terms of clearly defined linguistic elements, i.e. form-meaning pairings. Construction grammar can provide a rich inventory of terminology and tools to analyse linguistic elements as well as language change, shaped by a comparatively long and unified research tradition. Moreover, the network model of language, which is crucial to construction grammar and which allows for constructions to be linked without one having to be a transformation of the other as in generative accounts, matches with the evolutionary linguistic focus on competition between 'related' variants. Also, both usage-based construction grammar and evolutionary linguistics take frequency to play a fundamental part in language use and change; they are accordingly entirely compatible in this point. Last, the amount of psycho- and neuro-linguistic research compatible with constructionist, usage-based approaches that has gone into determining and detailing the cognitive factors which influence domain-general and linguistic processes is a clear benefit of using this particular framework. This is because evolutionary linguistics represents a meta-framework rather than a more concrete language-theoretic framework, subsuming a large variety of different sub-views.

In contrast to construction grammar, which was therefore used as a heuristic tool for description and analysis as well as for its theoretical underpinnings, evolutionary linguistics offers a means for explaining why certain patterns are present in a language. Presuming that they are there because they have been successful in being transmitted over time, the reasons for their success can be assessed in a much more analytic (rather than hermeneutic) way. This adds to the explanatory value of evolutionary linguistics as a framework and constitutes its major advantage over other approaches. Moreover, a distinct benefit of taking an evolutionary perspective is that it enables us to focus on the development of individual constructions or replicators without disregarding the constructional context of these patterns. In other words, surrounding, related constructions can be taken into account as part of the selective environment which determines the fitness of specific replicators. That way, constructions are not dealt with in isolation, but at the same time, we are to some extent saved from dealing with the complexity that is inherent to all language change. For instance, the success of double object constructions clearly depends on a variety of issues including the salience of case marking. Rather than attempting to account for the loss of case marking in general and treating the development of the DOC as part of this larger change, however, taking such a perspective allows us to assess the selective fitness of the DOC against the background of systemic, larger-scale changes at play. By drawing on concepts well-known from biology such as co-evolution and mutualism/cooperation, the interdependency of constructions and changes affecting them can be explained in a potentially more enlightening way.

An additional advantage in adopting an evolutionary view lies in the distinction between language systems and language strategies. While the former would correspond to (parts of) the constructional network as usually dealt with, the latter refers to strategies emerging from the collective behaviour of a speaker population without a cognitive basis. Like constructional variants, strategies are subject to linguistic selection as well, are influenced by the same factors, and are furthermore influenced by changes on the level of systems. Including this distinction in treatments of historical language change e.g. in English is interesting for two reasons: First, larger-scale changes such as the loss of case marking or the rise of prepositional patterns, potentially triggered by accumulations of smaller changes in the systems and spread through alignment in a population, can be addressed more realistically, without necessarily positing highly abstract strategy-like constructions in the minds of individual speakers. Second, even though not applied in the present study, adding a level of analysis by drawing on the concept of language strategies is useful for typological studies in that the strategies employed can be compared without having to concern oneself with the particular features of the systems maintained by the strategies.

Lastly, the benefit of evolutionary linguistics in introducing innovative tools and methodologies to historical linguistics was demonstrated in this study by a game theoretic model of certain issues in the history of ditransitives in English. This exploration of new tools also represents one of the main merits of the present book. Another is its innovative theoretical approach to issues in language change, and in particular to the diachrony of ditransitives in English in combining construction grammar and evolutionary linguistics. Concerning more concrete results on the specific issue of ditransitives, this study has proven to be more encompassing and therefore hopefully also more insightful than what has been presented so far. More precisely, by incorporating non-prototypical case frames and the entire range of prepositional (and other) paraphrases instead of focussing on the *to*-PRC, as well as paying attention to word order changes in the whole clause, the present book has aimed to provide a more conclusive picture of the processes at play in the history of the dative alternation. The chief contributions of this book are accordingly its theoretical grounding and its use of novel methodologies in addition to more established ones, by which it has provided a new perspective on the development of the dative alternation in English. Nonetheless, there have also been several limitations to the book, which could be remedied in future research. These are briefly discussed in the following section.

8.3 Open issues and possible directions for further research

There are two basic areas where I see a clear need for further research concerning the topics brought up in this book; the first is of a more methodological nature, while the second relates to theoretical implications and a need for further refinement.

As to the former, I believe that this book has yielded new insights into the as yet somewhat understudied history of ditransitives in English, and has put provided a firmer empirical basis for discussions of this issue. Still, it is evident that newer tools of analysis in (historical) corpus linguistics as well as more elaborate means of mathematical modelling have not been employed. A number of issues have also been dealt with in a rather speculative manner. For example, what has become clear is that even though Middle English certainly represents an important and highly remarkable period in the development of the structures in question, the changes within this time span cannot be adequately discussed without looking more closely at Old English. This is especially so because many of the changes visible in Middle English – such as the loss of case marking – can be assumed to have started well before that period or are at least highly dependent on the earlier situation. Above all, this concerns less prototypical ditransitive case frames such as [ACC-ACC] or [DAT-GEN], whose frequency distribution would be of great interest. Correspondingly, we know little about the distribution and precise formal and functional features of Old English prepositional competitors *not* involving *to*, e.g. *from-* or *of*-paraphrases (as well as PTC periphrases) of dispossession-DOCs, as well as PTCs or possessive patterns.

At the same time, it has been seen in the discussion above that several changes appear to have been only in progress, but far from completion during Middle English, meaning that an expansion of this research to cover Early Modern English or even later stages of the language would be beneficial. A special case in point is the establishment of the benefactive alternation, which is remarkably absent from Middle English, but definitely present in PDE – the emergence of this association is therefore likely located at some point in Early Modern English. An investigation of this issue could then possibly also help to unearth the reasons for this split in alternations, i.e. the fact that verbs of creation pattern together with a different (non-*to*) PRC despite still being used in the DOC.

Regardless of specific period, a more encompassing investigation of the network of ditransitive patterns is needed and would surely yield new insights. That is, following the assumption that constructions do not exist in isolation, but are always connected to a whole range of other constructions, I would certainly support a survey including all kinds of three-place predicate structures (cf. e.g. Mukherjee 2005). As has been seen, limiting the data in the way done in the present study e.g. prevents the detection of possible productivity asymmetries between different constructions (such as the DOC and the *to*-PRC; cf. Perek 2015). Similarly, the here excluded passives would clearly be important especially in regard to word order discussions. Closely connected to the question of the development impersonal or experiencer constructions, investigating passive ditransitives could possibly shed new light on the question of the emergence of prototypical 'subject' and 'object' slots/categories in the history of English (cf. Allen 1995). Finally, it appears that the diachrony of prepositional phrases, and their competition with NP-patterns, has not been dealt with empirically in more detail (except for the case of prepositional and phrasal verbs). Considering that PP-complements of various types constitute an integral part of the PDE language, such an undertaking would certainly be beneficial.

Last, what I have only very superficially addressed in this book is the influence of language contact on the various changes in question. While I would claim that the development of ditransitives in English can plausibly be explained by drawing on internal factors only, it can nevertheless not be denied that impact from Scandinavian or French may well have played a role. Even if contact between English and other languages did not constitute the ultimate trigger of the changes observed, it is still (more than) possible that a reinforcing effect could have been produced by it. A related matter is that of regional and social variation, which I have hardly dealt with. It is clear that much of what has been proposed in this book represents a simplification and generalisation over socio-linguistically very distinct situations. A good case in point is e.g. the retention of [TH-REC] orders in the DOC in some varieties of British English; since I have been largely concerned with change towards a standard, this issue (among others) has received little attention (but see Gerwin 2014).

On a more theoretical level, a refinement of what an integrated framework of construction grammar and evolutionary linguistics entails is still needed. Tying in with this, I have not been discussed the role of various types of factors influencing the success of variants, as well as of domain-general processes such as chunking or categorisation in adequate detail and with sufficient systematicity in this book. Even so, I hope to have shown here that taking an evolutionary approach to language change, combined with construction grammar principles, can be of advantage to the discipline. In general, I am optimistic that the present book has raised interesting issues and has come forward with plausible and fruitful suggestions. I look forward to 'cooperative' (rather than 'competitive') discussions on the many questions that remain.

References

Ackema, Peter & Ad Neeleman. 2010. *Beyond morphology*. Oxford: OUP.

Akimoto, Minoji. 1995. Grammaticalization and idiomatization. In Mava Powell (ed.), *The twenty–first LACUS forum 1994*, 583–590. Chapel Hill(NC): LACUS.

Akimoto, Minoji & Laurel Brinton. 1999. The origin of the composite predicate in Old English. In Laurel Brinton & Minoji Akimoto (eds.), *Collocational and idiomatic aspects of complex predicates in the history of English*, 21–58. Amsterdam: Benjamins.

Alcorn, Rhona. 2011. Pronouns, prepositions and probabilities: A multivariate study of Old English word order. Edinburgh: University of Edinburgh Ph.D. dissertation.

Allen, Cynthia. 1995. Case marking and reanalysis: Grammatical relations from Old to Early Modern English. Oxford: OUP.

Allen, Cynthia. 2003. Deflexion and the development of the genitive in English. *English Language and Linguistics* 7 (1). 1–28.

Allen, Cynthia. 2005. Changes in case marking in NP: From Old English to Middle English. In Mengistu Amberber & Helen de Hoop (eds.), *Competition and variation in natural languages: The case for case*, 223–249. Amsterdam: Elsevier.

Allen, Cynthia. 2006. Case syncretism and word order change. In Ans van Kemenade & Bettelou Los (eds.), *The handbook of the history of English*, 201–223. Malden, MA: Blackwell.

Allen, Cynthia. 2009. On the disappearance of genitive types in Middle English: Objective genitives with nouns of love and fear and the nature of syntactic change. In Monique Dufresne, Fernande Dupuis & Etleva Vocaj (eds.), *Historical linguistics 2007: Selected papers from the 18th International Conference on Historical Linguistics, Montreal, 6–11 August 2007*, 49–60. Amsterdam: Benjamins.

Allerton, David. 1978. Generating indirect objects in English. *Journal of Linguistics* 14 (1). 21–33.

Altenberg, Bengt. 1982. The genitive vs. the of-construction. A study of syntactic variation in 17th century English. Malmö: CWK Gleerup.

Ambridge, Ben & Elena Lieven. 2011. Child language acquisition: Contrasting theoretical approaches. Cambridge: CUP.

Ambridge, Ben, Julian Pine, Caroline Rowland, Rebecca Jones & Victoria Clark. 2009. A semantics-based approach to the 'no negative evidence' problem. *Cognitive Science* 33 (7). 1301–1316.

Anderson, John. 1988. The type of Old English impersonals. In John Anderson & Norman Macleod (eds.), *Edinburgh studies in the English language*, 1–32. Edinburgh: John Donald.

Anthony, Laurence. 2014. *AntConc (Version 3.4.3)* [Computer Software]. Tokyo: Waseda University. http://www.laurenceanthony.net/software/antconc/ (accessed 18 April 2019).

Anttila, Raimo. 2003. Analogy: The warp and woof of cognition. In Brian Joseph & Richard Janda (eds.), *The handbook of historical linguistics*, 435–440. Oxford: Blackwell.

Arbib, Michael. 2012. Mirror systems: Evolving imitation and the bridge from praxis to language. In Maggie Tallerman & Kathleen Gibson (eds.), *The Oxford handbook of language evolution*, 207–2015. Oxford: OUP.

Arnold, Jennifer, Thomas Wasow, Anthony Losoncgo & Ryan Ginstrom. 2000. Heaviness vs. newness: The effects of structural complexity and discourse status on constituent ordering. *Language* 76. 28–55.

https://doi.org/10.1515/9783110633856-009

Arndt-Lappe, Sabine. 2014. Synchronic and diachronic analogy in suffix rivalry: The case of *-ity* and *-ness* in English. *English Language and Linguistics* 18. 497–548.

Arppe, Antti, Gaëtanelle Gilquin, Dylan Glynn, Martin Hilpert & Arne Zeschel. 2010. Cognitive Corpus Linguistics: Five points of debate on current theory and methodology. *Corpora* 5 (1). 1–27.

Atkinson, Quentin D. & Russell Gray. 2005. Curious parallels and curious connection: Phylogenetic thinking in biology and historical linguistics. *Systematic Biology* 54. 513–526.

Aunger, Robert. 2002. *The electric meme: A new theory of how we think*. New York, NY: Free Press.

Baayen, Harald. 1993. On frequency, transparency, and productivity. In Geert Booij & Jaap van Marle (eds.), *Yearbook of morphology 1992*, 181–208. Dordrecht: Kluwer.

Baayen, Harald. 2009. Corpus linguistics in morphology: morphological productivity. In Anke Lüdeling & Merja Kytö (eds.), *Corpus Linguistics: An international handbook*, 900–919. Berlin: Mouton De Gruyter.

Baayen, Harald & Rochelle Lieber. 1991. Productivity and English derivation: A corpus-based study. *Linguistics* 29 (5). 801–844.

Bacquet, Paul. 1962. *La structure de la phrase verbale à l'époque Alfrédienne*. Paris: Publications de la Faculté des Lettres de l'Université de Strasbourg.

Baker, Peter. 2003-2012. The magic sheet of Old English inflections. http://faculty.virginia.edu/OldEnglish/courses/handouts/magic.pdf (accessed 18 April 2019).

Barlow, Michael & Suzanne Kemmer (eds.). 2000. *Usage based models of language*. Stanford, CA: CSLI Publications.

Barðdal, Jóhanna. 2006. Construction-specific properties of syntactic subjects in Icelandic and German. *Cognitive Linguistics* 17 (1). 39–106.

Barðdal, Jóhanna. 2007. The semantic and lexical range of the ditransitive construction in the history of (North) Germanic. *Functions of Language* 14. 9–30.

Barðdal, Jóhanna. 2008. Productivity: Evidence from case and argument structure in Icelandic. Amsterdam: Benjamins.

Barðdal, Jóhanna. 2009. The development of case in Germanic. In Jóhanna Barðdal & Shobhana Chelliah (eds.), *The role of semantic, pragmatic and discourse factors in the development of case*, 123–159. Amsterdam: Benjamins.

Barðdal, Jóhanna. 2011. Lexical vs. structural case: A false dichotomy. *Morphology* 21 (3-4). 619–659.

Barðdal, Jóhanna. 2012. Predicting the productivity of argument structure constructions. *Proceedings of the Annual Meeting of the Berkeley Linguistics Society* 32. 467–478.

Barðdal, Jóhanna & Spike Gildea. 2015. Diachronic Construction Grammar: Epistemological context, basic assumptions and historical implications. In Jóhanna Barðdal, Elena Smirnova, Lotte Sommerer & Spike Gildea (eds.), *Diachronic Construction Grammar*, 1–50. Amsterdam: Benjamins.

Barðdal, Jóhanna, Kristian Kristoffersen & Andreas Sveen. 2011. West Scandinavian ditransitives as a family of constructions: With a special attention to the Norwegian V–REFL–NP construction. *Linguistics* 49 (1). 53–104.

Barðdal, Jóhanna & Leonid Kulikov. 2009. Case in decline. In Andrej Malchukov & Andrew Spencer (eds.), *The Oxford handbook of case*, 470–478. Oxford: OUP.

Barðdal, Jóhanna, Elena Smirnova, Lotte Sommerer & Spike Gildea (eds.). 2015. *Diachronic Construction Grammar*. Amsterdam: Benjamins.

Barss, Andrew & Howard Lasnik. 1986. A note on anaphora and double objects. *Linguistic Inquiry* 17. 347–354.
Bates, Elizabeth & Brian MacWhinney. 1987. Competition, variation, and language learning. In Brian MacWhinney (ed.), *Mechanisms of language acquisition*, 157–193. Hillsdale, NJ: Erlbaum.
Bauer, Laurie. 2006. Competition in English word formation. In Ans van Kemenade & Bettelou Los (eds.), *The handbook of the history of English*, 177–198. Oxford: Blackwell.
Baugh, Albert & Thomas Cable. 2002. *A history of the English language*. (5th edn.). London: Routledge.
Baxter, Gareth, Richard Blythe, William Croft & Alan McKane. 2006. Utterance selection model of linguistic change. *Physical Review* 73 (4). 046118.
Baxter, Gareth, Richard Blythe, William Croft & Alan McKane. 2009. Modeling language change: an evaluation of Trudgill's theory of the emergence of New Zealand English. *Language Variation and Change* 21 (2). 257–296.
Bech, Kristin. 2001. Word order patterns in Old and Middle English: A syntactic and pragmatic study. Bergen: University of Bergen Ph.D. dissertation.
Beckner, Clay, Nick Ellis, Richard Blythe, John Holland, Joan Bybee, Jinyun Ke, Morten Christiansen, Diane Larsen-Freeman, William Croft & Tom Schoenemann. 2009. Language is a complex adaptive system: Position paper. *Language Learning* 59 (Suppl.1). 1–26.
Beekes, Robert. 1995. Comparative Indo–European linguistics: An introduction. Amsterdam: Benjamins.
Bencini, Giulia & Adele Goldberg 2000. The contribution of argument structure constructions to sentence meaning. *Journal of Memory and Language* 43 (4). 640–651.
Benz, Anton, Gerhard Jäger & Robert van Rooij. 2006. An introduction to game theory for linguists. In Anton Benz, Gerhard Jäger & Robert van Rooij (eds.), *Game theory and pragmatics*. Houndingsmill: Palgrave Macmillan.
Berg, Thomas. 2014. Competition as a unifying concept for the study of language. *The Mental Lexicon* 9 (2). 338–370.
Bergs, Alexander & Gabriele Diewald (eds.), 2008. *Constructions and language change*. Berlin: Mouton de Gruyter.
Bernaisch, Tobias, Stefan Gries & Joybrato Mukherjee. 2014. The dative alternation in South Asian English(es): Modelling predictors and predicting prototypes. *English World–Wide* 35 (1). 7–31.
Bertacca, Antonio. 2009. Natural morphology and the loss of nominal inflections in English. Pisa: PLUS-Pisa UP.
Beuls, Katrien & Luc Steels. 2013. Agent-based models of strategies for the emergence and evolution of grammatical agreement. *PLoS ONE* 8 (3). e58960.
Biber, Douglas, Bethany Gray, Stig Johansson, Geoffrey Leech, Susan Conrad & Edward Finegan. 1999. *Longman grammar of spoken and written English*. Harlow: Pearson Education.
Bisang, Walter. 2009. On the evolution of complexity – sometimes less is more in East and mainland Southeast Asia. In Geoffrey Sampson, David Gil & Peter Trudgill (eds.), *Language complexity as an evolving variable*, 34–49. Oxford: OUP.
Blackmore, Susan. 1999. *The meme machine*. Oxford: OUP.
Blackmore, Susan. 2000. The power of memes. *Scientific American* 283. 53–61.
Blake, Barry. 2001. *Case*. (2nd edn.). Cambridge: CUP.

Blevins, Juliette. 2004. Evolutionary phonology. The emergence of sound patterns. Cambridge: CUP.

Bleys, Joris & Luc Steels. 2011. Linguistic selection of language strategies: A case study for colour. In György Kampis, István Karsai & Eörs Szathmáry (eds.), *Advances in artificial life: Darwin meets von Neumann*, 150–157. Berlin: Springer.

Blumenthal-Dramé, Alice. 2012. Entrenchment in usage-based theories: What corpus data do and do not reveal about the mind. Berlin: Mouton de Gruyter.

Blythe, Richard & William Croft. 2009. The speech community in evolutionary language dynamics. *Language Learning* 59 (Suppl.1). 47–63.

Blythe, Richard & William Croft. 2012. S-curves and the mechanisms of propagation in language change. *Language* 88. 269–304.

Boas, Hans. 2003. *A constructional approach to resultatives*. Stanford, CA: CSLI Publications.

Boas, Hans. 2008. Determining the structure of lexical entries and grammatical constructions in construction grammar. *Annual Review of Cognitive Linguistics* 6. 113–144.

Boas, Hans. 2009. *The life and death of Texas German*. Durham: Duke University Press.

Boas, Hans. 2010. The syntax-lexicon continuum in construction grammar: A case study of English communication verbs. *Belgian Journal of Linguistics* 24. 54–92.

Boas, Hans. 2011. A frame–semantic approach to syntactic alternations with *build*–verbs. In Guerrero Medina, Pilar (ed.), *Morphosyntactic alternations in English*, 207–234. London: Equinox.

Boas, Hans. 2013. Cognitive construction grammar. In Thomas Hoffmann & Graeme Trousdale (eds.), *The Oxford handbook of construction grammar*, 233–254. Oxford: OUP.

Boas, Hans. 2014. Lexical and phrasal approaches to argument structure: Two sides of the same coin. *Theoretical Linguistics* 40 (1–2). 89–112.

Bock, Kathryn. 1986. Syntactic persistence in language production. *Cognitive Psychology* 18. 355–387.

Bock, Kathryn & Zenzi Griffin. 2000. The persistence of structural priming: transient activation or implicit learning? *Journal of Experimental Psychology: General* 129 (2). 177–192.

Bock, Kathryn & David Irwin. 1980. Syntactic effects of information availability in sentence production. *Journal of Verbal Learning and Verbal Behavior* 19 (4). 467–484.

Bock, Kathryn & Helga Loebell. 1990. Framing sentences. *Cognition* 35. 1–39.

Bock, Kathryn, Helga Loebell & Randal Morey. 1992. From conceptual roles to structural relations: Bridging the syntactic cleft. *Psychological review* 99 (1). 150–171.

Boogaart, Ronny, Timothy Colleman & Gijsbert Rutten (eds.). 2014. *Extending the scope of construction grammar*. Berlin: De Gruyter Mouton.

Booij, Geert. 2002a. Constructional idioms, morphology and the Dutch lexicon. *Journal of Germanic Linguistics* 14. 301–329.

Booij, Geert. 2002b. *The morphology of Dutch*. Oxford: OUP.

Booij, Geert. 2005. Compounding and derivation: Evidence for construction morphology. In Wolfgang Dressler, Dieter Kastovsky, Oskar Pfeiffer & Franz Rainer (eds.), *Morphology and its demarcations*, 109–132. Amsterdam: Benjamins.

Booij, Geert. 2013. Morphology in construction grammar. In Thomas Hoffmann & Graeme Trousdale (eds.), *The Oxford handbook of construction grammar*, 255–273. Oxford: OUP.

Börjars, Kersti, Nigel Vincent & George Walkden. 2015. On constructing a theory of grammatical change. *Transactions of the Philological Society* 113 (3). 363–382.

Bosworth–Toller = Bosworth, Joseph. 2010. *An Anglo–Saxon dictionary online*. Edited by Toller, Thomas Northcote & others. Compiled by Christ, Sean & Ondřej Tichý. Faculty of Arts, Charles University in Prague http://bosworth.ff.cuni.cz/026836 (accessed 18 April 2019).

Bowern, Claire. 2006. Punctuated equilibrium and language change. In Keith Brown (ed.), *Encyclopedia of language and linguistics*, 286–289. Amsterdam: Elsevier.

Boyd, Jeremy & Adele Goldberg. 2011. Learning what not to say: The role of statistical preemption and categorization in *a*-adjective production. *Language* 87 (1). 55–83.

Boyd, Jeremy, Erin Gottschalk & Adele Goldberg. 2009. Linking rule acquisition in novel phrasal constructions. *Language Learning* 93 (3). 418–429.

Branigan, Holly, Martin Pickering, Janet Mclean & Andrew Stewart. 2006. The role of local and global syntactic structure in language production: Evidence from syntactic priming. *Language and Cognitive Processes* 21 (7-8). 974–1010.

Breheny, Patrick & Woodrow Burchett. 2018. R Package 'visreg': Visualization of regression models.

Bresnan, Joan. 2007. Is syntactic knowledge probabilistic? Experiments with the English dative alternation. In Sam Featherston & Wolfgang Sternefeld (eds.), *Roots: Linguistics in search of its evidential base*, 77–96. Berlin: Mouton de Gruyter.

Bresnan, Joan, Anna Cueni, Tatiana Nikitina & Harald Baayen. 2007. Predicting the dative alternation. In Gerlof Bouma, Irene Kraemer & Joost Zwarts (eds.), *Cognitive foundations of interpretation*, 69–94. Amsterdam: Royal Netherlands Academy of Science.

Bresnan, Joan & Marilyn Ford. 2010. Predicting syntax: Processing dative constructions in American and Australian varieties of English. *Language* 86 (1). 186–213.

Bresnan, Joan & Jennifer Hay. 2008. Gradient grammar: An effect of animacy on the syntax of give in New Zealand and American English. *Lingua* 118 (2). 245–259.

Bresnan, Joan & Tatiana Nikitina. 2009. The gradience of the dative alternation. In Linda Uyechi & Lian Hee Wee (eds). *Reality exploration and discovery: Pattern interaction in language and life*, 161–184. Stanford: CSLI Publications.

Brinton, Laurel & Minoji Akimoto (eds.). 1999a. Collocational and idiomatic aspects of complex predicates in the history of English. Amsterdam: Benjamins.

Brinton, Laurel & Minoji Akimoto. 1999b. Introduction. In Laurel Brinton & Minoji Akimoto (eds.), *Collocational and idiomatic aspects of complex predicates in the history of English*, 1–20. Amsterdam: Benjamins.

Brinton, Laurel & Elizabeth Traugott. 2005. *Lexicalization and language change*. Cambridge: CUP.

Brown, William. 1970. *A syntax of King Alfred's Pastoral Care*. The Hague: Mouton.

Bruckmann, Karl. 1911. Vergleichende Laut-, Stammbildungs- und Flexionslehre der Indogermanischen Sprachen, Vol. 2. (2nd edn.). Strassburg: Trübner.

Bybee, Joan. 1985. Morphology: A study of the relation between meaning and form. Amsterdam: Benjamins.

Bybee, Joan. 1995. Regular morphology and the lexicon. *Language and Cognitive Processes* 10 (5). 425–455.

Bybee, Joan. 2006. From usage to grammar: The mind's response to repetition. *Language* 82. 711–733.

Bybee, Joan. 2010. *Language, usage and cognition*. Cambridge: CUP.

Bybee, Joan. 2013. Usage-based theory and exemplar representation. In Thomas Hoffmann & Graeme Trousdale (eds.), *The Oxford handbook of construction grammar*, 49–69. Oxford: OUP.

Bybee, Joan & Clay Beckner. 2011. Usage-based theory. In Bernd Heine & Heiko Narrog (eds.), *The Oxford handbook of linguistic analysis*, 827–855. Oxford: OUP.

Bybee, Joan & Clay Beckner. 2014. Language use, cognitive processes and linguistic change. In Claire Bowern & Bethwyn Evans (eds.), *The Routledge handbook of historical linguistics*, 503–518. London: Routledge.

Bybee, Joan & David Eddington. 2006. A usage-based approach to Spanish verbs of 'becoming'. *Language* 82 (2). 323–355.

Bybee, Joan & Paul Hopper (eds.). 2001. *Frequency and the emergence of linguistic structure.* Amsterdam: Benjamins.

Bybee, Joan & James McClelland. 2005. Alternatives to the combinatorial paradigm of linguistic theory based on domain general principles of human cognition. *The Linguistic* Review 22 (2-4). 381–410.

Campbell, Aimee & Michael Tomasello. 2001. The acquisition of dative constructions. *Applied Psycholinguistics* 22. 253–267.

Campbell, Alistair. 2001. *Old English grammar*. Oxford: OUP.

Cappelle, Bert. 2006. Particle placement and the case for "allostructions". In Doris Schönefeld (ed.), *Constructions Special Volume 1– Constructions all over: Case studies and theoretical implications*.
http://www.researchgate.net/publication/31590515_Particle_placement_and_the_case_for_allostructions (accessed 18 April 2019).

Carlton, Charles. 1970. Descriptive syntax of the Old English charters. The Hague: Mouton.

Carroll, John & Michael Tanenhaus. 1975. Prolegomena to a functional theory of word formation. In Robin Grossman, Timothy Vance & James San (eds.), *Papers from the parasession on functionalism*, Chicago, IL: Chicago Linguistic Society.

Casenhiser, Devin & Adele Goldberg. 2005. Fast mapping between a phrasal form and meaning. *Developmental Science* 8 (6). 500–508.

Cassidy, Frederic. 1938. The background in Old English of the modern English substitutes for the dative-object in the group verb + dative-object +accusative-object. Ann Arbor, MA: University of Michigan Ph.D. dissertation.

Cavalli-Sforza, Luigi & Marcus Feldman. 1973. Cultural versus biological inheritance: phenotypic transmission from parents to children. *Human Genetics* 25. 618–637.

Chang, Franklin, Kathryn Bock & Adele Goldberg. 2003. Can thematic roles leave traces of their places? *Cognition* 90. 29–49.

Chang, Franklin, Gary Dell & Kathryn Bock. 2006. Becoming syntactic. *Psychological Review* 113 (2). 234–272.

Chen, Ping. 1986. Discourse and particle movement in English. *Studies in Language* 10. 79–95.

Cheshire, Jenny, Viv Edwards & Pamela Whittle. 1993. Non-standard English and dialect levelling. In James Milroy & Lesley Milroy (eds.), *Real English: The grammar of English dialects in the British Isles*, 53–95. London: Longman.

Chomsky, Noam. 1981. *Lectures on government and binding*. Dordrecht: Foris.

Chomsky, Noam. 1986. Knowledge of language: Its nature, origin and use. Westport, CT: Praeger.

Chomsky, Noam. 2000. *On nature and language*. Cambridge: CUP.

Christiansen, Morten & Nick Chater. 2008. Language as shaped by the brain. *Behavioral and Brain Sciences* 31. 489–509.

Clark, Eve. 1995. *The lexicon in acquisition*. Cambridge: CUP.

Clark, Herbert. 1996. *Using language*. Cambridge: CUP.

Clark, Herbert & Jean Fox Tree. 2002. Using *uh* and *um* in spontaneous speaking. *Cognition* 84. 73–111.

Cloak, Ted. 1975. Is a cultural ethology possible? *Human Ecology* 3. 161–182.

Colleman, Timothy. 2006. De Nederlandse datiefalternantie: Een constructioneel en corpusgebaseerd onderzoek [The dative alternation in Dutch: A constructional and corpus-based study]. Ghent: Ghent University Ph.D. dissertation.

Colleman, Timothy. 2009. The semantic range of the Dutch double object construction: A collostructional perspective. *Constructions and Frames* 1 (2). 190–221.

Colleman, Timothy. 2010a. Lectal variation in constructional semantics: Benefactive ditransitives in Dutch. In Dirk Geeraerts, Gitte Kristiansen & Yves Peirsman (eds.), *Advances in cognitive sociolinguistics*, 191–221. Berlin: Mouton de Gruyter.

Colleman, Timothy. 2010b. The benefactive semantic potential of 'caused reception' constructions: A case study of English, German, French, and Dutch. In Fernando Zúñiga & Seppo Kittilä (eds.), *Benefactives and malefactives: Typological perspectives and case studies*, 219–244. Amsterdam: Benjamins.

Colleman, Timothy. 2011. Ditransitive verbs and the ditransitive construction: A diachronic perspective. *Zeitschrift für Anglistik und Amerikanistik* 59 (4). 387–410.

Colleman, Timothy. 2015. Constructionalization and post-constructionalization: The constructional semantics of the Dutch krijgen–passive from a diachronic perspective. In Jóhanna Barðdal, Elena Smirnova, Lotte Sommerer & Spike Gildea (eds.), *Diachronic Construction Grammar*, 213–256. Amsterdam: Benjamins.

Colleman, Timothy & Bernard De Clerck. 2008. Accounting for ditransitives with *envy* and *forgive*. *Functions of Language* 15. 187–215.

Colleman, Timothy & Bernard De Clerck. 2009. 'Caused motion'? The semantics of the English *to*-dative and the Dutch *aan*-dative. *Cognitive Linguistics* 20 (1). 5–42.

Colleman, Timothy & Bernard De Clerck. 2011. Constructional semantics on the move: On semantic specialization in the English double object construction. *Cognitive Linguistics* 22 (1). 183–209.

Colleman, Timothy, Bernard De Clerck & Davos. 2010. Prepositional dative constructions in English and Dutch: A contrastive semantic analysis. *Neuphilologische Mitteilungen* 111 (2). 129–150.

Collins, Peter. 1995. The indirect object construction in English: An informational approach. *Linguistics* 33. 35–49.

Conwell, Erin & Katherine Demuth. 2007. Early syntactic productivity: Evidence from dative shift. *Cognition* 103. 163–179.

Cooper, David. 1999. Linguistic attractors: The cognitive dynamics of language acquisition and change. Amsterdam: Benjamins.

Coppock, Elizabeth. 2009. The logical and empirical foundations of Baker's paradox. Stanford, CA: Stanford University, Ph.D. dissertation. http://eecoppock.info/CoppockThesis (accessed 18 April 2019).

Cox, Robert. 2006. Coevolution. Dartmouth College Lecture (EEOB 400). www.dartmouth.edu/~robertcox/Teaching_files/lecture16.ppt (accessed 18 April 2019).

Croft, William. 1990. *Typology and universals*. Cambridge: CUP.

Croft, William. 2000. Explaining language change: An evolutionary approach. Harlow: Longman.

Croft, William. 2001. Radical construction grammar: Syntactic theory in typological perspective. Oxford: OUP.

Croft, William. 2003. Lexical rules vs. constructions: A false dichotomy. In Hubert Cuyckens, Thomas Berg, René Dirven & Klaus–Uwe Panther (eds.), *Motivation in language: Studies in honour of Guenter Radden*, 49–68. Amsterdam: Benjamins.

Croft, William. 2006a. Evolutionary models and functional-typological theories of language change. In Ans van Kemenade & Bettelou Los (eds.), *Handbook of the History of English*, 68–91. Oxford: Blackwell.

Croft, William. 2006b. The relevance of an evolutionary model to historical linguistics. In Ole Nedergård Thomsen (ed.), *Different models of linguistic change*, 91–132. Amsterdam: Benjamins.

Croft, William. 2007. Construction grammar. In Dirk Geeraerts & Hubert Cuyckens (eds.), *Handbook of cognitive linguistics*, 463–508. Oxford: OUP.

Croft, William. 2008. Evolutionary Linguistics. *Annual Review of Anthropology* 37 (1). 219–234.

Croft, William. 2009. Toward a social cognitive linguistics. In Vyvyan Evans & Stéphanie Pourcel (eds.), *New directions in cognitive linguistics*, 395–420. Amsterdam: Benjamins.

Croft, William. 2010. The origin of grammaticalization in the verbalization of experience. *Linguistics* 48. 1–48.

Croft, William. 2012. *Verbs: Aspect and causal structure*. Oxford: OUP.

Croft, William. 2013a. *Explaining language change: An evolutionary approach*. (2nd edn.). Chapter 2: An evolutionary model of language change and language structure. Oxford: OUP. http://www.unm.edu/~wcroft/Papers/ELC2-Chap02.pdf (accessed 18 April 2019).

Croft, William. 2013b. Radical Construction Grammar. In Thomas Hoffmann & Graeme Trousdale (eds.), *The Oxford handbook of construction grammar*, 211–232. Oxford: OUP.

Croft, William & Alan Cruse 2004. *Cognitive linguistics*. Cambridge: CUP.

Culicover, Peter & Ray Jackendoff. 2005. *Simpler syntax*. New York, NY: OUP.

Cuyckens, Hubert & Marjolijn Verspoor. 1998. On the road to *to*. In Johan van der Auwera, Frank Durieux & Ludo Lejeune (eds.), *English as a human language*, 57–72. Munich: Lincom.

Cziko, Gary. 1995. Without miracles. Universal selection theory and the second Darwinian revolution. Cambridge, MA: MIT Press.

Cziko, Gary. 2000. The things we do: using the lessons of Bernard and Darwin to understand the what, how, and why of our behavior. Cambridge, MA: MIT Press.

Ciszek-Kiliszewska, Ewa. 2014a. Middle English preposition and adverb *twix*. *Token: A Journal of English Linguistics* 2. 75–91.

Ciszek-Kiliszewska, Ewa. 2014b. Middle English preposition *twēn(e)*. *Studia Anglica Posnaniensia* 49 (3). 91–111.

Ciszek-Kiliszewska, Ewa. 2014c. The preposition *yeond* in Layamon's Brut. In Michael Bilynsky (ed.), *Studies in Middle English: Words, structures, senses and texts*, 135–150. Frankfurt/Main: Lang.

Ciszek-Kiliszewska, Ewa. 2015. The Middle English preposition and adverb *atwēn*. In Fabienne Toupin & Brian Lowrey (eds.), *Studies in linguistic variation and change: From Old to Middle English*, 41–63. Cambridge: Cambridge Scholars.

Dąbrowska, Ewa. 1997. *Cognitive semantics and the Polish dative*. Berlin: Mouton de Gruyter.

Damer, Edward. 2009. *Attacking faulty reasoning: A practical guide to fallacy–free arguments*. (6th edn.). Belmont, CA: Wadsworth Cengage Learning.

Daniel, Michael. 2014. Against the addressee of speech - recipient metaphor: Evidence from East Caucasian. In Silvia Luraghi & Heiko Narrog (eds.), *Perspectives on semantic roles*, 205–240. Amsterdam: Benjamins.

Darwin, Charles. 1859. On the origins of the species by means of natural selection. London: Murray.
Davidse, Kristin. 1996. Functional dimensions of the dative in English. In William van Belle & Willy van Langendonck (eds.), *The dative. Vol. 1: Descriptive studies*, 289–338. Amsterdam: Benjamins.
Davies, Mark. 2008-. *The Corpus of Contemporary American English (COCA): 560 million words, 1990-present.* https://corpus.byu.edu/coca/ (accessed 18 April 2019).
Dawkins, Richard. 1976. *The selfish gene.* Oxford: OUP.
Dawkins, Richard. 1982. *The extended phenotype.* Oxford: OUP.
Dawkins, Richard. 1986. *The blind watchmaker.* Harmondsworth: Penguin.
Dawkins, Richard. 1989[2006]. *The selfish gene.* (2nd edn., 30th anniversary edn.). Oxford: OUP.
Dawkins, Richard. 1999. Foreword to Blackmore, Susan. 1999. *The meme machine.* Oxford: OUP, vii–xvii.
Dawkins, Richard & John Krebs. 1979. Arms races between and within species. *Proceedings of the Royal society of London* 205(1161). 489–511.
De Clerck, Bernard & Timothy Colleman. 2009. Latinate verbs and restrictions on the dative/benefactive alternation: Further pieces to the puzzle. Paper presented at *ICAME* 30, Lancaster, UK, May 27–31.
De Clerck, Bernard, Martine Delorge & Anne-Marie Simon-Vandenbergen. 2011. Semantic and pragmatic motivations for constructional preferences: A corpus–based study of *provide, supply,* and *present. Journal of English Linguistics* 39. 359–391.
De Clerck, Bernard, Filip Verroens, Dominique Willems & Timothy Colleman. 2011. The syntactic flexibility of (new) verbs of instrument of communication: A corpus–based study. *Functions of Language* 18 (1). 57–86.
De Cuypere, Ludovic. 2010. The Old English double object alternation: A discourse–based account. *Sprachwissenschaft* 35. 337–68.
De Cuypere, Ludovic. 2013. Debiasing semantic analysis: The case of the English preposition *to. Language Sciences* 37. 122–135.
De Cuypere, Ludovic. 2015a. A multivariate analysis of the Old English ACC+DAT double object alternation. *Corpus Linguistics and Linguistic Theory* 11 (2). 225–254.
De Cuypere, Ludovic. 2015b. The evolution of the English dative alternation from Old to Present Day English. Paper presented at the *GLIMS workshop*, Ghent, Belgium, February 24.
De Cuypere, Ludovic. 2015c. The Old English *to*–dative construction. *English Language and Linguistics* 19 (1). 1–26.
De Cuypere, Ludovic & Saartje Verbeke. 2013. Dative alternation in Indian English: A corpus-based analysis. *World Englishes* 32 (2). 169–184.
De Smet, Hendrik. 2005. A corpus of Late Modern English. *ICAME-Journal* 29. 69–82.
De Smet, Hendrik. 2009. Analysing reanalysis. *Lingua*, 119. 1728–1755.
De Smet, Hendrik. 2010. Grammatical interference: Subject marker *for* and phrasal verb particles *out* and *forth*. In Elizabeth Traugott & Graeme Trousdale (eds.), *Gradience, gradualness, and grammaticalization*, 75–104. Amsterdam: Benjamins.
De Smet Hendrik, Frauke D'hoedt, Lauren Fonteyn & Kristel van Goethem. 2018. The changing functions of competing forms: Attraction and differentiation. *Cognitive Linguistics* 29 (2). 197–234.
Deacon, Terrence. 1997. The symbolic species: The co-evolution of language and the brain. New York, NY: Norton.

De Marneffe, Marie-Catherine, Scott Grimm, Inbal Arnon, Susannah Kirby & Joan Bresnan. 2012. A statistical model of grammatical choices in child production of datives sentences. *Language and Cognitive Processes* 27 (1). 25–61.

Denis, Derek & Sali Tagliamonte. 2017. The changing future: Competition, specialization, and reorganization in the contemporary English future temporal reference system. *English Language and Linguistics*.

Denison, David. 1993. English historical syntax: Verbal constructions. London: Longman.

Dennett, Daniel C. 1990. The interpretation of texts, people and other artefacts. *Philosophy and Phenomenological Research* 50 (Suppl.). 177–194.

Dennett, Daniel. 1991. *Consciousness explained*. Boston, MA: Back Bay Books.

Dennett, Daniel. 1993. *Consciousness explained*. Harmondsworth: Penguin.

Dennett, Daniel. 1995. Darwin's dangerous idea. Evolution and the meanings of life. New York, NY: Simon and Schuster.

Dennett, Daniel. 1999. The evolution of culture. [Charles Simonyi Lecture, Oxford University, 17 February 1999]. https://www.edge.org/documents/archive/edge52.html (accessed 18 April 2019).

Deo, Ashwini. 2015. The semantic and pragmatic underpinnings of grammaticalization paths: The progressive and the imperfective. *Semantics and Pragmatics* 8 (14). 1–52.

Dercole, Fabio & Sergio Rinaldi. 2008. Analysis of evolutionary processes: The adaptive dynamics approach and its applications. Princeton, NJ: Princeton University Press.

Deumert, Ana. 2003. Bringing speakers back in? Epistemological reflections on speaker-oriented explanations of language change. *Language Sciences* 25. 15–76.

Diessel, Holger. 2007. Frequency effects in language acquisition, language use, and diachronic change. *New Ideas in Psychology* 25. 108–127.

Diessel, Holger. 2011. Review of Joan Bybee, Language, use and cognition. *Language* 87. 830–844.

Diessel, Holger. 2013. Construction Grammar and first language acquisition. In Thomas Hoffmann & Graeme Trousdale (eds.), *The Oxford handbook of construction grammar*, 347–364. Oxford: OUP.

Diessel, Holger. 2015. Usage-based construction grammar. In Ewa Dąbrowska & Dagmar Divjak (eds.), *Handbook of cognitive linguistics*, 295–321. Berlin: Mouton de Gruyter.

Diewald, Gabriele. 2008. The catalytic function of constructional restrictions in grammaticalization. In Elisabeth Verhoeven, Stavros Skopeteas, Yong-Min Shin, Yoko Nishina & Johannes Helmbrecht (eds.), *Studies on grammaticalization*, 219–240. Berlin: de Gruyter.

Diewald, Gabriele & Elena Smirnova. 2012. Paradigmatic integration: The fourth stage in an expanded grammaticalization scenario. In Kristin Davidse, Tine Breban, Lieselotte Brems & Tanja Mortelmans (eds.), *Grammaticalization and language change: New reflections*, 111–133. Amsterdam: Benjamins.

Dixon, Robert. 1997. *The rise and fall of languages*. Cambridge: CUP.

Dodson, Kelly & Michael Tomasello. 1998. Acquiring the transitive construction in English: The role of animacy and pronouns. *Journal of Child Language* 25. 555–574.

Du Bois, John. 1985. Competing motivations. In John Haiman (ed.), *Iconicity in syntax*, 343–365. Amsterdam: Benjamins.

Du Bois, John. 2014. Motivating competitions. In Brian MacWhinney, Andrej Malchukov & Edith Moravcsik (eds.), *Competing motivations in grammar and usage*, 263–281. Oxford: OUP.

Dunn, Michael. 2014. Language phylogenies. In Claire Bowern & Bethwyn Evans (eds.), *The Routledge handbook of historical linguistics*, 190–211. London: Routledge.

Durham, William. 1991. *Coevolution: genes, culture and human diversity*. Stanford, CA: Stanford University Press.

Eddington, David & Francisco Ruiz de Mendoza Ibáñez. 2010. Argument constructions and language processing: Evidence from a priming experiment and pedagogical implications. In Sabine De Knop, Frank Boers & Antoon De Rycker (eds.), *Fostering language teaching efficiency through cognitive linguistics*, 213–238. Berlin: Mouton de Gruyter.

Edelman, Gerald & Joseph Gally. 2001. Degeneracy and complexity in biological systems. *PNAS* 98(24). 13763–13768.

Ehrlich, Paul & Peter Raven. 1964. Butterflies and plants: A study in coevolution. *Evolution* 18 (4). 586–608.

Eldredge, Niles & Stephen Gould. 1972. Punctuated equilibria: An alternative to phyletic gradualism. In Thomas Schopf (ed.), *Models in paleobiology*, 82–115. San Francisco, CA: Freeman Cooper.

Ellis, Nick. 2002. Frequency effects in language processing: A review with implications for theories of implicit and explicit language acquisition. *Studies in Second Language Acquisition* 24(2). 143–188.

Ellis, Nick. 2013. Construction grammar and second language acquisition. In Thomas Hoffmann & Graeme Trousdale (eds.), *The Oxford handbook of construction grammar*, 365–378. Oxford: OUP.

Elsness, Johan. 1984. *That* or zero? A look at the choice of object clause connective in a corpus of American English. *English Studies 65*. 519–533.

Emonds, Joseph. 1976. A transformational approach to English syntax: Root, structure-preserving, and local transformations. New York, NY: Academic Press.

Emonds, Joseph. 1993. Projecting indirect objects. *The Linguistic Review* 10 (3). 211–263.

Ernst, Thomas. 2002. *The syntax of adjuncts*. Cambridge: CUP.

Erteschik-Shir, Nomi. 1979. Discourse constraints on dative movement. In Talmy Givón (ed.), *Syntax and semantics*, 441–467. New York, NY: Academic Press.

Evans, Nicholas. 2007. Insubordination and its uses. In Irina Nikolaeva (ed.), *Finiteness: Theoretical and empirical foundations*, 366–431. Oxford: OUP.

Evans, Nicholas & Stephen Levinson. 2009. The myth of language universals: language diversity and its importance for cognitive science. *Behavioral and Brain Sciences* 32 (5). 429–448.

Evans, Vyvyan & Andrea Tyler. 2007. Rethinking English 'prepositions of movement': The case of *to* and *through*. In Hubert Cuyckens, Walter De Mulder & Tanja Mortelmans (eds.), *Adpositions of movement*, 247-270. Amsterdam: Benjamins.

Faulhaber, Susen. 2011. Verb valency patterns: A challenge for semantics-based accounts. Berlin: Mouton de Gruyter.

Fay, David & Anne Cutler. 1977. Malapropisms and the structure of the mental lexicon. *Linguistic Inquiry* 8. 505–520.

Fay, Nicolas, Simon Garrod, Leo Roberts & Nik Swoboda. 2010. The interactive evolution of human communication systems. *Cognitive Science* 34 (3). 351–386.

Fehér, Olga, Nikolaus Ritt & Kenny Smith. 2017. Asymmetric accommodation during interaction leads to the regularisation of linguistic variants. *PsyArXiv Preprints*.

Fehér, Olga, Elizabeth Wonnacott & Kenny Smith. 2016. Structural priming in artificial languages and the regularization of unpredictable variation. *Journal of Memory and Language* 91. 158–180.

Ferreira, Victor & Gary Dell. 2000. Effect of ambiguity and lexical availability on syntactic and lexical production. *Cognitive Psychology* 40 (4). 296–340.

Ferrer-i-Cancho, Ramon. 2015. The placement of the head that minimizes online memory: A complex systems approach. *Language Dynamics and Change* 5 (1). 114–137.

Fillmore, Charles. 1965. Indirect object constructions in English and the ordering of transformations. The Hague: Mouton.

Fillmore, Charles. 1988. The mechanisms of 'construction grammar'. *Berkeley Linguistic Society* 14. 35–55.

Fillmore, Charles. 2007. Valency issues in Framenet. In Thomas Herbst & Karin Götzz-Votteler (eds.), *Valency: Theoretical, descriptive and cognitive issues*, 129–160. Berlin: Mouton de Gruyter.

Fillmore, Charles, Paul Kay & Mary Catherine O'Connor. 1988. Regularity and idiomaticity in grammatical constructions: The case of *let alone*. *Language* 64. 501–538.

Fischer, Olga. 1992. Syntax. In Norman Blake (ed.), *The Cambridge history of the English language, Vol.* 2, 207–408. Cambridge: CUP.

Fischer, Olga. 2000. Grammaticalisation: Unidirectional, non reversable? The case of *to* before the infinitive in English. In Anette Rosenbach, Dieter Stein & Olga Fischer (eds.), *Pathways of change: Grammaticalization in English*, 149–169. Amsterdam: Benjamins.

Fischer, Olga. 2007. Morphosyntactic change: Functional and formal perspectives. Oxford: OUP.

Fischer, Olga, Ans van Kemenade, Willem Koopman & Wim van der Wurff. 2000. *The syntax of Early English*. Cambridge: CUP.

Fischer Olga & Wim van der Wurff. 2006. Syntax. In Richard Hogg & David Denison (eds.), *A history of the English language*, 109–198. Cambridge: CUP.

Fitch, Tecumseh. 2010. *The evolution of language*. Cambridge: CUP.

Foraker, Stephani, Terry Regier, Naveen Khetarpal, Amy Perfors & Joshua Tenenbaum. 2007. Indirect evidence and the poverty of the stimulus: The case of anaphoric *one*. In Danielle McNamara & Gregory Trafton (eds.), *Proceedings of the twenty-ninth annual conference of the Cognitive Science Society*, 275–280. New York, NY: Lawrence Erlbaum.

Ford, Marilyn & Joan Bresnan. 2013. 'They whispered me the answer' in Australia and the US: A comparative experimental study. In Tracy Holloway King & Valeria de Paiva (eds.), *From quirky case to representing space: Papers in honor of Annie Zaenen*, 95–107. Stanford, CA: CSLI Publications.

Francis, Elaine & Laura Michaelis. 2003. Mismatch: A crucible for linguistic theory. In Elaine Francis & Laura Michaelis (eds.), *Mismatch: Form-function incongruity and the architecture of grammar*, 1–27. Stanford, CA: CSLI Publications.

Frank, Roslyn & Nathalie Gontier. 2010. On constructing a research model for historical cognitive linguistics (HCL): some theoretical considerations. In Margaret Winters, Heli Tissari & Kathryn Allan (eds.), *Historical cognitive linguistics*, 31–69. Berlin: Mouton de Gruyter.

Fried, Mirjam. 2010. Grammar and interaction: New directions in constructional research. *Constructions and Frames* 2. 125–133.

Friedrich, Paul. 1975. Proto-Indo-European syntax: The order of meaningful elements. Butte, MT: Montana.

Fries, Charles. 1940. On the development of the structural use of word-order in Modern English. *Language* 16. 199–208.

García Velasco, Daniel. 2011. The causative/inchoative alternation in functional discourse grammar. In Pilar Guerrero Medina (ed.), *Morphosyntactic alternations in English: Functional and cognitive perspectives*, 115–136. London: Equinox.

Garrod, Simon, Nicolas Fay, John Lee, Jon Oberlander & Tracy McLeod. 2007. Foundations of representation: Where might graphical symbol systems come from?. *Cognitive Science* 31 (6). 961–987.

Gaskell, Gareth & William Marslen-Wilson. 2002. Representation and competition in the perception of spoken words. *Cognitive Psychology* 45 (2). 220–266.

Gast, Volker. 2007. *I gave it him* – on the motivation of the 'alternative double object construction' in varieties of British English. *Functions of Language* 14(1). 31–56.

Geeraerts, Dirk. 1997. Diachronic prototype semantics: A contribution to historical lexicology. Oxford: Clarendon.

Geeraerts, Dirk. 1998. The semantic structure of the indirect object in Dutch. In Willy van Langendonck & William van Belle (eds.), *The Dative. Vol. 2: Theoretical and contrastive studies*, 185–210. Amsterdam: Benjamins.

Gell-Mann, Murray. 1994. *The quark and the jaguar*. New York, NY: Freeman.

Gerwin, Johanna. 2013. *Give it me*! Pronominal ditransitives in English dialects. *English Language and Linguistics* 17 (3). 445–463.

Gerwin, Johanna. 2014. *Ditransitives in British English dialects*. Berlin: De Gruyter Mouton.

Gisborne, Nikolas & Amanda Patten. 2011. Construction grammar and grammaticalization. In Heiko Narrog & Bernd Heine (eds.), *The Oxford handbook of grammaticalization*, 92–104. Oxford: OUP.

Givón, Talmy. 1984. Syntax. A functional-typological introduction, Vol. 1. Amsterdam: Benjamins.

Givón, Talmy. 2002. *Bio-linguistics. The Santa Barbara lectures*. Amsterdam: Benjamins.

Glossary Old English Aerobics = Baker, Peter. 2003-2012. Supplementary online material to Baker, Peter. 2012. *Introduction to Old English*. (3rd edn.). Hoboken, NJ: Wiley–Blackwell. http://glossary.oldenglishaerobics.net/ (accessed 18 April 2019).

Goldberg, Adele. 1992. The inherent semantics of argument structure: The case of the English ditransitive construction. *Cognitive Linguistics* 3 (1). 37–74.

Goldberg, Adele. 1995. Constructions: A construction grammar approach to argument structure. Chicago: University of Chicago Press.

Goldberg, Adele. 1999. The emergence of argument structure semantics. In Brian MacWhinney (ed.), *The emergence of language*, 197–212. Mahwah, NJ: Lawrence Erlbaum.

Goldberg, Adele. 2002. Surface generalizations: An alternative to alternations. *Cognitive Linguistics* 13 (4). 327–356.

Goldberg, Adele. 2003. Constructions: A new theoretical approach to language. *Trends in Cognitive Science* 7 (5). 219–224.

Goldberg, Adele. 2006. Constructions at work: The nature of generalization in language. Oxford: OUP.

Goldberg, Adele. 2011. Corpus evidence of the viability of statistical preemption. *Cognitive Linguistics* 22 (1). 131–153.

Goldberg, Adele. 2013. Constructionist approaches to language. In Thomas Hoffmann & Graeme Trousdale (eds.), *The Oxford handbook of construction grammar*, 15–31. Oxford: OUP.

Goldberg, Adele. 2014. Fitting a slim dime between the verb template and argument structure construction approaches. *Theoretical Linguistics* 40 (1–2). 113–135.

Goldberg, Adele, Devin Casenhiser & Nitya Sethuraman. 2004. Learning argument structure generalizations. *Cognitive Linguistics* 14 (3). 289–316.

Goldsmith, John. 1980. Meaning and mechanism in language. In Susumo Kuno (ed.), *Harvard studies in syntax and semantics, Vol. 3*, 423–449. Cambridge, MA: Harvard UP.

Goldwater, Micah, Marc Tomlinson, Catharine Echols & Bradley Love. 2011. Structural priming as structure-mapping: Children use analogies from previous utterances to guide sentence production. *Cognitive Science* 35. 156–170.

Gould, Stephen. 1983. Hen's teeth and horse's toes: Further reflections in natural history. New York, NY: Norton.

Gould, Stephen. 1989. Wonderful life: The Burgess Shale and the nature of history. New York, NY: Norton.

Gould, Stephen & Elizabeth Vrba. 1982. Exaptation – a missing term in the science of form. *Paleobiology* 8 (1). 4–15.

Green, Georgia. 1974. *Semantics and syntactic regularity*. Bloomington, IN: Indiana University Press.

Gries, Stefan. 1999. Particle movement: A cognitive and functional approach. *Cognitive Linguistics* 10. 105–145.

Gries, Stefan. 2003. Multifactorial analysis in corpus linguistics: A study of particle placement. London: Continuum Press.

Gries, Stefan. 2005. Syntactic priming: A corpus-based approach. *Journal of Psycholinguistic Research* 34 (4). 365–399.

Gries, Stefan. 2009. Statistics for linguistics with R: A practical introduction. Berlin: De Gruyter Mouton.

Gries, Stefan. 2010. Useful statistics for corpus linguistics. In Aquilino Sánchez & Moisés Almela (eds.), *A mosaic of corpus linguistics: Selected approaches*, 269–291. Frankfurt/Main: Lang.

Gries, Stefan. 2012. Frequencies, probabilities, and association measures in usage- / exemplar-based linguistics: Some necessary clarifications. *Studies in Language* 11 (3). 477–510.

Gries, Stefan. 2014. Coll.analysis 3.5. A script for R to compute perform collostructional analyses.

Gries, Stefan & Martin Hilpert. 2008. The identification of stages in diachronic data: Variability-based neighbor clustering. *Corpora* 3 (1). 59–81.

Gries, Stefan & Martin Hilpert. 2010. Modeling diachronic change in the third person singular: A multi-factorial, verb- and author-specific exploratory approach. *English Language and Linguistics* 14 (3). 293–320.

Gries, Stefan & Anatol Stefanowitsch. 2004. Extending collostructional analysis: A corpus-based perspective on 'alternations'. *International Journal of Corpus Linguistics* 9 (1). 97–129.

Gries, Stefan & Stefanie Wulff. 2005. Do foreign language learners also have constructions? Evidence from priming, sorting, and corpora. *Annual Review of Cognitive Linguistics* 3. 182–200.

Gries, Stefan & Stefanie Wulff. 2009. Psycholinguistic and corpus linguistic evidence for L2 constructions. *Annual Review of Cognitive Linguistics* 7. 163–186.

Grondelaers, Stefan, Dirk Speelman & Dirk Geeraerts. 2007. Lexical variation and change. In Dirk Geeraerts & Hubert Cuyckens (eds.), *The Oxford handbook of cognitive linguistics*, 988–1011. Oxford: OUP.

Gropen, Jess, Steven Pinker, Michelle Hollander, Richard Goldberg & Ronald Wilson. 1989. The learnability and acquisition of the dative alternation in English. *Language* 65. 205–257.

Haeberli, Eric. 2000. Adjuncts and the syntax of subjects in Old and Middle English. In Susan Pintzuk, George Tsoulas & Anthony Warner (eds.), *Diachronic syntax: Models and mechanisms*, 109–131. Oxford: OUP.

Hagège, Claude. 2010. *Adpositions*. Oxford: OUP.

Halliday, Michael. 1970. Language structure and language function. In John Lyons (ed.), *New horizons in linguistics*, 140–165. Harmondsworth: Penguin.

Harbert, Wayne. 2007. *The Germanic languages*. Cambridge: CUP.

Harley, Heidi. 2002. Possession and the double object construction. *Yearbook of Linguistic Variation* 2. 29–68.

Harley, Heidi. 2007. The bipartite structure of verbs cross–linguistically, or Why Mary can't 'exhibit John her paintings'. (unpublished ms.). http://ling.auf.net/lingbuzz/000435 (accessed 18 April 2019).

Harrell, Frank. 2018. R Package rms: Regression modeling strategies.

Harris, Alice & Lyle Campbell. 1995. *Historical syntax in cross-linguistic perspective*. Cambridge: CUP.

Hartsuiker, Robert, Martin Pickering & Eline Veltkamp. 2004. Is syntax separate or shared between languages? Cross-linguistic syntactic priming in Spanish-English bilinguals. *Psychological Science* 15. 409–414.

Haselow, Alexander. 2011. Typological changes in the lexicon: Analytic tendencies in English noun formation. Berlin: De Gruyter Mouton.

Haspelmath, Martin. 1999. Optimality and diachronic adaptation. *Zeitschrift für Sprachwissenschaft* 18 (2). 180–205.

Haspelmath, Martin. 2000. The relevance of extravagance: A reply to Bart Geurts. *Linguistics* 38 (4). 789–798.

Haspelmath, Martin. 2003. The geometry of grammatical meaning: Semantic maps and cross-linguistic comparison. In Michael Tomasello (ed.), *The new psychology of language, Vol. 2*, 211–43. New York, NY: Lawrence Erlbaum.

Haspelmath, Martin. 2006. *Ditransitive constructions in the world's languages*. Leipzig spring school on linguistic diversity. http://email.eva.mpg.de/~haspelmt/DitrLSSLD.pdf (accessed 18 April 2019).

Haspelmath, Martin. 2008. Parametric versus functional explanations of syntactic universals. In Theresa Biberauer (ed.), *The limits of syntactic variation*, 75–107. Amsterdam: Benjamins.

Haspelmath, Martin. 2015. Ditransitive constructions. *Annual Review of Linguistics* 1. 19–41.

Hauser, Marc, Noam Chomsky & Tecumseh Fitch. 2002. The language faculty: What is it, who has it, and how did it evolve? *Science* 298. 1569–1579.

Hawkins, John A. 1983. *Word order universals*. London: Academic Press.

Hawkins, John A. 1992. Syntactic weight versus information structure in word order variation. *Linguistische Berichte* (Special Issue) 4. 196–219.

Hawkins, John A. 1994. A performance theory of order and constituency. Cambridge: CUP.

Hawkins, John A. 2014. Patterns in competing motivations and the interaction of principles. In Brian MacWhinney, Andrej Malchukov & Edith Moravcsik (eds.), *Competing motivations in grammar and usage*, 54–69. Oxford: OUP.

Hawkins, John A. & Murray Gell-Mann (ed.). 1992. *The evolution of human languages*. Redwood City, CA: Addison Wesley.

Hay, Jennifer & Joan Bresnan. 2006. Spoken syntax: The phonetics of *giving a hand* in New Zealand English. *Linguistic Review* 23. 321–349.
Hebb, Donald. 1949. *The organization of behavior*. New York, NY: Wiley & Sons.
Heine, Bernd. 1994. Grammaticalization as an explanatory parameter. In William Pagliuca (ed.), *Perspectives on grammaticalization*, 255–287. Amsterdam: Benjamins.
Heine, Bernd & Christa König. 2010. On the linear order of ditransitive objects. *Language Sciences* 32. 87–131.
Heine, Bernd & Tania Kuteva. 2002. *World lexicon of grammaticalization*. Cambridge: CUP.
Herbst, Thomas. 2011. The status of generalizations: Valency and argument structure constructions. *Zeitschrift für Anglistik und Amerikanistik* 59 (4). 331–346.
Herriman, Jennifer. 1995. *The indirect object in Present-Day English*. Goeteborg: Acta Universitatis Gothoburgensis.
Hilpert, Martin. 2006. Distinctive collexeme analysis and diachrony. *Corpus Linguistics and Linguistic Theory* 2 (2). 243–257.
Hilpert, Martin. 2008. Germanic future constructions: A usage-based approach to language change. Amsterdam: Benjamins.
Hilpert, Martin. 2011. Dynamic visualizations of language change: Motion charts on the basis of bivariate and multivariate data from diachronic corpora. *International Journal of Corpus Linguistics* 16 (4). 435–461.
Hilpert, Martin. 2013. *Constructional change in English*. Cambridge: CUP.
Hilpert, Martin. 2014. Construction Grammar and its application to English. Edinburgh: EUP.
Hilpert, Martin. 2018. Three open questions in Diachronic Construction Grammar. In Evie Coussé, Peter Andersson & Joel Olofsson (eds.), *Grammaticalization meets Construction Grammar*, 21–39. Amsterdam: Benjamins.
Hilpert, Martin & Stefan Gries 2009. Assessing frequency changes in multi–stage diachronic corpora: Applications for historical corpus linguistics and the study of language acquisition. *Literary and Linguistic Computing* 24 (4). 385–401.
Hinterhölzl, Ronald & Ans van Kemenade. 2012. The interaction between syntax, information structure and prosody in word order change. In Terttu Nevalainen & Elizabeth Traugott (eds.), *The Oxford handbook of the history of English*, 803–821. Oxford: OUP.
Hirt, Hermann. 1927. *Indogermanische Grammatik. Vol. 3: Das Nomen*. Heidelberg: Carl Winter.
Hock, Hans-Heinrich. 1982. Aux-cliticizationas a motivation for word order change. *Studies in the Linguistic Sciences* 12. 91–101.
Hock, Hans-Heinrich. 1986. *Principles of historical linguistics*. Berlin: Mouton de Gruyter.
Hock, Hans-Heinrich. 2003. Analogical change. In Brian Joseph & Richard Janda (eds.), *The handbook of historical linguistics*, 441–460. Oxford: Blackwell.
Höder, Steffen. 2016. Phonological elements and Diasystematic Construction Grammar. In Martin Hilpert & Jan-Ola Östman (eds.), *Constructions across grammars*, 67–96. Amsterdam: Benjamins.
Hofbauer, Josef & Karl Sigmund. 1998. *Evolutionary games and population dynamics*. Cambridge: CUP.
Hofbauer, Joseph & Karl Sigmund. 2003. Evolutionary game dynamics. *Bulletin of the American Mathematical Society* 40 (4). 479–519.
Hoffmann, Sebastian. 2005. Grammaticalization and English complex prepositions: A corpus-based study. Abingdon: Routledge.

Hoffmann, Sebastian & Joybrato Mukherjee. 2007. Ditransitive verbs in Indian English and British English: A corpus-linguistic study. *Arbeiten aus Anglistik und Amerikanistik* 32 (1). 5–24.

Hoffmann, Thomas. 2005. Variable vs. categorical effects: Preposition pied piping and stranding in British English relative clauses. *Journal of English Linguistics* 33 (3). 257–297.

Hoffmann, Thomas. 2007. Complements versus adjuncts? A construction grammar account of English prepositional phrases. *Occasional Papers in Language and Linguistics (University of Nairobi)* 3. 92–119.

Hoffmann, Thomas. 2011. Preposition placement in English: A usage-based approach. Cambridge: CUP.

Hoffmann, Thomas. 2013. Abstract phrasal and clausal constructions. In Thomas Hoffmann & Graeme Trousdale (eds.), *The Oxford handbook of construction grammar*, 307–328. Oxford: OUP.

Hoffmann, Thomas & Graeme Trousdale. 2011. Variation, change and constructions in English. *Cognitive Linguistics* 22 (1). 1–23.

Hoffmann, Thomas & Graeme Trousdale. 2013. Introduction. In Thomas Hoffmann & Graeme Trousdale (eds.), *The Oxford handbook of construction grammar*, 1–14. Oxford: OUP.

Hogg, Richard. 2002. *An introduction to Old English*. Edinburgh: EUP.

Hopper, Paul. 1987. Emergent grammar. In Jon Aske, Natasha Berry, Laura Michaelis & Hana Filip (eds.), *Berkeley Linguistics Society 13: General session and parasession on grammar and cognition*, 139–157. Berkeley, CA: Berkeley Linguistics Society.

Hopper, Paul. 1991. On some principles of grammaticization. In Elizabeth Traugott & Bernd Heine (eds.), *Approaches to grammaticalization. Vol. 1: Theoretical and methodological issues*, 17–36. Amsterdam: Benjamins.

Hopper, Paul & Sandra Thompson. 1980. Transitivity in grammar and discourse. *Language* 56 (2). 251–299.

Hopper, Paul & Elizabeth Traugott. 2003. *Grammaticalization*. (2nd edn.). Cambridge: CUP.

Horn, Wilhelm. 1921. *Sprachkoerper und Sprachfunktion im Englischen*. Berlin: Mayer & Mueller.

Hosmer, David & Stanley Lemeshow. 2000. *Applied logistic regression*. New York, NY: Wiley.

Hruschka, Daniel, Morten Christiansen, Richard Blythe, William Croft, Paul Heggarty, Salikoko Mufwene, Janet Pierrehumbert & Shana Poplack. 2009. Building social cognitive models of language change. *Trends in Cognitive Sciences* 13 (11). 464–469.

Huddleston, Rodney & Geoffrey Pullum. 2002. *The Cambridge grammar of the English language*. Cambridge: CUP.

Huchon, René. 1923. *Histoire de la langue anglaise: Tome 1*. Paris: Armand Colin.

Hudson, Richard. 1990. English word grammar. Hoboken, NJ: Wiley-Blackwell.

Hudson, Richard. 1992. So-called 'double objects' and grammatical relations. *Language* 68. 251–276.

Hudson, Richard. 2010. *An introduction to word grammar*. Cambridge: CUP.

Hughes, Arthur & Peter Trudgill. 1996. English accents and dialects: An introduction to social and regional varieties of English in the British Isles. (3rd edn.). London: Arnold.

Hughes, Arthur, Peter Trudgill & Dominic Watt. 2012. English accents and dialects: An introduction to social and regional varieties of English in the British Isles. (5th edn.). London: Routledge.

Hull, David. 1988. Science as progress: An evolutionary account of the social and conceptual development of science. Chicago, IL: University of Chicago Press.

Hull, David. 2001. Taking memetics seriously: Memetics will be what we make it. In Robert Aunger (ed.), *Darwinizing culture*, 43–67. Oxford: OUP.

Hundt, Markus. 2001. Grammatikalisierungsphänomene bei Präpositionalobjekten in der deutschen Sprache. *Zeitschrift für germanistische Linguistik* 29 (2). 167–191.

Hundt, Marianne & Eva Zehentner. 2018. Prepositions in Early Modern English argument structure. Paper presented at the 20th *International Conference on English Historical Linguistics* (ICEHL), Edinburgh, UK, August 27.

Hunston, Susan & Gillian Francis. 2000. Pattern grammar: A corpus-driven approach to the lexical grammar of English. Amsterdam: Benjamins.

Hurford , James. 2007. The origins of meaning: Language in the light of evolution I. Oxford: OUP.

Hurford, James. 2012a. Linguistics from an evolutionary point of view. In Ruth Kempson, Tim Fernando & Nicholas Asher (eds.), *Handbook of the philosophy of science: Linguistics*, 473–498. Burlington: Elsevier.

Hurford, James. 2012b. The origins of grammar: Language in the light of evolution II. Oxford: OUP.

Hurford, James. 2014. *Origins of language: A slim guide*. Oxford: OUP.

Iglesias-Rábade, Luis. 2011. *Semantic erosion of Middle English prepositions*. Frankfurt/Main: Lang.

Ingham, Richard. subm. The Middle English prepositional dative: Grammaticalisation and contact with French. In Melanie Roethlisberger, Eva Zehentner & Timothy Colleman (eds.), *Ditransitive constructions in Germanic languages: Synchronic and diachronic aspects*. [Studies in Germanic Linguistics]. Amsterdam: Benjamins.

Israel, Michael. 1996. The *way* constructions grow. In Adele Goldberg (ed.), *Conceptual structure, discourse and language*, 217–230. Stanford, CA: CSLI Publications.

Iwata, Seizi. 2005. The role of verb meaning in locative alternations. In Mirjam Fried & Hans C. Boas (eds.), *Grammatical constructions: Back to the roots*, 101–118. Amsterdam: Benjamins.

Iwata, Seizi. 2008. Locative alternation: A lexical–constructional approach. Amsterdam: Benjamins.

Jackendoff, Ray. 1990. *Semantic structures*. Cambridge, MA: MIT Press.

Jackendoff, Ray & Steven Pinker. 2005. The nature of the language faculty and its implications for evolution of language (reply to Fitch, Hauser, and Chomsky). *Cognition* 97 (2). 211–225.

Jäger, Gerhard. 2004. *Evolutionary game theory for linguists: A primer*. (unpublished manuscript). University of Tübingen. http://www.sfs.uni-tuebingen.de/~gjaeger/publications/egtPrimer.pdf (accessed 18 April 2019).

Jäger, Gerhard. 2007. Evolutionary game theory and typology: A case study. *Language* 83 (1). 74–109.

Jäger, Gerhard. 2008. Applications of game theory in linguistics. *Language and Linguistics Compass* 2 (3). 408–421.

Jäger, Gerhard & Annette Rosenbach. 2008. Priming and unidirectional language change. *Theoretical Linguistics* 34. 85–113.

Jarad, Najib Ismail. 1997. *The origin and development of* for*-infinitives*. Bangor: University of Wales Ph.D. dissertation.

Jespersen, Otto. 1927. *A modern English grammar on historical principles*. Heidelberg: Carl Winter.

Johansson, Christine. 2002. Pied piping and stranding from a diachronic perspective. In Pam Peters, Peter Collins & Adam Smith (eds.), *New frontiers of corpus research: Papers from the Twenty First International Conference on English Language Research on Computerized Corpora, Sydney 2000*, 147–162. Amsterdam: Rodopi.

Jurafsky, Daniel. 1992. An on-line computational model of human sentence interpretation. In American Association for Artificial Intelligence (eds.), *Proceedings of the national conference on artificial intelligence*, 302–308. Cambridge, MA: MIT Press.

Kaschak, Michael. 2007. Long-term structural priming affects subsequent patterns of language production. *Memory and Cognition* 35 (5). 925–937.

Kaschak, Michael, Timothy Kutta & John Jones. 2011. Structural priming as implicit learning: Cumulative priming effects and individual differences. *Psychonomic bulletin and review* 18 (6). 1133–1139.

Kaschak, Michael, Timothy Kutta & John Jones. 2014. Long and short term cumulative structural priming effects. *Language, Cognition and Neuroscience* 29 (6). 728–743.

Kay, Paul. 1996. *Argument structure: Causative ABC-constructions*. (unpublished ms.). University of California, Berkeley. http://www.icsi.berkeley.edu/~kay/bcg/5/lec05.html (accessed 18 April 2019).

Kay, Paul. 2005. Argument structure constructions and the argument-adjunct distinction. In Mirjam Fried & Hans Boas (eds.), *Grammatical constructions: Back to the roots*, 71–100. Amsterdam: Benjamins.

Kay, Paul & Charles Fillmore. 1999. Grammatical constructions and linguistic generalizations: The *What's X Doing Y?* construction. *Language* 75. 1–34.

Kaźmierski, Kamil. 2015. Vowel-shifting in the English language: An evolutionary account. Berlin: De Gruyter Mouton.

Keenan, Edwards. 1976. Towards a universal definition of 'subject.' In Charles Li (ed.), *Subject and topic*, 303–334. New York, NY: Academic Press.

Keller, Rudi. 1990[1994]. On language change: The invisible hand in language. London: Routledge.

Kemmer, Suzanne. 1992. Grammatical prototypes and competing motivations in a theory of linguistic change. In Garry Davis & Gregory Iverson (eds.), *Explanation in historical linguistics*, 145–166. Amsterdam: Benjamins.

Kemmer, Suzanne. 2003. Schemas and lexical blends. In Hubert Cuyckens, Thomas Berg, René Dirven & Klaus-Uwe Panther (eds.), *Motivation in language: Studies in honor of Günter Radden*, 69–97. Amsterdam: Benjamins.

Kendall, Tyler, Joan Bresnan & Gerard Van Herk. 2011. The dative alternation in African American English: Researching syntactic variation and change across sociolinguistic datasets. *Corpus Linguistics and Linguistic Theory* 7 (2). 229–244.

Kiparsky, 1995. The phonological basis of sound change. In John Goldsmith (ed.), *Handbook of generative phonology*, 640–670. Oxford: Blackwell.

Kirby, Simon. 1994. Adaptive explanations for language universals: a model of Hawkins' performance theory. *Sprachtypologie und Universalienforschung* 47. 186–210.

Kirby, Simon. 1999. Function, selection, and innateness. Oxford: OUP.

Kirby, Simon. 2012. Language is an adaptive system: The role of cultural evolution in the origins of structure. In Maggie Tallerman & Kathleen Gibson (eds.), *The Oxford handbook of language evolution*, 589–604. Oxford: OUP.

Kirby, Simon. 2017. Culture and biology in the origins of linguistic structure. *Psychonomic Bulletin and Review* 24 (1). 118–137.

Kirby, Simon & James Hurford. 2002. The emergence of linguistic structure: An overview of the Iterated Learning Model. In Angelo Cangelosi & Domenico Parisi (eds.), *Simulating the evolution of language*, 121–148. London: Springer.

Kirby, Simon, Tamariz, Monica, Cornish, Hannah & Smith, Kenny. 2015. Compression and communication in the cultural evolution of linguistic structure. *Cognition* 141. 87–102.

Kirk, John. 1985. Linguistic atlases and grammar: The investigation and description of regional variation in English syntax. In John Kirk, Stewart Sanderson & John Widdowson (eds.), *Studies in linguistic geography: The dialects of English in Britain and Ireland*, 130–156. London: Croom Helm.

Kittilä, Seppo. 2005. Recipient-prominence vs. beneficiary-prominence. *Linguistic Typology* 9 (2). 269–297.

Kittilä, Seppo. 2006. The anomaly of the verb 'give' explained by its high (formal and semantic) transitivity. *Linguistics* 44 (3). 569–612.

Kittilä, Seppo; Västi, Katja; Ylikoski, Jussi. 2011. Introduction to case, animacy and semantic roles. In Seppo Kittilä, Katja Västi & Jussi Ylikoski (eds.), *Case, animacy and semantic roles*, 1–26. Amsterdam: Benjamins.

Kjellmer 2000. Auxiliary marginalities: The case of *try*. In John Kirk (ed.), *Corpora galore. Analyses and techniques in describing English*, 115–124. Amsterdam: Rodopi.

Kniesza, Veronika. 1991. Prepositional phrases expressing adverbs of time from late Old English to early Middle English. In Dieter Kastovsky (ed.), *Historical English syntax*, 221–231. Berlin: Mouton de Gruyter.

Kohonen, Viljo. 1978. On the development of English word order in religious prose around 1000 and 1200 A.D.: A quantitative study of word order in context. Turku: Abo Akademi Foundation.

Koopman, Willem. 1990. *Word order in Old English*. Amsterdam: University of Amsterdam Ph.D. dissertation.

Koopman, Willem & Wim van der Wurff. 2000. Two word order patterns in the history of English: Stability, variation, change. In Rosanna Sornicola, Erich Poppe & Ariel Shisha–Halevy (eds.), *Stability, variation and change of word-order patterns over time*, 259–283. Amsterdam: Benjamins.

Krifka, Manfred. 2004. Semantic and pragmatic conditions for the dative alternation. *Korean Journal of English Language and Linguistics* 4. 1–32.

Kroch, Anthony. 1989a. Function and grammar in the history of English periphrastic *do*. In Ralph Fasold & Deborah Schiffrin (eds.), *Language change and variation*, 133–172. Amsterdam: Benjamins.

Kroch, Anthony. 1989b. Reflexes of grammar in patterns of language change. *Language Variation and Change* 1. 199–244.

Kroch, Anthony. 1994. Morphosyntactic variation. In Katharine Beals (ed.), *Proceedings of the Thirtieth Annual Meeting of the Chicago Linguistic Society, Vol. 2*, 180–201. Chicago, IL: Chicago Linguistics Society.

Kroch, Anthony & Ann Taylor. 1994. The syntax of verb movement in Middle English: Dialect variation and language contact. *University of Pennsylvania Working Papers in Linguistics* 1 (1). http://repository.upenn.edu/pwpl/vol1/iss1/4 (accessed 18 April 2019).

Kroch, Anthony & Ann Taylor. 1997. Verb movement in Old and Middle English: Dialect variation and language contact. In Ans van Kemenade & Nigel Vincent (eds.), *Parameters of morphosyntactic change*, 297–325. Cambridge: CUP.

Kroch, Anthony & Ann Taylor. 2000a. *Penn–Helsinki Parsed Corpus of Middle English, second edition*. www.ling.upenn.edu/hist–corpora/PPCME2–RELEASE–3/index.html (accessed 18 April 2019).

Kroch, Anthony & Ann Taylor. 2000b. Verb-object order in Early Middle English. In Susan Pintzuk, George Tsoulas & Anthony Warner (eds.), *Diachronic syntax: Models and mechanisms*, 132–187. Oxford: OUP.

Kroch, Anthony & Ann Taylor. 2010. Corpus description/ Philological information. http://www.ling.upenn.edu/hist–corpora/PPCME2–RELEASE–3/index.html (accessed 18 April 2019).

Kulikov, Leonid. 2009. Evolution of case systems. In Andrej Malchukov & Andrew Spencer (eds.), *The Oxford handbook of case*, 439–457. Oxford: OUP.

Kytö, Merja & Matti Rissanen. 1992. General introduction. In Matti Rissanen, Merja Kytö, Minna Palander-Collin (eds.), *Early English in the computer age: Explorations through the Helsinki Corpus*, 1–17. Berlin: Mouton de Gruyter.

Labov, William. 1972. *Sociolinguistic patterns*. Philadelphia, PA: University of Pennsylvania Press.

Labov, William. 1994. *Principle of change, internal factors*. Oxford: Blackwell.

Lacalle Palacios, Miguel. 2016. Constructions and alternations with Old English verbs of depriving. Paper presented at the 19th *International Conference on English Historical Linguistics* (ICEHL), Essen, Germany, August 22.

Laing, Margaret. 2013. *A Linguistic Atlas of Early Middle English, 1150-1325*, Version 3.2. Edinburgh: The University of Edinburgh. http://www.lel.ed.ac.uk/ihd/laeme2/laeme2.html (accessed 18 April 2019).

Lakoff, George. 1987. Women, fire and dangerous things: What categories reveal about the mind. Chicago, IL: University of Chicago Press.

Lambert, Silke. 2010. *Beyond recipients: Towards a typology of dative uses*. Buffalo, NY: The State University of New York at Buffalo Ph.D. dissertation.

Lambrecht, Knud. 1994. Information structure and sentence form: A theory of topic, focus, and the mental representations of discourse referents. Cambridge: CUP.

Langacker, Ronald. 1987. *Foundations of cognitive grammar. Vol. 1: Theoretical prerequisites*. Stanford, CA: Stanford University Press.

Langacker, Ronald. 1988. A usage-based model. In Brygida Rudzka-Ostyn (ed.), *Topics in cognitive linguistics*, 127–161. Philadelphia: Benjamins.

Langacker, Ronald. 1991. Concept, image, and symbol: The cognitive basis of grammar. Berlin: Mouton de Gruyter.

Langacker, Ronald. 1992. Prepositions as grammatical(izing) elements. *Leuvense Bijdragen* 81. 287–309.

Langacker, Ronald. 2000. A dynamic usage-based model. In Michael Barlow & Suzanne Kemmer (eds.), 2000. *Usage based models of language*, 1–63. Stanford, CA: CSLI Publications.

Langacker, Ronald. 2008. *Cognitive grammar: A basic introduction*. New York, NY: OUP.

Langacker, Ronald. 2009. Constructions and constructional meaning. In Vyvyan Evans & Stéphanie Pourcel (eds.), *New directions in cognitive linguistics*, 225–267. Amsterdam: Benjamins.

Lansing, Stephen. 2003. Complex adaptive systems. *Annual Review of Anthropology* 32. 183–204.

Lapata, Maria. 1999. Acquiring lexical generalizations from corpora: A case study for diathesis alternations. *Proceedings of the North American Chapter of the Association for Computational Linguisics* 37. 397–404.

Larson, Richard. 1988. On the double object construction. *Linguistic Inquiry* 19 (3). 335–391.

Lass, Roger. 1980. *On explaining language change*. Cambridge: CUP.

Lass, Roger. 1990. How to do things with junk: Exaptation in language evolution. *Journal of Linguistics* 26. 79–102.

Lass, Roger. 1992. Phonology and morphology. In Norman Blake (ed.), *The Cambridge history of the English language. Vol. 2: 1066-1476*, 23–155. Cambridge: CUP.

Lass, Roger. 1996. Of emes and memes: On the trail of the wild replicator. *VIEWS* 5 (1&2). 3–11.

Lass, Roger. 1997. Historical linguistics and language change. Cambridge: CUP.

Lass, Roger. 2000. Remarks on (uni)directionality. In Olga Fischer, Anette Rosenbach & Dieter Stein (eds.), *Pathways of change: Grammaticalization in English*, 207–227. Amsterdam: Benjamins.

Lass, Roger. 2003. Genetic metaphor in historical linguistics. *Alternation* 10 (1). 47–62.

Lauwers, Peter & Dominique Willems. 2011. Coercion: Definition and challenges, current approaches, and new trends. *Linguistics* 49 (6). 1219–1235.

Lehmann, Christian. 2002. New reflections on grammaticalization and lexicalization. In Ilse Wischer & Gabriele Diewald (eds.), *New reflections on grammaticalization*, 1–18. Amsterdam: Benjamins.

Lehmann, Winfred. 1974. *Proto-Indo-European syntax*. Austin, TX: University of Texas Press.

Leino, Jaako. 2013. Information structure. In Thomas Hoffmann & Graeme Trousdale (eds.), *The Oxford handbook of construction grammar*, 329–346. Oxford: OUP.

Lestrade, Sander. 2016. The emergence of argument marking. In Seán Roberts, Christine Cuskley, Luke McCrohon, Lluís Barceló–Coblijn, Olga Fehér & Tessa Verhoef (eds.), *The evolution of language: Proceedings of the 11th international conference (EVOLANG11)*. http://evolang.org/neworleans/papers/36.html (accessed 18 April 2019).

Levin, Beth (ed.). 1985. *Lexical semantics in review*. Cambridge, MA: MIT Press.

Levin, Beth. 1993. English verb classes and alternations: A preliminary investigation. Chicago, IL: University of Chicago Press.

Levin, Beth & Malka Rappaport Hovav. 1995. *Unaccusativity: At the syntax-lexical semantics interface*. Cambridge, MA: MIT Press.

Levin, Beth & Malka Rappaport Hovav. 2005. *Argument realization*. Cambridge: CUP.

Levin, Beth & Malka Rappaport Hovav. 2008. The English dative alternation: The case for verb sensitivity. *Journal of Linguistics* 44. 129–167.

Levshina, Natalia. 2015. How to do linguistics with R: Data exploration and statistical analysis. Amsterdam: Benjamins.

Lightfoot, David. 1991. How to set parameters: Arguments from language change. Cambridge, MA: MIT Press.

Lightfoot, David. 1999. The development of language: Acquisition, change, and evolution. Malden, MA: Blackwell.

Lindblom, Björn. 1990. Explaining phonetic variation: A sketch of the H&H theory. In William Hardcastle & Alain Marchal (eds.), *Speech production and speech modelling*, 403–439. Dordrecht: Kluwer.

Lindquist, Hans. 2000. *Livelier* or *more lively*? Syntactic and contextual factors influencing the comparison of disyllabic adjectives. In John Kirk (ed.), *Corpora galore. Analyses and techniques in describing English*, 125–132. Amsterdam: Rodopi.

Lohmann, Arne. 2011. *Help* vs. *help to*: A multifactorial, mixed-effects account of infinitive marker omission. *English Language and Linguistics* 15. 499–521.

Lohse, Barbara, John Hawkins & Thomas Wasow. 2004. Domain minimization in English verb-particle constructions. *Language* 80. 238–261.

Los, Bettelou. 2009. The consequences of the loss of verb-second in English: Information structure and syntax in interaction. *English Language and Linguistics* 13 (1). 97–125.

Los, Bettelou. 2015. *A historical syntax of English*. Edinburgh: EUP.

Los, Bettelou & Gea Dreschler. 2012. The loss of local anchoring: From adverbial local anchors to permissive subjects. In Terttu Nevalainen & Elizabeth Traugott (eds.), *The Oxford handbook of the history of English*, 859–871. New York, NY: OUP.

Losiewicz, Beth. 1992. *The effect of duration on linguistic morphology*. Ph.D. dissertation, University of Texas, Austin, TX.

Lumsden, Charles & Edward Wilson. 1981. *Genes, mind and culture*. Cambridge, MA: Harvard UP.

Lundskær–Nielsen, Tom. 1993. *Prepositions in Old and Middle English* (NOWELE Supplement 9). Odense: Odense UP.

Luraghi, Silvia. 1987. Patterns of case syncretism in Indo-European languages. In Anna Giacalone Ramat, Onofrio Carruba & Giuliani Bernini (eds.), *Papers from the 7th international conference on historical linguistics*, 355–371. Amsterdam: Benjamins.

Luraghi, Silvia. 2003. On the meaning of prepositions and cases: A study of the expression of semantic roles in Ancient Greek. Amsterdam: Benjamins.

Malchukov, Andrej, Martin Haspelmath & Bernard Comrie. 2010. Ditransitive constructions: A typological overview. In Andrej Malchukov, Martin Haspelmath & Bernard Comrie (eds.), *Studies in ditransitive constructions*, 1–64. Berlin: De Gruyter Mouton.

Malkiel, Yakov. 1968. The inflectional paradigm as an occasional determinant of sound change. In Winfred Lehmann & Yakov Malkiel (eds.), *Directions for historical linguistics*, 21–64. Austin, TX: University of Texas Press.

Marcotte, Jean-Philippe. 2005. *Causative alternation errors in child language acquisition*. Stanford, CA, Stanford University Ph.D. dissertation. http://www.tc.umn.edu/~marco043/files/MarcotteThesis2005.pdf (accessed 18 April 2019).

Marcotte, Jean-Philippe. 2006. Causative alternation errors as event-driven construction paradigm completions. In Eve Clark & Barbara Kelly (eds.), *Constructions in acquisition*, 205–232. Stanford, CA: CSLI Publications.

Marten, Gerald. 2008. Human ecology: Basic concepts for sustainable development. London: Earthscan.

Maynard Smith, John. 1982. *Evolution and the theory of games*. Cambridge: CUP.

Maynard Smith, John & George Price. 1973. The logic of animal conflict. *Nature* 246. 15–18.

McCrohon, Luke. 2012. The two-stage life cycle of cultural replicators. *Theoria et historia scientiarum* 9. 151–172.

McEnery, Tony & Andrew Hardie. 2012. *Corpus linguistics: Method, theory and practice*. Cambridge: CUP.

McFadden, Thomas. 2002. The rise of the to-dative in Middle English. In David Lightfoot (ed.), *Syntactic effects of morphological change*, 107–123. Oxford: OUP.

McLaughlin, John. 1983. *Old English syntax: A handbook*. Tübigen: Niemeyer.

McMahon, April. 1994. *Understanding language change*. Cambridge: CUP.

McMahon, April. 2000. *Change, chance, and optimality*. Cambridge: CUP.

McMahon, April & Robert McMahon. 2013. *Evolutionary linguistics*. Cambridge: CUP.
Meillet, Antoine. 1949. *Caractères généraux des langues germaniques*. (4th edn.). Paris: Librairie Hachette.
Mesoudi, Alex, Andrew Whiten & Kevin Laland. 2004. Is human cultural evolution Darwinian? Evidence reviewed from the perspective of *The Origin of Species*. *Evolution* 58 (1). 1–11.
Michaelis, Laura. 2005. Entity and event coercion in a symbolic theory of syntax. In Jan-Ola Östman & Mirjam Fried (eds.), *Construction grammars: Cognitive grounding and theoretical extensions*, 45–87. Amsterdam: Benjamins.
Michaelis, Laura. 2013. Sign-based Construction Grammar. In Thomas Hoffman & Graeme Trousdale (eds.), *The Oxford handbook of Construction Grammar*, 133–152. Oxford: OUP.
Michaelis, Laura & Josef Ruppenhofer. 2001. *Beyond alternations: A constructional model of the German applicative pattern*. Stanford, CA: CSLI Publications.
Mitchell, Bruce. 1985. *Old English syntax, Vol. 1*. Oxford: Clarendon.
Möhlig-Falke, Ruth. 2012. The early English impersonal construction: An analysis of verbal and constructional meaning. Oxford: OUP.
Molencki, Rafał. 1991. *Complementation in Old English*. 1991. Katowice: Wydawnictwo Uniwersytetu Śląskiego.
Molencki, Rafał. 2005. On the syntactic and semantic development of after in medieval English. In Marcin Krygier & Liliana Sikorska (eds.), *Naked wordes in Englissh*, 47–67. Frankfurt/Main: Lang.
Molencki, Rafał. 2007. On the rise of the temporal preposition/conjunction before. In Marcin Krygier & Lliana Sikorska (eds.), *To make his Englissh sweete upon his tonge*, 37–54. Frankfurt/Main: Lang.
Molencki, Rafał. 2008. The rise of because in Middle English. In Masachiyo Amano, Michiko Ogura & Masayuki Ohkado (eds.), *Historical Englishes in varieties of texts and contexts*, 201–216. Frankfurt/Main: Peter Lang.
Molencki, Rafał. 2011a. New prepositions and subordinating conjunctions of Romance origin in Middle English. In Jacek Fisiak & Magdalena Bator (eds.), *Foreign influences on Medieval English*, 9–24. Frankfurt/Main: Lang.
Molencki, Rafał. 2011b. The evolution of forward in Mediaeval English. In Renate Bauer & Ulrike Krischke (eds.), *More than words: English lexicography past and present*, 225–244. Frankfurt/Main: Lang.
Mondorf, Britta. 2009. More support for more-support: The role of processing constraints on the choice between synthetic and analytic comparative forms. Amsterdam: Benjamins.
Moore, Randall & Sehoya Cotner. 2011. *Arguing for evolution: An encyclopedia for understanding science*. Santa Barbara, CA: Greenwood.
Mufwene, Salikoko. 2001. *The ecology of language evolution*. Cambridge: CUP.
Mufwene, Salikoko. 2002. Competition and selection in language evolution. *Selection* 3. 45–56.
Mufwene, Salikoko. 2008. Language evolution: Contact, competition and change. London: Continuum.
Mukherjee, Joybrato. 2005. English ditransitive verbs: Aspects of theory, description and a usage-based model. Amsterdam: Rodopi.
Mukherjee, Joybrato & Sebastian Hoffmann. 2006. Describing verb-complementational profiles of new Englishes: A pilot study of Indian English. *English World-Wide* 27 (2). 147–173.
Müller, Stefan & Stephen Wechsler. 2014. Lexical approaches to argument structure. *Theoretical Linguistics* 40 (1–2). 1–76.

Mustanoja, Tauno. 1960. *A Middle English syntax, Vol. 1.* Helsinki: Société Néophilologique.
Nash, John. 1950. Equilibrium points in n-person games. Proceedings of the National Academy of Sciences of the United States of America 36 (1). 48–49.
Nettle, Daniel. 1999. *Linguistic diversity*. Oxford: OUP.
Nevalainen, Terttu. 1999. Making the best use of 'bad' data: Evidence for sociolinguistic variation in Early Modern English. *Neuphilologische Mitteilungen* 100 (4). 499–533.
Newman, John. 1996. *Give: A cognitive linguistic study*. Berlin: Mouton de Gruyter.
Nisbet, Tim. 2005. Benefactives in English: Evidence against argumenthood. *Reading Working Papers in Linguistics* 8. 51–67.
Noël, Dirk. 2007. Diachronic construction grammar and grammaticalization theory. *Functions of Language* 14 (2). 177–202.
Norde, Muriel & Freek van de Velde (eds.). 2016. *Exaptation and language change*. Amsterdam: Benjamins.
Nowak, Martin A. 2000. The basic reproductive ratio of a word, the maximum size of a lexicon. *Journal of Theoretical Biology* 204. 179–189.
Nowak, Martin A. 2006. *Evolutionary dynamics: Exploring the equations of life*. Cambridge, MA: Belknap Harvard UP.
Nowak, Martin & David Krakauer. 1999. The evolution of language. *Proceedings of the National Academy of Sciences of the United States of America* 96 (14). 8028–8033.
OED = *Oxford English Dictionary*. 2016. Oxford: OUP.
Oehrle, Richard. 1976. *The grammatical status of the English dative alternation*. Cambridge, MA: MIT Ph.D. dissertation.
Ogura, Michiko. 1980. The syntactic and semantic rivalry of quoth, say and tell in medieval English. Japan: Kufs.
Ozón, Gabriel A. 2009. *Alternating ditransitives in English: A corpus-based study*. London: University College London Ph.D. dissertation.
Panther, Klaus-Uwe. 1997. Dative alternation from a cognitive perspective. In Birgit Smieja & Meike Tasch (eds.), *Human contact through language and linguistics*, 107–126. Frankfurt/Main: Lang.
Pasicki, Adam. 1998. Meanings of the dative case in Old English. In Willy van Langendonck & William van Belle (eds.), *The Dative. Vol 2: Theoretical and contrastive studies*, 113–142. Amsterdam: Benjamins.
Patten, Amanda. 2012. The English IT-cleft: A constructional account and a diachronic investigation. Berlin: de Gruyter Mouton.
Percillier, Michael. 2018. A Toolkit for lemmatising, analysing, and visualising Middle English Data. In Andrew Frank, Christine Ivanovic, Francesco Mambrini, Marco Passarotti, & Caroline Sporleder (eds.), *Proceedings of the Second Workshop on Corpus-Based Research in the Humanities CRH-2*, 153–160. Vienna: TU Wien.
Percillier, Michael. subm. Allostructions, homostructions, or a constructional family? Changes in the network of secondary predicate constructions in Middle English. In Lotte Sommerer & Elena Smirnova (eds.), *Nodes and links in the network: Advances in Diachronic Construction Grammar* [Constructional Approaches to Language (special issue)].
Perek, Florent. 2012. Alternation-based generalizations are stored in the mental grammar: Evidence from a sorting task experiment. *Cognitive Linguistics* 23 (3). 601–635.
Perek, Florent. 2014. Vector spaces for historical linguistics. Proceedings of the 52nd Annual Meeting of the Association for Computational Linguistics. 309–314.

Perek, Florent. 2015. Argument structure in usage-based construction grammar: Experimental and corpus–based perspectives. Amsterdam: Benjamins.

Perek, Florent. 2016. Using distributional semantics to study syntactic productivity in diachrony: A case study. *Linguistics* 54 (1). 149–188.

Perek, Florent & Adele Goldberg. 2015. Generalizing beyond the input: The functions of the constructions matter. *Journal of Memory and Language* 84. 108–127.

Perek, Florent & Martin Hilpert. 2017. A distributional semantic approach to the periodization of change in the productivity of constructions. *International Journal of Corpus Linguistics* 22 (4). 490–520.

Perek, Florent & Maarten Lemmens. 2010. Getting at the meaning of the English *at*-construction: The case of a constructional split. *CogniTextes* 5. http://cognitextes.revues.org/331 (accessed 18 April 2019).

Petré, Peter. 2012. General productivity: How *become* waxed and *wax* became a copula. *Cognitive Linguistics* 23 (1). 27–65.

Petré, Peter. 2014. Constructions and environments: Copular, passive, and related constructions in Old and Middle English. Oxford: OUP.

Petyt, K. M. 1985. Dialect and accent in industrial West Yorkshire. Amsterdam: Benjamins.

Pierrehumbert, Janet B. 2001. Exemplar dynamics: Word frequency, lenition and contrast. In Joan Bybee & Paul Hopper (eds.), *Frequency and the emergence of linguistic structure*, 137–157. Amsterdam: Benjamins.

Pinker, Steven. 1984. *Language learnability and language development*. Cambridge, MA: Harvard UP.

Pinker, Steven. 1989. Learnability and cognition: The acquisition of argument structure. Cambridge, MA: MIT Press.

Pinker, Steven & Paul Bloom. 1990. Natural language and natural selection. *Behavioral and Brain Sciences* 13 (4). 707–784.

Pinsker, Hans. 1959. *Historische englische Grammatik*. Munich: Hueber.

Pintzuk, Susan. 1991. *Phrase structures in competition: Variation and change in Old English word order*. Philadelphia, PA: University of Pennsylvania Ph.D. dissertation.

Pintzuk, Susan. 1995. Variation and change in Old English clause structure. *Language variation and change* 7. 229–260.

Pintzuk, Susan. 1996. Cliticization in Old English. In Aaron Halpern & Arnold Zwicky (eds.), *Approaching second: Second position clitics and related phemomena*, 375–409. Stanford, CA: CSLI Publications.

Pintzuk, Susan. 1999. Phrase structures in competition: Variation and change in Old English word order. New York, NY: Garland.

Pintzuk, Susan & Anthony Kroch. 1985. Reconciling an exceptional feature of Old English clause structure. In Jan Faarlund, Jan (ed.), *Germanic linguistics: Papers from a symposium at the University of Chicago*, 87–111. Indiana, IN: Indiana University Linguistics Club.

Pintzuk, Susan & Ann Taylor. 2006. The loss of OV order in the history of English. In Ans van Kemenade & Bettelou Los (eds.), *The handbook of the history of English*, 249–278. London: Blackwell.

Pleyer, Michael. 2014. Cognition, usage, and complex systems: Evolving theories of language and their relevance for evolutionary linguistics. In Luke McCrohon, Tessa Verhoef, Bill Thompson & Hajime Yamauchi (eds.), *The past, present and future of language evolution research student volume of the 9th international conference on the evolution of language*, 64–74. Evolang 9 Organizing Committee.

Pleyer, Michael & Nicolas Lindner 2014. Constructions, construal and cooperation in the evolution of language. In Erica Cartmill, Seán Roberts, Heidi Lyn & Hannah Cornish (eds.), *The evolution of language: Proceedings of the 10th international conference (EVOLANG10)*.

Pleyer, Michael & James Winters. 2015. Integrating cognitive linguistics and language evolution research. *Theoria et historia scientiarium* 11. 19–43.

Plotkin, Henry. 1994. Darwin machines and the nature of knowledge. London: Penguin.

Polinsky, Maria. 1998. A non-syntactic account of some asymmetries in the double object construction. In Adele Goldberg (ed.), *Conceptual structure, discourse and language*, 403–422. Chicago, IL: CSLI and University of Chicago Press.

Polo, Chiara. 2002. Double objects and morphological triggers for syntactic case. In David Lightfoot (ed.), *Syntactic effects of morphological change*, 124–142. Oxford: OUP.

Prat–Sala, Mercè & Holly Branigan. 2000. Discourse constraints on syntactic processing in language production: A cross-linguistic study in English and Spanish. *Journal of Memory and Language* 42 (2). 168–182.

Primus, Beatrice. 1997. The relative order of recipient and patient in the languages of Europe. In Anna Siewierska (ed.), *Constituent order in the languages of Europe*, 421–473. Berlin: Mouton de Gruyter.

Pulvermüller, Friedemann. 2002. *The neuroscience of language*. Cambridge: CUP.

Quinn, Heidi. 2005. *The distribution of case forms in English*. Amsterdam: Benjamins.

Quirk, Randolph, Sidney Greenbaum, Geoffrey Leech & Jan Svartvik. 1985. *A comprehensive grammar of the English language*. London: Longman.

Randall, Beth. 2009. *CorpusSearch 2: A tool for linguistic research*. Philadelphia: University of Pennsylvania. http://corpussearch.sourceforge.net/ (accessed 18 April 2019).

Ransom, Evelyn. 1979. Definiteness and animacy constraints on passive and double-object constructions in English. *Glossa* 13. 215–240.

Rappaport Hovav, Malka & Beth Levin. 2008. The English dative alternation: The case of verb sensitivity. *Journal of Linguistics* 44 (1). 129–167.

R Development Core Team. 2014. *R: A language and environment for statistical computing*. R Foundation for Statistical Computing. Vienna. www.R–project.org (accessed 18 April 2019).

Reddy, William. 1979. The conduit metaphor: A case of frame conflict in our language about language. In Andrew Ortony (ed.), *Metaphor and thought*, 284–324. Cambridge: CUP.

Rice, Sally & Kaori Kabata. 2007. Cross-linguistic grammaticalization patterns of the allative. *Linguistic Typology* 11 (3). 453–516.

Ringe, Don. 2006. A linguistic history of English. Vol. 1: From Proto-Indo-European to Proto-Germanic. Oxford: OUP.

Rissanen, Matti. 1999. Syntax. In Roger Lass (ed.), *The Cambridge history of the English language. Vol. 3: 1476-1776*, 187–331. Cambridge: CUP.

Ritt, Nikolaus. 1995. Language change as evolution: Looking for linguistic genes. *VIEWS* 4 (1). 43–57.

Ritt, Nikolaus. 1996. Darwinising historical linguistics: Applications of a dangerous idea. *VIEWS* 5 (1&2). 27–47.

Ritt, Nikolaus. 2004. Selfish sounds and linguistic evolution: A Darwinian approach to language change. Cambridge: CUP.

Ritt, Nikolaus. 2013a. Evolutionary theories of language: Theories and methods. In Bernd Kortmann & Johannes Kabatek (eds.), *Linguistic theory and methodology*. (WSK–Dictionaries of Language and Communication Science). Berlin: Mouton de Gruyter.

http://www.degruyter.com/databasecontent?dbf_0=wskfulltext&dbid=wsk&dbq_0=ritt&dbsource=%2Fdb%2Fwsk&dbt_0=fulltext&o_0=&&sort=title-sort (accessed 18 April 2019).

Ritt, Nikolaus. 2013b. Is it 'Speakers and their languages' or 'languages and their speakers'? – On biologism and speciesism in historical linguistic thought. Paper presented at the *46th meeting of the Societas Linguistica Europaea*, Split, Croatia, September 18-23.

Ritt, Nikolaus & Andreas Baumann. 2012. Transferring mathematics to English studies. In Manfred Markus & Herbert Schendl (eds.), *Transfer in English studies*, 219–237. Wien: Braumüller.

Ritt, Nikolaus & Andreas Baumann. 2014. Evolutionary game theory in historical language studies. Workshop abstract for the *10th International Conference on the Evolution of Language* (EVOLANG X), Vienna, April 14–17.

Roberts, Ian. 1997. Directionality and word order change in the history of English. In Ans van Kemenade & Nigel Vincent (eds.), *Parameters of morphosyntactic change*, 397–426. Cambridge: CUP.

Roberts, Ian. 2007. *Diachronic syntax*. Oxford: OUP.

Roberts, Jane. 2000. *Robbares and reuares þat ryche men despoilen*: Some competing forms. In Irma Taavitsainen, Terttu Nevalainen, Päivi Pahta & Matti Rissanen (eds.), *Placing Middle English in context*, 235–255. The Hague: Mouton de Gruyter.

Röthlisberger, Melanie. subm. Macro-and micro-level variationin the English dative alternation: The view from World Englishes. In Melanie Roethlisberger, Eva Zehentner & Timothy Colleman (eds.), *Ditransitive constructions in Germanic languages: Synchronic and diachronic aspects*. [Studies in Germanic Linguistics]. Amsterdam: Benjamins.

Rohdenburg, Günter. 1995. Betrachtungen zum Auf- und Abstieg einiger praepositionaler Konstruktionen im Englischen. *NOWELE* 26. 67–124.

Rohdenburg, Günter. 1996. Cognitive complexity and increased grammatical explicitness in English. *Cognitive Linguistics* 7 (2). 149–182.

Rohdenburg, Günter. 2007. Functional constraints in syntactic change: The rise and fall of prepositional constructions in Early and Late Modern English. *English Studies* 88 (2). 217–233.

Rohdenburg, Günter. 2009. Nominal complements. In Günter Rohdenburg & Julia Schlüter (eds.), *One language, two grammars? Differences between British and American English*, 194–211. Cambridge: CUP.

Rohdenburg, Günter. 2013. The construction *cannot help -ing* and its rivals in Modern English. In Hilde Hesselgård, Jarle Ebeling & Signe Oksefjell Ebeling (eds.), *Corpus perspectives on patterns of lexis*, 113–132. Amsterdam: Benjamins.

Ronneberger-Sibold, Elke. 1987. A performance model for a natural theory of linguistic change. In Anna Giacalone Ramat, Onofrio Corruba & Giuliano Bernini (eds.), *Papers from the 7th international conference on historical linguistics*, 517–533. Amsterdam: Benjamins.

Rosenbach, Anette. 2002. Genitive variation in English: Conceptual factors in synchronic and diachronic studies. Berlin: Mouton de Gruyter.

Rosenbach, Anette. 2007. Emerging variation: Determiner genitives and noun modifiers in English. *English Language and Linguistics* 11 (1). 143–189.

Rosenbach, Anette. 2008. Language change as cultural evolution: Evolutionary approaches to language change. In Regine Eckardt, Gerhard Jäger & Tonja Veenstra (eds.), *Variation, selection, development. Probing the evolutionary model of language change*, 23–72. Berlin: Mouton de Gruyter.

Rosenbach, Anette. 2010. How synchronic gradience gives rise to language change (and vice versa). In Elizabeth Traugott & Graeme Trousdale (eds.), *Gradience, gradualness and grammaticalization*, 149–179. Amsterdam: John Benjamins.

Rostila, Jouni. 2004. Lexicalization as a way to grammaticalization. In Fred Karlsson (ed.), *Proceedings of the 20th Scandinavian Conference of Linguistics*. http://www.ling.helsinki.fi/kielitiede/20scl/Rostila.pdf (accessed 18 April 2019).

Rostila, Jouni. 2006. Construction Grammar as a Functional Generative Grammar. In Piotr Chruszczewski, Michał Garcarz & Tomasz Górski (eds.), *Crossroads of linguistic sciences*, 365–367. Krakau: Tertium.

Rostila, Jouni. 2007. *Konstruktionsansaetze zur Argumentmarkierung im Deutschen*. Tampere: Juvenes Print. (University of Tampere Ph.D. dissertation).

Samara, Anna, Kenny Smith, Helen Brown & Elizabeth Wonnacott. 2017. Acquiring variation in an artificial language: Children and adults are sensitive to socially conditioned linguistic variation. *Cognitive Psychology* 94, 85–114.

Samuels, Michael. 1972. Linguistic evolution: With special reference to English. Cambridge: CUP.

Santa Fe Institute. 2015. Santa Fe Institute mission and scientific principles. http://www.santafe.edu/ (18 April 2019).

Sato, Kiriko. 2009. The development from case-forms to prepositional constructions in Old English prose. Bern: Lang.

Savit, Robert, Maria Riolo & Rick Riolo. 2013. Co-adaptation and the emergence of structure. *PLoS ONE* 8 (9). e71828. http://journals.plos.org/plosone/article?id=10.1371/journal.pone.0071828 (18 April 2019).

Schendl, Herbert. 1996. Who does the copying? Some thoughts on N. Ritt's Darwinian historical linguistics. *VIEWS* 5 (1&2). 47–49.

Schibsbye, Knud. 1977. *Origin and development of the English language, Vol. 3*. Copenhagen: Nordisk Sprog Kulturforlag.

Schilk, Marco, Joybrato Mukherjee, Christopher Nam & Sach Mukherjee. 2013. Complementation of ditransitive verbs in South Asian Englishes: A multifactorial analysis. *Corpus Linguistics and Linguistic Theory* 9 (2). 187–225.

Schleicher, August. 1863. *Die Darwinsche Theorie und die Sprachwissenschaft*. Weimar: Herrmann Böhlau.

Schlücker, Barbara & Matthias Hüning. 2009. Compounds and phrases. A functional comparison between German A + N compounds and corresponding phrases. *Italian Journal of Linguistics* 21. 209–234.

Schmid, Hans-Jörg. 2015. Does gender-related variation still have an effect, even when topic and (almost) everything else is controlled? In Jocelyne Daems, Eline Zenner, Kris Heylen, Dirk Speelman & Hubert Cuyckens (eds.), *Change of paradigms – New paradoxes. Recontextualizing language and linguistics*, 327–246. Berlin: de Gruyter Mouton.

Schwegler, Armin. 1990. Analyticity and syntheticity: A diachronic perspective with special reference to Romance languages. Berlin: Mouton de Gruyter.

Schwyter, Juerg. 2012. Old English legal language: The lexical field of theft. Amsterdam: Benjamins.

Seiler, Guido. 2006. The role of functional factors in language change: An evolutionary approach. In Ole Nedergård Thomsen (ed.), *Different models of linguistic change*, 163–182. Amsterdam: Benjamins.

Shallice, Tim & McGill. 1978. The origins of mixed errors. In Jean Requin (ed.), *Attention and performance VII*, 193–208. Hillsdale, NJ: Lawrence Erlbaum.

Shannon, Ann. 1964. A descriptive syntax of the Parker manuscript of the Anglo-Saxon Chronicle from 734 to 891. The Hague: Mouton & Co.

Siewierska, Anna & Willem Hollmann. 2007. Ditransitive clauses in English with special reference to Lancashire dialect. In Mike Hannay & Gerard Steen (eds.), *Structural-functional studies in English grammar*, 83–102. Amsterdam: Benjamins.

Slowiaczek, Louisa & David Pisoni. 1986. Effects of phonological similarity on priming in auditory lexical decision. *Memory and Cognition* 14. 230–237.

Smirnova, Elena. 2015. Constructionalization and constructional change: The role of context in the development of constructions. In Jóhanna Barðdal, Spike Gildea, Elena Smirnova & Lotte Sommerer (eds.), *Diachronic construction grammar*, 81–106. Amsterdam: Benjamins.

Smith, Jeremy & Simon Horobin. 2002. *An introduction to Middle English*. Edinburgh: EUP.

Smith, Kenny, Olga Fehér & Nikolaus Ritt. 2014. 2014. Eliminating unpredictable linguistic variation through interaction. In *Proceedings of the 36th Annual Conference of the Cognitive Science Society*, 1461–1466. Austin, TX: Cognitive Science Society.

Smith, Kenny, Monica Tamariz & Simon Kirby. 2013. Linguistic structure is an evolutionary trade-off between simplicity and expressivity. In Markus Knauff, Michael Pauen, Natalie Sebanz & Ipke Wachsmuth (eds.), *Proceedings of the 35th annual meeting of the cognitive science society*. Austin, TX: Cognitive Science Society, 1348–1353.

Smith, Kenny, Amy Perfors, Olga Féher, Anna Samara, Kate Swoboda & Elizabeth Wonnacott. 2017. Language learning, language use, and the evolution of linguistic variation. *Philosophical Transactions of the Royal Society* 372 (1711). 1–13.

Smyth, Ronald, John Hogan & Gary Prideaux. 1979. The effect of context on dative position. *Lingua* 47. 27–42.

Snyder, Kieran. 2003. *The relationship between form and function in ditransitive constructions*. Philadelphia, PA: University of Pennsylvania Ph.D. dissertation.

Solé, Ricard, Bernat Corominas Murtra, Sergi Valverde & Luc Steels. 2010. Language networks: Their structure, function and evolution. *Complexity* 15. 20–26.

Sommerer, Lotte. 2018. Article emergence in Old English: A constructionalist perspective. Berlin: De Gruyter Mouton.

Soskuthy, Marton & Jennifer Hay. 2017. Changing word usage predicts changing word durations in New Zealand English. *Cognition* 166. 298–313.

Sówka-Pietraszewska, Katarzyna. 2012. On the development of a prepositional object construction with give verbs, motion verbs & Latinate verbs in English. In Jukka Tyrkkö, Matti Kilpiö, Terttu Nevalainen & Matti Rissanen (eds.), *Studies in variation, contacts and change in English, Vol. 10*. http://www.helsinki.fi/varieng/series/volumes/10/sowka–pietraszewska/ (accessed 18 April 2019).

Sówka-Pietraszewska, Katarzyna. 2013. On the inherent semantic meaning of double object Latinate verbs in English in modern and historical perspective. *Questions and Answers in Linguistics* 1 (1). 21–32.

Spencer, Andrew. 2001. The paradigm-based model of norphosyntax. *Transactions of the Philological Society* 99 (2). 279–314.

Stefanowitsch, Anatol. 2006. Negative evidence and the raw frequency fallacy. *Corpus Linguistics and Linguistic Theory* 2 (1). 61–77.

Stefanowitsch, Anatol. 2008. Negative entrenchment: A usage-based approach to negative evidence. *Cognitive Linguistics* 19 (3). 513–531.
Stefanowitsch, Anatol. 2011. Constructional preemption by contextual mismatch: A corpus-linguistic investigation. *Cognitive Linguistics* 22 (1). 107–129.
Stefanowitsch, Anatol. 2013. Collostructional analysis. In Thomas Hoffmann & Graeme Trousdale (eds.), *The Oxford handbook of construction grammar*, 290–306. Oxford: OUP.
Stefanowitsch, Anatol & Stefan Gries. 2003. Collostructions: Investigating the interaction of words and constructions. *International Journal of Corpus Linguistics* 8 (2). 209–243.
Steels, Luc. 1998. The origins of syntax in visually grounded robotic agents. *Artificial Intelligence* 103. 133–156.
Steels, Luc. 2000. Language as a complex adaptive system. In Marc Schoenauer, Kalyanmoy Deb, Günter Rudolph, Xin Yao, Evelyne Lutton, Juan Merelo & Hans-Paul Schwefel (eds.), *Parallel problem solving from nature – PPSN VI*, 17–26. Berlin: Springer.
Steels, Luc. 2006. How to do experiments in artificial language evolution and why. In Angelo Cangelosi, Andrew Smith & Kenny Smith (eds.), *Proceedings of the 6th international conference (EVOLANG6)*, 323–332.
Steels, Luc. 2007. The recruitment theory of language origins. In Caroline Lyon, Chrystopher Nehaniv & Angelo Cangelosi (eds.), *Emergence of language and communication*, 129–151. Berlin: Springer.
Steels, Luc. 2010. Can evolutionary linguistics become a science? *Journal for Evolutionary Linguistics* 1 (1). 1–35.
Steels, Luc (ed.). 2011a. *Design patterns in fluid construction grammar*. Amsterdam: Benjamins.
Steels, Luc. 2011b. Modeling the cultural evolution of language. *Physics of Life Reviews* 8. 339–356.
Steels, Luc (ed.). 2012a. Computational issues in fluid construction grammar. Berlin: Springer.
Steels, Luc (ed.). 2012b. *Experiments in cultural language evolution*. Amsterdam: Benjamins.
Steels, Luc. 2012c. Introduction: Self-organization and selection in cultural language evolution. In Luc Steels (ed.), *Experiments in cultural language evolution*, 1–37. Amsterdam: Benjamins.
Steels, Luc. 2013. Fluid construction grammar. In Thomas Hoffmann & Graeme Trousdale (eds.), *The Oxford handbook of construction grammar*, 153–167. Oxford: OUP.
Steels, Luc. 2017. Basics of Fluid Construction Grammar. In Luc Steels & Katrien Beuls (eds.), *Verb phrase and Fluid Construction Grammar*, 178–225. Amsterdam: Benjamins.
Steels, Luc & Martin Loetzsch. 2012. The grounded naming game. In Luc Steels (ed.), *Experiments in cultural language evolution*, 41–59. Amsterdam: Benjamins.
Stemberger, Joseph & Brian MacWhinney. 1986. Frequency and the lexical storage of regularly inflected forms. *Memory and Cognition* 14. 17–26.
Strang, Barbara. 1970. *A history of English*. London: Methuen & Co.
Suttle, Laura & Adele Goldberg. 2011. The partial productivity of constructions as induction. *Linguistics* 49 (6). 1237–1269.
Sweet, Henry. 1874. A history of English sounds from the earliest period. Oxford: OUP.
Szmrecsanyi, Benedikt. 2007. Review of Joybrato Mukherjee, English ditransitive verbs: Aspects of theory, description and a usage–base model. *English Language and Linguistics* 11 (1). 240–246.

Szmrecsanyi, Benedikt. 2012. Analyticity and syntheticity in the history of English. In Terttu Nevalainen & Elizabeth Traugott (eds.), *The Oxford handbook of the history of English*, 654–665. Oxford: OUP.

Szmrecsanyi, Benedikt & Lars Hinrichs. 2008. Probabilistic determinants of genitive variation in spoken and written English. In Terttu Nevalainen, Irma Taavitsainen, Päivi Pahta & Minna Korhonen (eds.), *The dynamics of linguistic variation: Corpus evidence on English past and present*, 291–309. Amsterdam: Benjamins.

Szmrecsanyi, Benedikt, Jason Grafmiller, Benedikt Heller & Melanie Röthlisberger. 2016. Around the world in three alternations: Modeling syntactic variation in varieties of English. *English World-Wide* 37 (2). 109–37.

Szmrecsanyi, Benedikt, Jason Grafmiller, Joan Bresnan, Anette Rosenbach, Sali Tagliamonte & Simon Todd. 2017. Spoken syntax in a comparative perspective: The dative and genitive alternation in varieties of English. *Glossa* 2 (1). 1–17.

Tagliamonte, Sali. 2014. A comparative sociolinguistic analysis of the dative alternation. In Rena Torres-Cacoullos, Nathalie Dion & André Lapierre (eds.), *Linguistic variation: Confronting fact and theory*, 297–318. London: Routledge.

Takami, Ken-Ichi. 2003. A semantic constraint on the benefactive double object construction. *English Linguistics* 20. 197–224.

Tallerman, Maggie & Kathleen Gibson (eds.). 2012. *The Oxford handbook of language evolution*. Oxford: OUP.

Talmy, Leonard. 2000. Toward a cognitive linguistics. Vol. 1: Concept structuring systems. Cambridge, MA: MIT Press.

Taylor, Ann & Susan Pintzuk. 2012a. Rethinking the OV/VO alternation in Old English: The effect of complexity, grammatical weight, and information status. In Terttu Nevalainen & Elizabeth Traugott (eds.), *The Oxford handbook of the history of English*, 835–845. Oxford: OUP.

Taylor, Ann & Susan Pintzuk. 2012b. The effect of information structure on object position in Old English: A pilot study. In Anneli Meurman-Solin, María José López-Couso & Bettelou Los (eds.), *Information structure and syntactic change in the History of English*, 47–65. Oxford: OUP.

Taylor, Ann & Susan Pintzuk. 2014. Testing the theory: Information structure in Old English. In Kristin Bech & Kristinne Gunn Eide (eds.), *Information structure and syntactic change in Germanic and Romance languages*, 53–78. Amsterdam: Benjamins.

Taylor, Ann & Susan Pintzuk. 2015. Verb order, object position, and information status in Old English. In Theresa Biberauer & George Walkden (eds.), *Syntax over time: Lexical, morphological, and information-structural interactions*, 318–335. Oxford: OUP.

Taylor, John. 1993. Prepositions: patterns of polysemization and strategies of disambiguation. In Cornelia Zelinsky-Wibbelt (ed.), *The semantics of prepositions*, 151–178. Berlin: Mouton de Gruyter.

Taylor, Peter & Leo Jonker. 1978. Evolutionary stable strategies and game dynamics. *Mathematical Biosciences* 40. 145–156.

The British National Corpus, version 3 (BNC XML Edition). 2007. Distributed by Bodleian Libraries, University of Oxford, on behalf of the BNC Consortium. http://www.natcorp.ox.ac.uk/ (accessed 18 April 2019).

Theijssen, Daphne. 2008. Using the ICE–GB corpus to model the English dative alternation. *Online Proceedings of the Aston Postgraduate Conference on Corpus Linguistics*.

http://daphnetheijssen.ruhosting.nl/publications/Theijssen_2008_Using_ICE-GB_to_model_English_dative.pdf (accessed 18 April 2019).

Theijssen, Daphne, Joan Bresnan, Marilyn Ford & Lou Boves. 2011. In a land far far away... A probabilistic account of the dative alternation in British, American and Australian English. (unpublished manuscript). http://daphnetheijssen.ruhosting.nl/publications/Theijssen_et_al_2011_In_a_land_far_far_away.pdf (accessed 18 April 2019).

Theijssen, Daphne, Hans van Halteren, Karin Fikkers, Frederike Groothoff, Lian van Hoof, Eva van de Sande, Jorieke Tiems, Véronique Verhagen & Patrick van der Zande. 2010. A regression model for the English benefactive alternation: An efficient, practical, actually usable approach. In Barbara Plank, Erik Tjong Kim Sang & Tim van de Cruys (eds.), *Computational Linguistics in the Netherlands 2009* (LOT Occasional Series), 115–130. Utrecht.

Theijssen, Daphne, Louis ten Bosch, Lou Boves, Bert Cranen & Hans van Halteren. 2013. Choosing alternatives: Using Bayesian Networks and memory-based learning to study the dative alternation. *Corpus Linguistics and Linguistic Theory* 9 (2). 227–262.

Thompson, Sandra. 1995. The iconicity of "dative shift" in English: Considerations from information flow in discourse. In Marge Landsberg (ed.). *Syntactic iconicity and linguistic freezes. The human dimension*, 155–175. Berlin: De Gruyter Mouton.

Thompson, Sandra & Barbara Fox. 2004. Relative clauses in English conversation: Relativizers, frequency and the notion of construction. (unpublished manuscript). University of California, Santa Barbara, CA.

Thompson, Sandra & Yuka Koide. 1987. Iconicity and indirect objects in English. *Journal of Pragmatics* 11 (3). 399–406.

Thompson, Sandra & Anthony Mulac. 1991. The discourse conditions for the use of the complementizer *that* in conversational English. *Journal of Pragmatics* 15 (3). 237–251.

Tomasello, Michael. 1992. First verbs: A case study of early grammatical development. Cambridge, MA: CUP.

Tomasello, Michael. 2003. Constructing language: A usage-based theory of language acquisition. Cambridge, MA: Harvard UP.

Tomasello, Michael. 2008. *The origins of human communication*. Cambridge, MA: MIT Press.

Torrent, Tiago Timponi. 2011. The construction network hypothesis. *Special issue of Letras and Letras* 27. http://www.letraseletras.ileel.ufu.br/viewissue.php?id=21 (accessed 18 April 2019).

Torrent, Tiago Timponi. 2015. On the relation between inheritance and change: The construction network reconfiguration hypothesis. In Jóhanna Barðdal, Spike Gildea, Elena Smirnova & Lotte Sommerer (eds.), *Diachronic construction grammar*, 173–212. Amsterdam: Benjamins.

Torres Cacoullos, Rena & James Walker. 2009. The present of the English future: Grammatical variation and collocations in discourse. *Language* 85. 321–354.

Traugott, Elizabeth. 1972. *A history of English syntax*. New York, NY: Holt, Rinehart, and Winston.

Traugott, Elizabeth. 1982. From propositional to textual and expressive meanings: Some semantic-pragmatic aspects of grammaticalization. In Winfried Lehmann & Yakov Malkiel (eds.), *Perspectives on historical linguistics*, 245–271. Amsterdam: Benjamins.

Traugott, Elizabeth C. 1992. Syntax. In Richard Hogg (ed.), The *Cambridge history of the English language, Vol. 1*, 168–289. Cambridge: CUP.

Traugott, Elizabeth. 2004. Exaptation and grammaticalization. In Minoji Akimoto (ed.), *Linguistic studies based on corpora*, 133–156. Tokyo: Hituzi Syobo.

Traugott, Elizabeth. 2006. Constructions and language change revisited: Constructional emergence from the perspective of grammaticalization. Paper presented at *Directions in English Language Studies* (DELS), Manchester, UK, April 6-8.

Traugott, Elizabeth. 2008a. Grammaticalization, constructions and the incremental development of language: Suggestions from the development of degree modifiers in English. In Regine Eckardt, Gerhard Jäger & Tonjes Veenstra (eds.), *Variation, selection, development: Probing the evolutionary model of language change*, 219–250. Berlin: Mouton de Gruyter.

Traugott, Elizabeth. 2008b. The grammaticalization of NP of NP constructions. In Alexander Bergs & Gabriele Diewald (eds.), *Constructions and language change*, 21–43. Berlin: Mouton de Gruyter.

Traugott, Elizabeth. 2015. Towards a coherent account of grammatical constructionalization. In Jóhanna Barðdal, Spike Gildea,

Traugott, Elizabeth. 2016. Do semantic modal maps have a role in a constructionalization approach to modals? In Bert Cappelle & Ilse Depraetere (eds.), *Modal meaning in Construction Grammar*, 97–124. Amsterdam: Benjamins.

Traugott, Elizabeth. forthc. Modeling language change with constructional networks. In Salvador Pons Bordería, & Óscar Loureda (eds.), *Beyond grammaticalization and discourse markers: New issues in the study of language change*. Leiden: Brill.

Traugott, Elizabeth & Graeme Trousdale. 2013. *Constructionalization and constructional changes*. Oxford: OUP.

Trips, Carola. 2002. *From OV to VO in Early Middle English*. Amsterdam: Benjamins.

Trousdale, Graeme. 2008. Constructions in grammaticalization and lexicalization: Evidence from the history of a composite predicate construction in English. In Graeme Trousdale & Nikolas Gisborne (eds.), *Constructional approaches to English grammar*, 33–67. Berlin: Mouton de Gruyter.

Trousdale, Graeme. 2010. Issues in constructional approaches to grammaticalization in English. In Katerina Stathi, Elke Gehweiler & Ekkehard König (eds.), *Grammaticalization: Current views and issues*, 51–72. Amsterdam: Benjamins.

Tuggy, David. 1981. The transitivity-related morphology of Tetelcingo Náhuatl: An exploration in space grammar. San Diego, CA: University of California Ph.D. dissertation.

Tuggy, David. 2007. Schematicity. In Dirk Geeraerts & Hubert Cuyckens (eds.), *The Oxford handbook of cognitive linguistics*, 82–116. New York, NY: OUP.

Tungseth, Mai. 2008. Verbal prepositions and argument structure: Path, place and possession in Norwegian. Amsterdam: Benjamins.

Tyler, Andrea & Vyvyan Evans. 2003. The semantics of English prepositions: Spatial scenes, embodied meaning, and cognition. Cambridge: CUP.

University of Michigan Regents. 2013. *The electronic Middle English dictionary*. http://quod.lib.umich.edu/m/med/ (accessed 18 april 2019).

Välimaa-Blum, Riitta. 2011. Cognitive phonology in Construction Grammar: Analytic tools for students of English. Berlin: Mouton de Gruyter.

Van de Velde, Freek. 2014. Degeneracy: The maintenance of constructional networks. In Ronny Boogaart, Timothy Colleman & Gijsbert Rutten (eds.), *Extending the scope of Construction Grammar*, 141–180. Berlin: De Gruyter.

Van Gelderen, Elly. 1996. The reanalysis of grammaticalized prepositions in Middle English. *Studia linguistica* 50 (2). 106–124.
Van Kemenade, Ans. 1987. Syntactic case and morphological case in the history of English. Providence: Foris.
Van Kemenade, Ans. 1997. V2 and embedded topicalization in Old and Middle English. In Ans van Kemenade & Nigel Vincent (eds.), *Parameters of morphosyntactic change*, 326–352. Cambridge: CUP.
Van Kemenade, Ans. 1999. Sentential negation and word order in Old English. In Ingrid Tieken-Boon van Ostade, Gunnel Tottie & Wim van der Wurff (eds.), *Negation in the history of English*, 147–166. Berlin: Mouton de Gruyter.
Van Kemenade, Ans. 2002. Word order in Old English prose and poetry: The position of finite verbs and adverbs. In Donka Minkova & Robert Stockwell (eds.), *Studies in the history of the English language: A millennial perspective*, 355–373. Berlin: Mouton de Gruyter.
Van Kemenade, Ans. 2009. Discourse relations and word order change. In Roland Hinterhölzl & Svetlana Petrova (eds.), *Information structure and language change*, 91–120. Berlin: Mouton de Gruyter.
Van Kemenade, Ans. 2011. Secondary negation and information structure organization in the history of English. In Pierre Larrivee & Richard Ingham (eds.), *The evolution of negation: Beyond the Jespersen cycle*, 77–114. Berlin: Mouton de Gruyter.
Van Kemenade, Ans. 2012. Rethinking the loss of V2. In Terttu Nevalainen & Elizabeth Traugott (eds.), *The Oxford handbook of the history of English*, 1182–199. Oxford: OUP.
Van Kemenade, Ans & Bettelou Los. 2006. Discourse adverbs and clausal syntax in Old and Middle English. In Ans van Kemenade, Ans & Bettelou Los (eds.), *The handbook of the history of English*, 224–248. Oxford: Blackwell.
Van Reenen, Pieter & Lene Schøsler. 2000. Declension in Old and Middle French. Two opposing tendencies. In John Smith & Delia Bentley (eds.), *Historical linguistics 1995: Selected papers from the 12th International Conference on Historical Linguistics, Manchester, August 1995, Vol. 1*, 327–334. Amsterdam: Benjamins.
Van Trijp, Remi. 2010. Grammaticalization and semantic maps: Evidence from artificial language evolution. *Linguistic Discovery* 8 (1). 310–326.
Van Trijp, Remi. 2012. The evolution of case systems for marking event structure. In Luc Steels (ed.), *Experiments in cultural language evolution*, 169–205. Amsterdam: Benjamins.
Van Trijp, Remi. 2013. Linguistic assessment criteria for explaining language change: A case study on syncretism in German definite articles. *Language Dynamics and Change* 3. 105–132.
Van Valin, Robert & Randy LaPolla. 1997. *Syntax: Structure, meaning, and function*. Cambridge: CUP.
Vasilyeva, Marina & Heidi Waterfall. 2011. Beyond syntactic priming: Evidence for activation of alternative syntactic structures. *Journal of Child Language* 39 (2). 1–26.
Vázquez-González, Juan-Gabriel & Jóhanna Barðdal. subm. Reconstructing the ditransitive construction for Proto-Germanic: Gothic, Old English and Old Norse-Icelandic.
Vincent, Nigel. 1997. Synthetic and analytic structures. In Martin Maiden & Mair Parry (eds.), *The dialects of Italy*, 99–105. London: Routledge.
Visser, Fredericus. 1963. An historical syntax of the English language. Leiden: Brill.
Vitevitch, Michael. 1997. The neighbourhood characteristics of malapropisms. *Language and Speech* 40. 211–228.

Von Neumann, John & Oskar Morgenstern. 1944. *Theory of games and economic behavior*. Princeton, NJ: Princeton UP.

Von Seefranz-Montag, Ariane. 1983. Syntaktische Funktionen und Wortstellungsveränderung. Die Entwicklung ‚subjektloser' Konstruktionen in einigen Sprachen. Munich: Wilhelm Fink.

Von Seefranz-Montag, Ariane. 1984. 'Subjectless' constructions and syntactic change. In Jacek Fisiak (ed.), *Historical syntax*, 521–553. Berlin: Mouton.

Wang, William. 1969. Competing changes as a cause of residue. *Language* 45. 9–25.

Wasow, Thomas. 2002. *Postverbal behavior*. Stanford, CA: CSLI Publications.

Wasow, Thomas & Jennifer Arnold. 2003. Post-verbal constituent ordering in English. In Günter Rohdenburg & Britta Mondorf (eds.), *Determinants of grammatical variation in English*, 119–154. Berlin: Mouton de Gruyter.

Webelhuth, Gert & Clare Dannenberg. 2006. Southern American English personal datives: The theoretical significance of dialectal variation. *American Speech* 81 (1). 31–55.

Wechsler, Stephen. 1995. *The semantic basis of argument structure*. Stanford, CA: CSLI Publications.

Wedel, Andrew. 2006. Exemplar models, evolution and language change. *The Linguistics* 23. 247–274.

Wellens, Pieter, Remi van Trijp, Katrien Beuls & Luc Steels. 2013. Fluid construction grammar for historical and evolutionary linguistics. In The Association for Computational Linguistics (eds.), *Proceedings of the 51st Annual Meeting of the Association for Computational Linguistics*, 127–132. Madison, WI: Omnipress.

Werner, Otmar. 1987. Natürlichkeit und Nutzen morphologischer Irregularität. In Norbert Boretzky, Werner Enninger & Thomas Stolz (eds.), *Beiträge zum 3. Essener Kolloquium über Sprachwandel und seine bestimmenden Faktoren*, 289–316. Bochum: Brockmeyer.

Westergaard, Marit. 2010. Cue-based acquisition and information structure drift in diachronic language development. In Gisella Ferraresi & Rosemarie Lühr (eds.), *Diachronic studies on information structure: Language acquisition and change*, 87–116. Berlin: de Gruyter.

Whitacre, James. 2010. Degeneracy: A link between evolvability, robustness and complexity in biological systems. *Theoretical Biology and Medical Modelling* 7 (6). https://doi.org/10.1186/1742-4682-7-6 (18 April 2019).

Wickham, Hadley. 2016. *ggplot2: Elegant graphics for data analysis*. New York, NY: Springer.

Wierzbicka, Anna. 1986. The semantics of 'internal dative' in English. *Quaderni di Semantica* 7. 121–135.

Wierzbicka, Anna. 1988. *The semantics of grammar*. Amsterdam: Benjamins.

Winters, Margaret, Heli Tissari & Kathryn Allan (eds.). 2010. *Historical cognitive linguistics*. Berlin: Mouton de Gruyter.

Wolk, Christoph, Joan Bresnan, Anette Rosenbach & Benedikt Szmrecsanyi. 2013. Dative and genitive variability in Late Modern English. *Diachronica* 30 (3). 382–419.

Wonnacott, Elizabeth, Jeremy Boyd, Jennifer Thompson & Adele Goldberg. 2012. Input effects on the acquisition of a novel phrasal construction in 5 year olds. *Journal of Memory and Language* 66. 458–478.

Wonnacott, Elizabeth, Elissa Newport & Michael Tanenhaus. 2008. Acquiring and processing verb argument structure: Distributional learning in a miniature language. *Cognitive Psychology* 56. 165–209.

Yáñez-Bouza, Nuria. 2015. Grammar, rhetoric and usage in English: Preposition placement 1500-1900. Cambridge: CUP.

Yáñez–Bouza, Nuria & David Denison. 2015. Which comes first in the double object construction? Diachronic and dialectal variation. *English Language and Linguistics* 19 (2). 247–268.

Yang, Charles. 2001. Internal and external forces in language change. *Language Variation and Change* 12 (3). 231–250.

Yang, Charles. 2002. Grammar competition and language change. In David Lightfoot (ed.), *Syntactic effects of morphological change*, 367–380. Oxford: OUP.

Zehentner, Eva. 2018. Ditransitives in Middle English: on semantic specialisation and the rise of the dative alternation. *English Language and Linguistics* 22 (1). 149–175.

Zehentner, Eva & Elizabeth Traugott. forthc. Constructional networks and the development of benefactive ditransitives in English. In Lotte Sommerer & Elena Smirnova (eds.), *Nodes and links in the network: Advances in Diachronic Construction Grammar* [Constructional Approaches to Language (special issue)].

Zeschel, Arne. 2012. Incipient productivity: A construction-based approach to linguistic creativity. Berlin: De Gruyter Mouton.

Zipf, George. 1949. Human behaviour and the principle of least effort: An introduction to human ecology. Cambridge, MA: Addison–Wesley.

Ziv, Yael & Gloria Sheintuch. 1979. Indirect objects reconsidered. In Paul Clyne, William Hanks & Carol Hofbauer (eds.), *Papers from the fifteenth regional meeting of the Chicago Linguistics Society*, 390–403. Chicago, IL: Chicago Linguistics Society.

Zwicky, Arnold. 1992. Some choices in the theory of morphology. In Robert Levine (ed.), *Formal Grammar*, 327–371. Oxford: OUP.

Index

https://doi.org/10.1515/9783110633856-010